Great Writing:

A READER FOR WRITERS

Great Writing:
A READER FOR WRITERS

Harvey Wiener
Nora Eisenberg
**THE CITY UNIVERSITY OF NEW YORK,
LAGUARDIA**

McGRAW-HILL BOOK COMPANY

NEW YORK   ST. LOUIS   SAN FRANCISCO   AUCKLAND   BOGOTÁ   HAMBURG   JOHANNESBURG
LONDON   MADRID   MEXICO   MILAN   MONTREAL   NEW DELHI   PANAMA   PARIS   SÃO PAULO
SINGAPORE   SYDNEY   TOKYO   TORONTO

Great Writing: **A READER FOR WRITERS**

1 2 3 4 5 6 7 8 9 0 DOCDOC 8 9 4 3 2 1 0 9 8 7 6

ISBN 0-07-070167-9

This book was set in Times Roman by Better Graphics (ECU).
The editors were Emily G. Barrosse and David Dunham;
the designer was Scott Chelius; the production supervisors
were Joe Campanella and Fred Schulte.
Cover Illustration by Tom Lulevitch.
R. R. Donnelley & Sons Company was printer and binder.

Library of Congress Cataloging-in-Publication Data

Great writing.

   1. College readers.   2. English language—Rhetoric.
I. Wiener, Harvey S.   II. Eisenberg, Nora.
PE1417.G67   1987   808'.0427   86-10413
ISBN: 0-07-070167-9

About the Authors

Harvey S. Wiener, professor of English at LaGuardia Community College of the City University of New York, codirects the National Testing Network in Writing (NTNW) and College Assessment Program Evaluation (CAPE). He was founding president of the Council of Writing Program Administrators. Dr. Wiener is the author of many books on reading and writing for college students and their teachers, including *The Writing Room* (Oxford, 1981). He is coauthor with Richard Marius of *The McGraw Hill College Handbook*, a reference grammar and rhetoric text. Dr. Wiener is a member of the Standing Committee on Assessment for the National Council of Teachers of English, and he is chair of the Teaching of Writing Division of the Modern Language Association (1987). He has taught writing at every level of education from elementary school to graduate school. A Phi Beta Kappa graduate of Brooklyn College, he holds a Ph.D in Renaissance literature from Fordham University. Dr. Wiener has won grants from the National Endowment for the Humanities, the Fund for the Improvement of Postsecondary Education, and the Exxon Education Foundation.

Nora Eisenberg is a professor of English at LaGuardia Community College of the City University of New York, where she teaches courses in composition, creative writing, and literature and is associate director of the college's writing across the curriculum program. Dr. Eisenberg holds a Ph.D. from Columbia University and has taught at Brooklyn College, Stanford University, and Georgetown University. She has published numerous articles on Virginia Woolf and is the coauthor with Harvey Wiener of *Stepping Stones: A Course in Basic Writing* (Random House, 1985). Dr. Eisenberg is also a fiction writer; she has published short stories and poems and is at present working on a novel.

Contents

Chapter Six:
CLASSIFICATION 300

Chapter Seven:
CAUSATION 361

Chapter Eight:
DEFINITION 458

Preface

We believe in a number of important principles about learning to write, and these principles inform this book and establish its content, approach, and format.

We believe first in the primacy of text and in the enduring authority, intelligence, and joy in great writing. When aspiring writers read great writing carefully and attentively, they come closer to producing exceptional writing themselves. Aiming for contemporaneity, too many anthologies for writers avoid great writing; they may offer readable, serviceable samples, but they rarely show our language at its very best or address the great intellectual issues of our civilization. To use readings as guides for writing—as exercises in form, as explorations of style, as laboratories for the growth of ideas in words and sentences—students must read the very best our culture has to offer. Shakespeare, Swift, Virginia Woolf, Cather, Plato, Conrad, T. S. Eliot, Orwell, John Stuart Mill, Poe, Emerson, Emily Bronte, E. B. White, Langston Hughes, Sophocles, Keats, James Joyce, Thoreau, great writers of our civilization, help provide the models that teach the writer's craft.

With a title like *Great Writing* we know that we are going out on a limb, and we want to admit at the outset that our selections unabashedly proclaim our own subjective judgments, tastes, and prejudices. An experienced reader could grumble about our exclusions or could question some of the pieces or authors we chose to include. Still, we strove to make selections that many educated readers would identify as important writing by great figures. You will recognize most of the authors and many of the selections. Our goal was always to choose the most clearly written, the most elegantly and intelligently reasoned, the most sensitive and thought provoking pieces that suited the rhetorical strategies we believe best organize a course of study. We aimed for ethnic, geographical, and sexual diversity among our authors, and we tried to balance long pieces with short ones, humorous pieces with serious ones, and intense pieces with relaxed ones. We chose excerpts as rarely as possible, yet could not always avoid them when we drew from novels, plays, or long essays. Thus, we provide all of *Oedipus Rex* but only a scene from *Othello*. Where excerpts appear, we have explained the context so that what precedes or follows the selection is always clear. Of course, our wish is that students will like so much what they read here that they will choose to read or reread on their own the full-length works—all of *Huckleberry Finn*, *Native Son*, *Wuthering Heights*, *Othello*, and *Walden* to name a few.

We also believe that poets, dramatists, novelists, and short story writers have as much to teach about writing essays as do nonfiction writers. Certainly in regard to description, narration, imagery, style, tone, characterization, symbol, point of view, satire, irony, dialogue, diction, coherence, allusion, and analogy—basic terms that readers and writers use to talk about their efforts—our collection of poems, short stories, and scenes from novels and plays can speak to beginning writers and can teach them. To exclude poetry, fiction, and dramatic literature from a reader is to risk a loss of exposure to great minds at a critical point in a student's growth to knowledge.

More than offering great ideas and brilliant style, poets, fiction writers, and playwrights grapple with the same kinds of rhetorical principles that many people have too long insisted are the purview of essayists alone. Surely Dickens struggled with the rhetorical issues inherent in comparison and contrast when he wrote the first chapter of *A Tale of Two Cities*. Surely Marvell in "To His Coy Mistress" worked through the familiar conventions of argument and persuasion that face any writer who chooses to take a position and to win supporters. Certainly Carson McCullers in "A Tree. A Rock. A Cloud." faced the same need for clarity and personalized meaning, the same confusions of denotation and connotation, the same impulse to establish new lexical validity that any writer faces in attempting an important definition. This is not to say, of course, that we are challenging the rightful place of the expository essay in a program for developing writers; rather, we aim to complement that place by establishing for it a larger context that includes great writing in any genre. In fact, you will find many outstanding essays in this book.

Exploring the writer's craft through a consideration of rhetorical patterns is a useful way to study writing. We have chosen to organize this book by means of traditional rhetorical categories: description, narration, illustration, process analysis, comparison, classification, causation, definition, and argumentation. Our choice of selections demonstrates our conviction that elements of writing in all genres rely upon these categories. Every chapter contains poetry, fiction, essays, and occasionally drama—all within familiar rhetorical contexts. We're not offering these examples as pure or absolute models of their type, however. Sometimes the rhetorical strategy is a dominant mode in the selection and is easy to recognize. At other times the strategy may be more subtle. A single paragraph or two, even a couple of sentences, may demonstrate some particularly striking application of a rhetorical principle. Sometimes more than one strategy—say, description and narration, causality and process, or definition, illustration and argumentation—may work hand in hand.

The value in practicing rhetorical patterns is that they point the way to a range of available options for writers. We agree with many critics of rhetorically organized readers—it's the rare writer who chooses a rhetorical strategy and then sets out to fill it with ideas. No one says, "Today I'm going to write a classification essay." Ideas always come first for writers, and as these ideas develop, writers pay attention to audience, purpose, language, style, and all the varied, complex factors that help make an essay successful. Still, as ideas develop, writers cannot help but benefit from knowing rhetorical options and to use them creatively and intelligently. Thus, if a writer wanted to develop an essay about the Civil War, a knowledge of cause-and-effect strategies would help him or her present clearly a sense of why the war began; a knowledge of descriptive strategies would help breathe life into a Union hospital scene; a knowledge of comparison and contrast strategies would help in a consideration of the relative strengths of the North and South. The writer would not have to exclude one strategy for the other: powerful writing often relies upon a number of different rhetorical patterns within a single essay. Again, the key is choices. Learning to write within rhetorical contexts expands a writer's choices and, no matter what the assignment, improves dramatically the possible approaches to writing.

We want to thank our friends and colleagues who encouraged us to develop this text and who read proposals and early drafts. Don McQuade and Bob Atwan listened to early versions of our thoughts. John Wright saw the goals of our project immediately and gave us the support and energy we needed to carry it through. Elizabeth McMahan (Illinois State Univeristy), Lee Jacobus (University of Connecticut), and Gratia Murphey (Youngstown State University) did a thorough, thoughtful job of critiquing the manuscript. Phillip Butcher, Emily Barrosse, and David Dunham at McGraw Hill guided *Great Writing* to, and through, production with affection, respect, and care. To all the people who helped us along, including our families, we are deeply in debt.

Harvey S. Wiener
Nora Eisenberg

Great Writing:

A READER FOR WRITERS

INTRODUCTION: THE WRITING PROCESS

*A*ll public writing—whether fiction, nonfiction, drama, or poetry—is the endpoint of a creative process made permanent by language. Understanding the process of writing, that is, how a piece develops from start to finish, is an essential feature of learning how to write. Yet without digging in diaries, personal journals, biographies, or letters, when we read what great writers have written, we do not see any of that process. We see only a final product. The routes of access to it—the false starts, the wrong turns, the winding roadways—are not open to our inspection as we read.

If they share anything, though, great writers share an elaborate and often agonizing commitment to process. To produce a page of writing they follow a series of irregular, often undefinable steps that, despite some similarities, may differ from task to task and from writer to writer. If this seems paradoxical—writers doing the same thing differently—it is nonetheless true. The steps are different, are taken in no certain sequence, and vary dramatically; yet every writer follows some steps that take him or her from an emerging idea to a piece of finished prose or poetry. Of course, we can rarely arrive at a fully satisfactory response to the age-old question that attentive readers will ask, often incredulously, about the writer of a wonderful essay or story or poem: "How did she do that?" Still, by considering the ways writers get to where they want to go, we can uncover new paths to our own final products.

All writers begin with thinking. They may use pen, pencil, typewriter, or computer to pin down tentatively that thinking in language, before making any permanent commitment to an idea with polished, well-crafted sentences. A vague notion about your subject is frequently your only starting point, but you want to sharpen this notion in your own mind before trying to develop it fully in a draft. The point here is that writing even a first draft is an effort you should usually make *after* the idea starts to take its course. The various stages of thinking and writing in advance of a draft is called *prewriting*. Thus, you might prewrite by jotting ideas on a small slip of paper or writing a list of questions or a very rough outline that you'll subject to frequent revision. Some writers who have trouble generating ideas on a subject will try free association. They make a list of everything that enters their minds about the topic, or they write nonstop for a set time period. In either case, they censor nothing. These are useful strategies for bringing unconscious thoughts and ideas to the surface. Looking the list over, a writer can see just how he or she is thinking, can group together related ideas that appear on different parts of the page, or can identify some feature of the topic that limits it and makes it more clearly focused than before. To tease this feature out even further, a writer might try list-making, outlining, or free association again and again.

You can nurture an emerging idea by holding it up to someone else's thinking. What have others written about the topic? What do trusted people—a friend, a professor, a parent—believe about the issues? Has a recent television documentary or radio talk show addressed them? Ezra Pound, the great twentieth-century poet who along with T. S. Eliot and a number of others helped usher in the modern age of literature, called poets "the antennae of the race." We extend that neat label to all writers. Put out your antennae, consider how the world is thinking about your concerns, write about them freshly and with your own special insights. And don't hesitate to share your drafts *as drafts* with any sound thinker who will read what you've written. Pound tore apart Eliot's early drafts of *The Wasteland* and with trenchant commentary helped bring great poetry to birth.

By the time the first draft appears, then, a writer has already taken a number of definable steps. These steps may be recursive (writers go back and forth from their questions to their outlines to their drafts) and in no logical order; and many writers skip some steps altogether or replace them with other steps. One thing for sure, though, is that the trail leading to the draft, and the draft itself, are pretty messy affairs. You can always tell how intense the prewriting effort was from the scratch-outs, erasures, insertions, and loops and arrows on a page. A tidy early draft is probably a bad one. You've got to be struggling with word choice, syntax, emphasis, rhythm, and so many other issues that your page is often a battlefield of as many dead words as living ones to take up the charge. Don't aim for neatness. Slash foggy thinking. Snip imprecise words. Trim wordy sentences. Changing words and ideas while you write and after you write is absolutely vital for an emerging creative effort. Look at some of the changes that Virginia Woolf makes in a draft of the first three paragraphs of her brilliant novel *Mrs. Dalloway:*

> Mrs Dalloway said she would buy the flowers herself.
>
> For Lucy had her work cut ~~of~~ out for her. The doors would be taken off their hinges; Rumpelmayers men were coming. And then, thought Clarissa, what a day!
>
> What ~~an ecstasy~~! a ~~miracle~~! ~~ecstasy~~! <u>lark</u>! What a plunge! For so it had always seemed to her, when, with a little squeak of the hinges which she could hear now, she had burst open the French windows ~~as and stepped out on to the terrace at Bourton~~, and plunged at Bourton ~~into the terrace~~ into the open air. ~~Like waves, like~~ How fresh, how calm, stiller than this of course, ~~and~~ the air was in the early morning; rooks cawing, dogs barking; ~~and the ———, which naturally one lost later ——— and then, rooks cawing, dogs barking; and and with it all—but Peter Walsh she would say she~~ like the flap of a wave; like the kiss of a wave; ~~for~~—chill and sharp and yet, (for a girl of eighteen as she was then) ~~how~~ . ~~and~~ a ~~little~~ solemn, ~~yes, solemn~~. Peter Walsh would say—whatever Peter Walsh did say—~~when he found when he found her~~ "Musing among the vegetables?" Wasn't that it? Peter who didn't know a rose from a cauliflower, and "preferred men to

cabbages.'' She ''I prefer men to cabbages.'' He must have said it at breakfast, for her to be thinking of it on the terrace, in a morning, ~~and then going
she had~~ out ~~on to the terrace~~, and she had gone on to the terrace, as she
done over and over again, ~~with to escape~~, ~~to look~~, ~~to think it over~~,
~~what Peter said and how the morning looked~~ and stood there, just for a moment, and felt as she could not feel now, ~~at her~~ age, that something
tremendous was about to happen, but ~~that~~ and so stood, and so looked, at
the flowers, at the trees, and wondered why, then, ~~that~~ this young man,
whom they hardly knew, should begin like that, to Aunt Helena of all people, at breakfast. ~~Not to like flowers~~! It was very like him. And he would
be back from India one of these days, June or July, she forgot which, ~~and
to be perfectly honest~~ she ~~had~~ ~~for she~~ never ~~could~~ ~~not~~ read his letters; they
were awfully dry; it was his sayings one remembered, his big pocket knife,
his eyes; his ~~charm too~~; and his grumpiness; and ~~when~~ millions of things
~~were~~ had utterly vanished, a few ~~sayin~~things. like this. ~~which brought back
to her that~~ about cabbages.*

And that's not all by any means. The final draft shows many changes
from the earlier efforts as she struggles to root abstract concepts in
sensory diction:

Mrs. Dalloway said she would buy the flowers herself.

    For Lucy had her work cut out for her. The doors would be taken off
their hinges; Rumpelmayer's men were coming. And then, thought Clarissa
Dalloway, what a morning—fresh as if issued to children on a beach.

    What a lark! What a plunge! For so it had always seemed to her, when,
with a little squeak of the hinges, which she could hear now, she had burst
open the French windows and plunged at Bourton into the open air. How
fresh, how calm, stiller than this of course, the air was in the early morning;
like the flap of a wave; the kiss of a wave; chill and sharp and yet (for a girl
of eighteen as she then was) solemn, feeling as she did, standing there at the
open window, that something awful was about to happen; looking at the
flowers, at the trees with the smoke winding off them and the rooks rising,
falling; standing and looking until Peter Walsh said, ''Musing among the
vegetables?''—was that it?—''I prefer men to cauliflowers''—was that it?
He must have said it at breakfast one morning when she had gone out on to
the terrace—Peter Walsh. He would be back from India one of these days,
June or July, she forgot which, for his letters were awfully dull; it was his
sayings one remembered; his eyes, his pocket-knife, his smile, his grumpiness and, when millions of things had utterly vanished—how strange it
was!—a few sayings like this about cabbages.

One only can imagine the emotional energy, the intellectual vigor, the
agony of creation at play here as these early paragraphs develop. But
there is joy, too, in the process, an excitement of discovery, self-

*These paragraphs are reproduced from Wallace Hildick's *Word for Word* (New York:
Norton, 1965).

awareness, and pride as the words and sentences finally say what Woolf wants them to say. She reports that joy while writing her book; she reports plunging "deep into the richest strata of my mind. I can write & write & write now: the happiest feeling in the world." As you write you too will move from states of frustration and despair to states of exhilaration; that is all part of the roller coaster a writer will ride to a finished draft.

Among your most important concerns as you shape your drafts into efforts you'll want to make public is whether your thoughts cohere and whether they are unified. *Unity* and *coherence* are two of the most important aims writers can have for anything they write. Your writing is coherent if one idea leads smoothly and logically to the next. Your writing is unified if each idea relates clearly to your main point and to the other ideas you've presented. Transitional devices, repetitions, a constant focus on your thesis—these can help you produce unified, coherent writing. As you read the selections in this text, pay particular attention to the way great writers achieve the same goals you're after.

We've structured the chapters in this book and the questioning apparatus to reflect important principles we believe in: a commitment to great writing; enthusiasm for fiction, nonfiction, poetry, and drama as models that developing writers must study; a belief in rhetorical strategies as important and useful approaches to writing exercises; and strong support for attention to the writing process as a means for learning the writer's craft.

First, read the introduction to each chapter. Each introduction provides an overview of the rhetorical strategy at hand by defining it and by placing it in the larger context of human thought and expression. In this section we try to point out what you should be looking for in the essays, poems, plays, and stories you will read that will help you with your own writing. The introduction considers the reading selections that follow and calls attention to readers' expectations for the rhetorical mode. In addition, the introduction treats the general issues you must attend to as a writer practicing a particular rhetorical technique. In every chapter the section entitled Audience and Purpose focuses on these major elements in writing. Finally, in the section entitled Process, we try to help you think about how to produce your own writing in the mode we are exploring. Here we make suggestions about steps to take and pitfalls to avoid.

Once you finish the chapter introductions and turn to the selections themselves, you'll find a headnote before each selection. The first paragraph of the headnote provides biographical information on the writer, and the second paragraph provides any important information you might need to know about the selection in order to help you understand or appreciate it better. Study questions appear after each selection. The first group of questions asks you to test your literal understanding of the piece; the next group focuses your attention on the language, form, and structure that help make the piece great; and the final group offers ideas for writing that grow out of what you've read.

"A good book," John Milton wrote in the *Aereopogitica* (1644), "is the precious life-blood of a master-spirit, embalmed and treasured up on purpose to a life beyond life." We bring you many of those master spirits in *Great Writing* and wish only that their grand efforts help you develop your own craft and spur you to continue perfecting it.

Chapter One
DESCRIPTION

*I*n a famous and frequently quoted line, Joseph Conrad, one of the great novelists in the English language, asserts the preeminent role of description in the writer's craft. "My task which I am trying to achieve," he writes in the Preface to *The Nigger of the Narcissus* (1897), "is, by the power of the written word to make you hear, to make you feel—it is before all, to make you *see*. That—and no more, and it is everything."

The senses are the stock in trade for any writer, but particularly for the writer of description. The French novelist George Sand wrote to her friend Flaubert, "I believe that art needs a palette overflowing with colour, soft or violent according to the subject of the painting; that the artist is an instrument on which everything must play before he can play on others." To bring readers to sense what they themselves sense, writers turn to the language of the senses, to words that convey sight, sound, smell, taste, and touch. What, in fact, other than an image—a sketch, a photograph, a painting, a film sequence, a cluster of sentences—immediately links the mind of the creator of the image with the mind of the observer? In any kind of writing an image can create a sudden and immediate illumination that pages and pages of prose that lack sensory detail rarely achieve.

READING DESCRIPTION

Readers of description acknowledge the power of the image, the phrase or sentence that provides an indelible sensation in language. The image may appeal to the sense of sight with colors and with actions portrayed by energetic verbs. In a poem in this chapter, Tennyson writes of the eagle on a mountain, who, "ringed with the azure world," "clasps the crag with crooked hands," and with that picture, the poet fixes the majesty of the great bird in our minds forever. The image may appeal to the sense of sound with one of the multitude of English words that name sounds (onomatopoeia like *ring, whoosh, buzz,* and *roar*) or that describe them (*loud, groaning, shattering, hoarse*). The image may appeal to the sense of touch (*soft, wet, rough*), to the sense of smell (*acrid, perfumed, dusty*), to the sense of taste (*bitter, lemony, sweet*). Often a single image or a combination of images appeals to many senses. Conrad himself was a master of sensory diction. This brief passage opening Chapter Three of *Lord Jim* is only one of hundreds like it alive in color, action, sound, and touch.

> A marvellous stillness pervaded the world, and the stars, together with the serenity of their rays, seemed to shed upon the earth the assurance of ever- lasting security. The young moon recurved, and shining low in the west,

was like a slender shaving thrown up from a bar of gold, and the Arabian Sea, smooth and cool to the eye like a sheet of ice, extended its perfect level to the perfect circle of a dark horizon. The propeller turned without a check, as though its beat had been part of the scheme of a safe universe; and on each side of the *Patna* two deep folds of water, permanent and sombre on the unwrinkled shimmer, enclosed within their straight and diverging ridges a few white swirls of foam bursting in a low hiss, a few wavelets, a few ripples, a few undulations that, left behind, agitated the surface of the sea for an instant after the passage of the ship, subsided splashing gently, calmed down at last into the circular stillness of water and sky with the black speck of the moving hull remaining everlastingly in its centre.

Conrad does make us hear and feel, and above all see. We hear the hissing foam and the gentle splash as the ship passes; we feel the smooth, cool, Arabian sea and the marvelous stillness of the moment; we see the reflecting moon in the dark, the somber folds of water, the ripples and the undulations of the waves. It is Conrad's genius, of course, his photographic eye, as Galsworthy calls it, that records the scene and shapes it for his readers. But his language helps establish some general features to look for as we read description. First, the main goal of description is clarity, and toward that end the writer uses what Flaubert calls *le seul mot juste*, the single correct word. Notice the specificity of Conrad's nouns to signify the texture of the sea's surface—*ridges, swirls, foam, wavelets, ripples, undulations*. Specific words like these as opposed to a more general word like *waves*, for example, compel readers to see exactly what Conrad wants them to see. Modifiers sharpen the meaning of the nouns but do not overwhelm them. Only a fifth of the words in this passage are adjectives. Great writers resist using modifiers when specific nouns can create a clearer picture than any describing words could. Similarly, verbs show remarkable precision here, with minimal help from adverbs: *recurved, thrown up, turned, agitated, subsided, calmed*.

Among the nouns and verbs, you will notice a preponderance of concrete as opposed to abstract words. Conrad does not totally avoid language apart from perceivable experience—"everlasting security" and "safe universe" are abstractions certainly—but his description hangs more upon concrete images like the passage of the ship through the water than upon these theoretical words and concepts. A writer's purpose may demand a higher degree of abstraction than Conrad allows here, but more often than not the descriptive passage relies heavily upon concrete sensory diction. Concrete words make descriptions clear and easy to see in the imagination.

Memorable, accurate description relies on selectivity of detail, perhaps the most difficult goal for the writer. In observing anything, we are bombarded with sensory impressions, hundreds of them, that register on our minds. In recreating an object, a person, or a scene, what does the writer leave in? What does the writer leave out? Including everything is never the intention; we readers would be overwhelmed and would have no clue to what makes the scene special. The intention is to include only indispensable detail. Paul Claudel, a twentieth-century French writer, insists quite correctly that "nothing unessential is the first condition of art." Leaving out is as important as putting in. When we read, we look for the economy of expression and the originality of thought that immediately make an object clear, sharp, and alive. Being original and conveying that originality at just the right level of detail are part of the genius of the writer, and contribute to our judgments about the quality of a piece of prose or poetry.

In reaching for the clear and indelible image, writers often turn to figurative devices. Figurative devices compare. By likening one object in a description to some other object writers can bring an immediately sharp, visual quality to a scene. With Conrad's unusual simile of the moon shining low in the west "like a slender shaving thrown up from a bar of gold" the comparison between the moon and a sliver of gold makes us see this moon as we have seen no other. Similes, metaphors, personification (and other figures) are powerful descriptive tools, and you should be aware of them as you read. You should also note a writer's efforts to show you a scene, not just to tell you about it. Showing means drawing pictures; telling means offering judgments. Telling readers, for example, that a face is beautiful is very much different from showing details of the face so that readers infer its beauty. Critical readers like to draw their own conclusions, and writers can never be sure when they provide judgments that readers will see what the writer sees; in fact, without supporting details, how many people could agree on what a beautiful face was? No descriptive writer avoids judgments entirely, and as in every other case in writing, audience and purpose dictate the degree to which a writer will adhere to any principle, even one as sound as "show—don't tell" Even Conrad provides judgments—note how he starts his paragraph with a generalization that *tells* us about the scene: "A marvellous stillness pervaded the world, and the stars, together with the serenity of their rays, seemed to shed upon the earth the assurance of everlasting security." Yet we are not left to take Conrad's word for it. Every sentence after that judgment supports and enhances it, so that we are helpless to conclude anything other than "marvellous stillness" pervading the world he draws. In description the balance always tips in favor of details that show rather than tell. As you read selections in this chapter—selections like Tennyson's "The Eagle" and E. B. White's "Once More to the Lake"—you will experience what writers of description always strive for: concrete, sensory language that brings a person, an object, a scene immediately to life.

WRITING DESCRIPTION

Description will find its way into much of your writing as a means of supporting your ideas with detail. In papers that narrate, compare and contrast, explain a process, or argue, for example, concrete sensory images will help you make a point with clarity and force. In this chapter, however, we ask you to use description as the dominant mode of your writing so that you can practice a range of strategies that will make your writing clear and original in execution whenever you need to call upon your descriptive powers.

PURPOSE AND AUDIENCE

As you choose your topics for description, you must consider your reasons for writing and the people you intend to read your work. Textbooks often distinguish between *subjective* and *objective* description, and you would choose one or the other of these as a strategy, depending upon your purpose and your audience.

True, an individual writer's personal perceptions are embedded in the details he or she offers to the reader, and it is therefore hard to make a strong case for an absolute distinction between subjective and objective description. Still, the distinction is worthwhile. Objective descriptions are technical; the details the writer uses are impersonal, at a distance, independent of the perceiving mind. Scientific writing relies on such objective description in one sense so that experiments are replicable. The size and shape of a vein in a dogfish shark dissected in a tray, the color and odor of chemicals in a test tube, the texture of a lesion on human skin—nonsubjective descriptions of these sensory observations help students validate their views as part of a large community of observers who record the details in similar language. Of course, the quality of even the most ''objective'' observation depends upon the observer and his or her past experience, ability to see and to hear, talent for recognizing those details worth noting and those worth ignoring. Francis Bacon, the clarion of modern science, acknowledged the difficulties of sensory observation in science: ''The subtlety of nature,'' he writes in *The Great Instauration* (1620), is ''greater many times over than the subtlety of the senses and understanding.'' And he called repeatedly for aids to the senses: ''Neither the naked hand nor the understanding left to itself can effect much. It is by instruments and helps that the work is done, which are as much wanted for the understanding as for the hand.''

It is not so clear cut or simple, then, to achieve objective writing. Yet despite difficulties, objective description has its uses, and in areas other than the pure sciences. As we said before, a writer's purpose and the reaction of the audience may demand that he or she keep opinions, impressions, or subjective responses out of the prose. Thus, in describing a bedroom of a nursing home for a report on the aging, your writing would be detached: You would show what you observed, not your reactions to your observations. You'd measure the bed, and, focusing on impressions of sights, you'd measure the length of the window, you'd name the colors of the walls and the ceiling, you'd identify by name and with sensory detail the various pieces of equipment around the room. You'd use language that means just what it says, not language rich in associations and accrued meanings. Certainly, in an objective description you'd avoid stating your opinions: You might think the color of the walls a sickly green, the bed stand dilapidated, the blankets worn and tattered, but none of those impressions should slip into your prose.

If on the other hand, your purposes in writing were to show the deplorable conditions you saw in a nursing home to an audience unfamiliar with those conditions, you'd choose a much more subjective approach, allowing your personal attitudes and impressions to guide your selection of words and to shape your construction of images. You'd want people to know how you felt about the scene. You'd select words whose connotations you'd weighed carefully so that readers had precisely the impression you had. You'd be sensitive to shades of meaning. In the simile of the moon and the bar of gold that we commented on earlier, note how Conrad emphasizes the wonderful placid beauty of the moment on the sea with carefully chosen words like *marvellous, stillness, serenity, slender, smooth,* and *cool.* (Try substituting synonyms for some of these words in the image—*astonishing* for *marvellous, quiet* for *stillness, peacefulness* for *serenity, thin* for *slender, unbroken* for *smooth, moderately cold* for *cool*—to see how they alter the impact of the original.) Note too, the sound of the words to the ear, the repetition of the word *perfect,* the *s* or *sh* sound at the start of six words in the simile, the three coordinated structures with the word *and.* None of these is accidental. Especially in a subjective description, your words have the potential to compel your reader to see with your eyes, to hear with your ears, to touch with your fingers. All the selections in this chapter are examples of subjective descriptions, and you will see in them the care writers exercise in locating *le seul mot juste.*

PROCESS

To help focus your description you want to spend some time thinking about purpose and audience. Just what point will you make by means of your description? What is the overriding impression you wish to create? What will your readers expect to learn from the details you present? Freewriting or brainstorming will help you think on paper about those questions. Conversations with friends who can help you answer some of these questions now will be useful. Once you have selected a subject for description, think about how you will bring it to life. If you choose something you can visit before you write or that you can observe as you write—a quiet football field, say, or a child at play with her red wagon, or a taco on a paper plate—so much the better. Make lists of sensory images that contribute to the overall effect you are trying to convey; you might even group them in columns—"what I saw," "what I heard," "what I felt," and so on. Don't aim for completeness. You'll have to select carefully among your many sense impressions for those that give the best glimpse of the nature of your subject. If you choose a subject out of your memory of experiences, find some quiet place where you can concentrate and try to imagine your subject in the full richness of details, the colors, actions, sounds, and smells you associate with it. Listing your sense impressions will be very helpful here too.

When you're ready to write a draft, consider how you will arrange the details in your paper. Where do you, the observer, stand in relation to the object? Will you show it to the reader from a fixed position, presenting details spatially from left to right, front to back, top to bottom? Or, will you move with the reader as you describe the features of your subject? Will you present details according to importance, building from the least to the most significant? In a subjective description of a ward in a nursing home, for example, you might tour its contents from your entry point at the door, showing what you see and hear as you take the reader around or across the room. But if your interest is to show the run-down conditions of the place, you might show instead the minor inconveniences first, like its threadbare sheets and curtains, peeling paint, and exposed pipes, and then move to what you consider more serious features of neglect, like lumpy beds, dirty floors, broken nightstands. If you're adventurous, you might trust to an impressionistic portrait, allowing your imagination freedom to both create and organize details. Though this is a tricky and difficult plan to follow, it can sometimes produce a very interesting piece of writing.

Don't ever think of your draft as writing cut in stone. Put down as much as you can in your early efforts, but plan to revise carefully to achieve the goals of accurate description. Revise, edit, rewrite: In producing a public copy of your paper you must pay attention to these steps that all writers take whenever they write.

Tolstoy writes: "To evoke in oneself a feeling one has once experienced, then by means of movement, lines, colors, sounds, or forms expressed in words, so to transmit that feeling that others experience the same feeling—this is the activity of art." You can carry that activity forward as you write your descriptive paper.

E. B. White

ONCE MORE TO THE LAKE

Elwyn Brooks White was born in Mount Vernon, New York, in 1899. After graduating from Cornell University, he worked as a reporter, and in 1926, he joined the staff of *The New Yorker*. His delightful and insightful contributions to that magazine in great part helped set its past and present tone. White was a versatile writer whose descriptions have delighted readers of all ages. In addition to his *New Yorker* writing, his legacy includes *One Man's Meat* (1942), *Here Is New York* (1949), *Charlotte's Web* (1952), and the collected *Essays of E. B. White* (1977).

Taken from White's *Essays,* this reflective description of a scene first visited some thirty-seven years in the past, amply supports President Kennedy's evaluation of White as "an essayist whose concise comment on men and places has revealed to yet another age the vigor of the English sentence." His strongly subjective, yet precise, descriptions help bridge the gaps between the actual, physical changes he sees in the place and the emotional, perceptual changes he feels.

AUGUST 1941

*O*ne summer, along about 1904, my father rented a camp on a lake in Maine and took us all there for the month of August. We all got ringworm from some kittens and had to rub Pond's Extract on our arms and legs night and morning, and my father rolled over in a canoe with all his clothes on; but outside of that the vacation was a success and from then on none of us ever thought there was any place in the world like that lake in Maine. We returned summer after summer—always on August 1 for one month. I have since become a salt-water man, but sometimes in summer there are days when the restlessness of the tides and the fearful cold of the sea water and the incessant wind that blows across the afternoon and into the evening make me wish for the placidity of a lake in the woods. A few weeks ago this feeling got so strong I bought myself a couple of bass hooks and a spinner and returned to the lake where we used to go, for a week's fishing and to revisit old haunts.

I took along my son, who had never had any fresh water up his nose and who had seen lily pads only from train windows. On the journey over to the lake I began to wonder what it would be like. I wondered how time would have marred this unique, this holy spot—the coves and streams, the hills that the sun set behind, the camps and the paths behind the camps. I was sure that the tarred road would have found it out, and I wondered in what other ways it would be desolated. It is strange how much you can remember about places like that once you allow your mind to return into the grooves that lead back. You remember one thing, and that suddenly reminds you of another thing. I guess I remembered clearest of all the early mornings, when the lake was cool and motionless, remembered how the bedroom smelled of the lumber it was made of and of the wet woods whose scent entered through the screen. The partitions in the camp were thin and did not extend clear to the top of the rooms, and as I was always the first up I would dress softly so as not to wake the others, and sneak out into the sweet outdoors and start out in the canoe, keeping close along the shore in the long shadows of the pines. I remembered being very careful never to rub my paddle against the gunwale for fear of disturbing the stillness of the cathedral.

The lake had never been what you would call a wild lake. There were cottages sprinkled around the shores, and it was in farming country although the shores of the lake were quite heavily wooded. Some of the cottages were owned by nearby farmers, and you would live at the shore and eat your meals at the farmhouse. That's what our family did. But although it wasn't wild, it was a fairly large and undisturbed lake and there were places in it that, to a child at least, seemed infinitely remote and primeval.

I was right about the tar: it led to within half a mile of the shore. But when I got back there, with my boy, and we settled into a camp near a farmhouse and into the kind of summertime I had known, I could tell that it was going to be pretty much the same as it had been before—I knew it, lying in bed the first morning smelling the bedroom and hearing the boy sneak quietly out and go off along the shore in a boat. I began to sustain the illusion that he was I, and therefore, by simple transposition, that I was my father. This sensation persisted, kept cropping up all the time we were there. It was not an entirely new feeling, but in this setting it grew much stronger. I seemed to be living a dual existence. I would be in the middle of some simple act, I would be picking up a bait box or laying down a table fork, or I would be saying something and suddenly it would be not I but my father who was saying the words or making the gesture. It gave me a creepy sensation.

We went fishing the first morning. I felt the same damp moss covering the worms in the bait can, and saw the dragonfly alight on the tip of my rod as it hovered a few inches from the surface of the water. It was the arrival of this fly that convinced me beyond any doubt that everything was as it always had been, that the years were a mirage and that there had been no years. The small waves were the same, chucking the rowboat under the chin as we fished at anchor, and the boat was the same boat, the same color green and the ribs broken in the same places, and under the floorboards the same fresh water leavings and débris—the dead helgramite, the wisps of moss, the rusty discarded fishhook, the dried blood from yesterday's catch. We stared silently at the tips of our rods, at the dragonflies that came and went. I lowered the tip of mine into the water, tentatively, pensively dislodging the fly, which darted two feet away, poised, darted two feet back, and came to rest again a little farther up the rod. There had been no years between the ducking of this dragonfly and the other one—the one that was part of memory. I looked at the boy, who was silently watching his fly, and it was my hands that held his rod, my eyes watching. I felt dizzy and didn't know which rod I was at the end of.

We caught two bass, hauling them in briskly as though they were mackerel, pulling them over the side of the boat in a businesslike manner without any landing net, and stunning them with a blow on the back of the head. When we got back for a swim before lunch, the lake was exactly where we had left it, the same number of inches from the dock, and there was only the merest suggestion of a breeze. This seemed an utterly enchanted sea, this lake you could leave to its own devices for a few hours and come back to, and find that it had not stirred, this constant and trustworthy body of water. In the shallows, the dark, water-soaked sticks and twigs, smooth and old, were undulating in clusters on the bottom against the clean ribbed sand, and the track of the mussel was plain. A school of minnows swam by, each minnow with its small individual shadow, doubling the attendance, so clear and sharp in the sunlight. Some of the other campers were in swimming, along the shore, one of them with a cake of soap, and the water felt thin and clear and unsubstantial. Over the years there had been this person with the cake of soap, this cultist, and here he was. There had been no years.

Up to the farmhouse to dinner through the teeming dusty field, the road under our sneakers was only a two-track road. The middle track was missing, the one with the marks of the hooves and the splotches of dried, flaky manure. There had always been three tracks to choose from in choosing which track to walk in; now the choice was narrowed down to two. For a moment I missed terribly the middle alternative. But the way led past the tennis court, and something about the way it lay there in the sun reassured me; the tape had loosened along the backline, the alleys were green with plantains and other weeds, and the net (installed in June and removed in September) sagged in the dry noon, and the whole place steamed with midday heat and hunger and emptiness. There was a choice of pie for dessert, and one was blueberry and one was apple, and the waitresses were the same country girls, there having been no passage of time, only the illusion of it as in a dropped curtain—the waitresses were still fifteen; their hair had been washed, that was the only difference—they had been to the movies and seen the pretty girls with the clean hair.

Summertime, oh, summertime, pattern of life indelible with fade-proof lake, the wood unshatterable, the pasture with the sweetfern and the juniper forever and ever, summer without end; this was the background, and the life along the shore was the design, the cottages with their innocent and tranquil design, their tiny docks with the flagpole and the American flag floating against the white clouds in the blue sky, the little paths over the roots of the trees leading from camp to camp and the paths leading back to the outhouses and the can of lime for sprinkling, and at the souvenir counters at the store the miniature birch-bark canoes and the postcards that showed things looking a little better than they looked. This was the American family at play, escaping the city heat, wondering whether the newcomers in the camp at the head of the cove were "common" or "nice," wondering whether it was true that the people who drove up for Sunday dinner at the farmhouse were turned away because there wasn't enough chicken.

It seemed to me, as I kept remembering all this, that those times and those summers had been infinitely precious and worth saving. There had been jollity and peace and goodness. The arriving (at the beginning of August) had been so big a business in itself, at the railway station the farm wagon drawn up, the first smell of the pine-laden air, the first glimpse of the smiling farmer, and the great importance of the trunks and your father's enormous authority in such matters, and the feel of the wagon under you for the long ten-mile haul, and at the top of the last long hill catching the first view of the lake after eleven months of not seeing this cherished body of water. The shouts and cries of the other campers when they saw you, and the trunks to be unpacked, to give up their rich burden. (Arriving was less exciting nowadays, when you sneaked up in your car and parked it under a tree near the camp and took out the bags and in five minutes it was all over, no fuss, no loud wonderful fuss about trunks.)

Peace and goodness and jollity. The only thing that was wrong now, really, was the sound of the place, an unfamiliar nervous sound of the outboard motors. This was the note that jarred, the one thing that would sometimes break the illusion and set the years moving. In those other summertimes all motors were inboard; and when they were at a little distance, the noise they made was a sedative, an ingredient of summer sleep. They were one-cylinder and two-cylinder engines, and some were make-and-break and some were jump-spark, but they all made a sleepy sound across the lake. The one-lungers throbbed and fluttered, and the twin-cylinder ones purred and purred, and that was a quiet sound, too.

But now the campers all had outboards. In the daytime, in the hot mornings, these motors made a petulant, irritable sound; at night in the still evening when the afterglow lit the water, they whined about one's ears like mosquitoes. My boy loved our rented outboard, and his great desire was to achieve single-handed mastery over it, and authority, and he soon learned the trick of choking it a little (but not too much), and the adjustment of the needle valve. Watching him I would remember the things you could do with the old one-cylinder engine with the heavy flywheel, how you could have it eating out of your hand if you got really close to it spiritually. Motorboats in those days didn't have clutches, and you would make a landing by shutting off the motor at the proper time and coasting in with a dead rudder. But there was a way of reversing them, if you learned the trick, by cutting the switch and putting it on again exactly on the final dying revolution of the flywheel, so that it would kick back against compression and begin reversing. Approaching a dock in a strong following breeze, it was difficult to slow up sufficiently by the ordinary coasting method, and if a boy felt he had complete mastery over his motor, he was tempted to keep it running beyond its time and then reverse it a few feet from the dock. It took a cool nerve, because if you threw the switch a twentieth of a second too soon you would catch the flywheel when it still had speed enough to go up past center, and the boat would leap ahead, charging bull-fashion at the dock.

We had a good week at the camp. The bass were biting well and the sun shone endlessly, day after day. We would be tired at night and lie down in the accumulated heat of the little bedrooms after the long hot day and the breeze would stir almost imperceptibly outside and the smell of the swamp drift in through the rusty screens. Sleep would come easily and in the morning the red squirrel would be on the roof, tapping out his gay routine. I kept remembering everything, lying in bed in the mornings—the small steamboat that had a long rounded stern like the lip of a Ubangi, and how quietly she ran on the moonlight sails, when the older boys played their mandolins and the girls sang and we ate doughnuts dipped in sugar, and how sweet the music was on the water in the shining night, and what it had felt like to think about girls then. After breakfast we would go up to the store and the things were in the same place—the minnows in a bottle, the plugs and spinners disarranged and pawed over by the youngsters from the boys' camp, the Fig Newtons and the Beeman's gum. Outside, the road was tarred and cars stood in front of the store. Inside, all was just as it had always been, except there was more Coca-Cola and not so much Moxie and root beer and birch beer and sarsaparilla. We would walk out with the bottle of pop apiece and sometimes the pop would backfire up our noses and hurt. We explored the streams, quietly, where the turtles slid off the sunny logs and dug their way into the soft bottom; and we lay on the town wharf and fed worms to the tame bass. Everywhere we went I had trouble making out which was I, the one walking at my side, the one walking in my pants.

One afternoon while we were at that lake a thunderstorm came up. It was like the revival of an old melodrama that I had seen long ago with childish awe. The second-act climax of the drama of the electrical disturbance over a lake in America had not changed in any important respect. This was the big scene, still the big scene. The whole thing was so familiar, the first feeling of oppression and heat and a general air around camp of not wanting to go very far away. In midafternoon (it was all the same) a curious darkening of the sky, and a lull in everything that had made life tick; and then the way the boats suddenly swung the other way at their moorings with the coming of a breeze out of the new quarter, and the premonitory rumble. Then the kettle drum, then the snare, then the bass drum and cymbals, then crackling light against the dark, and the gods grinning and licking their chops in the hills. Afterward the calm, the rain steadily rustling in the calm lake, the return of light and hope and spirits, and the campers running out in joy and relief to go swimming in the rain, their bright cries perpetuating the deathless joke about how they were getting simply drenched, and the children screaming with delight at the new sensation of bathing in the rain, and the joke about getting drenched linking the generations in a strong indestructible chain. And the comedian who waded in carrying an umbrella.

When the others went swimming my son said he was going in, too. He pulled his dripping trunks from the line where they had hung all through the shower and wrung them out. Languidly, and with no thought of going in, I watched him, his hard little body, skinny and bare, saw him wince slightly as he pulled up around his vitals the small, soggy, icy garment. As he buckled the swollen belt, suddenly my groin felt the chill of death.

Meaning and Idea

1. Why does White go to the lake? When was he at the lake before? Whom does he bring with him now? With whom did he go to the lake on his earlier visit?

2. During what season do the visits take place? Describe the weather during White's return.

3. White's essay traces things that have changed at the lake and things that have not changed over the years. Identify what seems not to have changed. Identify the changes that White notes. Why do you think White devotes a paragraph to the change in motor boats? What effect do the new outboard motors have on White's feeling of the years not passing? Why?

4. What understanding does he develop from his trip to the lake as an adult?

Language, Form, Structure

1. In paragraph one White writes that he returned to the lake "for a week's fishing and to revisit old haunts." What are the denotations and connotations of the word *haunt?* In what way is "haunt" central to the essay?

2. What illusion does White try to sustain (paragraph four)? Why is the illusion "creepy" (paragraph four)? How successful is White in maintaining his illusion? Relate the last line to the rest of the essay.

3. List the images in the essay that most effectively render White's sense of sameness. What senses does White call upon in these images? Which images do you find most compelling?

4. White's use of language invites attention. He refers to his son as "my son" and "my boy." But sometimes he calls him simply "the boy" (paragraphs four and five). What effect does he achieve with this phrasing? How does this choice of words relate to the essay's meaning? White makes use of a simile in his discussion of the storm (paragraph twelve). To what event or events does he compare the storm? Do you feel the simile contributes to the essay's meanings about time and change? Why?

5. In this essay about time, White makes use of temporal organization. Consider the sequence of time from paragraph to paragraph and within each paragraph. How does White's organizational pattern add to the essay's ideas?

Ideas for Writing

1. Write a paragraph in which you describe a favorite place—a room, a park, a street, a corner. Choose details that convey the place's special features and qualities. Organize your description spatially, moving from one direction to another.

2. Write an essay in which you describe a place that strongly impressed you in childhood, either positively or negatively. Choose details that make the reader feel the place and its atmosphere.

3. Write a paragraph in which you discuss White's language. What phrases most impressed you? What in them seemed special?

Emily Bronte
WUTHERING HEIGHTS
CHAPTER 1

Born on July 30, 1818, in Yorkshire, as the fifth child of the Reverend and Mrs. Patrick Bronte, Emily Bronte attended Roe Head School with her sister Charlotte (author of *Jane Eyre*). Bronte worked as a governess and studied in Brussels, hoping to open a school in Haworth, where the Bronte family lived. In 1846, Emily, Charlotte, and their sister Anne published a collection of their poems under the pseudonyms Currer, Ellis, and Acton Bell. Ellis Bell is the author named for the 1847 edition of *Wuthering Heights*. (In the same year Emily Bronte's sisters published novels too, Charlotte's *Jane Eyre* and Anne's *Agnes Grey*.) Emily Bronte died of consumption at the age of 30.

Although *Wuthering Heights* is in the form of a journal written by the narrator Mr. Lockwood, the novel provides more than personal thoughts, speculations, and fantasy. Here we read a history of a household society, strange certainly, but so vividly described as to occupy a permanent place in western literature. In this first chapter Bronte pays careful attention to details of place and of people's actions to create a clear picture of some of the characters who dominate the book.

1801—I have just returned from a visit to my landlord—the solitary neighbour that I shall be troubled with. This is certainly, a beautiful country! In all England, I do not believe that I could have fixed on a situation so completely removed from the stir of society. A perfect misanthropist's Heaven—and Mr. Heathcliff and I are such a suitable pair to divide the desolation between us. A capital fellow! He little imagined how my heart warmed towards him when I beheld his black eyes withdraw so suspiciously under their brows, as I rode up, and when his fingers sheltered themselves, with a jealous resolution, still further in his waistcoat, as I announced my name.

"Mr. Heathcliff?" I said.

A nod was the answer.

"Mr. Lockwood your new tenant, sir—I do myself the honour of calling as soon as possible, after my arrival, to express the hope that I

have not inconvenienced you by my perseverance in soliciting the occupation of Thrushcross Grange: I heard, yesterday, you had had some
thoughts—''

''Thrushcross Grange is my own, sir,'' he interrupted wincing, ''I
should not allow any one to inconvenience me, if I could hinder it—walk
in!''

The ''walk in,'' was uttered with closed teeth and expressed the
sentiment, ''Go to the Deuce!'' even the gate over which he leant man-
ifested no sympathizing movement to the words; and I think that circumstance determined me to accept the invitation: I felt interested in a man
who seemed more exaggeratedly reserved than myself.

When he saw my horse's breast fairly pushing the barrier, he did pull
out his hand to unchain it, and then sullenly preceded me up the
causeway, calling, as we entered the court:

''Joseph, take Mr. Lockwood's horse; and bring up some wine.''

''Here we have the whole establishment of domestics, I suppose,'' was
the reflection, suggested by this compound order. ''No wonder the grass
grows up between the flags, and cattle are the only hedge-cutters.''

Joseph was an elderly, nay, an old man, very old, perhaps, though hale
and sinewy.

''The Lord help us!'' he soliloquised in an undertone of peevish dis-
pleasure, while relieving me of my horse: looking, meantime, in my face
so sourly that I charitably conjectured he must have need of divine aid to
digest his dinner, and his pious ejaculation had no reference to my
unexpected advent.

Wuthering Heights is the name of Mr. Heathcliff's dwelling. ''Wuthering'' being a significant provincial adjective, descriptive of the atmospheric tumult to which its station is exposed, in stormy weather. Pure,
bracing ventilation they must have up there, at all times, indeed: one may
guess the power of the north wind, blowing over the edge, by the excessive slant of a few, stunted firs at the end of the house; and by a range of
gaunt thorns all stretching their limbs one way, as if craving alms of the
sun. Happily, the architect had foresight to build it strong: the narrow
windows are deeply set in the wall; and the corners defended with large
jutting stones.

Before passing the threshold, I paused to admire a quantity of grotesque carving lavished over the front, and especially about the principal
door, above which, among a wilderness of crumbling griffins, and shame-
less little boys, I detected the date ''1500,'' and the name ''Hareton
Earnshaw.'' I would have made a few comments, and requested a short
history of the place, from the surly owner, but his attitude at the door
appeared to demand my speedy entrance, or complete departure, and I
had no desire to aggravate his impatience, previous to inspecting the
penetralium.

One step brought us into the family sitting-room, without any introductory lobby, or passage: they call it here "the house" preeminently. It includes kitchen, and parlor, generally, but I believe at Wuthering Heights, the kitchen is forced to retreat altogether, into another quarter, at least I distinguished a chatter of tongues, and a clatter of culinary utensils, deep within; and I observed no signs of roasting, boiling, or baking, about the huge fire-place; nor any glitter of copper saucepans and tin cullenders on the walls. One end, indeed, reflected splendidly both light and heat, from ranks of immense pewter dishes; interspersed with silver jugs, and tankards, towering row after row, in a vast oak dresser, to the very roof. The latter had never been under-drawn, its entire anatomy lay bare to an inquiring eye, except where a frame of wood laden with oatcakes, and clusters of legs of beef, mutton and ham, concealed it. Above the chimney were sundry villanous old guns, and a couple of horse-pistols, and, by way of ornament, three gaudily painted canisters disposed along its ledge. The floor was of smooth, white stone: the chairs, high-backed, primitive structures, painted green: one or two heavy black ones lurking in the shade. In an arch, under the dresser, reposed a huge, liver-coloured bitch pointer surrounded by a swarm of squealing puppies, and other dogs, haunted other recesses.

The apartment, and furniture would have been nothing extraordinary as belonging to a homely, northern farmer with a stubborn countenance, and stalwart limbs, set out to advantage in knee-breeches, and gaiters. Such an individual, seated in his arm-chair, his mug of ale frothing on the round table before him, is to be seen in any circuit of five or six miles among these hills, if you go at the right time, after dinner. But, Mr. Heathcliff forms a singular contrast to his abode and style of living. He is a dark skinned gypsy, in aspect, in dress, and manners, a gentleman, that is, as much a gentleman as many a country squire: rather slovenly, perhaps, yet not looking amiss, with his negligence, because he has an erect and handsome figure—and rather morose—possibly, some people might suspect him of a degree of under-bred pride—I have a sympathetic chord within that tells me it is nothing of the sort; I know, by instinct, his reserve springs from an aversion to showy displays of feeling—to manifestations of mutual kindliness. He'll love and hate, equally under cover, and esteem it a species of impertinence, to be loved or hated again—No, I'm running on too fast—I bestow my own attributes over liberally on him. Mr. Heathcliff may have entirely dissimilar reasons for keeping his hand out of the way, when he meets a would be acquaintance, to those which actuate me. Let me hope my constitution is almost peculiar: my dear mother used to say I should never have a comfortable home, and only last summer, I proved myself perfectly unworthy of one.

While enjoying a month of fine weather at the sea-coast, I was thrown into the company of a most fascinating creature, a real goddess, in my eyes, as long as she took no notice of me. I "never told my love" vocally; still, if looks have language, the merest idiot might have guessed I was over head and ears: she understood me, at last, and looked a return—the sweetest of all imaginable looks—and what did I do? I confess it with shame—shrunk icily into myself, like a snail, at every glance retired colder and farther; till, finally, the poor innocent was led to doubt her own senses, and, overwhelmed with confusion at her supposed mistake, persuaded her mamma to decamp.

By this curious turn of disposition I have gained the reputation of deliberate heartlessness, how undeserved, I alone can appreciate.

I took a seat at the end of the hearthstone opposite that towards which my landlord advanced, and filled up an interval of silence by attempting to caress the canine mother, who had left her nursery, and was sneaking wolfishly to the back of my legs, her lip curled up, and her white teeth watering for a snatch.

My caress provoked a long, guttural gnarl.

"You'd better let the dog alone," growled Mr. Heathcliff, in unison, checking fiercer demonstrations with a punch of his foot. "She's not accustomed to be spoiled—not kept for a pet."

Then, striding to a side-door, he shouted again.

"Joseph!"

Joseph mumbled indistinctly in the depths of the cellar; but, gave no intimation of ascending; so, his master dived down to him, leaving me *vis-à-vis* the ruffianly bitch, and a pair of grim, shaggy sheep dogs, who shared with her a jealous guardianship over all my movements.

Not anxious to come in contact with their fangs, I sat still—but, imagining they would scarcely understand tacit insults, I unfortunately indulged in winking and making faces at the trio, and some turn of my physiognomy so irritated madam, that she suddenly broke into a fury, and leapt on my knees. I flung her back, and hastened to interpose the table between us. This proceeding roused the whole hive. Half-a-dozen four-footed fiends, of various sizes, and ages, issued from hidden dens to the common centre. I felt my heels, and coat-laps peculiar subjects of assault; and, parrying off the larger combatants, as effectually as I could, with the poker, I was constrained to demand, aloud, assistance from some of the household, in re-establishing peace.

Mr. Heathcliff and his man climbed the cellar steps with vexatious phlegm. I don't think they moved one second faster than usual, though the hearth was an absolute tempest of worrying and yelping.

Happily, an inhabitant of the kitchen made more dispatch; a lusty dame, with tucked up gown, bare arms, and fire-flushed cheeks, rushed into the midst of us flourishing a fryingpan; and used that weapon, and her tongue to such purpose, that the storm subsided magically, and she only remained, heaving like a sea after a high wind, when her master entered on the scene.

"What the devil is the matter?" he asked, eyeing me in a manner that I could ill endure after this inhospitable treatment.

"What the devil, indeed!" I muttered. "The herd of possessed swine could have had no worse spirits in them than those animals of yours, sir. You might as well leave a stranger with a brood of tigers!"

"They wont meddle with persons who touch nothing," he remarked, putting the bottle before me, and restoring the displaced table. "The dogs do right to be vigilant. Take a glass of wine?"

"No, thank you."

"Not bitten, are you?"

"If I had been, I would have set my signet on the biter."

Heathcliff's countenance relaxed into a grin.

"Come, come," he said, "you are flurried, Mr. Lockwood. Here take a little wine. Guests are so exceedingly rare in this house that I and my dogs, I am willing to own, hardly know how to receive them. Your health, sir!"

I bowed and returned the pledge; beginning to perceive that it would be foolish to sit sulking for the misbehaviour of a pack of curs: besides, I felt loath to yield the fellow further amusement, at my expense; since his humour took that turn.

He—probably swayed by prudential considerations of the folly of offending a good tenant—relaxed, a little, in the laconic style of chipping of his pronouns, and auxiliary verbs; and introduced, what he supposed would be a subject of interest to me, a discourse on the advantages and disadvantages of my present place of retirement.

I found him very intelligent on the topics we touched; and, before I went home, I was encouraged so far as to volunteer another visit, to-morrow.

He evidently wished no repetition of my intrusion. I shall go, notwithstanding. It is astonishing how sociable I feel myself compared with him.

Meaning and Idea

1. Why has Lockwood chosen to live in Thrushcross Grange? Why has he come to visit Heathcliff? What impression does Bronte give us of Heathcliff? Of Joseph? Describe each of these men in your own words.

2. What impression does Bronte create of the narrator Lockwood? Why does he see himself as having the reputation of "deliberate heartlessness"? How do Lockwood and Heathcliff compare in temperament? How does Lockwood feel towards Heathcliff? What is the meaning of the last sentence?

3. Describe the outside and the family sitting room of "Wuthering Heights," Heathcliff's dwelling. Why does Lockwood not ask for a history of the place? Why is "Wuthering Heights" an appropriate name for it?

Language, Form, Structure

1. What is Bronte's purpose in the first chapter of her novel *Wuthering Heights*? In an essay you might expect a thesis to state the main idea of the piece, but not in a novel, certainly. What, however, is the point of this chapter? Write a sentence in which you state the main idea as precisely as you can.

2. Bronte provides a series of outstanding descriptions here—of the house, of Heathcliff and Joseph, of the dogs, of the "lusty dame" from the kitchen. What details stand out particularly? Where does Bronte appeal to the senses of sight, sound, and touch? What does she achieve by using specific words like *jugs* and *tankards* (instead of *vessels*, say) or *beef, mutton,* and *ham* (instead of *meat*)? In the description of the dwelling, what impression do the details of the scene seem to be creating?

3. Make a list of images that describe actions in this chapter. How appropriate are the words Bronte selects to the impressions she wishes us to have of the actors? How does the sentence that first describes Heathcliff's actions (paragraph 1, sentence 6) serve to establish his character? What is the effect of an image like "Mr. Heathcliff and his man climbed the cellar steps with vexatious phlegm"? How does the spoken conversation of the men help establish their character?

4. Reread the paragraph in which the dogs assault Lockwood. Which sensory details make their actions particularly clear and vivid to you? Why does Bronte dwell at such length on the dogs?

5. Use a dictionary to check meanings for any of the following words that you do not know: misanthrope, desolation, capital (paragraph 1); perseverance (4); sullenly (7); hale, sinewy (10); soliloquised, peevish, conjectured, pious, ejaculation (11); griffins, penetralium (13); cullenders, sundry (14); stalwart, singular, slovenly, morose, aversion, impertinence (15); decamp (16); *vis-a-vis,* ruffianly (23); physiognomy (24); vexatious phlegm (25); signet (32); prudential (36).

Ideas for Writing

1. Write a paragraph description of a room in your house or in some other house that you know well. Concentrate on rich sensory details of color, action, sound, smell, and touch.

2. Write an essay in which you describe someone in the setting of his or her home or apartment. Use sharp sensory details to paint a picture of the person and the scene. Try to make the details revolve about a single impression you want to give of the person or place. Perhaps, like Bronte, you might wish to show a kind of hostile moroseness, or cheerfulness, neatness, friendliness, indifference, and so on.

3. Write a paragraph in which you comment on Bronte's skills as a writer of description. How effective are the images she creates? What patterns, if any, do you discover?

Amy Lowell
WIND AND SILVER

Amy Lowell (1874–1925) was a leader among the group of British and American poets called *imagists* in the early part of this century. Lowell's imagist poetry concentrated on clear, hard, specific imagery as a reaction against the sentimentality that pervaded the previous century's poetry. Others in this group included Ezra Pound, Hilda Doolittle, and Richard Addington. Born in Brookline, Massachusetts, Lowell joined the imagists in England in 1913. She was the sister of Abbott Lawrence Lowell, a progressive president of Harvard University, and Percival Lowell, the discoverer of the planet Pluto. Lowell's volume of poems *What's O'Clock* won the Pulitzer Prize in 1925.

With almost haiku-like simplicity, Amy Lowell juxtaposes the particular against the universal. The poem is a simple statement, well within Lowell's imagist roots, which leaves the reader with a lovely picture of glittering ponds.

*G*reatly shining,
The Autumn moon floats in the thin sky;
And the fish-ponds shake their backs and flash their dragon
    scales
As she passes over them.

Meaning and Idea

1. Who or what is the "she" in the last line? Why "she" instead of "he"? To whom or to what does the pronoun *their* refer in line 3?

2. What is the weather of this poem? How do you know from the sparse description?

3. Describe the scene and action of this short poem in plain prose, as objectively as possible.

4. How does the title of the poem supplement the description?

Language, Form, Structure

1. What is Lowell's *purpose* in this poem? For what reasons do you think she chose to express that purpose in such a short poem? Do you think she was successful?

2. In line 3, Lowell relies on metaphoric description. Explain the meaning of the line in your own words. How is using metaphor here effective for the poem's impact? Why? Identify any other metaphors in the poem.

3. With what feeling does the poem leave you? To which of the reader's senses does it most appeal? Refer to specific elements of the poem to support your opinion.

4. What is the connection between the word *shining* in line 1 and *flash* in line 3? Is it an effective connection? How does it relate to the descriptive scene?

5. What is the significance of the title?

Ideas For Writing

1. The Japanese poem form of haiku makes use, like Lowell does, of extreme economy of description to create a dominant impression. Choose a limited scene to describe—perhaps a street corner or your favorite "hiding place"—and describe it two times: first, in an objectively detailed paragraph; second, in a three- to five-line impressionistic poem which relies on metaphoric description.

2. Imagine Lowell's scene as clearly as possible. Then, in either a short poem or a paragraph, describe the same scene during a summer day. Try to parallel her descriptive movement.

3. In writing a poem of an autumn night pond scene, Lowell selected just a few elements of the scene to describe. In a few paragraphs, discuss your response to the brevity and extreme selectivity of this poem. What is gained by it? What is lost by it? Does it represent any judgment about the scene on Lowell's part? Does it leave you feeling fulfilled or wanting more? Why?

Percy Bysshe Shelley
OZYMANDIAS

Percy Bysshe Shelley (1792–1822) is considered among the greatest poets of the romantic era. He was a sensitive nonconformist who as a boy at Eton was nicknamed "Mad Shelley." Later, he was dismissed from Oxford for writing *The Necessity of Atheism.* He was, however, a quiet and modest man. In 1816, he married Mary Gordon, who the next year wrote the classic horror story *Frankenstein.* In 1822, Shelley drowned in a boating accident, and in the romantic fashion, his body was burned on the beach by his friends.

"Ozymandias" displays Shelley's attraction to mythological legend as it combines with his self-proclaimed abhorrence of "religious, political, and domestic oppression." In this poem, he demonstrates the irony of tyrannical bravura while leaving us on a typically romantic landscape.

I met a traveller from an antique land   1
Who said: Two vast and trunkless legs of stone
Stand in the desert . . . Near them, on the sand,
Half sunk, a shattered visage lies, whose frown,
And wrinkled lip, and sneer of cold command,   5
Tell that its sculptor well those passions read
Which yet survive, stamped on these lifeless things,
The hand that mocked them, and the heart that fed:
And on the pedestal these words appear:
"My name is Ozymandias, king of kings: 10
Look on my works, ye Mighty, and despair!"
Nothing beside remains. Round the decay
Of that colossal wreck, boundless and bare
The lone and level sands stretch far away.

Meaning and Idea

1. Ozymandias is the Greek name for the Egyptian pharaoh Ramses II. According to the description in the poem, what physical characteristics do you know about Ozymandias? From what lines do you learn this? What kind of attitude did he project, according to Shelley's description?

2. What is the "antique land" mentioned here? What, exactly, does the traveller describe to the speaker of this poem?

3. Summarize, in your own words, the statement that appears on the pedestal.

Language, Form, Structure

1. *Irony* refers to the disparity between what is said and what is meant (verbal irony) or what should be and what actually is (situational irony). What is the main situational irony of this poem? What sort of verbal irony exists here as well?

2. Why is *lifeless* a particularly good descriptive word in line 8? Aside from its literal meaning for the poem, what ironic or connotative meanings does it carry here? What are the possible meanings for the word *mocked* in line 9?

3. What are the uses of the verb *survive* in line 7? How does it refer to the phrase that precedes it? How does it refer to the verbal constructions which follow it?

4. What are the special meanings in this poem for the following words: vast (line 2); visage (4); sneer (5); read (6); mocked (8); pedestal (9); despair (11); boundless (13).

Ideas for Writing

1. Choose a situation which you expected to turn out one way but which in fact turned out in some other way. Describe in detail your expectations; then, describe the actual outcome.

2. Write a description of some place or some thing you have seen which was either decayed, eroded, or destroyed. Concentrate on visual details.

3. Write a paragraph in which you discuss the effectiveness of Shelley's use of irony in this poem. How do you think it enhanced or detracted from the impact of the poem?

Ursula K. Le Guin
THE ONES WHO WALK AWAY
FROM OMELAS

Ursula K. Le Guin was born in Berkeley, California, in 1929. She is a novelist, an essayist, and a writer of children's books, though she is most successful as a science fiction writer. She has won the Hugo Award, the Science Fiction of America Nebula Award, a Newbury Silver Medal, and the National Book Award. Her best known works include *The Left Hand of Darkness* (1969), *The Tombs of Atuan* (1971), *The Farthest Shore* (1972), *The Dispossessed* (1974), *Malafrena* (1979), and *The Compass Rose* (1982).

As in the best of science fiction, Ursula K. Le Guin tells a story which has its roots in almost real possibilities. Omelas, as described by Le Guin, is a place that *almost* exists. (The name was suggested to her by spelling "Salem" backwards.) Through her exact and full detailing, she creates a place just one step past everyday reality.

With a clamor of bells that set the swallows soaring, the Festival of Summer came to the city Omelas, bright-towered by the sea. The rigging of the boats in harbor sparkled with flags. In the streets between houses with red roofs and painted walls, between old moss-grown gardens and under avenues of trees, past great parks and public buildings, processions moved. Some were decorous: old people in long stiff robes of mauve and gray, grave master workmen, quiet, merry women carrying their babies and chatting as they walked. In other streets the music beat faster, a shimmering of gong and tambourine, and the people went dancing, the procession was a dance. Children dodged in and out, their high calls rising like the swallows' crossing flights over the music and the singing. All the processions wound toward the north side of the city, where on the great water-meadow called the Green Fields boys and girls, naked in the bright air, with mudstained feet and ankles and long, lithe arms, exercised their restive horses before the race. The horses wore no gear at all but a halter without a bit. Their manes were braided with streamers of silver, gold, and green. They blew out their nostrils and pranced and boasted to one another; they were vastly excited, the horse being the only animal who has adopted our ceremonies as his own. Far off to the north and west the mountains stood up half-encircling Omelas on her bay. The air of morning was so clear that the snow still crowning the Eighteen Peaks burned with white-gold fire across the miles of sunlit air, under the dark blue of the sky. There was just enough wind to make the banners that marked the race course snap and flutter now and then. In the silence of the broad green meadows one could hear the music winding through the city streets, farther and nearer and ever approaching, a cheerful faint sweetness of the air that from time to time trembled and gathered together and broke out into the great joyous clanging of the bells.

Joyous! How is one to tell about joy? How describe the citizens of Omelas?

They were not simple folk, you see, though they were happy. But we do not say the words of cheer much any more. All smiles have become archaic. Given a description such as this one tends to make certain assumptions. Given a description such as this one tends to look next for the King, mounted on a splendid stallion and surrounded by his noble knights, or perhaps in a golden litter borne by great-muscled slaves. But there was no king. They did not use swords, or keep slaves. They were not barbarians. I do not know the rules and laws of their society, but I suspect that they were singularly few. As they did without monarchy and slavery, so they also got on without the stock exchange, the advertisement, the secret police, and the bomb. Yet I repeat that these were not simple folk, not dulcet shepherds, noble savages, bland utopians. They were not less complex than we. The trouble is that we have a bad habit, encouraged by pedants and sophisticates, of considering happiness as something rather stupid. Only pain is intellectual, only evil interesting. This is the treason of the artist: a refusal to admit the banality of evil and the terrible boredom of pain. If you can't lick 'em, join 'em. If it hurts, repeat it. But to praise despair is to condemn delight, to embrace violence is to lose hold of everything else. We have almost lost hold; we can no longer describe a happy man, nor make any celebration of joy. How can I tell you about the people of Omelas? They were not naive and happy children—though their children were, in fact, happy. They were mature, intelligent, passionate adults whose lives were not wretched. O miracle! But I wish I could describe it better. I wish I could convince you. Omelas sounds in my words like a city in a fairytale, long ago and far away, once upon a time. Perhaps it would be best if you imagined it as your own fancy bids, assuming it will rise to the occasion, for certainly I cannot suit you all. For instance, how about technology? I think that there would be no cars or helicopters in and above the streets; this follows from the fact that the people of Omelas are happy people. Happiness is based on a just discrimination of what is necessary, what is neither necessary nor destructive, and what is destructive. In the middle category, however—that

of the unnecessary but undestructive, that of comfort, luxury, exuberance, etc.—they could perfectly well have central heating, subway trains,
washing machines, and all kinds of marvelous devices not yet invented
here, floating lightsources, fuelless power, a cure for the common cold.
Or they could have none of that: it doesn't matter. As you like it. I incline
to think that people from towns up and down the coast have been coming
in to Omelas during the last days before the Festival on very fast little
trains and doubledecked trams, and that the train station of Omelas is
actually the handsomest building in town, though plainer than the magnificent Farmers Market. But even granted trains, I fear that Omelas so far
strikes some of you as goody-goody. Smiles, bells, parades, horses, bleh.
If so, please add an orgy. If an orgy would help, don't hesitate. Let us not,
however, have temples from which issue beautiful nude priests and
priestesses already half in ecstasy and ready to copulate with whosoever,
man or woman, lover or stranger, desires union with the deep godhead of
the blood, although that was my first idea. But really it would be better
not to have any temples in Omelas—at least, not manned temples. Religion yes, clergy no. Surely the beautiful nudes can just wander about,
offering themselves like divine soufflés to the hunger of the needy and the
rapture of the flesh. Let them join the processions. Let tambourines be
struck above the copulations, and the glory of desire be proclaimed upon
the gongs, and (a not unimportant point) let the offspring of these delightful rituals be beloved and looked after by all. One thing I know there is
none of in Omelas is guilt. But what else should there be? I thought at first
there were no drugs, but that is puritanical. For those who like it, the faint
insistent sweetness of *drooz* may perfume the ways of the city, *drooz*
which first brings a great lightness and brilliance to the mind and limbs,
and then after some hours a dreamy languor, and wonderful visions at last
of the very arcana and inmost secrets of the Universe, as well as exciting
the pleasure of sex beyond all belief; and it is not habit-forming. For more
modest tastes I think there ought to be beer. What else, what else belongs
in the joyous city? The sense of victory, surely, the celebration of courage. But as we did without clergy, let us do without soldiers. The joy built
upon successful slaughter is not the right kind of joy; it will not do; it is
fearful and it is trivial. A boundless and generous contentment, a magnanimous triumph felt not against some outer enemy but in communion with
the finest and fairest in the souls of all men everywhere and the splendor
of the world's summer: this is what swells the hearts of the people of
Omelas, and the victory they celebrate is that of life. I really don't think
many of them need to take *drooz*.

Most of the processions have reached the Green Fields by now. A
marvelous smell of cooking goes forth from the red and blue tents of the
provisioners. The faces of small children are amiably sticky; in the benign
gray beard of a man a couple of crumbs of rich pastry are entangled. The

youths and girls have mounted their horses and are beginning to group around the starting line of the course. An old woman, small, fat, and laughing, is passing out flowers from a basket, and tall young men wear her flowers in their shining hair. A child of nine or ten sits at the edge of the crowd, alone, playing on a wooden flute. People pause to listen, and they smile, but they do not speak to him, for he never ceases playing and never sees them, his dark eyes wholly rapt in the sweet, thin magic of the tune.

He finishes, and slowly lowers his hands holding the wooden flute.

As if that little private silence were the signal, all at once a trumpet sounds from the pavilion near the starting line: imperious, melancholy, piercing. The horses rear on their slender legs, and some of them neigh in answer. Sober-faced, the young riders stroke the horses' necks and soothe them, whispering, "Quiet, quiet, there my beauty, my hope . . ." They begin to form in rank along the starting line. The crowds along the race course are like a field of grass and flowers in the wind. The Festival of Summer has begun.

Do you believe? Do you accept the festival, the city, the joy? No? Then let me describe one more thing.

In a basement under one of the beautiful buildings of Omelas, or perhaps in the cellar of one of its spacious private homes, there is a room. It has one locked door, and no window. A little light seeps in dustily between cracks in the boards, secondhand from a cobwebbed window somewhere across the cellar. In one corner of the little room a couple of mops, with stiff, clotted, foul-smelling heads, stand near a rusty bucket. The floor is dirt, a little damp to the touch, as cellar dirt usually is. The room is about three paces long and two wide: a mere broom closet or disused toolroom. In the room a child is sitting. It might be a boy or a girl. It looks about six, but actually is nearly ten. It is feebleminded. Perhaps it was born defective, or perhaps it has become imbecile through fear, malnutrition, and neglect. It picks its nose and occasionally fumbles vaguely with its toes or genitals, as it sits hunched in the corner farthest from the bucket and the two mops. It is afraid of the mops. It finds them horrible. It shuts its eyes, but it knows the mops are still standing there; and the door is locked; and nobody will come. The door is always locked, and nobody ever comes, except that sometimes—the child has no under-standing of time or interval—sometimes the door rattles terribly and opens, and a person, or several people, are there. One of them may come in and kick the child to make it stand up. The others never come close, but peer in at it with frightened, disgusted eyes. The food bowl and the water jug are hastily filled, the door is locked, the eyes disappear. The people at the door never say anything, but the child, who has not always lived in the toolroom, and can remember sunlight and its mother's voice, sometimes speaks, "I will be good," it says. "Please let me out. I will be good!"

They never answer. The child used to scream for help at night, and cry a good deal, but now it only makes a kind of whining, "eh-haa, eh-haa," and it speaks less and less often. It is so thin there are no calves to its legs; its belly protrudes; it lives on a half-bowl of cornmeal and grease a day. It is naked. Its buttocks and thighs are a mass of festered sores, as it sits in its own excrement continually.

They all know it is there, all the people of Omelas. Some of them have come to see it, others are content merely to know it is there. They all know that it has to be there. Some of them understand why, and some do not, but they all understand that their happiness, the beauty of their city, the tenderness of their friendships, the health of their children, the wisdom of their scholars, the skill of their makers, even the abundance of their harvest and the kindly weathers of their skies, depend wholly on this child's abominable misery.

This is usually explained to children when they are between eight and twelve, whenever they seem capable of understanding; and most of those who come to see the child are young people, though often enough an adult comes, or comes back, to see the child. No matter how well the matter has been explained to them, these young spectators are always shocked and sickened at the sight. They feel disgust, which they had thought themselves superior to. They feel anger, outrage, impotence, despite all the explanations. They would like to do something for the child. But there is nothing they can do. If the child were brought up into the sunlight out of that vile place, if it were cleaned and fed and comforted, that would be a good thing, indeed; but if it were done, in that day and hour all the prosperity and beauty and delight of Omelas would wither and be destroyed. Those are the terms. To exchange all the goodness and grace of every life in Omelas for that single, small improvement: to throw away the happiness of thousands for the chance of the happiness of one: that would be to let guilt within the walls indeed.

The terms are strict and absolute; there may not even be a kind word spoken to the child.

Often the young people go home in tears, or in a tearless rage, when they have seen the child and faced this terrible paradox. They may brood over it for weeks or years. But as time goes on they begin to realize that even if the child could be released, it would not get much good of its freedom: a vague pleasure of warmth and food, no doubt, but little more. It is too degraded and imbecile to know any real joy. It has been afraid too long ever to be free of fear. Its habits are too uncouth for it to respond to humane treatment. Indeed after so long it would probably be wretched without walls about it to protect it, and darkness for its eyes, and its own excrement to sit in. Their tears at the bitter injustice dry when they begin to perceive the terrible justice of reality, and to accept it. Yet it is their tears and anger, the trying of their generosity and the acceptance of their helplessness, which are perhaps the true source of the splendor of their lives. Theirs is no vapid, irresponsible happiness. They know that they, like the child, are not free. They know compassion. It is the existence of the child, and their knowledge of its existence, that makes possible the nobility of their architecture, the poignancy of their music, the profundity of their science. It is because of the child that they are so gentle with children. They know that if the wretched one were not there sniveling in the dark, the other one, the flute player, could make no joyful music as the young riders line up in their beauty for the race in the sunlight of the first morning of summer.

Now do you believe in them? Are they not more credible? But there is one more thing to tell, and this is quite incredible.

At times one of the adolescent girls or boys who go to see the child does not go home to weep or rage, does not, in fact, go home at all. Sometimes also a man or woman much older falls silent for a day or two, and then leaves home. These people go out into the street, and walk down the street alone. They keep walking, and walk straight out of the city of Omelas, through the beautiful gates. They keep walking across the farmlands of Omelas. Each one goes alone, youth or girl, man or woman. Night falls; the traveler must pass down village streets, between the houses with yellow-lit windows, and on out into the darkness of the fields. Each alone, they go west or north, toward the mountains. They go on. They leave Omelas, they walk ahead into the darkness, and they do not come back. The place they go toward is a place even less imaginable to most of us than the city of happiness. I cannot describe it at all. It is possible that it does not exist. But they seem to know where they are going, the ones who walk away from Omelas.

Meaning and Idea

1. What is the physical setting of Omelas? What season is it in the story? What event is about to take place?

2. Is the narrator of this story from Omelas? How do you know? Select and state in your own words at least two differences between the life of the narrator and the life of the people of Omelas.

3. What is the "bad habit" which the narrator attributes to him/herself and the reader? Summarize it in your own words.

4. For the people of Omelas, what is the value of the neglected child who is kept in the small room? What is the reaction of most people to the child? What do you suppose is the reaction of those who see the child and then "walk away from Omelas"?

5. What do you call a person who serves the purpose served by the child in Omelas?

Language, Form, Structure

1. This story is rich in sensory descriptions and images. For each of the five senses, choose three sensory images which you feel are particularly effective. How do these sensory images enhance the telling of the story?

2. What is the intended audience for this story? How does the narrator use description to involve the audience in the development of the story? Mention at least three such attempts to make the reader participate in the telling of the story.

3. Throughout the story, the narrator uses conditional constructions such as "could be," "ought to be," and so on. Select some instances of such usage and tell what effect they have on the story's development.

4. List and define five new vocabulary words from this story.

Ideas for Writing

1. In a short essay, describe your ideal community. What physical, cultural, social, religious, or political aspects would it include? Be sure to be as detailed as possible in your description of this ideal place.

2. Describe as though you were writing to a foreigner the events of a recent festival or celebration you attended.

3. Describe your feelings as you read and finished this story. Did they change at any points? Did you imagine Omelas to be a real place? Why or why not? How did the quality of the description influence your feelings and reactions?

Alfred Kazin
THE KITCHEN

Alfred Kazin is a literary and social critic who was born in Brooklyn, New York, in 1915. His studies on American literature include *On Native Grounds* (1942), *Contemporaries* (1962), and *Bright Book of Life* (1973). His various volumes of autobiography have provided a valuable social history, particularly of life among Jewish immigrants to this country at the beginning of the century. The most recent, and perhaps well-known of these volumes is *New York Jew,* published in 1978.

In this touching selection from his 1951 autobiographical work *A Walker in the City,* Alfred Kazin uses precise visual images to recapture "the aliveness of the moment" in his childhood. Through his intimate description of just one room, Kazin evokes all the people and places of the Jewish immigrant section of Brownsville, Brooklyn, as they appeared years ago.

*I*n Brownsville tenements the kitchen is always the largest room and the center of the household. As a child I felt that we lived in a kitchen to which four other rooms were annexed. My mother, a "home" dressmaker, had her workshop in the kitchen. She told me once that she had begun dressmaking in Poland at thirteen; as far back as I can remember, she was always making dresses for the local women. She had an innate sense of design, a quick eye for all the subtleties in the latest fashions, even when she despised them, and great boldness. For three or four dollars she would study the fashion magazines with a customer, go with the customer to the remnants store on Belmont Avenue to pick out the material, argue the owner down—all remnants stores, for some reason, were supposed to be shady, as if the owners dealt in stolen goods—and then for days would patiently fit and baste and sew and fit again. Our apartment was always full of women in their housedresses sitting around the kitchen table waiting for a fitting. My little bedroom next to the kitchen was the fitting room. The sewing machine, an old nut-brown Singer with golden scrolls painted along the black arm and engraved along the two tiers of little drawers massed with needles and thread on each side of the treadle, stood next to the window and the great coalblack stove which up to my last year in college was our main source of heat. By December the two outer bedrooms were closed off, and used to chill bottles of milk and cream, cold borscht and jellied calves' feet.

The kitchen held our lives together. My mother worked in it all day long, we ate in it almost all meals except the Passover *seder,* I did my homework and first writing at the kitchen table, and in winter I often had a bed made up for me on three kitchen chairs near the stove. On the wall just over the table hung a long horizontal mirror that sloped to a ship's prow at each end and was lined in cherry wood. It took up the whole wall, and drew every object in the kitchen to itself. The walls were a fiercely stippled white-wash, so often rewhitened by my father in slack seasons that the paint looked as if it had been squeezed and cracked into the walls. A large electric bulb hung down the center of the kitchen at the end of a chain that had been hooked into the ceiling; the old gas ring and key still jutted out of the wall like antlers. In the corner next to the toilet was the sink at which we washed, and the square tub in which my mother did our clothes. Above it, tacked to the shelf on which were pleasantly ranged square, blue-bordered white sugar and spice jars, hung calendars from the Public National Bank on Pitkin Avenue and the Minsker Progressive Branch of the Workman's Circle; receipts for the payment of insurance premiums, and household bills on a spindle; two little boxes engraved with Hebrew letters. One of these was for the poor, the other to buy back the Land of Israel. Each spring a bearded little man would suddenly appear in our kitchen, salute us with a hurried Hebrew blessing, empty the boxes (sometimes with a sidelong look of disdain if they were not full), hurriedly bless us again for remembering our less fortunate Jewish brothers and sisters, and so take his departure until the next spring, after vainly trying to persuade my mother to take still another box. We did occasionally remember to drop coins in the boxes, but this was usually only on the dreaded morning of "mid-terms" and final examinations, because my mother thought it would bring me luck. She was extremely superstitious, but embarrassed about it, and always laughed at herself whenever, on the morning of an examination, she counseled me to leave the house on my right foot. "I know it's silly," her smile seemed to say, "but what harm can it do? It may calm God down."

The kitchen gave a special character to our lives; my mother's character. All my memories of that kitchen are dominated by the nearness of my mother sitting all day long at her sewing machine, by the clacking of the treadle against the linoleum floor, by the patient twist of her right shoulder as she automatically pushed at the wheel with one hand or lifted the foot to free the needle where it had got stuck in a thick piece of material. The kitchen was her life. Year by year, as I began to take in her fantastic capacity for labor and her anxious zeal, I realized it was ourselves she kept stitched together. I can never remember a time when she was not working. She worked because the law of her life was work, work and anxiety; she worked because she would have found life meaningless without work. She read almost no English; she could read the Yiddish paper, but never felt she had time to. We were always talking of a time when I would teach her how to read, but somehow there was never time. When I awoke in the morning she was already at her machine, or in the great morning crowd of housewives at the grocery getting fresh rolls for breakfast. When I returned from school she was at her machine, or conferring over *McCall's* with some neighborhood woman who had come in pointing hopefully to an illustration—"Mrs. Kazin! Mrs. Kazin! Make me a dress like it shows here in the picture!" When my father came home from work she had somehow mysteriously interrupted herself to make supper for us, and the dishes cleared and washed, was back at her machine. When I went to bed at night, often she was still there, pounding away at the treadle, hunched over the wheel, her hands steering a piece of gauze under the needle with a finesse that always contrasted sharply with her swollen hands and broken nails. Her left hand had been pierced through when as a girl she had worked in the infamous Triangle Shirtwaist Factory on the East Side. A needle had gone straight through the palm, severing a large vein. They had sewn it up for her so clumsily that a tuft of flesh always lay folded over the palm.

The kitchen was the great machine that set our lives running; it whirred down a little only on Saturdays and holy days. From my mother's kitchen I gained my first picture of life as a white, overheated, starkly lit work-shop redolent with Jewish cooking, crowded with women in house-dresses, strewn with fashion magazines, patterns, dress material, spools of thread—and at whose center, so lashed to her machine that bolts of energy seemed to dance out of her hands and feet as she worked, my mother stamped the treadle hard against the floor, hard, hard, and silently, grimly at war, beat out the first rhythm of the world for me.

Every sound from the street roared and trembled at our windows—a mother feeding her child on the doorstep, the screech of the trolley cars on Rockaway Avenue, the eternal smash of a handball against the wall of our house, the clatter of *"der Italyéner"*'s cart packed with watermelons, the sing-song of the old-clothes men walking Chester Street, the cries *"Árbes! Árbes! Kinder! Kinder! Heyse gute árbes!"* All day long people streamed into our apartment as a matter of course—"customers," up-stairs neighbors, downstairs neighbors, women who would stop in for a half-hour's talk, salesmen, relatives, insurance agents. Usually they came in without ringing the bell—everyone knew my mother was always at home. I would hear the front door opening, the wind whistling through our front hall, and then some familiar face would appear in our kitchen with the same bland, matter-of-fact inquiring look: no need to stand on ceremony: my mother and her kitchen were available to everyone all day long.

At night the kitchen contracted around the blaze of light on the cloth, the patterns, the ironing board where the iron had burned a black border around the tear in the muslin cover; the finished dresses looked so frilly as they jostled on their wire hangers after all the work my mother had put into them. And then I would get that strangely ominous smell of tension from the dress fabrics and the burn in the cover of the ironing board—as if each piece of cloth and paper crushed with light under the naked bulb might suddenly go up in flames. Whenever I pass some small tailoring shop still lit up at night and see the owner hunched over his steam press; whenever in some poorer neighborhood of the city I see through a window some small crowded kitchen naked under the harsh light glittering in the ceiling, I still smell that fiery breath, that warning of imminent fire. I was always holding my breath. What I must have felt most about ourselves, I see now, was that we ourselves were like kindling—that all the hard-pressed pieces of ourselves and all the hard-used objects in that kitchen were like so many slivers of wood that might go up in flames if we came too near the white-blazing filaments in that naked bulb. Our tension itself was fire, we ourselves were forever burning—to live, to get down the foreboding in our souls, to make good.

Twice a year, on the anniversaries of her parents' deaths, my mother placed on top of the ice-box an ordinary kitchen glass packed with wax, the *yortsayt,* and lit the candle in it. Sitting at the kitchen table over my homework, I would look across the threshold to that mourning-glass, and sense that for my mother the distance from our kitchen to *der heym,* from life to death, was only a flame's length away. Poor as we were, it was not poverty that drove my mother so hard; it was loneliness—some endless bitter brooding over all those left behind, dead or dying or soon to die; a loneliness locked up in her kitchen that dwelt every day on the hazardousness of life and the nearness of death, but still kept struggling in the lock, trying to get us through by endless labor.

With us, life started up again only on the last shore. There seemed to be no middle ground between despair and the fury of our ambition. Whenever my mother spoke of her hopes for us, it was with such unbelievingness that the likes of us would ever come to anything, such abashed hope and readiness for pain, that I finally came to see in the flame burning on top of the ice-box death itself burning away the bones of poor Jews, burning out in us everything but courage, the blind resolution to live. In the light of that mourning-candle, there were ranged around me how many dead and dying—how many eras of pain, of exile, of dispersion, of cringing before the powers of this world!

It was always at dusk that my mother's loneliness came home most to me. Painfully alert to every shift in the light at her window, she would suddenly confess her fatigue by removing her pince-nez, and then wearily pushing aside the great mound of fabrics on her machine, would stare at the street as if to warm herself in the last of the sun. "How sad it is!" I once heard her say. "It grips me! It grips me!" Twilight was the bottommost part of the day, the chillest and loneliest time for her. Always so near to her moods, I knew she was fighting some deep inner dread, struggling against the returning tide of darkness along the streets that invariably assailed her heart with the same foreboding—Where? Where now? Where is the day taking us now?

Yet one good look at the street would revive her. I see her now, perched against the windowsill, with her face against the glass, her eyes almost asleep in enjoyment, just as she starts up with the guilty cry—"What foolishness is this in me!"—and goes to the stove to prepare supper for us: a moment, only a moment, watching the evening crowd of women gathering at the grocery for fresh bread and milk. But between my mother's pent-up face at the window and the winter sun dying in the fabrics—"Alfred, see how beautiful!"—she has drawn for me one single line of sentience.

Meaning and Idea

1. What is the setting for this description? What is the approximate time period described? How do you know? What is the nature of the environment in which Kazin grew up?

2. What does the kitchen look like? Why does the family have a sewing machine? Why is it in the kitchen?

3. Describe the mother's life. What did she do for a living at home? What did she do for a living earlier in her life? What is the Triangle Shirtwaist Factory? Why is it "infamous"?

4. What is the significance of the two boxes in the kitchen? What are the *yortsayt* candles for?

Language, Form, Structure

1. One of the necessities of good descriptive writing is to maintain a main focus for the description. This allows the writer to keep *unity* within the essay or story. Here, Kazin relies on two interrelated descriptive focuses. What are they? How do they relate to each other? What unifying transition word appears in the first sentence of nearly each paragraph?

2. *Allusions* in writing are figurative devices which make references to historical, cultural, or literary things. In this essay, Kazin makes a great deal of allusions, especially to Jewish culture, as in his allusion to the *seder* (the feast to celebrate the Jewish festival of Passover). List and explain at least five other allusions in this essay.

3. Kazin makes use of a number of words or expressions from the Yiddish language in this essay. List them all; then, if you do not know their meanings, write, relying on context clues, what you think the meanings are.

4. Kazin uses some extended images in this essay. Discuss how he uses many images of fire, burning, and light. Which does he use literally? Which metaphorically? How does he use sound imagery literally and metaphorically?

5. In your own words, explain Kazin's last sentence in the essay.

6. Write definitions for the following words: innate, baste (par. 1); stippled (2); zeal (3); redolent (4); ominous, imminent (6); dispersion (8); pince-nez (9); sentience (10).

Ideas for Writing

1. Describe the kitchen of your own childhood in as much detail as possible. If possible, try to link the physical description to a description of another family member.

2. Describe a person who you think feels great loneliness or despair. In your description, make use of the person's environment to help describe the nature of the person's emotions.

3. Kazin's essay is so full of description as to make the reader feel he or she has actually visited this kitchen and felt its many joys and sorrows. In a paragraph, discuss which description had the greatest emotional impact on you. What was that emotional effect? Why was it so strong?

Alfred, Lord Tennyson
THE EAGLE

Alfred, Lord Tennyson (1809–1892), along with Robert Browning, is considered the major poet of the early Victorian age. He was the son of a conservative clergyman and was educated at Cambridge where he early on dedicated himself to poetics. The publication in 1842 of his two-volume *Poems* established his early popularity, and by 1850 he could claim to be England's most popular poet. In that year, he was named Poet Laureate of England. Among his most noted works are his tribute to friendship, *In Memoriam* (1850), his patriotic "The Charge of the Light Brigade" (1854), and his Arthurian verse romance, *The Idylls of the King* (1859–1885).

"The Eagle" is typical of Tennyson's—and the early Victorians'—reliance on smooth, metrical constructions in an attempt to blend romanticism and realism in a way to take them away from pure emotionalism. Notice how, despite the grandeur of the description, the poem is emotionally quite controlled.

*H*e clasps the crag with crooked hands;   1
Close to the sun in lonely lands,
Ringed with the azure world, he stands.

The wrinkled sea beneath him crawls;
He watches from his mountain walls,   5
And like a thunderbolt he falls.

Meaning and Idea

1. What is the "azure world"? Who is the "he" in the poem?

2. Where is the eagle situated in this poem? What three descriptions in stanza one uphold this placement?

3. What does the eagle do at the end of the poem?

Language, Form, Structure

1. What is the effect of the patterning set up by ending stanza one with "he stands" and stanza two with "he falls"?

2. A *simile* is a figure of speech which compares two things with the use of the words *like* or *as*. A *metaphor* makes a descriptive comparison directly, without *like* or *as*. Where does Tennyson use simile in this poem? Where does he use metaphor?

3. *Personification* is the poetic technique of attributing human feelings or characteristics to inanimate objects or things in nature. Where in his description of the eagle does Tennyson rely on personification? What is its effect? How would the poem be different if he had used *she* or *it* instead of *he* to describe the eagle?

4. Write synonyms for the following words: crag (1); ringed, azure (3).

Ideas for Writing

1. Describe a pet you've had or any animal you've observed closely. Make use of personification to enhance your description. Place the animal in its most natural environment.

2. Watch an animal in a park or anywhere outdoors for a few minutes. List objectively five actions the animal performed. Then, write a simile for each action.

3. In this poem, Tennyson's description enables the reader to have a kind of *participation* in the eagle's experience. How is this accomplished? How is this description different from a dictionary definition of an eagle? Write a short analysis of the participatory effect of this poem.

John Keats
TO AUTUMN

John Keats (1795–1821) was the son of a stable hand and an innkeeper's daughter. Unlike his fellow romantic poets, he was little inclined towards cynical or revolutionary statements; instead, he strove only to capture the "people" in nature and in people. Keats originally studied medicine after being orphaned at age 15. Sadly, he contracted tuberculosis—the same disease which had killed his mother and brother—at age 26. It was from that point on that he wrote some of his masterpieces, including "Ode on a Grecian Urn" and "Ode to a Nightingale."

"To Autumn" exemplifies the lyric mastery with which Keats expressed his devotion to beauty and nature. It is a finely crafted poem rich in picturesque and sensory imagery.

*S*eason of mists and mellow fruitfulness,   1
    Close bosom-friend of the maturing sun;
Conspiring with him how to load and bless
    With fruit the vines that round the thatch-eves run;
To bend with apples the mossed cottage-trees,   5
    And fill all fruit with ripeness to the core;
        To swell the gourd, and plump the hazel shells
With a sweet kernel; to set budding more,
    And still more, later flowers for the bees,
    Until they think warm days will never cease,   10
        For summer has o'er-brimmed their clammy cells.

Who hath not seen thee oft amid thy store?
    Sometimes whoever seeks abroad may find
Thee sitting careless on a granary floor,
    Thy hair soft-lifted by the winnowing wind;   15
Or on a half-reaped furrow sound asleep,
    Drowsed with the fume of poppies, while thy hook
        Spares the next swath and all its twined flowers:
And sometimes like a gleaner thou dost keep
    Steady thy laden head across a brook;   20
    Or by a cider-press, with patient look,
        Thou watchest the last oozings hours by hours.

Where are the songs of Spring? Ay, where are they?
    Think not of them, thou hast thy music too,—
While barred clouds bloom the soft-dying day,   25
    And touch the stubble-plains with, rosy hue;
Then in a wailful choir the small gnats mourn
    Among the river sallows, borne aloft
        Or sinking as the light wind lives or dies;
And full-grown lambs loud bleat from hilly bourn;   30
    Hedge-crickets sing; and now with treble soft
    The red-breast whistles from a garden-croft;
        And gathering swallows twitter in the skies.

Meaning and Idea

1. The speaker is addressing autumn in the poem. Why does he call autumn a friend of the sun? How do autumn and the sun conspire?

2. Explain stanza two in your own words. How is autumn "like a gleaner"?

3. What, according to Keats, is autumn's music?

Language, Form, Structure

1. What is Keats's theme in this poem?

2. What is the focus of imagery in each stanza? How does Keats arrange the imagery within the poem?

3. To which of the five senses does the imagery of this poem appeal? Give an example of an image for each sense you list. Explain each image in your own words.

4. How does Keats use *personification* in the poem? Which stanza makes the most use of personification?

5. Look up the following words in a dictionary: granary (par. 14); winnowing (15); furrow (16); hook (17); swath (18); barred (25); sallow (28); bleat, bourn (30); twitter (33).

Ideas for Writing

1. Write a description, either in prose or verse, of your favorite season. Try to use images that appeal to each of the five senses.

2. Describe and evaluate the syntax and diction of this nineteenth-century poem.

Melville Cane
SNOW TOWARD EVENING

> Melville Cane (1879–1980) was born in Plattsburg, New York, and educated at Columbia University, where he received his law degree. He was primarily a lawyer, yet found enough time to concentrate on his poetry, so that in 1971 he received the Poetry Society of America's gold medal. His collections include *And Pastures New* (1956) and *Snow Toward Evening* (1974).
>
> Melville Cane blends direct statement description ("the sky turned gray") with metaphoric description ("From some invisible blossoming tree") to describe a simple, natural event.

*S*uddenly the sky turned gray,   1
The day,
Which had been bitter and chill,
Grew soft and still.
Quietly   5
From some invisible blossoming tree
Millions of petals cool and white
Drifted and blew,
Lifted and flew,
Fell with the falling night.   10

Meaning and Idea

1. What is the season described in this poem?

2. During what time of day does this poem occur? Aside from the title, what evidence do you have for your answer? How do you know it's not late at night, for example?

Language, Form, Structure

1. This poem is composed of two sentences, each beginning with an adverb. What are these adverbs? How do they help establish the dominant impression in the poem?

2. How does the use of rhyme contribute to the overall feeling of the poem?

3. How does Cane use *metaphor* as a descriptive technique in this poem? What are the "millions of petals"? What is the "invisible blossoming tree"?

Ideas for Writing

1. Describe an evening snow scene that particularly impressed you.

2. Describe the beginning moments of a simple, natural occurrence. Attempt to use some metaphoric description.

3. Both Cane's poem and Keat's "Autumn" describe seasonal scenes in nature. Which do you find more effective and evocative? Why?

George Orwell

MARRAKECH

George Orwell (1903–1950) was the pseudonym for Eric Blair, the English essayist, novelist, and journalist who was perhaps best known for his scathing political fictions *Animal Farm* (1945) and *1984* (1949). His life was as fascinating as his works: He was born in India, educated at Eton, served in Burma from 1922–1927, and was wounded fighting with the International Brigade during the Spanish Civil War.

In this sharp description of a city still known for its vibrant mix of social and economic classes, George Orwell brings to life his observations of poverty, prejudice, and injustice. Notice how he mixes unrelenting descriptions of human suffering (such as the funeral) with seemingly unrelated, lighthearted descriptions (such as the gazelle). Throughout the essay he uses such descriptive juxtapositions to create a full and intense view of what he witnesses and analyzes.

---

*A*s the corpse went past the flies left the restaurant table in a cloud and rushed after it, but they came back a few minutes later.

The little crowd of mourners—all men and boys, no women—threaded their way across the market-place between the piles of pomegranates and the taxis and the camels, wailing a short chant over and over again. What really appeals to the flies is that the corpses here are never put into coffins, they are merely wrapped in a piece of rag and carried on a rough wooden bier on the shoulders of four friends. When the friends get to the burying-ground they hack an oblong hole a foot or two deep, dump the body in it and fling over it a little of the dried-up, lumpy earth, which is like broken brick. No gravestone, no name, no identifying mark of any kind. The burying-ground is merely a huge waste of hummocky earth, like a derelict building-lot. After a month or two no one can even be certain where his own relatives are buried.

When you walk through a town like this—two hundred thousand inhabitants, of whom at least twenty thousand own literally nothing except the rags they stand up in—when you see how people live, and still more how easily they die, it is always difficult to believe that you are walking among human beings. All colonial empires are in reality founded upon that fact. The people have brown faces—besides, there are so many of them! Are they really the same flesh as yourself? Do they even have names? Or are they merely a kind of undifferentiated brown stuff, about as individual as bees or coral insects? They rise out of the earth, they sweat and starve for a few years, and then they sink back into the nameless mounds of the graveyard and nobody notices that they are gone. And even the graves themselves soon fade back into the soil. Sometimes, out for a walk, as you break your way through the prickly pear, you notice that it is rather bumpy underfoot, and only a certain regularity in the bumps tells you that you are walking over skeletons.

I was feeding one of the gazelles in the public gardens.

Gazelles are almost the only animals that look good to eat when they are still alive, in fact, one can hardly look at their hindquarters without thinking of mint sauce. The gazelle I was feeding seemed to know that this thought was in my mind, for though it took the piece of bread I was holding out it obviously did not like me. It nibbled rapidly at the bread, then lowered its head and tried to butt me, then took another nibble and then butted again. Probably its idea was that if it could drive me away the bread would somehow remain hanging in mid-air.

An Arab navvy working on the path nearby lowered his heavy hoe and sidled towards us. He looked from the gazelle to the bread and from the bread to the gazelle, with a sort of quiet amazement, as though he had never seen anything quite like this before. Finally he said shyly in French:

"I could eat some of that bread."

I tore off a piece and he stowed it gratefully in some secret place under his rags. This man is an employee of the Municipality.

When you go through the Jewish quarters you gather some idea of what the medieval ghettoes were probably like. Under their Moorish rulers the Jews were only allowed to own land in certain restricted areas, and after centuries of this kind of treatment they have ceased to bother about overcrowding. Many of the streets are a good deal less than six feet wide, the houses are completely windowless, and sore-eyed children cluster everywhere in unbelievable numbers, like clouds of flies. Down the centre of the street there is generally running a little river of urine.

In the bazaar huge families of Jews, all dressed in the long black robe and little black skull-cap, are working in dark fly-infested booths that look like caves. A carpenter sits cross-legged at a prehistoric lathe, turning chair-legs at lightning speed. He works the lathe with a bow in his right hand and guides the chisel with his left foot, and thanks to a lifetime of sitting in this position his left leg is warped out of shape. At his side his grandson, aged six, is already starting on the simpler parts of the job.

I was just passing the coppersmiths' booths when somebody noticed that I was lighting a cigarette. Instantly, from the dark holes all round, there was a frenzied rush of Jews, many of them old grandfathers with flowing grey beards, all clamouring for a cigarette. Even a blind man somewhere at the back of one of the booths heard a rumour of cigarettes and came crawling out, groping in the air with his hand. In about a minute I had used up the whole packet. None of these people, I suppose, works less than twelve hours a day, and every one of them looks on a cigarette as a more or less impossible luxury.

As the Jews live in self-contained communities they follow the same trades as the Arabs, except for agriculture. Fruit-sellers, potters, silversmiths, blacksmiths, butchers, leather-workers, tailors, water-carriers, beggars, porters—whichever way you look you see nothing but Jews. As a matter of fact there are thirteen thousand of them, all living in the space of a few acres. A good job Hitler isn't here. Perhaps he is on his way, however. You hear the usual dark rumours about the Jews, not only from the Arabs but from the poorer Europeans.

"Yes, *mon vieux,* they took my job away from me and gave it to a Jew. The Jews! They're the real rulers of this country, you know. They've got all the money. They control the banks, finance—everything."

"But," I said, "isn't it a fact that the average Jew is a labourer working for about a penny an hour?"

"Ah, that's only for show! They're all moneylenders really. They're cunning, the Jews."

In just the same way, a couple of hundred years ago, poor old women used to be burned for witchcraft when they could not even work enough magic to get themselves a square meal.

All people who work with their hands are partly invisible, and the more important the work they do, the less visible they are. Still, a white skin is always fairly conspicuous. In northern Europe, when you see a labourer ploughing a field, you probably give him a second glance. In a hot country, anywhere south of Gibraltar or east of Suez, the chances are that you don't even see him. I have noticed this again and again. In a tropical landscape one's eye takes in everything except the human beings. It takes in the dried-up soil, the prickly pear, the palm-tree and the distant mountain, but it always misses the peasant hoeing at his patch. He is the same colour as the earth, and a great deal less interesting to look at.

It is only because of this that the starved countries of Asia and Africa are accepted as tourist resorts. No one would think of running cheap trips to the Distressed Areas. But where the human beings have brown skins their poverty is simply not noticed. What does Morocco mean to a Frenchman? An orange-grove or a job in government service. Or to an Englishman? Camels, castles, palm-trees, Foreign Legionnaires, brass trays and bandits. One could probably live here for years without noticing that for nine-tenths of the people the reality of life is an endless, back-breaking struggle to wring a little food out of an eroded soil.

Most of Morocco is so desolate that no wild animal bigger than a hare can live on it. Huge areas which were once covered with forest have turned into a treeless waste where the soil is exactly like broken-up brick. Nevertheless a good deal of it is cultivated, with frightful labour. Every-thing is done by hand. Long lines of women, bent double like inverted capital Ls, work their way slowly across the fields, tearing up the prickly weeds with their hands, and the peasant gathering lucerne for fodder pulls it up stalk by stalk instead of reaping it, thus saving an inch or two on each stalk. The plough is a wretched wooden thing, so frail that one can easily carry it on one's shoulder, and fitted underneath with a rough iron spike which stirs the soil to a depth of about four inches. This is as much as the strength of the animals is equal to. It is usual to plough with a cow and a donkey yoked together. Two donkeys would not be quite strong enough, but on the other hand two cows would cost a little more to feed. The peasants possess no harrows, they merely plough the soil several times over in different directions, finally leaving it in rough furrows, after which the whole field has to be shaped with hoes into small oblong patches, to conserve water. Except for a day or two after the rare rainstorms there is never enough water. Along the edges of the fields channels are hacked out to a depth of thirty or forty feet to get at the tiny trickles which run through the subsoil.

Every afternoon a file of very old women passes down the road outside my house, each carrying a load of firewood. All of them are mummified with age and the sun, and all of them are tiny. It seems to be generally the case in primitive communities that the women, when they get beyond a certain age, shrink to the size of children. One day a poor old creature who could not have been more than four feet tall crept past me under a vast load of wood. I stopped her and put a five-sou piece (a little more than a farthing) into her hand. She answered with a shrill wail, almost a scream, which was partly gratitude but mainly surprise. I suppose that from her point of view, by taking any notice of her, I seemed almost to be violating a law of nature. She accepted her status as an old woman, that is to say as a beast of burden. When a family is travelling it is quite usual to see a father and a grown-up son riding ahead on donkeys, and an old woman following on foot, carrying the baggage.

But what is strange about these people is their invisibility. For several weeks, always at about the same time of day, the file of old women had hobbled past the house with their firewood, and though they had registered themselves on my eyeballs I cannot truly say that I had seen them. Firewood was passing—that was how I saw it. It was only that one day I happened to be walking behind them, and the curious up-and-down motion of a load of wood drew my attention to the human being underneath it. Then for the first time I noticed the poor old earth-coloured bodies, bodies reduced to bones and leathery skin, bent double under the crushing weight. Yet I suppose I had not been five minutes on Moroccan soil before I noticed the overloading of the donkeys and was infuriated by it. There is no question that the donkeys are damnably treated. The Moroccan donkey is hardly bigger than a St. Bernard dog, it carries a load which in the British army would be considered too much for a fifteen-hands mule, and very often its pack-saddle is not taken off its back for weeks together. But what is peculiarly pitiful is that it is the most willing creature on earth, it follows its master like a dog and does not need either bridle or halter. After a dozen years of devoted work it suddenly drops dead, whereupon its master tips it into the ditch and the village dogs have torn its guts out before it is cold.

This kind of thing makes one's blood boil, whereas—on the whole—the plight of the human beings does not. I am not commenting, merely pointing to a fact. People with brown skins are next door to invisible. Anyone can be sorry for the donkey with its galled back, but it is generally owing to some kind of accident if one even notices the old woman under her load of sticks.

As the storks flew northward the Negroes were marching southward—a long, dusty column, infantry, screw-gun batteries and then more infantry, four or five thousand men in all, winding up the road with a clumping of boots and a clatter of iron wheels.

They were Senegalese, the blackest Negroes in Africa, so black that sometimes it is difficult to see whereabouts on their necks the hair begins. Their splendid bodies were hidden in reach-me-down khaki uniforms, their feet squashed into boots that looked like blocks of wood, and every tin hat seemed to be a couple of sizes too small. It was very hot and the men had marched a long way. They slumped under the weight of their packs and the curiously sensitive black faces were glistening with sweat.

As they went past a tall, very young Negro turned and caught my eye. But the look he gave me was not in the least the kind of look you might expect. Not hostile, not contemptuous, not sullen, not even inquisitive. It was the shy, wide-eyed Negro look, which actually is a look of profound respect. I saw how it was. This wretched boy, who is a French citizen and has therefore been dragged from the forest to scrub floors and catch syphilis in garrison towns, actually has feelings of reverence before a white skin. He has been taught that the white race are his masters, and he still believes it.

But there is one thought which every white man (and in this connection it doesn't matter twopence if he calls himself a Socialist) thinks when he sees a black army marching past. "How much longer can we go on kidding these people? How long before they turn their guns in the other direction?"

It was curious, really. Every white man there has this thought stowed somewhere or other in his mind. I had it, so had the other onlookers, so had the officers on their sweating chargers and the white NCOs marching in the ranks. It was a kind of secret which we all knew and were too clever to tell; only the Negroes didn't know it. And really it was almost like watching a flock of cattle to see the long column, a mile or two miles of armed men, flowing peacefully up the road, while the great white birds drifted over them in the opposite direction, glittering like scraps of paper.

Meaning and Idea

1. In what part of the world is Marrakech? During which historical period (decade) do you think the essay was written? What details place the essay in time?

2. From reading the essay, what can you say about its narrator? Where does he come from? What color is his skin? What are his political leanings?

3. What event does the essay deal with? Briefly describe this event.

Language, Form, Structure

1. Summarize the essay's main point about the way white people "see" nonwhite people. Where in the essay does Orwell come closest to stating his thesis?

2. What general impression of death and burial in this part of the world does the essay convey? How does opening the essay with a description of death help to convey the author's main idea?

3. The essay makes its point through well-chosen anecdotes, images, and details. Which do you find most indelible?

4. Orwell offers arresting descriptions of mourners, animals, Arabs, Jews, women, soldiers. Which descriptions are most impressive? Identify.

5. Use a dictionary to check meanings for any of the following words that you do not know: derelict, hummocky (paragraph 2); ghettoes (9); lucerne, fodder (19).

Ideas for Writing

1. Write a descriptive essay illuminating the most "foreign" or "exotic" place you've ever visited (even if it is just another neighborhood or another section of the United States). Attempt to create a deep feeling for the place by concentrating mostly on details about the people you encountered.

2. In a few paragraphs, describe what you know about a cultural, religious, or ethnic group other than your own. As much as possible, concentrate your details on how the group's appearance and activities differ from those with which you are familiar.

3. Orwell once wrote of insincere writing that "When there is a gap between one's real and one's declared aims, one turns as it were instinctively to long words and exhausted idioms." Write a short essay in which you discuss Orwell's aims in this essay. Using specific descriptive examples from "Marrakech," explain how Orwell's use of description does or does not fulfill those aims.

Chapter Two
NARRATION

*I*n most cultures we find an exalted place for the story, the narrative with a clear march of scene that reports a notable sequence of events in vivid language. Stories reflect the reaches of human experience. People delight in narratives—whether fiction or fact, imagined or historical. Even our modern sensibilities, so obviously in flux as a result of the entertainment technologies and the media explosion, show no diminished love of stories. Afternoon soap operas, prime-time comedy and adventure series, the popular films of our decade build their appeals upon narrative frameworks. The fictions we read too, of course, the novels, short stories, and plays of our age, take much of their life from narrative as do popular songs and poems. Essays also rely upon narrative structures; when Aristotle identified narration as one of the four categories of prose forms (including description, exposition, and argumentation) it was clearly an acknowledgment of the value of the story for its own sake.

READING NARRATIVE

As speakers, listeners, readers, and writers, we are tireless narrators. We're always telling and listening to stories just for the fun of them. The Canadian novelist Alice Munro identifies this impulse in *Lives of Girls and Women*: "Aunt Elspeth and Auntie Grace told stories. It did not seem as if they were telling them to me, to entertain me, but as if they would have told them anyway, for their own pleasure, even if they had been alone." In this spirit, narratives in this chapter are appealing because they give pleasure to readers. This is not to say that the narratives here have no further goal. Certainly "A Wagner Matinée" delights us by stating the precise sensory details that arouse Aunt Georgiana's joy at hearing a concert after many years; but the dramatic final sentence of the story brings her sacrifices into sudden and shocking perspective. With the contrast between Aunt Georgiana's life of deprivation and a life in which musical performances are familiar ecstasies, Willa Cather is asserting the centrality of art to human experience. Similarly, Raymond Carver's accretion of details in his narrative essay, "My Father's Life," forces us to think again about fate, life, and reminiscence. The essay is great writing because it provides a stirring commentary on human nature, and the narrative structure makes the point more forcefully than any other. All narratives whether fiction or fact, prose or poetry, share the common bond of purpose. Readers seek out the point of the story and use it as a mark of the story's success. Today's stories may no longer have a moral, in the narrow sense, but the effective story will still, at the very least, present an understanding or raise a question, even if it offers no easy solution. "Why is this writer telling us this?" is the most important question we can ask about any piece of narration.

What in fact does a story do? A story breaks the ice: "It's great being back here talking to this Kiwanis Club in Charleston. Why, twenty years ago, when I was a small girl growing up in Parkersburg Virginia I. . . ." A story gives essential information: "My car was parked on the corner of Clark and Wabash, officer, when I saw a man leap out the door of Friendly's and. . . ." Stories connect us to other people and provide a frame or a mirror to our own lives. Stories prod our imaginations, our consciousness, our humanity. They win us over. They wear us down. Sometimes they push us to action.

Experienced readers of narrative can identify two general approaches. One is the *narrative summary* where the writer covers large segments of time, skips over some events to highlight others, and aims for broad comprehensive impressions in the minds of readers more than for a highly detailed vision of discrete scenes. Writers of history, memoirs, and biography, as well as news and sports reporters, often will rely upon narrative summaries. Essayists, too, will use this technique and so will novelists, poets, and short story writers. When you read Carver's essay in this chapter, you will see narrative summary in one of its best forms. The other approach is the *narrative moment* where the writer chooses a limited time frame and explores all its details for an intense, comprehensive view of a flash of time. Most selections here follow this format. Relying upon character, dialogue, plot, and concrete sensory language, the narrative moment is like a sequence of frames on a piece of film that presents carefully chosen details for the viewer. The selection from *Native Son,* along with many others in this chapter, underscores how effective this method is in holding a reader's attention. We're not suggesting any single approach here—writers may use both narrative summary and narrative moments in a novel or poem or story or essay—but as alert readers we want to be aware of how we arrive where writers want to take us. Hence, the distinction between narrative summary and narrative moment is useful.

Also when we read, we must be aware of the temporal sequence upon which the flesh of the story hangs. Most narratives procede through an orderly *chronology*: first this happened, then that, then some other thing. In using narrative to make a dramatic point most essayists and fiction writers use this simple arrangement. But experienced writers can and do take great liberties with sequence. A story can begin *in medias res*—in the midst of things—where readers suddenly find themselves in the heat of an event that does not evolve from an orderly march of hours and minutes and seconds. With such stories we often must fill in details on our own, reconstructing pieces as we go along, or waiting for information that may be revealed later on about earlier events. Or skillful writers may rely upon *flashback,* where they freeze the current narrative, whisking us back in time to explore an earlier event, then returning to the present moment. Yet even in the hands of the most talented writer, the flashback risks confusing readers. Note when you read "A Wagner Matinée" how Cather moves you back and forth in time with great skill, but how you must nonetheless concentrate carefully on these temporal shifts in order to keep the story properly focused. The heart of narrative is time—the writer's vision of reality is inseparable from the way he or she views time and its impact upon characters, events, and ideas—and you want to pay particular attention to sequence as you read.

WRITING NARRATIVE

To encourage practice in writing narrative, this chapter asks you to concentrate on the story pretty much for its own sake. Later on, you will use narrative as a means for advancing ideas in expository frameworks, but here the story itself is the thing. Your objective is to transform events into clear, vivid prose.

PURPOSE AND AUDIENCE

At least once, we have all sat almost transfixed by boredom as we listened to a rambling, pointless story. As soon as someone has to ask about a piece of writing, "What is this all about?" you've exhausted whatever patience your readers may possess. Thus in choosing your narrative you must be very clear yourself on why you are telling about this particular event. Ask yourself this question as you are brainstorming: "What am I trying to demonstrate with this story?" Write down your answer so that your purpose does not escape you and so that you can see if it holds up. Stating your purpose too generally will not help much: "to answer," "to shock," "to stimulate"—these are not particularly useful statements of purpose because they provide little guidance as you develop the narrative framework. Suppose you saw close up a fire blazing through a section of your town and you wanted to write a narrative about it. Notice how each of the purposes below would stimulate a different story line about the same event.

Topic: The October 1984 fire on Walker Street
Purpose:
1. To show the bravery of an understaffed volunteer fire department
2. To follow the actions of a suspicious bystander
3. To show how people clutching their possessions poured from the houses and shops engulfed in flames
4. To trace the events from the first sparks at the corner grocery store to the conflagration that swept through the neighborhood

5. To show the orderly evacuation of 600 children from Birch Lane Elementary School

Not all of these are mutually exclusive. You could combine 1 and 3, for example, or 3 and 4. The point is that your narrative should focus on some purpose that is absolutely clear to you and that you finally make clear to your reader. You might want to state your purpose in a *thesis sentence,* sometimes called a *main idea sentence,* somewhere in your introduction. "Three racing figures in yellow slickers and black boots (this is all there is to the Lewis Valley Volunteer Fire Department) contained the worst fire in our town in twenty years, saving more than a dozen lives before Walker Street lay in a heap of ashes." Or, you may choose not to state a thesis or main idea; instead you may want readers to be able to discover your purpose on their own by concentrating thoughtfully on your story. In either case you must *be able to* state your purpose even if it is just as a check on the integrity of your narrative.

Very much related to the purpose of your narrative is the audience you want to read it. Many of the writing exercises in this chapter suggest an audience, and your instructor may define a readership too. But you should be prepared to identify your own audience. For whom are you writing this narrative? If you wrote about the fire in a report to the mayor of Lewis Valley, in a front page news story for the *Lewis Valley Gazette,* or in a letter to your sister back East, your narrative in each case would differ sharply from the other. Thinking about your audience as you shape your story will help you select appropriate details and eliminate extraneous ones. Also, a good sense of audience will help you develop an appropriate point of view. Would your readers expect you to be as objective as possible? Would they want you to place yourself in the scene as a participant-observer sharing subjective feelings and reactions? Either of these points of view would have a major impact upon the tone and structure of your narrative.

PROCESS

Your first step is to find a story worth telling. But it's not accurate to think only in terms of dazzling incidents in the lives of superstars. In simple, everyday activities the sensitive, observing eye can find terrific stories. Walter Prichard Eaton, as a freshman at Harvard more than thirty years ago, recalls how his instructors encouraged him to develop "the daily theme eye." He writes, "It became needful, then, to watch for and treasure incidents that were sharply dramatic or poignant, moods that were clear and definite, pictures that created a single clean impression. . . . By training the daily theme eye, we watched for and found in the surroundings of our life, as it passed, a heightened picturesqueness, a constant wonder, and added significance."

Like Eaton, we remind you to look around for the best stories and to make today the starting point for a fresh view of the events in your life. Also like Eaton, you might wish to keep a notebook of your impressions, jotting down incidents you see that can open a floodgate of narrative when you sit at your chair ready to develop a draft. Selecting a moment you've only recently experienced almost always assures a high level of intensity in your paper: You'll see the events clearly in your mind's eye because they are fresh and vivid to you, and you'll be able to convey that freshness and vividness to your readers. But memorable past events too can etch themselves on your consciousness, and you'll want to comb the past experiences of your life for narrative worth sharing with your readers.

As you think and write with your audience and purpose in mind, be aware of the nature and quantity of detail you need to include. Obviously you cannot cover every minute event in the story you are reporting; such thoroughness would simply overwhelm your readers. You have to select details carefully so that they reinforce your objective and so that they keep your readers interested. What you learned about concrete sensory detail in the last chapter will be useful here. Much of your narrative will draw upon images of sound, color, action, smell, and touch.

You must be particularly attentive to time and sequence when you write narrative. Events should follow each other logically, if not chronologically, and readers should never feel adrift in a sea of unconnected events. If you are bold enough to try flashback, be careful not to bounce back and forth from present to past; it will jar your readers. You might wish to make a time line or a simple list of chronological events so that you have at your fingertips the exact order of actions, no matter how you finally present them.

As you link events together, *transitions* will be very useful. Words like *then, later, now, before, after, soon, in a moment*—there are hundreds of others—can help you move from beginning to middle to end. But you must use these connectors judiciously and selectively. A clearly told story makes its own internal connections; events flow naturally from one to the other, and a mechanical use of transitions will obstruct that natural flow.

A last point to consider: dialogue. Almost all stories about people draw upon the natural conversations among characters in the narrative. Listen to the rhythms in everyday speech, and when your characters speak, make their words sound as if real people spoke them. Dialogue, like other details, requires selectivity. Let all spoken language in your story advance the special point you wish to make.

Willa Cather
A WAGNER MATINÉE

Willa Cather (1876–1947) was amply familiar with the changing social values about which she wrote. Born in Virginia, she was soon on "foreign soil" when her family moved to the Nebraska immigrant town of Red Cloud. Here she gained an abiding respect for the land and the people who made something from it. Her best known novel is *My Antonia* (1918), the story of the struggles of the prairie girl, Antonia Shimerda.

In "A Wagner Matinée," Willa Cather tells us the story of a life seemingly fulfilled, but inwardly longing. In this story of a woman who appears to have everything, Cather blends flashback with chronological narration to show us what was, what is, and what could have been.

I received one morning a letter, written in pale ink on glossy blue-lined notepaper, and bearing the postmark of a little Nebraska village. This communication, worn and rubbed, looking as if it had been carried for some days in a coat pocket that was none too clean, was from my Uncle Howard, and informed me that his wife had been left a small legacy by a bachelor relative, and that it would be necessary for her to go to Boston to attend the settling of the estate. He requested me to meet her at the station and render her whatever services might be necessary. On examining the date indicated as that of her arrival, I found it to be no later than tomorrow. He had characteristically delayed writing until, had I been away from home for a day, I must have missed my aunt altogether.

The name of my Aunt Georgiana opened before me a gulf of recollection so wide and deep that, as the letter dropped from my hand, I felt suddenly a stranger to all the present conditions of my existence, wholly ill at ease and out of place amid the familiar surroundings of my study. I became, in short, the gangling farmboy my aunt had known, scourged with chilblains and bashfulness, my hands cracked and sore from the corn husking. I sat again before her parlor organ fumbling the scales with my stiff red fingers, while she, beside me, made canvas mittens for the huskers. The next morning, after preparing my landlady for a visitor, I set out for the station. When the train arrived I had some difficulty in finding my aunt. She was the last of the passengers to alight, and it was not until I got her into the carriage that she seemed really to recognize me. She had come all the way in a day coach; her linen duster had become black with soot and her black bonnet gray with dust during the journey. When we arrived at my boarding house the landlady put her to bed at once and I did not see her again until the next morning.

Whatever shock Mrs. Springer experienced at my aunt's appearance, she considerately concealed. As for myself, I saw my aunt's battered figure with that feeling of awe and respect with which we behold explorers who have left their ears and fingers north of Franz-Joseph Land or their health somewhere along the Upper Congo. My Aunt Georgiana had been a music teacher at the Boston Conservatory, somewhere back in the later sixties. One summer, while visiting in the little village among the Green Mountains where her ancestors had dwelt for generations, she had kindled the callow fancy of my uncle, Howard Carpenter, then an idle, shiftless boy of twenty-one. When she returned to her duties in Boston, Howard followed her, and the upshot of this infatuation was that she eloped with him, eluding the reproaches of her family and the criticism of her friends by going with him to the Nebraska frontier. Carpenter, who, of course, had no money, took up a homestead in Red Willow County, fifty miles from the railroad. There they had measured off their land themselves, driving across the prairie in a wagon, to the wheel of which they had tied a red cotton handkerchief, and counting its revolutions. They built a dug-out in the red hillside, one of those cave dwellings whose inmates so often reverted to primitive conditions. Their water they got from the lagoons where the buffalo drank, and their slender stock of provisions was always at the mercy of roving Indians. For thirty years my aunt had not been farther than fifty miles from the homestead.

I owed to this woman most of the good that ever came my way in my boyhood, and had a reverential affection for her. During the years when I was riding herd for my uncle, my aunt, after cooking the three meals—the first of which was ready at six o'clock in the morning—and putting the six children to bed, would often stand until midnight at her ironing-board with me at the kitchen table beside her, hearing me recite Latin declensions and conjugations, gently shaking me when my drowsy head sank down over a page of irregular verbs. It was to her, at her ironing or mending, that I read my first Shakespeare, and her old textbook on mythology was the first that ever came into my empty hands. She taught me my scales and exercises on the little parlor organ which her husband had bought her after fifteen years during which she had not so much as seen a musical instrument. She would sit beside me by the hour, darning and counting, while I struggled with the "Joyous Farmer." She seldom talked to me about music and I understood why. Once when I had been doggedly beating out some easy passages from an old score of *Euryanthe* I had found among her music books, she came up to me and, putting her hands over my eyes, gently drew my head back upon her shoulder, saying tremulously, "Don't love it so well, Clark, or it may be taken from you."

When my aunt appeared on the morning after her arrival in Boston, she was still in a semi-somnambulant state. She seemed not to realize that she was in the city where she had spent her youth, the place longed for hungrily half a lifetime. She had been so wretchedly train-sick throughout the journey that she had no recollection of anything but her discomfort, and, to all intents and purposes, there were but a few hours of nightmare between the farm in Red Willow County and my study on Newbury Street. I had planned a little pleasure for her that afternoon, to repay her for some of the glorious moments she had given me when we used to milk together in the straw-thatched cowshed and she, because I was more than usually tired, or because her husband had spoken sharply to me, would tell me of the splendid performance of the *Huguenots* she had seen in Paris, in her youth.

At two o'clock the Symphony Orchestra was to give a Wagner program, and I intended to take my aunt; though, as I conversed with her, I grew doubtful about her enjoyment of it. I suggested our visiting the Conservatory and the Common before lunch, but she seemed altogether too timid to wish to venture out. She questioned me absently about various changes in the city, but she was chiefly concerned that she had forgotten to leave instructions about feeding half-skimmed milk to a certain weakling calf, "old Maggie's calf, you know, Clark," she explained, evidently having forgotten how long I had been away. She was further troubled because she had neglected to tell her daughter about the freshly opened kit of mackerel in the cellar, which would spoil if it were not used directly.

I asked her whether she had ever heard any of the Wagnerian operas, and found that she had not, though she was perfectly familiar with their respective situations, and had once possessed the piano score of *The Flying Dutchman*. I began to think it would be best to get her back to Red Willow County without waking her, and regretted having suggested the concert.

From the time we entered the concert hall, however, she was a trifle less passive and inert, and for the first time seemed to perceive her surroundings. I had felt some trepidation lest she might become aware of her queer country clothes, or might experience some painful embarrassment at stepping suddenly into the world to which she had been dead for a quarter of a century. But again, I found how superficially I had judged her. She sat looking about her with eyes as impersonal, almost as stony, as those with which the granite Rameses in a museum watches the froth and fret that ebbs and flows about his pedestal. I have seen this same aloofness in old miners who drift into the Brown Hotel at Denver, their pockets full of bullion, their linen soiled, their haggard faces unshaven;

standing in the thronged corridors as solitary as though they were still in a
frozen camp on the Yukon.

The matinée audience was made up chiefly of women. One lost the
contour of faces and figures, indeed any effect of line whatever, and there
was only the color of bodies past counting, the shimmer of fabrics soft and
fine, silky and sheer; red, mauve, pink, blue, lilac, purple, ecru, rose,
yellow, cream, and white, all the colors that an impressionist finds in a
sunlight landscape, with here and there the dead shadow of a frock coat.
My Aunt Georgiana regarded them as though they had been so many
daubs of tube-paint on a palette.

When the musicians came out and took their places, she gave a little
stir of anticipation, and looked with quickening interest down over the rail
at that invariable grouping, perhaps the first wholly familiar thing that had
greeted her eye since she had left old Maggie and her weakling calf. I
could feel how all those details sank into her soul, for I had not forgotten
how they had sunk into mine when I came fresh from plowing forever and
forever between green aisles of corn, where, as in a treadmill, one might
walk from daybreak to dusk without perceiving a shadow of change. The
clean profiles of the musicians, the gloss of their linen, the dull black of
their coats, the beloved shapes of the instruments, the patches of yellow
light on the smooth, varnished bellies of the 'cellos and the bass viols in
the rear, the restless, wind-tossed forest of fiddle necks and bows—I
recalled how, in the first orchestra I ever heard, those long bow-strokes
seemed to draw the heart out of me, as a conjurer's stick reels out yards of
paper ribbon from a hat.

The first number was the *Tannhauser* overture. When the horns drew
out the first strain of the "Pilgrims' Chorus," Aunt Georgiana clutched
my coat sleeve. Then it was I first realized that for her this broke a silence
of thirty years. With the battle between the two motives, with the frenzy
of the Venusberg theme and its ripping of strings, there came to me an
overwhelming sense of the waste and wear we are so powerless to
combat; and I saw again the tall, naked house on the prairie, black and
grim as a wooden fortress; the black pond where I had learned to swim, its
margin pitted with sun-dried cattle tracks; the rain gullied clay banks
about the naked house, the four dwarf ash seedlings where the dishcloths
were always hung to dry before the kitchen door. The world there was the
flat world of the ancients; to the east, a cornfield that stretched to
daybreak; to the west, a corral that reached to sunset; between, the
conquests of peace, dearer-bought than those of war.

The overture closed, my aunt released my coat sleeve, but she said
nothing. She sat staring dully at the orchestra. What, I wondered, did she
get from it? She had been a good pianist in her day, I knew, and her
musical education had been broader than that of most music teachers of a
quarter of a century ago. She had often told me of Mozart's operas and

Meyerbeer's, and I could remember her sing, years ago, certain melodies of Verdi. When I had fallen ill with a fever in her house she used to sit by my cot in the evening—when the cool night wind blew in through the faded mosquito netting tacked over the window and I lay watching a certain bright star that burned red above the cornfield—and sing "Home to our mountain, O let us return!" in a way fit to break the heart of a Vermont boy near dead of homesickness already.

I watched her closely through the prelude to *Tristan and Isolde,* trying vainly to conjecture what that seething turmoil of strings and winds might mean to her, but she sat mutely staring at the violin bows that drove obliquely downward, like the pelting streaks of rain in a summer shower. Had this music any message for her? Had she enough left to at all comprehend this power which had kindled the world since she had left it? I was in a fever of curiosity, but Aunt Georgiana sat silent upon her peak in Darien. She preserved this utter immobility throughout the number from *The Flying Dutchman,* though her fingers worked mechanically upon her black dress, as if, of themselves, they were recalling the piano score they had once played. Poor hands! They had been stretched and twisted into mere tentacles to hold and lift and knead with; on one of them a thin worn band that had once been a wedding ring. As I pressed and gently quieted one of these groping hands, I remembered with quivering eyelids their services for me in other days.

Soon after the tenor began the "Prize Song," I heard a quick drawn breath, and turned to my aunt. Her eyes were closed, but the tears were glistening on her cheeks, and I think, in a moment more, they were in my eyes as well. It never really dies, then—the soul which can suffer so excruciatingly and so interminably; it withers to the outward eye only; like that strange moss which can lie on a dusty shelf half a century, and yet, if placed in water, grows green again. She wept so throughout the development and elaboration of the melody.

During the intermission before the second half, I questioned my aunt and found that the "Prize Song" was not new to her. Some years before there had drifted to the farm in Red Willow County a young German, a tramp cow-puncher, who had sung in the chorus at Bayreuth when he was a boy, along with the other peasant boys and girls. On a Sunday morning he used to sit on his gingham-sheeted bed in the hands' bedroom which opened off the kitchen, cleaning the leather of his boots and saddle, singing the "Prize Song," while my aunt went about her work in the kitchen. She had hovered over him until she had prevailed upon him to join the country church, though his sole fitness for this step, in so far as I could gather, lay in his boyish face, and his possession of this divine melody. Shortly afterward, he had gone to town on the Fourth of July, been drunk for several days, lost his money at a faro table, ridden a saddled Texas steer on a bet, and disappeared with a fractured collarbone. All this my aunt told me huskily, wanderingly, as though she were talking in the weak lapses of illness.

"Well, we have come to better things than the old *Trovatore,* at any rate, Aunt Georgie?" I queried, with a well-meant effort at jocularity.

Her lip quivered and she hastily put her handkerchief up to her mouth. From behind it she murmured, "And you have been hearing this ever since you left me, Clark?" Her question was the gentlest and saddest of reproaches.

The second half of the program consisted of four numbers from the *Ring,* and closed with Siegfried's funeral march. My aunt wept quietly but almost continuously, as a shallow vessel overflows in a rain-storm. From time to time her dim eyes looked up at the lights, burning softly under their dull glass globes.

The deluge of sound poured on and on; I never knew what she found in the shining current of it; I never knew how far it bore her, or past what happy islands. From the trembling of her face, I could well believe that before the last number she had been carried out where the myriad graves are, into the gray, nameless burying grounds of the sea, or into some world of death vaster yet, where, from the beginning of the world, hope has lain down with hope and dream with dream and, renouncing, slept.

The concert was over; the people filed out of the hall chattering and laughing, glad to relax and find the living level again, but my kinswoman made no effort to rise. The harpist slipped the green felt cover over his instrument; the flute-players shook the water from their mouth-pieces; the men of the orchestra went out one by one, leaving the stage to the chairs and music stands, empty as a winter cornfield.

I spoke to my aunt. She burst into tears and sobbed pleadingly. "I don't want to go, Clark, I don't want to go!"

I understood. For her, just outside the concert hall, lay the black pond with the cattle-tracked bluffs; the tall, unpainted house, with weather-curled boards, naked as a tower; the crook-backed ash seedlings where the dishcloths hung to dry; the gaunt, moulting turkeys picking up refuse about the kitchen door.

Meaning and Ideas

1. Where was Aunt Georgiana born? Where did she live at the time of the story? For how long? Why did she move there? What is her attitude towards that place? Does that attitude change at all during the course of the story?

2. Why did Aunt Georgiana seldom talk about music?

3. What kind of relationship do you think Aunt Georgiana had with her husband? How can you tell?

4. Who is Wagner? Which of his musical works are played at the matinée? How do Aunt Georgiana's reactions change with each piece? How does Cather use different pieces to further the narrative?

5. At one point, Clark states, "I began to think it would be best to get her back to Red Willow County without waking her. . . ." What is the meaning of this statement? Why does he think it?

6. Towards the end of the story, the narrator states, "It never really dies, then." What is the "it" in this statement?

Language, Form, Structure

1. To what does Clark compare his aunt's trip? To what does he compare her weeping? How else are comparisons used in this story?

2. What is the conflict in this story? How does Cather develop it? How is it resolved?

3. How is the technique of *flashback* used here? For what purpose? How does Cather maintain narrative unity with the flashbacks?

4. How is color imagery used in the narrative? Give specific examples.

5. Explain each of the following adjectival phrases from the story: reverential affection; gangling farmboy; semi-somnambulant state; wretching train-sick; quivering eyelids.

Ideas for Writing

1. Tell about an experience with a member of your family whom you hadn't seen in a number of years, but recently saw. How did you behave in this situation? How had you both changed? How had you stayed the same?

2. Narrate a particularly emotional experience of yours that centered on a musical performance, a play, a film, a poetry reading, or an art or museum exhibit.

3. Write a short commentary on your reaction to Cather's portrayal of the two characters. Do you feel you have sufficient knowledge of either or both of the characters to believe their actions and reactions? Do you have a clear visual impression of the characters? Why?

She didn't want to leave the matina. It gives her a pleasant + unpleasant stress.

Richard Wright
NATIVE SON
CHAPTER 1

Richard Wright (1908–1960) was one of America's foremost black writers, alternately praised or scorned for his dramatic, often angry accounts of black life and radical politics. Born on a cotton plantation near Natchez, Mississippi, Wright grew up impoverished and orphaned. His decision to join the American Communist Party in Chicago during the great depression significantly influenced his outlook in such books as *Native Son* (1940), which he wrote under the auspices of a Guggenheim Fellowship, the autobiographical *Black Boy* (1945), and the chronicle of his eventual dissatisfaction with communism, *The God That Failed* (1950).

When *Native Son* first appeared in 1940, it shook the literary world with its brutally realistic account of anger, alienation, and violence within the black community. The novel's dramatic climax, a murder, is foreshadowed in this selection when the narrator writes of the protagonist, Bigger: "He knew that the moment he allowed what his life meant to enter fully into his consciousness, he would either kill himself or someone else."

B rrrrrriiiiiiiiiiiiiiiiiiiiiiiing!

An alarm clock clanged in the dark and silent room. A bed spring creaked. A woman's voice sang out impatiently:

"Bigger, shut that thing off!"

A surly grunt sounded above the tinny ring of metal. Naked feet swished dryly across the planks in the wooden floor and the clang ceased abruptly.

"Turn on the light, Bigger."

"Awright," came a sleepy mumble.

Light flooded the room and revealed a black boy standing in a narrow space between two iron beds, rubbing his eyes with the backs of his hands. From a bed to his right, the woman spoke again:

"Buddy, get up from there! I got a big washing on my hands today, and I want you all out of here."

Another black boy rolled from bed and stood up. The woman also rose and stood in her nightgown.

"Turn your heads so I can dress," she said.

The two boys averted their eyes and gazed into a far corner of the room.

The woman rushed out of her nightgown and put on a pair of step-ins. She turned to the bed from which she had risen and called:

"Vera! Get up from there!"

"What time is it, Ma?" asked a muffled, adolescent voice from beneath a quilt.

"Get up from there, I say!"

"O.K., Ma."

A brown-skinned girl in a cotton gown got up and stretched her arms above her head and yawned. Sleepily, she sat on a chair and fumbled with her stockings. The two boys kept their faces averted while their mother and sister put on enough clothes to keep them from feeling ashamed; and the mother and sister did the same while the boys dressed. Abruptly, they all paused, holding their clothes in their hands, their attention caught by a light tapping in the thinly plastered walls of the room. They forgot their conspiracy against shame and their eyes strayed apprehensively over the floor.

"There he is again, Bigger!" the woman screamed, and the tiny one-room apartment galvanized into violent action. A chair toppled as the woman, half-dressed and in her stocking feet, scrambled breathlessly upon the bed. Her two sons, barefoot, stood tense and motionless, their eyes searching anxiously under the bed and chairs. The girl ran into a corner, half-stooped and gathered the hem of her slip into both of her hands and held it tightly over her knees.

"Oh! Oh!" she wailed.

"There he goes!"

The woman pointed a shaking finger. Her eyes were round with fascinated horror.

"Where?"

"I don't see 'im!"

"Bigger, he's behind the trunk!" the girl whimpered.

"Vera!" the woman screamed. "Get up here on the bed! Don't let that thing *bite* you!"

Frantically, Vera climbed upon the bed and the woman caught hold of her. With their arms entwined about each other, the black mother and the brown daughter gazed open-mouthed at the trunk in the corner.

Bigger looked round the room wildly, then darted to a curtain and swept it aside and grabbed two heavy iron skillets from a wall above a gas stove. He whirled and called softly to his brother, his eyes glued to the trunk.

"Buddy!"

"Yeah?"

"Here; take this skillet."

"O.K."

"Now, get over by the door!"

"O.K."

Buddy crouched by the door and held the iron skillet by its handle, his arm flexed and poised. Save for the quick, deep breathing of the four people, the room was quiet. Bigger crept on tiptoe toward the trunk with the skillet clutched stiffly in his hand, his eyes dancing and watching every inch of the wooden floor in front of him. He paused and, without moving an eye or muscle, called:

"Buddy!"

"Hunh?"

"Put that box in front of the hole so he can't get out!"

"O.K."

Buddy ran to a wooden box and shoved it quickly in front of a gaping hole in the molding and then backed again to the door, holding the skillet ready. Bigger eased to the trunk and peered behind it cautiously. He saw nothing. Carefully, he stuck out his bare foot and pushed the trunk a few inches.

"There he is!" the mother screamed again.

A huge black rat squealed and leaped at Bigger's trouser-leg and snagged it in his teeth, hanging on. "Goddamn!" Bigger whispered fiercely, whirling and kicking out his leg with all the strength of his body. The force of his movement shook the rat loose and it sailed through the air and struck a wall. Instantly, it rolled over and leaped again. Bigger dodged and the rat landed against a table leg. With clenched teeth, Bigger held the skillet; he was afraid to hurl it, fearing that he might miss. The rat squeaked and turned and ran in a narrow circle, looking for a place to hide; it leaped again past Bigger and scurried on dry rasping feet to one side of the box and then to the other, searching for the hole. Then it turned and reared upon its hind legs.

"Hit 'im, Bigger!" Buddy shouted.

"Kill 'im!" the woman screamed.

The rat's belly pulsed with fear. Bigger advanced a step and the rat emitted a long thin song of defiance, its black beady eyes glittering, its tiny forefeet pawing the air restlessly. Bigger swung the skillet; it skidded over the floor, missing the rat, and clattered to a stop against a wall.

"Goddamn!"

The rat leaped. Bigger sprang to one side. The rat stopped under a chair and let out a furious screak. Bigger moved slowly backward toward the door.

"Gimme that skillet, Buddy," he asked quietly, not taking his eyes from the rat.

Buddy extended his hand. Bigger caught the skillet and lifted it high in the air. The rat scuttled across the floor and stopped again at the box and searched quickly for the hole; then it reared once more and bared long yellow fangs, piping shrilly, belly quivering.

Bigger aimed and let the skillet fly with a heavy grunt. There was a shattering of wood as the box caved in. The woman screamed and hid her face in her hands. Bigger tiptoed forward and peered.

"I got 'im," he muttered, his clenched teeth bared in a smile. "By God, I got 'im."

He kicked the splintered box out of the way and the flat black body of the rat lay exposed, its two long yellow tusks showing distinctly. Bigger took a shoe and pounded the rat's head, crushing it, cursing hysterically:

"You sonofabitch!"

The woman on the bed sank to her knees and buried her face in the quilts and sobbed:

"Lord, Lord, have mercy. . . ."

"Aw, Mama," Vera whimpered, bending to her. "Don't cry. It's dead now."

The two brothers stood over the dead rat and spoke in tones of awed admiration.

"Gee, but he's a big bastard."

"That sonofabitch could cut your throat."

"He's over a foot long."

"How in hell do they get so big?"

"Eating garbage and anything else they can get."

"Look, Bigger, there's a three-inch rip in your pant-leg."

"Yeah; he was after me, all right."

"Please, Bigger, take 'im out," Vera begged.

"Aw, don't be so scary," Buddy said.

The woman on the bed continued to sob. Bigger took a piece of newspaper and gingerly lifted the rat by its tail and held it out at arm's length.

"Bigger, take 'im out," Vera begged again.

Bigger laughed and approached the bed with the dangling rat, swinging it to and fro like a pendulum, enjoying his sister's fear.

"Bigger!" Vera gasped convulsively; she screamed and swayed and closed her eyes and fell headlong across her mother and rolled limply from the bed to the floor.

"Bigger, for God's sake!" the mother sobbed, rising and bending over Vera. "Don't do that! Throw that rat out!"

He laid the rat down and started to dress.

"Bigger, help me lift Vera to the bed," the mother said.

He paused and turned round.

"What's the matter?" he asked, feigning ignorance.

"Do what I asked you, will you, boy?"

He went to the bed and helped his mother lift Vera. Vera's eyes were closed. He turned away and finished dressing. He wrapped the rat in a newspaper and went out of the door and down the stairs and put it into a garbage can at the corner of an alley. When he returned to the room his mother was still bent over Vera, placing a wet towel upon her head. She straightened and faced him, her cheeks and eyes wet with tears and her lips tight with anger.

"Boy, sometimes I wonder what makes you act like you do."

"What I do now?" he demanded belligerently.

"Sometimes you act the biggest fool I ever saw."

"What you talking about?"

"You scared your sister with that rat and she *fainted!* Ain't you got no sense at all?"

"Aw, I didn't know she was that scary."

"Buddy!" the mother called.

"Yessum."

"Take a newspaper and spread it over that spot."

"Yessum."

Buddy opened out a newspaper and covered the smear of blood on the floor where the rat had been crushed. Bigger went to the window and stood looking out abstractedly into the street. His mother glared at his back.

"Bigger, sometimes I wonder why I birthed you," she said bitterly.

Bigger looked at her and turned away.

"Maybe you oughtn't've. Maybe you ought to left me where I was."

"You shut your sassy mouth!"

"Aw, for chrissakes!" Bigger said, lighting a cigarette.

"Buddy, pick up them skillets and put 'em in the sink," the mother said.

"Yessum."

Bigger walked across the floor and sat on the bed. His mother's eyes followed him.

"We wouldn't have to live in this garbage dump if you had any manhood in you," she said.

"Aw, don't start that again."

"How you feel, Vera?" the mother asked.

Vera raised her head and looked about the room as though expecting to see another rat.

"Oh, Mama!"

"You poor thing!"

"I couldn't help it. Bigger scared me."

"Did you hurt yourself?"

"I bumped my head."

"Here; take it easy. You'll be all right."

"How come Bigger acts that way?" Vera asked, crying again.

"He's just crazy," the mother said. "Just plain dumb black crazy."

"I'll be late for my sewing class at the Y.W.C.A.," Vera said.

"Here; stretch out on the bed. You'll feel better in a little while," the mother said.

She left Vera on the bed and turned a pair of cold eyes upon Bigger.

"Suppose you wake up some morning and find your sister dead? What would you think then?" she asked. "Suppose those rats cut our veins at night when we sleep? Naw! Nothing like that ever bothers you! All you care about is your own pleasure! Even when the relief offers you a job you won't take it till they threaten to cut off your food and starve you! Bigger, honest, you the most no-countest man I ever seen in all my life!"

"You done told me that a thousand times," he said, not looking round.

"Well, I'm telling you agin! And mark my word, some of these days you going to set down and cry. Some of these days you going to wish you had made something out of yourself, instead of just a tramp. But it'll be too late then."

"Stop prophesying about me," he said.

"I prophesy much as I please! And if you don't like it, you can get out. We can get along without you. We can live in one room just like we living now, even with you gone," she said.

"Aw, for chrissakes!" he said, his voice filled with nervous irritation.

"You'll regret how you living some day," she went on. "If you don't stop running with that gang of yours and do right you'll end up where you never thought you would. You think I don't know what you boys is doing, but I do. And the gallows is at the end of the road you traveling, boy. Just remember that." She turned and looked at Buddy. "Throw that box outside, Buddy."

"Yessum."

There was silence. Buddy took the box out. The mother went behind the curtain to the gas stove. Vera sat up in bed and swung her feet to the floor.

"Lay back down, Vera," the mother said.

"I feel all right now, Ma. I got to go to my sewing class."

"Well, if you feel like it, set the table," the mother said, going behind the curtain again. "Lord, I get so tired of this I don't know what to do," her voice floated plaintively from behind the curtain. "All I ever do is try to make a home for you children and you don't care."

"Aw, Ma," Vera protested. "Don't say that."

"Vera sometimes I just want to lay down and quit."

"Ma, please don't say that."

"I can't last many more years, living like this."

"I'll be old enough to work soon, Ma."

"I reckon I'll be dead then. I reckon God'll call me home."

Vera went behind the curtain and Bigger heard her trying to comfort his mother. He shut their voices out of his mind. He hated his family because he knew that they were suffering and that he was powerless to help them. He knew that the moment he allowed himself to feel to its fullness how they lived, the shame and misery of their lives, he would be swept out of himself with fear and despair. So he held toward them an attitude of iron reserve; he lived with them, but behind a wall, a curtain. And toward himself he was even more exacting. He knew that the moment he allowed what his life meant to enter fully into his consciousness, he would either kill himself or someone else. So he denied himself and acted tough.

He got up and crushed his cigarette upon the window sill. Vera came into the room and placed knives and forks upon the table.

"Get ready to eat, you-all," the mother called.

He sat at the table. The odor of frying bacon and boiling coffee drifted to him from behind the curtain. His mother's voice floated to him in song.

Life is like a mountain railroad
  With an engineer that's brave
We must make the run successful
  From the cradle to the grave. . . .

The song irked him and he was glad when she stopped and came into the room with a pot of coffee and a plate of crinkled bacon. Vera brought the bread in and they sat down. His mother closed her eyes and lowered her head and mumbled,

"Lord, we thank Thee for the food You done placed before us for the nourishment of our bodies. Amen." She lifted her eyes and without changing her tone of voice, said, "You going to have to learn to get up earlier than this, Bigger, to hold a job."

He did not answer or look up.

"You want me to pour you some coffee?" Vera asked.

"Yeah."

"You going to take the job, ain't you, Bigger?" his mother asked.

He laid down his fork and stared at her.

"I told you last night I was going to take it. How many times you want to ask me?"

"Well, don't bite her head off," Vera said. "She only asked you a question."

"Pass the bread and stop being smart."

"You know you have to see Mr. Dalton at five-thirty," his mother said.

"You done said that ten times."

"I don't want you to forget, son."

"And you know how you can forget," Vera said.

"Aw, lay off Bigger," Buddy said. "He told you he was going to take the job."

"Don't tell 'em nothing," Bigger said.

"You shut your mouth, Buddy, or get up from this table," the mother said. "I'm not going to take any stinking sass from you. One fool in the family's enough."

"Lay off, Ma," Buddy said.

"Bigger's setting here like he ain't glad to get a job," she said.

"What you want me to do? Shout?" Bigger asked.

"Oh, Bigger!" his sister said.

"I wish you'd keep your big mouth out of this!" he told his sister.

"If you get that job," his mother said in a low, kind tone of voice, busy slicing a loaf of bread, "I can fix up a nice place for you children. You could be comfortable and not have to live like pigs."

"Bigger ain't decent enough to think of nothing like that," Vera said.

"God, I wish you-all would let me eat," Bigger said.

His mother talked on as though she had not heard him and he stopped listening.

"Ma's talking to you, Bigger," Vera said.

"So what?"

"Don't be that way, Bigger!"

He laid down his fork and his strong black fingers gripped the edge of the table; there was silence save for the tinkling of his brother's fork against a plate. He kept staring at his sister till her eyes fell.

"I wish you'd let me eat," he said again.

As he ate he felt that they were thinking of the job he was to get that evening and it made him angry; he felt that they had tricked him into a cheap surrender.

"I need some carfare," he said.

"Here's all I got," his mother said, pushing a quarter to the side of his plate.

He put the quarter in his pocket and drained his cup of coffee in one long swallow. He got his coat and cap and went to the door.

"You know, Bigger," his mother said, "if you don't take that job the relief'll cut us off. We won't have any food."

"I told you I'd take it!" he shouted and slammed the door.

Meaning and Idea

1. Why does the family practice a "conspiracy against shame" as they dress each morning? What is their morning routine? What does the scene tell us about their living conditions?

2. What accounts for Bigger's "sassiness"? Why has he "denied himself and acted tough"? From whom do we get that information, the narrator or a character? What is the difference in the information gathered from each? Quote exact lines in your answer.

3. What is the main reason the mother wants Bigger to get a job? Do you think that this is her only reason? Why? What other reasons might she have?

Language, Form, Structure

1. How is *sound imagery* used in the opening of this selection? Why is it an effective beginning? List specific sound words drawn from the first few paragraphs.

2. This selection is a good example of the use of *narrative moment*. Trace Wright's development of this narrative moment. How is it realistic or not? Complete or not? How does Wright use transitions to keep the story line flowing smoothly and swiftly?

3. The rat is not actually named as such until well into the narration of the incident. How do we know that it actually *is* a rat from the very beginning? What are the clues, both obvious and subtle, to its identity?

4. How does the use of *dialogue* affect the pacing and feeling of the story? *Dialect* is a special regional or cultural use of a language. How does Wright use dialect in this selection? Why does he do so?

5. Use each of the following words correctly in a sentence of your own: surly; averted; entwined; poised; rasping; pendulum; irked.

Ideas for Writing

1. Following the pattern of a narrative moment, write about a single dangerous incident that you, or someone you know, recently experienced.

2. Narrate an angry interaction among three people—either people you know or characters you create. Try to write the entire narration using dialogue almost exclusively.

3. In this selection, Wright uses a few distinct voices—those of the four characters as well as that of the narrator. How is the narrator's voice significantly different from those of the characters? Do you think that this difference is appropriate or not? How does it affect your reading of the selection?

poor - living in a one room place.
4 people
Bigger sort of father figure ; hes insecur
Sisters taking Sewing class
Contrast between real feelings + outer proje
family has hope

Countee Cullen
INCIDENT

—happening, incurrence

unpleasant lasting effect

Countee Cullen (1903–1946) was born in New York City. He is considered, along with W. E. B. Du Bois, Langston Hughes, Claude McKay, and Jean Toomer, among the leading writers of the Harlem Renaissance of the 1920s. The Renaissance was a literary and arts movement which chronicled black life and celebrated black pride. Cullen's contribution was his poetry, in which he intertwined traditional forms with black themes and syntax. Among his best known volumes of poetry are *Color* (1925) and *Copper Sun* (1927).

In this rhymed, simple three-stanza poem, Countee Cullen tells of a single event, which was in fact indicative of a cultural attitude that fostered millions of similar "incidents." As you read, think of how the idea of the poem reflects common moments in our everyday life.

Once riding in old Baltimore   1
    Heart-filled, head-filled with glee,
I saw a Baltimorean
    Keep looking straight at me.

Now I was eight and very small,   5
    And he was no whit bigger,
And so I smiled, but he poked out
    His tongue, and called me, "Nigger."

I saw the whole of Baltimore
    From May until December;   10
Of all the things that happened there
    That's all that I remember.

Meaning and Idea

1. The "incident" here is very straightforward. Tell what actually happened in a single sentence.

2. About how old was the person who called the narrator "Nigger"? How do you know?

3. What is the effect of the incident on the narrator? What is the immediate change in his attitude? He says he was in Baltimore "From May until December," but how can you tell that effects were longer lasting than that?

Language, Form, Structure

1. How does stanza three differ from the first two stanzas? From what does it derive its effectiveness?

2. Comment on the meaning and tone of the phrase "no whit bigger." What does it tell us about the time frame of this incident?

3. What is the relation between the poem's title and its story? What transitions does the poet use to make the narrative structure clear?

Ideas for Writing

1. Tell of a seemingly simple incident or comment that deeply affected you. What were the circumstances? What were the results?

2. Tell about a time when you intentionally or inadvertently insulted someone. Why did you insult the person? How did you feel, and what did you do afterwards?

3. Write a brief paper to explain whether or not you are satisfied with the format of a poem for telling this story. Do you think it would have been more effective written as a prose narrative? Why or why not?

E. E. Cummings
IN JUST-

Born in Cambridge, Massachusetts, in 1894, E. E. Cummings took his B.A. and M.A. degrees at Harvard, lived in Paris in the 1920s, then settled in New York's bohemian Greenwich Village. His travels spurred him to write the semifictional, semi-sociological *The Enormous Room* (1922) and *Eimi* (1933). Cummings is best known, however, for his whimsical play with typography and syntax, as well as for his near abhorrence of capital letters (he did not use capitals even for his name). He died in New Hampshire in 1962.

This is a poem of simple images, which succinctly tell of a world that is happy and wonderful but that simultaneously contains a sad edge. Cummings was a master at establishing such juxtapositions in seemingly silly and superficial verse.

*i*n Just-
spring   when the world is mud-
luscious the little
lame balloonman

whistles   far   and wee   5

and eddieandbill come
running from marbles and
piracies and it's
spring

when the world is puddle-wonderful   10

the queer
old balloonman whistles
far   and   wee
and bettyandisbel come dancing

from hop-scotch and jump-rope and   15

it's
spring
and
    the

        goat-footed   20

balloonMan   whistles
far
and
wee

Meaning and Idea

1. Who are the characters in this poem? Describe the balloon man.

2. What do Cummings's "made-up" adjectives (*mud-luscious* and *puddle-wonderful*) tell us about the weather in the poem?

3. In a single sentence, summarize the action of the poem.

Language, Form, Structure

1. The phrase which opens the poem ("in-Just-/spring") suggests a double meaning. What are the two possible meanings? Why is the double meaning effective?

2. What are the effects on the look, rhythm, and meaning of the poem of joining the names *eddieandbill* and *bettyandisbel*? The phrase "far and wee" is a

variation on the expected expression "far and wide." What is the purpose or effect of this variation? Why is the balloon man "goat-footed"? An *allusion* is a reference to some earlier literary or historical situation. To what does *goat-footed* allude?

3.   In what sense is this poem a narrative? From whose point of view is the narrative told?

Ideas for Writing

1.   Try to remember a time when you were very happy as a child, but suddenly became aware of a sad or less fortunate condition around you. In a paragraph, narrate what happened at that moment.

2.   Write a short narrative about your favorite play activity when you were young.

3.   Write a one-paragraph reaction to the *format* of this poem. How does the lack of regular syntax and the odd spacing of words affect your feeling for this poem? Does your feeling change with two or three readings? Do you find this any easier or harder to read than most poetry? Why?

James Welch
WINTER IN THE BLOOD
CHAPTER 36

- West, dusk

- accidents can happen anytime

- moving cattle to different place because the change in seasons

- 14, 12 yrs

- It should have been easy

- Conflict is accomplishing task before dark

- Boys are indians

- want father to be proud

- family not rich/poor closeknit

Born in Browning, Montana, in 1940, Welch is an American Indian descended from Blackfeet and Cross Ventre. He graduated from a Minneapolis high school after attending schools on Montana reservations, and received his B.A. from the University of Montana. "I have seen works written about Indians by whites . . ." he says, "but only an Indian knows who he is."

In this scene the 12-year-old narrator and his older brother Mose are in the midst of running cows and bulls back from grazing on prairie grass on the summer range. Welch devotes many chapters to this story of an event long past and interweaves them with chapters in the narrator's current life so that you learn only gradually of the trauma of Mose's death and the way memories haunt his brother and his father, First Raise. The rich descriptive details here and the clear narrative line draw the reader immediately into the scene.

- younger boy feels like a failure

*B*ut it was getting dark and we still had to get them across the highway. So we had them racing full tilt down the hill into the valley, both of us swearing and swatting at their behinds with the end of our ropes. The wild-eyed spinster was stretched flat-out, running low to the ground like some ungainly antelope which the others chased. Behind them came the bulls, their short legs almost a blur in the dusk, their heads swinging from side to side, hooking the wind, and the bucking calves, the white of their faces, necks and underbellies almost dead white.

Down in the valley they slowed to a trot, and Mose loped around them to open the gates.

I had lost track of the cold in our wild rush down the hill, but now as we trotted across the valley floor toward the highway, I felt the wind sing through my clothes. The tops of my thighs were numb beneath the worn Levi's and long johns. Tears rolled back away from my eyes.

Mose skirted the cows and rode up beside me. He wiped his nose with his coat sleeve.

"Okay, we've got to keep them moving—through this gate, over the highway and down through the other gate. Got that?" He tried to sound confident. "We've got to keep them moving. Okay?"

"Roger," I said.

Mose was fourteen.

It should have been easy. All of the cows had been through the routine before. They knew that when the weather turned cold and the sky gray, it was time to come in. After grazing the dry prairie grass, they were anxious to get at the alfalfa and bluejoint stubble.

It was dusk, that time of day the light plays tricks on you, when you think you can see better than you actually can, or see things that aren't there. The time of day your eyes, ears, nose become confused, all become one gray blur in the brain, so you step outside your body and watch the movie of a scene you have seen before. So it seemed, as I cut back and forth behind the herd, that I was somewhere else, not far, a hawk circling above or a beetle tracing corridors in the earth below the stamping hooves.

We pushed them through the first gate, up the incline and onto the highway. Screaming and swearing, we flailed at the stragglers with the ends of our ropes. The cows clattered on the hard surface of the highway, milling, circling, shying. My eyes watered in the gray wind until Mose seemed a crystal motion, no more or less distinct than the smell of fresh crap or the squeak of leather. The cows were spooked by the sound of their own hooves on the unfamiliar asphalt. The bulls swayed behind them, tensely, waiting to see which way the herd would move. We struck at them, but they wouldn't move without a direction.

Suddenly the spinster raced headlong down the incline. The other cows plunged after her and the bulls began to lumber across the highway.

It should have been easy. All we had to do was get them through the gate, close it and push them back a ways, away from the highway. Then we could go home to a plateful of meat and potatoes, and drink hot coffee, and tell First Raise all about it. He would listen and be pleased that we had done our job, surprised that we had done it in one day. And he would tell us how to be smart, how he had charged the white man from Dodson twenty dollars to kick his baler awake, "One dollar for the kick . . ." By now the light was almost gone and these thoughts were as real to me as the cows bunched up on the incline.

But the spinster wouldn't go through the gate. She stopped before it and lowered her head. I could see only the bulk of her back in front of the others, but in my movie I saw how she was standing, legs spread and stiff, head cocked to one side, the skin on her shoulders rippling in spasms as though she were trying to shake off a horsefly.

It was at this instant that I felt Bird quiver beneath me and gather his weight in his hindquarters. Then I saw the small shape of a calf break from the herd. I barely had time to grab the saddle horn before Bird leaped forward, chasing the calf along the fence line. We stayed on the shoulder of the highway, keeping the calf between the barbed wire and us. Mose yelled but I couldn't stop. With one hand I pushed with all my strength against the saddle horn; with the other I pulled back on the reins until I was standing, my legs stiff against the stirrups which were forward around Bird's shoulders. I couldn't raise his head, I had no strength, and so I clung helplessly to the horn.

Through a prism of tears I saw the searching yellow lights, heard the gray whine of metal, and it was past me, a scream of air whipping the hat off my head, the stinging blast against my face.

I couldn't have seen it—we were still moving in the opposite direction, the tears, the dark and wind in my eyes—the movie exploded whitely in my brain, and I saw the futile lurch of the car as the brake lights popped, the horse's shoulder caving before the fender, the horse spinning so that its rear end smashed into the door, thver the top of the car to land with the hush of a stuffed doll.

The calf stopped at the sound of collision. Bird jolted down the slope of the shoulder and I tumbled from his back, down into the dark weeds. I felt my knee strike something hard, a rock maybe, or a culvert, then the numbness.

Mose - thought killed

Meaning and Idea

1. Where are the characters physically as the chapter opens? Where are they intending to go?

2. Why does the narrator think that the job he and his brother are doing "should have been easy"?

3. What problems arise when the cattle reach the highway? Why does Bird, the narrator's horse, quiver and gather his weight in his hindquarters?

4. Summarize the last three paragraphs in your own words.

Language, Form, Structure

1. Which sensory images are most intense? Identify images of sight, sound, smell, and touch that bring you into the moment. Also, find sentences that best convey actions. What, for example, is the effect of the three participles *milling, circling, shying* at the end of the third sentence in paragraph ten? Where else do you find a concentrated use of participles?

2. The accident described in the last few paragraphs is sudden and shocking; yet Welch prepares us for it subtly in several places before we reach the end. Which sentences imply the coming catastrophe? What is the effect of the sentence "It should have been easy" at the start of paragraph eight? What effect does repeating the sentence at the start of paragraph twelve achieve? What is the effect of the one-sentence paragraph, paragraph seven, "Mose was fourteen"? What is the effect of the narrator's thoughts about what awaits Mose and him when they finish the job (paragraph twelve)?

3. Outline briefly the chronological sequence of events in this chapter. What transitional devices does Welch use to tie the events together?

4. Check these words in a dictionary and explain their meanings: spinster, ungainly (par. 1); skirted (4); bluejoint (8); flail (10); futile, lurch (16); culvert (17).

Ideas for Writing

1. Write an essay in which you narrate some accident that you had or that you witnessed. Follow a clear chronological sequence; use concrete sensory language to make the scene clear; concentrate on lively, specific verbs.

2. Narrate an unforgettable moment that you experienced with a relative—a brother, sister, parent, an aunt or uncle, a cousin.

3. On the book jacket of Welch's novel his publisher points to his "taut prose and powerfully understated vision of the reservation experience." Using this chapter, write a paragraph or two in which you comment upon Welch's skills as a prose stylist. What examples of "taut prose and powerfully understated vision" do you find here? Or, if you disagree with this assessment, make your own and provide evidence from the text to support your opinion.

William Blake
THE CHIMNEY SWEEPER

> By trade, William Blake (1757–1827) was a painter and an engraver. Yet, he was also an eccentric poet; much of his poetry derives from mystical visions and communications which he trusted as much as—or more than—his conscious reality. The "romantic school" shunned him because of his mysticism and abstruseness, and his poetry was all but ignored in his time. Today, however, we count his two major collections of poetry, *Songs of Innocence* (1789) and *Songs of Experience* (1794), among the most lyrical, profound delvings into human existence.
>
> Collected in Blake's later major volume, *Songs of Experience,* "The Chimney Sweeper" is indicative of the poet's indignation at society's treatment of poor and homeless children. Blake's concerns, in general, are with social evils, and these concerns pervade the whole collection.

When my mother died I was very young,   1
And my father sold me while yet my tongue
Could scarcely cry "'weep! 'weep! 'weep! 'weep!"
So your chimneys I sweep, and in soot I sleep.

There's little Tom Dacre, who cried when his head,   5
That curled like a lamb's back, was shaved; so I said,
"Hush, Tom! never mind it, for, when your head's bare,
You know that the soot cannot spoil your white hair."

And so he was quiet, and that very night,
As Tom was sleeping, he had such a sight!   10
That thousands of sweepers, Dick, Joe, Ned, and Jack,
Were all of them locked up in coffins of black.

And by came an Angel who had a bright key,
And he opened the coffins and set them all free;
Then down a green plain leaping, laughing, they run,   15
And wash in a river, and shine in the sun.

Then naked and white, all their bags left behind,
They rise upon clouds and sport in the wind;
And the Angel told Tom, if he'd be a good boy,
He'd have God for his father, and never want joy.   20

And so Tom awoke, and we rose in the dark,
And got with our bags and our brushes to work.
Though the morning was cold, Tom was happy and warm;
So if all do their duty they need not fear harm.

Meaning and Idea

1. What sort of boy narrates this poem? What can you discern about his character and his attitude towards life?

2. What is the "sight" of line 10?

3. Summarize the boy's dream (lines 11–20) in your own words.

Language, Form, Structure

1. *Dramatic irony* is the difference between what a narrator says and what the writer intends or knows. How is this poem an example of dramatic irony? How do you interpret the boy's dream? If a *symbol* is something that is both what it is and something else with a larger, more important meaning, how may the dream be viewed as *symbolic*?

2. What is the effect of the repetition of *weep* in line 3?

3. How does Blake use images of lightness and darkness to heighten the drama of this poem?

Ideas for Writing

1. Write a narrative of how a recent dream led you to some resolution of a difficult situation. Be sure to narrate the dream as well.

2. Write a short story—or write a poem—about an unfortunate person you have met.

3. This poem comes from Blake's *Songs of Experience*. Write a paragraph or two that tell in what ways you might consider this poem a "song." Draw specific examples from "The Chimney Sweeper" to support your point.

Emily Dickinson
THERE'S BEEN A DEATH IN THE OPPOSITE HOUSE

"The recluse of Amherst," Emily Dickinson (1830–1886) became one of the world's most renowned poets without ever leaving her home in Amherst, Massachusetts. Critics argue still whether Dickinson, most of whose poems were not published until after her death, wrote from a life fully lived or from one almost fully repressed. She wrote eloquently of love and devotion, yet she did not sustain an intimate romantic relationship nor did she ever marry. In all, Dickinson's collected poems leave us a rich expression of universal values and meanings.

Dickinson's "There's Been a Death in the Opposite House" tells readers both of the closeness of death and of the transparency of events in a small, country town. Though a simple narrative, the poem leaves one with a deep feeling and respect for the event.

There's been a death in the opposite house   1
As lately as today.
I know it by the numb look
Such houses have alway.

The neighbors rustle in and out,   5
The doctor drives away.
A window opens like a pod,
Abrupt, mechanically;

Somebody flings a mattress out,
The children hurry by;   10
They wonder if it died on that,
I used to when a boy.

The minister goes stiffly in
As if the house were his,
And he owned all the mourners now,   15
And little boys besides;

And then the milliner, and the man
Of the appalling trade,

To take the measure of the house.   20
There'll be that dark parade

Of tassels and of coaches soon;
It's easy as a sign,
The intuition of the news
In just a country town.

Meaning and Idea

1. How does the speaker know that a death has occurred? What images support this knowledge? How does the speaker feel about death?

2. What is a *milliner*? Why is the milliner important to the scene? Who is "the man/ of the appalling trade"?

3. According to the poem, why is it so easy to tell that a death has occurred in a country town?

Language, Form, Structure

1. Who is the audience for this poem? How do you know? The narrative structure here is extraordinarily simple. How does Dickinson take the reader from event to event? What transitions help the narrative movement?

2. Which verbs best convey simple crisp actions? Which adjectives best reflect the issue of death?

3. Contrast the meaning of the word *house* in lines 1 and 19.

4. Which lines in the poem come closest to stating Dickinson's main point?

5. Look up the following words in a dictionary: numb; rustle; flings; measure (noun); intuition.

Ideas for Writing

1. Write a page or two in which you narrate an early experience with death. Try to recreate the scene as clearly as possible.

2. Tell a story of an incident that you think is either uniquely rural or uniquely urban. In other words, tell of an incident that probably would not occur in the same way in the opposite environment.

3. The speaker of this poem is a man (refer to line 12), yet the poet is a woman. Do you feel Dickinson adequately portrays a man's point of view? Would there be any difference between a man's and a woman's point of view about this scene? In general, do you think writers can easily write through the eyes of a character of the opposite sex? Draw on examples from your reading.

James Joyce
ARABY

Deservedly considered the writer who forever changed the face of modern fiction, James Joyce (1882–1942) was born into a middle-class family in Dublin, Ireland. Educated at Jesuit boarding schools and later at University College, Dublin, James Joyce soon divorced himself physically (though not emotionally) from Irish nationalism and Irish Catholicism. He spent almost all his postcollege years outside of Ireland, living and working in such places as Paris, Zurich, and Trieste. His works, some of which are marked by such radical experiments in form and content as "stream of consciousness" narration, include the eloquent *Dubliners* (1914), the semiautobiographical *A Portrait of the Artist as a Young Man* (1916), the monumental *Ulysses* (1922), and the grandiose (if a little abstruse) *Finnegan's Wake* (1939). Unfortunately, Joyce's creative genius was not justly recognized until after his death.

"Araby" is one of the fifteen literary gems that comprise Joyce's collection of short stories, *Dubliners,* written between 1904 and 1907. Although some readers may be awed by the creative ambiguities of Joyce's other works, *Dubliners,* his early fiction, is easily accessible. In "Araby" he tells the story of a young man overcome by his confusions of love and infatuation, imagination and reality, freedom and commitment.

*N*orth Richmond Street, being blind, was a quiet street except at the hour when the Christian Brothers School set the boys free. An uninhabited house of two storeys stood at the blind end, detached from its neighbours in a square ground. The other houses of the street, conscious of decent lives within them, gazed at one another with brown imperturbable faces.

The former tenant of our house, a priest, had died in the back drawing-room. Air, musty from having been long enclosed, hung in all the rooms, and the waste room behind the kitchen was littered with old useless papers. Among these I found a few paper-covered books, the pages of which were curled and damp: *The Abbott,* By Walter Scott, *The Devout Communicant* and *The Memoirs of Vidocq.* I liked the last best because its leaves were yellow. The wild garden behind the house contained a central apple-tree and a few straggling bushes under one of which I found the late tenant's rusty bicycle-pump. He had been a very charitable priest; in his will he had left all his money to institutions and the furniture of his house to his sister.

When the short days of winter came dusk fell before we had well eaten our dinners. When we met in the street the houses had grown sombre. The space of sky above us was the colour of ever-changing violet and towards it the lamps of the street lifted their feeble lanterns. The cold air stung us and we played till our bodies glowed. Our shouts echoed in the silent street. The career of our play brought us through the dark muddy lanes behind the houses where we ran the gauntlet of the rough tribes from the cottages, to the back doors of the dark dripping gardens where odours arose from the ashpits, to the dark odorous stables where a coachman smoothed and combed the horse or shook music from the buckled harness. When we returned to the street light from the kitchen windows had filled the areas. If my uncle was seen turning the corner we hid in the shadow until we had seen him safely housed. Or if Mangan's sister came out on the doorstep to call her brother in to his tea we watched her from our shadow peer up and down the street. We waited to see whether she would remain or go in and, if she remained, we left our shadow and walked up to Mangan's steps resignedly. She was waiting for us, her figure defined by the light from the half-opened door. Her brother always teased her before he obeyed and I stood by the railings looking at her. Her dress swung as she moved her body and the soft rope of her hair tossed from side to side.

Every morning I lay on the floor in the front parlour watching her door. The blind was pulled down to within an inch of the sash so that I could not be seen. When she came out on the doorstep my heart leaped. I ran to the hall, seized my books and followed her. I kept her brown figure always in my eye and, when we came near the point at which our ways diverged, I quickened my pace and passed her. This happened morning after morning. I had never spoken to her, except for a few casual words, and yet her name was like a summons to all my foolish blood.

Her image accompanied me even in places the most hostile to romance. On Saturday evenings when my aunt went marketing I had to go to carry some of the parcels. We walked through the flaring streets, jostled by drunken men and bargaining women, amid the curses of labourers, the shrill litanies of shop-boys who stood on guard by the barrels of pigs' cheeks, the nasal chanting of street-singers, who sang a *come-all-you* about O'Donovan Rossa, or a ballad about the troubles in our native land. These noises converged in a single sensation of life for me: I imagined that I bore my chalice safely through a throng of foes. Her name sprang to my lips at moments in strange prayers and praises which I myself did not understand. My eyes were often full of tears (I could not tell why) and at times a flood from my heart seemed to pour itself out into my bosom. I thought little of the future. I did not know whether I would ever speak to her or not or, if I spoke to her, how I could tell her of my confused adoration. But my body was like a harp and her words and gestures were like fingers running upon the wires.

One evening I went into the back drawing-room in which the priest had died. It was a dark rainy evening and there was no sound in the house. Through one of the broken panes I heard the rain impinge upon the earth, the fine incessant needles of water playing in the sodden beds. Some distant lamp or lighted window gleamed below me. I was thankful that I could see so little. All my senses seemed to desire to veil themselves and, feeling that I was about to slip from them, I pressed the palms of my hands together until they trembled, murmuring: *"O love! O love!"* many times.

At last she spoke to me. When she addressed the first words to me I was so confused that I did not know what to answer. She asked me was I going to *Araby*. I forgot whether I answered yes or no. It would be a splendid bazaar, she said she would love to go.

"And why can't you?" I asked.

While she spoke she turned a silver bracelet round and round her wrist. She could not go, she said, because there would be a retreat that week in her convent. Her brother and two other boys were fighting for their caps and I was alone at the railings. She held one of the spikes, bowing her head towards me. The light from the lamp opposite our door caught the white curve of her neck, lit up her hair that rested there and, falling, lit up the hand upon the railing. It fell over one side of her dress and caught the white border of a petticoat, just visible as she stood at ease.

"It's well for you," she said.

"If I go," I said, "I will bring you something."

What innumerable follies laid waste my waking and sleeping thoughts after that evening! I wished to annihilate the tedious intervening days. I chafed against the work of school. At night in my bedroom and by day in the classroom her image came between me and the page I strove to read. The syllables of the word *Araby* were called to me through the silence in which my soul luxuriated and cast an Eastern enchantment over me. I asked for leave to go to the bazaar on Saturday night. My aunt was surprised and hoped it was not some Freemason affair. I answered few questions in class. I watched my master's face pass from amiability to sternness; he hoped I was not beginning to idle. I could not call my wandering thoughts together. I had hardly any patience with the serious work of life which, now that it stood between me and my desire, seemed to me child's play, ugly monotonous child's play.

On Saturday morning I reminded my uncle that I wished to go to the bazaar in the evening. He was fussing at the hallstand, looking for the hat-brush, and answered me curtly:

"Yes, boy, I know."

As he was in the hall I could not go into the front parlour and lie at the window. I left the house in bad humour and walked slowly towards the school. The air was pitilessly raw and already my heart misgave me.

When I came home to dinner my uncle had not yet been home. Still it was early. I sat staring at the clock for some time and, when its ticking began to irritate me, I left the room. I mounted the staircase and gained the upper part of the house. The high cold empty gloomy rooms liberated me and I went from room to room singing. From the front window I saw my companions playing below in the street. Their cries reached me weakened and indistinct and, leaning my forehead against the cool glass, I looked over at the dark house where she lived. I may have stood there for an hour, seeing nothing but the brown-clad figure cast by my imagination, touched discreetly by the lamplight at the curved neck, at the hand upon the railings and at the border below the dress.

When I came downstairs again I found Mrs. Mercer sitting at the fire. She was an old garrulous woman, a pawnbroker's widow, who collected used stamps for some pious purpose. I had to endure the gossip of the tea-table. The meal was prolonged beyond an hour and still my uncle did not come. Mrs. Mercer stood up to go: she was sorry she couldn't wait any longer, but it was after eight o'clock and she did not like to be out late, as the night air was bad for her. When she had gone I began to walk up and down the room, clenching my fists. My aunt said:

"I'm afraid you may put off your bazaar for this night of Our Lord."

At nine o'clock I heard my uncle's latchkey in the halldoor. I heard him talking to himself and heard the hallstand rocking when it had received the weight of his overcoat. I could interpret these signs. When he was midway through his dinner I asked him to give me the money to go to the bazaar. He had forgotten.

"The people are in bed and after their first sleep now," he said.

I did not smile. My aunt said to him energetically:

"Can't you give him the money and let him go? You've kept him late enough as it is."

My uncle said he was very sorry he had forgotten. He said he believed in the old saying: "All work and no play makes Jack a dull boy." He asked me where I was going and, when I had told him a second time he asked me did I know *The Arab's Farewell to his Steed*. When I left the kitchen he was about to recite the opening lines of the piece to my aunt.

I held a florin tightly in my hand as I strode down Buckingham Street towards the station. The sight of the streets thronged with buyers and glaring with gas recalled to me the purpose of my journey. I took my seat in a third-class carriage of a deserted train. After an intolerable delay the train moved out of the station slowly. It crept onward among ruinous houses and over the twinkling river. At Westland Row Station a crowd of people pressed to the carriage doors; but the porters moved them back, saying that it was a special train for the bazaar. I remained alone in the bare carriage. In a few minutes the train drew up beside an improvised wooden platform. I passed out on the road and saw by the lighted dial of a clock that it was ten minutes to ten. In front of me was a large building which displayed the magical name.

I could not find any sixpenny entrance and, fearing that the bazaar would be closed, I passed in quickly through a turnstile, handing a shilling to a weary-looking man. I found myself in a big hall girdled at half its height by a gallery. Nearly all the stalls were closed and the greater part of the hall was in darkness. I recognised a silence like that which pervades a church after a service. I walked into the centre of the bazaar timidly. A few people were gathered about the stalls which were still open. Before a curtain, over which the words *Café Chantant* were written in coloured lamps, two men were counting money on a salver. I listened to the fall of the coins.

Remembering with difficulty why I had come I went over to one of the stalls and examined porcelain vases and flowered tea-sets. At the door of the stall a young lady was talking and laughing with two young gentlemen. I remarked their English accents and listened vaguely to their conversation.

"O, I never said such a thing!"

"O, but you did!"

"O, but I didn't!"

"Didn't she say that?"

"Yes. I heard her."

"O, there's a . . . fib!"

Observing me the young lady came over and asked me did I wish to buy anything. The tone of her voice was not encouraging; she seemed to have spoken to me out of a sense of duty. I looked humbly at the great jars that stood like eastern guards at either side of the dark entrance to the stall and murmured:

"No, thank you."

The young lady changed the position of one of the vases and went back to the two young men. They began to talk of the same subject. Once or twice the young lady glanced at me over her shoulder.

I lingered before her stall, though I knew my stay was useless, to make my interest in her wares seem the more real. Then I turned away slowly and walked down the middle of the bazaar. I allowed the two pennies to fall against the sixpence in my pocket. I heard a voice call from one end of the gallery that the light was out. The upper part of the hall was now completely dark.

Gazing up into the darkness I saw myself as a creature driven and derided by vanity; and my eyes burned with anguish and anger.

Meaning and Idea

1. Describe the environment in which the narrator lives. What does he find special about it? What is the significance of the details which he chooses to emphasize, especially in the opening paragraphs?

2. What are the narrator's feelings towards Mangan's sister? On what are they based? What image of her does his imagination create? How close is it to her reality? Why is she always referred to as "Mangan's sister" rather than by her own name?

3. Is Mangan's sister older or younger than the narrator? How do you know?

4. What promise does the narrator make to Mangan's sister? Does he keep it? Why? Describe what happens. What do you think will be the consequences to the narrator?

5. How old do you think the narrator is when he is telling this story? How can you tell?

Language, Form, Structure

1. How is personification (see page 44) used in the beginning paragraphs of the story? How does it bear on the narrator's character and his choices? What is the theme of this story? How does the title support the theme?

2. Trace the uses of color imagery in the story. What are the predominant colors? How do they help set the tone of the story? What is the special significance of the colors used to describe Mangan's sister?

3. Joyce wrote of his stories as having "moments of epiphany"—that is, sudden, great realizations that change the course of the protagonist's actions. What is the "moment of epiphany" in this story? How is it foreshadowed? Imagine this story without its special moment. What does the moment of epiphany contribute to the story as a whole?

4. What is the theme of this story? How does the title support the theme?

5. Select ten words from this story which were unfamiliar to you and use them in sentences of your own.

Ideas for Writing

1. Write a narrative about a time you made a promise to someone, one which you decided not to keep. Why didn't you keep it? What were the consequences?

2. Write a narrative of a moment in which you felt alone, although you may have been in the midst of a crowd. Concentrate on details of the environment.

3. In *Dubliners,* the book of stories in which "Araby" was collected, Joyce wanted to write about the "paralysis"—or emotional immobilization—of the life in Dublin as he knew it. Write a short analysis of this story in relation to the theme of paralysis. Who or what is paralyzed here?

Langston Hughes
SALVATION

Langston Hughes (1902–1967) was one of America's fore-most poets, essayists, dramatists, and fiction writers whose self-proclaimed desire as a writer was "to explain and illuminate the Negro condition in America." Once elected class poet in gram-mar school in Lincoln, Illinois, Hughes first gained adult recogni-tion as a poet when he was a busboy at a hotel in Washington, D.C. He left some poems by the plate of the poet Vachel Lindsay, who fortunately recognized his talent.

"Salvation" is a selection from Hughes's autobiography *The Big Sea* (1940). In it, he tells of his "conversion" to Christ in the midst of peer and community pressure. The narrative informs us of young Hughes's difficult situation, his fanciful reaction to it, and both the short- and long-term effects of his actions.

I was saved from sin when I was going on thirteen. But not really saved. It happened like this. There was a big revival at my Auntie Reed's church. Every night for weeks there had been much preaching, singing, praying, and shouting, and some very hardened sinners had been brought to Christ, and the membership of the church had grown by leaps and bounds. Then just before the revival ended, they held a special meeting for children, "to bring the young lambs to the fold." My aunt spoke of it for days ahead. That night I was escorted to the front row and placed on the mourners' bench with all the other young sinners, who had not yet been brought to Jesus.

My aunt told me that when you were saved you saw a light, and something happened to you inside! And Jesus came into your life! And

God was with you from then on! She said you could see and hear and feel Jesus in your soul. I believed her. I had heard a great many old people say the same thing and it seemed to me they ought to know. So I sat there calmly in the hot, crowded church, waiting for Jesus to come to me.

The preacher preached a wonderful rhythmical sermon, all moans and shouts and lonely cries and dire pictures of hell, and then he sang a song about the ninety and nine safe in the fold, but one little lamb was left out in the cold. Then he said: "Won't you come? Won't you come to Jesus? Young lambs, won't you come?" And he held out his arms to all us young sinners there on the mourners' bench. And the little girls cried. And some of them jumped up and went to Jesus right away. But most of us just sat there.

A great many old people came and knelt around us and prayed, old women with jet-black faces and braided hair, old men with work-gnarled hands. And the church sang a song about the lower lights are burning, some poor sinners to be saved. And the whole building rocked with prayer and song.

Still I kept waiting to *see* Jesus.

Finally all the young people had gone to the altar and were saved, but one boy and me. He was a rounder's son named Westley. Westley and I were surrounded by sisters and deacons praying. It was very hot in the church, and getting late now. Finally Westley said to me in a whisper: "God damn! I'm tired o' sitting here. Let's get up and be saved." So he got up and was saved.

Then I was left all alone on the mourners' bench. My aunt came and knelt at my knees and cried, while prayers and songs swirled all around me in the little church. The whole congregation prayed for me alone, in a mighty wail of moans and voices. And I kept waiting serenely for Jesus, waiting, waiting—but he didn't come. I wanted to see him, but nothing happened to me. Nothing! I wanted something to happen to me, but nothing happened.

I heard the songs and the minister saying: "Why don't you come? My dear child, why don't you come to Jesus? Jesus is waiting for you. He wants you. Why don't you come? Sister Reed, what is this child's name?"

"Langston," my aunt sobbed.

"Langston, why don't you come? Why don't you come and be saved? Oh, Lamb of God! Why don't you come?"

Now it was really getting late. I began to be ashamed of myself, holding everything up so long. I began to wonder what God thought about Westley, who certainly hadn't seen Jesus either, but who was now sitting proudly on the platform, swinging his knickerbockered legs and grinning down at me, surrounded by deacons and old women on their knees praying. God had not struck Westley dead for taking his name in vain or for lying in the temple. So I decided that maybe to save further trouble, I'd better lie, too, and say that Jesus had come, and get up and be saved.

So I got up.

Suddenly the whole room broke into a sea of shouting, as they saw me rise. Waves of rejoicing swept the place. Women leaped in the air. My aunt threw her arms around me. The minister took me by the hand and led me to the platform.

When things quieted down, in a hushed silence, punctuated by a few ecstatic "Amens," all the new young lambs were blessed in the name of God. Then joyous singing filled the room.

That night, for the last time in my life but one—for I was a big boy twelve years old—I cried. I cried, in bed alone, and couldn't stop. I buried my head under the quilts, but my aunt heard me. She woke up and told my uncle I was crying because the Holy Ghost had come into my life, and because I had seen Jesus. But I was really crying because I couldn't bear to tell her that I had lied, that I had deceived everybody in the church, that I hadn't seen Jesus, and that now I didn't believe there was a Jesus any more, since he didn't come to help me.

the outcome was good in the eyes of everyone else but bad for Langston because he didn't believe anymore

Meaning and Idea

1. In your own words, describe the atmosphere of the revival meeting. What was its purpose?

2. Who are the "lambs" to be saved?

3. Who is most concerned about Langston's "salvation"? Why? Do you think they are sincere?

4. Why does Westley get "saved"? Why does Langston decide to be saved, too?

5. What are the immediate consequences of Langston's actions? What are the long-range consequences?

Language, Form, Structure

1. How do the first two sentences serve as a thesis for this essay? What conflict do they present which must be resolved within the narrative?

2. About midway through the essay, what *allusion* (see page 42) helps place the time period of this narrative? Approximately what time period is it?

3. What is the value of *dialogue* in this selection? Where is it used most effectively? How would paragraph six, for example, be different if Hughes had omitted Westley's lines of dialogue?

4. How is sound imagery used in this essay? Where is it used most vibrantly?

5. How does Hughes change slightly the time frame of the essay in the last sentence?

6. Check the dictionary meanings for: dire (par. 3); gnarled (4); rounder, deacons (6). Use each word in an original sentence.

Ideas for Writing

1. Tell about a time when you told a lie. Be sure to set the situation, tell about the actual event of the lie, and discuss the consequences.

2. Narrate an incident in which you did something you thought you *had to* do but didn't really *want* to do. Explain why you did it—what pressures affected you most strongly. Tell about your feelings afterward.

3. What do you consider the most effective prose narrative techniques in this essay? You might consider, for example, language, sentence structure, temporal sequencing, characterization, or dialogue. In a paragraph or two, explain your choice by analyzing examples from the text.

Edgar Allan Poe
THE TELL-TALE HEART

Edgar Allan Poe (1809–1849) was born in Boston. After his mother died when he was only 2 years old, he was adopted by John Allan of Richmond, Virginia. Poe eventually returned to Boston, then made homes in New York and Baltimore. Known mostly for his macabre and tormented stories and poems, Poe was also a literary critic of some merit. In fact, in one critical essay, he set down guidelines for the writing of a short story which are still relevant over a hundred years later. In 1835, Poe became editor of the *Southern Literary Messenger,* and for much of his life held similar editorial positions. However, his life was beset with difficulties and tragedies: poverty; the illness and death of his 13-year-old bride; bitter personal battles; his own physical and mental dissolution. Poe was found unconscious in a gutter in Baltimore in 1849, where he died soon after.

First published in the January 1843 edition of *The Pioneer,* "The Tell-Tale Heart" is Poe's classic of a gothic horror tale. Colored by the obviously deranged mind of its narrator, this story is a good example of an interior dramatic monologue, in which one character speaks to himself alone.

*T*rue!—nervous—very, very dreadfully nervous I had been and am; but why *will* you say that I am mad? The disease had sharpened my senses—not destroyed—not dulled them. Above all was the sense of hearing acute. I heard all things in the heaven and in the earth. I heard many things in hell. How, then, am I mad? Hearken! and observe how healthily—how calmly I can tell you the whole story.

It is impossible to say how first the idea entered my brain; but once conceived, it haunted me day and night. Object there was none. Passion there was none. I loved the old man. He had never wronged me. He had never given me insult. For his gold I had no desire. I think it was his eye! yes, it was this! One of his eyes resembled that of a vulture—a pale blue eye, with a film over it. Whenever it fell upon me, my blood ran cold; and so by degrees—very gradually—I made up my mind to take the life of the old man, and thus rid myself of the eye for ever.

Now this is the point. You fancy me mad. Madmen know nothing. But you should have seen *me*. You should have seen how wisely I pro-ceeded—with what caution—with what foresight—with what dissimula-tion I went to work! I was never kinder to the old man than during the whole week before I killed him. And every night, about midnight, I turned the latch of his door and opened it—oh, so gently! And then, when I had made an opening sufficient for my head, I put in a dark lantern, all closed, closed, so that no light shone out, and then I thrust in my head. Oh, you would have laughed to see how cunningly I thrust it in! I moved it slowly—very, very slowly, so that I might not disturb the old man's sleep. It took me an hour to place my whole head within the opening so far that I could see him as he lay upon his bed. Ha!—would a madman have been so wise as this? And then, when my head was well in the room, I undid the lantern cautiously—oh, so cautiously—cautiously (for the hinges creaked)—I undid it just so much that a single thin ray fell upon the vulture eye. And this I did for seven long nights—every night just at midnight—but I found the eye always closed; and so it was impossible to do the work; for it was not the old man who vexed me, but his Evil Eye. And every morning, when the day broke, I went boldly into the chamber, and spoke courageously to him, calling him by name in a hearty tone, and inquiring how he had passed the night. So you see he would have been a very profound old man, indeed, to suspect that every night, just at twelve, I looked in upon him while he slept.

Upon the eighth night I was more than usually cautious in opening the door. A watch's minute hand moves more quickly than did mine. Never before that night had I *felt* the extent of my own powers—of my sagacity. I could scarcely contain my feelings of triumph. To think that there I was, opening the door, little by little, and he not even to dream of my secret deeds or thoughts. I fairly chuckled at the idea; and perhaps he heard me;

for he moved on the bed suddenly, as if startled. Now you may think that I drew back—but no. His room was as black as pitch with the thick darkness (for the shutters were close fastened, through fear of robbers), and so I knew that he could not see the opening of the door, and I kept pushing it on steadily, steadily.

I had my head in, and was about to open the lantern, when my thumb slipped upon the tin fastening, and the old man sprang up in the bed, crying out—"Who's there?"

I kept quite still and said nothing. For a whole hour I did not move a muscle, and in the meantime I did not hear him lie down. He was still sitting up in the bed listening;—just as I have done, night after night, hearkening to the death watches in the wall.

Presently I heard a slight groan, and I knew it was the groan of mortal terror. It was not a groan of pain or of grief—oh, no!—it was the low stifled sound that arises from the bottom of the soul when overcharged with awe. I knew the sound well. Many a night, just at midnight, when all the world slept, it was welled up from my own bosom, deepening, with its dreadful echo, the terrors that distracted me. I say I knew it well. I knew what the old man felt, and pitied him, although I chuckled at heart. I knew that he had been lying awake ever since the first slight noise, when he had turned in the bed. His fears had been ever since growing upon him. He had been trying to fancy them causeless, but could not. He had been saying to himself—"It is nothing but the wind in the chimney—it is only a mouse crossing the floor," or "it is merely a cricket which has made a single chirp." Yes, he has been trying to comfort himself with these suppositions; but he had found all in vain. *All in vain;* because Death, in approaching him, had stalked with his black shadow before him, and enveloped the victim. And it was the mournful influence of the unper-ceived shadow that caused him to feel—although he neither saw nor heard—to *feel* the presence of my head within the room.

When I had waited a long time, very patiently, without hearing him lie down, I resolved to open a little—a very, very little crevice in the lantern. So I opened it—you cannot imagine how stealthily, stealthily—until, at length, a single dim ray, like the thread of a spider, shot from out the crevice and full upon the vulture eye.

It was open—wide, wide open—and I grew furious as I gazed upon it. I saw it with perfect distinctness—all a dull blue, with a hideous veil over it that chilled the very marrow in my bones; but I could see nothing else of the old man's face or person: for I had directed the ray as if by instinct, precisely upon the damned spot.

And now have I not told you that what you mistake for madness is but over-acuteness of the senses?—now, I say, there came to my ears a low, dull, quick sound, such as a watch makes when enveloped in cotton. I knew *that* sound well too. It was the beating of the old man's heart. It increased my fury, as the beating of a drum stimulates the soldier into courage.

But even yet I refrained and kept still. I scarcely breathed. I held the lantern motionless. I tried how steadily I could maintain the ray upon the eye. Meantime the hellish tattoo of the heart increased. It grew quicker and quicker, and louder and louder every instant. The old man's terror *must* have been extreme! It grew louder, I say, louder every moment!— do you mark me well? I have told you that I am nervous: so I am. And now at the dead hour of the night, amid the dreadful silence of that old house, so strange a noise as this excited me to uncontrollable terror. Yet, for some minutes longer I refrained and stood still. But the beating grew louder, louder! I thought the heart must burst. And now a new anxiety seized me—the sound would be heard by a neighbor! The old man's hour had come! With a loud yell, I threw open the lantern and leaped into the room. He shrieked once—once only. In an instant I dragged him to the floor, and pulled the heavy bed over him. I then smiled gaily, to find the deed so far done. But, for many minutes, the heart beat on with a muffled sound. This, however, did not vex me; it would not be heard through the wall. At length it ceased. The old man was dead. I removed the bed and examined the corpse. Yes, he was stone, stone dead. I placed my hand upon the heart and held it there many minutes. There was no pulsation. He was stone dead. His eye would trouble me no more.

If still you think me mad, you will think so no longer when I describe the wise precautions I took for the concealment of the body. The night waned and I worked hastily, but in silence. First of all I dismembered the corpse. I cut off the head and the arms and the legs.

I then took up three planks from the flooring of the chamber, and deposited all between the scantlings. I then replaced the boards so cleverly, so cunningly, that no human eye—not even *his*—could have detected any thing wrong. There was nothing to wash out—no stain of any kind—no blood-spot whatever. I had been too wary for that. A tub had caught all—ha! ha!

When I had made an end of these labors, it was four o'clock—still dark as midnight. As the bell sounded the hour, there came a knocking at the street door. I went down to open it with a light heart,—for what had I *now* to fear? There entered three men, who introduced themselves, with perfect suavity, as officers of the police. A shriek had been heard by a neighbor during the night; suspicion of foul play had been aroused; information had been lodged at the police office, and they (the officers) had been deputed to search the premises.

I smiled,—for *what* had I to fear? I bade the gentlemen welcome. The shriek, I said, was my own in a dream. The old man, I mentioned, was absent in the country. I took my visitors all over the house. I bade them search—search *well*. I led them, at length, to *his* chamber. I showed them his treasures, secure, undisturbed. In the enthusiasm of my confidence, I brought chairs into the room, and desired them *here* to rest from their fatigues, while I myself, in the wild audacity of my perfect triumph, placed my own seat upon the very spot beneath which reposed the corpse of the victim.

The officers were satisfied. My *manner* had convinced them. I was singularly at ease. They sat, and while I answered cheerily, they chatted familiar things. But, ere long, I felt myself getting pale and wished them gone. My head ached, and I fancied a ringing in my ears: but still they sat and still chatted. The ringing became more distinct:—it continued and became more distinct: I talked more freely to get rid of the feeling: but it continued and gained definitiveness—until, at length, I found that the noise was *not* within my ears.

No doubt I now grew *very* pale;—but I talked more fluently, and with a heightened voice. Yet the sound increased—and what could I do? It was *a low, dull, quick sound—much such a sound as a watch makes when enveloped in cotton*. I gasped for breath—and yet the officers heard it not. I talked more quickly—more vehemently; but the noise steadily increased. I arose and argued about trifles, in a high key and with violent gesticulations, but the noise steadily increased. Why *would* they not be gone? I paced the floor to and fro with heavy strides, as if excited to fury by the observation of the men—but the noise steadily increased. Oh God! what *could* I do? I foamed—I raved—I swore! I swung the chair upon which I had been sitting, and grated it upon the boards, but the noise arose over all and continually increased. It grew louder—louder—*louder!* And still the men chatted pleasantly, and smiled. Was it possible they heard not? Almighty God!—no, no! They heard!—they suspected!—they *knew!*—they were making a mockery of my horror!—this I thought, and this I think. But any thing was better than this agony! Any thing was more tolerable than this derision! I could bear those hypocritical smiles no longer! I felt that I must scream or die!—and now—again!—hark! louder! louder! louder! *louder!*—

"Villains!" I shrieked, "dissemble no more! I admit the deed!—tear up the planks!—here, here!—it is the beating of his hideous heart!"

Meaning and Idea

1. If not madness, what does the narrator claim is the effect of his disease? How does he try to convince the reader that he is not mad?

2. Throughout the story, the narrator claims to know well the old man's feelings. How can the narrator actually know those feelings?

3. How does the narrator explain the shriek that brought the police to the house? How does he deal with the police?

4. Given the events as related by the narrator, could he indeed still be haunted by the heart beating? Why? How does this assertion influence one's belief in the rest of the story?

5. In the last paragraph, the narrator describes his actions at trying to drown out the noise of the heart. What does he do? If these actions were true, would the three men still have "chatted pleasantly"? What do you suspect was the truth of the incident? Why?

Language, Form, Structure

1. This story is an example of the *I-narrative* form, or first-person narrative, in which the protagonist tells the events that happen to him and others. Also, this I-narrative is an example of a dramatic monologue. To whom does the narrator address himself? Why?

2. In the first paragraph, the narrator claims, "Above all was the sense of hearing acute." Poe then makes use of numerous auditory images throughout the story. Go through the tale again and list, in order, all the auditory imagery you find. How does this acute sense of hearing eventually cause the narrator's downfall?

3. The narrator's madness causes him to make certain highly ironic statements. Reread the opening three paragraphs; then choose and explain what you consider the most ironic statements.

4. There is a great deal of repetition of words and phrases in this narrative. What is the purpose of these repetitions? What do they indicate about the narrator's emotional state? How do they affect the rhythm of the story?

5. Look up the meanings of the following words: acute; sagacity; stealthily; hideous; vex; waned; suavity; audacity; trifles; gesticulations. Then use each of these words in a sentence of your own.

Ideas for Writing

1. Make up a horror story of your own and narrate it through an unreliable first-person narrator. Try to make it as dramatic as possible.

2. Narrate the most horrible true incident you've ever witnessed. Attempt to create a fearful tone.

3. Write an essay in which you analyze the narrator of "A Tell-Tale Heart." Unlike a third-person narrative where the reader can generally trust the narrator with no reservations, in any I-narrative the reader must apply certain tests to the narrator's reliability. For example, we must ascertain whether or not the narrator is crazy, drunk, in a heightened emotional state, a habitual liar, and so on. Clearly the I-narrator in this story is *un*reliable. In that case, what information *can* you obtain from this story? Why would Poe choose to write in this motif? Do you believe any of the story? Which part? Why? What do you suppose *is* the true story here?

In what other stories or books have you questioned the narrator's veracity? How did they compare with this story?

Raymond Carver
MY FATHER'S LIFE

Raymond Carver was born in 1939 in Clatskanie, Oregon. He studied at Humboldt State College and the University of Iowa and then worked a variety of jobs—janitor, stockboy, editor, creative writing instructor—to support his family. All the time, he wrote and began to earn the critical acclaim he now receives. Among other awards, he has been the recipient of a National Endowment for the Arts "Discovery" Award, a Guggenheim Fellowship, and the prestigious Strauss Living Award. His poems, essays, and stories have been widely published in magazines, and his narrative sparseness has caused some to compare him to Hemingway. His collections of fiction include *Will You Please Be Quiet, Please* (1976), *What We Talk About When We Talk About Love* (1981), and *Cathedral* (1983).

"My Father's Life" first appeared in the "First Person" column of *Esquire Magazine* in September, 1984. In it, Carver remembers his father, senses the convergences and divergences of their lives, and at last, consigns his father to memory.

My dad's name was Clevie Raymond Carver. His family called him Raymond and friends called him C.R. I was named Raymond Clevie Carver Jr. I hated the "Junior" part. When I was little my dad called me Frog, which was okay. But later, like everybody else in the family, he began calling me Junior. He went on calling me this until I was thirteen or fourteen and announced that I wouldn't answer to that name any longer. So he began calling me Doc. From then until his death, on June 17, 1967, he called me Doc, or else Son.

When he died, my mother telephoned my wife with the news. I was away from my family at the time, between lives, trying to enroll in the School of Library Science at the University of Iowa. When my wife answered the phone, my mother blurted out, "Raymond's dead!" For a moment, my wife thought my mother was telling her that I was dead. Then my mother made it clear *which* Raymond she was talking about and my wife said, "Thank God. I thought you meant *my* Raymond."

My dad walked, hitched rides, and rode in empty boxcars when he went from Arkansas to Washington State in 1934, looking for work. I don't know whether he was pursuing a dream when he went out to Washington. I doubt it. I don't think he dreamed much. I believe he was simply looking for steady work at decent pay. Steady work was meaningful work. He picked apples for a time and then landed a construction laborer's job on the Grand Coulee Dam. After he'd put aside a little money, he bought a car and drove back to Arkansas to help his folks, my grandparents, pack up for the move west. He said later that they were about to starve down there, and this wasn't meant as a figure of speech. It was during that short while in Arkansas, in a town called Leola, that my mother met my dad on the sidewalk as he came out of a tavern.

"He was drunk," she said. "I don't know why I let him talk to me. His eyes were glittery. I wish I'd had a crystal ball." They'd met once, a year or so before, at a dance. He'd had girlfriends before her, my mother told me. "Your dad always had a girlfriend, even after we married. He was my first and last. I never had another man. But I didn't miss anything."

They were married by a justice of the peace on the day they left for Washington, this big, tall country girl and a farmhand-turned-construction worker. My mother spent her wedding night with my dad and his folks, all of them camped beside the road in Arkansas.

In Omak, Washington, my dad and mother lived in a little place not much bigger than a cabin. My grandparents lived next door. My dad was still working on the dam, and later, with the huge turbines producing electricity and the water backed up for a hundred miles into Canada, he stood in the crowd and heard Franklin D. Roosevelt when he spoke at the construction site. "He never mentioned those guys who died building that dam," my dad said. Some of his friends had died there, men from Arkansas, Oklahoma, and Missouri.

He then took a job in a sawmill in Clatskanie, Oregon, a little town alongside the Columbia River. I was born there, and my mother has a picture of my dad standing in front of the gate to the mill, proudly holding me up to face the camera. My bonnet is on crooked and about to come untied. His hat is pushed back on his forehead, and he's wearing a big grin. Was he going in to work or just finishing his shift? It doesn't matter. In either case, he had a job and a family. These were his salad days.

In 1941 we moved to Yakima, Washington, where my dad went to work as a saw filer, a skilled trade he'd learned in Clatskanie. When war broke out, he was given a deferment because his work was considered necessary to the war effort. Finished lumber was in demand by the armed services, and he kept his saws so sharp they could shave the hair off your arm.

After my dad had moved us to Yakima, he moved his folks into the same neighborhood. By the mid-1940s the rest of my dad's family—his brother, his sister, and her husband, as well as uncles, cousins, nephews, and most of their extended family and friends—had come out from Arkansas. All because my dad came out first. The men went to work at Boise Cascade, where my dad worked, and the women packed apples in the canneries. And in just a little while, it seemed—according to my mother—everybody was better off than my dad. "Your dad couldn't keep money," my mother said. "Money burned a hole in his pocket. He was always doing for others."

The first house I clearly remember living in, at 1515 South Fifteenth Street, in Yakima, had an outdoor toilet. On Halloween night, or just any night, for the hell of it, neighbor kids, kids in their early teens, would carry our toilet away and leave it next to the road. My dad would have to get somebody to help him bring it home. Or these kids would take the toilet and stand it in somebody else's backyard. Once they actually set it on fire. But ours wasn't the only house that had an outdoor toilet. When I was old enough to know what I was doing, I threw rocks at the other toilets when I'd see someone go inside. This was called bombing the toilets. After a while, though, everyone went to indoor plumbing until, suddenly, our toilet was the last outdoor one in the neighborhood. I remember the shame I felt when my third-grade teacher, Mr. Wise, drove me home from school one day. I asked him to stop at the house just before ours, claiming I lived there.

I can recall what happened one night when my dad came home late to find that my mother had locked all the doors on him from the inside. He was drunk, and we could feel the house shudder as he rattled the door. When he'd managed to force open a window, she hit him between the eyes with a colander and knocked him out. We could see him down there on the grass. For years afterward, I used to pick up this colander—it was as heavy as a rolling pin—and imagine what it would feel like to be hit in the head with something like that.

It was during this period that I remember my dad taking me into the bedroom, sitting me down on the bed, and telling me that I might have to go live with my Aunt LaVon for a while. I couldn't understand what I'd done that meant I'd have to go away from home to live. But this, too—whatever prompted it—must have blown over, more or less, anyway, because we stayed together, and I didn't have to go live with her or anyone else.

I remember my mother pouring his whiskey down the sink. Sometimes she'd pour it all out and sometimes, if she was afraid of getting caught, she'd only pour half of it out and then add water to the rest. I tasted some of his whiskey once myself. It was terrible stuff, and I don't see how anybody could drink it.

After a long time without one, we finally got a car, in 1949 or 1950, a 1938 Ford. But it threw a rod the first week we had it, and my dad had to have the motor rebuilt.

"We drove the oldest car in town," my mother said. "We could have had a Cadillac for all he spent on car repairs." One time she found someone else's tube of lipstick on the floorboard, along with a lacy handkerchief. "See this?" she said to me. "Some floozy left this in the car."

Once I saw her take a pan of warm water into the bedroom where my dad was sleeping. She took his hand from under the covers and held it in the water. I stood in the doorway and watched. I wanted to know what was going on. This would make him talk in his sleep, she told me. There were things she needed to know, things she was sure he was keeping from her.

Every year or so, when I was little, we would take the North Coast Limited across the Cascade Range from Yakima to Seattle and stay in the Vance Hotel and eat, I remember, at a place called the Dinner Bell Cafe. Once we went to Ivar's Acres of Clams and drank glasses of warm clam broth.

In 1956, the year I was to graduate from high school, my dad quit his job at the mill in Yakima and took a job in Chester, a little sawmill town in northern California. The reasons given at the time for his taking the job had to do with a higher hourly wage and the vague promise that he might, in a few years' time, succeed to the job of head filer in this new mill. But I think, in the main, that my dad had grown restless and simply wanted to try his luck elsewhere. Things had gotten a little too predictable for him in Yakima. Also, the year before, there had been the deaths, within six months of each other, of both his parents.

But just a few days after graduation, when my mother and I were packed to move to Chester, my dad penciled a letter to say he'd been sick for a while. He didn't want us to worry, he said, but he'd cut himself on a saw. Maybe he'd got a tiny sliver of steel in his blood. Anyway, something had happened and he'd had to miss work, he said. In the same mail was an unsigned postcard from somebody down there telling my mother that my dad was about to die and that he was drinking "raw whiskey."

When we arrived in Chester, my dad was living in a trailer that belonged to the company. I didn't recognize him immediately. I guess for a moment I didn't want to recognize him. He was skinny and pale and looked bewildered. His pants wouldn't stay up. He didn't look like my dad. My mother began to cry. My dad put his arm around her and patted her shoulder vaguely, like he didn't know what this was all about, either. The three of us took up life together in the trailer, and we looked after him as best we could. But my dad was sick, and he couldn't get any better. I worked with him in the mill that summer and part of the fall. We'd get up in the mornings and eat eggs and toast while we listened to the radio, and then go out the door with our lunch pails. We'd pass through the gate together at eight in the morning, and I wouldn't see him again until quitting time. In November I went back to Yakima to be closer to my girlfriend, the girl I'd made up my mind I was going to marry.

He worked at the mill in Chester until the following February, when he collapsed on the job and was taken to the hospital. My mother asked if I would come down there and help. I caught a bus from Yakima to Chester, intending to drive them back to Yakima. But now, in addition to being physically sick, my dad was in the midst of a nervous breakdown, though none of us knew to call it that at the time. During the entire trip back to Yakima, he didn't speak, not even when asked a direct question. ("How do you feel, Raymond?" "You okay, Dad?") He'd communicate, if he communicated at all, by moving his head or by turning his palms up as if to say he didn't know or care. The only time he said anything on the trip, and for nearly a month afterward, was when I was speeding down a gravel road in Oregon and the car muffler came loose. "You were going too fast," he said.

Back in Yakima a doctor saw to it that my dad went to a psychiatrist. My mother and dad had to go on relief, as it was called, and the county paid for the psychiatrist. The psychiatrist asked my dad, "Who is the President?" He'd had a question put to him that he could answer. "Ike," my dad said. Nevertheless, they put him on the fifth floor of Valley Memorial Hospital and began giving him electroshock treatments. I was married by then and about to start my own family. My dad was still locked up when my wife went into this same hospital, just one floor down, to have our first baby. After she had delivered, I went upstairs to give my dad the news. They let me in through a steel door and showed me where I could find him. He was sitting on a couch with a blanket over his lap. *Hey,* I thought. *What in hell is happening to my dad?* I sat down next to him and told him he was a grandfather. He waited a minute and then he said, "I feel like a grandfather." That's all he said. He didn't smile or move. He was in a big room with a lot of other people. Then I hugged him, and he began to cry.

Somehow he got out of there. But now came the years when he couldn't work and just sat around the house trying to figure what next and what he'd done wrong in his life that he'd wound up like this. My mother went from job to crummy job. Much later she referred to that time he was in the hospital, and those years just afterward, as "when Raymond was sick." The word *sick* was never the same for me again.

In 1964, through the help of a friend, he was lucky enough to be hired on at a mill in Klamath, California. He moved down there by himself to see if he could hack it. He lived not far from the mill, in a one-room cabin not much different from the place he and my mother had started out living in when they went west. He scrawled letters to my mother, and if I called she'd read them aloud to me over the phone. In the letters, he said it was touch and go. Every day that he went to work, he felt like it was the most important day of his life. But every day, he told her, made the next day that much easier. He said for her to tell me he said hello. If he couldn't sleep at night, he said, he thought about me and the good times we used to have. Finally, after a couple of months, he regained some of his confidence. He could do the work and didn't think he had to worry that he'd let anybody down ever again. When he was sure, he sent for my mother.

He'd been off from work for six years and had lost everything in that time—home, car, furniture, and appliances, including the big freezer that had been my mother's pride and joy. He'd lost his good name too—Raymond Carver was someone who couldn't pay his bills—and his self-respect was gone. He'd even lost his virility. My mother told my wife, "All during that time Raymond was sick we slept together in the same bed, but we didn't have relations. He wanted to a few times, but nothing happened. I didn't miss it, but I think he wanted to, you know."

During those years I was trying to raise my own family and earn a living. But, one thing and another, we found ourselves having to move a lot. I couldn't keep track of what was going down in my dad's life. But I did have a chance one Christmas to tell him I wanted to be a writer. I might as well have told him I wanted to become a plastic surgeon. "What are you going to write about?" he wanted to know. Then as if to help me out, he said, "Write about stuff you know about. Write about some of those fishing trips we took." I said I would, but I knew I wouldn't. "Send me what you write," he said. I said I'd do that, but then I didn't. I wasn't writing anything about fishing, and I didn't think he'd particularly care about, or even necessarily understand, what I was writing in those days. Besides, he wasn't a reader. Not the sort, anyway, I imagined I was writing for.

Then he died. I was a long way off, in Iowa City, with things still to say to him. I didn't have the chance to tell him goodbye, or that I thought he was doing great at his new job. That I was proud of him for making a comeback.

My mother said he came in from work that night and ate a big supper. Then he sat at the table by himself and finished what was left of a bottle of whiskey, a bottle she found hidden in the bottom of the garbage under some coffee grounds a day or so later. Then he got up and went to bed, where my mother joined him a little later. But in the night she had to get up and make a bed for herself on the couch. "He was snoring so loud I couldn't sleep," she said. The next morning when she looked in on him, he was on his back with his mouth open, his cheeks caved in. *Gray-looking,* she said. She knew he was dead—she didn't need a doctor to tell her that. But she called one anyway, and then she called my wife.

Among the pictures my mother kept of my dad and herself during those early days in Washington was a photograph of him standing in front of a car, holding a beer and a stringer of fish. In the photograph he is wearing his hat back on his forehead and has this awkward grin on his face. I asked her for it and she gave it to me, along with some others. I put it up on my wall, and each time we moved, I took the picture along and put it up on another wall. I looked at it carefully from time to time, trying to figure out some things about my dad, and maybe myself in the process. But I couldn't. My dad just kept moving further and further away from me and back into time. Finally, in the course of another move, I lost the photograph. It was then that I tried to recall it, and at the same time make an attempt to say something about my dad, and how I thought that in some important ways we might be alike. I wrote the poem when I was living in an apartment house in an urban area south of San Francisco, at a time when I found myself, like my dad, having trouble with alcohol. The poem was a way of trying to connect up with him.

Photograph of my Father in His Twenty-Second Year

October. Here in this dank, unfamiliar kitchen
I study my father's embarrassed young man's face.
Sheepish grin, he holds in one hand a string
of spiny yellow perch, in the other a bottle of Carlsberg beer.

In jeans and flannel shirt, he leans against the front fender of a
1934 Ford.
He would like to pose brave and hearty for his posterity,
wear his old hat cocked over his ear.
All his life my father wanted to be bold.

But the eyes give him away, and the hands
that limply offer the string of dead perch
and the bottle of beer. Father, I love you,
yet how can I say thank you, I who can't hold my liquor either
and don't even know the places to fish.

The poem is true in its particulars, except that my dad died in June and not October, as the first word of the poem says. I wanted a word with more than one syllable to it to make it linger a little. But more than that, I wanted a month appropriate to what I felt at the time I wrote the poem—a month of short days and failing light, smoke in the air, things perishing. June was summer nights and days, graduations, my wedding anniversary, the birthday of one of my children. June wasn't a month your father died in.

After the service at the funeral home, after we had moved outside, a woman I didn't know came over to me and said, "He's happier where he is now." I stared at this woman until she moved away. I still remember the little knob of a hat she was wearing. Then one of my dad's cousins—I didn't know the man's name—reached out and took my hand. ''We all miss him,'' he said, and I knew he wasn't saying it just to be polite.

I began to weep for the first time since receiving the news. I hadn't been able to before. I hadn't had the time, for one thing. Now, suddenly, I couldn't stop. I held my wife and wept while she said and did what she could do to comfort me there in the middle of that summer afternoon.

I listened to people say consoling things to my mother, and I was glad that my dad's family had turned up, had come to where he was. I thought I'd remember everything that was said and done that day and maybe find a way to tell it sometime. But I didn't. I forgot it all, or nearly. What I do remember is that I heard our name used a lot that afternoon, my dad's name and mine. But I knew they were talking about my dad. *Raymond,* these people kept saying in their beautiful voices out of my childhood. *Raymond.*

Meaning and Idea

1. How did Carver's mother and father meet? What was her reaction to him? How did she feel about him in later life?

2. Why was Carver embarrassed about his home in Yakima?

3. Trace the geographic movement of Carver's father.

4. How does Carver's father get sick? What are the results of that sickness?

5. What parallels between his own life and his father's life does Carver write about? What is his opinion of these similarities?

6. What sort of person was Carver's father? What is your reaction to him? What was Carver's?

Language, Form, Structure

1. How does Carver use *narrative summary* (see page 65) throughout this essay? How does it affect the tone of the writing? How does Carver maintain unity throughout the essay? What words or phrases are often repeated?

2. What is the use of *dialogue* in this essay? How does it enhance the narration?

3. Essentially, this essay is a chronological narrative of the life of Carver's father. Yet, the paragraph just after the poem seems to break the chronology momentarily. What is the purpose of this break?

4. What is the effect of the terse line: "Then he died"?

5. Why does Carver include the full text of the poem in this essay? How is its tone different from the narrative tone? Could he have summarized the poem's contents just as easily?

6. Throughout the essay, Carver uses various colloquialisms such as *floozy, raw whiskey,* and *crummy.* Explain the meanings of these, and find and explain three other colloquialisms.

Ideas for Writing

1. Narrate the history of one of your closest family members. Attempt to follow Carver's pattern of highlighting through narrative summary.

2. Select one incident from the narration you wrote in response to question one in this section, and expand it to a two or three paragraph narration of its own.

3. Write a brief analysis of Carver's style as evidenced in "My Father's Life." Carver, who is primarily a fiction writer, is known for his terse, compact, narrative summary style. Do the same stylistic qualities emerge here? What are the effects of this style upon the reader? Draw specific examples from the selection to make your point.

Chapter Three
EXEMPLIFICATION

*7*he process of exemplification is such an essential part of the way we think, the way we talk and argue and respond, that it may seem odd to consider it as a writer's option. Simply put, exemplification means providing examples to illustrate an idea with particulars.

As a case in point, if you wanted to illustrate Dickens's skill at characterization, you could present a single well-developed example—the example of Pip, say, the main character in *Great Expectations*. Or, to make a point about the extraordinary defensive playing by the Mets and the Cubs you might provide a blow-by-blow retelling of the pitching duel in the last inning of some crucial game between them. In each case you'd probably infuse the one example with details. In the first, you'd draw upon paraphrases and quotations from the novel. In the second, you'd provide concrete sensory images and narrative particulars to bring to life the final breathless moments of play.

A single extended example can make a strong case; yet we are equally impressed with cumulative exemplification. Here, you provide a series of illustrations, the accretion of related yet different instances making the original point grow and solidify. Thus if you wanted to use *Great Expectations* to demonstrate Dickens's talent for character development, you might deal with Miss Haversham, the convict Magwitch, and Estella, as well as with Pip. Similarly, if you were touting the Cubs's defense, you might want to point to instances of skillful fielding by the third baseman, the shortstop, and the right fielder, as well as to the masterful job on the mound. Cumulative exemplification provides the reader with many illustrations of the writer's point.

Examples move readers beyond generalizations. As a means for anchoring general ideas in specifics, examples are essential rhetorical strategies to writers of stories, novels, essays, and poems.

READING EXEMPLIFICATION

As you read instances to support a writer's position, your critical faculties should engage this question: Are these examples solid illustrations of the point? No matter how clever or amusing they may be, the examples must pertain to the writer's purpose in the essay. Sometimes the writer will list examples, expecting through accumulation of supporting information to win you over, as Orwell does here, in order to convince us to acknowledge his good memories of Crossgates School:

> I have good memories of Crossgates, among a horde of bad ones. Sometimes on summer afternoons there were wonderful expeditions across the Downs, or to Beachy Head, where one bathed dangerously among the chalk

boulders and came home covered with cuts. And there were still more wonderful midsummer evenings when, as a special treat, we were not driven off
to bed as usual but allowed to wander about the grounds in the long twilight, ending up with a plunge into the swimming bath at about nine o'clock.
There was the joy of waking early on summer mornings and getting in an
hour's undisturbed reading (Ian Hay, Thackeray, Kipling and H. G. Wells
were the favourite authors of my boyhood) in the sunlit, sleeping dormitory.
There was also cricket, which I was no good at but with which I conducted
a sort of hopeless love affair up to the age of about eighteen. And there was
the pleasure of keeping caterpillars—the silky green and purple puss-moth,
the ghostly green poplar-hawk, the privet hawk, large as one's third finger,
specimens of which could be illicitly purchased for sixpence at a shop in the
town—and, when one could escape long enough from the master who was
"taking the walk," there was the excitement of dredging the dew-ponds on
the Downs for enormous newts with orange-coloured bellies. This business
of being out for a walk, coming across something of fascinating interest and
then being dragged away from it by a yell from the master, like a dog jerked
onwards by the leash, is an important feature of school life, and helps to
build up the conviction, so strong in many children, that the things you
most want to do are always unattainable.

To support the general statement in the first sentence, each subsequent
sentence in the paragraph provides a different example. The last sentence
develops yet another generalization from the examples. Drawing upon
personal experiences, Orwell advances his examples with concrete sensory details—"bathed dangerously among the chalk boulders," "in the
silent, sleeping dormitory," "the silky green and purple puss-moth"—
but he does not expand any one example to any particular degree. Notice
how deftly he moves us from one instance to the next. Words and phrases
like "And then there were still more," "there was also," "And then there
was" link the instances by repetition and transitions.

In this selection from *Manchild in the Promised Land,* Claude Brown
wants to convince us of the strange things he saw down South, but he uses
only a few examples, each somewhat more expanded than Orwell's:

Down South seemed like a dream when I was on the train going back to
New York. I saw a lot of things down South that I never saw in my whole
life before and most of them I didn't ever want to see again. I saw a great
big old burly black man hit a pig in the head with the back of an ax. The pig
screamed, oink-oinked a few times, lay down, and started kicking and
bleeding . . . and died. When he was real little, I used to chase him, catch
him, pick him up, and play catch with him. He was a greedy old pig, but I
used to like him. One day when it was real cold, I ate a piece of that pig,
and I still liked him. One day I saw Grandma kill a rattlesnake with a hoe.
She chopped the snake's head off in the front yard, and I sat on the porch
and watched the snake's body keep wiggling till it was nighttime. And I saw

an old brown hound dog named Old Joe eat a rat one day, right out in the front yard. He caught the rat in the woodpile and started tearing him open. Old Joe was eating everything in the rat. He ate something that looked like the yellow part in an egg, and I didn't eat eggs for a long time after that. I saw a lady rat have a lot of little baby rats on a pile of tobacco leaves. She had to be a lady, because my first-grade teacher told a girl that ladies don't cry about little things, and the rat had eleven little hairless pink rats, and she didn't even squeak about it.

I made a gun down South out of a piece of wood, some tape, a piece of tire-tube rubber, a nail, some wire, a piece of pipe, and a piece of door hinge. And I saw nothing but blood where my right thumbnail used to be after I shot it for the first time. That nail grew back, little by little. I saw a lot of people who had roots worked on them, but I never saw anybody getting roots worked on them.

Down South sure was a crazy place, and it was good to be going back to New York.

Here too, images of color, sound, and action make the instances come alive. Note how Brown develops the example of the pig by jerking us back and forth in time. In wrenching the chronology, he sustains the shock of the pig's death. The example takes on special significance because of the temporally disconnected memories the writer associates with the murdered animal. Brown uses *and* as a transitional device at the start of several sentences. The repeated phrase "down South" also helps to connect the examples smoothly.

Both Orwell and Brown write from personal experience and support their examples with concrete sensory details. However, many writers do not call exclusively upon events in their lives; and they use other kinds of details to support a point through exemplification. You should be aware of some of these techniques as you read. Writers will draw upon facts, the language of numbers, statistics, and cases. They will draw upon quotations or paraphrases chosen from experts in the field. They will summarize. They will cite historical or scientific evidence to advance their ideas. Whatever the nature of the details, good writing always provides them, and you should pay careful attention to the kind of concrete support that a writer will use to make the instances come alive. Note the details in this paragraph from Theodore Ziolkowski's essay "The Existential Anxieties of Engineering" in a recent issue of *The American Scholar* (Spring 1984, Vol. 53, Num. 2, p. 207):

Novels portraying the moral anxiety of engineering did not cease to be written after World War I, of course. Literary genres do not disappear so quickly. Some thirty years later Frederick Philip Grove's *Master of the Mill* (1944) recapitulates all the characteristics of the genre. In this powerful Canadian classic, the engineer Samuel Clark learns that his family's milling empire, which supplies 90 percent of the nation's flour, was founded by a criminal act of his father. Clark is unsuccessful in his efforts to assume the responsibility, to compensate for the crime by social welfare, and to protect his own son from the inherited guilt. His plans for social reform fail; the workers are displaced by technology; and his son is shot during a strike of the enraged millers. By the time Clark dies, he realizes that the great pyramidal mill of seventeen stories had always ruled his destiny and determined his every action. "The history of the mill had been his history"—as much so as the submarines, tunnels, and bridges of the earlier novels. Having destroyed its creator and disenfranchised its former workers, it survives as a symbol of the engineer's moral anxiety.

In the first two sentences Ziolkowski asserts that post-World War I novels about "the moral anxiety of engineering" did not vanish. As an example, he presents Grove's 1944 *Master of the Mill;* and then, to support, the example, Ziolkowski provides specific details from that novel, including a quotation in the next to the last sentence. It is interesting to see here how only one example, richly expanded with detail, serves very nicely to make the point.

Which writer—Orwell, Brown, Ziolknowski—has used the right number of examples and the appropriate degree of detail? Of course, there is no answer to that question. As a critical reader, you need to decide for yourself whether the examples and supporting details clarify the point. If you're left just short of being convinced or are overwhelmed with more than you need, the writer may have seriously misjudged his audience.

In addition to the quantity and quality of the examples, you should look also for their manner of arrangement. Does the writer present the instances chronologically—in the order in which they occurred? Does he or she present them according to importance, building from the least to the most significant example? Do you detect any logic in the scheme of arrangement that the writer has used? Why are the examples presented in the order that you see them? As you read the selections in this chapter, in particular Whitman's "There Was a Child Went Forth," Maxine Kingston's "Family Ghosts," and James Thurber's "Courtship through the Ages," you should consider the relation between the examples and their method of arrangement.

WRITING EXEMPLIFICATION

Many topics lend themselves to development through examples, and as you think about your topic, you should be able to list a number of instances to use as possible means of support in your essay. Suppose you wanted to write about the personality of your old family car, a 74 Chevy, with which you associate many happy memories. You could develop an essay through description alone, showing your reader with careful, loving details all the memorable features of this automobile. Or, you could narrate one particular trip you took in which your beat-up sedan served as vehicle, living room, dining room, and bedroom on a slow trip to Maine from your home in Dallas. Or, if you wanted to point to a number of pleasant associations, you would reach for exemplification, showing two or three instances to show readers the range of memories this car provides for you. The point here is that the topic and your view of how to develop it will suggest an appropriate rhetorical scheme. You start with a sense of your topic and an idea of your purpose in writing about it, and then you consider the strategy that will help you best achieve your goal.

As with all the rhetorical models you're exploring in this book, try not to think of exemplification as an isolated form. Often you see it working hand in hand with description, narration, comparison and contrast, or definition. In writing an exemplification paper about your memories of your old auto, no doubt you'd weave in concrete sensory details. You might tell two or three brief stories about the car; and you might compare and contrast the instances with each other. Again, the rhetorical form you choose always should serve your purpose and suit your intended audience.

AUDIENCE AND PURPOSE

The nature of the instances you choose for your exemplification paper will depend upon what your aim is in your essay and upon who your intended reader is. As we pointed out earlier, it's hard to find a topic that cannot be approached through exemplification, so you probably won't have much trouble in identifying an appropriate subject or in generating examples to support your ideas. Sources for examples are many. The most familiar, of course, is personal experience. Thus, as a start, you might want to search your memory, your own personal past history, to identify instances you could expand with details. Or, you could use a topic idea to stimulate new experiences that you could record accurately and share with your readers. To provide examples of the crush of holiday shoppers at a local mall, you could try to recall those harried buyers who'd impressed you during your last shopping spree; but you might tap a fresher source of details if you returned to the mall, pencil in hand, to observe carefully the hustle and bustle around you. Many writers will draw upon their imaginations for details, spinning hypotheses, metaphors, or analogies to support an issue with a pointed example. Comparing one shopper's trail down the aisle in a clothing store to a long-necked crane poking and pecking and staring at racks of blouses and dresses might make your point creatively and delight your readers.

In addition to personal experience, all you read in books, newspapers, and magazines, all you hear on the radio, in class, out on the street, all you see in the movies and on television are remarkable sources for examples to use in your writing. When you've identified a topic, have thought of what you wish to say about it, and have considered what your audience might expect in your essay, don't hesitate to talk your idea over with friends, to watch some local programs on your Public Broadcasting System or on network television, or to check your topic in the card catalog, the *Readers' Guide for Periodical Literature,* or the *Social Science and Humanities Index* in your library. Your audience might expect solid details drawn from nonexperiential sources, and your own purpose in writing might be served by examples taken from careful investigation. If you wanted to write about those holiday shoppers for the Chamber of Commerce, a group you wanted to convince of the need for a better safety plan during peak shopping hours, you'd want to draw upon statistics of accidents and crimes in former years, upon testimony by store owners, managers, and customers at the mall, upon public records of supplemental budgets for part-time police protection in the mall parking lot and in open areas during December. Intent on persuading your readers to take some course of action, and knowing them to respond to hard data, you might be making a mistake to draw only upon your own personal experiences to make your point.

PROCESS

Jot down some ideas in a list or a scratch outline to help you decide on a topic and a purpose for writing. With some record of your thoughts on paper, you might find an informal outline or some other grouping system useful before you try a draft. Cluster together any ideas that are related to the same example. As in most writing tasks, a thesis sentence will be very helpful, and you should spend considerable time writing a clear one even though you may decide ultimately not to use it in your final draft. In most cases your thesis will be a generalization that your examples will expand.

Keeping audience and purpose in mind, decide on how many examples you need to hold your reader's attention. Will you offer one single instance expanded with precise and appropriate details? Will you offer three or four examples each with some supporting information? Will you offer a simple listing in which you provide numerous examples, none of which is backed up to any large degree with details? Take into account too the nature of the kinds of examples and the details your essay will require. Will you use images of concrete sensory details to anchor your examples? Will you use statistics, cases, or other data? Will you quote from a book, a television program, or an actual interview? Will you summarize a song or a short story or a lab report? Will you *invent* an example? When you give a draft of your paper to a friend, ask him or her to tell you if your examples are believable, if they suit your point, and if you've developed them with adequate detail.

As we suggested before, you'll have to make a decision about how to arrange the examples for the strongest presentation. If they involve narration, a simple chronological arrangement might serve you best. In order to build slowly to the most dramatic instance, many writers will choose an arrangement by importance, saving the most crucial example for last. Whatever your method of arrangement, aim for coherence by linking your examples so that readers move smoothly from instance to instance. To achieve a coherent essay you'll find that transitions, used moderately, will be useful, as will other connecting devices, such as pronouns, repetition, and coordinate structures.

Keep in mind that the particulars in your essay will hold your readers' attention. No matter how thoughtful or original or surprising your generalizations may be, specific instances make those generalizations more immediate, interesting, and, finally, understandable.

Maxine Hong Kingston
FAMILY GHOSTS

Maxine Hong Kingston was born in Stockton, California, in 1940, the daughter of a scholar who has also been a laundry worker and of a midwife who has done field work. Kingston's writing, which focuses on the Chinese and Chinese-American experience, has been aptly described by Susan Cinner as a blend of "myth, legend, history and autobiography into a genre of her own invention." Her honors include the National Book Critics' Circle Award in 1976 for *The Woman Warrior,* which was also named by *Time* magazine as among the top ten nonfiction works of the decade 1970–1980. Her latest book is *China Men* (1980).

In "Family Ghosts," Maxine Hong Kingston uses description, narration, and flashback to set the stage for a ghost story. She derives her tale from ancient Chinese legends, of *Sit Dom Kuei*—semimagical words for which she can better give examples than translations or definitions.

W hen the thermometer in our laundry reached one hundred and eleven degrees on summer afternoons, either my mother or my father would say that it was time to tell another ghost story so that we could get some good chills up our backs. My parents, my brothers, sisters, great-uncle, and "Third Aunt," who wasn't really our aunt but a fellow villager, someone else's third aunt, kept the presses crashing and hissing and shouted out the stories. Those were our successful days, when so much laundry came in, my mother did not have to pick tomatoes. For breaks we changed from pressing to sorting.

"One twilight," my mother began, and already the chills travelled my back and crossed my shoulders; the hair rose at the nape and the back of the legs, "I was walking home after doctoring a sick family. To get home I had to cross a footbridge. In China the bridges are nothing like the ones in Brooklyn and San Francisco. This one was made from rope, laced and knotted as if by magpies. Actually it had been built by men who had returned after harvesting sea swallow nests in Malaya. They had had to swing over the faces of the Malayan cliffs in baskets they had woven themselves. Though this bridge pitched and swayed in the updraft, no one had ever fallen into the river, which looked like a bright scratch at the bottom of the canyon, as if the Queen of Heaven had swept her great silver hairpin across the earth as well as the sky."

One twilight, just as my mother stepped on the bridge, two smoky columns spiraled up taller than she. Their swaying tops hovered over her head like white cobras, one at either handrail. From stillness came a wind rushing between the smoke spindles. A high sound entered her temple bones. Through the twin whirlwinds she could see the sun and the river, the river twisting in circles, the trees upside down. The bridge moved like a ship, sickening. The earth dipped. She collapsed to the wooden slats, a ladder up the sky, her fingers so weak she could not grip the rungs. The wind dragged her hair behind her, then whipped it forward across her face. Suddenly the smoke spindles disappeared. The world righted itself, and she crossed to the other side. She looked back, but there was nothing there. She used the bridge often, but she did not encounter those ghosts again.

"They were Sit Dom Kuei," said Great-Uncle. "Sit Dom Kuei."

"Yes, of course," said my mother. "Sit Dom Kuei."

I keep looking in dictionaries under those syllables. "Kuei" means "ghost," but I don't find any other words that make sense. I only hear my great-uncle's river-pirate voice, the voice of a big man who had killed someone in New York or Cuba, make the sounds—"Sit Dom Kuei." How do they translate?

When the Communists issued their papers on techniques for combating ghosts, I looked for "Sit Dom Kuei." I have not found them described anywhere, although now I see that my mother won in ghost battle because she can eat anything—quick, pluck out the carp's eyes, one for Mother and one for Father. All heroes are bold toward food. In the research against ghost fear published by the Chinese Academy of Science is the story of a magistrate's servant, Kao Chung, a capable eater who in 1683 ate five cooked chickens and drank ten bottles of wine that belonged to the sea monster with branching teeth. The monster had arranged its food around a fire on the beach and started to feed when Kao Chung attacked. The swan-feather sword he wrested from this monster can be seen in the Wentung County Armory in Shantung today.

Another big eater was Chou Yi-han of Changchow, who fried a ghost. It was a meaty stick when he cut it up and cooked it. But before that it had been a woman out at night.

Chen Luan-feng, during the Yuan Ho era of the T'ang dynasty (A.D. 806–820), ate yellow croaker and pork together, which the thunder god had forbidden. But Chen wanted to incur thunderbolts during drought. The first time he ate, the thunder god jumped out of the sky, its legs like old trees. Chen chopped off the left one. The thunder god fell to the earth, and the villagers could see that it was a blue pig or bear with horns and fleshy wings. Chen leapt on it, prepared to chop its neck and bite its throat, but the villagers stopped him. After that, Chen lived apart as a rainmaker, neither relatives nor the monks willing to bring lightning upon themselves. He lived in a cave, and for years whenever there was drought the villagers asked him to eat yellow croaker and pork together, and he did.

The most fantastic eater of them all was Wei Pang, a scholar-hunter of the Ta Li era of the T'ang dynasty (A.D. 766–779). He shot and cooked rabbits and birds, but he could also eat scorpions, snakes, cockroaches, worms, slugs, beetles, and crickets. Once he spent the night in a house that had been abandoned because its inhabitants feared contamination from the dead man next door. A shining, twinkling sphere came flying through the darkness at Wei. He felled it with three true arrows—the first making the thing crackle and flame; the second dimming it; and the third putting out its lights, sputter. When his servant came running in with a lamp, Wei saw his arrows sticking in a ball of flesh entirely covered with eyes, some rolled back to show the dulling whites. He and the servant pulled out the arrows and cut up the ball into little pieces. The servant cooked the morsels in sesame oil, and the wonderful aroma made Wei laugh. They ate half, saving half to show the household, which would return now.

Big eaters win. When other passers-by stepped around the bundle wrapped in white silk, the anonymous scholar of Hanchow took it home. Inside were three silver ingots and a froglike evil, which sat on the ingots. The scholar laughed at it and chased it off. That night two frogs the size of year-old babies appeared in his room. He clubbed them to death, cooked them, and ate them with white wine. The next night a dozen frogs, together the size of a pair of year-old babies, jumped from the ceiling. He ate all twelve for dinner. The third night thirty small frogs were sitting on his mat and staring at him with their frog eyes. He ate them too. Every night for a month smaller but more numerous frogs came so that he always had the same amount to eat. Soon his floor was like the healthy banks of a pond in spring when the tadpoles, having just turned, sprang in the wet grass. "Get a hedgehog to help eat," cried his family. "I'm as good as a hedgehog," the scholar said, laughing. And at the end of the month the frogs stopped coming, leaving the scholar with the white silk and silver ingots.

Meaning and Idea

1. What was the occasion for Kingston's mother telling a ghost story? What was the desired effect? Summarize the ghost story in your own words.

2. Why did her mother "win" the ghost battle? What generalization does Kingston make about those who conquer ghosts? How many examples of "ghost conquerors" does she offer?

3. Not only does Kingston provide examples of "ghost conquerors," but also within each example she gives instances of different ghost manifestations. List them in the order that they appear. Where does she provide examples of what the "ghosts" really may have been?

Language, Form, Structure

1. How does Kingston arrange her examples of "heroes" against ghosts? Name the examples she provides.

2. Midway through her mother's story, the narrator shifts. From whom to whom does it shift? What is the effect of this change? There is also a significant shift in the time sequence in this essay. Where does it occur? What grammatical change signals the shift? Why does it occur?

3. What transitions appear between each example? How does the first sentence of the last paragraph act as a transition?

4. List and define five unusual animal names used in this essay.

Ideas for Writing

1. Have you ever had a supernatural experience, or do you know someone who has? Tell about it and provide examples of what was seen, heard, or felt as supernatural.

2. What was your favorite kind of story when you were a child? Write an essay in which you exemplify this type of story and the purposes it served for you besides pure enjoyment.

3. Kingston's writing often demonstrates a clash of cultures, an old-world Chinese culture and a new-world American culture. Using examples drawn from "Family Ghosts" show whether or not you agree with this point.

James Thurber
COURTSHIP THROUGH THE AGES

James Thurber (1894–1961) was perhaps best known and loved by the American public for his stories, essays, and line drawings in *The New Yorker* magazine, where he was employed after being hired by E. B. White in 1925. Always casting a humorously ironic eye on the human condition, his best known collections include *Is Sex Necessary?* (with E. B. White, 1929), *The Seal in the Bedroom and Other Predicaments* (1932), *The Thurber Carnival* (1945), and *Thurber Country* (1953).

"Courtship Through the Ages," Thurber's accumulation of examples of "love displays" by the male species toward the opposite sex, first appeared in *The New Yorker* in 1939; that same year it was also collected in Thurber's book *My World— and Welcome to It.*

Surely nothing in the astonishing scheme of life can have nonplussed Nature so much as the fact that none of the females of any of the species she created really cared very much for the male, as such. For the past ten million years Nature has been busily inventing ways to make the male attractive to the female, but the whole business of courtship, from the marine annelids up to man, still lumbers heavily along, like a complicated musical comedy. I have been reading the sad and absorbing story in Volume 6 (Cole to Dama) of the *Encyclopaedia Britannica*. In this volume you can learn all about cricket, cotton, costume designing, crocodiles, crown jewels, and Coleridge, but none of these subjects is so interesting as the Courtship of Animals, which recounts the sorrowful lengths to which all males must go to arouse the interest of a lady.

We all know, I think, that Nature gave man whiskers and a mustache with the quaint idea in mind that these would prove attractive to the female. We all know that, far from attracting her, whiskers and mustaches only made her nervous and gloomy, so that man had to go in for somersaults, tilting with lances, and performing feats of parlor magic to win her attention; he also had to bring her candy, flowers, and the furs of animals. It is common knowledge that in spite of all these "love displays" the male is constantly being turned down, insulted, or thrown out of the house. It is rather comforting, then, to discover that the peacock, for all his gorgeous plumage, does not have a particularly easy time in courtship; none of the males in the world do. The first peahen, it turned out, was only faintly stirred by her suitor's beautiful train. She would often go quietly to sleep while he was whisking it around. The *Britannica* tells us that the peacock actually had to learn a certain little trick to wake her up and revive her interest: he had to learn to vibrate his quills so as to make a rustling sound. In ancient times man himself, observing the ways of the peacock, probably tried vibrating his whiskers to make a rustling sound; if so, it didn't get him anywhere. He had to go in for something else; so, among other things, he went in for gifts. It is not unlikely that he got this idea from certain flies and birds who were making no headway at all with rustling sounds.

One of the flies of the family Empidae, who had tried everything, finally hit on something pretty special. He contrived to make a glistening transparent balloon which was even larger than himself. Into this he would put sweetmeats and tidbits and he would carry the whole elaborate envelope through the air to the lady of his choice. This amused her for a time, but she finally got bored with it. She demanded silly little colorful presents, something that you couldn't eat but that would look nice around the house. So the male Empis had to go around gathering flower petals and pieces of bright paper to put into his balloon. On a courtship flight a male Empis cuts quite a figure now, but he can hardly be said to be happy. He never knows how soon the female will demand heavier presents, such as Roman coins and gold collar buttons. It seems probable that one day the courtship of the Empidae will fall down, as man's occasionally does, of its own weight.

The bowerbird is another creature that spends so much time courting the female that he never gets any work done. If all the male bowerbirds became nervous wrecks within the next ten or fifteen years, it would not surprise me. The female bowerbird insists that a playground be built for her with a specially constructed bower at the entrance. This bower is much more elaborate than an ordinary nest and is harder to build; it costs a lot more, too. The female will not come to the playground until the male has filled it up with a great many gifts: silvery leaves, red leaves, rose petals, shells, beads, berries, bones, dice, buttons, cigar bands, Christmas seals, and the Lord knows what else. When the female finally condescends to visit the playground, she is in a coy and silly mood and has to be chased in and out of the bower and up and down the playground before she will quit giggling and stand still long enough even to shake hands. The male bird is, of course, pretty well done in before the chase starts, because he has worn himself out hunting for eyeglass lenses and begonia blossoms. I imagine that many a bowerbird, after chasing a female for two or three hours, says the hell with it and goes home to bed. Next day, of course, he telephones someone else and the same trying ritual is gone through again. A male bowerbird is as exhausted as a night-club habitué before he is out of his twenties.

The male fiddler crab has a somewhat easier time, but it can hardly be said that he is sitting pretty. He has one enormously large and powerful claw, usually brilliantly colored, and you might suppose that all he had to do was reach out and grab some passing cutie. The very earliest fiddler crabs may have tried this, but, if so, they got slapped for their pains. A female crab will not tolerate any caveman stuff; she never has and she doesn't intend to start now. To attract a female, a fiddler crab has to stand on tiptoe and brandish his claw in the air. If any female in the neighborhood is interested—and you'd be surprised how many are not—she comes over and engages him in light badinage, for which he is not in the mood. As many as a hundred females may pass the time of day with him and go on about their business. By nightfall of an average courting day, a fiddler crab who has been standing on tiptoe for eight or ten hours waving a heavy claw in the air is in pretty sad shape. As in the case of the males of all species, however, he gets out of bed next morning, dashes some water on his face, and tries again.

The next time you encounter a male web-spinning spider, stop and reflect that he is too busy worrying about his love life to have any desire to bite you. Male web-spinning spiders have a tougher life than any other males in the animal kingdom. This is because the female web-spinning spiders have very poor eyesight. If a male lands on a female's web, she kills him before he has time to lay down his cane and gloves, mistaking him for a fly or a bumblebee who has tumbled into her trap. Before the species figured out what to do about this, millions of males were murdered by ladies they called on. It is the nature of spiders to perform a little dance in front of the female, but before a male spinner could get near enough for the female to see who he was and what he was up to, she would lash out at him with a flat-iron or a pair of garden shears. One night, nobody knows when, a very bright male spinner lay awake worrying about calling on a lady who had been killing suitors right and left. It came to him that this business of dancing as a love display wasn't getting anybody anywhere except the grave. He decided to go in for web-twitching, or strand-vibrating. The next day he tried it on one of the nearsighted girls. Instead of dropping in on her suddenly, he stayed outside the web and began monkeying with one of its strands. He twitched it up and down and in and out with such a lilting rhythm that the female was charmed. The serenade worked beautifully; the female let him live. The *Britannica*'s spider-watchers, however, report that this system is not always successful. Once in a while, even now, a female will fire three bullets into a suitor or run him through with a kitchen knife. She keeps threatening him from the moment he strikes the first low notes on the outside strings, but usually by the time he has got up to the high notes played around the center of the web, he is going to town and she spares his life.

Even the butterfly, as handsome a fellow as he is, can't always win a mate merely by fluttering around and showing off. Many butterflies have to have scent scales on their wings. Hepialus carries a powder puff in a perfumed pouch. He throws perfume at the ladies when they pass. The male tree cricket, Oecanthus, goes Hepialus one better by carrying a tiny bottle of wine with him and giving drinks to such doxies as he has designs on. One of the male snails throws darts to entertain the girls. So it goes, through the long list of animals, from the bristle worm and his rudimentary dance steps to man and his gift of diamonds and sapphires. The golden-eye drake raises a jet of water with his feet as he flies over a lake; Hepialus has his powder puff, Oecanthus his wine bottle, man his etchings. It is a bright and melancholy story, the age-old desire of the male for the female, the age-old desire of the female to be amused and entertained. Of all the creatures on earth, the only males who could be figured as putting any irony into their courtship are the grebes and certain other diving birds. Every now and then a courting grebe slips quietly down to the bottom of a lake and then, with a mighty "Whoosh!," pops out suddenly a few feet from his girl friend, splashing water all over her. She seems to be persuaded that this is a purely loving display, but I like to think that the grebe always has a faint hope of drowning her or scaring her to death.

I will close this investigation into the mournful burdens of the male with the *Britannica*'s story about a certain Argus pheasant. It appears that the Argus displays himself in front of a female who stands perfectly still without moving a feather. . . . The male Argus the *Britannica* tells about was confined in a cage with a female of another species, a female who kept moving around, emptying ashtrays and fussing with lampshades all the time the male was showing off his talents. Finally, in disgust, he stalked away and began displaying in front of his water trough. He reminds me of a certain male (Homo sapiens) of my acquaintance who one night after dinner asked his wife to put down her detective magazine so that he could read her a poem of which he was very fond. She sat quietly enough until he was well into the middle of the thing, intoning with great ardor and intensity. Then suddenly there came a sharp, disconcerting *slap!* It turned out that all during the male's display, the female had been intent on a circling mosquito and had finally trapped it between the palms of her hands. The male in this case did not stalk away and display in front of a water trough; he went over to Tim's and had a flock of drinks and recited the poem to the fellas. I am sure they all told bitter stories of their own about how their displays had been interrupted by females. I am also sure that they all ended up singing "Honey, Honey, Bless Your Heart."

Meaning and Idea

1.   On what other piece of writing does Thurber hinge his essay? Why?

2.   In paragraph two, Thurber gives examples of the things men had to do to attract females because their whiskers and mustaches weren't enough. What are those other things? What is the ultimate substitute—the "something else"—mentioned in that paragraph? What examples of it does Thurber include in subsequent paragraphs?

3.   Who does Thurber think ultimately has the upper hand in male-female relations? How do you know? How does the last line of the essay fit in with his evaluation?

Language, Form, Structure

1.   What is the initial generalization that Thurber sets out to support through exemplification? Do you agree with this generalization? Why is exemplification a suitable technique for this essay?

2.   Thurber tends to use *hyperbole* (the deliberate exaggeration of an idea or description) quite freely throughout the essay. Give three examples of the most hyperbolic statements. To what purpose does he use hyperbole?

3.   An *analogy* is a comparison of two subjects drawn from divergent areas. If you showed point by point the similarities between an ant hill and a crowded train station, you'd be writing an analogy. What is the implicit *analogy* throughout this essay? Where in each paragraph is that analogy made most explicitly? What purpose does that explicit analogy serve?

4.   How does Thurber arrange his examples in paragraphs 3 through 6? In paragraph 7? Why does he change his arrangement in paragraph 7? Briefly outline Thurber's use of transitions between paragraphs 2 through 7.

5.   What is Thurber's attitude toward his topic in this essay? How can you tell? Does he maintain the same attitude throughout the essay?

6.   Make certain that you know the meanings of the following words: nonplussed; feats; habitue; badinage; doxies; intoning; ardor.

Ideas for Writing

1.   Write a paragraph using examples in which you explain your favorite means of attracting the opposite sex. Which are most effective? Which are least effective?

2.   Go to a place where men and women gather socially—a cafeteria, a pub, a lecture hall, for example—and observe their behavior toward each other, especially their means of attracting each other. Write a single generalization about your observation of the scene and support it in an essay of exemplification.

3. Clearly, Thurber uses *irony* here almost to the limits of *sarcasm*. Write a short essay in which you analyze the positive and negative sides of the use of irony in this essay. Support your ideas with specific examples drawn from the text.

Walt Whitman
THERE WAS A CHILD WENT FORTH

> Whitman's effect on American poetry has been profound, not only because of his wide-ranging subject matter but also because of his experimental verse. Born on New York's Long Island in 1819, he wrote poems infused with such divergent forces as democratic idealism, opera, Shakespeare, Quaker religious philosophy, sexual openness, and the rhythms of city life. His magnum opus, *Leaves of Grass* (1855), proclaimed the great freedom of the human mind, body, and spirit.
>
> In this poem Whitman provides a series of indelible images in an effort to define the personality of a child. Critics point to many autobiographical lines in "There Was a Child Went Forth." But the poem goes beyond the concrete experiential world of the poet, a world so vividly recreated here, to a statement on the relation between human character and experience and the unity of all in nature.

There was a child went forth every day,   1
And the first object he look'd upon, that object he became,
And that object became part of him for the day or a certain part
    of the day,
Or for many years or stretching cycles of years.   5

The early lilacs became part of this child.
And grass and white and red morning-glories, and white and
    red clover, and the song of the phoebe-bird,
And the Third-month lambs and the sow's pink-faint litter, and
    the mare's foal and the cow's calf,   10
And the noisy brood of the barnyard or by the mire of the
    pond-side,

And the fish suspending themselves so curiously below there,
and the beautiful curious liquid,
And the water-plants with their graceful flat heads, all became   15
part of him.
The field-sprouts of Fourth-month and Fifth-month became
part of him,
Winter-grain sprouts and those of the light-yellow corn, and
the esculent roots of the garden,   20
And the apple-trees cover'd with blossoms and the fruit after-
ward, and wood-berries, and the commonest weeds by
the road,
And the old drunkard staggering home from the outhouse of
the tavern whence he had lately risen,   25
And the schoolmistress that pass'd on her way to the school,
And the friendly boys that pass'd, and the quarrelsome boys,
And the tidy and fresh-cheek'd girls, and the barefoot negro
boy and girl,
And all the changes of city and country wherever he went.   30

His own parents, he that had father'd him and she that had
conceiv'd him in her womb and birth'd him,
They gave this child more of themselves than that,
They gave him afterward every day, they became part of him.

The mother at home quietly placing the dishes on the supperta-   35
ble,
The mother with mild words, clean her cap and gown, a wholesome odor falling off her person and clothes as she walks
by,
The father, strong, self-sufficient, manly, mean, anger'd, un-   40
just,
The blow, the quick loud word, the tight bargain, the crafty
lure,
The family usages, the language, the company, the furniture,
the yearning and swelling heart,   45
Affection that will not be gainsay'd, the sense of what is real,
the thought if after all it should prove unreal,
The doubts of day-time and the doubts of night-time, the
curious whether and how,
Whether that which appears so is so, or is it all flashes and   50
specks?
Men and women crowding fast in the streets, if they are not
flashes and specks what are they?
The streets themselves and the facades of houses, and goods in
the windows,   55

Vehicles, teams, the heavy-plank'd wharves, the huge cross-
    ing at the ferries,
The village on the highland seen from afar at sunset, the river
    between,
Shadows, aureola and mist, the light falling on roofs and gables   60
    of white or brown two miles off,
The schooner near by sleepily dropping down the tide, the
    little boat slack-tow'd astern,
The hurrying tumbling waves, quick-broken crests, slapping,
The strata of color'd clouds, the long bar of maroon-tint away   65
    solitary by itself, the spread of purity it lies motionless in,
The horizon's edge, the flying sea-crow, the fragrance of salt
    marsh and shore mud,
These became part of that child who went forth every day, and
    who now goes, and will always go forth every day.   70

Meaning and Idea

1. State in your own words the point Whitman is trying to make with this poem. Where does he come closest to stating his purpose? What is the value to the poem of the last line in the first stanza?

2. What experiences with nature, family, and city are most vivid to you? What is the character of the child that Whitman is attempting to draw for us here?

3. What are the doubts and questions aroused by the child's experiences? Would you call them typical of a child growing up? Why?

4. Describe the child's father and mother.

Language, Form, Structure

1. Which images are richest in concrete sensory detail? Whitman has a special knack of sketching characters with a series of single words or short phrases. Why are the modifiers describing the father particularly well chosen? What is the effect of placing all the modifiers after the noun *father*?

2. How is this poem an instance of exemplification? Why does Whitman provide a listing of so many details? Why didn't he just choose five or six examples instead of all that you see here? How does the use of all of these examples reinforce the purpose and meaning of the poem?

3. Why does Whitman repeat from line 3 the phrase "part of him" (or variations of that phrase) in lines 5, 10, 11, 21, and 40? What other words or phrases does he repeat? What is your reaction to the last line of the poem? (Compare its meaning to the meaning of the first stanza.)

4. How has Whitman used sentence structure as a unifying element? What is the advantage of beginning so many sentences with the word *and?* With the word *the?*

5. Explain the meanings of the following words: mire (par. 8); gainsay'd (27); facades (31); aureola (34); strata (37). Why has Whitman used the terms Third-month (7) and Fourth-month and Fifth-month (11)?

Ideas for Writing

1. Write a paragraph entitled "What Am I?" in which you provide a series of concrete sensory images that show the various experiences that helped to shape your personality.

2. Check library resources to investigate the life of some person who interests you. Try to find an identifiable element of character or personality. Then, in an essay use exemplification to show how experiences in the person's life demonstrate that element of character.

3. A critic of nineteenth-century American literature, F. O. Matthiessen, writes about Whitman: "He understood that language was not 'an abstract construction' made by the learned, but that it had arisen out of the work and needs, the joys and struggles and desires of long generations of humanity, and that it had 'its bases broad and low, close to the ground.' Words are not arbitrary inventions, but the product of human events and customs, the progeny of folkways." Consider the validity of this statement in regard to "There Was a Child Went Forth." Use specific examples from the poem to support your point.

E. E. Cummings
NOBODY LOSES ALL THE TIME

The poet Edward Estlin Cummings, who was born in 1894 in Cambridge, Massachusetts, used the signature "e. e. cummings." Cummings's strange use of typography, combined with his lyrical language, is viewed by many as one of the most important keys to the "free style" of contemporary poetry. *Is 5* (1926) and *95 Poems* (1958) are foremost among his verse collections, and his *The Enormous Room* (1922) is a forceful prose account of World War I. Cummings died in 1962.

Cummings's wry exemplification in this poem affords us insight into the general nature of failure and success rather than causing us great anguish about Uncle Sol's failed life.

i had an uncle named   1
Sol who was a born failure and
nearly everybody said he should have gone
into vaudeville perhaps because my Uncle Sol could
sing McCann He Was A Diver on Xmas Eve like Hell Itself   5
    which
may or may not account for the fact that my Uncle

Sol indulged in that possibly most inexcusable
of all to use a highfalootin phrase
luxuries that is or to   10
wit farming and be
it needlessly
added

my Uncle Sol's farm
failed because the chickens   15
ate the vegetables so
my Uncle Sol had a
chicken farm till the
skunks ate the chickens when

my Uncle Sol   20
had a skunk farm but
the skunks caught cold and
died and so
my Uncle Sol imitated the
skunks in a subtle manner   25

or by drowning himself in the watertank
but somebody who'd given my Uncle Sol a Victor
Victrola and records while he lived presented to
him upon the auspicious occasion of his decease a
scrumptious not to mention splendiferous funeral with   30
tall boys in black gloves and flowers and everything and

i remember we all cried like the Missouri
when my Uncle Sol's coffin lurched because
somebody pressed a button
(and down went   35
my Uncle
Sol

and started a worm farm)

Meaning and Idea

1. What examples in the poem support the assertion that Uncle Sol was "a born failure"?

2. What is the speaker's attitude toward Uncle Sol? Can you really categorize it as sorrow even at the funereal ending?

3. What is the relation between Sol's vaudevillian talents and his failures? Might Cummings be trying to impart a message to us? If so, what is it?

Language, Form, Structure

1. What is the relation between the title of the poem and the examples it sets forth? If "nobody loses all the time," is there any example of Uncle Sol's "success" in life?

2. What is the tone of this poem? How does the way it is set up on the page contribute to that tone? Do any words or expressions especially effect the tone?

3. How does Cummings connect the various illustrations here? Are the transitions smooth? Which ones do you think serve the poem best?

4. Write definitions for the following words: subtle; auspicious; decease (as a noun); scrumptious; lurched.

Ideas for Writing

1. Choose any person you know (not a celebrity) whom you consider to be a success. Write a short character sketch that focuses on the person's success using the cumulative technique of exemplification.

2. Choose any aspect of human nature and write a paragraph to define that aspect through extended exemplification.

3. The introduction to this chapter of the textbook states that "The process of exemplification is such an essential part of the way we talk and argue and respond." What elements of Cummings's poem make his use of exemplification seem very commonplace, very *un*literary?

4. Analyze Cummings's use of everyday words and idioms in this poem. What effect does his language have on the idea of the poem? On your appreciating it?

Mark Twain
I DISCOVER MOSES AND
THE BULRUSHERS

Mark Twain, the pen name for Samuel Langhorne Clemens (1835–1910), was a teller of tales of and for the people. Additionally, he was a perceptive journalist, a biting satirist, and a world traveller (by his mid-thirties he'd already been throughout the United States, Hawaii, Europe, and Palestine). Born in Hannibal, Missouri, he was the first major American writer born and raised west of the Mississippi River, which became the lifeblood of so much of his writing. His works exhibit the full range of his talents, as well as the breadth of his experiences and emotions. His major books include *Roughing It* (1872), *The Adventures of Tom Sawyer* (1876), *Life on the Mississippi* (1883), *Adventures of Huckleberry Finn* (1885), *The Prince and the Pauper* (1882), *A Connecticut Yankee in King Arthur's Court* (1889), and *The Mysterious Stranger* (1916).

"I Discover Moses and the Bulrushers" is the opening chapter of Twain's *Adventures of Huckleberry Finn*. *Huck Finn* was the third in a series of books about the Mississippi, which also included *Tom Sawyer* and *Life on the Mississippi*. *Huckleberry Finn* is generally considered the most complex and mature of the three—a kind of folk epic written by one of America's major humorists who did not ignore the dark side of our civilization. Twain's style in *Huck Finn* is rarely polemical; he opts instead for the rich descriptive details and examples evidenced in this first chapter.

You ou don't know about me without you have read a book by the name of *The Adventures of Tom Sawyer;* but that ain't no matter. That book was made by Mr. Mark Twain, and he told the truth, mainly. There was things which he stretched, but mainly he told the truth. That is nothing. I never seen anybody but lied one time or another, without it was Aunt Polly, or the widow, or maybe Mary. Aunt Polly—Tom's Aunt Polly, she is—and Mary, and the Widow Douglas is all told about in that book, which is mostly a true book, with some stretchers, as I said before.

Now the way that the book winds up is this: Tom and me found the money that the robbers hid in the cave, and it made us rich. We got six thousand dollars apiece—all gold. It was an awful sight of money when it was piled up. Well, Judge Thatcher he took it and put it out at interest, and it fetched us a dollar a day apiece all the year round—more than a body could tell what to do with. The Widow Douglas she took me for her son, and allowed she would sivilize me; but it was rough living in the house all the time, considering how dismal regular and decent the widow was in all her ways; and so when I couldn't stand it no longer I lit out. I got into my old rags and my sugar-hogshead again, and was free and satisfied. But Tom Sawyer he hunted me up and said he was going to start a band of robbers, and I might join if I would go back to the widow and be respectable. So I went back.

The widow she cried over me, and called me a poor lost lamb, and she called me a lot of other names, too, but she never meant no harm by it. She put me in them new clothes again, and I couldn't do nothing but sweat and sweat, and felt all cramped up. Well, then, the old thing commenced again. The widow rung a bell for supper, and you had to come to time. When you got to the table you couldn't go right to eating, but you had to wait for the widow to tuck down her head and grumble a little over the victuals, though there warn't really anything the matter with them—that is, nothing only everything was cooked by itself. In a barrel of odds and ends it is different; things get mixed up, and the juice kind of swaps around, and the things go better.

After supper she got out her book and learned me about Moses and the Bulrushers, and I was in a sweat to find out all about him; but by and by she let it out that Moses had been dead a considerable long time; so then I didn't care no more about him, because I don't take no stock in dead people.

Pretty soon I wanted to smoke, and asked the widow to let me. But she wouldn't. She said it was a mean practice and wasn't clean, and I must try to not do it any more. That is just the way with some people. They get down on a thing when they don't know nothing about it. Here she was a-bothering about Moses, which was no kin to her, and no use to anybody, being gone, you see, yet finding a power of fault with me for doing a thing that had some good in it. And she took snuff, too; of course that was all right, because she done it herself.

Her sister, Miss Watson, a tolerable slim old maid, with goggles on, had just come to live with her, and took a set at me now with a spelling book. She worked me middling hard for about an hour, and then the widow made her ease up. I couldn't stood it much longer. Then for an hour it was deadly dull, and I was fidgety. Miss Watson would say, "Don't put your feet up there, Huckleberry"; and "Don't scrunch up like that, Huckleberry—set up straight"; and pretty soon she would say, "Don't gap and stretch like that, Huckleberry—why don't you try to behave?" Then she told me all about the bad place, and I said I wished I was there. She got mad then, but I didn't mean no harm. All I wanted was to go somewheres; all I wanted was a change, I warn't particular. She said it was wicked to say what I said; said she wouldn't say it for the whole world; *she* was going to live so as to go to the good place. Well, I couldn't see no advantage in going where she was going, so I made up my mind I wouldn't try for it. But I never said so, because it would only make trouble, and wouldn't do no good.

Now she had got a start, and she went on and told me all about the good place. She said all a body would have to do there was to go around all day long with a harp and sing, forever and ever. So I didn't think much of it. But I never said so. I asked her if she reckoned Tom Sawyer would go there, and she said not by a considerable sight. I was glad about that, because I wanted him and me to be together.

Miss Watson she kept pecking at me, and it got tiresome and lonesome. By and by they fetched the niggers in and had prayers, and then everybody was off to bed. I went up to my room with a piece of candle, and put it on the table. Then I set down in a chair by the window and tried to think of something cheerful, but it warn't no use. I felt so lonesome I most wished I was dead. The stars were shining, and the leaves rustled in the woods ever so mournful; and I heard an owl, away off, who-whooing about somebody that was dead, and a whippowill and a dog crying about somebody that was going to die; and the wind was trying to whisper something to me, and I couldn't make out what it was, and so it made the cold shivers run over me. Then away out in the woods I heard that kind of a sound that a ghost makes when it wants to tell about something that's on its mind and can't make itself understood, and so can't rest easy in its grave, and has to go about that way every night grieving. I got so downhearted and scared I did wish I had some company. Pretty soon a spider went crawling up my shoulder, and I flipped it off and it lit in the candle; and before I could budge it was all shriveled up. I didn't need anybody to tell me that that was an awful bad sign and would fetch me some bad luck, so I was scared and most shook the clothes off of me. I got up and turned around in my tracks three times and crossed my breast every time; and then I tied up a little lock of my hair with a thread to keep witches away. But I hadn't no confidence. You do that when you've lost a horseshoe that you've found, instead of nailing it up over the door, but I hadn't ever heard anybody say it was any way to keep off bad luck when you'd killed a spider.

I set down again, a-shaking all over, and got out my pipe for a smoke; for the house was all as still as death now, and so the widow wouldn't know. Well, after a long time I heard the clock away off in the town go boom—boom—boom—twelve licks; and all still again—stiller than ever. Pretty soon I heard a twig snap down in the dark amongst the trees— something was a-stirring. I set still and listened. Directly I could just barely hear a *"me-yow! me-yow!"* down there. That was good! Says I, *"me-yow! me-yow!"* as soft as I could, and then I put out the light and scrambled out of the window on to the shed. Then I slipped down to the ground and crawled in among the trees, and, sure enough, there was Tom Sawyer waiting for me.

Meaning and Idea

1. What is the biblical story of Moses and the Bulrushes (note the difference in spelling)? What is the significance of that story to Huck's narration?

2. Throughout this chapter, how does Huck exemplify "how dismal regular and decent" the Widow Douglas was? List the examples and paraphrase each. What is the worst example of her righteousness? What are Huck's reactions to her decency?

3. What is meant by "the bad place"? Why does Huck tell the Widow Douglas that he wishes she were there? What is "the good place"? Why doesn't Huck want to be there?

4. What causes Huck's lonesomeness? How does he deal with it?

5. What examples of superstitious behavior and belief does Huck provide? What do his superstitions tell you about his character?

Language, Form, Structure

1. What sort of narration is this? How is the point of view appropriate to the story?
How does Twain use exemplification in this chapter from *Huckleberry Finn*? How does he use narrative summary? What is the advantage of using narrative summary here?

2. How does the narrator arrange the examples in this selection? How does time sequence influence the arrangement?

3. How is dialect important in this story? List five examples of dialectical usage. For each, write a standard English equivalent.

Ideas for Writing

1. Select an authority figure whose sense of propriety or decorum you question. Summarize the person's attitudes, then proceed to explain them through exemplification.

2. Do you believe in any particular superstition? If so, write a paragraph in which you explain your belief through cumulative exemplification.

3. If you define *tone* as the author's attitude toward his subject, write a reaction to the *tone* of this selection, especially as it is affected by Huck's dialectical usage. How does the dialect, which continues throughout the book, affect your understanding or enjoyment of the selection? How does Twain feel about Huck? About the Widow Douglas? Miss Watson? Huck's milieu in general?

Robert Frost
THE ROSE FAMILY

Robert Frost (1874–1963) has often been called "America's unofficial Poet Laureate." Born in San Francisco, he was raised in the East and later settled in New Hampshire. He studied at Harvard for a while, then moved to England, though he returned to the United States in 1915. He led a hard life, and his demanding nature often made life difficult for his family and friends as well. Nevertheless, he received worldwide honors, not the least of which was the invitation from President John F. Kennedy to read the poem "Mending Wall" at the 1963 inauguration ceremony.

In this rather tongue-in-cheek imitation of Robert Burns's often-quoted poem, "A Red, Red Rose," Robert Frost uses examples to define *rose* on both literal and metaphoric levels.

The rose is a rose,   1
And was always a rose.
But the theory now goes
That the apple's a rose,
And the pear is, and so's   5
The plum, I suppose.
The dear only knows
What will next prove a rose.
You, of course, are a rose—
But were always a rose.   10

Meaning and Idea

1.   Why does Frost assert that the apple, the pear, and the plum are all roses? To what theory does he refer? (Hint: Try to find the scientific names for each.)

2. Who is the "dear" of line 7? Who is the "You" of line 9?

3. What attitude toward scientific theory in general does Frost express in this poem?

Language, Form, Structure

1. What is the tone of this poem? Why is it appropriate? How does the tone change in the poem? Why? Where?

2. How does Frost use exemplification as a rhetorical device in this poem? What is the relation in the poem between exemplification and definition? What is being defined?

3. How many times does Frost use the word *rose* in this poem? What is the advantage of the repetition?

4. What metaphor is used in this poem?

Ideas for Writing

1. Begin a paragraph with the sentence: "A _____ is a _____." (Fill in the same word in both blanks.) Develop the paragraph by exemplification in an effort to define the term you chose.

2. Choose an emotion and create a personal metaphor for it. Then write a short poem or a paragraph in which you place the metaphor at the end and lead up to it with literal examples.

3. This poem is a parody of the poem "A Red, Red Rose" by the eighteenth-century Scottish poet Robert Burns. Read Burns's poem, then write an essay in which you compare the two poems. Which do you like better? Why? What are the best elements of each?

Robert Browning
MY LAST DUCHESS
FERRARA

> Along with Tennyson, Robert Browning (1812–1889) is considered the shining poet of the late Victorian period. He was raised in an artistic and cultured family of nonconformists—a sort of "preBohemian" English intellectual group. Browning's own education was excellent and well-rounded, and in his early teens he began to write poetry, heavily influenced by Shelley. Browning is considered the master of the dramatic monologue, the three most popular of which are *My Last Duchess, Fra Lippo Lippi,* and *Andrea Del Sarto.* His other well-known works include *Rabbi Ben Ezra* (1864) and the popular children's classic *The Pied Piper of Hamelin* (1842). He was happily married to the poet Elizabeth Barrett Browning.
>
> Browning's "My Last Duchess" is considered one of the best crafted and consistent revelations of character in all of English poetry. Browning has the Duke of Ferrara (a man probably as powerful as a monarch in sixteenth-century Italy) choose just the right descriptive details and examples to reveal to us the full extent of his massive egotism.

*T*hat's my last duchess painted on the wall,   1
Looking as if she were alive. I call
That piece a wonder, now; Fra Pandolf's hands
Worked busily a day, and there she stands.
Will't please you sit and look at her? I said   5
"Fra Pandolf" by design, for never read
Strangers like you that pictured countenance,
The depth and passion of its earnest glance,
But to myself they turned (since none puts by
The curtain I have drawn for you, but I)   10
And seemed as they would ask me, if they durst,
How such a glance came there; so, not the first
Are you to turn and ask thus. Sir, 'twas not

Her husband's presence only, called that spot
Of joy into the Duchess' cheek; perhaps   15
Fra Pandolf chanced to say, "Her mantle laps
Over my lady's wrist too much," or, "Paint
Must never hope to reproduce the faint
Half-blush that dies along her throat." Such stuff
Was courtesy, she thought, and cause enough   20
For calling up that spot of joy. She had
A heart—how shall I say?—too soon made glad,
Too easily impressed; she liked whate'er
She looked on, and her looks went everywhere.
Sir, 'twas all one! My favor at her breast,   25
The dropping of the daylight in the West,
The bough of cherries some officious fool
Broke in the orchard for her, the white mule
She rode with round the terrace—all and each
Would draw from her alike the approving speech,   30
Or blush, at least. She thanked men—good! but thanked
Somehow—I know not how—as if she ranked
My gift of a nine-hundred-years-old name
With anybody's gift. Who'd stoop to blame
This sort of trifling? Even had you skill   35
In speech—which I have not—to make your will
Quite clear to such an one, and say, "Just this
Or that in you disgusts me; here you miss,
Or there exceed the mark"—and if she let
Herself be lessoned so, nor plainly set   40
Her wits to yours, forsooth, and made excuse—
E'en then would be some stooping; and I choose
Never to stoop. Oh, sir, she smiled, no doubt,
Whene'er I passed her; but who passed without
Much the same smile? This grew; I gave commands;   45
Then all smiles stopped together. There she stands
As if alive. Will 't please you rise? We'll meet
The company below, then. I repeat,
The Count your master's known munificence
Is ample warrant that no just pretense   50
Of mine for dowry will be disallowed;
Though his fair daughter's self, as I avowed
At starting, is my object. Nay, we'll go
Together down, sir. Notice Neptune, though,
Taming a sea-horse, thought a rarity,   55
Which Claus of Innsbruck cast in bronze for me.

Meaning and Idea

1. "My Last Duchess" is considered one of the foremost examples of dramatic monologue in English. A *dramatic monologue* is a form of lyric poetry in which a character reveals—to another person, but without dialogue—his inner self at a particular moment and situation. What is the situation in this monologue? To whom is the Duke of Ferrara speaking? What does the Duke reveal about himself to the speaker?

2. What does the Duke think was *right* about his Duchess? What does he think was *wrong* with her?

3. What is the meaning of lines 21–23: "She had/ A heart—how shall I say?— too soon made glad,/ Too easily impressed"? How does the Duke support his allegation?

4. Within the poem's dramatic context, what do you suppose were the "commands" of line 45? Why did all smiles stop after their fulfillment?

5. What, according to the Duke, was his ultimate gift to the Duchess? How did she receive it?

Language, Form, Structure

1. Within the dramatic context of the monologue, what is the Duke's purpose in relating this story? Do you think he has any ulterior motives? What are they? What is the significance of the word *last* in the first line of the poem?

2. How does *exemplification* operate in this poem? How are the examples important in revealing the meaning?

3. What is the use of *dramatic irony* in this poem? (Dramatic irony refers to a condition where the reader knows the truth of a situation to be other than what is presented.)

4. Write dictionary definitions for the following words: countenance (line 7); durst (11); mantle (16); bough, officious (27); lessoned (40); munificence (49); pretense (50); dowry (51).

Ideas for Writing

1. Choose a nonabstract painting which you enjoy, and make a narrative generalization about it. Then describe the painting in a paragraph supporting your generalization with examples drawn from the painting.

2. Write a paragraph in which you attempt to convince someone of the rightness or wrongness of an action by using exemplification as your support technique.

3. Although this poem is about the Duke's wife, we learn a great deal about the Duke himself as he speaks his mind to his visitor. Write a paper in which you analyze the Duke's character. Draw specific examples from the poem in order to support your position.

Sara Teasdale

BARTER

> Sara Teasdale, born in St. Louis, was one of the best-known American poets at the beginning of this century. Unlike her contemporary, Amy Lowell, Teasdale preferred more traditionally shaped, personal lyrics about the fragility of love. Her collections include *Love Songs* (1917), for which she won a Pulitzer Prize, *Flame and Shadow* (1920), and *Strange Victory* (1933). Teasdale committed suicide at the age of 48.
>
> Sara Teasdale's "Barter" provides a series of illuminating examples in support of a very concrete, mercantile term. Notice the balance between concreteness and abstraction, the use of vivid sensory detail on the one hand and of abstract ideas like *peace* and *wonder* on the other.

*L*ife has loveliness to sell,   1
    All beautiful and splendid things,
Blue waves whitened on a cliff,
    Soaring fire that sways and sings,
And children's faces looking up   5
Holding wonder like a cup.

Life has loveliness to sell,
    Music like a curve of gold,
Scent of pine trees in the rain,
    Eyes that love you, arms that hold,   10
And for your spirit's still delight,
Holy thoughts that star the night.

Spend all you have for loveliness,
    Buy it and never count the cost;
For one white singing hour of peace   15
    Count many a year of strife well lost,
And for a breath of ecstasy
Give all you have been, or could be.

Meaning and Idea

1. What does Teasdale feel about the "cost" of life's joys? Quote specific lines in your answer.

2. What does Teasdale consider life's most valuable loveliness? What does she say it's worth? What examples or images lead up to that "most valuable" example?

3. From what aspect of existence does the poet draw most of her imagery? Give examples.

Language, Form, Structure

1. What is the meaning of the word *barter*? How is the title appropriate to the theme and examples of the poem?

2. How does this poem demonstrate the use of exemplification? How do the examples cohere?

3. How is the intended audience of the two stanzas different? How does the difference in intended audience affect the nature of the examples? How are the two stanzas unified?

4. How does Teasdale use *simile* in the poem? How does she use *metaphor*? Make a list of each. Which predominates?

Ideas for Writing

1. Write a paragraph in which you exemplify the best "deal" or "trade" you have ever made. Use the technique of a single, extended example.

2. Select any abstract notion (freedom; desire; fairness, for example) and, using the technique of exemplification, write a paper about that concept. Use many examples, just as Teasdale has.

3. What do you think of the quality of Teasdale's imagery in this poem? How does it affect you emotionally?

Lucille Clifton
GOOD TIMES

> Lucille Clifton was born in 1936 in upstate New York and graduated from Howard University. She is the recipient of a National Endowment for the Arts grant among other awards and has taught at the Columbia University School of the Arts. She says of herself, "I am a black woman poet, and I sound like one." Her poetry is characterized by understatement and succinctness, and although her poems often deal with the nitty-gritty difficulties of life, they are essentially affirmative and optimistic. Clifton's collections of poetry include *Good Times* (1969), *Good News About the Earth* (1972), and *An Ordinary Woman* (1974).
>
> Lucille Clifton's "Good Times" is ultimately a social commentary in which the examples are often ironically double-edged.

My Daddy has paid the rent   1
and the insurance man is gone
and the lights is back on
and my uncle Brud has hit
for one dollar straight   5
and they is good times
good times
good times

My Mama has made bread
and Grampaw has come   10
and everybody is drunk
and dancing in the kitchen
and singing in the kitchen
oh these is good times
good times   15
good times

oh children think about the
good times

Meaning and Idea

1. In a single sentence, state the main point of this poem. Is Clifton writing about good times or its opposite?

2. What is the meaning of the lines "and my uncle Brud has hit/ for one dollar straight"?

3. What examples of "good times" does the speaker give? How do the examples convey the social status of the speaker?

4. At the end of the poem, why does the speaker tell the children to "think about the/ good times"?

Language, Form, Structure

1. What is the general tone of this poem? Does that tone seem at all to contradict the title? How?

2. What is the significance of the stanza divisions of this poem? How does it allow Clifton to arrange her examples?

3. Is there irony in this poem? If so, what kind of irony is it? How does the poet achieve it? What is its purpose?

4. What is the role of repetition in this poem? What does it contribute to the poem's meaning? Notice how the only transition is the word *and*. Why does Clifton use this word eight times? What is the purpose of repeating the words *good times* seven times?

Ideas for Writing

1. Write an exemplification essay called "Good Times" or "Bad Times." Draw upon your own experiences to illustrate your point.

2. Write a paragraph in which you exemplify "success." Attempt to be ironic, and end your paragraph with a caution to your readers.

3. This poem is written in very colloquial language. Some "purist" readers of poetry still object to such "unexalted" language being used for poetry. In general, how do you react to poetry of this sort? What else have you read with similar language use (either poetry or prose)? In your answer, make specific references to this and other works.

Paule Marshall
FROM THE POETS IN THE KITCHEN

Paule Marshall, a well-respected commentator on the black experience and on black literature, has written fiction and nonfiction and has lectured at Columbia and Oxford Universities. Born in Brooklyn, in 1929, the daughter of immigrant parents from Barbados, Marshall graduated from Brooklyn College. Her novels include *Brown Girl, Brownstones* (1959) and *Praisesong for the Widow* (1983).

In this essay, which first appeared in the January 9, 1983, *New York Times Book Review,* Paule Marshall accumulates a plethora of examples—both direct and indirect—to explain how influenced she was by her mother's friends who were the unknowing poets of her childhood.

$\mathcal{S}$ ome years ago, when I was teaching a graduate seminar in fiction at Columbia University, a well-known male novelist visited my class to speak on his development as a writer. In discussing his formative years, he didn't realize it but he seriously endangered his life by remarking that women writers are luckier than those of his sex because they usually spend so much time as children around their mothers and their mothers' friends in the kitchen.

What did he say that for? The women students immediately forgot about being in awe of him and began readying their attack for the question and answer period later on. Even I bristled. There again was that awful image of women locked away from the world in the kitchen with only each other to talk to, and their daughters locked in with them.

But my guest wasn't really being sexist or trying to be provocative or even spoiling for a fight. What he meant—when he got around to examining himself more fully—was that, given the way children are (or were) raised in our society, with little girls kept closer to home and their mothers, the woman writer stands a better chance of being exposed, while growing up, to the kind of talk that goes on among women, more often than not in the kitchen; and that this experience gives her an edge over her male counterpart by instilling in her an appreciation for ordinary speech.

It was clear that my guest lecturer attached great importance to this, which is understandable. Common speech and the plain, workaday words that make it up are, after all, the stock in trade of some of the best fiction writers. They are the principal means by which a character in a novel or story reveals himself and gives voice sometimes to profound feelings and complex ideas about himself and the world. Perhaps the proper measure of a writer's talent is his skill in rendering everyday speech—when it is appropriate to his story—as well as his ability to tap, to exploit, the beauty, poetry and wisdom it often contains.

"If you say what's on your mind in the language that comes to you from your parents and your street and friends you'll probably say something beautiful." Grace Paley tells this, she says, to her students at the beginning of every writing course.

It's all a matter of exposure and a training of the ear for the would-be writer in those early years of his or her apprenticeship. And, according to my guest lecturer, this training, the best of it, often takes place in as unglamorous a setting as the kitchen.

He didn't know it, but he was essentially describing my experience as a little girl. I grew up among poets. Now they didn't look like poets—whatever that breed is supposed to look like. Nothing about them suggested that poetry was their calling. They were just a group of ordinary housewives and mothers, my mother included, who dressed in a way (shapeless housedresses, dowdy felt hats and long, dark, solemn coats) that made it impossible for me to imagine they had ever been young.

Nor did they do what poets were supposed to do—spend their days in an attic room writing verses. They never put pen to paper except to write occasionally to their relatives in Barbados. "I take my pen in hand hoping these few lines will find you in health as they leave me fair for the time being," was the way their letters invariably began. Rather, their day was spent "scrubbing floor," as they described the work they did.

Several mornings a week these unknown bards would put an apron and a pair of old house shoes in a shopping bag and take the train or streetcar from our section of Brooklyn out to Flatbush. There, those who didn't have steady jobs would wait on certain designated corners for the white housewives in the neighborhood to come along and bargain with them over pay for a day's work cleaning their houses. This was the ritual even in the winter.

Later, armed with the few dollars they had earned, which in their vocabulary became "a few raw-mouth pennies," they made their way back to our neighborhood, where they would sometimes stop off to have a cup of tea or cocoa together before going home to cook dinner for their husbands and children.

The basement kitchen of the brownstone house where my family lived was the usual gathering place. Once inside the warm safety of its walls the women threw off the drab coats and hats, seated themselves at the large center table, drank their cups of tea or cocoa, and talked. While my sister and I sat at a smaller table over in a corner doing our homework, they talked—endlessly, passionately, poetically, and with impressive range. No subject was beyond them. True, they would indulge in the usual gossip: whose husband was running with whom, whose daughter looked slightly ''in the way'' (pregnant) under her bridal gown as she walked down the aisle. That sort of thing. But they also tackled the great issues of the time. They were always, for example, discussing the state of the economy. It was the mid and late 30's then, and the aftershock of the Depression, with its soup lines and suicides on Wall Street, was still being felt.

Some people, they declared, didn't know how to deal with adversity. They didn't know that you had to ''tie up your belly'' (hold in the pain, that is) when things got rough and go on with life. They took their image from the bellyband that is tied around the stomach of a newborn baby to keep the navel pressed in.

They talked politics. Roosevelt was their hero. He had come along and rescued the country with relief and jobs, and in gratitude they christened their sons Franklin and Delano and hoped they would live up to the names.

If F.D.R. was their hero, Marcus Garvey was their God. The name of the fiery, Jamaican-born black nationalist of the 20's was constantly invoked around the table. For he had been their leader when they first came to the United States from the West Indies shortly after World War I. They had contributed to his organization, the United Negro Improvement Association (UNIA), out of their meager salaries, bought shares in his ill-fated Black Star Shipping Line, and at the height of the movement they had marched as members of his ''nurses' brigade'' in their white uniforms up Seventh Avenue in Harlem during the great Garvey Day parades. Garvey: He lived on through the power of their memories.

And their talk was of war and rumors of wars. They raged against World War II when it broke out in Europe, blaming it on the politicians. ''It's these politicians. They're the ones always starting up all this lot of war. But what they care? It's the poor people got to suffer and mothers with their sons.'' If it was *their* sons, they swore they would keep them out of the Army by giving them soap to eat each day to make their hearts sound defective. Hitler? He was for them ''the devil incarnate.''

Then there was home. They reminisced often and at length about home. The old country. Barbados—or Bimshire, as they affectionately called it. The little Caribbean island in the sun they loved but had to leave. ''Poor—poor but sweet'' was the way they remembered it.

And naturally they discussed their adopted home. America came in for both good and bad marks. They lashed out at it for the racism they encountered. They took to task some of the people they worked for, especially those who gave them only a hard-boiled egg and a few spoon-fuls of cottage cheese for lunch. ''As if anybody can scrub floor on an egg and some cheese that don't have no taste to it!''

Yet although they caught H in "this man country," as they called America, it was nonetheless a place where "you could at least see your way to make a dollar." That much they acknowledged. They might even one day accumulate enough dollars, with both them and their husbands working, to buy the brownstone houses which, like my family, they were only leasing at that period. This was their consuming ambition: to "buy house" and to see the children through.

There was no way for me to understand it at the time, but the talk that filled the kitchen those afternoons was highly functional. It served as therapy, the cheapest kind available to my mother and her friends. Not only did it help them recover from the long wait on the corner that morning and the bargaining over their labor, it restored them to a sense of themselves and reaffirmed their self-worth. Through language they were able to overcome the humiliations of the work-day.

But more than therapy, that freewheeling, wide-ranging, exuberant talk functioned as an outlet for the tremendous creative energy they possessed. They were women in whom the need for self-expression was strong, and since language was the only vehicle readily available to them they made of it an art form that—in keeping with the African tradition in which art and life are one—was an integral part of their lives.

And their talk was a refuge. They never really ceased being baffled and overwhelmed by America—its vastness, complexity and power. Its strange customs and laws. At a level beyond words they remained fearful and in awe. Their uneasiness and fear were even reflected in their attitude toward the children they had given birth to in this country. They referred to those like myself, the little Brooklyn-born Bajans (Barbadians), as "these New York children" and complained that they couldn't discipline us properly because of the laws here. "You can't beat these children as you would like, you know, because the authorities in this place will dash you in jail for them. After all, these is New York children." Not only were we different, American, we had, as they saw it, escaped their ultimate authority.

Confronted therefore by a world they could not encompass, which even limited their rights as parents, and at the same time finding themselves permanently separated from the world they had known, they took refuge in language. "Language is the only homeland," Czeslaw Milosz, the emigré Polish writer and Nobel Laureate, has said. This is what it became for the women at the kitchen table.

It served another purpose also, I suspect. My mother and her friends were after all the female counterpart of Ralph Ellison's invisible man. Indeed, you might say they suffered a triple invisibility, being black, female and foreigners. They really didn't count in American society except as a source of cheap labor. But given the kind of women they were, they couldn't tolerate the fact of their invisibility, their powerlessness. And they fought back, using the only weapon at their command: the spoken word.

Those late afternoon conversations on a wide range of topics were a way for them to feel they exercised some measure of control over their lives and the events that shaped them. "Soully-gal, talk yuh talk!" they were always exhorting each other. "In this man world you got to take yuh mouth and make a gun!" They were in control, if only verbally and if only for the two hours or so that they remained in our house.

For me, sitting over in the corner, being seen but not heard, which was the rule for children in those days, it wasn't only what the women talked about—the content—but the way they put things—their style. The insight, irony, wit and humor they brought to their stories and discussions and their poet's inventiveness and daring with language—which of course I could only sense but not define back then.

They had taken the standard English taught them in the primary schools of Barbados and transformed it into an idiom, an instrument that more adequately described them—changing around the syntax and imposing their own rhythm and accent so that the sentences were more pleasing to their ears. They added the few African sounds and words that had survived, such as the derisive suck-teeth sound and the word "yam," meaning to eat. And to make it more vivid, more in keeping with their expressive quality, they brought to bear a raft of metaphors, parables, Biblical quotations, sayings and the like:

"The sea ain' got no back door," they would say, meaning that it wasn't like a house where if there was a fire you could run out the back. Meaning that it was not to be trifled with. And meaning perhaps in a larger sense that man should treat all of nature with caution and respect.

"I has read hell by heart and called every generation blessed!" They sometimes went in for hyperbole.

A woman expecting a baby was never said to be pregnant. They never used that word. Rather, she was "in the way" or, better yet, "tumbling big." "Guess who I butt up on in the market the other day tumbling big again!"

And a woman with a reputation of being too free with her sexual favors was known in their book as a "thoroughfare"—the sense of men like a steady stream of cars moving up and down the road of her life. Or she might be dubbed "a free-bee," which was my favorite of the two. I liked the image it conjured up of a woman scandalous perhaps but independent, who flitted from one flower to another in a garden of male beauties, sampling their nectar, taking her pleasure at will, the roles reversed.

And nothing, no matter how beautiful, was ever described as simply beautiful. It was always "beautiful-ugly": the beautiful-ugly dress, the beautiful-ugly house, the beautiful-ugly car. Why the word "ugly," I used to wonder, when the thing they were referring to was beautiful, and they knew it. Why the antonym, the contradiction, the linking of opposites? It used to puzzle me greatly as a child.

There is the theory in linguistics which states that the idiom of a people, the way they use language, reflects not only the most fundamental views they hold of themselves and the world but their very conception of reality. Perhaps in using the term "beautiful-ugly" to describe nearly everything, my mother and her friends were expressing what they believed to be a fundamental dualism in life: the idea that a thing is at the same time its opposite, and that these opposites, these contradictions make up the whole. But theirs was not a Manichaean brand of dualism that sees matter, flesh, the body, as inherently evil, because they constantly addressed each other as "soully-gal"—soul: spirit; gal: the body, flesh, the visible self. And it was clear from their tone that they gave one as much weight and importance as the other. They had never heard of the mind/body split.

As for God, they summed up His essential attitude in a phrase. "God," they would say, "don' love ugly and He ain' stuck on pretty."

Using everyday speech, the simple commonplace words—but always with imagination and skill—they gave voice to the most complex ideas. Flannery O'Connor would have approved of how they made ordinary language work, as she put it, "double-time," stretching, shading, deepening its meaning. Like Joseph Conrad they were always trying to infuse new life in the "old old words worn thin . . . by . . . careless usage." And the goals of their oral art were the same as his: "to make you hear, to make you feel . . . to make you *see*." This was their guiding esthetic.

By the time I was 8 or 9, I graduated from the corner of the kitchen to the neighborhood library, and thus from the spoken to the written word. The Macon Street Branch of the Brooklyn Public Library was an imposing half block long edifice of heavy gray masonry, with glass-paneled doors at the front and two tall metal torches symbolizing the light that comes of learning flanking the wide steps outside.

The inside was just as impressive. More steps—of pale marble with gleaming brass railings at the center and sides—led up to the circulation desk, and a great pendulum clock gazed down from the balcony stacks that faced the entrance. Usually stationed at the top of the steps like the guards outside Buckingham Palace was the custodian, a stern-faced West Indian type who for years, until I was old enough to obtain an adult card, would immediately shoo me with one hand into the Children's Room and with the other threaten me into silence, a finger to his lips. You would have thought he was the chief librarian and not just someone whose job it was to keep the brass polished and the clock wound. I put him in a story called "Barbados" years later and had terrible things happen to him at the end.

I was sheltered from the storm of adolescence in the Macon Street library, reading voraciously, indiscriminately, everything from Jane Austen to Zane Grey, but with a special passion for the long, full-blown, richly detailed 18th- and 19th-century picaresque tales: *Tom Jones. Great Expectations. Vanity Fair.*

But although I loved nearly everything I read and would enter fully into the lives of the characters—indeed, would cease being myself and become them—I sensed a lack after a time. Something I couldn't quite define was missing. And then one day, browsing in the poetry section, I came across a book by someone called Paul Laurence Dunbar, and opening it I found the photograph of a wistful, sad-eyed poet who to my surprise was black. I turned to a poem at random. "Little brown-baby wif spa'klin'/eyes/Come to yo' pappy an' set on his knee." Although I had a little difficulty at first with the words in dialect, the poem spoke to me as nothing I had read before of the closeness, the special relationship I had had with my father, who by then had become an ardent believer in Father Divine and gone to live in Father's "kingdom" in Harlem. Reading it helped to ease somewhat the tight knot of sorrow and longing I carried around in my chest that refused to go away. I read another poem. "Lias! Lias! Bless de Lawd!/Don' you know de day's/erbroad?/Ef you don' get up, you scamp/Dey'll be trouble in dis camp." I laughed. It reminded me of the way my mother sometimes yelled at my sister and me to get out of bed in the mornings.

And another: "Seen my lady home las' night/Jump back, honey, jump back./Hel' huh han' an' sque'z it tight . . ." About love between a black man and a black woman. I had never seen that written about before and it roused in me all kinds of delicious feelings and hopes.

And I began to search then for books and stories and poems about "The Race" (as it was put back then), about my people. While not abandoning Thackeray, Fielding, Dickens and the others, I started asking the reference librarian, who was white, for books by Negro writers, although I must admit I did so at first with a feeling of shame—the shame I and many others used to experience in those days whenever the word "Negro" or "colored" came up.

No grade school literature teacher of mine had ever mentioned Dunbar or James Weldon Johnson or Langston Hughes. I didn't know that Zora Neale Hurston existed and was busy writing and being published during those years. Nor was I made aware of people like Frederick Douglass and Harriet Tubman—their spirit and example—or the great 19th-century abolitionist and feminist Sojourner Truth. There wasn't even Negro History Week when I attended P.S. 35 on Decatur Street!

What I needed, what all the kids—West Indian and native black American alike—with whom I grew up needed, was an equivalent of the

Jewish shul, someplace where we could go after school—the schools that were shortchanging us—and read works by those like ourselves and learn about our history.

It was around that time also that I began harboring the dangerous thought of someday trying to write myself. Perhaps a poem about an apple tree, although I had never seen one. Or the story of a girl who could magically transplant herself to wherever she wanted to be in the world—such as Father Divine's kingdom in Harlem. Dunbar—his dark, eloquent face, his large volume of poems—permitted me to dream that I might someday write, and with something of the power with words my mother and her friends possessed.

When people at readings and writers' conferences ask me who my major influences were, they are sometimes a little disappointed when I don't immediately name the usual literary giants. True, I am indebted to those writers, white and black, whom I read during my formative years and still read for instruction and pleasure. But they were preceded in my life by another set of giants whom I always acknowledge before all others: the group of women around the table long ago. They taught me my first lesson in the narrative art. They trained my ear. They set a standard of excellence. This is why the best of my work must be attributed to them; it stands as testimony to the rich legacy of language and culture they so freely passed on to me in the wordshop of the kitchen.

Meaning and Idea

1. Who are "the poets in the kitchen"? What is Marshall's attitude toward them? What does she feel she gained from them? How? Would they have ever called themselves "poets"? Why or why not?

2. According to Marshall, why was language so important to the women who sat around the kitchen? Why was it especially important for them as immigrants? What example of a famous immigrant writer does she quote to support her opinion?

3. Who does Marshall cite as her major literary influence? Is this the greatest influence on her as a writer? If not, what is?

4. How does Marshall explain the use of descriptions such as "the beautiful-ugly dress"?

5. List at least five examples of the "poetry talk" of the "unknown bards" of the kitchen which Marshall most appreciated.

Language, Form, Structure

1. What is Marshall's thesis in this essay? Try to state it in a single sentence of your own.

2. List at least five of the purposes of language as these "kitchen poets" used it. For each, cite an example given by Marshall. What was the *main* goal of their conversations?

3. Marshall uses a great number of *allusions* in this essay. List and identify ten allusions, at least half of which must *not* be writers.

4. What examples of the value of language does she quote from other writers? Find all and list them.

5. Look up the following words in a dictionary: bristled; to tap; nationalist; functional; exuberant; idiom; a raft of; esthetic; picaresque; shul.

Ideas for Writing

1. Write a paper in which you recount gatherings of your parents' friends during your childhood. What were they like? For what purposes did they gather? Who were they? Devise a name for the group that met most often, and then write a short essay in which you use cumulative examples to support that name.

2. Write an essay in which you discuss the major influences on your use of language, verbal or written. Exemplify as fully as possible.

3. At the beginning of this essay, Marshall quotes the writer Grace Paley: "If you say what's on your mind in the language that comes to you from your parents and your street and friends you'll probably say something beautiful."

Comment on this statement. How true or not true is it in your own reading and writing experiences?

Chapter Four
PROCESS

*I*n early recorded literature we can identify the impulse to explain and to understand how to perform some task. "Make thee an ark of gopher wood," proclaims the voice of the Lord of the Old Testament to Noah; "rooms shalt thou make in the ark, and shalt pitch it within and without with pitch."

> And this is how thou shalt make it: the length of the ark three hundred cubits, the breadth of it fifty cubits, and the height of it thirty cubits. A light shalt thou make to the ark, and to a cubit shalt thou finish it upward; and the door of the ark shalt thou set in the side thereof; with lower, second, and third stories shalt thou make it. And I, behold, I do bring the flood of waters upon the earth, to destroy all flesh, wherein is the breath of life, from under heaven; every thing that is in the earth shall perish. But I will establish My covenant with thee; and thou shalt come into the ark, thou, and thy sons, and thy wife, and thy sons' wives, with thee. And of every living thing of all flesh, two of every sort shalt thou bring into the ark, to keep them alive with thee; they shall be male and female. Of the fowl after their kind, and of the cattle after their kind, of every creeping thing of the ground after its kind, two of every sort shall come unto thee, to keep them alive. And take thou unto thee of all food that is eaten and gather it to thee; and it shall be for food for thee, and for them. Thus did Noah; according to all that God commanded him, so did he.

Certainly, the simplicity of language and the precise sequence of events belie the complexity of the tasks here—it would be no easy task to make an ark simply by following these instructions—but in this explanation from the Book of Genesis you have a striking example of *process analysis* as a key element in early creative literature.

Simply put, the general concept of analysis is the attempt to break something down into parts in an effort to make the whole clear and understandable. When you analyze a novel or a poem, for example, you look carefully at the words and sentences, the chapters or stanzas to give you insights into the total work. Sometimes *causal analysis* motivates your exploration; when you examine a historical event—the Boxer Rebellion, say, or the invasion of Cambodia—you may be looking for the chain of causes and effects that make the situation comprehensible. (See Chapter 7.) *Process analysis* states and explains the steps required to do or to make something or to show how something is (or was) done or is (or was) made.

READING PROCESS ANALYSIS

The distinction above between learning how to do or make something and learning how it is done or made is not simply semantic. Rather the distinction lies at the heart of process analysis as a reflection of thought and as a means of broadening knowledge for readers.

The modern reading public has an ongoing love affair with "how to" books; these books line shelf after shelf in trade book stores everywhere. The cover of a recent issue of *Publisher's Weekly,* the journal of the book industry, showed for one publisher more than twenty "do-it-yourself" volumes issued in a single year: how to design and build deck patios, basic remodeling techniques, how to build and use greenhouses, and how to design and install outdoor lighting, just to name a few. As a further indication of our seemingly endless attraction to books on process, *The New York Times Book Review* recently added the category "Advice, How-to, and Miscellaneous" to the list of weekly best sellers, a list that for years and years reported on only the two familiar groups, "Fiction" and "Nonfiction." We all want instructions on how to perform some process so that we ourselves can perform it in our backyards, under the hoods of our automobiles, in the solitude of our homes. When Hemingway writes to his 1920 *Toronto Star* readers, (see pp. 164 to 167) he tells them exactly what steps to take in order to camp out successfully. Even today we can follow the process and duplicate it. Hemingway wrote this piece so that anyone interested in a short stay in the great outdoors could get the most out of it.

Yet as readers we are equally interested in learning about processes that we have no intention of duplicating. We simply want to see a thing from the inside out, so to speak. We read with rapt attention about how homemade bombs are built or about how flappers made bathtub gin, never thinking for a moment to try schemes like these ourselves. When we read about how music boxes work, how the FBI captured one of its most wanted criminals, or how a woman born in the slums of Chicago became a multimillionaire as a banker, we are seeking information for its own sake, our joy here simply in learning the steps that produced some situation that fascinates us. Thoreau's goal in the selection from *Walden* reprinted here is to tell you how, not how to. Similarly, Ovid explains step-by-step procedures without the slightest interest in getting his readers to try to copy them. Sometimes writers explain a process so clearly that it could be copied, even if the author had not so intended it. Anthony Trollope wants you to understand how *he* goes about writing, but he lays out the process so clearly that *you* might easily use his techniques to become a prolific, if obsessive, writer.

Despite the array of topics that face a reader interested in processes, good "how-to" writing shares a common ground, and alert readers have certain expectations. Perhaps the first here (as for all writing) is clarity. Does the writer make the steps comprehensible? An omitted step, an undefined term, an inappropriate assumption of the reader's prior knowledge can turn a process into mayhem. What frustration is greater then trying to put together a utility cabinet, a gas grill, or a motorized toy from accompanying instructions and finding some abstruse technical term at a critical stage in the assembly? Or wondering with consternation how anyone other than a genius in engineering could advance from one step to the next simply by following the available instructions?

Readers of process analysis, like readers of narrative, usually expect to find a clear chronological sequence, although there are other possibilities. If we expect to carry out the steps ourselves, the relation of the steps to each other is especially important. When we read about process for pleasure and for information—as opposed to reading simply as the fastest and most efficient way to do something (the way we read recipes, for example, or instructions for assembling a stereo)—we also expect the writing to be interesting. Often a writer will depart from chronology to give an example, to provide some relevant background details, to define terms, or to give a lively example. But no matter how much the narrative sequence may recede, its framework is usually there as a necessary guide to the steps being explained.

WRITING PROCESS ANALYSIS

In writing process analysis, perhaps more than in any other kind of writing, you, the writer, become a teacher, and you have to be as well informed about your subject as the best teacher always is. When you explain how something is done or made, you are showing the complexities of an operation to someone who may have little knowledge about your subject. Thus, if you're revealing a process that you know how to perform quite well, have performed often, and hope to stimulate someone else to duplicate, your experience should shine in your prose. Readers should recognize with ease how much you are a master of this process. If you're analyzing a process you've investigated but have not ever attempted, readers should have no questions about your authority to write. Your explanations must be securely grounded in relevant, up-to-date, comprehensive information. In advance of selecting a topic to explore through process analysis, then, you should address these questions:

1. What process can I perform well enough to explain to people who might want to try it themselves or who just might want to know how the process is carried out?

2. What process interests me enough to make me want to research it adequately and to present it clearly in an explanation readers can follow easily?

AUDIENCE AND PURPOSE

You have options in regard to your purpose for writing as you consider a topic for development through process analysis. You should decide whether you want primarily to give instructions or to give information. Certainly these two purposes overlap, but it's important to acknowledge some differences. Giving instructions implies a desire on behalf of reader and writer alike to take action. If you're explaining how to plant a garden of perennials, for example, you'd want the reader to be able to follow your directions on a piece of land in his or her own backyard, and the reader would have the same expectations. If you're writing essentially to give information, on the other hand, you'll be explaining a process you probably would not expect anyone to act upon. Nevertheless, your reader should see easily how this process is achieved and should understand fully how an orderly procedure leads to a realistic end. A consideration of your purpose in writing a process paper is incomplete without considerable thought about your audience. It's comfortable, and sometimes accurate, to assume that anyone who chooses to read *instructions* has a need or a desire for them, and so the writer can count on the readers' loyal interest in the subject right from the start. It's true that most people who choose to read a book called *How to Build a Deck Patio* would have ambitions in the future for expanding their outdoor living space. Such people want to build a deck, and, already motivated and charged with self interest, they turn to a book for help in realizing their goal.

But it's not always true that instructions are read by captive audiences only. Assume for a moment that you're leafing through a popular magazine and you come across a piece called "How to Tune Up Your Car: Ten Simple Steps for People with Ten Thumbs and Two Left Hands." Being unmechanical, you might be one of those who ordinarily shiver and turn the page when you see anything that requires taking things apart and putting them together. But this essay, from its title at least, may be talking your language. You're fed up with the high costs of car maintenance at a service station, and you'll take a chance on reading this essay to see if in fact even a clod like you can follow the process and master it. Here, then, the writer would have been wrong to assume only a captive readership. A good part of this essay would have to go toward capturing and engaging the reader. It's certain that a writer who chose a title like the one we've mentioned above knows how little his audience understands about tuning cars and how important it is to woo that audience from the start.

Furthermore, assuming that you have only an eager, dedicated audience for your instructions can make for sloppy writing. In some cases the easiest way to present a set of instructions is just to number and list them briefly with accompanying illustrations and be done with it. But if you've ever struggled with supposedly simple lists and pictures on the cartons of do it yourself products, you know what it means to long for fuller explanations—complete sentences, detailed paragraphs!—when there is no slot into which an equally nonexistent flap A must fit, or when four nuts and three bolts remain to complete a unit that demands three nuts and four bolts. Even interested readers deserve clear, careful prose.

Besides, for the kind of process paper you will write to give instructions at school or on the job, the real audience—your instructor, your fellow classmates, or your coworkers—will almost certainly not have a passion for or an interest in your essay topic. You might be able to tick off fifteen quick steps for curing ick in tropical fish; and if you were writing for an amateur collector who had lost a tank of mollies and swordtails to the disease, she might be reading your essay with rapt attention. But if your teacher or the fellow in the next row has no interest in home aquariums, your essay will have to win these people over as much as it will have to teach them how to carry out those basic steps for bacteria-free fish. Although *your* purpose might be to give directions, readers who have no special interest in advance of following them may, despite your goals, be reading only for information. Your paper should acknowledge both readerships by avoiding complaisance at all costs.

When you analyze a process essentially to convey information, as opposed to writing essentially to give directions, you should always work to draw your reader in, and that rule of thumb should guide a process essay of any kind. You should be weighing your audience's stake in reading your paper. What chord can you strike that will hold your reader's interest? How can you convince your readers that what you say will amuse or inform or surprise them to a high enough degree to warrant their taking the time to read?

Consideration of (and for) your audience raises another question that you must face as you plan and develop your paper. How much can you assume that your audience knows about your topic? This is an important question because the response will guide your level of vocabulary and the scope and depth of detail you must include. Suppose you wanted to explain a quick method you'd developed for adding cuffs to trouser legs or coat sleeves. If your intended audience were a group of young, single males or females who had never held a needle in their hands, you'd have to consider as technical vocabulary some of the basic language required to explain the process, words like *hem, hemline, basting, thimble, finish, blind stitch,* just to name a few. If you didn't provide definitions at least for some of these, you couldn't be sure that your readers would understand what you were talking about. And for such an audience you couldn't assume much advanced knowledge of any steps in the process. You'd have to spell out everything from how to hold the garment to how to knot the thread at the end of the needle. However, for an audience of experienced homemakers who had sewn lots of hems and seams before, you could assume a thorough working knowledge of sewing vocabulary and could skip the most elementary steps, fairly confident that your readers knew the basics of needlework.

You can see even from this brief section how complex an issue audience is for the writer of process analysis. It's never easy to know exactly what your audience is like, even when you might know pretty well who they are—your teacher, say, or the group of fellow writers with whom you've been working in class. Professional writers have similar problems: For example, a writer doing a piece for *Mademoiselle,* a magazine ostensibly for fashion-conscious, upper middle-class young women, has no guarantee that every reader is equal in knowledge, language, and background to understand an article on the use of weight machines to firm up flabby muscles, or on the process of buying good wines, or on planting a window garden. Some writers of process, then, will define their own audience and refer overtly to it in the paper, weaving their assumptions about the readership into the essay itself. Hemingway makes clear in the first couple of paragraphs of "Camping Out" that he is writing not to experienced campers and fishing enthusiasts but to *bona fide* amateurs. The writer whose title is "How to Tune Up Your Car: Ten Simple Steps for People with Ten Thumbs and Two Left Hands" has defined his audience directly in the title. The strategy of naming your audience for all to see can help you draw in otherwise reluctant readers. Your audience may not in fact be the audience you've defined; but once they know exactly for whom you're aiming, they might be willing to suspend disbelief, so to speak, and to join temporarily the group you're trying to reach. Aware of the readers that Hemingway is addressing, even long-time fishermen could enjoy the good-humored recommendations the writer offers to novices.

PROCESS

Spend some time identifying a process you want to write about by considering the two questions raised on page 159. If you choose to give directions for a process you know how to do well, you'll have to reflect a while on the various steps required to carry it out. The more experienced you are, the more automatic your actions become; you may have to bring to a level of conscious thought some of the steps you haven't dwelled on for years. If you choose to give information about a process that interests you, you may have to spend some time in the library looking at books and magazines that will fill in any gaps of knowledge.

Once you have a topic and have duly considered audience and purpose, perhaps the best way to begin is to make a rough list of all the steps required in the process. Once you have your list, look it over carefully. Be sure that you have not left anything out. Are there preparatory steps to take, for example? Is there equipment that must be gathered together before beginning? Should objects be measured or counted beforehand? Should you provide an overview or some background information, including, perhaps, a history of the process, the reasons for your interest in it, the ultimate goals of the process, or your intention to examine in great detail only certain phases of the analysis?

You'll also need to examine as objectively as you can the terminology that appears on your list. Identify specialized terms, and plan to define them for your readers.

Look too with special attention at the sequence of steps you've listed. Do they follow each other chronologically? Most process analyses proceed through an orderly sequence of time: Readers have to know what to do first, what to do next, and what to do after that. But you do have other options, and you might want to rearrange the steps on your list. In explaining how you clean a six-room apartment efficiently, you might reject the apparent chronological sequence—"First I clean the bedrooms. . . . Then I wash the bathroom floor. . . . Last I do the kitchen." Instead you might arrange information by importance or by level of difficulty. "The easiest part of the job is vacuuming the carpet on all the floors. . . . The most difficult task is dusting the top corners in the rooms with high ceilings." (This order may be chronological as well, that is, if you do the simple work first and the tough work last, but it does not have to be.) Another option is to arrange the information in order of physical location. Here you'd move the reader from place to place in the house, your organizing principle based on the spacial relationship of the rooms. Or, you could decide on some other logical sequence, sorting information according to an interesting scheme you've worked out. "I have learned that cleaning a six-room house is best viewed in one of these ways, the 'once-over-lightly' approach, the 'I'm starting to get serious about this mess' approach, and the 'pull out the stops because the folks are coming tonight' approach." Whatever order you choose should be meaningful, however, and should help the reader understand the process. A revised version of your list should guide you as you develop your drafts. Remember that you're trying to engage your reader's interest, so you should resist writing your process paper as a mere list of steps. You might relate a personal incident that sheds light on why you chose to analyze this particular process or that taught you the quickest and the simplest way to do the job. You might investigate the effects or consequences of the process. You might draw upon concrete sensory language to give an immediacy and drama to the steps you're explaining. You might insist upon the importance of knowing how to master this process or of understanding how it is achieved. You might develop an appropriate comparison or analogy. You might provide diagrams, drawings, photographs, maps, charts, or graphs to illustrate the text of your essay.

And don't ignore your style. Prune from early drafts any details that risk making your paper wordy or unnecessarily complicated. Check your vocabulary for jargon, excessively technical terms, or key words that you failed to define. Pay particular attention to transitions. It's easy to overdo time or step markers—"*first* do this, *then* do that, *next* do something else"—but you will need some of them to help your readers know when one step ends and another begins.

Ernest Hemingway
CAMPING OUT

Ernest Hemingway (1898–1961) is perhaps America's best-known and most widely read modern writer. He was born in Oak Park, Illinois, and started his career as a journalist for the *Kansas City Star.* Wounded while serving as a volunteer ambulance driver in France, Hemingway became part of the "lost generation" of American expatriate writers in Paris in the 1920s. Nick Adams, his alter-ego fictional hero, first appeared in Hemingway's collection of stories, *In Our Time,* in 1924. That book was followed by, among others, *The Sun Also Rises* (1926), *A Farewell to Arms* (1929), *For Whom the Bell Tolls* (1940), and *The Old Man and the Sea* (1952)—all characterized by Hemingway's renowned crisp simplicity. After leaving Paris, Hemingway lived, wrote, hunted, and caroused in Key West, Cuba, Montana, and Africa. He received the Nobel Prize for Literature in 1954. A despondent Hemingway shot himself in 1961.

This piece originally appeared in the *Toronto Star,* for which Hemingway was the Paris correspondent, in the 1920s *before* he established himself as a major writer. In this process analysis, we can observe the roots of the author's well-known fascination with outdoor life and his simplicity in writing.

*T*housands of people will go into the bush this summer to cut the high cost of living. A man who gets his two weeks' salary while he is on vacation should be able to put those two weeks in fishing and camping and be able to save one week's salary clear. He ought to be able to sleep comfortably every night, to eat well every day and to return to the city rested and in good condition.

But if he goes into the woods with a frying pan, an ignorance of black flies and mosquitoes, and a great and abiding lack of knowledge about cookery the chances are that his return will be very different. He will come back with enough mosquito bites to make the back of his neck look like a relief map of the Caucasus. His digestion will be wrecked after a valiant battle to assimilate half-cooked or charred grub. And he won't have had a decent night's sleep while he has been gone.

He will solemnly raise his right hand and inform you that he has joined the grand army of never-agains. The call of the wild may be all right, but it's a dog's life. He's heard the call of the tame with both ears. Waiter, bring him an order of milk toast.

In the first place he overlooked the insects. Black flies, no-see-ums, deer flies, gnats and mosquitoes were instituted by the devil to force people to live in cities where he could get at them better. If it weren't for them everybody would live in the bush and he would be out of work. It was a rather successful invention.

But there are lots of dopes that will counteract the pests. The simplest perhaps is oil of citronella. Two bits' worth of this purchased at any pharmacist's will be enough to last for two weeks in the worst fly and mosquito-ridden country.

Rub a little on the back of your neck, your forehead and your wrists before you start fishing, and the blacks and skeeters will shun you. The odor of citronella is not offensive to people. It smells like gun oil. But the bugs do hate it.

Oil of pennyroyal and eucalyptol are also much hated by mosquitoes, and with citronella they form the basis for many proprietary preparations. But it is cheaper and better to buy the straight citronella. Put a little on the mosquito netting that covers the front of your pup tent or canoe tent at night, and you won't be bothered.

To be really rested and get any benefit out of a vacation a man must get a good night's sleep every night. The first requisite for this is to have plenty of cover. It is twice as cold as you expect it will be in the bush four nights out of five, and a good plan is to take just double the bedding that you think you will need. An old quilt that you can wrap up in is as warm as two blankets.

Nearly all outdoor writers rhapsodize over the browse bed. It is all right for the man who knows how to make one and has plenty of time. But in a succession of one-night camps on a canoe trip all you need is level ground for your tent floor and you will sleep all right if you have plenty of covers under you. Take twice as much cover as you think that you will need, and then put two-thirds of it under you. You will sleep warm and get your rest.

When it is clear weather you don't need to pitch your tent if you are only stopping for the night. Drive four stakes at the head of your made-up bed and drape your mosquito bar over that, then you can sleep like a log and laugh at the mosquitoes.

Outside of insects and bum sleeping the rock that wrecks most camping trips is cooking. The average tyro's idea of cooking is to fry everything and fry it good and plenty. Now, a frying pan is a most necessary thing to any trip, but you also need the old stew kettle and the folding reflector baker.

A pan of fried trout can't be bettered and they don't cost any more than ever. But there is a good and bad way of frying them.

The beginner puts his trout and his bacon in and over a brightly burning fire, the bacon curls up and dries into a dry tasteless cinder and the trout is burned outside while it is still raw inside. He eats them and it is all right if he is only out for the day and going home to a good meal at night. But if he is going to face more trout and bacon the next morning and other equally well-cooked dishes for the remainder of two weeks he is on the pathway to nervous dyspepsia.

The proper way is to cook over coals. Have several cans of Crisco or Cotosuet or one of the vegetable shortenings along that are as good as lard and excellent for all kinds of shortening. Put the bacon in and when it is about half cooked lay the trout in the hot grease, dipping them in corn meal first. Then put the bacon on top of the trout and it will baste them as it slowly cooks.

The coffee can be boiling at the same time and in a smaller skillet pancakes being made that are satisfying the other campers while they are waiting for the trout.

With the prepared pancake flours you take a cupful of pancake flour and add a cup of water. Mix the water and flour and as soon as the lumps are out it is ready for cooking. Have the skillet hot and keep it well greased. Drop the batter in and as soon as it is done on one side loosen it in the skillet and flip it over. Apple butter, syrup or cinnamon and sugar go well with the cakes.

While the crowd have taken the edge from their appetites with flap-jacks the trout have been cooked and they and the bacon are ready to serve. The trout are crisp outside and firm and pink inside and the bacon is well done—but not too done. If there is anything better than that combination the writer has yet to taste it in a lifetime devoted largely and studiously to eating.

The stew kettle will cook you dried apricots when they have resumed their predried plumpness after a night of soaking, it will serve to concoct a mulligan in, and it will cook macaroni. When you are not using it, it should be boiling water for the dishes.

In the baker, mere man comes into his own, for he can make a pie that to his bush appetite will have it all over the product that mother used to make, like a tent. Men have always believed that there was something mysterious and difficult about making a pie. Here is a great secret. There is nothing to it. We've been kidded for years. Any man of average office intelligence can make at least as good a pie as his wife.

All there is to a pie is a cup and a half of flour, one-half teaspoonful of salt, one-half cup of lard and cold water. That will make pie crust that will bring tears of joy into your camping partners' eyes.

Mix the salt with the flour, work the lard into the flour, make it up into a good workmanlike dough with cold water. Spread some flour on the back of a box or something flat, and pat the dough around a while. Then roll it out with whatever kind of round bottle you prefer. Put a little more lard on the surface of the sheet of dough and then slosh a little flour on and roll it up and then roll it out again with the bottle.

Cut out a piece of the rolled out dough big enough to line a pie tin. I like the kind with holes in the bottom. Then put in your dried apples that have soaked all night and been sweetened, or your apricots, or your blueberries, and then take another sheet of the dough and drape it gracefully over the top, soldering it down at the edges with your fingers. Cut a couple of slits in the top dough sheet and prick it a few times with a fork in an artistic manner.

Put it in the baker with a good slow fire for forty-five minutes and then take it out and if your pals are Frenchmen they will kiss you. The penalty for knowing how to cook is that the others will make you do all the cooking.

It is all right to talk about roughing it in the woods. But the real woodsman is the man who can be really comfortable in the bush.

Meaning and Idea

1. Explain in your own words the overall process that Hemingway analyzes in this essay. What subprocesses does he explain as parts of the overall process? Choose one of those subprocesses and explain it fully.

2. According to the essay, what are some of the advantages of spending your vacation camping out?

3. What are the best ways "to counteract the pests"?

4. What are the bad and good ways to cook trout? What other cooking preparations does Hemingway explain?

5. Is Hemingway in favor of "roughing it"? How do you know? Analyze the first and last paragraphs in light of your answer.

Language, Form, Structure

1. Which sentences best state Hemingway's purpose in this essay? Where does he define his audience?

2. How do the first two paragraphs establish the organization of this process analysis? Where does the process analysis actually begin? What is the purpose of the writing up to that point?

3. How does Hemingway use exemplification in this essay? How does he use description?

4. Write sentences showing that you know the meaning of the following words: assimilate; valiant; requisite; rhapsodize; tyro; dyspepsia; mulligan; concoct; soldering.

Ideas for Writing

1. What is your favorite vacation activity? Write a process analysis telling others how to enjoy a similar vacation experience.

2. Choose some common activity—commuting to work, studying, working out, making a pie crust—and write an essay that tells how to do it correctly as opposed to how to do it incorrectly.

3. The intended audience for "Camping Out" was originally urban newspaper readers in the 1920s. Write an essay in which you analyze Hemingway's use of language. Is the word choice appropriate to his audience? How appropriate is the style of the essay to a 1980s newspaper readership? Would you suggest any modifications if the essay were to be published in a newspaper today?

Anthony Trollope

250 WORDS EVERY QUARTER OF AN HOUR

Anthony Trollope (1815–1882) is known for his realistic novels about the lives of ordinary middle- and upper-middle-class people of Victorian England. Though his later novels became more politically and sociologically oriented, his most famous works are the series of Barsetshire novels about daily life in that fictional county, which include *The Warden* (1855), *The Small House at Allington* (1864), and *The Last Chronicle of Barset* (1867).

In this section from Trollope's *Autobiography,* he gives us an intimate view of the processes and results of his own writing habits. In this way, he suggests a daily process which "will produce as much as a man ought to write."

*A*ll those who have lived as literary men,—working daily as literary labourers,—will agree with me that three hours a day will produce as much as a man ought to write. But then, he should so have trained himself that he shall be able to work continuously during those three hours,—so have tutored his mind that it shall not be necessary for him to sit nibbling his pen, and gazing at the wall before him, till he shall have found the words with which he wants to express his ideas. It had at this time become my custom,—and it still is my custom, though of late I have become a little lenient with myself,—to write with my watch before me, and to require from myself 250 words every quarter of an hour. I have found that the 250 words have been forthcoming as regularly as my watch went. But my three hours were not devoted entirely to writing. I always began my task by reading the work of the day before, an operation which would take me half an hour, and which consisted chiefly in weighing with my ear the sound of the words and phrases. I would strongly recommend this practice to all tyros in writing. That their work should be read after it has been written is a matter of course,—that it should be read twice at least before it goes to the printers, I take to be a matter of course. But by reading what he has last written, just before he recommences his task, the writer will catch the tone and spirit of what he is then saying, and will avoid the fault of seeming to be unlike himself. This division of time allowed me to produce over ten pages of an ordinary novel volume a day, and if kept up through ten months, would have given as its results three novels of three volumes each in the year. . . .

I have never written three novels in a year, but by following the plan above described I have written more than as much as three volumes; and by adhering to it over a course of years, I have been enabled to have always on hand,—for some time back now,—one or two or even three unpublished novels in my desk beside me. Were I to die now there are three such,—besides *The Prime Minister,* half of which only has as yet been issued. One of these has been six years finished, and has never seen the light since it was first tied up in the wrapper which now contains it. I look forward with some grim pleasantry to its publication after another period of six years, and to the declaration of the critics that it has been the work of a period of life at which the power of writing novels has passed from me.

Meaning and Idea

1.   Outline, in your own words, Trollope's daily writing process.

2.   According to the author, how many hours each day should a writer write? What special procedure should begin that time period? How long does this procedure take Trollope?

3.   Explain what Trollope considers the minimal revision process. What is its

main purpose? Explain the meaning of "avoid the fault of seeming to sound unlike himself."

4. What for Trollope were the results of adhering to the process he describes?

Language, Form, Structure

1. About whom is Trollope writing? For whom is he writing? What word in the essay helps to identify his intended audience?

2. How does Trollope organize the steps of his process?

3. What is the tone of this selection? Do you detect any tonal change in the last sentence. What is it?

4. Where does the writer use metaphors? Identify them.

5. Write the dictionary meanings of the following words: lenient; tyros; recommences; grim; pleasantry.

Ideas for Writing

1. Choose an activity which you do daily for a limited period of time. Write a short process analysis which would be beneficial to others desiring to do the same activity.

2. Write a process analysis of some intellectual pursuit, other than writing, which you practice. You might choose reading, thinking, or solving a mathematical problem, for example. Gear your analysis to novices to the pursuit.

3. Write a paper in which you evaluate Trollope's advice on writing. How realistic or effective do you find his advice? You might wish to compare his suggestions to the processes of other writers which you have read or heard about. What further advice would you add?

Ovid
THE CREATION

Ovid, the name by which we know Publius Ovidius Naso, was born to a wealthy family in the hill country outside Rome in 43 B.C. He began writing verse at age 12 and a few years later moved to Rome. In the year A.D. 8, Emperor Augustus exiled Ovid to a small town on the Black Sea for various scandalous indiscretions. He died in that town in A.D. 18, survived by his third wife and his writings, among them *The Art of Love, Heroines, On Make-Up,* and the *Metamorphoses.*

This selection, translated by Rolfe Humphries, is the opening poem of Book I of Ovid's *Metamorphoses,* or *Stories of Changing Forms,* which is a novel-length series of poems described by John Crowe Ransom as "a key to the literary and religious culture of the ancients." This selection describes the most fundamental process of all, a version of which appears in every mythology and culture.

*B*efore the ocean was, or earth, or heaven,   1
Nature was all alike, a shapelessness,
Chaos, so-called, all rude and lumpy matter,
Nothing but bulk, inert, in whose confusion
Discordant atoms warred: there was no sun   5
To light the universe; there was no moon
With slender silver crescents filling slowly;
No earth hung balanced in surrounding air;
No sea reached far along the fringe of shore.
Land, to be sure, there was, and air, and ocean,   10
But land on which no man could stand, and water
No man could swim in, air no man could breathe,
Air without light, substance forever changing,
Forever at war: within a single body
Heat fought with cold, wet fought with dry, the hard   15
Fought with the soft, things having weight contended
With weightless things.
            Till God, or kindlier Nature,
Settled all argument, and separated
Heaven from earth, water from land, our air   20
From the high stratosphere, a liberation

So things evolved, and out of blind confusion
Found each its place, bound in eternal order.
The force of fire, that weightless element,
Leaped up and claimed the highest place in heaven;   25
Below it, air; and under them the earth
Sank with its grosser portions; and the water,
Lowest of all, held up, held in, the land.

Whatever god it was, who out of chaos
Brought order to the universe, and gave it   30
Division, subdivision, he molded earth,
In the beginning, into a great globe,
Even on every side, and bade the waters
To spread and rise, under the rushing winds,
Surrounding earth; he added ponds and marshes,   35
He banked the river-channels, and the waters
Feed earth or run to sea, and that great flood
Washes on shores, not banks. He made the plains
Spread wide, the valleys settle, and the forest
Be dressed in leaves; he made the rocky mountains   40
Rise to full height, and as the vault of Heaven
Has two zones, left and right, and one between them
Hotter than these, the Lord of all Creation
Marked on the earth the same design and pattern.
The torrid zone too hot for men to live in,   45
The north and south too cold, but in the middle
Varying climate, temperature and season.
Above all things the air, lighter than earth,
Lighter than water, heavier than fire,
Towers and spreads; there mist and cloud assemble,   50
And fearful thunder and lightning and cold winds,
But these, by the Creator's order, held
No general dominion; even as it is,
These brothers brawl and quarrel; though each one
Has his own quarter, still, they come near tearing   55
The universe apart. Eurus is monarch
Of the lands of dawn, the realms of Araby,
The Persian ridges under the rays of morning.
Zephyrus holds the west that glows at sunset,
Boreas, who makes men shiver, holds the north,   60
Warm Auster governs in the misty southland,
And over them all presides the weightless ether,
Pure without taint of earth.

These boundaries given,
Behold, the stars, long hidden under darkness,   65
Broke through and shone, all over the spangled heaven,
Their home forever, and the gods lived there,
And shining fish were given the waves for dwelling
And beasts the earth, and birds the moving air.

But something else was needed, a finer being,   70
More capable of mind, a sage, a ruler,
So Man was born, it may be, in God's image,
Or Earth, perhaps, so newly separated
From the old fire of Heaven, still retained
Some seed of the celestial force which fashioned   75
Gods out of living clay and running water.
All other animals look downward; Man,
Alone, erect, can raise his face toward Heaven.

Meaning and Idea

1. Paraphrase Ovid's description of the universe before creation.

2. Describe the process of chaos becoming order as it is presented in this poem.

3. What was the relationship among universal opposing forces before the creation? What examples does Ovid provide to support this theory? How does that condition change after the creation? What brought about the change?

4. Identify the following Roman gods whom Ovid alludes to: Eurus; Zephyrus; Boreas; Auster.

5. What, according to the poem, was the purpose for humankind in the creation? At what point in the creation does humanity appear?

Language, Form, Structure

1. In a four-line preface to the *Metamorphoses,* Ovid wrote:

My intention is to tell of bodies changed
To different forms; the gods, who made the changes,
Will help me—or I hope so—with a poem
That runs from the world's beginning to our own days.

How does this short poem serve as an appropriate beginning to the process described in "The Creation"?

2. What is the use of description and narration in this poem? How do they enhance the process analysis?

3. Look up the following words in a dictionary: rude; inert; fringe; stratosphere; bade; torrid; dominion; ether; taint; celestial.

Ideas for Writing

1. Write a process essay that analyzes a creative process with which you are familiar. Attempt to use imagery as much as possible.

2. Select some natural process (leaves turning color; for example), and write a process analysis explaining it to readers.

3. Read the account of creation in the Old Testament Book of Genesis. Write a paper in which you compare Ovid's version with the Old Testament story. What are the main similarities? What is the major difference? How do they compare in terms of style and tone?

Emily Dickinson

CRUMBLING IS NOT AN INSTANT'S ACT

Emily Dickinson is known as one of the oddities and wonders of modern poetry. Born into a fairly well-to-do family in Amherst, Massachusetts, in 1830, she died there in 1886 having spent virtually all her fifty-six years there. She left over 1,000 poems dealing with love and death, religion and nature. Like William Blake, an earlier master of simple imagery and emotion, Dickinson was not well known during her lifetime, although her posthumous volumes have exerted a tremendous influence on the direction of poetry. Although small volumes were published in the 1890s, a definitive collected works did not appear until 1955.

By fixing her process description onto a natural process, Dickinson is able to distance herself somewhat from one of the most painful of human experiences. At the same time, she is able to universalize the experience.

C rumbling is not an instant's Act   1
A fundamental pause
Delapidation's processes
Are organized Decays.

'Tis first a Cobweb on the Soul   5
A Cuticle of Dust
A Borer in the Axis
An Elemental Rust—

Ruin is formal—Devils work
Consecutive and slow—   10
Fail in an instant, no man did
Slipping—is Crashe's law.

Meaning and Idea

1. What is Dickinson's meaning here for "crumbling"? How does she use it and other images to communicate something about human experience? What, then, is the poem's theme?

2. In a single sentence, summarize what Dickinson says about the *process* of "crumbling."

3. By whom are "Delapidation's processes" organized? Why?

4. What is "Crashe's law"?

Language, Form, Structure

1. Who is the poet's audience for this poem? How do you know?

2. What is Dickinson trying to communicate in this poem? In the context of this chapter—Process Analysis—what is her purpose in communicating that message?

3. What is the effect of the seemingly random capitalization of words?

4. Write meanings for the following words: fundamental (line 2); delapidation (3); cuticle (6); axis (7); elemental (8).

Ideas for Writing

1. Select a natural process, such as physical growth, boiling of liquids. Write a process paragraph in which you use this natural process as a metaphor for a human emotional experience.

2. Relate the process by which you pulled yourself out of a negative emotional state at some time in your life.

3. Dickinson is renowned as a stylist for her ability to pack complex meanings into brief and, on the surface, simple lines and stanzas and for her surprising use of words in unexpected contexts. Write a brief paper in which you analyze and evaluate Dickinson's style as it appears to you from "Crumbling Is Not an Instant's Act."

Henry David Thoreau
ON ECONOMY

Henry David Thoreau (1817–1862) along with Ralph Waldo Emerson helped move the mid-nineteenth-century American literary center from New York to Boston. Thoreau was a man of deeds, a nonconformist, a social critic. He graduated from Harvard, though he eschewed the professional opportunities that education provided him, choosing instead a quiet life in Concord, Massachusetts, where he was born. His most famous writings are *Walden* (1854), his account of natural living at Walden Pond, and the essay "Civil Disobedience," which significantly influenced the philosophy and tactics of Mahatma Ghandi.

In *Walden* Thoreau describes his experiment in living the solitary, self-sufficient, somewhat ascetic life at Walden Pond. In this selection from that book, he addresses the processes by which he learned to live a life of fiscal and emotional economy. He readily admits personal pride in his accomplishments, but also hopes that what he learned will benefit his readers.

*N*ear the end of March, 1845, I borrowed an axe and went down to the woods by Walden Pond, nearest to where I intended to build my house, and began to cut down some tall, arrowy white pines, still in their youth, for timber. It is difficult to begin without borrowing, but perhaps it is the most generous course thus to permit your fellow-men to have an interest in your enterprise. The owner of the axe, as he released his hold on it, said that it was the apple of his eye; but I returned it sharper than I received it. It was a pleasant hillside where I worked, covered with pine woods, through which I looked out on the pond, and a small open field in the woods where pines and hickories were springing up. The ice in the pond was not yet dissolved, though there were some open spaces, and it was all dark-colored and saturated with water. There were some slight flurries of snow during the days that I worked there; but for the most part when I came out on to the railroad, on my way home, its yellow sand-heap stretched away gleaming in the hazy atmosphere, and the rails shone in the spring sun, and I heard the lark and pewee and other birds already come to commence another year with us. They were pleasant spring days, in which the winter of man's discontent was thawing as well as the earth, and the life that had lain torpid began to stretch itself. One day, when my axe had come off and I had cut a green hickory for a wedge, driving it with a stone, and had placed the whole to soak in a pond-hole in order to swell the wood, I saw a striped snake run into the water, and he lay on the bottom, apparently without inconvenience, as long as I stayed there, or more than a quarter of an hour; perhaps because he had not yet fairly come out of the torpid state. It appeared to me that for a like reason men remain in their present low and primitive condition; but if they should feel the influence of the spring of springs arousing them, they would of necessity rise to a higher and more ethereal life. I had previously seen the snakes in frosty mornings in my path with portions of their bodies still numb and inflexible, waiting for the sun to thaw them. On the 1st of April it rained and melted the ice, and in the early part of the day, which was very foggy, I heard a stray goose groping about over the pond and cackling as if lost, or like the spirit of the fog.

So I went on for some days cutting and hewing timber, and also studs and rafters, all with my narrow axe, not having many communicable or scholar-like thoughts, singing to myself,—

Men say they know many things;
But lo! they have taken wings,—
The arts and sciences,
And a thousand appliances:
The wind that blows
Is all that anybody knows.

I hewed the main timbers six inches square, most of the studs on two sides only, and the rafters and floor timbers on one side, leaving the rest of the bark on, so that they were just as straight and much stronger than sawed ones. Each stick was carefully mortised or tenoned by its stump, for I had borrowed other tools by this time. My days in the woods were not very long ones; yet I usually carried my dinner of bread and butter, and read the newspaper in which it was wrapped, at noon, sitting amid the green pine boughs which I had cut off, and to my bread was imparted some of their fragrance, for my hands were covered with a thick coat of pitch. Before I had done I was more the friend than the foe of the pine tree, though I had cut down some of them having become better acquainted with it. Sometimes a rambler in the wood was attracted by the sound of my axe, and we chatted pleasantly over the chips which I had made.

By the middle of April, for I made no haste in my work, but rather made the most of it, my house was framed and ready for the raising. I had already bought the shanty of James Collins, an Irishman who worked on the Fitchburg Railroad, for boards. James Collins' shanty was considered an uncommonly fine one. When I called to see it he was not at home. I walked about the outside, at first unobserved from within, the window was so deep and high. It was of small dimensions, with a peaked cottage roof, and not much else to be seen, the dirt being raised five feet all around as if it were a compost heap. The roof was the soundest part, though a good deal warped and made brittle by the sun. Doorsill there was none, but a perennial passage for the hens under the door-board. Mrs. C. came to the door and asked me to view it from the inside. The hens were driven in by my approach. It was dark, and had a dirt floor for the most part, dank, clammy, and aguish, only here a board and there a board which would not bear removal. She lighted a lamp to show me the inside of the roof and the walls, and also that the board floor extended under the bed, warning me not to step into the cellar, a sort of dust hole two feet deep. In her own words, they were "good boards overhead, good boards all around, and a good window,"—of two whole squares originally, only the cat had passed out that way lately. There was a stove, a bed, and a place to sit, an infant in the house where it was born, a silk parasol, gilt-framed looking-glass, and a patent new coffee-mill nailed to an oak sapling, all told. The bargain was soon concluded, for James had in the meanwhile returned. I to pay four dollars and twenty-five cents to-night, he to vacate at five to-morrow morning, selling to nobody else meanwhile: I to take possession at six. It were well, he said, to be there early, and anticipate certain indistinct but wholly unjust claims on the score of ground rent and fuel. This he assured me was the only encumbrance. At six I passed him and his family on the road. One large bundle held their all,—bed, coffee-mill, looking-glass, hens,—all but the cat; she took to the woods and became a wild cat, and, as I learned afterward, trod in a trap set for woodchucks, and so became a dead cat at last.

I took down this dwelling the same morning, drawing the nails, and removed it to the pond-side by small cartloads, spreading the boards on the grass there to bleach and warp back again in the sun. One early thrush gave me a note or two as I drove along the woodland path. I was informed treacherously by a young Patrick that neighbor Seeley, an Irishman, in the intervals of the carting, transferred the still tolerable, straight, and drivable nails, staples, and spikes to his pocket, and then stood when I came back to pass the time of day, and look freshly up, unconcerned, with spring thoughts, at the devastation; there being a dearth of work, as he said. He was there to represent spectatordom, and help make this seemingly insignificant event one with the removal of the gods of Troy.

I dug my cellar in the side of a hill sloping to the south, where a woodchuck had formerly dug his burrow, down through sumach and blackberry roots, and the lowest stain of vegetation, six feet square by seven deep, to a fine sand where potatoes would not freeze in any winter. The sides were left shelving, and not stoned; but the sun having never shone on them, the sand still keeps its place. It was but two hours' work. I took particular pleasure in this breaking of ground, for in almost all latitudes men dig into the earth for an equable temperature. Under the most splendid house in the city is still to be found the cellar where they store their roots as of old, and long after the superstructure has disappeared posterity remark its dent in the earth. The house is still but a sort of porch at the entrance of a burrow.

At length, in the beginning of May, with the help of some of my acquaintances, rather to improve so good an occasion for neighborliness than from any necessity, I set up the frame of my house. No man was ever more honored in the character of his raisers than I. They are destined, I trust, to assist at the raising of loftier structures one day. I began to occupy my house on the 4th of July, as soon as it was boarded and roofed, for the boards were carefully feather-edged and lapped, so that it was perfectly impervious to rain, but before boarding I laid the foundation of a chimney at one end, bringing two cartloads of stones up the hill from the pond in my arms. I built the chimney after my hoeing in the fall, before a fire became necessary for warmth, doing my cooking in the meanwhile out of doors on the ground, early in the morning: which mode I still think is in some respects more convenient and agreeable than the usual one. When it stormed before my bread was baked, I fixed a few boards over the fire, and sat under them to watch my loaf, and passed some pleasant hours in that way. In those days, when my hands were much employed, I read but little, but the least scraps of paper which lay on the ground, my holder, or tablecloth, afforded me as much entertainment, in fact answered the same purpose as the Iliad.

It would be worth the while to build still more deliberately than I did, considering, for instance, what foundation a door, a window, a cellar, a garret, have in the nature of man, and perchance never raising any superstructure until we found a better reason for it than our temporal necessities even. There is some of the same fitness in a man's building his own house that there is in a bird's building its own nest. Who knows but if men constructed their dwellings with their own hands, and provided food

for themselves and families simply and honestly enough, the poetic faculty would be universally developed, as birds universally sing when they
are so engaged? But alas! we do like cowbirds and cuckoos, which lay
their eggs in nests which other birds have built, and cheer no traveller
with their chattering and unmusical notes. Shall we forever resign the
pleasure of construction to the carpenter? What does architecture amount
to in the experience of the mass of men? I never in all my walks came
across a man engaged in so simple and natural an occupation as building
his house. We belong to the community. It is not the tailor alone who is
the ninth part of a man; it is as much the preacher, and the merchant, and
the farmer. Where is this division of labor to end? and what object does it
finally serve? No doubt another *may* also think for me; but it is not
therefore desirable that he should do so to the exclusion of my thinking
for myself.

True, there are architects so called in this country, and I have heard of
one at least possessed with the idea of making architectural ornaments
have a core of truth, a necessity, and hence a beauty, as if it were a
revelation to him. All very well perhaps from his point of view, but only a
little better than the common dilettantism. A sentimental reformer in
architecture, he began at the cornice, not at the foundation. It was only
how to put a core of truth within the ornaments, that every sugarplum, in
fact, might have an almond or caraway seed in it,—though I hold that
almonds are most wholesome without the sugar,—and not how the inhabitant, the indweller, might build truly within and without, and let the
ornaments take care of themselves. What reasonable man ever supposed
that ornaments were something outward and in the skin merely,—that the
tortoise got his spotted shell, or the shell-fish its mother-o'-pearl tints, by
such a contract as the inhabitants of Broadway their Trinity Church? But
a man has no more to do with the style of architecture of his house than a
tortoise with that of its shell: nor need the soldier be so idle as to try to
paint the precise *color* of his virtue on his standard. The enemy will find it
out. He may turn pale when the trial comes. This man seemed to me to
lean over the cornice, and timidly whisper his half truth to the rude
occupants who really knew it better than he. What of architectural beauty
I now see, I know has gradually grown from within outward, out of the
necessities and character of the indweller, who is the only builder,—out
of some unconscious truthfulness, and nobleness, without ever a thought
for the appearance; and whatever additional beauty of this kind is destined to be produced will be preceded by a like unconscious beauty of life.
The most interesting dwellings in this country, as the painter knows, are
the most unpretending, humble log huts and cottages of the poor commonly; it is the life of the inhabitants whose shells they are, and not any
peculiarity in their surfaces merely, which makes them *picturesque;* and
equally interesting will be the citizen's suburban box, when his life shall
be as simple and as agreeable to the imagination, and there is as little

straining after effect in the style of his dwelling. A great proportion of architectural ornaments are literally hollow, and a September gale would strip them off, like borrowed plumes, without injury to the substantials. They can do without *architecture* who have no olives nor wines in the cellar. What if an equal ado were made about the ornaments of style in literature, and the architects of our Bibles spent as much time about their cornices as the architects of our churches do? So are made the *belles-lettres* and the *beaux-arts* and their professors. Much it concerns a man, forsooth, how a few sticks are slanted over him or under him, and what colors are daubed upon his box. It would signify somewhat, if, in any earnest sense, *he* slanted them and daubed it; but the spirit having departed out of the tenant, it is of a piece with constructing his own coffin,— the architecture of the grave,—and "carpenter" is but another name for "coffin-maker." One man says, in his despair or indifference to life, take up a handful of the earth at your feet, and paint your house that color. Is he thinking of his last and narrow house? Toss up a copper for it as well. What an abundance of leisure he must have! Why do you take up a handful of dirt? Better paint your house your own complexion; let it turn pale or blush for you. An enterprise to improve the style of cottage architecture! When you have got my ornaments ready, I will wear them.

Before winter I built a chimney, and shingled the sides of my house, which were already impervious to rain, with imperfect and sappy shingles made of the first slice of the log, whose edges I was obliged to straighten with a plane.

I have thus a tight shingled and plastered house, ten feet wide by fifteen long, and eight-feet posts, with a garret and a closet, a large window on each side, two trap-doors, one door at the end, and a brick fireplace opposite. The exact cost of my house, paying the usual price for such materials as I used, but not counting the work, all of which was done by myself, was as follows; and I give the details because very few are able to tell exactly what their houses cost, and fewer still, if any, the separate cost of the various materials which compose them:—

Boards	$8 03½,	mostly shanty boards.
Refuse shingles for roof and sides	4 00	
Laths	1 25	
Two second-hand windows with glass	2 43	
One thousand old brick	4 00	
Two casks of lime	2 40	That was high.
Hair	0 31	More than I needed.
Mantle-tree iron	0 15	
Nails	3 90	
Hinges and screws	0 14	

Latch	0 10	
Chalk	0 01	
Transportation	1 40	{ I carried a good part on my back.

In all	$28 12½

These are all the materials, excepting the timber, stones, and sand, which I claimed by squatter's right. I have also a small woodshed adjoining, made chiefly of the stuff which was left after building the house.

I intend to build me a house which will surpass any on the main street in Concord in grandeur and luxury, as soon as it pleases me as much and will cost me no more than my present one.

I thus found that the student who wishes for a shelter can obtain one for a lifetime at an expense not greater than the rent which he now pays annually. If I seem to boast more than is becoming, my excuse is that I brag for humanity rather than for myself; and my shortcomings and inconsistencies do not affect the truth of my statement. Notwithstanding much cant and hypocrisy,—chaff which I find it difficult to separate from my wheat, but for which I am as sorry as any man,—I will breathe freely and stretch myself in this respect, it is such a relief to both the moral and physical system; and I am resolved that I will not through humility become the devil's attorney. I will endeavor to speak a good word for the truth. At Cambridge College the mere rent of a student's room, which is only a little larger than my own, is thirty dollars each year, though the corporation had the advantage of building thirty-two side by side and under one roof, and the occupant suffers the inconvenience of many and noisy neighbors, and perhaps a residence in the fourth story. I cannot but think that if we had more true wisdom in these respects, not only less education would be needed, because, forsooth, more would already have been acquired, but the pecuniary expense of getting an education would in a great measure vanish. Those conveniences which the student requires at Cambridge or elsewhere cost him or somebody else ten times as great a sacrifice of life as they would with proper management on both sides. Those things for which the most money is demanded are never the things which the student most wants. Tuition, for instance, is an important item in the term bill, while for the far more valuable education which he gets by associating with the most cultivated of his contemporaries no charge is made. The mode of founding a college is, commonly, to get up a subscription of dollars and cents, and then, following blindly the principles of a division of labor to its extreme,—a principle which should never be followed but with circumspection,—to call in a contractor who makes this a subject of speculation, and he employs Irishmen or other operatives actually to lay the foundations, while the students that are to be are said to

be fitting themselves for it; and for these oversights successive generations have to pay. I think that it would be *better than this,* for the
students, or those who desire to be benefited by it, even to lay the
foundation themselves. The student who secures his coveted leisure and
retirement by systematically shirking any labor necessary to man obtains
but an ignoble and unprofitable leisure, defrauding himself of the experience which alone can make leisure fruitful. "But," says one, "you do not
mean that the students should go to work with their hands instead of their
heads?" I do not mean that exactly, but I mean something which he might
think a good deal like that; I mean that they should not *play* life, or *study* it
merely, while the community supports them at this expensive game, (but
earnestly *live* it from beginning to end.) How could youths better learn to
live than by at once trying the experiment of living? Methinks this would
exercise their minds as much as mathematics. If I wished a boy to know
something about the arts and sciences, for instance, I would not pursue
the common course, which is merely to send him into the neighborhood of
some professor, where anything is professed and practised but the art of
life;—to survey the world through a telescope or a microscope, and never
with his natural eye; to study chemistry, and not learn how his bread is
made, or mechanics, and not learn how it is earned; to discover new
satellites to Neptune, and not detect the motes in his eyes, or to what
vagabond he is a satellite himself; or to be devoured by the monsters that
swarm all around him, while contemplating the monsters in a drop of
vinegar. Which would have advanced the most at the end of a month,—
the boy who had made his own jackknife from the ore which he had dug
and smelted, reading as much as would be necessary for this—or the boy
who had attended the lectures on metallurgy at the Institute in the meanwhile, and had received a Rodgers penknife from his father? Which would
be most likely to cut his fingers? . . . To my astonishment I was informed
on leaving college that I had studied navigation!—why, if I had taken one
turn down the harbor I should have known more about it. Even the *poor*
student studies and is taught only *political* economy, while that economy
of living which is synonymous with philosophy is not even sincerely
professed in our colleges. The consequence is, that while he is reading
Adam Smith, Ricardo, and Say, he runs his father in debt irretrievably.

As with our colleges, so with a hundred "modern improvements;"
there is an illusion about them; there is not always a positive advance.
The devil goes on exacting compound interest to the last for his early
share and numerous succeeding investments in them. Our inventions are
wont to be pretty toys, which distract our attention from serious things.
They are but improved means to an unimproved end, an end which it was
already but too easy to arrive at; as railroads lead to Boston or New York.
We are in great haste to construct a magnetic telegraph from Maine to
Texas; but Maine and Texas, it may be, have nothing important to

communicate. Either is in such a predicament as the man who was earnest to be introduced to a distinguished deaf woman, but when he was presented, and one end of her ear trumpet was put into his hand, had nothing to say. As if the main object were to talk fast and not to talk sensibly. We are eager to tunnel under the Atlantic and bring the Old World some weeks nearer to the New; but perchance the first news that will leak through into the broad, flapping American ear will be that the Princess Adelaide has the whooping cough. After all, the man whose horse trots a mile a minute does not carry the most important messages; he is not an evangelist, nor does he come round eating locusts and wild honey. I doubt if Flying Childers ever carried a peck of corn to mill.

One says to me, "I wonder that you do not lay up money; you love to travel; you might take the cars and go to Fitchburg today and see the country." But I am wiser than that. I have learned that the swiftest traveller is he that goes afoot. I say to my friend, Suppose we try who will get there first. The distance is thirty miles; the fare ninety cents. That is almost a day's wages. I remember when wages were sixty cents a day for laborers on this very road. Well, I start now on foot, and get there before night; I have travelled at that rate by the week together. You will in the meanwhile have earned your fare, and arrive there sometime to-morrow, or possibly this evening, if you are lucky enough to get a job in season. Instead of going to Fitchburg, you will be working here the greater part of the day. And so, if the railroad reached round the world, I think that I should keep ahead of you; and as for seeing the country and getting experience of that kind, I should have to cut your acquaintance altogether.

Such is the universal law, which no man can ever outwit, and with regard to the railroad even we may say it is as broad as it is long. To make a railroad round the world available to all mankind is equivalent to grading the whole surface of the planet. Men have an indistinct notion that if they keep up this activity of joint stocks and spades long enough all will at length ride somewhere, in next to no time, and for nothing; but though a crowd rushes to the depot, and the conductor shouts "All aboard!" when the smoke is blown away and the vapor condensed, it will be perceived that a few are riding, but the rest are run over,—and it will be called, and will be, "A melancholy accident." No doubt they can ride at last who shall have earned their fare, that is, if they survive so long, but they will probably have lost their elasticity and desire to travel by that time. This spending of the best part of one's life earning money in order to enjoy a questionable liberty during the least valuable part of it reminds me of the Englishman who went to India to make a fortune first, in order that he might return to England and live the life of a poet. He should have gone up garret at once. "What!" exclaim a million Irishmen starting up from all the shanties in the land, "is not this railroad which we have built a good thing?" Yes, I answer, *comparatively* good, that is, you might have done worse; but I wish, as you are brothers of mine, that you could have spent your time better than digging in this dirt.

Before I finished my house, wishing to earn ten or twelve dollars by some honest and agreeable method, in order to meet my unusual expenses, I planted about two acres and a half of light and sandy soil near it chiefly with beans, but also a small part with potatoes, corn, peas, and turnips. The whole lot contains eleven acres, mostly growing up to pines and hickories, and was sold the preceding season for eight dollars and eight cents an acre. One farmer said that it was "good for nothing but to raise cheeping squirrels on." I put no manure whatever on this land, not being the owner, but merely a squatter, and not expecting to cultivate so much again, and I did not quite hoe it all once. I got out several cords of stumps in plowing, which supplied me with fuel for a long time, and left small circles of virgin mould, easily distinguishable through the summer by the greater luxuriance of the beans there. The dead and for the most part unmerchantable wood behind my house, and the drift wood from the pond, have supplied the remainder of my fuel. I was obliged to hire a team and a man for the plowing, though I held the plow myself. My farm outgoes for the first season were, for implements, seed, work, etc., $14.72½. The seed corn was given me. This never costs anything to speak of unless you plant more than enough. I got twelve bushels of beans, and eighteen bushels of potatoes, beside some peas and sweet corn. The yellow corn and turnips were too late to come to anything. My whole income from the farm was

	$23 44
Deducting the outgoes	14 72½
There are left	$8 71½,

beside produce consumed and on hand at the time this estimate was made of the value of $4.50,—the amount on hand much more than balancing a little grass which I did not raise. All things considered, that is, considering the importance of a man's soul and of to-day, notwithstanding the short time occupied by my experiment, nay, partly even because of its transient character, I believe that that was doing better than any farmer in Concord did that year.

The next year I did better still, for I spaded up all the land which I required, about a third of an acre, and I learned from the experience of both years, not being in the least awed by many celebrated works on husbandry, Arthur Young among the rest, that if one would live simply and eat only the crop which he raised, and raise no more than he ate, and not exchange it for an insufficient quantity of more luxurious and expensive things, he would need to cultivate only a few rods of ground, and that it would be cheaper to spade up that than to use oxen to plow it, and to select a fresh spot from time to time than to manure the old, and he could do all his necessary farm work as it were with his left hand at odd hours in the summer; and thus he would not be tied to an ox, or horse, or cow, or pig, as at present. I desire to speak impartially on this point, and as one not interested in the success or failure of the present economical and social arrangements. I was more independent than any farmer in Concord, for I was not anchored to a house or farm, but could follow the bent of my genius, which is a very crooked one, every moment. Beside being better off than they already, if my house had been burned or my crops had failed, I should have been nearly as well off as before.

I am wont to think that men are not so much the keepers of herds as herds are the keepers of men, the former are so much the freer. Men and oxen exchange work; but if we consider necessary work only, the oxen will be seen to have greatly the advantage, their farm is so much the larger. Man does some of his part of the exchange work in his six weeks of haying, and it is no boy's play. Certainly no nation that lived simply in all respects, that is, no nation of philosophers, would commit so great a blunder as to use the labor of animals. True, there never was and is not likely soon to be a nation of philosophers, nor am I certain it is desirable that there should be. However, *I* should never have broken a horse or bull and taken him to board for any work he might do for me, for fear I should become a horse-man or a herds-man merely; and if society seems to be the gainer by so doing, are we certain that what is one man's gain is not another's loss, and that the stable-boy has equal cause with his master to be satisfied? Granted that some public works would not have been constructed without this aid, and let man share the glory of such with the ox and horse; does it follow that he could not have accomplished works yet more worthy of himself in that case? When men begin to do, not merely unnecessary or artistic, but luxurious and idle work, with their assistance, it is inevitable that a few do all the exchange work with the oxen, or, in other words, become the slaves of the strongest. Man thus not only works for the animal within him, but, for a symbol of this, he works for the animal without him. Though we have many substantial houses of brick or stone, the prosperity of the farmer is still measured by the degree to which the barn overshadows the house. This town is said to have the largest houses for oxen, cows, and horses hereabouts, and it is not behindhand in its public buildings; but there are very few halls for free worship or free speech in this county. It should not be by their architecture, but why not even by their power of abstract thought, that nations should seek to commemorate themselves? How much more admirable the Bhagvat-Geeta than all the ruins of the East! Towers and temples are the luxury of princes. A simple and independent mind does not toil at the bidding of any prince. Genius is not a retainer to any emperor, nor is its material silver, or gold, or marble, except to a trifling extent. To what end, pray, is so much stone hammered? In Arcadia, when I was there, I did not see any hammering stone. Nations are possessed with an insane ambition to perpetuate the memory of themselves by the amount of hammered stone they leave. What if equal pains were taken to smooth and polish their manners? One piece of good sense would be more memorable than a monument as high as the moon. I love better to see stones in place. The grandeur of Thebes was a vulgar grandeur. More sensible is a rod of stone wall that bounds an honest man's field than a hundred-gated Thebes that has wandered farther from the true end of life. The religion and civiliza-tion which are barbaric and heathenish build splendid temples; but what you might call Christianity does not. Most of the stone a nation hammers goes toward its tomb only. It buries itself alive. As for the Pyramids, there is nothing to wonder at in them so much as the fact that so many men could be found degraded enough to spend their lives constructing a tomb for some ambitious booby, whom it would have been wiser and manlier to have drowned in the Nile, and then given his body to the dogs. I might possibly invent some excuse for them and him, but I have no time for it. As for the religion and love of art of the builders, it is much the same all the world over, whether the building be an Egyptian temple or the United States Bank. It costs more than it comes to. The mainspring is vanity, assisted by the love of garlic and bread and butter. Mr. Balcom, a promising young architect, designs it on the back of his Vitruvius, with hard pencil and ruler, and the job is let out to Dobson & Sons, stonecut-ters. When the thirty centuries begin to look down on it, mankind begin to look up at it. As for your high towers and monuments, there was a crazy fellow once in this town who undertook to dig through to China, and he got so far that, as he said, he heard the Chinese pots and kettles rattle; but I think that I shall not go out of my way to admire the hole which he made. Many are concerned about the monuments of the West and the East,—to know who built them. For my part, I should like to know who in those days did not build them,—who were above such trifling. But to proceed with my statistics.

By surveying, carpentry, and day-labor of various other kinds in the village in the meanwhile, for I have as many trades as fingers, I had earned $13.34. The expense of food for eight months, namely, from July 4th to March 1st, the time when these estimates were made, though I lived there more than two years,—not counting potatoes, a little green corn, and some peas, which I had raised, nor considering the value of what was on hand at the last date,—was

Rice	$1 73½	
Molasses	1 73	Cheapest form of the saccharine.
Rye meal	1 04¾	
Indian meal	0 99¾	Cheaper than rye.
Pork	0 22	
Flour	0 88	{ Costs more than Indian meal, both money and trouble.
Sugar	0 80	
Lard	0 65	
Apples	0 25	
Dried apple	0 22	
Sweet potatoes	0 10	
One pumpkin	0 6	
One watermelon . . .	0 2	
Salt	0 3	

Yes, I did eat $8.74, all told; but I should not thus unblushingly publish my guilt, if I did not know that most of my readers were equally guilty with myself, and that their deeds would look no better in print. The next year I sometimes caught a mess of fish for my dinner, and once I went so far as to slaughter a woodchuck which ravaged my bean-field,—effect his transmigration, as a Tartar would say,—and devour him, partly for experiment's sake; but though it afforded me a momentary enjoyment, notwithstanding a musky flavor, I saw that the longest use would not make that a good practice, however it might seem to have your woodchucks ready dressed by the village butcher.

Clothing and some incidental expenses within the same dates, though little can be inferred from this item, amounted to

$8 40¾

Oil and some household utensils 2 00

So that all the pecuniary outgoes, excepting for washing and mending, which for the most part were done out of the house, and their bills have not yet been received,—and these are all and more than all the ways by which money necessarily goes out in this part of the world,—were

House	$28 12½
Farm one year	14 72½
Food eight months	8 74

Clothing, etc., eight months	8 40¾
Oil, etc., eight months	2 00
	$61 99¾

I address myself now to those of my readers who have a living to get. And to meet this I have for farm produce sold

	$23 44
Earned by day-labor	13 34
In all	$36 78,

which subtracted from the sum of the outgoes leaves a balance of $25.21¾ on the one side,—this being very nearly the means with which I started, and the measure of expenses to be incurred,—and on the other, beside the leisure and independence and health thus secured, a comfortable house for me as long as I choose to occupy it.

These statistics, however accidental and therefore uninstructive they may appear, as they have a certain completeness, have a certain value also. Nothing was given me of which I have not rendered some account. It appears from the above estimate, that my food alone cost me in money about twenty-seven cents a week. It was, for nearly two years after this, rye and Indian meal without yeast, potatoes, rice, a very little salt pork, molasses, and salt; and my drink, water. It was fit that I should live on rice, mainly, who loved so well the philosophy of India. To meet the objections of some inveterate cavillers, I may as well state, that if I dined out occasionally, as I always had done, and I trust shall have opportunities to do again, it was frequently to the detriment of my domestic arrangements. But the dining out, being, as I have stated, a constant element, does not in the least affect a comparative statement like this.

I learned from my two years' experience that it would cost incredibly little trouble to obtain one's necessary food, even in this latitude; that a man may use as simple a diet as the animals, and yet retain health and strength. I have made a satisfactory dinner, satisfactory on several accounts, simply off a dish of purslane (*Portulaca oleracea*) which I gathered in my cornfield, boiled and salted. I give the Latin on account of the savoriness of the trivial name. And pray what more can a reasonable man desire, in peaceful times, in ordinary noons, than a sufficient number of ears of green sweet corn boiled, with the addition of salt? Even the little variety which I used was a yielding to the demands of appetite, and not of health. Yet men have come to such a pass that they frequently starve, not for want of necessaries, but for want of luxuries; and I know a good woman who thinks that her son lost his life because he took to drinking water only.

The reader will perceive that I am treating the subject rather from an economic than a dietetic point of view, and he will not venture to put my abstemiousness to the test unless he has a well-stocked larder.

Bread I at first made of pure Indian meal and salt, genuine hoe-cakes, which I baked before my fire out of doors on a shingle or the end of a stick of timber sawed off in building my house; but it was wont to get smoked and to have a piny flavor. I tried flour also; but have at last found a mixture of rye and Indian meal most convenient and agreeable. In cold weather it was no little amusement to bake several small loaves of this in succession, tending and turning them as carefully as an Egyptian his hatching eggs. They were a real cereal fruit which I ripened, and they had to my senses a fragrance like that of other noble fruits, which I kept in as long as possible by wrapping them in cloths. I made a study of the ancient and indispensable art of bread-making, consulting such authorities as offered, going back to the primitive days and first invention of the un-leavened kind, when from the wildness of nuts and meats men first reached the mildness and refinement of this diet, and travelling gradually down in my studies through that accidental souring of the dough which, it is supposed, taught the leavening process, and through the various fer-mentations thereafter, till I came to "good, sweet, wholesome bread," the staff of life. Leaven, which some deem the soul of bread, the *spiritus* which fills its cellular tissue, which is religiously preserved like the vestal fire,—some precious bottleful, I suppose, first brought over in the May-flower, did the business for America, and its influence is still rising, swelling, spreading, in cerealian billows over the land,—this seed I regu-larly and faithfully procured from the village, till at length one morning I forgot the rules, and scalded my yeast; by which accident I discovered that even this was not indispensable,—for my discoveries were not by the synthetic but analytic process,—and I have gladly omitted it since, though most housewives earnestly assured me that safe and wholesome bread without yeast might not be, and elderly people prophesied a speedy decay of the vital forces. Yet I find it not to be an essential ingredient, and after going without it for a year am still in the land of the living; and I am glad to escape the trivialness of carrying a bottleful in my pocket, which would sometimes pop and discharge its contents to my discomfiture. It is simpler and more respectable to omit it. Man is an animal who more than any other can adapt himself to all climates and circumstances. Neither did I put any sal-soda, or other acid or alkali, into my bread. It would seem that I made it according to the recipe which Marcus Porcius Cato gave about two centuries before Christ. "Panem depsticium sic facito. Manus mortariumque bene lavato. Farinam in mortarium indito, aquae paulatim addito, subigitoque pulchre. Ubi bene subegeris, defingito, coquitoque sub testu." Which I take to mean, "Make kneaded bread thus. Wash your hands and trough well. Put the meal into the trough, add water gradually, and knead it thoroughly. When you have kneaded it well, mould it, and bake it under a cover," that is, in a baking-kettle. Not a word about leaven. But I did not always use this staff of life. At one time, owing to the emptiness of my purse, I saw none of it for more than a month.

Every New Englander might easily raise all his own breadstuffs in this land of rye and Indian corn, and not depend on distant and fluctuating markets for them. Yet so far are we from simplicity and independence that, in Concord, fresh and sweet meal is rarely sold in the shops, and hominy and corn in a still coarser form are hardly used by any. For the most part the farmer gives to his cattle and hogs the grain of his own producing, and buys flour, which is at least no more wholesome, at a greater cost, at the store. I saw that I could easily raise my bushel or two of rye and Indian corn, for the former will grow on the poorest land, and the latter does not require the best, and grind them in a hand-mill, and so do without rice and pork; and if I must have some concentrated sweet, I found by experiment that I could make a very good molasses either of pumpkins or beets, and I knew that I needed only to set out a few maples to obtain it more easily still, and while these were growing I could use various substitutes beside those which I have named. "For," as the Forefathers sang,—

> "we can make liquor to sweeten our lips
> Of pumpkins and parsnips and walnut-tree chips."

Finally, as for salt, that grossest of groceries, to obtain this might be a fit occasion for a visit to the seashore, or, if I did without it altogether, I should probably drink the less water. I do not learn that the Indians ever troubled themselves to go after it.

Thus I could avoid all trade and barter, so far as my food was concerned, and having a shelter already, it would only remain to get clothing and fuel. The pantaloons which I now wear were woven in a farmer's family,—thank Heaven there is so much virtue still in man; for I think the fall from the farmer to the operative as great and memorable as that from the man to the farmer;—and in a new country, fuel is an encumbrance. As for a habitat, if I were not permitted still to squat, I might purchase one acre at the same price for which the land I cultivated was sold—namely, eight dollars and eight cents. But as it was, I considered that I enhanced the value of the land by squatting on it.

There is a certain class of unbelievers who sometimes ask me such questions as, if I think that I can live on vegetable food alone; and to strike at the root of the matter at once,—for the root is faith,—I am accustomed to answer such, that I can live on board nails. If they cannot understand that, they cannot understand much that I have to say. For my part, I am glad to hear of experiments of this kind being tried; as that a young man tried for a fortnight to live on hard, raw corn on the ear, using his teeth for all mortar. The squirrel tribe tried the same and succeeded. The human race is interested in these experiments, though a few old women who are incapacitated for them, or who own their thirds in mills, may be alarmed.

Meaning and Idea

1. What does Thoreau mean by *economy?* (You may want to check a dictionary definition of the word and compare Thoreau's use of it.) Briefly summarize what Thoreau considers the importance of economy.

2. What is the "experiment" Thoreau mentions? What does Thoreau identify as the nonmonetary personal gains of his experiment?

3. Towards the end of the essay, Thoreau claims, "Thus I could avoid all trade and barter, so far as my food was concerned." Describe the process by which he achieved this condition. What are Thoreau's general suggestions to his audience about economizing on food?

4. What is the author's attitude toward modernization? How does he exemplify his attitude?

5. Thoreau writes in this essay: ". . . my discoveries were not by the synthetic but analytic process." Interpret the meaning of this statement in light of your reading of the essay.

Language, Form, Structure

1. What is the main process which Thoreau explains in this essay? Outline the steps he describes. How does he accomplish the transitions between these steps? How does he arrange them? What is the time span covered by the essay? What stages of the overall process occur at different points in this time span?

2. What is the overall purpose of this selection? In other words, what is Thoreau trying to teach his audience about the process of their lives? Into what categories of daily life and necessities does he divide his overall process analysis?

3. How does Thoreau use description in this essay? Which descriptive details do you find freshest? Which sensory appeals are particularly vivid? Where does Thoreau use data to support his point? Why do you think he uses data?

4. Throughout the essay, Thoreau makes numerous comparisons of the steps of his process to the processes of nature. Identify some of these comparisons. What do they add to the tone and style of the essay?

He also makes several comparisons to Greek mythology. Identify them and explain their purpose.

5. How does Thoreau analyze the process of human beings becoming subservient to their work animals? How might this section be read metaphorically?

6. Identify the meanings of ten of the following words from the essay. Then add five more definitions of words unfamiliar to you in the reading that do not appear on this list: ethereal; perennial; dank; dearth; posterity; revelation; dilettantism; ado; *belles-lettres;* cant; pecuniary; coveted; perpetuate; heathenish; transmigration.

Ideas for Writing

1. Write about a long-term project you attempted either recently or in the past. Analyze the process by which you approached and carried out this project.

2. In the form of a letter, write to a friend who has trouble managing money and propose a process by which he or she could be more financially responsible.

3. In an essay respond to the following question: Would you classify "Economy" as a *How* or a *How-to* process analysis? Support your answer with specific references to Thoreau's essay.

D. H. Lawrence
THE ROCKING-HORSE WINNER

D. H. Lawrence was born in 1885 in the English Midlands coal-mining town of Eastwood, the son of a coal miner. Lawrence was ambivalent about his background—he found it overly materialistic and repressive, yet he used it as the basis for nearly all his fiction. In 1912, he ran off with his wife-to-be, Frieda, and they lived outside of England for most of their lives—in Australia, Italy, Germany, Mexico, and the United States. Lawrence's fiction—including *Sons and Lovers* (1913), *The Rainbow* (1915), *Women in Love* (1920), and *Lady Chatterley's Lover* (1928)—created great uproars for their literary daring and their so-called immorality. Lawrence, who was also a prolific critical and travel writer, died of tuberculosis in southern France in 1930, and his ashes rest in Taos, New Mexico.

"The Rocking-Horse Winner" shows us how need—real or imagined—can sometimes overcome life itself. Notice how Lawrence uses processes of both building up and deterioration to develop the narrative line.

*T*here was a woman who was beautiful, who started with all the advantages, yet she had no luck. She married for love, and the love turned to dust. She had bonny children, yet she felt they had been thrust upon her, and she could not love them. They looked at her coldly, as if they were finding fault with her. And hurriedly she felt she must cover up some fault in herself. Yet what it was that she must cover up she never knew. Nevertheless, when her children were present, she always felt the centre of her heart go hard. This troubled her, and in her manner she was all the more gentle and anxious for her children, as if she loved them very much. Only she herself knew that at the centre of her heart was a hard little place that could not feel love, no, not for anybody. Everybody else said of her: "She is such a good mother. She adores her children." Only she herself, and her children themselves, knew it was not so. They read it in each other's eyes.

There were a boy and two little girls. They lived in a pleasant house, with a garden, and they had discreet servants, and felt themselves superior to anyone in the neighbourhood.

Although they lived in style, they felt always an anxiety in the house. There was never enough money. The mother had a small income, and the father had a small income, but not nearly enough for the social position which they had to keep up. The father went into town to some office. But though he had good prospects, these prospects never materialised. There was always the grinding sense of the shortage of money, though the style was always kept up.

At last the mother said: "I will see if *I* can't make something." But she did not know where to begin. She racked her brains, and tried this thing and the other, but could not find anything successful. The failure made deep lines come into her face. Her children were growing up, they would have to go to school. There must be more money, there must be more money. The father, who was always very handsome and expensive in his tastes, seemed as if he never *would* be able to do anything worth doing. And the mother, who had a great belief in herself, did not succeed any better, and her tastes were just as expensive.

And so the house came to be haunted by the unspoken phrase: *There must be more money! There must be more money!* The children could hear it all the time, though nobody said it aloud. They heard it at Christmas, when the expensive and splendid toys filled the nursery. Behind the shining modern rocking-horse, behind the smart doll's house, a voice would start whispering: "There *must* be more money! There *must* be more money!" And the children would stop playing, to listen for a moment. They would look into each other's eyes, to see if they had all heard. And each one saw in the eyes of the other two that they too had heard. "There *must* be more money! There *must* be more money!"

It came whispering from the springs of the still-swaying rocking-horse, and even the horse, bending his wooden, champing head, heard it. The big doll, sitting so pink and smirking in her new pram, could hear it quite plainly, and seemed to be smirking all the more self-consciously because of it. The foolish puppy, too, that took the place of the teddy-bear, he was looking so extraordinarily foolish for no other reason but that he heard the secret whisper all over the house: "There _must_ be more money!"

Yet nobody ever said it aloud. The whisper was everywhere, and therefore no one spoke it. Just as no one ever says: "We are breathing!" in spite of the fact that breath is coming and going all the time.

"Mother," said the boy Paul one day, "why dWhy do we always use uncle's, or else a taxi?"

"Because we're the poor members of the family," said the mother.

"But why _are_ we, mother?"

"Well—I suppose," she said slowly and bitterly, "it's because your father has no luck."

The boy was silent for some time.

"Is luck money, mother?" he asked, rather timidly.

"No, Paul. Not quite. It's what causes you to have money."

"Oh!" said Paul vaguely. "I thought when Uncle Oscar said _filthy lucker,_ it meant money."

"_Filthy lucre_ does mean money," said the mother. "But it's lucre, not luck."

"Oh!" said the boy. "Then what _is_ luck, mother?"

"It's what causes you to have money. If you're lucky you have money. That's why it's better to be born lucky than rich. If you're rich, you may lose your money. But if you're lucky, you will always get more money."

"Oh! Will you? And is father not lucky?"

"Very unlucky, I should say," she said bitterly.

The boy watched her with unsure eyes.

"Why?" he asked.

"I don't know. Nobody ever knows why one person is lucky and another unlucky."

"Don't they? Nobody at all? Does _nobody_ know?"

"Perhaps God. But He never tells."

"He ought to, then. And aren't you lucky either, mother?"

"I can't be, if I married an unlucky husband."

"But by yourself, aren't you?"

"I used to think I was, before I married. Now I think I am very unlucky indeed."

"Why?"

"Well—never mind! Perhaps I'm not really," she said.

The child looked at her to see if she meant it. But he saw, by the lines of her mouth, that she was only trying to hide something from him.

"Well, anyhow," he said stoutly, "I'm a lucky person."

"Why?" said his mother, with a sudden laugh.

He stared at her. He didn't even know why he had said it.

"God told me," he asserted, brazening it out.

"I hope He did, dear!" she said, again with a laugh, but rather bitter.

"He did, mother!"

"Excellent!" said the mother, using one of her husband's exclamations.

The boy saw she did not believe him; or rather, that she paid no attention to his assertion. This angered him somewhere, and made him want to compel her attention.

He went off by himself, vaguely, in a childish way, seeking for the clue to "luck." Absorbed, taking no heed of other people, he went about with a sort of stealth, seeking inwardly for luck. He wanted luck, he wanted it, he wanted it. When the two girls were playing dolls in the nursery, he would sit on his big rocking-horse, charging madly into space, with a frenzy that made the little girls peer at him uneasily. Wildly the horse careered, the waving dark hair of the boy tossed, his eyes had a strange glare in them. The little girls dared not speak to him.

When he had ridden to the end of his mad little journey, he climbed down and stood in front of his rocking-horse, staring fixedly into its lowered face. Its red mouth was slightly open, its big eye was wide and glassy-bright.

"Now!" he would silently command the snorting steed. "Now, take me to where there is luck! Now take me!"

And he would slash the horse on the neck with the little whip he had asked Uncle Oscar for. He *knew* the horse could take him to where there was luck, if only he forced it. So he would mount again and start on his furious ride, hoping at last to get there. He knew he could get there.

"You'll break your horse, Paul!" said the nurse.

"He's always riding like that! I wish he'd leave off!" said his elder sister Joan.

But he only glared down on them in silence. Nurse gave him up. She could make nothing of him. Anyhow, he was growing beyond her.

One day his mother and his Uncle Oscar came in when he was on one of his furious rides. He did not speak to them.

"Hallo, you young jockey! Riding a winner?" said his uncle.

"Aren't you growing too big for a rocking-horse? You're not a very little boy any longer, you know," said his mother.

But Paul only gave a blue glare from his big, rather close-set eyes. He would speak to nobody when he was in full tilt. His mother watched him with an anxious expression on her face.

At last he suddenly stopped forcing his horse into the mechanical gallop and slid down.

"Well, I got there!" he announced fiercely, his blue eyes still flaring, and his sturdy long legs straddling apart.

"Where did you get to?" asked his mother.

"Where I wanted to go," he flared back at her.

"That's right, son!" said Uncle Oscar. "Don't you stop till you get there. What's the horse's name?"

"He doesn't have a name," said the boy.

"Gets on without all right?" asked the uncle.

"Well, he has different names. He was called Sansovino last week."

"Sansovino, eh? Won the Ascot. How did you know this name?"

"He always talks about horse-races with Bassett," said Joan.

The uncle was delighted to find that his small nephew was posted with all the racing news. Bassett, the young gardener, who had been wounded in the left foot in the war and had got his present job through Oscar Cresswell, whose batman he had been, was a perfect blade of the "turf." He lived in the racing events, and the small boy lived with him.

Oscar Cresswell got it all from Bassett.

"Master Paul comes and asks me, so I can't do more than tell him, sir," said Bassett, his face terribly serious, as if he were speaking of religious matters.

"And does he ever put anything on a horse he fancies?"

"Well—I don't want to give him away—he's a young sport, a fine sport, sir. Would you mind asking him himself? He sort of takes a pleasure in it, and perhaps he'd feel I was giving him away, sir, if you don't mind."

Bassett was serious as a church.

The uncle went back to his nephew and took him off for a ride in the car.

"Say, Paul, old man, do you ever put anything on a horse?" the uncle asked.

The boy watched the handsome man closely.

"Why, do you think I oughtn't to?" he parried.

"Not a bit of it! I thought perhaps you might give me a tip for the Lincoln."

The car sped on into the country, going down to Uncle Oscar's place in Hampshire.

"Honour bright?" said the nephew.

"Honour bright, son!" said the uncle.

"Well, then, Daffodil."

"Daffodil! I doubt it, sonny. What about Mirza?"

"I only know the winner," said the boy. "That's Daffodil."

"Daffodil, eh?"

There was a pause. Daffodil was an obscure horse comparatively.

"Uncle!"

"Yes, son?"

"You won't let it go any further, will you? I promised Bassett."

"Bassett be damned, old man! What's he got to do with it?"

"We're partners. We've been partners from the first. Uncle, he lent me my first five shillings, which I lost. I promised him, honour bright, it was only between me and him; only you gave me that ten-shilling note I started winning with, so I thought you were lucky. You won't let it go any further, will you?"

The boy gazed at his uncle from those big, hot, blue eyes, set rather close together. The uncle stirred and laughed uneasily.

"Right you are, son! I'll keep your tip private. Daffodil, eh? How much are you putting on him?"

"All except twenty pounds," said the boy. "I keep that in reserve."

The uncle thought it a good joke.

"You keep twenty pounds in reserve, do you, you young romancer? What are you betting, then?"

"I'm betting three hundred," said the boy gravely. "But it's between you and me, Uncle Oscar! Honour bright?"

The uncle burst into a roar of laughter.

"It's between you and me all right, you young Nat Gould," he said, laughing. "But where's your three hundred?"

"Bassett keeps it for me. We're partners."

"You are, are you! And what is Bassett putting on Daffodil?"

"He won't go quite as high as I do, I expect. Perhaps he'll go a hundred and fifty."

"What, pennies?" laughed the uncle.

"Pounds," said the child, with a surprised look at his uncle. "Bassett keeps a bigger reserve than I do."

Between wonder and amusement Uncle Oscar was silent. He pursued the matter no further, but he determined to take his nephew with him to the Lincoln races.

"Now, son," he said, "I'm putting twenty on Mirza, and I'll put five on for you on any horse you fancy. What's your pick?"

"Daffodil, uncle."

"No, not the fiver on Daffodil!"

"I should if it was my own fiver," said the child.

"Good! Good! Right you are! A fiver for me and a fiver for you on Daffodil."

The child had never been to a race-meeting before, and his eyes were blue fire. He pursed his mouth tight and watched. A Frenchman just in front had put his money on Lancelot. Wild with excitement, he flayed his arms up and down, yelling *"Lancelot! Lancelot!"* in his French accent.

Daffodil came in first, Lancelot second, Mirza third. The child, flushed and with eyes blazing, was curiously serene. His uncle brought him four five-pound notes, four to one.

"What am I do with these?" he cried, waving them before the boy's eyes.

"I suppose we'll talk to Bassett," said the boy. "I expect I have fifteen hundred now; and twenty in reserve; and this twenty."

His uncle studied him for some moments.

"Look here, son!" he said. "You're not serious about Bassett and that fifteen hundred, are you?"

"Yes, I am. But it's between you and me, uncle. Honour bright?"

"Honour bright all right, son! But I must talk to Bassett."

"If you'd like to be a partner, uncle, with Bassett and me, we could all be partners. Only, you'd have to promise, honour bright, uncle, not to let it go beyond us three. Bassett and I are lucky, and you must be lucky, because it was your ten shillings I started winning with. . . ."

Uncle Oscar took both Bassett and Paul into Richmond Park for an afternoon, and there they talked.

"It's like this, you see, sir," Bassett said. "Master Paul would get me talking about racing events, spinning yarns, you know, sir. And he was always keen on knowing if I'd made or if I'd lost. It's about a year since, now, that I put five shillings on Blush of Dawn for him: and we lost. Then the luck turned, with that ten shillings he had from you: that we put on Singhalese. And since that time, it's been pretty steady, all things considering. What do you say, Master Paul?"

"We're all right when we're sure," said Paul. "It's when we're not quite sure that we go down."

"Oh, but we're careful then," said Bassett.

"But when are you *sure?*" smiled Uncle Oscar.

"It's Master Paul, sir," said Bassett in a secret, religious voice. "It's as if he had it from heaven. Like Daffodil, now, for the Lincoln. That was as sure as eggs."

"Did you put anything on Daffodil?" asked Oscar Cresswell.

"Yes, sir. I made my bit."

"And my nephew?"

Bassett was obstinately silent, looking at Paul.

"I made twelve hundred, didn't I, Bassett? I told uncle I was putting three hundred on Daffodil."

"That's right," said Bassett, nodding.

"But where's the money?" asked the uncle.

"I keep it safe locked up, sir. Master Paul he can have it any minute he likes to ask for it."

"What, fifteen hundred pounds?"

"And twenty! And *forty,* that is, with the twenty he made on the course."

"It's amazing!" said the uncle.

"If Master Paul offers you to be partners, sir, I would, if I were you: if you'll excuse me," said Bassett.

Oscar Cresswell thought about it.

"I'll see the money," he said.

They drove home again, and, sure enough, Bassett came round to the garden-house with fifteen hundred pounds in notes. The twenty pounds reserve was left with Joe Glee, in the Turf Commission deposit.

"You see, it's all right, uncle, when I'm *sure!* Then we go strong, for all we're worth. Don't we, Bassett?"

"We do that, Master Paul."

"And when are you sure?" said the uncle, laughing.

"Oh, well, sometimes I'm *absolutely* sure, like about Daffodil," said the boy; "and sometimes I have an idea; and sometimes I haven't even an idea, have I, Bassett? Then we're careful, because we mostly go down."

"You do, do you! And when you're sure, like about Daffodil, what makes you sure, sonny?"

"Oh, well, I don't know," said the boy uneasily. "I'm sure, you know, uncle; that's all."

"It's as if he had it from heaven, sir," Bassett reiterated.

"I should say so!" said the uncle.

But he became a partner. And when the Leger was coming on Paul was "sure" about Lively Spark, which was a quite inconsiderable horse. The boy insisted on putting a thousand on the horse, Bassett was for five hundred, and Oscar Cresswell two hundred. Lively Spark came in first, and the betting had been ten to one against him. Paul had made ten thousand.

"You see," he said, "I was absolutely sure of him."

Even Oscar Cresswell had cleared two thousand.

"Look here, son," he said, "this sort of thing makes me nervous."

"It needn't, uncle! Perhaps I shan't be sure again for a long time."

"But what are you going to do with your money?" asked the uncle.

"Of course," said the boy, "I started it for mother. She said she had no luck, because father is unlucky, so I thought if *I* was lucky, it might stop whispering."

"What might stop whispering?"

"Our house. I *hate* our house for whispering."

"What does it whisper?"

"Why—why"—the boy fidgeted—"why, I don't know. But it's always short of money, you know, uncle."

"I know it, son, I know it."

"You know people send mother writs, don't you, uncle?"

"I'm afraid I do," said the uncle.

"And then the house whispers, like people laughing at you behind your back. It's awful, that is! I thought if I was lucky——"

"You might stop it," added the uncle.

The boy watched him with big blue eyes, that had an uncanny cold fire in them, and he said never a word.

"Well, then!" said the uncle. "What are we doing?"

"I shouldn't like mother to know I was lucky," said the boy.

"Why not, son?"

"She'd stop me."

"I don't think she would."

"Oh!"—and the boy writhed in an odd way—"I *don't* want her to know, uncle."

"All right, son! We'll manage it without her knowing."

They managed it very easily. Paul, at the other's suggestion, handed over five thousand pounds to his uncle, who deposited it with the family lawyer, who was then to inform Paul's mother that a relative had put five thousand pounds into his hands, which sum was to be paid out a thousand pounds at a time, on the mother's birthday, for the next five years.

"So she'll have a birthday present of a thousand pounds for five successive years," said Uncle Oscar. "I hope it won't make it all the harder for her later."

Paul's mother had her birthday in November. The house had been "whispering" worse than ever lately, and, even in spite of his luck, Paul could not bear up against it. He was very anxious to see the effect of the birthday letter, telling his mother about the thousand pounds.

When there were no visitors, Paul now took his meals with his parents, as he was beyond the nursery control. His mother went into town nearly every day. She had discovered that she had an odd knack of sketching furs and dress materials, so she worked secretly in the studio of a friend who was the chief "artist" for the leading drapers. She drew the figures of ladies in furs and ladies in silk and sequins for the newspaper advertisements. This young woman artist earned several thousand pounds a year, but Paul's mother only made several hundreds, and she was again dissatisfied. She so wanted to be first in something, and she did not succeed, even in making sketches for drapery advertisements.

She was down to breakfast on the morning of her birthday. Paul watched her face as she read her letters. He knew the lawyer's letter. As his mother read it, her face hardened and became more expressionless. Then a cold, determined look came on her mouth. She hid the letter under the pile of others, and said not a word about it.

"Didn't you have anything nice in the post for your birthday, mother?" said Paul.

"Quite moderately nice," she said, her voice cold and absent.

She went away to town without saying more.

But in the afternoon Uncle Oscar appeared. He said Paul's mother had had a long interview with the lawyer, asking if the whole five thousand could not be advanced at once, as she was in debt.

"What do you think, uncle?" said the boy.

"I leave it to you, son."

"Oh, let her have it, then! We can get some more with the other," said the boy.

"A bird in the hand is worth two in the bush, laddie!" said Uncle Oscar.

"But I'm sure to *know* for the Grand National; or the Lincolnshire; or else the Derby. I'm sure to know for *one* of them," said Paul.

So Uncle Oscar signed the agreement, and Paul's mother touched the whole five thousand. Then something very curious happened. The voices in the house suddenly went mad, like a chorus of frogs on a spring evening. There were certain new furnishings, and Paul had a tutor. He was *really* going to Eton, his father's school, in the following autumn. There were flowers in the winter, and a blossoming of the luxury Paul's mother had been used to. And yet the voices in the house, behind the sprays of mimosa and almondblossom, and from under the piles of iridescent cushions, simply trilled and screamed in a sort of ecstasy: "There *must* be more money! Oh-h-h; there *must* be more money. Oh, now, now-w! Now-w-w—there *must* be more money!—more than ever! More than ever!"

It frightened Paul terribly. He studied away at his Latin and Greek with his tutor. But his intense hours were spent with Bassett. The Grand National had gone by: he had not "known," and had lost a hundred pounds. Summer was at hand. He was in agony for the Lincoln. But even for the Lincoln he didn't "know," and he lost fifty pounds. He became wild-eyed and strange, as if something were going to explode in him.

"Let it alone, son! Don't you bother about it!" urged Uncle Oscar. But it was as if the boy couldn't really hear what his uncle was saying.

"I've got to know for the Derby! I've got to know for the Derby!" the child reiterated, his big blue eyes blazing with a sort of madness.

His mother noticed how overwrought he was.

"You'd better go to the seaside. Wouldn't you like to go now to the seaside, instead of waiting? I think you'd better," she said, looking down at him anxiously, her heart curiously heavy because of him.

But the child lifted his uncanny blue eyes.

"I couldn't possibly go before the Derby, mother!" he said. "I couldn't possibly!"

"Why not?" she said, her voice becoming heavy when she was opposed. "Why not? You can still go from the seaside to see the Derby with your Uncle Oscar, if that's what you wish. No need for you to wait here. Besides, I think you care too much about these races. It's a bad sign. My family has been a gambling family, and you won't know till you grow up how much damage it has done. But it has done damage. I shall have to send Bassett away, and ask Uncle Oscar not to talk racing to you, unless you promise to be reasonable about it: go away to the seaside and forget it. You're all nerves!''

"I'll do what you like, mother, so long as you don't send me away till after the Derby," the boy said.

"Send you away from where? Just from this house?"

"Yes," he said, gazing at her.

"Why, you curious child, what makes you care about this house so much, suddenly? I never knew you loved it."

He gazed at her without speaking. He had a secret within a secret, something he had not divulged, even to Bassett or to his Uncle Oscar.

But his mother, after standing undecided and a little bit sullen for some moments, said:

"Very well, then! Don't go to the seaside till after the Derby, if you don't wish it. But promise me you won't let your nerves go to pieces. Promise you won't think so much about horse-racing and *events*, as you call them!''

"Oh no," said the boy casually. "I won't think much about them, mother. You needn't worry. I wouldn't worry, mother, if I were you."

"If you were me and I were you," said his mother, "I wonder what we *should* do!''

"But you know you needn't worry, mother, don't you?" the boy repeated.

"I should be awfully glad to know it," she said wearily.

"Oh, well, you *can,* you know. I mean, you *ought* to know you needn't worry," he insisted.

"Ought I? Then I'll see about it," she said.

Paul's secret of secrets was his wooden horse, that which had no name. Since he was emancipated from a nurse and a nursery-governess, he had had his rocking-horse removed to his own bedroom at the top of the house.

"Surely you're too big for a rocking-horse!" his mother had remonstrated.

"Well, you see, mother, till I can have a *real* horse, I like to have *some* sort of animal about," had been his quaint answer.

"Do you feel he keeps you company?" she laughed.

"Oh yes! He's very good, he always keeps me company, when I'm there," said Paul.

So the horse, rather shabby, stood in an arrested prance in the boy's bedroom.

The Derby was drawing near, and the boy grew more and more tense. He hardly heard what was spoken to him, he was very frail, and his eyes were really uncanny. His mother had sudden strange seizures of uneasiness about him. Sometimes, for half an hour, she would feel a sudden anxiety about him that was almost anguish. She wanted to rush to him at once, and know he was safe.

Two nights before the Derby, she was at a big party in town, when one of her rushes of anxiety about her boy, her first-born, gripped her heart till she could hardly speak. She fought with the feeling, might and main, for she believed in common sense. But it was too strong. She had to leave the dance and go downstairs to telephone to the country. The children's nursery-governess was terribly surprised and startled at being rung up in the night.

"Are the children all right, Miss Wilmot?"

"Oh yes, they are quite all right."

"Master Paul? Is he all right?"

"He went to bed as right as a trivet. Shall I run up and look at him?"

"No," said Paul's mother reluctantly. "No! Don't trouble. It's all right. Don't sit up. We shall be home fairly soon." She did not want her son's privacy intruded upon.

"Very good," said the governess.

It was about one o'clock when Paul's mother and father drove up to their house. All was still. Paul's mother went to her room and slipped off her white fur cloak. She had told her maid not to wait up for her. She heard her husband downstairs, mixing a whisky and soda.

And then, because of the strange anxiety at her heart, she stole upstairs to her son's room. Noiselessly she went along the upper corridor. Was there a faint noise? What was it?

She stood, with arrested muscles, outside his door, listening. There was a strange, heavy, and yet not loud noise. Her heart stood still. It was a soundless noise, yet rushing and powerful. Something huge, in violent, hushed motion. What was it? What in God's name was it? She ought to know. She felt that she knew the noise. She knew what it was.

Yet she could not place it. She couldn't say what it was. And on and on it went, like a madness.

Softly, frozen with anxiety and fear, she turned the doorhandle.

The room was dark. Yet in the space near the window, she heard and saw something plunging to and fro. She gazed in fear and amazement.

Then suddenly she switched on the light, and saw her son, in his green pyjamas, madly surging on the rocking-horse. The blaze of light suddenly lit him up, as he urged the wooden horse, and lit her up, as she stood, blonde, in her dress of pale green and crystal, in the doorway.

"Paul!" she cried. "Whatever are you doing?"

"It's Malabar!" he screamed in a powerful, strange voice. "It's Malabar!"

His eyes blazed at her for one strange and senseless second, as he ceased urging his wooden horse. Then he fell with a crash to the ground, and she, all her tormented motherhood flooding upon her, rushed to gather him up.

But he was unconscious, and unconscious he remained, with some brain-fever. He talked and tossed, and his mother sat stonily by his side.

"Malabar! It's Malabar! Bassett, Bassett, I *know!* It's Malabar!"

So the child cried, trying to get up and urge the rocking-horse that gave him his inspiration.

"What does he mean by Malabar?" asked the heart-frozen mother.

"I don't know," said the father stonily.

"What does he mean by Malabar?" she asked her brother Oscar.

"It's one of the horses running for the Derby," was the answer.

And, in spite of himself, Oscar Cresswell spoke to Bassett, and himself put a thousand on Malabar: at fourteen to one.

The third day of the illness was critical: they were waiting for a change. The boy, with his rather long, curly hair, was tossing ceaselessly on the pillow. He neither slept nor regained consciousness, and his eyes were like blue stones. His mother sat, feeling her heart had gone, turned actually into a stone.

In the evening, Oscar Cresswell did not come, but Bassett sent a message, saying could he come up for one moment, just one moment? Paul's mother was very angry at the intrusion, but on second thoughts she agreed. The boy was the same. Perhaps Bassett might bring him to consciousness.

The gardener, a shortish fellow with a little brown moustache and sharp little brown eyes, tiptoed into the room, touched his imaginary cap to Paul's mother, and stole to the bedside, staring with glittering, smallish eyes at the tossing, dying child.

"Master Paul!" he whispered. "Master Paul! Malabar came in first all right, a clean win. I did as you told me. You've made over seventy thousand pounds, you have; you've got over eighty thousand. Malabar came in all right, Master Paul."

"Malabar! Malabar! Did I say Malabar, mother? Did I say Malabar? Do you think I'm lucky, mother? I knew Malabar, didn't I? Over eighty thousand pounds! I call that lucky, don't you, mother? Over eighty thousand pounds! I knew, didn't I know I knew? Malabar came in all right. If I ride my horse till I'm sure, then I tell you, Bassett, you can go as high as you like. Did you go for all you were worth, Bassett?"

"I went a thousand on it, Master Paul."

"I never told you, mother, that if I can ride my horse, and *get there,* then I'm absolutely sure—oh, absolutely! Mother, did I ever tell you? I *am* lucky!"

"No, you never did," said his mother.

But the boy died in the night.

And even as he lay dead, his mother heard her brother's voice saying to her: "My God, Hester, you're eighty-odd thousand to the good, and a poor devil of a son to the bad. But, poor devil, poor devil, he's best gone out of a life where he rides his rocking-horse to find a winner."

Meaning and Idea

1. Describe Paul's character. How does his home environment affect him? What does he hope to accomplish in this story? Does he manage it? How and why does he die?

2. Who are the other main characters in this story? How does each of them contribute to the overall process of the story?

3. According to Paul's mother, what is the relation between luck and money? What process derives from that relation?

4. What do the voices in the house say? Why? How do they change after the first windfall of money? Why?

Language, Form, Structure

1. What is the overall process described in this story? Who is most responsible for enacting that process? What are his or her motivations to follow through on that process?

2. What is the theme of this story? What is its tone? Describe the relation between theme and tone here. Why is process analysis used as one of the organizing techniques?

3. The overall process here is divided into smaller processes, among them Paul's ritual on the rocking horse and the process of placing bets. Describe these two processes. What other smaller processes help form the overall process? Describe at least two of them.

4. How does repetition function in this story?

5. Write meanings for each of the following figurative expressions from this story: "prospects never materialised"; "racked her brains"; *filthy lucre*"; "unsure eyes"; "compel her attention"; "brazening it out"; "in full tilt"; "spinning yarns"; "an odd knack"; "an arrested prance." Then use each phrase in a sentence of your own.

Ideas for Writing

1. Explain a process that you used to get something you wanted very much. Be sure to indicate your motivations for beginning the process and tell if you actually got what you wanted.

2. Describe a process by which you solved a major problem for yourself or someone else. Use narration and dialogue to enhance your analysis.

3. In interpreting this story, critics have often read the overall process involved as a metaphor either for Paul's "coming of age" (that is, his adolescence) or for what Lawrence viewed as the corruptness of the society in which it takes place. What is your response to these interpretations? Do you think either, or both, is valid? If so, in what ways? If not, why? Do you think there are any other metaphoric values attached to the processes of the story?

Ved Mehta

THE BABY MYNA

Ved Mehta was born in Lahore, India (now Pakistan), in 1934, and became an American citizen in 1975. Educated at Oxford and Harvard, Mehta began his schooling at schools for the blind in Bombay, India, and Little Rock, Arkansas, where his father had sent him to escape the life of degradation and poverty so often the fate of Asian blind children. The main part of Mehta's essay and story writing was accomplished while he was a contributing editor to *The New Yorker* magazine. His explanations of Indian lifestyles are collected in such works as *Walking the Indian Streets* (1960), the biographical *Daddyji* (1972) and *Mamaji* (1979), *The Photographs of Chachji* (1980), and the autobiographical *Vedi* (1984). Among Mehta's honors are a Guggenheim fellowship and a Ford Foundation grant.

In this vignette from his autobiographical *Vedi* (1982), Ved Mehta skillfully blends description and narration to explain the various processes involved in his getting, training, and ultimately losing his pet myna bird, Sweetie.

*O*ne day, Sher Singh returned from leave in his village in the Kangara District, in the hills, with a baby myna for me. "I have brought you a friend," he said. "It's a baby myna. It's one of the only birds in the world that can talk. It's just the right age to learn to talk."

I was excited. I went with Sher Singh to the Mozang Chowk and bought a wire cage with a door, a metal floor, and a little swing. The cage had a hook at the top, and I hung it in my room. (We were temporarily living in our own house, at 11 Temple Road.) I got a couple of brass bowls—one for water, the other for grain—and filled them up and put them in the cage. I got a brush for cleaning out the cage. I named the myna Sweetie. The name came to me just out of the sky.

"How do you catch a baby myna?" I asked Sher Singh.

"It's difficult, Vedi Sahib. There are very few of them around, and you have to know where a baby myna is resting with her mother. You have to slip up on them in the middle of the night, when they are sleeping in their nest, and throw a cover over them and hope that you catch the baby, because only a baby myna can learn to talk. Sometimes the mother myna will nip at your finger, and there are people in my village who are constantly getting their fingers nipped at because they have been trying to catch a baby myna."

At first, Sweetie was so small that she could scarcely fly even a few inches. I would sit her on my shoulder and walk around the room. She would dig her nervous, trembling claws through my shirt and into my shoulder as she tried to keep her balance, fluttering around my ear and sending off little ripples of air. But Sweetie grew fast, and soon she was flying around my room. Before I opened her cage to fill up the bowls or clean the floor, I would have to shut the door. She would often nip at my finger and escape from the cage. She would go and perch on the mantelpiece. When I ran to the mantelpiece to catch her, she would fly up to the curtain rod. When I climbed up onto the windowsill and shook the curtain, she would fly back to the mantelpiece. Sometimes she would be so silent that I would wonder if she was still in the room. Other times, I would hear her flying all around the room—now she would be by the window, now by the overhead light, her wings beating against the pane and the lampshade. I would make kissing sounds, as I had heard Sher Singh make them. I would call to her—"Sweetie! Sweetie!" I would whistle affectionately. I would run frenetically from one end of the room to the other. I would scream with rage. But she wouldn't come to me. I would somehow have to summon Sher Singh through the closed door, and then give him a cue to come in when I thought she wasn't near the door, and he would have to prance around the room and somehow catch her with his duster.

"She's a real hill girl, all right, flying around like that," he would say.

When we had finally got her back in the cage, I would scold her roundly, but it didn't seem to do much good.

"Vedi Sahib, you'll lose her, like your eyes, if you don't keep her always in the cage," Sher Singh said.

"But then how can I feed her? How can I clean out her cage?"

"I will do all that, Vedi Sahib. And, because I can see, I can watch her."

"But I like looking after her," I said.

"You'll lose her, Vedi Sahib," he said. "And mind your finger. She's getting big."

I devised a way of filling her bowls and cleaning some of the cage's floor by surreptitiously sticking my fingers between the wires. But now and again I would want to feel her on her swing or take her out and hold her, and then she would nip at my finger and sometimes draw blood. She would escape and give me a real run around the room.

Every time I passed Sweetie's cage, I would say "Hello, Sweetie," and wait for her to talk. But she would only flutter in the cage or, at most, make her swing squeak.

"Are you sure Sweetie can talk?" I asked Sher Singh.

"All baby mynas from Kangara can learn to talk," he said.

"Are you sure she is from Kangara?"

"Only mynas from Kangara have a black patch on the throat. You can feel it, and you can ask anyone—it's as black as coal."

I took Sweetie out of her cage. I held her tight in one hand and tried to feel the patch on her throat with the other. She screamed and tried to bite my finger, but I finally found the patch. It was a little soft, downy raised circle that throbbed with her pulse.

"What do mynas sound like when they talk?" I later asked Sher Singh.

"They have the voice of the Kangara, of a Kangara hill girl."

"What is that?"

"The Punjab hills, the leaves in the wind, the waterfall on a mountainside—you know, Vedi Sahib, it's the sound of a peacock spreading its wings in Kangara at dawn."

One day, I passed her cage and said, "Hello. Sweetie."

"Hello, Sweetie," she answered.

I jumped. I don't know how I had expected her voice to sound, but it was thin, sharp, and defiant—at once whiny and abrasive—like three treble notes on the harmonium played very fast. Her words assaulted my ears—"Sweetie" was something that film stars called each other on the screen, and sounded very naughty.

I had scarcely taken in the fact that Sweetie could really speak when she repeated "Hello, Sweetie." She kept on repeating it, hour after hour. "Hello, Sweetie" would suddenly explode into the air like a firecracker.

Try as I would, I couldn't teach her to say anything else. All the same, there was something thrilling and comforting in having my own film star in the cage, and I got so used to her enticing outbursts that I missed them when she kept quiet or was dozing.

Every evening, at the time when my big sisters and my big brother went to play hockey or some other game with their school friends, it was Sher Singh's duty to take me for a walk to Lawrence Gardens. There I would ride the merry-go-round—a big, creaky thing with wooden seats and a metal railing—while Sher Singh ran alongside. It would revolve and lurch, tipping this way and that way, filling me with terror and excitement. On the ground, I would throw off my shoes and run up and down the hillocks. They were covered with damp, soft grass and occasional patches of dead grass. The grass would caress, tickle, and prick my feet. All around, there were the light, cheerful sounds of sighted children running and playing and of birds flying and perching and calling. In the distance, there was the solitary, mournful song of a nightingale.

I felt sorry that Sweetie, shut up in the house, couldn't enjoy the company of other birds, and one evening I insisted that we take her along in her cage and let her enjoy the fresh air and the life of Lawrence Gardens, even if it was only through the wires of her cage.

"But don't let her out of the cage," Sher Singh said. "She is a spirit from the hills. She will fly back to Kangara."

"Fly all the way to Kangara! She would die without food or water. Besides, she is my friend. She wouldn't leave me."

"Vedi Sahib, you know how loyal Kangara servants are?"

"No one could be more loyal than you, Sher Singh."

"Well, Kangara mynas are as disloyal as Kangara servants are loyal. You can love a beloved myna all you want to, give her all the grain to eat you want to, give her all the water to drink you want to, and at the first opportunity she will nip at your finger and fly away. But you can kick a servant from Kangara and he will still give you first-class service."

"Why is that?"

"Because servants from Kangara, like mynas, have breathed the Himalayan air and are free spirits. A Kangara servant is a servant by choice—but no myna is in a cage by choice."

I couldn't follow exactly what Sher Singh was saying, but I laughed. Anyway, I insisted that we take Sweetie with us.

At Lawrence Gardens, I had no intention of taking Sweetie out of her cage, but when she heard the other birds she set up such a racket that children and servants who usually took little notice of me wandered toward us to find out what I was doing to the poor myna. They said all kinds of things:

"She is lonely."

"He's keeping her a prisoner."

"Tch, tch! He can't play with other children, so he won't let his myna play with other birds."

"She'll fly away to Kangara!" I cried.

People laughed, hooted, and jeered. "She's so small she probably can't even fly up to that tree."

"Why are you pointing? He doesn't know how high that tree is."

I suddenly got an idea. I had with me a ball of strong, fortified string that Brother Om used for flying kites. I took Sweetie out of the cage and, while I held her screaming and biting in my hands, I had Sher Singh tie up her legs with the string. Then I caught hold of the ball and let her go, and the people about us clapped and cheered. I started giving her string, and she flew high up and pulled and tugged. I gave her more string and let her lead me where she would around the grass. I thought it was a wonderful game. Before I knew what had happened, her weight at the end of the string was gone, and the limp string had fluttered down on me.

"She's bitten through the string! Look, she's bitten through the string!" everyone shouted, running away.

"Sher Singh, catch her! Catch her!" I cried. "Bring Sweetie back!"

"I think I see her!" he called, running off.

A few minutes later, Sher Singh came back. "She's nowhere to be found, Vedi Sahib. She's gone, Sahib—gone straight back to Kangara. You will now have to get along without Sweetie."

Sher Singh and I looked for her all over Lawrence Gardens, calling "Sweetie! Sweetie!" until it was dark and everyone had left. Then Sher Singh and I walked home with the empty cage.

Meaning and Idea

1. What is a myna? Why would it be a particularly attractive pet for a child?

2. What problems does the blind child Vedi have with the infant bird? What advice does Sher Singh give him? Why is Vedi reluctant to accept it?

3. How does Sher Singh's description of what the bird's voice would sound like compare with what Vedi actually hears once Sweetie learns to talk?

4. What plan does Vedi put into action for releasing Sweetie at Lawrence Gardens? How does it fail?

Language, Form, Structure

1. How does Ved Mehta use narration as the organizing technique for this selection? How does narration enhance the analysis of the various processes?

2. What is the main point of the selection? As part of a chapter from a long book, "The Baby Myna" understandably lacks a thesis sentence. What might a thesis sentence for this selection include? Write one that you think would be appropriate.

3. What does the tone of this essay tell you about Mehta's feelings about his childhood? How?

4. Identify meanings for the following words: frenetically; prance; roundly; surreptitiously; defiant; abrasive; harmonium; enticing; lurch; fortified.

Ideas for Writing

1. If you have ever had a pet, explain the process by which you trained it to do something. Be sure to include any failures you experienced in this process before you were successful.

2. Using narration as your organizing principle, write a process analysis of how you learned to do something during your childhood.

3. Ved Mehta, as you might have picked up from context clues, has been blind since his childhood. How does this knowledge affect your reading of this selection? Does it make you reevaluate the descriptive passages or the overall tone and development of the process analysis? What other famous writers can you think of who were blind? How do you think their blindness affected their writing?

Camara Laye
THE GOLD WORKER

Camara Laye (1928–1980) was born the son of a goldsmith in Kouroussa, French Guinea. His writings focus on the sharp contrast between traditional rural culture and modern urban lifestyles, a relationship that mirrors his own experience of leaving a tribal system to study and work in Paris. Among his best known works are *The Dark Child* (1953) and *A Dream of Africa* (1971). Laye was also a contributor to numerous African, European, and American journals.

In *The Dark Child,* drawn from his childhood memory, Camara Laye explains the "magical" process of his father's work as a goldsmith. Technical process, though easily identifiable in this selection, is artfully crafted into a vivid narration.

*O*f all the different kinds of work my father engaged in, none fascinated me so much as his skill with gold. No other occupation was so noble, no other needed such a delicate touch. And then, every time he worked in gold it was like a festival—indeed it *was* a festival—that broke the monotony of ordinary working days.

So, if a woman, accompanied by a go-between, crossed the threshold of the workshop, I followed her in at once. I knew what she wanted: she had brought some gold, and had come to ask my father to transform it into a trinket. She had collected it in the placers of Siguiri where, crouching over the river for months on end, she had patiently extracted grains of gold from the mud.

These women never came alone. They knew my father had other things to do than make trinkets. And even when he had the time, they knew they were not the first to ask a favor of him, and that, consequently, they would not be served before others.

Generally they required the trinket for a certain date, for the festival of Ramadan or the Tabaski or some other family ceremony or dance.

Therefore, to enhance their chances of being served quickly and to more easily persuade my father to interrupt the work before him, they used to request the services of an official praise-singer, a go-between, arranging in advance the fee they were to pay him for his good offices.

The go-between installed himself in the workshop, tuned up his *cora*, which is our harp, and began to sing my father's praises. This was always a great event for me. I heard recalled the lofty deeds of my father's ancestors and their names from the earliest times. As the couplets were reeled off it was like watching the growth of a great genealogical tree that spread its branches far and wide and flourished its boughs and twigs before my mind's eye. The harp played an accompaniment to this vast utterance of names, expanding it with notes that were now soft, now shrill.

I could sense my father's vanity being inflamed, and I already knew that after having sipped this milk-and-honey he would lend a favorable ear to the woman's request. But I was not alone in my knowledge. The woman also had seen my father's eyes gleaming with contented pride. She held out her grains of gold as if the whole matter were settled. My father took up his scales and weighed the gold.

"What sort of trinket do you want?" he would ask.

"I want. . . ."

And then the woman would not know any longer exactly what she wanted because desire kept making her change her mind, and because she would have liked all the trinkets at once. But it would have taken a pile of gold much larger than she had brought to satisfy her whim, and from then on her chief purpose in life was to get hold of it as soon as she could.

"When do you want it?"

Always the answer was that the trinket was needed for an occasion in the near future.

"So! You are in that much of a hurry? Where do you think I shall find the time?"

"I am in a great hurry, I assure you."

"I have never seen a woman eager to deck herself out who wasn't in a great hurry! Good! I shall arrange my time to suit you. Are you satisfied?"

He would take the clay pot that was kept specially for smelting gold, and would pour the grains into it. He would then cover the gold with powdered charcoal, a charcoal he prepared by using plant juices of exceptional purity. Finally, he would place a large lump of the same kind of charcoal over the pot.

As soon as she saw that the work had been duly undertaken, the woman, now quite satisfied, would return to her household tasks, leaving her go-between to carry on with the praise-singing which had already proved so advantageous.

At a sign from my father the apprentices began working two sheepskin bellows. The skins were on the floor, on opposite sides of the forge, connected to it by earthen pipes. While the work was in progress the apprentices sat in front of the bellows with crossed legs. That is, the younger of the two sat, for the elder was sometimes allowed to assist. But the younger—this time it was Sidafa—was only permitted to work the bellows and watch while waiting his turn for promotion to less rudimentary tasks. First one and then the other worked hard at the bellows: the flame in the forge rose higher and became a living thing, a genie implacable and full of life.

Then my father lifted the clay pot with his long tongs and placed it on the flame.

Immediately all activity in the workshop almost came to a halt. During the whole time that the gold was being smelted, neither copper nor aluminum could be worked nearby, lest some particle of these base metals fall into the container which held the gold. Only steel could be worked on such occasions, but the men, whose task that was, hurried to finish what they were doing, or left it abruptly to join the apprentices gathered around the forge. There were so many, and they crowded so around my father, that I, the smallest person present, had to come near the forge in order not to lose track of what was going on.

If he felt he had inadequate working space, my father had the apprentices stand well away from him. He merely raised his hand in a simple gesture: at that particular moment he never uttered a word, and no one else would: no one was allowed to utter a word. Even the go-between's voice was no longer raised in song. The silence was broken only by the panting of the bellows and the faint hissing of the gold. But if my father never actually spoke, I know that he was forming words in his mind. I could tell from his lips, which kept moving, while, bending over the pot, he stirred the gold and charcoal with a bit of wood that kept bursting into flame and had constantly to be replaced by a fresh one.

What words did my father utter? I do not know. At least I am not certain what they were. No one ever told me. But could they have been anything but incantations? On these occasions was he not invoking the genies of fire and gold, of fire and wind, of wind blown by the blast-pipes of the forge, of fire born of wind, of gold married to fire? Was it not their assistance, their friendship, their espousal that he besought? Yes. Almost certainly he was invoking these genies, all of whom are equally indispensable for smelting gold.

The operation going on before my eyes was certainly the smelting of gold, yet something more than that: a magical operation that the guiding spirits could regard with favor or disfavor. That is why, all around my father, there was absolute silence and anxious expectancy. Though only a child, I knew there could be no craft greater than the goldsmith's. I expected a ceremony; I had come to be present at a ceremony; and it actually was one, though very protracted. I was still too young to understand why, but I had an inkling as I watched the almost religious concentration of those who followed the mixing process in the clay pot.

When finally the gold began to melt I could have shouted aloud—and perhaps we all would have if we had not been forbidden to make a sound. I trembled, and so did everyone else watching my father stir the mixture—it was still a heavy paste—in which the charcoal was gradually consumed. The next stage followed swiftly. The gold now had the fluidity of water. The genies had smiled on the operation!

"Bring me the brick!" my father would order, thus lifting the ban that until then had silenced us.

The brick, which an apprentice would place beside the fire, was hollowed out, generously greased with Galam butter. My father would take the pot off the fire and tilt it carefully while I would watch the gold flow into the brick, flow like liquid fire. True, it was only a very sparse trickle of fire, but how vivid, how brilliant! As the gold flowed into the brick the grease sputtered and flamed and emitted a thick smoke that caught in the throat and stung the eyes, leaving us all weeping and coughing.

But there were times when it seemed to me that my father ought to turn this task over to one of his assistants. They were experienced, had assisted him hundreds of times, and could certainly have performed the work well. But my father's lips moved and those inaudible, secret words, those incantations he addressed to one we could not see or hear, was the essential part. Calling on the genies of fire, of wind, of gold and exorcising the evil spirits—this was a knowledge he alone possessed.

By now the gold had been cooled in the hollow of the brick, and my father began to hammer and stretch it. This was the moment when his work as a goldsmith really began. I noticed that before embarking on it he never failed to stroke the little snake stealthily as it lay coiled up under the sheepskin. I can only assume that this was his way of gathering strength for what remained to be done, the most trying part of his task.

But was it not extraordinary and miraculous that on these occasions the little black snake was always coiled under the sheepskin? He was not always there. He did not visit my father every day. But he was always present whenever there was gold to be worked. His presence was no surprise to *me*. After that evening when my father had spoken of the guiding spirit of his race I was no longer astonished. The snake was there intentionally. He knew what the future held. Did he tell my father? I think that he most certainly did. Did he tell him everything? I have another reason for believing firmly that he did.

The craftsman who works in gold must first of all purify himself. That is, he must wash himself all over and, of course, abstain from all sexual commerce during the whole time. Great respecter of ceremony as he was, it would have been impossible for my father to ignore these rules. Now, I never saw him make these preparations. I saw him address himself to his work without any apparent preliminaries. From that moment it was obvious that, forewarned in a dream by his black guiding spirit of the task which awaited him in the morning, my father must have prepared for it as soon as he arose, entering his workshop in a state of purity, his body smeared with the secret potions hidden in his numerous pots of magical substances; or perhaps he always came into his workshop in a state of ritual purity. I am not trying to make him out a better man than he was—he was a man and had his share of human frailties—but he was always uncompromising in his respect for ritual observance.

The woman for whom the trinket was being made, and who had come often to see how the work was progressing, would arrive for the final time, not wanting to miss a moment of this spectacle—as marvelous to her as to us—when the gold wire, which my father had succeeded in drawing out from the mass of molten gold and charcoal, was transformed into a trinket.

There she would be. Her eyes would devour the fragile gold wire, following it in its tranquil and regular spiral around the little slab of metal which supported it. My father would catch a glimpse of her and I would see him slowly beginning to smile. Her avid attention delighted him.

"Are you trembling?" he would ask.

"Am I trembling?"

And we would all burst out laughing at her. For she would be trembling! She would be trembling with covetousness for the spiral pyramid in which my father would be inserting, among the convolutions, tiny grains of gold. When he had finally finished by crowning the pyramid with a heavier grain, she would dance in delight.

No one—no one at all—would be more enchanted than she as my father slowly turned the trinket back and forth between his fingers to display its perfection. Not even the praise-singer whose business it was to register excitement would be more excited than she. Throughout this metamorphosis he did not stop speaking faster and ever faster, increasing his tempo, accelerating his praises and flatteries as the trinket took shape, shouting to the skies my father's skill.

For the praise-singer took a curious part—I should say rather that it was direct and effective—in the work. He was drunk with the joy of creation. He shouted aloud in joy. He plucked his *cora* like a man inspired. He sweated as if he were the trinket-maker, as if he were my father, as if the trinket were his creation. He was no longer a hired censer-bearer, a man whose services anyone could rent. He was a man who created his song out of some deep inner necessity. And when my father, after having soldered the large grain of gold that crowned the summit, held out his work to be admired, the praise-singer would no longer be able to contain himself. He would begin to intone the *douga,* the great chant which is sung only for celebrated men and which is danced for them alone.

But the *douga* is a formidable chant, a provocative chant, a chant which the praise-singer dared not sing, and which the man for whom it is sung dared not dance before certain precautions had been taken. My father had taken them as soon as he woke, since he had been warned in a dream. The praise-singer had taken them when he concluded his arrangements with the woman. Like my father he had smeared his body with magic substances and had made himself invulnerable to the evil genies whom the *douga* inevitably set free; these potions made him invulnerable also to rival praise-singers, perhaps jealous of him, who awaited only this song and the exaltation and loss of control which attended it, in order to begin casting their spells.

At the first notes of the *douga* my father would arise and emit a cry in which happiness and triumph were equally mingled; and brandishing in his right hand the hammer that was the symbol of his profession and in his left a ram's horn filled with magic substances, he would dance the glorious dance.

No sooner had he finished, than workmen and apprentices, friends and customers in their turn, not forgetting the woman for whom the trinket had been created, would flock around him, congratulating him, showering praises on him and complimenting the praise-singer at the same time. The latter found himself laden with gifts—almost his only means of support, for the praise-singer leads a wandering life after the fashion of the troubadours of old. Aglow with dancing and the praises he had received, my father would offer everyone cola nuts, that small change of Guinean courtesy.

Now all that remained to be done was to redden the trinket in a little water to which chlorine and sea salt had been added. I was at liberty to leave. The festival was over! But often as I came out of the workshop my mother would be in the court, pounding millet or rice, and she would call to me:

"Where have you been?" although she knew perfectly well where I had been.

"In the workshop."

"Of course. Your father was smelting gold. Gold! Always gold!"

And she would beat the millet or rice furiously with her pestle.

"Your father is ruining his health!"

"He danced the *douga*."

"The *douga!* The *douga* won't keep him from ruining his eyes. As for you, you would be better off playing in the courtyard instead of breathing dust and smoke in the workshop."

My mother did not like my father to work in gold. She knew how dangerous it was: a trinket-maker empties his lungs blowing on the blowpipe and his eyes suffer from the fire. Perhaps they suffer even more from the microscopic precision which the work requires. And even if there had been no such objections involved, my mother would scarcely have relished this work. She was suspicious of it, for gold can not be smelted without the use of other metals, and my mother thought it was not entirely honest to put aside for one's own use the gold which the alloy had displaced. However, this was a custom generally known, and one which she herself had accepted when she took cotton to be woven and received back only a piece of cotton cloth half the weight of the original bundle.

Meaning and Idea

1. What function does the official praise-singer serve in negotiations between the woman and the narrator's father? How does the praise-singer continue to participate in the creation of the trinket?

2. Why is there "absolute silence and anxious expectancy" in the workshop?

3. When does the work of the skillful goldsmith really begin? How does the snake figure in the work?

4. What elements of ceremony and superstition do you note here? Why does the narrator say that his father "was always uncompromising in his respect for ritual observance"? How, in fact, is the day for working the gold "like a festival"?

5. What is the *douga*? How does the father prepare himself for it?

Language, Form, Structure

1. How does the author make this highly technical process lively and enjoyable for his readers?

2. How does the first paragraph serve as an appropriate introduction to the selection? Which sentence in the introduction might be considered as a thesis sentence?

3. How do description and narration serve as transitional devices here? What transitional words and phrases help link the elements of the selection together?

4. Explain the following simile from the essay: "As the couplets were reeled off it was like watching the growth of a great genealogical tree." Explain the following metaphor: "after having sipped this milk-and-honey, he would lend a favorable ear to the woman's request." Find and explain at least two other metaphors and two other similes in the selection.

5. Choose ten of the following words and write definitions for them: trinket; shrill; vanity; smelting; apprentices; bellows; rudimentary; incantations; invoke; espousal; inaudible; covetousness; metamorphosis; intone.

Ideas for Writing

1. Describe the process by which you learned to do something in your childhood. Try to include how your perception of the process now is different from what it was then.

2. Explain any technical process with which you are familiar. Use narration and description to make the process analysis lively.

3. This selection is a childhood memory explained from the perspective of an adult. Evaluate Laye's ability to connect those two perspectives in this essay. What other writing have you read which relies on this connection, and how does it compare to Laye's essay? (You may want to reread Langston Hughes's "Salvation" in Chapter Two or Ved Mehta's "The Baby Myna" in this chapter.)

Chapter Five
COMPARISON

*W*here would we be without the ability to see things in relation to other things? Making comparisons, seeing similarities or differences (or both) is essential for making the judgments we live by. Is he large or small, beautiful or ugly, kind or cruel? Is she attentive or blasé, energetic or lethargic, coy or ostentatious? To answer such questions intelligently we often ask another question: "*Compared* to whom?" Making comparisons allows us to think more deeply. Indeed thought without comparisons is not really thought as we know it. A mind overtaken by an obsession, for example, is a mind stuck in a single vision, unable to look about with an eye open to relationships and comparisons.

Comparative thinking is a particularly human gift that enables us to organize experience, and to make the serious and fanciful connections that help us evaluate the conditions of our daily lives.

READING COMPARISONS

Careful readers know that for the best writers, the comparative faculty is a steady apparatus. The writer of fiction or drama develops one character with another in mind and depends on readers or viewers seeing these created people in relation to one another. We appreciate the nobility of an Othello, for example, more clearly in relation to the vile actions of an Iago, or the vulnerable youth of Romeo and Juliet in relation to their ruling elders.

The world of comedy and tragedy alike is populated with characters meant for the reader to compare—Mutt and Jeff, Felix and Oscar, Lenny and George, and the list goes on—clear opposites meant to illuminate each other. Many writers, then, make generous use of explicit and implicit comparisons. This is as true for the writer of essays as for the writer of imaginative literature. Patterns emerge and generalizations are drawn as the essayist in "Once More to the Lake" (see Chapter 2), considers subjects relatively. E. B. White's trip to the lake with his son gains meaning for both the writer and the reader as White *compares* the stay to those of his earlier childhood. Without the pressure of these other memories, White's descriptions might have evoked a sense of place, but could never have conveyed the rich sense of time and of life passing by. Similarly, readers confronted with Susan Sontag's comparison in this chapter between the public's perceptions about cancer and tuberculosis learn much about our entrenched habits in thinking about and dealing with disease. The primitive dread, shame, and disgust that for centuries marked attitudes toward TB have attached themselves in the modern age to our attitude toward cancer and cancer patients. Sontag's comparison urges us to review our thinking, to cast off old prejudices and phobias, and to assume the enlightened consciousness and behavior permitted by the advancing science of our century. Her historical perspective allows us to view cancer with increased hope as well. Like TB, so long the dreaded "killer," cancer too can be understood and conquered, both mentally and physically. The essay deepens from the apt comparison.

In reading poetry, we are confronted again and again with comparisons. Poets can structure their poems with comparisons, exploring two subjects at once. Such basic comparisons are seen in poems like "The Little Black Boy" and "Richard Corey." These comparisons help readers see subjects dynamically—white people versus black people, town patrician versus town folk. But poets work in fanciful comparisons as well, comparing a lover to a summer's day, life to a staircase, life to a road.

Figurative devices help us compare things in an imaginative fashion. Through metaphor, for example, we can make statements that tell special truths. In Tennyson's "The Eagle" we read about the eagle's "hands" and accept this, though, in actuality, the eagle doesn't have hands but talons. By writing "hands," however, the poet is able to convey to us the bird's extraordinarily strong, firm grasp and to suggest to the reader that his subject is human, or is as important as a human. Had Tennyson written _claws,_ we might have found ourselves thinking in a more mundane context—chicken feet and so on. Poems, like our daily lives, are filled with metaphors (a thing is said to be something it really is not—but really _is_ if you think about it) and similes (a thing is said to be _like_ something it really is not—but really _is_ if you think about it). In poetry, as in life, these comparisons can be fresh, or they can be overused—big as a house, long as the day, eats like a bird, he's a monster, he's an animal, and so on. The similes and metaphors that we use daily may be trite, but they reflect nonetheless our very human desire to see elements in our lives comparatively. In the comparisons offered by figurative language (metaphor, simile, and others) something from one class of things (or people or ideas) is set against something from another class of things. Such comparisons are the opposites of those comparisons we spoke of earlier in which two or more things of the _same_ class are compared—two trips, two diseases, two people, two newspapers. Hence, with figurative language a person is compared to an animal—a horse, let's say, because of the qualities shared with horses—largeness, endurance, strength, appetite, range of feelings. Or a person is compared to something superhuman in order to emphasize some extraordinary features—she sings like an angel, he's built like a god, and so on. There is pleasure in breaking down barriers between classifications in order to see our world more vividly: combs have teeth, shoes have tongues, corn grows in ears, trees have arms. The metaphors and similes we use again and again in our daily lives might show wear from overuse, but they reflect our desire to see comparisons, to make connections, to play with seeing and saying.

Reading good poetry gives us the chance to enjoy unique comparisons—the poet's similes and metaphors. Langston Hughes's "Dream Deferred," a poem you will read in a later chapter, is a prime example of the use of figurative device to shock us into awareness about both language and the human condition. Who would ever think, for example, of a deferred dream as being like an infected wound? And yet by making this comparison, Hughes makes us see its validity and makes us see as well the ability of language to transport us to new areas of feeling and thought.

The comparisons presented in this chapter are both sensible—comparing within classes—and fanciful—comparing things from different classes. Each in its way will help you to see subjects freshly with the understanding that comes from comparative thinking.

WRITING COMPARISONS

In writing comparisons, more perhaps than in any other writing, you must plan with care. The comparison paper presents you with a double challenge: to discuss two things at once. Therefore as you approach your discussion of these two things—two ideas, two people, two places—you must reflect at length upon matters such as purpose, audience, and organization.

AUDIENCE AND PURPOSE

Often as you write in college, the assignment itself will clarify your purpose. Indeed some instructors use the term *compare* to mean "to state likenesses," and *contrast* to mean "to state differences." For our purpose, however, we are using the term compare to mean both or either (similarities and differences) depending on your subject and your thinking.

When the two items in your comparison are very different on the surface—separated by time, nationality, or what-have-you—stressing likenesses would seem more appropriate because the differences are already so apparent. A paper comparing horses and humans would require little attention to the contrasting features of the animals. Everyone knows the two differ dramatically; what readers want to know is what the writer sees as similarities.

But when the two items you wish to compare are on the surface very similar, stressing differences makes for a more enlightening discussion. In comparing manual and electric typewriters, you would spend most of your time detailing the differences between the old and the new technologies. But there are no absolutes. If your employer asked you to compare the IBM PC and the Apple IIe, you would probably pay careful attention to likenesses as well as differences.

Often, however, subjects are both alike and not alike. Rock groups like the Beatles and the Rolling Stones, for example, share much—the time they began, their popularity, the death of group members, and so on. However, the groups are very different in tone, image, and style. To give your writing a purpose, you must decide which way to go. If you stress differences, it does not mean you will not deal with likenesses at all, only that you won't dwell on them. Perhaps an introductory paragraph can state the obvious similarities and the rest of the paper can explore distinctions. Or, if you find similarities most interesting, then you may wish to consider obvious differences first in a paragraph or two and then move on to your main concern and purpose: that the two groups, for example, had more in common than they knew they had; that they each in their own way, however unwittingly, fell prey to the violence of the times.

An effective, persuasive comparison paper must have a purpose—to show likenesses or differences *primarily*. Without this purpose, you risk providing a mere catalogue of features and qualities to no good end. And you want to consider the value of expressing the purpose of your comparison paper in an original statement of thesis. For example, the comparison paper built on thesis statements such as "There are many similarities between X and Y but also many differences," may be a clear enough paper, but one bound to bore the reader. The paper that rests on a daring thesis like Sontag's for example—that our *similar* responses to two very *different* diseases reflect a continuing negative impulse in our psyche and culture—grabs the reader's attention and holds it. The purpose of comparison, then, is to stress similarities *or* differences *in order to make a point*. It's the additional point that distinguishes the humdrum sorting of qualities from the engaging essay.

As for audience—again as in other kinds of essays, the reader makes a big difference for the writer. How much does the reader know about the subject? How much background must you give? What are the readers' social or political or aesthetic inclinations? What are their cultural backgrounds? How old are they? For example, your analysis of the Beatles or the Rolling Stones for an American or British audience would be very different from your analysis for an Asian audience. Your analysis will differ too, depending on whether the reader was listening to pop music when these groups were in their heydey, or whether the reader was "tuned in to" other music at the time or was possibly not yet alive!

PROCESS

First determine what two subjects you wish to compare in your paper. As you consider your subjects, make sure that you have a sound basis for comparison. Ask yourself, are they of the same class of things—two music groups, two plays, two heroes, two books, two treaties? If you find that the subjects you're thinking of comparing are *not* of the same class, then ask yourself if the "stretch" pays off. Does the fanciful comparison allow you to present something in a new light, or is it simply the result of a quick or an idiosyncratic idea?

Once you have two items for your comparison and have assured yourself that you have a sound basis for comparison, you are ready to identify the features to consider in the comparison. Some writers find a grid a useful tool for this stage of prewriting. Use a grid like the accompanying one or some other note-taking system that allows you to generate the points in your comparison and the details and examples that develop or illustrate these points.

	Topics for Comparison	
Points of Comparison	A. _____	B. _____

Next, look over the notes on your grid to see what you can say about your two topics. Where you have the most detail should give you a clue about where you have the most to say.

Formulate a thesis sentence that joins the two subjects in an interesting formulation: Despite obvious differences . . . X and Y's similarities show them both to be expressions of popular urges, or some such sentence.

With your thesis and your points of comparison developed, you are ready to organize your essay. Organization is critical for any essay, but in the comparison essay it is doubly important. Without careful planning, your essay can end up being an analysis of one of your subjects on a few points and then an analysis of the other on some other points—two separate analyses with no comparisons drawn. Or your essay, without proper planning, can easily become a lopsided affair, with ample discussion of one subject and a race through the next.

The effective comparison paper is balanced and consistent. If you discuss the history of one subject, you should discuss the history of the other; if you discuss the appearance of one subject, you should discuss the appearance of the other.

As you plan, you must decide on an appropriate scheme. Do you wish to discuss one subject covering all the points of comparison and then go on to the next subject covering the same points? Then your paper might look like this:

A.

1.
2.
3.

B.

1.
2.
3.

Or do you wish to allow the points of comparison to structure your discussion? Then your paper might look like this:

1. History	A.
	B.
2. Appearance	A.
	B.
3. Sound	A.
	B.

The first way allows for a fuller presentation of each of the topics on its own terms and for a more inductive approach. The second permits a more dynamic discussion with the relationship being stated throughout. If you choose the first arrangement, you will need to plan to make some more explicit statements of comparison at the end of the essay once you have laid out the different points for each of the two subjects.

Finally, as you write your comparison paper, you will want to make use of the transitional phrases that ease movement from one topic to the other—*similarly, likewise, in contrast, on the other hand, however,* and so on. These phrases will help you and the reader to navigate the complicated process of comparative analysis.

Virginia Woolf

SHAKESPEARE'S GIFTED SISTER

Virginia Woolf (1882–1941) is today considered one of the most important writers in the development of modernist fiction. She lived with her husband, editor and publisher Leonard Woolf, and her sister Vanessa (a painter), and Vanessa's husband Clive Bell (an art critic) as a part of the famous Bloomsbury group in England. This group was to include people such as novelist E. M. Forster, poet T. S. Eliot, art historian Roger Fry, and economist John Maynard Keynes, all of whom became renowned, in one way or another, for their progressive thought and lifestyles. Virginia and Leonard founded the Hogarth Press, which published her work, Eliot's, and Freud's (the first editions in English), among other great writers. Her widely admired fiction includes *Mrs. Dalloway* (1925), *To the Lighthouse* (1927), *Orlando* (1928), and *The Waves* (1931). She also left us a rich repository of essays when, after years of battling mental illness, she committed suicide in 1941.

This selection, from her 1929 feminist book *A Room of One's Own,* sets an imaginative, fictional context allowing Woolf to explore the inequities between men and women. Notice how she manages to balance description and exemplification of the real with the abstract as she looks at Elizabethan literature.

For it is a perennial puzzle why no woman wrote a word of that extraordinary literature when every other man, it seemed, was capable of song or sonnet. What were the conditions in which women lived, I asked myself; for fiction, imaginative work that is, is not dropped like a pebble upon the ground, as science may be; fiction is like a spider's web, attached ever so lightly perhaps, but still attached to life at all four corners. Often the attachment is scarcely perceptible; Shakespeare's plays, for instance, seem to hang there complete by themselves. But when the web is pulled askew, hooked up at the edge, torn in the middle, one remembers that these webs are not spun in mid-air by incorporeal creatures, but are the work of suffering human beings, and are attached to grossly material things, like health and money and the houses we live in. . . .

But what I find deplorable . . . is that nothing is known about women before the eighteenth century. I have no model in my mind to turn about this way and that. Here am I asking why women did not write poetry in the Elizabethan age, and I am not sure how they were educated; whether they were taught to write; whether they had sitting-rooms to themselves; how many women had children before they were twenty-one; what, in short, they did from eight in the morning till eight at night. They had no money, evidently; according to Professor Trevelyan they were married whether they liked it or not before they were out of the nursery, at fifteen or sixteen very likely. It would have been extremely odd, even upon this showing, had one of them suddenly written the plays of Shakespeare, I concluded, and I thought of that old gentleman, who is dead now, but was a bishop, I think, who declared that it was impossible for any woman, past, present, or to come, to have the genius of Shakespeare. He wrote to the papers about it. He also told a lady who applied to him for information that cats do not as a matter of fact go to heaven, though they have, he added, souls of a sort. How much thinking those old gentlemen used to save one! How the borders of ignorance shrank back at their approach! Cats do not go to heaven. Women cannot write the plays of Shakespeare.

Be that as it may, I could not help thinking, as I looked at the works of Shakespeare on the shelf, that the bishop was right at least in this; it would have been impossible, completely and entirely, for any woman to have written the plays of Shakespeare in the age of Shakespeare. Let me imagine, since facts are so hard to come by, what would have happened had Shakespeare had a wonderfully gifted sister, called Judith, let us say. Shakespeare himself went, very probably—his mother was an heiress—to the grammar school, where he may have learnt Latin—Ovid, Virgil and Horace—and the elements of grammar and logic. He was, it is well known, a wild boy who poached rabbits, perhaps shot a deer, and had, rather sooner than he should have done, to marry a woman in the neighbourhood, who bore him a child rather quicker than was right. That escapade sent him to seek his fortune in London. He had, it seemed, a taste for the theatre; he began by holding horses at the stage door. Very soon he got work in the theatre, became a successful actor, and lived at the hub of the universe, meeting everybody, knowing everybody, practising his art on the boards, exercising his wits in the streets, and even getting access to the palace of the queen. Meanwhile his extraordinarily gifted sister, let us suppose, remained at home. She was as adventurous, as imaginative, as agog to see the world as he was. But she was not sent to school. She had no chance of learning grammar and logic, let alone of reading Horace and Virgil. She picked up a book now and then, one of her brother's perhaps, and read a few pages. But then her parents came in and told her to mend the stockings or mind the stew and not moon about with books and papers. They would have spoken sharply but kindly, for they were substantial people who knew the conditions of life for a woman and loved their daughter—indeed, more likely than not she was the apple of her father's eye. Perhaps she scribbled some pages up in an apple loft on the sly, but was careful to hide them or set fire to them. Soon, however, before she was out of her teens, she was to be betrothed to the son of a neighbouring wool-stapler. She cried out that marriage was hateful to her, and for that she was severely beaten by her father. Then he ceased to scold her. He begged her instead not to hurt him, not to shame him in this matter of her marriage. He would give her a chain of beads or a fine petticoat, he said; and there were tears in his eyes. How could she disobey him? How could she break his heart? The force of her own gift alone drove her to it. She made up a small parcel of her belongings, let herself down by a rope one summer's night and took the road to London. She was not seventeen. The birds that sang in the hedge were not more musical than she was. She had the quickest fancy, a gift like her brother's, for the tune of words. Like him, she had a taste for the theatre. She stood at the stage door; she wanted to act, she said. Men laughed in her face. The manager—a fat, loose-lipped man—guffawed. He bellowed something about poodles dancing and women acting—no woman, he said, could possibly be an actress. He hinted—you can imagine what. She could get no training in her craft. Could she even seek her dinner in a tavern or roam the streets at midnight? Yet her genius was for fiction and lusted to feed abundantly upon the lives of men and women and the study of their ways. At last—for she was very young, oddly like Shakespeare the poet in her face, with the same grey eyes and rounded brows—at last Nick Greene the actor-manager took pity on her; she found herself with child by that gentleman and so—who shall measure the heat and violence of the poet's heart when caught and tangled in a woman's body?—killed herself one winter's night and lies buried at some cross-roads where the omnibuses now stop outside the Elephant and Castle.

That, more or less, is how the story would run, I think, if a woman in Shakespeare's day had had Shakespeare's genius. But for my part, I agree with the deceased bishop, if such he was—it is unthinkable that any woman in Shakespeare's day should have had Shakespeare's genius. For genius like Shakespeare's is not born among labouring, uneducated, servile people. It was not born in England among the Saxons and the Britons. It is not born today among the working classes. How, then, could it have been born among women whose work began, according to Professor Trevelyan, almost before they were out of the nursery, who were forced to it by their parents and held to it by all the power of law and custom? Yet genius of a sort must have existed among women as it must have existed among the working classes.

Meaning and Idea

1. What is Woolf's specific thesis about Shakespeare and his imaginary sister? How is that specific thesis indicative of her overall thesis comparing the lives and creative endeavors of men and women? Summarize briefly what that overall thesis says.

2. What is Woolf's opinion of the contrast between scientific and creative works?

3. How do Woolf's references to the "deceased bishop" exemplify her views concerning how men generally think about women? What other specific examples of such thinking does she offer?

4. What is the Elephant and Castle? What does the last line of the third paragraph indicate about Shakespeare's sister's relative importance?

5. Why does Woolf agree that it would have been "unthinkable" for a woman in Elizabethan times to have achieved Shakespeare's genius? How is she using the term *genius*? Is this a conclusion with which she is happy?

Language, Form, Structure

1. Which developmental pattern for a comparison essay does Woolf follow here? How does she balance the two sides of her comparison? Prepare a point-by-point outline of Woolf's comparison between William and "Judith" Shakespeare. What does she say about their comparative schooling? Writing? Marriages? Results of creative impulses?

2. What generally is Woolf's tone in this essay—sorrowful, angry, comic, sarcastic, ironic? Find three examples from the essay which contribute to that tone.

3. Interpret the following lines as a generalization of Woolf's attitude about the relationship between men and women throughout the ages: ". . . at last Nick Greene the actor-manager took pity on her; she found herself with child by that gentleman and so—"

4. Identify the paragraphs which constitute the introduction, body, and conclusion to this essay.

5. Look up dictionary definitions for the following words: perennial; perceptible; askew; incorporeal; poached; escapade; hub; guffawed; betrothed; lusted; servile. Then choose any five and use them in original sentences.

Ideas for Writing

1. Write an essay in which you compare the life and achievements of a famous man with the life and achievements of his imaginary sister. Use the block method of organization, taking care to balance both sections.

2. Write a short essay in which you compare how you and your best friend approach a similar task.

3. Virginia Woolf wrote this piece in the 1920s, whereas Shakespeare wrote in the late-1500s to mid-1600s. How does she make her ideas applicable to twentieth-century life? Do you feel her analysis is relevant to the relations between women and men in the mid-1980s? Explain.

Joseph Conrad
THE SECRET SHARER

Joseph Conrad (1857–1924), who was born in Poland as Jozef Teodor Konrad Nalecz Korzeniowski, did not speak a word of English until he was 21. At the age of 14, he went to sea for the first time as a gunrunner, and by 1884 he was a master mariner in the British Merchant Service (having become a naturalized British citizen in 1886). In all, he spent twenty years at sea all over the globe, surviving shipwrecks and observing the rich details of life which we find in his fiction. Conrad is considered one of the most important cross-over writers from the Victorian to the modern era, and his importance in shaping both the technical and thematic course of modern literature can never be underestimated. Quite popular in his own lifetime, he left a legacy of such works as *The Nigger of "Narcissus"* (1897), *Heart of Darkness* (1899), *Lord Jim* (1900), *Nostromo* (1904), *The Secret Agent* (1907), *Victory* (1915), and a number of short story collections.

Some critics claim that Conrad's psychologically subtle and hauntingly symbolic "The Secret Sharer," published in 1907, is among the most important shapers of the course of modernist fiction. The basis of the overriding comparison—a man versus his "other self"—set the stage for the twentieth-century fascination with split personalities (pathological or not), the struggle to find one's "true self," and the necessity of resolving opposing forces in order to attain freedom. As you read, pay special attention to the intricate, multilevel weaving of the fabric of contrasts and comparisons.

I

*O*n my right hand there were lines of fishing-stakes resembling a mysterious system of half-submerged bamboo fences, incomprehensible in its division of the domain of tropical fishes, and crazy of aspect as if abandoned for ever by some nomad tribe of fishermen now gone to the other end of the ocean; for there was no sign of human habitation as far as the eye could reach. To the left a group of barren islets, suggesting ruins of stone walls, towers, and blockhouses, had its foundations set in a blue sea that itself looked solid, so still and stable did it lie below my feet; even the track of light from the westering sun shone smoothly, without that animated glitter which tells of an imperceptible ripple. And when I turned my head to take a parting glance at the tug which had just left us anchored outside the bar, I saw the straight line of the flat shore joined to the stable sea, edge to edge, with a perfect and unmarked closeness, in one levelled floor half brown, half blue under the enormous dome of the sky. Corresponding in their insignificance to the islets of the sea, two small clumps of trees, one on each side of the only fault in the impeccable joint, marked the mouth of the river Meinam we had just left on the first preparatory stage of our homeward journey; and, far back on the inland level, a larger and loftier mass, the grove surrounding the great Paknam pagoda, was the only thing on which the eye could rest from the vain task of exploring the monotonous sweep of the horizon. Here and there gleams as of a few scattered pieces of silver marked the windings of the great river; and on the nearest of them, just within the bar, the tug steaming right into the land became lost to my sight, hull and funnel and masts, as though the impassive earth had swallowed her up without an effort, without a tremor. My eye followed the light cloud of her smoke, now here, now there, above the plain, according to the devious curves of the stream, but always fainter and farther away, till I lost it at last behind the mitre-shaped hill of the great pagoda. And then I was left alone with my ship, anchored at the head of the Gulf of Siam.

She floated at the starting-point of a long journey, very still in an immense stillness, the shadows of her spars flung far to the eastward by the setting sun. At that moment I was alone on her decks. There was not a sound in her—and around us nothing moved, nothing lived, not a canoe on the water, not a bird in the air, not a cloud in the sky. In this breathless pause at the threshold of a long passage we seemed to be measuring our fitness for a long and arduous enterprise, the appointed task of both our existences to be carried out, far from all human eyes, with only sky and sea for spectators and for judges.

There must have been some glare in the air to interfere with one's sight, because it was only just before the sun left us that my roaming eyes made out beyond the highest ridge of the principal islet of the group something which did away with the solemnity of perfect solitude. The tide of darkness flowed on swiftly; and with tropical suddenness a swarm of stars came out above the shadowy earth, while I lingered yet, my hand resting lightly on my ship's rail as if on the shoulder of a trusted friend. But, with all that multitude of celestial bodies staring down at one, the comfort of quiet communion with her was gone for good. And there were also disturbing sounds by this time—voices, footsteps forward; the steward flitted along the maindeck, a busily ministering spirit; a hand-bell tinkled urgently under the poop-deck. . . .

I found my two officers waiting for me near the supper table, in the lighted cuddy. We sat down at once, and as I helped the chief mate, I said:

"Are you aware that there is a ship anchored inside the islands? I saw her mastheads above the ridge as the sun went down."

He raised sharply his simple face, overcharged by a terrible growth of whisker, and emitted his usual ejaculations: "Bless my soul, sir! You don't say so!"

My second mate was a round-cheeked, silent young man, grave beyond his years, I thought; but as our eyes happened to meet I detected a slight quiver on his lips. I looked down at once. It was not my part to encourage sneering on board my ship. It must be said, too, that I knew very little of my officers. In consequence of certain events of no particular significance, except to myself, I had been appointed to the command only a fortnight before. Neither did I know much of the hands forward. All these people had been together for eighteen months or so, and my position was that of the only stranger on board. I mention this because it has some bearing on what is to follow. But what I felt most was my being a stranger to the ship; and if all the truth must be told, I was somewhat of a stranger to myself. The youngest man on board (barring the second mate), and untried as yet by a position of the fullest responsibility, I was willing to take the adequacy of the others for granted. They had simply to be equal to their tasks; but I wondered how far I should turn out faithful to that ideal conception of one's own personality every man sets up for himself secretly.

Meantime the chief mate, with an almost visible effect of collaboration on the part of his round eyes and frightful whiskers, was trying to evolve a theory of the anchored ship. His dominant trait was to take all things into earnest consideration. He was of a painstaking turn of mind. As he used to say, he "liked to account to himself" for practically everything that came in his way, down to a miserable scorpion he had found in his cabin a week before. The why and the wherefore of that scorpion—how it got on board and came to select his room rather than the pantry (which was a dark place and more what a scorpion would be partial to), and how on earth it managed to drown itself in the inkwell of his writing-desk—had exercised him infinitely. The ship within the islands was much more easily accounted for; and just as we were about to rise from table he made his pronouncement. She was, he doubted not, a ship from home lately arrived. Probably she drew too much water to cross the bar except at the top of spring tides. Therefore she went into that natural harbour to wait for a few days in preference to remaining in an open roadstead.

"That's so," confirmed the second mate, suddenly, in his slightly hoarse voice. "She draws over twenty feet. She's the Liverpool ship *Sephora* with a cargo of coal. Hundred and twenty-three days from Cardiff."

We looked at him in surprise.

"The tugboat skipper told me when he came on board for your letters, sir," explained the young man. "He expects to take her up the river the day after tomorrow."

After thus overwhelming us with the extent of his information he slipped out of the cabin. The mate observed regretfully that he "could not account for that young fellow's whims." What prevented him telling us all about it at once, he wanted to know.

I detained him as he was making a move. For the last two days the crew had had plenty of hard work, and the night before they had very little sleep. I felt painfully that I—a stranger—was doing something unusual when I directed him to let all hands turn in without setting an anchor-watch. I proposed to keep on deck myself till one o'clock or thereabouts. I would get the second mate to relieve me at that hour.

"He will turn out the cook and the steward at four," I concluded, "and then give you a call. Of course at the slightest sign of any sort of wind we'll have the hands up and make a start at once."

He concealed his astonishment. "Very well, sir." Outside the cuddy he put his head in the second mate's door to inform him of my unheard-of caprice to take a five hours' anchor-watch on myself. I heard the other raise his voice incredulously—"What? The Captain himself?" Then a few more murmurs, a door closed, then another. A few moments later I went on deck.

My strangeness, which had made me sleepless, had prompted that unconventional arrangement, as if I had expected in those solitary hours of the night to get on terms with the ship of which I knew nothing, manned by men of whom I knew very little more. Fast alongside a wharf, littered like any ship in port with a tangle of unrelated things, invaded by unrelated shore people, I had hardly seen her yet properly. Now, as she lay cleared for sea, the stretch of her main-deck seemed to me very fine under the stars. Very fine, very roomy for her size, and very inviting. I descended the poop and paced the waist, my mind picturing to myself the coming passage through the Malay Archipelago, down the Indian Ocean, and up the Atlantic. All its phases were familiar enough to me, every characteristic, all the alternatives which were likely to face me on the high seas—everything! . . . except the novel responsibility of command. But I took heart from the reasonable thought that the ship was like other ships, the men like other men, and that the sea was not likely to keep any special surprises expressly for my discomfiture.

Arrived at that comforting conclusion, I bethought myself of a cigar and went below to get it. All was still down there. Everybody at the after end of the ship was sleeping profoundly. I came out again on the quarter-deck, agreeably at ease in my sleeping-suit on that warm breathless night, barefooted, a glowing cigar in my teeth, and, going forward, I was met by the profound silence of the fore end of the ship. Only as I passed the door of the forecastle I heard a deep, quiet, trustful sigh of some sleeper inside. And suddenly I rejoiced in the great security of the sea as compared with the unrest of the land, in my choice of that untempted life presenting no disquieting problems, invested with an elementary moral beauty by the absolute straightforwardness of its appeal and by the singleness of its purpose.

The riding-light in the fore-rigging burned with a clear, untroubled, as if symbolic, flame, confident and bright in the mysterious shades of the night. Passing on my way aft along the other side of the ship, I observed that the rope side-ladder, put over, no doubt, for the master of the tug when he came to fetch away our letters, had not been hauled in as it should have been. I became annoyed at this, for exactitude in small matters is the very soul of discipline. Then I reflected that I had myself peremptorily dismissed my officers from duty, and by my own act had prevented the anchor-watch being formally set and things properly attended to. I asked myself whether it was wise ever to interfere with the established routine of duties even from the kindest of motives. My action might have made me appear eccentric. Goodness only knew how that absurdly whiskered mate would "account" for my conduct, and what the whole ship thought of that informality of their new captain. I was vexed with myself.

Not from compunction certainly, but, as it were mechanically, I proceeded to get the ladder in myself. Now a side-ladder of that sort is a light affair and comes in easily, yet my vigorous tug, which should have brought it flying on board, merely recoiled upon my body in a totally unexpected jerk. What the devil! . . . I was so astounded by the immovableness of that ladder that I remained stock-still, trying to account for it to myself like that imbecile mate of mine. In the end, of course, I put my head over the rail.

The side of the ship made an opaque belt of shadow on the darkling glassy shimmer of the sea. But I saw at once something elongated and pale floating very close to the ladder. Before I could form a guess a faint flash of phosphorescent light, which seemed to issue suddenly from the naked body of a man, flickered in the sleeping water with the elusive, silent play of summer lightning in a night sky. With a gasp I saw revealed to my stare a pair of feet, the long legs, a broad livid back immersed right up to the neck in a greenish cadaverous glow. One hand, awash, clutched the bottom rung of the ladder. He was complete but for the head. A headless corpse! The cigar dropped out of my gaping mouth with a tiny plop and a short hiss quite audible in the absolute stillness of all things under heaven. At that I suppose he raised up his face, a dimly pale oval in the shadow of the ship's side. But even then I could only barely make out down there the shape of his black-haired head. However, it was enough for the horrid, frost-bound sensation which had gripped me about the chest to pass off. The moment of vain exclamations was past, too. I only climbed on the spare spar and leaned over the rail as far as I could, to bring my eyes nearer to that mystery floating alongside.

As he hung by the ladder, like a resting swimmer, the sea-lightning played about his limbs at every stir; and he appeared in it ghastly, silvery, fish-like. He remained as mute as a fish, too. He made no motion to get out of the water, either. It was inconceivable that he should not attempt to come on board, and strangely troubling to suspect that perhaps he did not want to. And my first words were prompted by just that troubled incertitude.

"What's the matter?" I asked in my ordinary tone, speaking down to the face upturned exactly under mine.

"Cramp," it answered, no louder. Then slightly anxious, "I say, no need to call any one."

"I was not going to," I said.

"Are you alone on deck?"

"Yes."

I had somehow the impression that he was on the point of letting go the ladder to swim away beyond my ken—mysterious as he came. But, for the moment, this being appearing as if he had risen from the bottom of the sea (it was certainly the nearest land to the ship) wanted only to know the time. I told him. And he, down there, tentatively:

"I suppose your captain's turned in?"

"I am sure he isn't," I said.

He seemed to struggle with himself, for I heard something like the low, bitter murmur of doubt. "What's the good?" His next words came out with a hesitating effort.

"Look here, my man. Could you call him out quietly?"

I thought the time had come to declare myself.

"*I* am the captain."

I heard a "By Jove!" whispered at the level of the water. The phosphorescence flashed in the swirl of the water all about his limbs, his other hand seized the ladder.

"My name's Leggatt."

The voice was calm and resolute. A good voice. The self-possession of that man had somehow induced a corresponding state in myself. It was very quietly that I remarked:

"You must be a good swimmer."

"Yes. I've been in the water practically since nine o'clock. The question for me now is whether I am to let go this ladder and go on swimming till I sink from exhaustion, or—to come on board here."

I felt this was no mere formula of desperate speech, but a real alternative in the view of a strong soul. I should have gathered from this that he was young; indeed, it is only the young who are ever confronted by such clear issues. But at the time it was pure intuition on my part. A mysterious communication was established already between us two—in the face of that silent, darkened tropical sea. I was young, too; young enough to make no comment. The man in the water began suddenly to climb up the ladder, and I hastened away from the rail to fetch some clothes.

Before entering the cabin I stood still, listening in the lobby at the foot of the stairs. A faint snore came through the closed door of the chief mate's room. The second mate's door was on the hook, but the darkness in there was absolutely soundless. He, too, was young and could sleep like a stone. Remained the steward, but he was not likely to wake up before he was called. I got a sleeping-suit out of my room and, coming back on deck, saw the naked man from the sea sitting on the main-hatch, glimmering white in the darkness, his elbows on his knees and his head in his hands. In a moment he had concealed his damp body in a sleeping-suit of the same grey-stripe pattern as the one I was wearing and followed me like my double on the poop. Together we moved right aft, barefooted, silent.

"What is it?" I asked in a deadened voice, taking the lighted lamp out of the binnacle, and raising it to his face.

"An ugly business."

He had rather regular features; a good mouth; light eyes under somewhat heavy, dark eyebrows; a smooth, square forehead; no growth on his cheeks; a small, brown moustache, and a well-shaped, round chin. His expression was concentrated, meditative, under the inspecting light of the lamp I held up to his face; such as a man thinking hard in solitude might wear. My sleeping-suit was just right for his size. A well-knit young fellow of twenty-five at most. He caught his lower lip with the edge of white, even teeth.

"Yes," I said, replacing the lamp in the binnacle. The warm, heavy tropical night closed upon his head again.

"There's a ship over there," he murmured.

"Yes, I know. The *Sephora*. Did you know of us?"

"Hadn't the slightest idea. I am the mate of her——" He paused and corrected himself. "I should say I *was*."

"Aha! Something wrong?"

"Yes. Very wrong indeed. I've killed a man."

"What do you mean? Just now?"

"No, on the passage. Weeks ago. Thirty-nine south. When I say a man——"

"Fit of temper," I suggested, confidently.

The shadowy, dark head, like mine, seemed to nod imperceptibly above the ghostly grey of my sleeping-suit. It was, in the night, as though I had been faced by my own reflection in the depths of a sombre and immense mirror.

"A pretty thing to have to own up to for a Conway boy," murmured my double, distinctly.

"You're a Conway boy?"

"I am," he said, as if startled. Then, slowly . . . "Perhaps you too——"

It was so; but being a couple of years older I had left before he joined. After a quick interchange of dates a silence fell; and I thought suddenly of my absurd mate with his terrific whiskers and the "Bless my soul—you don't say so" type of intellect. My double gave me an inkling of his thoughts by saying: "My father's a parson in Norfolk. Do you see me before a judge and jury on that charge? For myself I can't see the necessity. There are fellows that an angel from heaven——And I am not that. He was one of those creatures that are just simmering all the time with a silly sort of wickedness. Miserable devils that have no business to live at all. He wouldn't do his duty and wouldn't let anybody else do theirs. But what's the good of talking! You know well enough the sort of ill-conditioned snarling cur——"

He appealed to me as if our experiences had been as identical as our clothes. And I knew well enough the pestiferous danger of such a character where there are no means of legal repression. And I knew well enough also that my double there was no homicidal ruffian. I did not think of asking him for details, and he told me the story roughly in brusque, disconnected sentences. I needed no more. I saw it all going on as though I were myself inside that other sleeping-suit.

"It happened while we were setting a reefed foresail, at dusk. Reefed foresail! You understand the sort of weather. The only sail we had left to keep the ship running; so you may guess what it had been like for days. Anxious sort of job, that. He gave me some of his cursed insolence at the sheet. I tell you I was overdone with this terrific weather that seemed to have no end to it. Terrific, I tell you—and a deep ship. I believe the fellow himself was half crazed with funk. It was no time for gentlemanly reproof, so I turned round and felled him like an ox. He up and at me. We closed just as an awful sea made for the ship. All hands saw it coming and took to the rigging, but I had him by the throat, and went on shaking him like a rat, the men above us yelling, 'Look out! look out!'" Then a crash as if the sky had fallen on my head. They say that for over ten minutes hardly anything was to be seen of the ship—just the three masts and a bit of the forecastle head and of the poop all awash driving along in a smother of foam. It was a miracle that they found us, jammed together behind the forebits. It's clear that I meant business, because I was holding him by the throat still when they picked us up. He was black in the face. It was too much for them. It seems they rushed us aft together, gripped as we were, screaming 'Murder!' like a lot of lunatics, and broke into the cuddy. And the ship running for her life, touch and go all the time, any minute her last in a sea fit to turn your hair grey only a-looking at it. I understand that the skipper, too, started raving like the rest of them. The man had been deprived of sleep for more than a week, and to have this sprung on him at the height of a furious gale nearly drove him out of his mind. I wonder they didn't fling me overboard after getting the carcass of their precious ship-mate out of my fingers. They had rather a job to separate us, I've been told. A sufficiently fierce story to make an old judge and a respectable jury sit up a bit. The first thing I heard when I came to myself was the maddening howling of that endless gale, and on that the voice of the old man. He was hanging on to my bunk, staring into my face out of his sou'wester.

" 'Mr. Leggatt, you have killed a man. You can act no longer as chief mate of this ship.'"

His care to subdue his voice made it sound monotonous. He rested a hand on the end of the skylight to steady himself with, and all that time did not stir a limb, so far as I could see. "Nice little tale for a quiet tea-party," he concluded in the same tone.

One of my hands, too, rested on the end of the skylight; neither did I stir a limb, so far as I knew. We stood less than a foot from each other. It occurred to me that if old "Bless my soul—you don't say so" were to put his head up the companion and catch sight of us, he would think he was seeing double, or imagine himself come upon a scene of weird witchcraft; the strange captain having a quiet confabulation by the wheel with his own grey ghost. I became very much concerned to prevent anything of the sort. I heard the other's soothing undertone.

"My father's a parson in Norfolk," it said. Evidently he had forgotten he had told me this important fact before. Truly a nice little tale.

"You had better slip down into my stateroom now," I said, moving off stealthily. My double followed my movements; our bare feet made no sound; I let him in, closed the door with care, and, after giving a call to the second mate, returned on deck for my relief.

"Not much sign of any wind yet," I remarked when he approached.

"No, sir. Not much," he assented, sleepily, in his hoarse voice, with just enough deference, no more, and barely suppressing a yawn.

"Well, that's all you have to look out for. You have got your orders."

"Yes, sir."

I paced a turn or two on the poop and saw him take up his position face forward with his elbow in the ratlines of the mizzenrigging before I went below. The mate's faint snoring was still going on peacefully. The cuddy lamp was burning over the table on which stood a vase with flowers, a polite attention from the ship's provision merchant—the last flowers we should see for the next three months at the very least. Two bunches of bananas hung from the beam symmetrically, one on each side of the rudder-casing. Everything was as before in the ship—except that two of her captain's sleeping-suits were simultaneously in use, one motionless in the cuddy, the other keeping very still in the captain's stateroom.

It must be explained here that my cabin had the form of the capital letter L the door being within the angle and opening into the short part of the letter. A couch was to the left, the bed-place to the right; my writing-desk and the chronometers' table faced the door. But any one opening it, unless he stepped right inside, had no view of what I call the long (or vertical) part of the letter. It contained some lockers surmounted by a bookcase; and a few clothes, a thick jacket or two, caps, oilskin coat, and such like, hung on hooks. There was at the bottom of that part a door opening into my bathroom, which could be entered also directly from the saloon. But that way was never used.

The mysterious arrival had discovered the advantage of this particular shape. Entering my room, lighted strongly by a big bulkhead lamp swung on gimbals above my writing-desk, I did not see him anywhere till he stepped out quietly from behind the coats hung in the recessed part.

"I heard somebody moving about, and went in there at once," he whispered.

I, too, spoke under my breath.

"Nobody is likely to come in here without knocking and getting permission."

He nodded. His face was thin and the sunburn faded, as though he had been ill. And no wonder. He had been, I heard presently, kept under arrest in his cabin for nearly seven weeks. But there was nothing sickly in his eyes or in his expression. He was not a bit like me, really; yet, as we stood leaning over my bed-place, whispering side by side, with our dark heads together and our backs to the door, anybody bold enough to open it stealthily would have been treated to the uncanny sight of a double captain busy talking in whispers with his other self.

"But all this doesn't tell me how you came to hang on to our side-ladder," I inquired, in the hardly audible murmurs we used, after he had told me something more of the proceedings on board the *Sephora* once the bad weather was over.

"When we sighted Java Head I had had time to think all those matters out several times over. I had six weeks of doing nothing else, and with only an hour or so every evening for a tramp on the quarter-deck."

He whispered, his arms folded on the side of my bed-place, staring through the open port. And I could imagine perfectly the manner of this thinking out—a stubborn if not a steadfast operation; something of which I should have been perfectly incapable.

"I reckoned it would be dark before we closed with the land," he continued, so low that I had to strain my hearing, near as we were to each other, shoulder touching shoulder almost. "So I asked to speak to the old man. He always seemed very sick when he came to see me—as if he could not look me in the face. You know, that foresail saved the ship. She was too deep to have run long under bare poles. And it was I that managed to set it for him. Anyway, he came. When I had him in my cabin—he stood by the door looking at me as if I had the halter round my neck already—I asked him right away to leave my cabin door unlocked at night while the ship was going through Sunda Straits. There would be the Java coast within two or three miles, off Angier Point. I wanted nothing more. I've had a prize for swimming my second year in the Conway."

"I can believe it," I breathed out.

"God only knows why they locked me in every night. To see some of their faces you'd have thought they were afraid I'd go about at night strangling people. Am I a murdering brute? Do I look it? By Jove! if I had been he wouldn't have trusted himself like that into my room. You'll say I might have chucked him aside and bolted out, there and then—it was dark already. Well, no. And for the same reason I wouldn't think of trying to smash the door. There would have been a rush to stop me at the noise, and I did not mean to get into a confounded scrimmage. Somebody else might have got killed—for I would not have broken out only to get chucked back, and I did not want any more of that work. He refused, looking more sick than ever. He was afraid of the men, and also of that old second mate of his who had been sailing with him for years—a grey-headed old humbug; and his steward, too, had been with him devil knows how long—seventeen years or more—a dogmatic sort of loafer who hated me like poison, just because I was the chief mate. No chief mate ever made more than one voyage in the *Sephora,* you know. Those two old chaps ran the ship. Devil only knows what the skipper wasn't afraid of (all his nerve went to pieces altogether in that hellish spell of bad weather we had)—of what the law would do to him—of his wife, perhaps. Oh, yes! she's on board. Though I don't think she would have meddled. She would have been only too glad to have me out of the ship in any way. The 'brand of Cain' business, don't you see. That's all right. I was ready enough to go off wandering on the face of the earth—and that was price enough to pay for an Abel of that sort. Anyhow, he wouldn't listen to me. 'This thing must take its course. I represent the law here.' He was shaking like a leaf. 'So you won't?' 'No!' 'Then I hope you will be able to sleep on that,' I said, and turned my back on him. 'I wonder that *you* can,' cries he, and locks the door.

"Well, after that, I couldn't. Not very well. That was three weeks ago. We have had a slow passage through the Java Sea; drifted about Carimata for ten days. When we anchored here they thought, I suppose, it was all right. The nearest land (and that's five miles) is the ship's destination; the consul would soon set about catching me; and there would have been no object in bolting to these islets there. I don't suppose there's a drop of water on them. I don't know how it was, but to-night that steward, after bringing me my supper, went out to let me eat it, and left the door unlocked. And I ate it—all there was, too. After I had finished I strolled out on the quarter-deck. I don't know that I meant to do anything. A breath of fresh air was all I wanted, I believe. Then a sudden temptation came over me. I kicked off my slippers and was in the water before I had made up my mind fairly. Somebody heard the splash and they raised an awful hullabaloo. 'He's gone! Lower the boats! He's committed suicide! No, he's swimming.' Certainly I was swimming. It's not so easy for a swimmer like me to commit suicide by drowning. I landed on the nearest islet before the boat left the ship's side. I heard them pulling about in the dark, hailing, and so on, but after a bit they gave up. Everything quieted down and the anchorage became as still as death. I sat down on a stone and began to think. I felt certain they would start searching for me at daylight. There was no place to hide on those stony things—and if there had been, what would have been the good? But now I was clear of that ship, I was not going back. So after a while I took off all my clothes, tied them up in a bundle with a stone inside, and dropped them in the deep water on the outer side of that islet. That was suicide enough for me. Let them think what they liked, but I didn't mean to drown myself. I meant to swim till I sank—but that's not the same thing. I struck out for another of these little islands, and it was from that one that I first saw your riding-light. Something to swim for. I went on easily, and on the way I came upon a flat rock a foot or two above water. In the daytime, I dare say, you might make it out with a glass from your poop. I scrambled up on it and rested myself for a bit. Then I made another start. That last spell must have been over a mile."

His whisper was getting fainter and fainter, and all the time he stared straight out through the port-hole, in which there was not even a star to be seen. I had not interrupted him. There was something that made comment impossible in his narrative, or perhaps in himself; a sort of feeling, a quality, which I can't find a name for. And when he ceased, all I found was a futile whisper: "So you swam for our light?"

"Yes—straight for it. It was something to swim for. I couldn't see any stars low down because the coast was in the way, and I couldn't see the land, either. The water was like glass. One might have been swimming in a confounded thousand-feet deep cistern with no place for scrambling out anywhere; but what I didn't like was the notion of swimming round and round like a crazed bullock before I gave out; and as I didn't mean to go back . . . No. Do you see me being hauled back, stark naked, off one of these little islands by the scruff of the neck and fighting like a wild beast? Somebody would have got killed for certain, and I did not want any of that. So I went on. Then your ladder——"

"Why didn't you hail the ship?" I asked, a little louder.

He touched my shoulder lightly. Lazy footsteps came right over our heads and stopped. The second mate had crossed from the other side of the poop and might have been hanging over the rail, for all we knew.

"He couldn't hear us talking—could he?" My double breathed into my very ear, anxiously.

His anxiety was an answer, a sufficient answer, to the question I had put to him. An answer containing all the difficulty of that situation. I closed the porthole quietly, to make sure. A louder word might have been overheard.

"Who's that?" he whispered then.

"My second mate. But I don't know much more of the fellow than you do."

And I told him a little about myself. I had been appointed to take charge while I least expected anything of the sort, not quite a fortnight ago. I didn't know either the ship or the people. Hadn't had the time in port to look about me or size anybody up. And as to the crew, all they knew was that I was appointed to take the ship home. For the rest, I was almost as much of a stranger on board as himself, I said. And at the moment I felt it most acutely. I felt that it would take very little to make me a suspect person in the eyes of the ship's company.

He had turned about meantime; and we, the two strangers in the ship, faced each other in identical attitudes.

"Your ladder——" he murmured, after a silence. "Who'd have thought of finding a ladder hanging over at night in a ship anchored out here! I felt just then a very unpleasant faintness. After the life I've been leading for nine weeks, anybody would have got out of condition. I wasn't capable of swimming round as far as your rudderchains. And, lo and behold! there was a ladder to get hold of. After I gripped it I said to myself, 'What's the good?' When I saw a man's head looking over I thought I would swim away presently and leave him shouting—in whatever language it was. I didn't mind being looked at. I—I liked it. And then you speaking to me so quietly—as if you had expected me—made me hold on a little longer. It had been a confounded lonely time—I don't mean while swimming. I was glad to talk a little to somebody that didn't belong to the *Sephora*. As to asking for the captain, that was a mere impulse. It could have been no use, with all the ship knowing about me and the other people pretty certain to be round here in the morning. I don't know—I wanted to be seen, to talk with somebody, before I went on. I don't know what I would have said. . . . 'Fine night, isn't it?' or something of the sort."

"Do you think they will be round here presently?" I asked with some incredulity.

"Quite likely," he said, faintly.

He looked extremely haggard all of a sudden. His head rolled on his shoulders.

"H'm. We shall see then. Meantime get into that bed," I whispered. "Want help? There."

It was a rather high bed-place with a set of drawers underneath. This amazing swimmer really needed the lift I gave him by seizing his leg. He tumbled in, rolled over on his back, and flung one arm across his eyes. And then, with his face nearly hidden, he must have looked exactly as I used to look in that bed. I gazed upon my other self for a while before drawing across carefully the two green serge curtains which ran on a brass rod. I thought for a moment of pinning them together for greater safety, but I sat down on the couch, and once there I felt unwilling to rise and hunt for a pin. I would do it in a moment. I was extremely tired, in a peculiarly intimate way, by the strain of stealthiness, by the effort of whispering and the general secrecy of this excitement. It was three o'clock by now and I had been on my feet since nine, but I was not sleepy; I could not have gone to sleep. I sat there, fagged out, looking at the curtains, trying to clear my mind of the confused sensation of being in two places at once, and greatly bothered by an exasperating knocking in my head. It was a relief to discover suddenly that it was not in my head at all, but on the outside of the door. Before I could collect myself the words "Come in" were out of my mouth, and the steward entered with a tray, bringing in my morning coffee. I had slept, after all, and I was so frightened that I shouted, "This way! I am here, steward," as though he had been miles away. He put down the tray on the table next the couch and only then said, very quietly, "I can see you are here, sir." I felt him give me a keen look, but I dared not meet his eyes just then. He must have wondered why I had drawn the curtains of my bed before going to sleep on the couch. He went out, hooking the door open as usual.

I heard the crew washing decks above me. I knew I would have been told at once if there had been any wind. Calm, I thought, and I was doubly vexed. Indeed, I felt dual more than ever. The steward reappeared suddenly in the doorway. I jumped up from the couch so quickly that he gave a start.

"What do you want here?"

"Close your port, sir—they are washing decks."

"It is closed," I said, reddening.

"Very well, sir." But he did not move from the doorway and returned my stare in an extraordinary, equivocal manner for a time. Then his eyes wavered, all his expression changed, and in a voice unusually gentle, almost coaxingly:

"May I come in to take the empty cup away, sir?"

"Of course!" I turned my back on him while he popped in and out. Then I unhooked and closed the door and even pushed the bolt. This sort of thing could not go on very long. The cabin was as hot as an oven, too. I took a peep at my double, and discovered that he had not moved, his arm was still over his eyes; but his chest heaved; his hair was wet; his chin glistened with perspiration. I reached over him and opened the port.

"I must show myself on deck," I reflected.

Of course, theoretically, I could do what I liked, with no one to say nay to me within the whole circle of the horizon; but to lock my cabin door and take the key away I did not dare. Directly I put my head out of the companion I saw the group of my two officers, the second mate barefooted, the chief mate in long india-rubber boots, near the break of the poop, and the steward half-way down the poopladder talking to them eagerly. He happened to catch sight of me and dived, the second ran down on the main-deck shouting some order or other, and the chief mate came to meet me, touching his cap.

There was a sort of curiosity in his eye that I did not like. I don't know whether the steward had told them that I was "queer" only, or downright drunk, but I know the man meant to have a good look at me. I watched him coming with a smile which, as he got into point-blank range, took effect and froze his very whiskers. I did not give him time to open his lips.

"Square the yards by lifts and braces before the hands go to breakfast."

It was the first particular order I had given on board that ship; and I stayed on deck to see it executed, too. I had felt the need of asserting myself without loss of time. That sneering young cub got taken down a peg or two on that occasion, and I also seized the opportunity of having a good look at the face of every foremast man as they filed past me to go to the after braces. At breakfast time, eating nothing myself, I presided with such frigid dignity that the two mates were only too glad to escape from the cabin as soon as decency permitted; and all the time the dual working of my mind distracted me almost to the point of insanity. I was constantly watching myself, my secret self, as dependent on my actions as my own personality, sleeping in that bed, behind that door which faced me as I sat at the head of the table. It was very much like being mad, only it was worse because one was aware of it.

I had to shake him for a solid minute, but when at last he opened his eyes it was in the full possession of his senses, with an inquiring look.

"All's well so far," I whispered. "Now you must vanish into the bathroom."

He did so, as noiseless as a ghost, and then I rang for the steward, and facing him boldly, directed him to tidy up my stateroom while I was having my bath—"and be quick about it." As my tone admitted of no excuses, he said, "Yes, sir," and ran off to fetch his dust-pan and brushes. I took a bath and did most of my dressing, splashing, and whistling softly for the steward's edification, while the secret sharer of my life stood drawn up bolt upright in that little space, his face looking very sunken in daylight, his eyelids lowered under the stern, dark line of his eyebrows drawn together by a slight frown.

When I left him there to go back to my room the steward was finishing dusting. I sent for the mate and engaged him in some insignificant conversation. It was, as it were, trifling with the terrific character of his whiskers; but my object was to give him an opportunity for a good look at my cabin. And then I could at last shut, with a clear conscience, the door of my stateroom and get my double back into the recessed part. There was nothing else for it. He had to sit still on a small folding stool, half smothered by the heavy coats hanging there. We listened to the steward going into the bathroom out of the saloon, filling the water-bottles there, scrubbing the bath, setting things to rights, whisk, bang, clatter—out again into the saloon—turn the key—click. Such was my scheme for keeping my second self invisible. Nothing better could be contrived under the circumstances. And there we sat; I at my writing-desk ready to appear busy with some papers, he behind me out of sight of the door. It would not have been prudent to talk in daytime; and I could not have stood the excitement of that queer sense of whispering to myself. Now and then, glancing over my shoulder, I saw him far back there, sitting rigidly on the low stool, his bare feet close together, his arms folded, his head hanging on his breast—and perfectly still. Anybody would have taken him for me.

I was fascinated by it myself. Every moment I had to glance over my shoulder. I was looking at him when a voice outside the door said:

"Beg pardon, sir."

"Well!" . . . I kept my eyes on him, and so when the voice outside the door announced, "There's ship's boat coming our way, sir," I saw him give a start—the first movement he had made for hours. But he did not raise his bowed head.

"All right. Get the ladder over."

I hesitated. Should I whisper something to him? But what? His immobility seemed to have been never disturbed. What could I tell him he did not know already? . . . Finally I went on deck.

II

The skipper of the *Sephora* had a thin red whisker all round his face, and the sort of complexion that goes with hair of that colour; also the particular, rather smeary shade of blue in the eyes. He was not exactly a showy figure; his shoulders were high, his stature but middling—one leg slightly more bandy than the other. He shook hands, looking vaguely around. A spiritless tenacity was his main characteristic, I judged. I behaved with a politeness which seemed to disconcert him. Perhaps he was shy. He mumbled to me as if he were ashamed of what he was saying; gave his name (it was something like Archbold—but at this distance of years I hardly am sure), his ship's name, and a few other particulars of that sort, in the manner of a criminal making a reluctant and doleful confession. He had had terrible weather on the passage out—terrible—terrible—wife aboard, too.

By this time we were seated in the cabin and the steward brought in a tray with a bottle and glasses. "Thanks! No." Never took liquor. Would have some water, though. He drank two tumblerfuls. Terrible thirsty work. Ever since daylight had been exploring the islands round his ship.

"What was that for—fun?" I asked, with an appearance of polite interest.

"No!" He sighed. "Painful duty."

As he persisted in his mumbling and I wanted my double to hear every word, I hit upon the notion of informing him that I regretted to say I was hard of hearing.

"Such a young man, too!" he nodded, keeping his smeary blue, unintelligent eyes fastened upon me. "What was the cause of it—some disease?" he inquired, without the least sympathy and as if he thought that, if so, I'd got no more than I deserved.

"Yes; disease," I admitted in a cheerful tone which seemed to shock him. But my point was gained, because he had to raise his voice to give me his tale. It is not worth while to record that version. It was just over two months since all this had happened, and he had thought so much about it that he seemed completely muddled as to its bearings, but still immensely impressed.

"What would you think of such a thing happening on board your own ship? I've had the *Sephora* for these fifteen years. I am a well-known shipmaster."

He was densely distressed—and perhaps I should have sympathised with him if I had been able to detach my mental vision from the unsuspected sharer of my cabin as though he were my second self. There he was on the other side of the bulkhead, four or five feet from us, no more, as we sat in the saloon. I looked politely at Captain Archbold (if that was his name), but it was the other I saw, in a grey sleeping-suit, seated on a low stool, his bare feet close together, his arms folded, and every word said between us falling into the ears of his dark head bowed on his chest.

"I have been at sea now, man and boy, for seven-and-thirty years, and I've never heard of such a thing happening in an English ship. And that it should be my ship. Wife on board, too."

I was hardly listening to him.

"Don't you think," I said, "that the heavy sea which, you told me, came aboard just then might have killed the man? I have seen the sheer weight of a sea kill a man very neatly, by simply breaking his neck."

"Good God!" he uttered, impressively, fixing his smeary blue eyes on me. "The sea! No man killed by the sea ever looked like that." He seemed positively scandalised at my suggestion. And as I gazed at him, certainly not prepared for anything original on his part, he advanced his head close to mine and thrust his tongue out at me so suddenly that I couldn't help starting back.

After scoring over my calmness in this graphic way he nodded wisely. If I had seen the sight, he assured me, I would never forget it as long as I lived. The weather was too bad to give the corpse a proper sea burial. So next day at dawn they took it up on the poop, covering its face with a bit of bunting; he read a short prayer, and then, just as it was, in its oilskins and long boots, they launched it amongst those mountainous seas that seemed ready every moment to swallow up the ship herself and the terrified lives on board of her.

"That reefed foresail saved you," I threw in.

"Under God—it did," he exclaimed fervently. "It was by a special mercy, I firmly believe, that it stood some of those hurricane squalls."

"It was the setting of that sail which——" I began.

"God's own hand in it," he interrupted me. "Nothing less could have done it. I don't mind telling you that I hardly dared give the order. It seemed impossible that we could touch anything without losing it, and then our last hope would have been gone."

The terror of that gale was on him yet. I let him go on for a bit, then said, casually—as if returning to a minor subject:

"You were very anxious to give up your mate to the shore people, I believe?"

He was. To the law. His obscure tenacity on that point had in it something incomprehensible and a little awful; something, as it were, mystical, quite apart from his anxiety that he should not be suspected of "countenancing any doings of that sort." Seven-and-thirty virtuous years at sea, of which over twenty of immaculate command, and the last fifteen in the *Sephora,* seemed to have laid him under some pitiless obligation.

"And you know," he went on, groping shamefacedly amongst his feelings, "I did not engage that young fellow. His people had some interest with my owners. I was in a way forced to take him on. He looked very smart, very gentlemanly, and all that. But do you know—I never liked him, somehow. I am a plain man. You see, he wasn't exactly the sort for the chief mate of a ship like the *Sephora.*"

I had become so connected in thoughts and impressions with the secret sharer of my cabin that I felt as if I, personally, were being given to understand that I, too, was not the sort that would have done for the chief mate of a ship like the *Sephora.* I had no doubt of it in my mind.

"Not at all the style of man. You understand," he insisted, super-fluously, looking hard at me.

I smiled urbanely. He seemed at a loss for a while.

"I suppose I must report a suicide."

"Beg pardon?"

"Sui-cide! That's what I'll have to write to my owners directly I get in."

"Unless you manage to recover him before to-morrow," I assented, dispassionately. . . . "I mean, alive."

He mumbled something which I really did not catch, and I turned my ear to him in a puzzled manner. He fairly bawled:

"The land—I say, the mainland is at least seven miles off my anchorage."

"About that."

My lack of excitement, of curiosity, of surprise, of any sort of pronounced interest, began to arouse his distrust. But except for the felicitous pretence of deafness I had not tried to pretend anything. I had felt utterly incapable of playing the part of ignorance properly, and therefore was afraid to try. It is also certain that he had brought some ready-made suspicions with him, and that he viewed my politeness as a strange and unnatural phenomenon. And yet how else could I have received him? Not heartily! That was impossible for psychological reasons, which I need not state here. My only object was to keep off his inquiries. Surlily? Yes, but surliness might have provoked a point-blank question. From its novelty to him and from its nature, punctilious courtesy was the manner best calculated to restrain the man. But there was the danger of his breaking through my defence bluntly. I could not, I think, have met him by a direct lie, also for psychological (not moral) reasons. If he had only known how afraid I was of his putting my feeling of identity with the other to the test! But, strangely enough—(I thought of it only afterwards)—I believe that he was not a little disconcerted by the reverse side of that weird situation, by something in me that reminded him of the man he was seeking—suggested a mysterious similitude to the young fellow he had distrusted and disliked from the first.

However that might have been, the silence was not very prolonged. He took another oblique step.

"I reckon I had no more than a two-mile pull to your ship. Not a bit more."

"And quite enough, too, in this awful heat," I said.

Another pause full of mistrust followed. Necessity, they say, is mother of invention, but fear, too, is not barren of ingenious suggestions. And I was afraid he would ask me point-blank for news of my other self.

"Nice little saloon, isn't it?" I remarked, as if noticing for the first time the way his eyes roamed from one closed door to the other. "And very well fitted out, too. Here, for instance," I continued, reaching over the back of my seat negligently and flinging the door open, "is my bath-room."

He made an eager movement, but hardly gave it a glance. I got up, shut the door of the bath-room, and invited him to have a look around, as if I were very proud of my accommodation. He had to rise and be shown around, but he went through the business without any raptures whatever.

"And now we'll have a look at my stateroom," I declared, in a voice as loud as I dared to make it, crossing the cabin to the starboard side with purposely heavy steps.

He followed me in and gazed around. My intelligent double had vanished. I played my part.

"Very convenient—isn't it?"

"Very nice. Very comf . . . " He didn't finish and went out brusquely as if to escape from some unrighteous wiles of mine. But it was not to be. I had been too frightened not to feel vengeful; I felt I had him on the run, and I meant to keep him on the run. My polite insistence must have had something menacing in it, because he gave in suddenly. And I did not let him off a single item; mate's room, pantry, storerooms, the very sail-locker which was also under the poop—he had to look into them all. When at last I showed him out on the quarter-deck he drew a long, spiritless sigh, and mumbled dismally that he must really be going back to his ship now. I desired my mate, who had joined us, to see to the captain's boat.

The man of whiskers gave a blast on the whistle which he used to wear hanging round his neck, and yelled, "*Sephora*'s away!" My double down there in my cabin must have heard, and certainly could not feel more relieved than I. Four fellows came running out from somewhere forward and went over the side, while my own men, appearing on deck too, lined the rail. I escorted my visitor to the gangway ceremoniously, and nearly overdid it. He was a tenacious beast. On the very ladder he lingered, and in that unique, guiltily conscientious manner of sticking to the point:

"I say . . . you . . . you don't think that——"

I covered his voice loudly:

"Certainly not. . . . I am delighted. Goodbye."

I had an idea of what he meant to say, and just saved myself by the privilege of defective hearing. He was too shaken generally to insist, but my mate, close witness of that parting, looked mystified and his face took on a thoughtful cast. As I did not want to appear as if I wished to avoid all communication with my officers, he had the opportunity to address me.

"Seems a very nice man. His boat's crew told our chaps a very extraordinary story, if what I am told by the steward is true. I suppose you had it from the captain, sir?"

"Yes. I had a story from the captain."

"A very horrible affair—isn't it, sir?"

"It is."

"Beats all these tales we hear about murders in Yankee ships."

"I don't think it beats them. I don't think it resembles them in the least."

"Bless my soul—you don't say so! But of course I've no acquaintance whatever with American ships, not I, so I couldn't go against your knowledge. It's horrible enough for me . . . But the queerest part is that those fellows seemed to have some idea the man was hidden aboard here. They had really. Did you ever hear of such a thing?"

"Preposterous—isn't it?"

We were walking to and fro athwart the quarter-deck. No one of the crew forward could be seen (the day was Sunday), and the mate pursued:

"There was some little dispute about it. Our chaps took offence. 'As if we would harbour a thing like that,' they said. 'Wouldn't you like to look for him in our coal-hole?' Quite a tiff. But they made it up in the end. I suppose he did drown himself. Don't you, sir?"

"I don't suppose anything."

"You have no doubt in the matter, sir?"

"None whatever."

I left him suddenly. I felt I was producing a bad impression, but with my double down there it was most trying to be on deck. And it was almost as trying to be below. Altogether a nerve-trying situation. But on the whole I felt less torn in two when I was with him. There was no one in the whole ship whom I dared take into my confidence. Since the hands had got to know his story, it would have been impossible to pass him off for any one else, and an accidental discovery was to be dreaded now more than ever. . . .

The steward being engaged in laying the table for dinner, we could talk only with our eyes when I first went down. Later in the afternoon we had a cautious try at whispering. The Sunday quietness of the ship was against us; the stillness of air and water around her was against us; the elements, the men were against us—everything was against us in our secret partnership; time itself—for this could not go on forever. The very trust in Providence was, I suppose, denied to his guilt. Shall I confess that this thought cast me down very much? And as to the chapter of accidents which counts for so much in the book of success, I could only hope that it was closed. For what favourable accident could be expected?

"Did you hear everything?" were my first words as soon as we took up our position side by side, leaning over my bed-place.

He had. And the proof of it was his earnest whisper, "The man told you he hardly dared to give the order."

I understood the reference to be to that saving foresail.

"Yes. He was afraid of it being lost in the setting."

"I assure you he never gave the order. He may think he did, but he never gave it. He stood there with me on the break of the poop after the maintopsail blew away, and whimpered about our last hope—positively whimpered about it and nothing else—and the night coming on! To hear one's skipper go on like that in such weather was enough to drive any fellow out of his mind. It worked me up into a sort of desperation. I just took it into my own hands and went away from him, boiling, and——But what's the use telling you? *You* know! . . . Do you think that if I had not been pretty fierce with them I should have got the men to do anything? Not it! The bo's'n perhaps? Perhaps! It wasn't a heavy sea—it was a sea gone mad! I suppose the end of the world will be something like that; and a man may have the heart to see it coming once and be done with it—but to have to face it day after day——I don't blame anybody. I was precious little better than the rest. Only—I was an officer of that old coal-wagon, anyhow——"

"I quite understand," I conveyed that sincere assurance into his ear. He was out of breath with whispering; I could hear him pant slightly. It was all very simple. The same strung-up force which had given twenty-four men a chance, at least, for their lives, had, in a sort of recoil, crushed an unworthy mutinous existence.

But I had no leisure to weigh the merits of the matter—footsteps in the saloon, a heavy knock. "There's enough wind to get under way with, sir." Here was the call of a new claim upon my thoughts and even upon my feelings.

"Turn the hands up," I cried through the door. "I'll be on deck directly."

I was going out to make the acquaintance of my ship. Before I left the cabin our eyes met—the eyes of the only two strangers on board. I pointed to the recessed part where the little camp-stool awaited him and laid my finger on my lips. He made a gesture—somewhat vague—a little mysterious, accompanied by a faint smile, as if of regret.

This is not the place to enlarge upon the sensations of a man who feels for the first time a ship move under his feet to his own independent word.

In my case they were not unalloyed. I was not wholly alone with my command; for there was that stranger in my cabin. Or rather, I was not completely and wholly with her. Part of me was absent. That mental feeling of being in two places at once affected me physically as if the mood of secrecy had penetrated my very soul. Before an hour had elapsed since the ship had begun to move, having occasion to ask the mate (he stood by my side) to take a compass bearing of the Pagoda, I caught myself reaching up to his ear in whispers. I say I caught myself, but enough had escaped to startle the man. I can't describe it otherwise than by saying that he shied. A grave, preoccupied manner, as though he were in possession of some perplexing intelligence, did not leave him henceforth. A little later I moved away from the rail to look at the compass with such a stealthy gait that the helmsman noticed it—and I could not help noticing the unusual roundness of his eyes. These are trifling instances, though it's to no commander's advantage to be suspected of ludicrous eccentricities. But I was also more seriously affected. There are to a seaman certain words, gestures, that should in given conditions come as naturally, as instinctively as the winking of a menaced eye. A certain order should spring on to his lips without thinking; a certain sign should get itself made, so to speak, without reflection. But all unconscious alertness had abandoned me. I had to make an effort of will to recall myself back (from the cabin) to the conditions of the moment. I felt that I was appearing an irresolute commander to those people who were watching me more or less critically.

And, besides, there were the scares. On the second day out, for instance, coming off the deck in the afternoon (I had straw slippers on my bare feet) I stopped at the open pantry door and spoke to the steward. He was doing something there with his back to me. At the sound of my voice he nearly jumped out of his skin, as the saying is, and incidentally broke a cup.

"What on earth's the matter with you?" I asked, astonished.

He was extremely confused. "Beg your pardon, sir. I made sure you were in your cabin."

"You see I wasn't."

"No, sir. I could have sworn I had heard you moving in there not a moment ago. It's most extraordinary . . . very sorry, sir."

I passed on with an inward shudder. I was so identified with my secret double that I did not even mention the fact in those scanty, fearful whispers we exchanged. I suppose he had made some slight noise of some kind or other. It would have been miraculous if he hadn't at one time or another. And yet, haggard as he appeared, he looked always perfectly self-controlled, more than calm—almost invulnerable. On my suggestion he remained almost entirely in the bathroom, which, upon the whole, was the safest place. There could be really no shadow of an excuse for any one ever wanting to go in there, once the steward had done with it. It was a very tiny place. Sometimes he reclined on the floor, his legs bent, his head sustained on one elbow. At others I would find him on the campstool, sitting in his grey sleeping-suit and with his cropped dark hair like a patient, unmoved convict. At night I would smuggle him into my bed-place, and we would whisper together, with the regular footfalls of the officer of the watch passing and repassing over our heads. It was an infinitely miserable time. It was lucky that some tins of fine preserves were stowed in a locker in my stateroom; hard bread I could always get hold of; and so he lived on stewed chicken, paté de foie gras, asparagus, cooked oysters, sardines—on all sorts of abominable sham delicacies out of tins. My early morning coffee he always drank; and it was all I dared do for him in that respect.

Every day there was the horrible manoeuvring to go through so that my room and then the bath-room should be done in the usual way. I came to hate the sight of the steward, to abhor the voice of that harmless man. I felt that it was he who would bring on the disaster of discovery. It hung like a sword over our heads.

The fourth day out, I think (we were then working down the east side of the Gulf of Siam, tack for tack, in light winds and smooth water)—the fourth day, I say, of this miserable juggling with the unavoidable, as we sat at our evening meal, that man, whose slightest movement I dreaded, after putting down the dishes ran up on deck busily. This could not be dangerous. Presently he came down again; and then it appeared that he had remembered a coat of mine which I had thrown over a rail to dry after having been wetted in a shower which had passed over the ship in the afternoon. Sitting stolidly at the head of the table I became terrified at the sight of the garment on his arm. Of course he made for my door. There was no time to lose.

"Steward," I thundered. My nerves were so shaken that I could not govern my voice and conceal my agitation. This was the sort of thing that made my terrifically whiskered mate tap his forehead with his forefinger. I had detected him using that gesture while talking on deck with a confidential air to the carpenter. It was too far to hear a word, but I had no doubt that this pantomime could only refer to the strange new captain.

"Yes, sir," the pale-faced steward turned resignedly to me. It was this maddening course of being shouted at, checked without rhyme or reason, arbitrarily chased out of my cabin, suddenly called into it, sent flying out of his pantry on incomprehensible errands, that accounted for the growing wretchedness of his expression.

"Where are you going with that coat?"

"To your room, sir."

"Is there another shower coming?"

"I'm sure I don't know, sir. Shall I go up again and see, sir?"

"No! never mind."

My object was attained, as of course my other self in there would have heard everything that passed. During this interlude my two officers never raised their eyes off their respective plates; but the lip of that confounded cub, the second mate, quivered visibly.

I expected the steward to hook my coat on and come out at once. He was very slow about it; but I dominated my nervousness sufficiently not to shout after him. Suddenly I became aware (it could be heard plainly enough) that the fellow for some reason or other was opening the door of the bath-room. It was the end. The place was literally not big enough to swing a cat in. My voice died in my throat and I went stony all over. I expected to hear a yell of surprise and terror, and made a movement, but had not the strength to get on my legs. Everything remained still. Had my second self taken the poor wretch by the throat? I don't know what I could have done next moment if I had not seen the steward come out of my room, close the door, and then stand quietly by the sideboard.

"Saved," I thought. "But, no! Lost! Gone! He was gone!"

I laid my knife and fork down and leaned back in my chair. My head swam. After a while, when sufficiently recovered to speak in a steady voice, I instructed my mate to put the ship round at eight o'clock himself.

"I won't come on deck," I went on. "I think I'll turn in, and unless the wind shifts I don't want to be disturbed before midnight. I feel a bit seedy."

"You did look middling bad a little while ago," the chief mate remarked without showing any great concern.

They both went out, and I stared at the steward clearing the table. There was nothing to be read on that wretched man's face. But why did he avoid my eyes, I asked myself. Then I thought I should like to hear the sound of his voice.

"Steward!"

"Sir!" Startled as usual.

"Where did you hang up that coat?"

"In the bath-room, sir." The usual anxious tone. "It's not quite dry yet, sir."

For some time longer I sat in the cuddy. Had my double vanished as he had come? But of his coming there was an explanation, whereas his disappearance would be inexplicable . . . I went slowly into my dark room, shut the door, lighted the lamp, and for a time dared not turn round. When at last I did I saw him standing bolt-upright in the narrow recessed part. It would not be true to say I had a shock, but an irresistible doubt of his bodily existence flitted through my mind. Can it be, I asked myself, that he is not visible to other eyes than mine? It was like being haunted. Motionless, with a grave face, he raised his hands slightly at me in a gesture which meant clearly, "Heavens! what a narrow escape!" Narrow indeed. I think I had come creeping quietly as near insanity as any man who has not actually gone over the border. That gesture restrained me, so to speak.

The mate with the terrific whiskers was now putting the ship on the other tack. In the moment of profound silence which follows upon the hands going to their stations I heard on the poop his raised voice: "Hard alee!" and the distant shout of the order repeated on the maindeck. The sails, in that light breeze, made but a faint fluttering noise. It ceased. The ship was coming round slowly; I held my breath in the renewed stillness of expectation; one wouldn't have thought that there was a single living soul on her decks. A sudden brisk shout, "Mainsail haul!" broke the spell, and in the noisy cries and rush overhead of the men running away with the main-brace we two, down in my cabin, came together in our usual position by the bed-place.

He did not wait for my question. "I heard him fumbling here and just managed to squat myself down in the path," he whispered to me. "The fellow only opened the door and put his arm in to hang the coat up. All the same——"

"I never thought of that," I whispered back, even more appalled than before at the closeness of the shave, and marvelling at that something unyielding in his character which was carrying him through so finely. There was no agitation in his whisper. Whoever was being driven distracted, it was not he. He was sane. And the proof of his sanity was continued when he took up the whispering again.

"It would never do for me to come to life again."

It was something that a ghost might have said. But what he was alluding to was his old captain's reluctant admission of the theory of suicide. It would obviously serve his turn—if I had understood at all the view which seemed to govern the unalterable purpose of his action.

"You must maroon me as soon as ever you can get amongst these islands off the Cambodge shore," he went on.

"Maroon you! We are not living in a boy's adventure tale," I protested. His scornful whispering took me up.

"We aren't indeed! There's nothing of a boy's tale in this. But there's nothing else for it. I want no more. You don't suppose I am afraid of what can be done to me? Prison or gallows or whatever they may please. But you don't see me coming back to explain such things to an old fellow in a wig and twelve respectable tradesmen, do you? What can they know whether I am guilty or not—or of *what* I am guilty, either? That's my affair. What does the Bible say? 'Driven off the face of the earth.' Very well. I am off the face of the earth now. As I came at night so I shall go."

"Impossible!" I murmured. "You can't."

"Can't? . . . Not naked like a soul on the Day of Judgment. I shall freeze on to this sleeping-suit. The Last Day is not yet—and . . . you have understood thoroughly. Didn't you?"

I felt suddenly ashamed of myself. I may say truly that I understood—
and my hesitation in letting that man swim away from my ship's side had
been a mere sham sentiment, a sort of cowardice.

"It can't be done now till next night," I breathed out. "The ship is on
the off-shore tack and the wind may fail us."

"As long as I know that you understand," he whispered. "But of
course you do. It's a great satisfaction to have got somebody to understand. You seem to have been there on purpose." And in the same
whisper, as if we two whenever we talked had to say things to each other
which were not fit for the world to hear, he added, "It's very wonderful."

We remained side by side talking in our secret way—but sometimes
silent or just exchanging a whispered word or two at long intervals. And
as usual he stared through the port. A breath of wind came now and again
into our faces. The ship might have been moored in dock, so gently and on
an even keel she slipped through the water, that did not murmur even at
our passage, shadowy and silent like a phantom sea.

At midnight I went on deck, and to my mate's great surprise put the
ship round on the other tack. His terrible whiskers flitted round me in
silent criticism. I certainly should not have done it if it had been only a
question of getting out of that sleepy gulf as quickly as possible. I believe
he told the second mate, who relieved him, that it was a great want of
judgment. The other only yawned. That intolerable cub shuffled about so
sleepily and lolled against the rails in such a slack, improper fashion that I
came down on him sharply.

"Aren't you properly awake yet?"

"Yes, sir! I am awake."

"Well, then, be good enough to hold yourself as if you were. And keep
a look-out. If there's any current we'll be closing with some islands before
daylight."

The east side of the gulf is fringed with islands, some solitary, others in
groups. On the blue background of the high coast they seem to float on
silvery patches of calm water, arid and grey, or dark green and rounded
like clumps of evergreen bushes, with the larger ones, a mile or two long,
showing the outlines of ridges, ribs of grey rock under the dank mantle of
matted leafage. Unknown to trade, to travel, almost to geography, the
manner of life they harbour is an unsolved secret. There must be villages—settlements of fishermen at least—on the largest of them, and
some communication with the world is probably kept up by native craft.
But all that forenoon, as we headed for them, fanned along by the faintest
of breezes, I saw no sign of man or canoe in the field of the telescope I
kept on pointing at the scattered group.

At noon I gave no orders for a change of course, and the mate's
whiskers became much concerned and seemed to be offering themselves
unduly to my notice. At last I said:

"I am going to stand right in. Quite in—as far as I can take her."

The stare of extreme surprise imparted an air of ferocity also to his eyes, and he looked truly terrific for a moment.

"We're not doing well in the middle of the gulf," I continued, casually. "I am going to look for the land breezes to-night."

"Bless my soul! Do you mean, sir, in the dark amongst the lot of all them islands and reefs and shoals?"

"Well—if there are any regular land breezes at all on this coast one must get close inshore to find them, mustn't one?"

"Bless my soul!" he exclaimed again under his breath. All that afternoon he wore a dreamy, contemplative appearance which in him was a mark of perplexity. After dinner I went into my stateroom as if I meant to take some rest. There we two bent our dark heads over a half-unrolled chart lying on my bed.

"There," I said. "It's got to be Koh-ring. I've been looking at it ever since sunrise. It has got two hills and a low point. It must be inhabited. And on the coast opposite there is what looks like the mouth of a biggish river—with some town, no doubt, not far up. It's the best chance for you that I can see."

"Anything. Koh-ring let it be."

He looked thoughtfully at the chart as if surveying chances and distances from a lofty height—and following with his eyes his own figure wandering on the blank land of Cochin-China, and then passing off that piece of paper clean out of sight into uncharted regions. And it was as if the ship had two captains to plan her course for her. I had been so worried and restless running up and down that I had not had the patience to dress that day. I had remained in my sleeping-suit, with straw slippers and a soft floppy hat. The closeness of the heat in the gulf had been most oppressive, and the crew were used to see me wandering in that airy attire.

"She will clear the south point as she heads now," I whispered into his ear. "Goodness only knows when, though, but certainly after dark. I'll edge her in to half a mile, as far as I may be able to judge in the dark——"

"Be careful," he murmured, warningly—and I realised suddenly that all my future, the only future for which I was fit, would perhaps go irretrievably to pieces in any mishap to my first command.

I could not stop a moment longer in the room. I motioned him to get out of sight and made my way on the poop. That unplayful cub had the watch. I walked up and down for a while thinking things out, then beckoned him over.

"Send a couple of hands to open the two quarter-deck ports," I said, mildly.

He actually had the impudence, or else so forgot himself in his wonder at such an incomprehensible order, as to repeat:

"Open the quarter-deck ports! What for, sir?"

"The only reason you need concern yourself about is because I tell you to do so. Have them opened wide and fastened properly."

He reddened and went off, but I believe made some jeering remark to the carpenter as to the sensible practice of ventilating a ship's quarter-deck. I know he popped into the mate's cabin to impart the fact to him because the whiskers came on deck, as it were by chance, and stole glances at me from below—for signs of lunacy or drunkenness, I suppose.

A little before supper, feeling more restless than ever, I rejoined, for a moment, my second self. And to find him sitting so quietly was surprising, like something against nature, inhuman.

I developed my plan in a hurried whisper.

"I shall stand in as close as I dare and then put her round. I will presently find means to smuggle you out of here into the sail-locker, which communicates with the lobby. But there is an opening, a sort of square for hauling the sails out, which gives straight on the quarter-deck and which is never closed in fine weather, so as to give air to the sails. When the ship's way is deadened in stays and all the hands are aft at the main-braces you will have a clear road to slip out and get overboard through the open quarter-deck port. I've had them both fastened up. Use a rope's end to lower yourself into the water so as to avoid a splash—you know. It could be heard and cause some beastly complication."

He kept silent for a while, then whispered, "I understand."

"I won't be there to see you go," I began with an effort. "The rest . . . I only hope I have understood, too."

"You have. From first to last"—and for the first time there seemed to be a faltering, something strained in his whisper. He caught hold of my arm, but the ringing of the supper bell made me start. He didn't, though; he only released his grip.

After supper I didn't come below again till well past eight o'clock. The faint, steady breeze was loaded with dew; and the wet, darkened sails held all there was of propelling power in it. The night, clear and starry, sparkled darkly, and the opaque, lightless patches shifting slowly against the low stars were the drifting islets. On the port bow there was a big one more distant and shadowily imposing by the great space of sky it eclipsed.

On opening the door I had a back view of my very own self looking at a chart. He had come out of the recess and was standing near the table.

"Quite dark enough," I whispered.

He stepped back and leaned against my bed with a level, quiet glance. I sat on the couch. We had nothing to say to each other. Over our heads the officer of the watch moved here and there. Then I heard him move quickly. I knew what that meant. He was making for the companion; and presently his voice was outside my door.

"We are drawing in pretty fast, sir. Land looks rather close."

"Very well," I answered. "I am coming on deck directly."

I waited till he was gone out of the cuddy, then rose. My double moved too. The time had come to exchange our last whispers, for neither of us was ever to hear each other's natural voice.

"Look here!" I opened a drawer and took out three sovereigns. "Take this anyhow. I've got six and I'd give you the lot, only I must keep a little money to buy some fruit and vegetables for the crew from native boats as we go through Sunda Straights."

He shook his head.

"Take it," I urged him, whispering desperately. "No one can tell what——"

He smiled and slapped meaningly the only pocket of the sleeping-jacket. It was not safe, certainly. But I produced a large old silk hand-kerchief of mine, and tying the three pieces of gold in a corner, pressed it on him. He was touched, I suppose, because he took it at last and tied it quickly round his waist under the jacket, on his bare skin.

Our eyes met; several seconds elapsed, till, our glances still mingled, I extended my hand and turned the lamp out. Then I passed through the cuddy, leaving the door of my room wide open. . . . "Steward!"

He was still lingering in the pantry in the greatness of his zeal, giving a rub-up to a plated cruet stand the last thing before going to bed. Being careful not to wake up the mate, whose room was opposite, I spoke in an undertone.

He looked round anxiously. "Sir!"

"Can you get me a little hot water from the galley?"

"I am afraid, sir, the galley fire's been out for some time now."

"Go and see."

He flew up the stairs.

"Now," I whispered, loudly, into the saloon—too loudly, perhaps, but I was afraid I couldn't make a sound. He was by my side in an instant—the double captain slipped past the stairs—through a tiny dark passage . . . a sliding door. We were in the sail-locker, scrambling on our knees over the sails. A sudden thought struck me. I saw myself wandering barefooted, bareheaded, the sun beating on my dark poll. I snatched off my floppy hat and tried hurriedly in the dark to ram it on my other self. He dodged and fended off silently. I wonder what he thought had come to me before he understood and suddenly desisted. Our hands met gropingly, lingered united in a steady, motionless clasp for a second. . . . No word was breathed by either of us when they separated.

I was standing quietly by the pantry door when the steward returned.

"Sorry, sir. Kettle barely warm. Shall I light the spirit-lamp?"

"Never mind."

I came out on deck slowly. It was now a matter of conscience to shave the land as close as possible—for now he must go overboard whenever the ship was put in stays. Must! There could be no going back for him. After a moment I walked over to leeward and my heart flew into my mouth at the nearness of the land on the bow. Under any other circumstances I would not have held on a minute longer. The second mate had followed me anxiously.

I looked on till I felt I could command my voice.

"She will weather," I said then in a quiet tone.

"Are you going to try that, sir?" he stammered out incredulously.

I took no notice of him and raised my tone just enough to be heard by the helmsman.

"Keep her good full."

"Good full, sir."

The wind fanned my cheek, the sails slept, the world was silent. The strain of watching the dark loom of the land grow bigger and denser was too much for me. I had shut my eyes—because the ship must go closer. She must! The stillness was intolerable. Were we standing still?

When I opened my eyes the second view started my heart with a thump. The black southern hill of Koh-ring seemed to hang right over the ship like a towering fragment of the everlasting night. On that enormous mass of blackness there was not a gleam to be seen, not a sound to be heard. It was gliding irresistibly towards us and yet seemed already within reach of the hand. I saw the vague figures of the watch grouped in the waist, gazing in awed silence.

"Are you going on, sir?" inquired an unsteady voice at my elbow.

I ignored it. I had to go on.

"Keep her full. Don't check her way. That won't do now," I said, warningly.

"I can't see the sails very well," the helmsman answered me, in strange, quavering tones.

Was she close enough? Already she was, I won't say in the shadow of the land, but in the very blackness of it, already swallowed up as it were, gone too close to be recalled, gone from me altogether.

"Give the mate a call," I said to the young man who stood at my elbow as still as death. "And turn all hands up."

My tone had a borrowed loudness reverberated from the height of the land. Several voices cried out together: "We are all on deck, sir."

Then stillness again, with the great shadow gliding closer, towering higher, without a light, without a sound. Such a hush had fallen on the ship that she might have been a bark of the dead floating in slowly under the very gate of Erebus.

"My God! Where are we?"

It was the mate moaning at my elbow. He was thunderstruck, and as it were deprived of the moral support of his whiskers. He clapped his hands and absolutely cried out, "Lost!"

"Be quiet," I said, sternly.

He lowered his tone, but I saw the shadowy gesture of his despair. "What are we doing here?"

"Looking for the land wind."

He made as if to tear his hair, and addressed me recklessly.

"She will never get out. You have done it, sir. I knew it'd end in something like this. She will never weather, and you are too close now to stay. She'll drift ashore before she's round. O my God!''

I caught his arm as he was raising it to batter his poor devoted head, and shook it violently.

"She's ashore already,'' he wailed, trying to tear himself away.

"Is she? . . . Keep good full there!''

"Good full, sir,'' cried the helmsman in a frightened, thin, childlike voice.

I hadn't let go the mate's arm and went on shaking it. "Ready about, do you hear? You go forward''—shake—"and stop there''—shake—"and hold your noise''—shake—"and see these headsheets properly overhauled''—shake, shake—shake.

And all the time I dared not look towards the land lest my heart should fail me. I released my grip at last and he ran forward as if fleeing for dear life.

I wondered what my double there in the sail-locker thought of this commotion. He was able to hear everything—and perhaps he was able to understand why, on my conscience, it had to be thus close—no less. My first order "Hard alee!'' re-echoed ominously under the towering shadow of Koh-ring as if I had shouted in a mountain gorge. And then I watched the land intently. In that smooth water and light wind it was impossible to feel the ship coming-to. No! I could not feel her. And my second self was making now ready to slip out and lower himself overboard. Perhaps he was gone already . . .?

The great black mass brooding over our very mastheads began to pivot away from the ship's side silently. And now I forgot the secret stranger ready to depart, and remembered only that I was a total stranger to the ship. I did not know her. Would she do it? How was she to be handled?

I swung the mainyard and waited helplessly. She was perhaps stopped, and her very fate hung in the balance, with the black mass of Koh-ring like the gate of the everlasting night towering over her taffrail. What would she do now? Had she way on her yet? I stepped to the side swiftly, and on the shadowy water I could see nothing except a faint phosphorescent flash revealing the glassy smoothness of the sleeping surface. It was impossible to tell—and I had not learned yet the feel of my ship. Was she moving? What I needed was something easily seen, a piece of paper, which I could throw overboard and watch. I had nothing on me. To run down for it I didn't dare. There was no time. All at once my strained, yearning stare distinguished a white object floating within a yard of the ship's side. White on the black water. A phosphorescent flash passed under it. What was that thing? . . . I recognised my own floppy hat. It must have fallen off his head . . . and he didn't bother. Now I had what I wanted—the saving mark for my eyes. But I hardly thought of my other self, now gone from the ship, to be hidden for ever from all friendly faces, to be a fugitive and a vagabond on the earth, with no brand of the curse on his sane forehead to stay a slaying hand . . . too proud to explain.

And I watched the hat—the expression of my sudden pity for his mere flesh. It had been meant to save his homeless head from the dangers of the sun. And now—behold—it was saving the ship, by serving me for a mark to help out the ignorance of my strangeness. Ha! It was drifting forward, warning me just in time that the ship had gathered sternway.

"Shift the helm," I said in a low voice to the seaman standing still like a statue.

The man's eyes glistened wildly in the binnacle light as he jumped round to the other side and spun round the wheel.

I walked to the break of the poop. On the overshadowed deck all hands stood by the forebraces waiting for my order. The stars ahead seemed to be gliding from right to left. And all was so still in the world that I heard the quiet remark, "She's round," passed in a tone of intense relief between two seamen.

"Let go and haul."

The foreyards ran round with a great noise, amidst cheery cries. And now the frightful whiskers made themselves heard giving various orders. Already the ship was drawing ahead. And I was alone with her. Nothing! no one in the world should stand now between us, throwing a shadow on the way of silent knowledge and mute affection, the perfect communion of a seaman with his first command.

Walking to the taffrail, I was in time to make out, on the very edge of a darkness thrown by a towering black mass like the very gateway of Erebus—yes, I was in time to catch an evanescent glimpse of my white hat left behind to mark the spot where the secret sharer of my cabin and of my thoughts, as though he were my second self, had lowered himself into the water to take his punishment: a free man, a proud swimmer striking out for a new destiny.

Meaning and Idea

1. Who is the narrator of the story? What is his post on the boat? How does he feel about his responsibilities?

2. Where is the ship at the start of the story? At sea? At port? In what part of the world? Where is it headed?

3. What is the *Sephora*? What is Leggatt's relation to the *Sephora*? What crime has Leggatt committed? How? Why? What is his background?

4. Describe the narrator's room. What shape is it? Of what importance are these details to the story?

5. What does the narrator do at the end of the story? What does Leggatt do? Why does the narrator go along with this?

Language, Form, Structure

1. What is the main point of this story? What comparisons and contrasts does Conrad use to advance his theme? Pay particular attention to the characters and to the setting as you answer this question.

2. Conrad relies on repetitive devices in this story. For example, he repeats the word *stranger* throughout the first few pages. Also, throughout the story, the captain continuously refers to Leggatt as "my double"—or some variation of that description. What is the effect of the repetitions?

3. Find specific references that indicate the sensory reality of Leggatt for the captain. Find specific references to Leggatt's possible "ghostliness." How do the two interpretations of Leggatt compare? Why is it important that throughout the story Leggatt is dressed in the captain's sleep suit?

4. How does the description in the first paragraph foreshadow the more important comparisons and contrasts to come? What does it tell us about the captain's situation?

5. Interpret the possible meaning of the title "The Secret Sharer." About midway through the story, the captain actually names Leggatt "the secret sharer," yet towards the end he calls Leggatt "the secret stranger." Compare these two descriptions.

6. Select fifteen words from this story with which you were unfamiliar and write dictionary definitions for them. Select your words on this basis: five descriptive words; five nouns; five verbs.

Ideas for Writing

1. Compare two crucial choices that you have made concerning love. Show how the nature, enactment or process, and results of these choices compare.

2. Write a comparison of two very different feelings you have had about yourself at different times in your life. You may want to consider feelings about your personality, your goals, your looks, etc. Which perspective now seems more important to you? Why?

3. The great critical controversy about "The Secret Sharer" is, quite simply, whether or not Leggatt is real. Write an analysis, drawing on specific references to the text, in which you explain your point of view on this matter. You may want to consider if it is indeed possible to read the story on two levels simultaneously.

Thomas Hardy
THE RUINED MAID

Thomas Hardy (1840–1928) was born in Dorset, Wessex, England, and there received a liberal education with special concentration in Latin and Greek. His father having been a master mason, Hardy chose architecture as his intended profession and moved to London in 1862 to apprentice. He practiced as an architect until 1874 when his first critically acclaimed novel, *Far from the Madding Crowd,* appeared. His four best, and most widely read, novels followed closely: *The Return of the Native* (1878), *The Mayor of Casterbridge* (1886), *Tess of the D'Urbervilles* (1891), and *Jude the Obscure* (1896). Unfortunately, the strongly passionate *Jude* shocked Victorian critical circles, and Hardy's response was to abandon writing novels in favor of composing poetry. He is buried in "Poets' Corner" in Westminster Abbey in London.

In "The Ruined Maid" Hardy uses dialogue to express two views of what, because of moral considerations, is an ambiguous condition. As you finish this poem, consider whether the two speakers' opinions are ultimately more the same or more different.

" *O* 'Melia, my dear, this does everything crown!   1
Who could have supposed I should meet you in Town?
And whence such fair garments, such prosperi-ty?"—
"O didn't you know I'd been ruined?" said she.

—"You left us in tatters, without shoes or socks,   5
Tired of digging potatoes, and spudding up docks;
And now you've gay bracelets and bright feathers three!"—
"Yes: that's how we dress when we're ruined," said she.

—"At home in the barton you said 'thee' and 'thou,'
And 'thik oon,' and 'theäs oon,' and 't'other'; but now   10
Your talking quite fits 'ee for high compa-ny!"—
"Some polish is gained with one's ruin," said she.

—"Your hands were like paws then, your face blue and bleak
But now I'm bewitched by your delicate cheek,
And your little gloves fit as on any la-dy!"—   15
"We never do work when we're ruined," said she.

—"You used to call home-life a hag-ridden dream,
And you'd sigh, and you'd sock; but at present you seem
To know not of megrims or melancho-ly!"—
"True. One's pretty lively when ruined," said she.   20

—"I wish I had feathers, a fine sweeping gown,
And a delicate face, and could strut about Town!"—
"My dear—a raw country girl, such as you be,
Cannot quite expect that. You ain't ruined," said she.

Meaning and Idea

1.   What is the setting for this conversation? Who are the two speakers? What is their relationship?

2.   What is the first speaker's attitude toward 'Melia? What is 'Melia's attitude toward the speaker? Where and how do we learn of these attitudes?

3.   Why does 'Melia call herself "ruined"? Is she using that term ironically? How do her old and new lives compare? What is Hardy's attitude about her "ruination"? What is his attitude toward the first speaker?

Language, Form, Structure

1.   How is comparison an appropriate format for the theme of this poem? Why is dialogue an effective means to support the comparison? What main point does the poem make?

2.   What words suggest 'Melia's newfound sophistication? What words suggest that this sophistication is only a veneer?

3.   See if you can find meanings for the following words. Use a collegiate-sized dictionary, since several have archaic, specialized, or dialectical meanings: crown (line 1); spudding up docks (6); barton (9); sock (18); megrims (19).

Ideas for Writing

1.   Write an imaginary dialogue in which one person "sizes up" an old acquaintance after not seeing him or her for a long time. Be sure to keep a consistent point of view throughout.

2.   Write a short essay in which you discuss the friend you've known longest in terms of how he or she has changed since five (more or less) years ago. You should include two specific bases of comparison.

3.   In this poem, Hardy expresses a comparison in dialogue. Do you feel that dialogue adequately supports the theme here? Making allowances for the fact that the poem was written over eighty years ago, how realistic do you find the dialogue?

Langston Hughes
MOTHER TO SON

Langston Hughes (1902–1967) was one of America's fore-most poets, essayists, dramatists, and fiction writers, whose self-proclaimed desire as a writer was "to explain and illuminate the Negro condition in America." Once elected class poet in grammar school in Lincoln, Illinois, Hughes first gained adult recognition as a poet when he was a busboy at a hotel in Washington, D.C. He left some poems by the plate of the poet Vachel Lindsay, who fortunately recognized his talent.

In "Mother to Son," Langston Hughes uses extended meta-phor to portray a dramatic comparison between two generations and to convey a heartfelt plea.

Well, son, I'll tell you: 1
Life for me ain't been no crystal stair.
It's had tacks in it,
And splinters,
And boards torn up,   5
And places with no carpet on the floor—
Bare.
But all the time
I'se been a-climb'n' on,
And reachin' landin's,   10
And turnin' corners,
And sometimes goin' in the dark
Where there ain't been no light.
So, boy, don't you turn back.
Don't you set down on the steps   15
'Cause you finds it kinder hard.
Don't you fall now—
For I'se still goin', honey,
I'se still climbin',
And life for me ain't been no crystal stair.   20

Meaning and Idea

1. Who is the speaker of the poem? To whom is she speaking? What sort of life has the speaker had? What sort of life does she imagine her son will have?

2. Characterize the poem exchange: Is it a lesson? A lecture? A scolding? Loving advice? Explain your answer.

Language, Form, Structure

1. What comparisons does the mother imply between her life and her son's? How does she tie their lives together?

2. Do you get the feeling that this is actually a *specific* mother talking to a *specific* son? Why or why not? Explain your answer in terms of Hughes's purpose for this poem.

3. For what audience is Hughes writing? How do you know?

4. What extended metaphor does Hughes use throughout this poem? On what two levels are we meant to interpret this metaphor?

5. What is the purpose of the dialect in this poem? Give three obvious examples of dialectical usage and paraphrase them in standard English.

Ideas for Writing

1. Write a poem or a paragraph in which you give advice to someone younger than you. Base your advice on a comparison of your two lives.

2. Compare your lifestyle with that of someone you know from another culture or social group. Be specific in your bases for comparison.

3. Write an analysis of the nature of Hughes's extended metaphor in this poem. How does he get the comparison to work?

Susan Sontag
TWO DISEASES

Susan Sontag, born in New York City in 1933, is known for her astute writings about contemporary culture. She has continually surprised readers and critics alike with her range of subject and interpretation, which defy any one "label." Her work has taken the form of fiction, essays, and films. Sontag's fiction includes the novels *The Benefactor* and *Death Kit,* and the short story collection *I, etcetera.* Her essay collections include *Against Interpretation* (1966), *About Photography* (1977), *Illness as Metaphor* (1978), and *Under the Sign of Saturn* (1980).

In "Two Diseases" (taken from Chapters 1 and 2 of her *Illness as Metaphor*) Sontag uses comparison and contrast techniques to demystify the "trappings of metaphor" which have surrounded two of the worst killers of this and the past centuries—cancer and tuberculosis. Pay close attention to the ways in which Sontag uses historical development, allusions, and exemplification.

*T*wo diseases have been spectacularly, and similarly, encumbered by the trappings of metaphor: tuberculosis and cancer.

The fantasies inspired by TB in the last century, by cancer now, are responses to a disease thought to be intractable and capricious—that is, a disease not understood—in an era in which medicine's central premise is that all diseases can be cured. Such a disease is, by definition, mysterious. For as long as its cause was not understood and the ministrations of doctors remained so ineffective, TB was thought to be an insidious, implacable theft of a life. Now it is cancer's turn to be the disease that doesn't knock before it enters, cancer that fills the role of an illness experienced as a ruthless, secret invasion—a role it will keep until, one day, its etiology becomes as clear and its treatment as effective as those of TB have become.

Although the way in which disease mystifies is set against a backdrop of new expectations, the disease itself (once TB, cancer today) arouses thoroughly old-fashioned kinds of dread. Any disease that is treated as a mystery and acutely enough feared will be felt to be morally, if not literally, contagious. Thus, a surprisingly large number of people with cancer find themselves being shunned by relatives and friends and are the object of practices of decontamination by members of their household, as if cancer, like TB, were an infectious disease. Contact with someone afflicted with a disease regarded as a mysterious malevolency inevitably feels like a trespass; worse, like the violation of a taboo. The very names of such diseases are felt to have a magic power. In Stendhal's *Armance* (1827), the hero's mother refuses to say "tuberculosis," for fear that pronouncing the word will hasten the course of her son's malady. And Karl Menninger has observed (in *The Vital Balance*) that "the very word 'cancer' is said to kill some patients who would not have succumbed (so quickly) to the malignancy from which they suffer." This observation is offered in support of anti-intellectual pieties and a facile compassion all too triumphant in contemporary medicine and psychiatry. "Patients who consult us because of their suffering and their distress and their disability," he continues, "have every right to resent being plastered with a damning index tab." Dr. Menninger recommends that physicians generally abandon "names" and "labels" ("our function is to help these people, not to further afflict them")—which would mean, in effect, increasing secretiveness and medical paternalism. It is not naming as such that is pejorative or damning, but the name "cancer." As long as a particular disease is treated as an evil, invincible predator, not just a disease, most people with cancer will indeed be demoralized by learning what disease they have. The solution is hardly to stop telling cancer patients the truth, but to rectify the conception of the disease, to demythicize it.

When, not so many decades ago, learning that one had TB was tantamount to hearing a sentence of death—as today, in the popular imagination, cancer equals death—it was common to conceal the identity of their disease from tuberculars and, after they died, from their children. Even with patients informed about their disease, doctors and family were reluctant to talk freely. "Verbally I don't learn anything definite," Kafka wrote to a friend in April 1924 from the sanatorium where he died two months later, "since in discussing tuberculosis . . . everybody drops into a shy, evasive, glassy-eyed manner of speech." Conventions of concealment with cancer are even more strenuous. In France and Italy it is still the rule for doctors to communicate a cancer diagnosis to the patient's family but not to the patient; doctors consider that the truth will be intolerable to all but exceptionally mature and intelligent patients. (A leading French oncologist has told me that fewer than a tenth of his patients know they have cancer.) In America—in part because of the doctors' fear of malpractice suits—there is now much more candor with patients, but the country's largest cancer hospital mails routine communications and bills to outpatients in envelopes that do not reveal the sender, on the assumption that the illness may be a secret from their families. Since getting cancer can be a scandal that jeopardizes one's love life, one's chance of promotion, even one's job, patients who know what they have tend to be extremely prudish, if not outright secretive, about their disease. And a federal law, the 1966 Freedom of Information Act, cites "treatment for cancer" in a clause exempting from disclosure matters whose disclosure "would be an unwarranted invasion of personal privacy." It is the only disease mentioned.

All this lying to and by cancer patients is a measure of how much harder it has become in advanced industrial societies to come to terms with death. As death is now an offensively meaningless event, so that disease widely considered a synonym for death is experienced as something to hide. The policy of equivocating about the nature of their disease with cancer patients reflects the conviction that dying people are best spared the news that they are dying, and that the good death is the sudden one, best of all if it happens while we're unconscious or asleep. Yet the modern denial of death does not explain the extent of the lying and the wish to be lied to; it does not touch the deepest dread. Someone who has had a coronary is at least as likely to die of another one within a few years as someone with cancer is likely to die soon from cancer. But no one thinks of concealing the truth from a cardiac patient: there is nothing shameful about a heart attack. Cancer patients are lied to, not just because the disease is (or is thought to be) a death sentence, but because it is felt to be obscene—in the original meaning of that word: ill-omened, abominable, repugnant to the senses. Cardiac disease implies a weakness, trouble, failure that is mechanical; there is no disgrace, nothing of the taboo that once surrounded people afflicted with TB and still surrounds those who have cancer. The metaphors attached to TB and to cancer imply living processes of a particularly resonant and horrid kind.

Throughout most of their history, the metaphoric uses of TB and cancer crisscross and overlap. The *Oxford English Dictionary* records "consumption" in use as a synonym for pulmonary tuberculosis as early as 1398. (John of Trevisa: "Whan the blode is made thynne, soo folowyth consumpcyon and wastying.") But the pre-modern understanding of cancer also invokes the notion of consumption. The OED gives as the early figurative definition of cancer: "Anything that frets, corrodes, corrupts, or consumes slowly and secretly." (Thomas Paynell in 1528: "A canker is a melancolye impostume eatynge partes of the bodye.") The earliest literal definition of cancer is a growth, lump, or protuberance, and the disease's name—from the Greek *karkinos* and the Latin *cancer,* both meaning crab—was inspired, according to Galen, by the resemblance of an external tumor's swollen veins to a crab's legs, not, as many people think, because a metastatic disease crawls or creeps like a crab. But etymology indicates that tuberculosis was also once considered a type of abnormal extrusion: the word tuberculosis—from the Latin *tūberculum,* the diminutive of *tūber,* bump, swelling—means a morbid swelling, protuberance, projection, or growth. Rudolf Virchow, who founded the science of cellular pathology in the 1850s, thought of the tubercle as a tumor.

Thus, from late antiquity until quite recently, tuberculosis was—typologically—cancer. And cancer was described, like TB, as a process in which the body was consumed. The modern conceptions of the two diseases could not be set until the advent of cellular pathology. Only with the microscope was it possible to grasp the distinctiveness of cancer, as a type of cellular activity, and to understand that the disease did not always take the form of an external or even palpable tumor. (Before the mid-nineteenth century, nobody could have identified leukemia as a form of cancer.) And it was not possible definitively to separate cancer from TB until after 1882, when tuberculosis was discovered to be a bacterial infection. Such advances in medical thinking enabled the leading metaphors of the two diseases to become truly distinct and, for the most part, contrasting. The modern fantasy about the cancer could then begin to take shape—a fantasy which from the 1920s on would inherit most of the problems dramatized by the fantasies about TB, but with the two diseases and their symptoms conceived in quite different, almost opposing, ways.

TB is understood as a disease of one organ, the lungs, while cancer is understood as a disease that can turn up in any organ and whose outreach is the whole body.

TB is understood as a disease of extreme contrasts: white pallor and red flush, hyperactivity alternating with languidness. The spasmodic course of the disease is illustrated by what is thought of as the prototypical TB symptom, coughing. The sufferer is wracked by coughs, then sinks back, recovers breath, breathes normally; then coughs again. Cancer is a disease of growth (sometimes visible; more characteristically, inside), of abnormal, ultimately lethal growth that is measured, incessant, steady. Although there may be periods in which tumor growth is arrested (remissions), cancer produces no contrasts like the oxymorons of behavior—febrile activity, passionate resignation—thought to be typical of TB. The tubercular is pallid some of the time; the pallor of the cancer patient is unchanging.

TB makes the body transparent. The X-rays, which are the standard diagnostic tool, permit one, often for the first time, to see one's insides—to become transparent to oneself. While TB is understood to be, from early on, rich in visible symptoms (progressive emaciation, coughing, languidness, fever), and can be suddenly and dramatically revealed (the blood on the handkerchief), in cancer the main symptoms are thought to be, characteristically, invisible—until the last stage, when it is too late. The disease, often discovered by chance or through a routine medical checkup, can be far advanced without exhibiting any appreciable symptoms. One has an opaque body that must be taken to a specialist to find out if it contains cancer. What the patient cannot perceive, the specialist will determine by analyzing tissues taken from the body. TB patients may see their X-rays or even possess them: the patients at the sanatorium in *The Magic Mountain* carry theirs around in their breast pockets. Cancer patients don't look at their biopsies.

TB was—still is—thought to produce spells of euphoria, increased appetite, exacerbated sexual desire. Part of the regimen for patients in *The Magic Mountain* is a second breakfast, eaten with gusto. Cancer is thought to cripple vitality, make eating an ordeal, deaden desire. Having TB was imagined to be an aphrodisiac, and to confer extraordinary powers of seduction. Cancer is considered to be de-sexualizing. But it is characteristic of TB that many of its symptoms are deceptive—liveliness that comes from enervation, rosy cheeks that look like a sign of health but come from fever—and an upsurge of vitality may be a sign of approaching death. (Such gushes of energy will generally be self-destructive, and may be destructive of others: recall the Old West legend of Doc Holliday, the tubercular gunfighter released from moral restraints by the ravages of his disease.) Cancer has only true symptoms.

TB is disintegration, febrilization, dematerialization; it is a disease of liquids—the body turning to phlegm and mucus and sputum and, finally, blood—and of air, of the need for better air. Cancer is degeneration, the body tissues turning to something hard. Alice James, writing in her journal a year before she died from cancer in 1892, speaks of "this unholy granite substance in my breast." But this lump is alive, a fetus with its own will. Novalis, in an entry written around 1798 for his encyclopedia project, defines cancers, along with gangrene, as "full-fledged *parasites*—they grow, are engendered, engender, have their structure, secrete, eat." Cancer is a demonic pregnancy. St. Jerome must have been thinking of a cancer when he wrote: "The one there with his swollen belly is pregnant with his own death" (*"Alius tumenti aqualiculo mortem parturit"*). Though the course of both diseases is emaciating, losing weight from TB is understood very differently from losing weight from cancer. In TB the person is "consumed," burned up. In cancer, the patient is "invaded" by alien cells, which multiply, causing an atrophy or blockage of bodily functions. The cancer patient "shrivels" (Alice James's word) or "shrinks" (Wilhelm Reich's word).

TB is a disease of time; it speeds up life, highlights it, spiritualizes it. In both English and French, consumption "gallops." Cancer has stages rather than gaits; it is (eventually) "terminal." Cancer works slowly, insidiously: the standard euphemism in obituaries is that someone has "died after a long illness." Every characterization of cancer describes it as slow, and so it was first used metaphorically. "The word of hem crepith as a kankir," Wyclif wrote in 1382 (translating a phrase in II

Timothy 2:17); and among the earliest figurative uses of cancer are as a metaphor for "idleness" and "sloth." Metaphorically, cancer is not so much a disease of time as a disease or pathology of space. Its principal metaphors refer to topography (cancer "spreads" or "proliferates" or is "diffused"; tumors are surgically "excised"), and its most dreaded consequence, short of death, is the mutilation or amputation of part of the body.

TB is often imagined as a disease of poverty and deprivation—of thin garments, thin bodies, unheated rooms, poor hygiene, inadequate food. The poverty may not be as literal as Mimi's garret in *La Bohème;* the tubercular Marguerite Gautier in *La Dame aux camélias* lives in luxury, but inside she is a waif. In contrast, cancer is a disease of middle-class life, a disease associated with affluence, with excess. Rich countries have the highest cancer rates, and the rising incidence of the disease is seen as resulting, in part, from a diet rich in fat and proteins and from the toxic effluvia of the industrial economy that creates affluence. The treatment of TB is identified with the stimulation of appetite, cancer treatment with nausea and the loss of appetite. The undernourished nourishing themselves—alas, to no avail. The overnourished, unable to eat.

The TB patient was thought to be helped, even cured, by a change in environment. There was a notion that TB was a wet disease, a disease of humid and dank cities. The inside of the body became damp ("moisture in the lungs" was a favored locution) and had to be dried out. Doctors advised travel to high, dry places—the mountains, the desert. But no change of surroundings is thought to help the cancer patient. The fight is all inside one's own body. It may be, is increasingly thought to be, something in the environment that has caused the cancer. But once cancer is present, it cannot be reversed or diminished by a move to a better (that is, less carcinogenic) environment.

TB is thought to be relatively painless. Cancer is thought to be, invariably, excruciatingly painful. TB is thought to provide an easy death, while cancer is the spectacularly wretched one. For over a hundred years TB remained the preferred way of giving death a meaning—an edifying, refined disease. Nineteenth-century literature is stocked with descriptions of almost symptomless, unfrightened, beatific deaths from TB, particularly of young people, such as Little Eva in *Uncle Tom's Cabin* and Dombey's son Paul in *Dombey and Son* and Smike in *Nicholas Nickleby,* where Dickens described TB as the "dread disease" which "refines" death.

> if its grosser aspect . . . in which the struggle between soul and body is so gradual, quiet, and solemn, and the result so sure, that day by day, and grain by grain, the mortal part wastes and withers away, so that the spirit grows light and sanguine with its lightening load. . . .

Contrast these ennobling, placid TB deaths with the ignoble, agonizing cancer deaths of Eugene Gant's father in Thomas Wolfe's *Of Time and the River* and of the sister in Bergman's film *Cries and Whispers*. The dying tubercular is pictured as made more beautiful and more soulful; the person dying of cancer is portrayed as robbed of all capacities of self-transcendence, humiliated by fear and agony.

Meaning and Idea

1. What two diseases does the essay explore? How does Sontag characterize each of them?

2. What is Sontag's main point about the relation between the two diseases?

3. How, according to Sontag, have we formed our ideas about the diseases? What do you think she hopes to accomplish with this essay?

4. What does Sontag say about the realities of the relation between social standing or economic condition and the two diseases she is exploring? What does she say about the images we have of these relations? What is the common connection among cancer, death, and dying in our society?

Language, Form, Structure

1. As you know, this essay comes from Sontag's book *Illness as Metaphor*. Explain how the title of the book applies to this selection.

2. How does Sontag move back and forth between her two subjects? She uses few transitional expressions, and yet the essay holds together. How do you explain this coherence?

3. Throughout the essay, Sontag uses numerous historical references and literary allusions. Identify a few of them. How are they selected? What is their nature? For what purpose does Sontag include them? Which do you consider more effective, the literary or the statistical allusions?

4. Sontag calls attention to the metaphoric uses of the terms *tuberculosis* and *cancer*. Why?

5. What is the meaning of Sontag's final sentences (after the Dickens quote)? How do they serve as a fitting conclusion?

6. Make a list of any unfamiliar words from this essay and write definitions for them.

Ideas for Writing

1. Write a comparison of the two things that you fear most. Describe how they affect you, and attempt to blend both similarities and differences without losing your focus.

2. Select a social condition (for example, poverty, gentrification, child abuse) about which you have first-hand knowledge or experience over the past five to ten years. Compare the manifestations and processes of that condition as it existed five to ten years ago with its present existence. In your essay, make the process of change (or lack of change) clear to your reader.

3. Sontag's essay is very complete, almost encyclopedic. What might that completeness say about her attitude toward the subject? Bear in mind that Sontag herself had recently fought cancer when she wrote this essay. Does that fact color your opinion of this essay? How?

Plato

THE ALLEGORY OF THE CAVE

The Greek philosopher Plato (427?–347 B.C.) is considered to be among the greatest of world philosophers and the ancestor of much of modern philosophy. He was a student of Socrates, and his dialogues—including *Phaedo, Symposium,* and *Phaedrus*—are thought to be records of his conversations with Socrates and other students.

"The Allegory of the Cave" comes from the *Republic,* Plato's work about an ideal world. This allegory relies on the traditional Socratic method of a dialectic—that is, a questioning dialogue—aimed at arriving at a general truth or Platonic Form (Ideal Truth). Notice how through comparison, Plato attempts to make that Ideal a part of the world of "human affairs" as well as of "the upper world."

*A*nd now, I said, let me show in a figure how far our nature is enlightened or unenlightened: Behold! human beings living in an underground den, which has a mouth open towards the light and reaching all along the den; here they have been from their childhood, and have their legs and necks chained so that they cannot move, and can only see before them, being prevented by the chains from turning round their heads. Above and behind them a fire is blazing at a distance, and between the fire and the prisoners there is a raised way; and you will see, if you look, a low wall built along the way, like the screen which marionette players have in front of them, over which they show the puppets.

I see.

And do you see, I said, men passing along the wall carrying all sorts of vessels, and statues and figures of animals made of wood and stone and various materials, which appear over the wall? Some of them are talking, others silent.

You have shown me a strange image, and they are strange prisoners.

Like ourselves, I replied; and they see only their own shadows, or the shadows of one another, which the fire throws on the opposite wall of the cave?

True, he said; how could they see anything but the shadows if they were never allowed to move their heads?

And of the objects which are being carried in like manner they would only see the shadows?

Yes, he said.

And if they were able to converse with one another, would they not suppose that they were naming what was actually before them?

Very true.

And suppose further that the prison had an echo which came from the other side, would they not be sure to fancy when one of the passers-by spoke that the voice which they heard came from the passing shadow?

No question, he replied.

To them, I said, the truth would be literally nothing but the shadows of the images.

That is certain.

And now look again, and see what will naturally follow if the prisoners are released and disabused of their error. At first, when any of them is liberated and compelled suddenly to stand up and turn his neck round and walk and look towards the light, he will suffer sharp pains; the glare will distress him and he will be unable to see the realities of which in his former state he had seen the shadows; and then conceive some one saying to him, that what he saw before was an illusion, but that now, when he is approaching nearer to being and his eye is turned towards more real existence, he has a clearer vision—what will be his reply? And you may further imagine that his instructor is pointing to the objects as they pass and requiring him to name them—will he not be perplexed? Will he not fancy that the shadows which he formerly saw are truer than the objects which are now shown to him?

Far truer.

And if he is compelled to look straight at the light, will he not have a pain in his eyes which will make him turn away to take refuge in the objects of vision which he can see, and which he will conceive to be in reality clearer than the things which are now being shown to him?

True, he said.

And suppose once more, that he is reluctantly dragged up a steep and rugged ascent, and held fast until he is forced into the presence of the sun himself, is he not likely to be pained and irritated? When he approaches the light his eyes will be dazzled and he will not be able to see anything at all of what are now called realities.

Not all in a moment, he said.

He will require to grow accustomed to the sight of the upper world. And first he will see the shadows best, next the reflections of men and other objects in the water, and then the objects themselves; then he will gaze upon the light of the moon and the stars and the spangled heaven; and he will see the sky and the stars by night better than the sun or the light of the sun by day?

Certainly.

Last of all he will be able to see the sun, and not mere reflections of him in the water, but he will see him in his own proper place, and not in another; and he will contemplate him as he is.

Certainly.

He will then proceed to argue that this is he who gives the season and the years, and is the guardian of all that is in the visible world, and in a certain way the cause of all things which he and his fellows have been accustomed to behold?

Clearly, he said, he would first see the sun and then reason about him.

And when he remembered his old habitation, and the wisdom of the den and his fellow-prisoners, do you not suppose that he would felicitate himself on the change, and pity them?

Certainly, he would.

And if they were in the habit of conferring honors among themselves on those who were quickest to observe the passing shadows and to remark which of them went before, and which followed after, and which were together; and who were therefore best able to draw conclusions as to the future, do you think that he would care for such honors and glories, or envy the possessors of them? Would he not say with Homer,

> Better to be the poor servant of a poor master,

and to endure anything, rather than their manner?

Yes, he said, I think that he would rather suffer anything than entertain these false notions and live in this miserable manner.

Imagine once more, I said, such an one coming suddenly out of the sun to be replaced in his old situation; would he not be certain to have his eyes full of darkness?

To be sure, he said.

And if there were a contest, and he had to compete in measuring the shadows with the prisoners who had never moved out of the den, while his sight was still weak, and before his eyes had become steady (and the time which would be needed to acquire this new habit of sight might be very considerable) would he not be ridiculous? Men would say of him that up he went and down he came without his eyes; and that it was better not even to think of ascending; and if any one tried to loose another and lead him up to the light, let them only catch the offender, and they would put him to death.

No question, he said.

This entire allegory, I said, you may now append, dear Glaucon, to the previous argument; the prison-house is the world of sight, the light of fire is the sun, and you will not misapprehend me if you interpret the journey upwards to be the ascent of the soul into the intellectual world according to my poor belief, which, at your desire, I have expressed—whether rightly or wrongly God knows. But, whether true or false, my opinion is that in the world of knowledge the idea of good appears last of all, and is seen only with an effort; and, when seen, is also inferred to be the universal author of all things beautiful and right, parent of light and of the lord of light in this visible world, and the immediate source of reason and truth in the intellectual; and that this is the power upon which he who would act rationally either in public or private life must have his eye fixed.

I agree, he said, as far as I am able to understand you.

Moreover, I said, you must not wonder that those who attain to this beatific vision are unwilling to descend to human affairs; for their souls are ever hastening into the upper world where they desire to dwell; which desire of theirs is very natural, if our allegory may be trusted.

Yes, very natural.

And is there anything surprising in one who passes from divine con-templations to the evil state of man, misbehaving himself in a ridiculous manner; if, while his eyes are blinking and before he has become ac-customed to the surrounding darkness, he is compelled to fight in courts of law, or in other places, about the images or the shadows of images of justice, and is endeavouring to meet the conceptions of those who have never yet seen absolute justice?

Anything but surprising, he replied.

Any one who has common sense will remember that the bewilderments of the eyes are of two kinds, and arise from two causes, either from coming out of the light or from going into the light, which is true of the mind's eye, quite as much as of the bodily eye; and he who remembers this when he sees any one whose vision is perplexed and weak, will not be too ready to laugh; he will first ask whether that soul of man has come out of the brighter life, and is unable to see because unaccustomed to the dark, or having turned from darkness to the day is dazzled by excess of light. And he will count the one happy in his condition and state of being, and he will pity the other; or, if he have a mind to laugh at the soul which comes from below into the light, there will be more reason in this than in the laugh which greets him who returns from above out of the light into the den.

That, he said, is a very just distinction.

Meaning and Idea

1. Who is speaking to whom in this selection? What are they talking about? Do the two speakers maintain similar or dissimilar opinions?

2. Describe the conditions and activities of the prisoners in the cave. What is the contrast in perceptions of things between remaining prisoners and newly released ones? Between prisoners and those who have been outside the cave for a while? Compare the attitude of a prisoner toward his fellow prisoners before and after leaving the cave.

3. How, according to Plato, does someone learn truth?

4. Toward the end of this allegory, with what are the two realms compared or contrasted? How does Plato compare the process of coming out of the light to going into the light? Which does he feel is preferable? Why?

Language, Form, Structure

1. Plato makes use of *allegory* in this selection. What is an allegory? How is this dialogue allegorical?

2. In what ways does Plato use process analysis here? Briefly outline the processes described. Which is, overall, the most important process?

3. Look up the meanings of the following words: enlightened; glare; perplexed; ascent; dazzled; felicitate; append; misapprehend; rationally; endeavoring.

Ideas for Writing

1. Write a dialogue in which two speakers argue opposing sides of an issue. Write only in dialogue with no authorial commentary or analysis.

2. Choose an abstract concept and write a comparison essay in which you explore two points of view concerning that abstraction.

3. How effective is the allegory in helping Plato make his point? Write an analysis in which you draw on specific references to the text.

William Shakespeare
MY MISTRESS' EYES ARE NOTHING LIKE THE SUN

> The world's most acknowledged literary figure is William Shakespeare (1564–1616). Born in Stratford-on-Avon, England, on April 26, 1564, he never attended university and was, by his own admission, a poor and unmotivated student. After moving to London with his wife Ann Hathaway, Shakespeare became involved as a dramatist and actor with the Globe Theatre there. He was extremely popular in his day, though somewhat careless with the manuscripts of his now invaluable plays and sonnets. In fact, if not for the efforts of his friends, we might not today have many of his masterpieces which include, of course, *Hamlet, Macbeth, King Lear, Othello, The Comedy of Errors, The Merchant of Venice, Romeo and Juliet,* and *The Tempest*—the list goes on and on! Shakespeare returned to Stratford-on-Avon at the age of 50 and he died there two years later.
>
> In this love sonnet, Shakespeare uses comparison in such a way that we might at first think of it as a "hate sonnet." Notice how he begins to change course in lines 11–12, then makes his purpose clear in lines 13–14.

*M*y mistress' eyes are nothing like the sun;   1
Coral is far more red than her lips' red:
If snow be white, why then her breasts are dun;
If hairs be wires, black wires grow on her head.
I have seen roses damasked, red and white,   5

But no such roses see I in her cheeks;
And in some perfumes is there more delight
Than in the breath that from my mistress reeks.
I love to hear her speak, yet well I know
That music hath a far more pleasing sound: 10
I grant I never saw a goddess go,—
My mistress, when she walks, treads on the ground.
   And yet, by heaven, I think my love as rare
   As any she belied with false compare.

Meaning and Idea

1. Who is the speaker of the poem? To whom is he speaking?

2. About whom does the speaker speak? What qualities does he stress about that person?

Language, Form, Structure

1. In this sonnet does Shakespeare rely primarily on similarities or on differences? How does the speaker arrange his descriptive comparisons of his mistress? What is the nature of most of the comparisons?

2. What do the last two lines of the sonnet say about Shakespeare's reasoning in the poem? For what purpose did he use the comparisons which preceded the last two lines?

3. How does Shakespeare use negatives to make what is ultimately a highly positive statement?

4. To learn the meanings of some of the following words, it may be necessary to consult a dictionary such as the *Oxford English Dictionary,* since many of the meanings are archaic: dun; damasked; reeks; grant; belied.

Ideas for Writing

1. Write a description of some person you like very much, but develop your description using negative comparisons of that person's features to other objects. Be sure that at the end of the description, your real purpose is clear.

2. In a paragraph, describe the ugliest person you know (either physically or emotionally ugly). Then, in another paragraph, describe that same person through the eyes of someone who loves him or her.

3. Some commentators on this poem have suggested that Shakespeare wrote the sonnet not to his mistress, but with a more metaphoric idea in mind. Write a piece in which you explore another meaning or value of the poem. Support your response with specific analyses of references in the poem.

Ogden Nash
VERY LIKE A WHALE

Ogden Nash (1902–1971) was born in Rye, New York, just north of New York City. His poetry (though some critics would call it verse) is marked by his humor and sometimes absurd rhyming. Despite their light nature, Nash's poems often deal with concerns close to all. His volumes of poetry include *I'm a Stranger Here Myself* (1938), *You Can't Get There from Here* (1957), and *Bed Riddance* (1970).

The title of this poem derives from Act III, scene 2, of *Hamlet* where the prince, pretending to be crazy, compares the shape of a cloud to a whale. Ever solicitous, Polonius instantly agrees with the comparison which Hamlet meant to be awful. Polonius, however, says, "Very like a whale," a comment which Nash obviously thought made Polonius perhaps more of a fool than even Shakespeare intended him to be.

O ne thing that literature would be greatly the better for 1
Would be a more restricted employment by authors of simile
    and metaphor.
Authors of all races, be they Greeks, Romans, Teutons or
    Celts, 5
Can't seem just to say that anything is the thing it is but have to
    go out of their way to say that it is like something else.
What does it mean when we are told
That the Assyrian came down like a wolf on the fold?
In the first place, George Gordon Byron had had enough 10
    experience
To know that it probably wasn't just one Assyrian, it was a lot
    of Assyrians.
However, as too many arguments are apt to induce apoplexy
    and thus hinder longevity, 15
We'll let it pass as one Assyrian for the sake of brevity.
Now then, this particular Assyrian, the one whose cohorts
    were gleaming in purple and gold,
Just what does the poet mean when he says he came down like
    a wolf on the fold? 20

In heaven and earth more than is dreamed of in our philosophy
    there are a great many things,
But I don't imagine that among them there is a wolf with purple
    and gold cohorts or purple and gold anythings.
No, no, Lord Byron, before I'll believe that this Assyrian was   25
    actually like a wolf I must have some kind of proof;
Did he run on all fours and did he have a hairy tail and a big red
    mouth and big white teeth and did he say Woof woof
    woof?
Frankly I think it very unlikely, and all you were entitled to   30
    say, at the very most,
Was that the Assyrian cohorts came down like a lot of As-
    syrian cohorts about to destroy the Hebrew host.
But that wasn't fancy enough for Lord Byron, oh dear me no,
    he had to invent a lot of figures of speech and then   35
    interpolate them,
With the result that whenever you mention Old Testament
    soldiers to people they say Oh yes, they're the ones that a
    lot of wolves dressed up in gold and purple ate them.
That's the kind of thing that's being done all the time by poets,   40
    from Homer to Tennyson;
They're always comparing ladies to lilies and veal to venison.
How about the man who wrote,
Her little feet stole in and out like mice beneath her petticoat?
Wouldn't anybody but a poet think twice   45
Before stating that his girl's feet were mice?
Then they always say things like that after a winter storm
The snow is a white blanket. Oh it is, is it, all right then, you
    sleep under a six-inch blanket of snow and I'll sleep
    under a half-inch blanket of unpoetical blanket material   50
    and we'll see which one keeps warm,
And after that maybe you'll begin to comprehend dimly
What I mean by too much metaphor and simile.

Meaning and Idea

  1. What is Nash's main purpose in this poem?

  2. To whom does Nash address this poem? Might he have had a secondary audience in mind as well?

  3. What does Nash suggest as a concrete way of testing his theories about poetry?

Language, Form, Structure

1. State specifically how Nash makes use of comparison to prove his point in this poem.

2. Lines 5–20 refer to the following two lines from Lord Byron's poem, "The Destruction of Sennacherib":

The Assyrian came down like a wolf on the fold,
And his cohorts were gleaming in purple and gold;

Lines 23–26 refer to the following lines from Sir John Suckling's poem, "A Ballad Upon a Wedding":

Her feet beneath her petticoat,
Like little mice stole in and out,
As if they feared the light;

How are such references particularly valuable to Nash's argument?

3. One might say that Nash's entire poem uses hyperbole or overstatement to make its point. Select two instances here of overstatement. How do these help the poem work?

4. Look up and write definitions for the following words from the poem: restricted; apt; apoplexy; brevity; cohorts; host; interpolate.

Ideas for Writing

1. Select something with which you are familiar that you feel is done wrong by most people. Write a few paragraphs in which you compare the established method with a way you think would be better.

2. Write an analysis of Nash's poem. Is his point valid? Why or why not?

Robert Frost
FIRE AND ICE

> Although Robert Frost is well-known as a New England poet, he was in fact born in San Francisco in 1874. After a brief stay in England (1912–1914), where he first gained fame as a poet, Frost settled in New Hampshire, where he lived most of his days until his death in 1963. Frost the poet is sometimes deceptively simple; underlying his dramatic accounts of the New England people and landscape, there often lies deep symbolism and lyricism. His collected poems were published posthumously in 1967; he had already received four Pulitzer Prizes for poetry in 1924, 1931, 1937, and 1943.
>
> In this short, almost deceptively singsong poem, Robert Frost compares two notions of the way the world will end.

Some say the world will end in fire,   1
Some say in ice.
From what I've tasted of desire
I hold with those who favor fire.
But if it had to perish twice,   5
I think I know enough of hate
To say that for destruction ice
Is also great
And would suffice.

Meaning and Idea

1. Who, literally, are those who "say the world will end in fire"? Who are those who say "in ice"? Which group does Frost favor? Why?

2. What impossible occurrence does the poet describe? Why?

3. State, in a single sentence, Frost's meaning in this poem.

Language, Form, Structure

1. Refer back to your answer to question 1 in the Meaning and Idea section above. Then, state how Frost uses the two groups to symbolize other things. Explain this symbolic meaning.

2.   This poem is quite sparse, yet Frost implicitly creates very graphic images. Describe them and explain how he creates them.

3.   What special meanings does Frost employ when he writes "tasted" and "hold with"?

Ideas for Writing

1.   What do you consider the most negative social trend among your peers? Write an essay in which you compare two ways in which this trend manifests itself.

2.   Write a paragraph in which you compare two methods of doing something creative—either a natural process (such as growing sprouts) or an abstract process (such as writing a poem).

3.   The Bauhaus school of design is famous for its edict: "Less is more." Write a short essay in which you respond to Frost's poem within the context of the Bauhaus statement.

Sylvia Plath
A COMPARISON

Sylvia Plath (1932–1963) was born in Boston to well-educated immigrant parents. She graduated from Smith College and took a master's degree at Cambridge University on a Fulbright Scholarship. She was a melancholy person, as reflected in her poetry collections such as *The Collossus* (1960), *Ariel* (1965), and *Winter Trees* (1972). She was married to the British poet Ted Hughes with whom she lived in England and the United States. Her autobiographical novel *The Bell-Jar* (1963) records her emotional ups and downs, which culminated finally in her suicide at the age of 30.

This essay, written just a year before Plath's suicide, playfully compares the life and art of novelists and poets. Notice how she fully details the difficulties of each, and comes out clearly on the side of her first love.

*H*ow I envy the novelist! I imagine him—better say her, for it is the women I look to for . . . a parallel—I imagine her, then, pruning a rose-bush with a large pair of shears, adjusting her spectacles, shuffling about among the teacups, humming, arranging ashtrays or babies, absorbing a slant of light, a fresh edge to the weather, and piercing, with a kind of modest, beautiful X-ray vision, the psychic interiors of her neighbors— her neighbors on trains, in the dentist's waiting room, in the corner teashop. To her, this fortunate one, what is there that *isn't* relevant! Old shoes can be used, doorknobs, air letters, flannel nightgowns, cathedrals, nail varnish, jet planes, rose arbors and budgerigars; little mannerisms— the sucking at a tooth, the tugging at a hemline—any weird or warty or fine or despicable thing. Not to mention emotions, motivations—those rumbling, thunderous shapes. Her business is Time, the way it shoots forward, shunts back, blooms, decays and double-exposes itself. Her business is people in Time. And she, it seems to me, has all the time in the world. She can take a century if she likes, a generation, a whole summer.

I can take about a minute.

I'm not talking about epic poems. We all know how long *they* can take. I'm talking about the smallish, unofficial garden-variety poem. How shall I describe it?—a door opens, a door shuts. In between you have had a glimpse: a garden, a person, a rainstorm, a dragonfly, a heart, a city. I think of those round glass Victorian paperweights which I remember, yet can never find—a far cry from the plastic mass-productions which stud the toy counters in Woolworth's. This sort of paperweight is a clear globe, self-complete, very pure, with a forest or village or family group within it. You turn it upside down, then back. It snows. Everything is changed in a minute. It will never be the same in there—not the fir trees, nor the gables, nor the faces.

So a poem takes place.

And there is really so little room! So little time! The poet becomes an expert packer of suitcases:

The apparition of these faces in the crowd;
Petals on a wet black bough.

There it is: the beginning and the end in one breath. How would the novelist manage that? In a paragraph? In a page? Mixing it, perhaps, like paint, with a little water, thinning it, spreading it out.

Now I am being smug, I am finding advantages.

If a poem is concentrated, a closed fist, then a novel is relaxed and expansive, an open hand: it has roads, detours, destinations; a heart line, a head line; morals and money come into it. Where the fist excludes and stuns, the open hand can touch and encompass a great deal in its travels.

I have never put a toothbrush in a poem.

I do not like to think of all the things, familiar, useful and worthy things, I have never put into a poem. I did, once, put a yew tree in. And that yew tree began, with astounding egotism, to manage and order the whole affair. It was not a yew tree by a church on a road past a house in a town where a certain woman lived . . . and so on, as it might have been in a novel. Oh, no. It stood squarely in the middle of my poem, manipulating its dark shades, the voices in the churchyard, the clouds, the birds, the tender melancholy with which I contemplated it—everything! I couldn't subdue it. And, in the end, my poem was a poem about a yew tree. That yew tree was just too proud to be a passing black mark in a novel.

Perhaps I shall anger some poets by implying that the *poem* is proud. The poem, too, can include everything, they will tell me. And with far more precision and power than those baggy, disheveled and undiscriminate creatures we call novels. Well, I concede these poets their steamshovels and old trousers. I really *don't* think poems should be all that chaste. I would, I think, even concede a toothbrush, if the poem was a real one. But these apparitions, these poetical toothbrushes, are rare. And when they do arrive, they are inclined, like my obstreperous yew tree, to think themselves singled out and rather special.

Not so in novels.

There the toothbrush returns to its rack with beautiful promptitude and is forgot. Time flows, eddies, meanders, and people have leisure to grow and alter before our eyes. The rich junk of life bobs all about us: bureaus, thimbles, cats, the whole much-loved, well-thumbed catalog of the miscellaneous which the novelist wishes us to share. I do not mean that there is no pattern, no discernment, no rigorous ordering here.

I am only suggesting that perhaps the pattern does not insist so much. The door of the novel, like the door of the poem, also shuts.

But not so fast, nor with such manic, unanswerable finality.

Meaning and Idea

1. Why does Plath choose to make her imaginary novelist a woman? How does that make her comparison more relevant and genuine?

2. What does Plath mean by "the smallish, unofficial garden-variety poem"? To what does she compare it? Why does she call it "unofficial"?

3. Summarize briefly how Plath contrasts the process of poetry writing with the process of novel writing. Are they more alike or more different?

4. What is the significance of the "toothbrush" mentioned frequently throughout Plath's essay? Explain the line, in terms of the comparison, "I have not put a toothbrush in a poem."

5. Whom do you think Plath intended as an audience for this essay?

Language, Form, Structure

1. What organizational techniques does Plath use to compare her likes and dislikes for poems versus novels? What transitions help move the essay along smoothly?

2. Explain how Plath uses a single-sentence paragraph ("I can take about a minute.") to balance a richly detailed paragraph such as the one which precedes it.

3. The two lines quoted in paragraph six constitute a *complete,* famous imagist poem by Ezra Pound called "In a Station of the Metro." How does Plath use it to support her poem-novel comparison?

4. How does Plath use the poetic technique of *personification* in this essay? How does personification support process analysis in the essay? What other techniques of poetry does she use?

5. Identify the following words from the essay: budgerigars; mannerisms; despicable; egotism; chaste; concede; obstreperous; promptitude; meanders; discernment; manic.

Ideas for Writing

1. Select a poem and a work of fiction that deal with similar themes or subjects. Write a brief essay to compare them. In your conclusion, indicate which you like better and why.

2. Select an activity you enjoy and compare it to another activity in the same category; for example, playing soccer versus playing football (sports); growing flowers versus growing vegetables (gardening); fixing cars versus fixing televisions (mechanical repair).

3. Plath was almost exclusively a poet, though she is perhaps most widely known for her autobiographical novel *The Bell-Jar.* Identify what you see as poetic elements in "A Comparison." What evidences do you find of a poet behind the prose in this essay?

Toni Morrison
A SLOW WALK OF TREES

Toni Morrison, an editor at Random House and a much admired novelist, was born near Cleveland in 1931. In 1953 she received her B.A. from Howard University, and in 1955 she earned her M.A. at Cornell. Her novels focus on the black experience, historical and modern, using a unique blend of historical fact and personal mythos. *Sula* (1973) was nominated for the National Book Award in 1975, and *Song of Solomon* (1977) won the National Book Critics Circle Award for fiction. *Tar Baby* was published in 1981 to critical acclaim.

Grandmother Ardelia Willis had it one way, grandfather John Solomon Willis another. This contrast helped formulate Toni Morrison's views on the historical and modern-day fortunes and misfortunes of black people in America. Notice how the author keeps offering yet "another slant" on this issue. This article was first published in the July 4, 1976, *New York Times Magazine*.

*H*is name was John Solomon Willis, and when at age 5 he heard from the old folks that "the Emancipation Proclamation was coming," he crawled under the bed. It was his earliest recollection of what was to be his habitual response to the promises of white people: horror and an instinctive yearning for safety. He was my grandfather, a musician who managed to hold on to his violin but not his land. He lost all 88 acres of his Indian mother's inheritance to legal predators who built their fortunes on the likes of him. He was an unreconstructed black pessimist who, in spite of or because of emancipation, was convinced for 85 years that there was no hope whatever for black people in this country. His rancor was legitimate, for he, John Solomon, was not only an artist but a first-rate carpenter and farmer, reduced to sending home to his family money he made playing the violin because he was not able to find work. And this during the years when almost half the black male population were skilled craftsmen who lost their jobs to white ex-convicts and immigrant farmers.

His wife, however, was of a quite different frame of mind and believed that all things could be improved by faith in Jesus and an effort of the will. So it was she, Ardelia Willis, who sneaked her seven children out of the back window into the darkness, rather than permit the patron of their sharecropper's existence to become their executioner as well, and headed north in 1912, when 99.2 percent of all black people in the U.S. were native-born and only 60 percent of white Americans were. And it was Ardelia who told her husband that they could not stay in the Kentucky town they ended up in because the teacher didn't know long division.

They have been dead now for 30 years and more and I still don't know which of them came closer to the truth about the possibilities of life for black people in this country. One of their grandchildren is a tenured professor at Princeton. Another, who suffered from what the Peruvian poet called "anger that breaks a man into children," was picked up just as he entered his teens and emotionally lobotomized by the reformatories and mental institutions specifically designed to serve him. Neither John Solomon nor Ardelia lived long enough to despair over one or swell with pride over the other. But if they were alive today each would have selected and collected enough evidence to support the accuracy of the other's original point of view. And it would be difficult to convince either one that the other was right.

Some of the monstrous events that took place in John Solomon's America have been duplicated in alarming detail in my own America. There was the public murder of a President in a theater in 1865 and the public murder of another President on television in 1963. The Civil War of 1861 had its encore as the civil-rights movement of 1960. The torture and mutilation of a black West Point Cadet (Cadet Johnson Whittaker) in 1880 had its rerun with the 1970's murders of students at Jackson State College, Texas Southern and Southern University in Baton Rouge. And in 1976 we watch for what must be the thousandth time a pitched battle between the children of slaves and the children of immigrants—only this time, it is not the New York draft riots of 1863, but the busing turmoil in Paul Revere's home town, Boston.

Hopeless, he'd said. Hopeless. For he was certain that white people of every political, religious, geographical and economic background would band together against black people everywhere when they felt the threat of our progress. And a hundred years after he sought safety from the white man's "promise," somebody put a bullet in Martin Luther King's brain. And not long before that some excellent samples of the master race demonstrated their courage and virility by dynamiting some little black girls to death. If he were here now, my grandfather, he would shake his head, close his eyes and pull out his violin—too polite to say, "I told you so." And his wife would pay attention to the music but not to the sadness in her husband's eyes, for she would see what she expected to see—not the occasional historical repetition, but, *like the slow walk of certain species of trees from the flatlands up into the mountains,* she would see the signs of irrevocable and permanent change. She, who pulled her girls out of an inadequate school in the Cumberland Mountains, knew all along that the gentlemen from Alabama who had killed the little girls would be rounded up. And it wouldn't surprise her in the least to know that the number of black college graduates jumped 12 percent in the last three years; 47 percent in 20 years. That there are 140 black mayors in this country; 14 black judges in the District Circuit, 4 in the Courts of Appeals and one on the Supreme Court. That there are 17 blacks in Congress, one in the Senate; 276 in state legislatures—223 in state houses, 53 in state senates. That there are 112 elected black police chiefs and sheriffs, 1 Pulitizer Prize winner; 1 winner of the Prix de Rome; a dozen or so winners of the Guggenheim; 4 deans of predominently white colleges. . . . Oh, her list would go on and on. But so would John Solomon's sweet sad music.

While my grandparents held opposite views on whether the fortunes of black people were improving, my own parents struck similarly opposed postures, but from another slant. They differed about whether the moral fiber of white people would ever improve. Quite a different argument. The old folks argued about how and if black people could improve themselves, who could be counted on to help us, who would hinder us and so on. My parents took issue over the question of whether it was possible for white people to improve. They assumed that black people were the humans of the globe, but had serious doubts about the quality and existence of white humanity. Thus my father, distrusting every word and every gesture of every white man on earth, assumed that the white man who crept up the stairs one afternoon had come to molest his daughters and threw him down the stairs and then our tricycle after him. (I think my father was wrong, but considering what I have seen since, it may have been very healthy for me to have witnessed that as my first black-white encounter.) My mother, however, *believed* in them—their possibilities. So when the meal we got on relief was bug-ridden, she wrote a long letter to Franklin Delano Roosevelt. And when white bill collectors came to our door, it was she who received them civilly and explained in a sweet voice that we were people of honor and that the debt would be taken care of. Her message to Roosevelt got through—our meal improved. Her message to the bill collectors did not always get through and there was occasional violence when my father (self-exiled to the bedroom for fear he could not hold his temper) would hear that her reasonableness had failed. My mother was always wounded by these scenes, for she thought the bill collector knew that she loved good credit more than life and that being in arrears on a payment horrified her probably more than it did him. So she thought he was rude because he was white. For years she walked to utility companies and department stores to pay bills in person and even now she does not seem convinced that checks are legal tender. My father loved excellence, worked hard (he held three jobs at once for 17 years) and was so outraged by the suggestion of personal slackness that he could explain it to himself only in terms of racism. He was a fastidious worker who was frightened of one thing: unemployment. I can remember now the dooms-day-cum-graveyard sound of "laid off" and how the minute school was out he asked us, "Where you workin'?" Both my parents believed that all succor and aid came from themselves and their neighborhood, since "they"—white people in charge and those not in charge but in obstructionist positions—were in some way fundamentally, genetically corrupt.

So I grew up in a basically racist household with more than a child's share of contempt for white people. And for each white friend I acquired who made a small crack in that contempt, there was another who repaired it. For each one who related to me as a person, there was one who in my presence at least, became actively "white." And like most black people of my generation, I suffer from racial vertigo that can be cured only by taking what one needs from one's ancestors. John Solomon's cynicism and his deployment of his art as both weapon and solace, Ardelia's faith in the magic that can be wrought by sheer effort of the will; my mother's openmindedness in each new encounter and her habit of trying reasonableness first; my father's temper, his impatience and his efforts to keep "them" (throw them) out of his life. And it is out of these learned and selected attitudes that I look at the quality of life for my people in this country now. These widely disparate and sometimes conflicting views, I suspect, were held not only by me, but by most black people. Some I know are clearer in their positions, have not sullied their anger with optimism or dirtied their hope with despair. But most of us are plagued by a sense of being worn shell-thin by constant repression and hostility as well as the impression of being buoyed by visible testimony of tremendous strides. There *is* repetition of the grotesque in our history. And there *is* the miraculous walk of trees. The question is whether our walk is progress or merely movement. O.J. Simpson leaning on a Hertz car *is* better than the Gold Dust Twins on the back of a soap box. But is "Good Times" better than Stepin Fetchit? Has the first order of business been taken care of? Does the law of the land work for us?

Are white people who murder black people punished with at least the same dispatch that sends black teen-age truants to Coxsackie? Can we relax now and discuss "The Jeffersons" instead of genocide? Or is the difference between the two only the difference between a greedy pointless white life-style and a messy pointless black death? Now that Mr. Poitier and Mr. Belafonte have shot up all the racists in "Buck and the Preacher," have they all gone away? Can we really move into better neighborhoods and not be set on fire? Is there anybody who will lay me a $5 bet on it?

The past decade is a fairly good index of the odds at which you lay your money down.

Ten years ago in Queens, as black people like me moved into a neighborhood 20 minutes away from the Triborough Bridge, "for sale" signs shot up in front of white folks' houses like dandelions after a hot spring rain. And the black people smiled. "Goody, goody," said my neighbor. "Maybe we can push them on out to the sea. You think?"

Now I live in another neighborhood, 20 minutes away from the George Washington Bridge, and again the "for sale" signs are pushing up out of the ground. Fewer, perhaps, and for different reasons, perhaps. Still the Haitian lady and I smile at each other. "My, my," she says "they goin' on up to the hills? Seem like they just come from there." "The woods," I say. "They like to live in the woods." She nods with infinite understanding, then shrugs. The Haitians have already arranged for one mass in the church to be said in French, already have their own newspaper, stores, community center. That's not movement. That's progress.

But the decade has other revelations. Ten years ago, young, bright, energetic blacks were sought out, pursued and hired into major corporations, major networks, and onto the staffs of newspapers and national magazines. *Many survived that courtship, some even with their souls intact*. Newscasters, corporate lawyers, marketing specialists, journalists, production managers, plant foreman, college deans. But many more spend a lot of time on the telephone these days, or at the typewriter preparing résumés, which they send out (mostly to friends now) with little notes attached: "Is there anything you know of?" Or they think there is a good book in the story of what happened to them, the great hoax that was played on them. They are right, of course, about the hoax, for many of them were given elegant executive jobs with the work drained out. Work minus power. Work minus decision-making. Work minus dominion. Affirmative Action Make Believe that a lot of black people *did* believe because they also believed that the white people in those nice offices were not like the ones in the general store or in the plumbers' union—that they were fundamentally kind, or fair, or something. Anything but the desperate prisoners of economics they turned out to be, holding on to their dominion with a tenacity and sang-froid that can only be described as Nixonian. So the bright and the black (architects, reporters, vice-presidents in charge of public relations) walk the streets right along with that astounding 38 percent of the black teen-aged female work force that does not have and never has had a job. So the black female college graduate earns two-thirds of what a white male high-school dropout earns. So the black people who put everything into community-action programs supported by Government funds have found themselves bereft of action bereft of funds and all but bereft of community.

This decade has been rife with disappointment in practically every place where we thought we saw permanent change: Hostos, CUNY, and the black-studies departments that erupted like minivolcanoes on campuses all over the nation; easy integrations of public-school systems; acceleration of promotion in factories and businesses. But now when we describe what has happened we cannot do it without using the verbs of upheaval and destruction: Open admission *closes;* minority-student quotas *fall* or *discontinue;* salary gaps between blacks and whites *widen;* black-studies departments *merge.* And the only growth black people can count on is in the prison population and the unemployment line. Even busing, which used to be a plain, if emotional, term at best, has now taken on an adjective normally reserved for rape and burglary—it is now called "forced" busing.

All of that counts, but I'm not sure that in the long haul it matters. Maybe Ardelia Willis had the best idea. One sees signs of her vision and the fruits of her prophecy in spite of the dread-lock statistics. The trees *are* walking, albeit slowly and quietly and without the fanfare of a cross-country run. It seems that at last black people have abandoned our foolish dependency on the Government to do the work that we once thought all of its citizenry would be delighted to do. Our love affair with the Federal Government is over. We misjudged the ardor of its attention. We thought its majority constituency would *prefer* having their children grow up among happy, progressive, industrious, contented black children rather than among angry, disenchanted and dangerous ones. That the profit motive of industry alone would keep us employed and therefore spending, and that our poverty was bad for business. We thought landlords wanted us to have a share in our neighborhoods and therefore love and care for them. That city governments wanted us to control our schools and therefore preserve them.

We were wrong. And now, having been eliminated from the lists of urgent national priorities, from TV documentaries and the platitudes of editorials, black people have chosen, or been forced to seek safety from the white man's promise, but happily not under a bed. More and more, there is the return to Ardelia's ways: the exercise of the will, the recognition of obstacles as only that—obstacles, not fixed stars. Black judges are fixing appropriate rather than punitive bail for black "offenders" and letting the rest of the community of jurisprudence scream. Young black women are leaving plush Northern jobs to sit in their living rooms and teach black children, work among factory women and spend months finding money to finance the college education of young blacks. Groups of blacks are buying huge tracts of land in the South and cutting off entirely the dependency of whole communities on grocery chains. For the first time, significant numbers of black people are returning or migrating to the South to focus on the acquisition of land, the transferral of crafts and skills, and the sharing of resources, the rebuilding of neighborhoods.

In the shambles of closing admissions, falling quotas, widening salary gaps and merging black-studies departments, builders and healers are working quietly among us. They are not like the heroes of old, the leaders we followed blindly and upon whom we depended for everything, or the blacks who had accumulated wealth for its own sake, fame, medals or some public acknowledgment of success. These are the people whose work is real and pointed and clear in its application to the race. Some are old and have been at work for a long time in and out of the public eye. Some are new and just finding out what their work is. But they are unmistakably the natural aristocrats of the race. The ones who refuse to imitate, to compromise, and who are indifferent to public accolade. Whose work is free or priceless. They take huge risks economically and personally. They are not always popular, even among black people, but they are the ones whose work black people respect. They are the healers. Some are nowhere near the public eye: Ben Chavis, preacher and political activist languishing now in North Carolina prisons; Robert Moses, a pioneering activist; Sterling Brown, poet and teacher; Father Al McKnight, land reformer; Rudy Lombard, urban sociologist; Lerone Bennett, historian; C.L.R. James, scholar; Alyce Gullattee, psychologist and organizer. Others are public legends: Judge Crockett, Judge Bruce Wright, Stevie Wonder, Ishmael Reed, Miles Davis, Richard Pryor, Muhammad Ali, Fannie Lou Hamer, Eubie Blake, Angela Davis, Bill Russell. . . .

But a complete roll-call is neither fitting nor necessary. They know who they are and so do we. They clarify our past, make livable our present and are certain to shape our future. And since the future is where our immortality as a race lies, no overview of the state of black people at this time can ignore some speculation on the only ones certain to live it— the children.

They are both exhilarating and frightening, those black children, and a source of wonderment to me. Although statistics about black teen-age crime and the "failure" of the courts to gut them are regularly printed and regularly received with outrage and fear, the children I know and see, those born after 1960, do not make such great copy. They are those who have grown up with nothing to prove to white people, whose perceptions of themselves are so new, so different, so focused they appear to me to be either magnificent hybrids or throwbacks to the time when our ancestors were called "royal." They are the baby sisters of the sit-in generation, the sons of the neighborhood blockbusters, the nephews of jailed revolution-aries, and a huge number who have had college graduates in their families for three and four generations. I thought we had left them nothing to love and nothing to want to know. I thought that those who exhibited some excitement about their future had long ago looked into the eyes of their teachers and were either saddened or outraged by the death of possibility they found there. I thought that those who were interested in the past had looked into the faces of their parents and seen betrayal. I thought the state had deprived them of a land and the landlords and banks had deprived them of a turf. So how is it that, with nothing to love, nothing they need to know, landless, turfless, minus a future and a past, these black children look us dead in the eye? They seem not to know how to apologize. And even when they are wrong they do not ask for forgiveness. It is as though they are waiting for us to apologize to them, to beg their pardon, to seek their approval. What species of black is this that not only does not choose to grovel, but doesn't know how? How will they keep jobs? How will they live? Won't they be killed before they reproduce? But they are unafraid. Is it because they refuse to see the world as we did? Is it because they have rejected both land and turf to seek instead a world? Maybe they finally got the message that we had been shouting into their faces; that they *live* here, *belong* here on this planet earth and that it is *theirs.* So they watch us with the eyes of poets and carpenters and musicians and scholars and other people who know who they are because they have invented themselves and know where they are going because they have envisioned it. All of which would please Ardelia—and John Solomon, too, I think. After all, he did hold on to his violin.

Meaning and Idea

1.   Summarize the grandfather's thinking about the progress of black people. Summarize the grandmother's thinking. How do they compare? Whose thinking does the writer favor?

2.   Briefly describe each of the grandparents' backgrounds.

3.   How does Morrison compare the status and conditions of blacks from ten years ago with those today? What is her point in that comparison? Why does she call the "prisoners of economics" *Nixonian?* How does this section fit in with her overall historical comparison?

4.   On the first list of "the ones whose work black people respect," how many names do you recognize? Do you think Morrison meant those names to be recognizable? What is her point?

Language, Form, Structure

1.   What is Morrison's thesis in this essay? Does she ever state it exactly? If so, where? If not, how can you tell what her main point is?

2.   What is the initial comparison developed in this essay? How does Morrison use it as the seed to develop a comparison in a larger context? What is that comparison?

3.   How does Morrison use data in this essay? Give three examples and analyze each for its significance and use in the essay. What generalization is each used to support?

4. How does Morrison use references to popular culture in this essay? Why are they effective? How do they influence the organization and coherence of the essay?

5. In the conclusion to this essay, the author makes use of a series of questions. What is their purpose? Does she mean for them to be answered? Why or why not? What tone do they create? How do they serve as a fitting conclusion to the essay?

6. Define the following words from the essay: predators; rancor; fastidious; succor; vertigo; solace; disparate; sang-froid; rife; albeit; accolade; grovel. Choose five of these terms and use them in sentences of your own.

Ideas for Writing

1. Write a comparison between your parents' and your own outlook on a key political, social, or historical issue. Attempt to blend objective data with vivid, sometimes metaphoric descriptions.

2. Do you remember any time in your childhood when your grandparents, parents, or a close older relative told you how something *would be* when you grew up? Compare what you were told with what you now know to be true.

3. What is the relation between Morrison's intended audience and her style, outlook, choice of information, and use of language. Remember that this piece was written for the *New York Times Magazine.* How do you think her audience influenced her? How do you think they received the article? What significance is added in that the article first appeared on the day of the United States Bicentennial? In your analysis make specific references to the text.

Chapter Six
CLASSIFICATION

*A*s thinking animals we are forever dividing things up in our minds and putting them back together in a new way. Basic to much of this analytic thinking is the effort to classify myriad experiences and phenomena into meaningful categories. Related objects look clearer and more sensible when sorted into like groups.

Classification usually works hand in hand with division (or analysis). In *division,* you break something down into discrete elements. In *classification,* you place like members of a group into categories. Generally, the intent of division is to take one large object, concept, or idea and to split it so that its parts are clear. To understand the structure of a newspaper, you might divide it into departments—news, sports, advertising, human interest, and so on. The intent of classification is to identify groups by putting together items with common properties. You'd come closer to understanding newspaper advertisements if you looked at specific examples of personal ads, want ads, department store ads, supermarket ads, and so on. Division breaks a large unit down into its pieces; classification builds groups up by collecting common examples.

Think of almost any subject and imagine where we would be without our well-honed habits of division and classification for mental sorting. Take the simple but necessary task of housekeeping, for example. Faced with items piled high during a busy week, we must turn to division and classification as an aid. We divide the items in our pile—clothing, books, papers, sports equipment, records, games. Then we put similar items together into a large category, building to a group identity so to speak. Thus, a deflated soccer ball, a worn pair of Nikes, a catcher's mitt, two stained sweatbands, a surfboard—these specific objects help us create the category of "sports equipment." Classifying our housekeeping objects even further, we can see other possibilities for groupings. Clothing falls into categories—dirty and clean, sports and dressy, daytime and evening, and so on. These categories can be even further split: You might classify the clean clothing, for example, into underwear, slacks, shirts; the dirty into nonwashable and washable; the washable into cold, warm, and hot, or bleach and no bleach.

Classification, in short, helps us order our lives, and this ordering can be both humble, as you saw above, or more lofty as, for example, when we group countries by their economic or political systems, people by their learning styles or creative talents, colleges by their courses of study. Through classification, we can make sensible groupings not only of our daily lives, but also of the complex issues that emerge in every area of human activity and study. Indeed without classification, advanced and systematic thinking could not exist. The chemists divide the world first into organic and inorganic objects and then proceed to subdivide each of these categories further. The biologists classify living things into large groups that are further subdivided to link common creatures. The literary critics classify writing—fiction, poetry, drama, essays—and then make smaller groups within the larger ones.

For the writer, in any area or discipline, classification is essential. Rich details, observations, and examples may be the writer's stock-in-trade, but through appropriate groupings, the writer can link ideas that otherwise might lose force.

READING CLASSIFICATION

As we read classification we are reminded of the human invention involved in the undertaking. All of the selections in this chapter eschew common categories and offer the reader instead fresh mental containers for classifying the various subjects at hand.

Malcolm Cowley's essay "The National Heartbeat: 'We-ness' and 'Me-ness'" allows us to see our age under a modern political microscope. Through his classification of this century's politics as "me"-oriented or "we"-oriented, conservative and then progressive, a back-and-forth pendulum swing between two poles, Cowley helps us to see our century as patterned and to predict the tone of our next era. The two groups and the characteristics of their members enrich our understanding of contemporary politics. Similarly, George Orwell's by now classic essay "Politics and the English Language," uses classification to help us view politics from a fresh perspective. Orwell categorizes the "tricks" that many modern prose writers, especially political writers, use to cover over truth, and his classification helps us both to read with greater awareness of demagoguery in print and to write purer and truer prose ourselves.

Classification is a particularly powerful tool for helping us see the patterns and habits of political and social life. But through classification we can also come to a greater understanding of life at its most personal. Dylan Thomas's poem "Do Not Go Gentle into That Good Night" classifies dying men into types. Thomas shows the ways of men as they face death—wise men, good men, wild men, and grave men. By means of his classification, he brings us to a unique view—for his dying father and for us, the readers—of how to face the end of life.

The selections included in this chapter suggest the wide range of subjects that the strategy of classification can help to illuminate, the fresh and novel categories we can use to help us see patterns in personal, public, and artistic life.

WRITING CLASSIFICATION ANALYSIS

Much of what you are called upon to write requires some classification—breaking down your subject into classes or groups of similar members. You want to write about a poem; well, then chances are you will want to explore the *kind* of poem it is. Is it a sonnet, a ballad, a haiku? How can you classify it according to stanzaic form? Or you might try classifying the poem according to literary genre—epic, lyric, dramatic monologue—or according to subject—a love poem, a war poem, a historical poem. You may do much more besides classifying the poem in your paper, certainly, but writing on almost any topic, in almost any discipline, you will see that classification plays an important role. And it is not just in determining where your subject stands—what class of thing it is—that you call upon classification as a writer. Further analysis of your subject may compel you to make steady use of classification by grouping and categorizing your ideas and observations. In writing about a poem, let's say, you may prepare for the task by jotting down your many thoughts as you read. But then you use some rudimentary classification system to help you sort your many thoughts into different groups: thoughts on imagery, thoughts on word choice, thoughts on characters in the poem perhaps. And then within each of these groups you may find yourself using classification again. In discussing word choice you may classify into denotative meanings (dictionary meanings) and connotative meanings (the meanings that have clustered about the word through usage), or Latinate and Anglo-Saxon words, or abstract and concrete words, and so on—classifying within each of your categories.

Because categorization is a much-used tool in thinking and writing, it is worthwhile to practice writing classification. Again, as with writing of any kind, in preparing the classifications paper you will draw on many of the writer's strategies—description, exemplification, and so on. In this writing exercise, however, you will use classification as the controlling strategy.

PURPOSE AND AUDIENCE

Classification by definition reflects an act of individual judgment. People, chemicals, flora, and fauna do not come into the world neatly fitting into categories; *people* put them into categories in order to make better sense of them and to make the world more orderly through these understandings.

You must make many decisions as you think about exploring a topic through classification. Do you want to be funny or serious? Do you want simply to give information or to criticize or to persuade? Classification is an able tool and lends itself to many purposes. You want to write about your family, let's say. Well, classifying family members into ranters and ravers, whimperers, pouters, and pounders—categorizing their behavior when hurt or angry—will help you to develop your thoughts along a comic vein, to think about your family in humorous terms, and to make your reader laugh. But perhaps it's a very serious matter to you when your family is angry or hurt. Well, then you would classify very differently: You'd discuss those in your family who hold their anger in and those in your family who let their anger go. How you classify depends on how you see your subject.

Readers naturally take to classification because readers, being human, like to see the world made comprehensible and like to see the sorts of arrangements others can make. But without sufficient planning and invention on the part of the writer, classification, like comparison, can grow tedious. Beware then of papers whose ideas are merely informational, with little point of view expressed. An essay with the following thesis risks boring the reader terribly: "My teachers fall into three categories: those with degrees in science, those with degrees in humanities, and those with degrees in the social sciences." True, some lively description of teachers and their habits might make such a thesis come to life. But if the writer settles simply for cataloging information in this cinical way, readers, unless they are especially interested in the subject, will soon lose interest. How much more engaging, then, to build your own special perception into your classification. "My teachers fall into three categories: friend, mother-surrogate, confessor." Or if you're using a common classification scheme to group them—science, humanities, social science, say—then chances are that you can heighten your reader's attention if you build a point of view into your thesis. "Here at Dovery College my teachers in major academic areas—science, humanities, social science— operate from the same educational assumption: that writing is learning and learning is writing." As we said, the reader with special interest or knowledge in a subject may be tolerant or even enthusiastic about a classification essay that is purely informational. But your own lively perspective will add a unique tone to the essay and will engage your audience. Be sure, then, to think about your audience and its relation to your subject, as well as your own relation to the subject, as you prepare your classification essay.

PROCESS

Your first step in designing an essay in classification is to select the principle by which you will classify. Many subjects you might choose to write about lend themselves to varied classification systems. You want to write a classification essay on microcomputers, let's say. You should decide whether you want to classify by price, make, power, availability of software, compatibility, or what have you. Once you've decided on the principle that goes best with your interests, as well as your audience's knowledge and interest, stick with this principle as you develop your paper. Keep your categories discrete and do not overlap them. Classifying microcomputers as low-priced, main frame, medium-priced, microcomputers, IBMs, and high-priced reflects confused thinking and would lead to a confusing paper.

You also must be careful to be as complete as possible when you develop your categories. A classification of urban public transportation into automobiles and buses is a clearly incomplete classification. A complete classification would have to include trains, subways, and taxis as well. Although Cowley's two large groups are complex and original, you should be aware of the pitfalls in simplistic divisions into two groups only, these and everything else. Classifying films into the successful and the unsuccessful or foods into the nutritious and the nonnutritious creates categories too large and diffuse to be meaningful. A good rule of thumb to help you achieve a relatively complete classification system is to present at least three groups. Depending on your purpose, you might have to approach your topic exhaustively, omitting no categories whatsoever. And, you should pay some attention to exceptions: Do examples exist that defy the orderly system you have created? To ignore them is to stack the deck, and an intelligent reader will mistrust you for it. If as you plan your classification paper you find you have too many categories to manage, then modify your subject so that you and your reader don't feel either overwhelmed by too much material or cheated by a big purpose not successfully developed.

When your categories are set, decide on how you will arrange them in your paper. If you're classifying literary genre, will you move chronologically, referring as you name the groups to their origins in time? Will you present them by considering the simpler forms first and then the more complex? Or, will you follow public sensibilities by organizing your categories from the least to the most popular forms?

Classifications require the writer to attend to a good deal at once. The effective classification is one whose sections get more or less equal attention. If you devote lots of space to one or two of your categories and skimp on another, your essay will be unsatisfactory in shape and consistency.

Writing classification demands rigorous thinking and careful planning. The rewards of this effort, however, are many, as you and your readers see a subject illuminated by this important reflective act.

George Orwell
POLITICS AND THE ENGLISH LANGUAGE

George Orwell was the name adopted by the English writer Eric Arthur Blair (1903–1950). Although a socialist, Orwell is perhaps best known for his fable-novel *Animal Farm* (1946), which is highly critical of communism, and for his *1984* (1949), which presented a frightening view of a totalitarian world society. His autobiographical *Down and Out in Paris and London* (1933) and his literary criticism are considered among the best European writing of the first half of the century.

Orwell published "Politics and the English Language" in 1945; it is now considered among the finest contemporary treatises on the use of language. In this essay Orwell makes connections among thought and language processes, social corruption, and politics, employing classification as an organizational technique for his many examples and astute analyses.

*M*ost people who bother with the matter at all would admit that the English language is in a bad way, but it is generally assumed that we cannot by conscious action do anything about it. Our civilisation is decadent, and our language—so the argument runs—must inevitably share in the general collapse. It follows that any struggle against the abuse of language is a sentimental archaism, like preferring candles to electric light or hansom cabs to aeroplanes. Underneath this lies the half-conscious belief that language is a natural growth and not an instrument which we shape for our own purposes.

Now, it is clear that the decline of a language must ultimately have political and economic causes: it is not due simply to the bad influence of this or that individual writer. But an effect can become a cause, reinforcing the original cause and producing the same effect in an intensified form, and so on indefinitely. A man may take to drink because he feels himself to be a failure, and then fail all the more completely because he drinks. It is rather the same thing that is happening to the English language. It becomes ugly and inaccurate because our thoughts are foolish, but the slovenliness of our language makes it easier for us to have foolish thoughts. The point is that the process is reversible. Modern English, especially written English, is full of bad habits which spread by imitation and which can be avoided if one is willing to take the necessary trouble. If one gets rid of these habits one can think more clearly, and to think clearly is a necessary first step towards political regeneration: so that the fight against bad English is not frivolous and is not the exclusive concern of professional writers. I will come back to this presently, and I hope that by that time the meaning of what I have said here will have become clearer. Meanwhile, here are five specimens of the English language as it is now habitually written.

These five passages have not been picked out because they are especially bad—I could have quoted far worse if I had chosen—but because they illustrate various of the mental vices from which we now suffer. They are a little below the average, but are fairly representative samples. I number them so that I can refer back to them when necessary:

1. I am not, indeed, sure whether it is not true to say that the Milton who once seemed not unlike a seventeenth-century Shelley had not become, out of an experience ever more bitter in each year, more alien (sic) to the founder of that Jesuit sect which nothing could induce him to tolerate.

Professor Harold Laski (Essay in Freedom of Expression).

2. Above all, we cannot play ducks and drakes with a native battery of idioms which prescribes such egregious collocations of vocables as the Basic *put up with* for *tolerate* or *put at a loss* for *bewilder*.

Professor Lancelot Hogben (Interglossa).

3. On the one side we have the free personality: by definition it is not neurotic, for it has neither conflict nor dream. Its desires, such as they are, are transparent, for they are just what institutional approval keeps in the forefront of consciousness; another institutional pattern would alter their number and intensity; there is little in them that is natural, irreducible, or culturally dangerous. But *on the other side,* the social bond itself is nothing but the mutual reflection of these self-secure integrities. Recall the definition of love. Is not this the very picture of a small academic? Where is there a place in this hall of mirrors for either personality or fraternity?

Essay on psychology in Politics (New York).

4. All the ''best people'' from the gentlemen's clubs, and all the frantic Fascist captains, united in common hatred of Socialism and bestial horror of the rising tide of the mass revolutionary movement, have turned to acts of provocation, to foul incendiarism, to medieval legends of poisoned wells, to legalise their own destruction to proletarian organisations, and rouse the agitated petty-bourgeoisie to chauvinistic fervour on behalf of the fight against the revolutionary way out of the crisis.

Communist pamphlet.

5. If a new spirit *is* to be infused into this old country, there is one thorny and contentious reform which must be tackled, and that is the humanisation and galvanisation of the BBC. Timidity here will bespeak canker and atrophy of the soul. The heart of Britain may be sound and of strong beat, for instance, but the British lion's roar at present is like that of Bottom in Shakespeare's *Midsummer Night's Dream*—as gentle as any sucking dove. A virile new Britain cannot continue indefinitely to be traduced in the eyes, or rather ears, of the world by the effete languors of Langham Place, brazenly masquerading as ''standard English''. When the Voice of Britain is heard at nine o'clock,

better far and infinitely less ludicrous to hear aitches honestly dropped than the present priggish, inflated, inhibited, school-ma'amish arch braying of blameless bashful mewing maidens!

Letter in *Tribune*.

Each of these passages has faults of its own, but, quite apart from avoidable ugliness, two qualities are common to all of them. The first is staleness of imagery: the other is lack of precision. The writer either has a meaning and cannot express it, or he inadvertently says something else, or he is almost indifferent as to whether his words mean anything or not. This mixture of vagueness and sheer incompetence is the most marked characteristic of modern English prose, and especially of any kind of political writing. As soon as certain topics are raised, the concrete melts into the abstract and no one seems able to think of turns of speech that are not hackneyed: prose consists less and less of *words* chosen for the sake of their meaning, and more of *phrases* tacked together like the sections of a prefabricated hen-house. I list below, with notes and examples, various of the tricks by means of which the work of prose construction is habitually dodged:

Dying metaphors.   A newly invented metaphor assists thought by evoking a visual image, while on the other hand a metaphor which is technically "dead" (e.g. *iron resolution*) has in effect reverted to being an ordinary word and can generally be used without loss of vividness. But in between these two classes there is a huge dump of worn-out metaphors which have lost all evocative power and are merely used because they save people the trouble of inventing phrases for themselves. Examples are: *Ring the changes on, take up the cudgels for, toe the line, ride roughshod over, stand shoulder to shoulder with, play into the hands of, no axe to grind, grist to the mill, fishing in troubled waters, rift within the lute, on the order of the day, Achilles' heel, swan song, hotbed.* Many of these are used without knowledge of their meaning (what is a "rift", for instance?), and incompatible metaphors are frequently mixed, a sure sign that the writer is not interested in what he is saying. Some metaphors now current have been twisted out of their original meaning without those who use them even being aware of the fact. For example, *toe the line* is sometimes written *tow the line*. Another example is *the hammer and the anvil,* now always used with the implication that the anvil gets the worst of it. In real life it is always the anvil that breaks the hammer, never the other way about: a writer who stopped to think what he was saying would be aware of this, and would avoid perverting the original phrase.

Operators, or verbal false limbs.   These save the trouble of picking out appropriate verbs and nouns, and at the same time pad each sentence with extra syllables which give it an appearance of symmetry. Characteristic phrases are: *render inoperative, militate against, prove unacceptable, make contact with, be subjected to, give rise to, give grounds for, have the effect of, play a leading part (rôle) in, make itself felt, take effect, exhibit a tendency to, serve the purpose of,* etc. etc. The keynote is the elimination of simple verbs. Instead of being a single word, such as *break, stop, spoil, mend, kill,* a verb becomes a *phrase,* made up of a noun or adjective tacked on to some general-purposes verb such as *prove, serve, form, play, render.* In addition, the passive voice is wherever possible used in preference to the active, and noun constructions are used instead of gerunds (*by examination of* instead of *by examining*). The range of verbs is further cut down by means of the *-ise* and *de-* formations, and banal statements are given an appearance of profundity by means of the *not un-* formation. Simple conjunctions and prepositions are replaced by such phrases as *with respect to, having regard to, the fact that, by dint of, in view of, in the interests of, on the hypothesis that;* and the ends of sentences are saved from anticlimax by such resounding commonplaces as *greatly to be desired, cannot be left out of account, a development to be expected in the near future, deserving of serious consideration, brought to a satisfactory conclusion,* and so on and so forth.

Pretentious diction. Words like *phenomenon, element, individual* (as noun), *objective, categorical, effective, virtual, basic, primary, promote, constitute, exhibit, exploit, utilise, eliminate, liquidate,* are used to dress up simple statements and give an air of scientific impartiality to biased judgements. Adjectives like *epoch-making, epic, historic, unforgettable, triumphant, age-old, inevitable, inexorable, veritable,* are used to dignify the sordid processes of international politics, while writing that aims at glorifying war usually takes on an archaic colour, its characteristic words being: *realm, throne, chariot, mailed fist, trident, sword, shield, buckler, banner, jackboot, clarion.* Foreign words and expressions such as *cul de sac, ancien régime, deus ex machina, mutatis mutandis, status quo, Gleichschaltung, Weltanschauung,* are used to give an air of culture and elegance. Except for the useful abbreviations *i.e., e.g.,* and *etc.,* there is no real need for any of the hundreds of foreign phrases now current in English. Bad writers, and especially scientific, political and sociological writers, are nearly always haunted by the notion that Latin or Greek words are grander than Saxon ones, and unnecessary words like *expedite, ameliorate, predict, extraneous, deracinated, clandestine, sub-aqueous* and hundreds of others constantly gain ground from their Anglo-Saxon opposite numbers.[1] The jargon peculiar to Marxist writing (*hyena, hangman, cannibal, petty bourgeois, these gentry, lacquey, flunkey, mad dog,*

---

[1]An interesting illustration of this is the way in which the English flower names which were in use till very recently are being ousted by Greek ones; *snapdragon,* becoming *antirrhinum, forget-me-not* becoming *myosotis,* etc. It is hard to see any practical reason for this change of fashion: it is probably due to an instinctive turning-away from the more homely word and a vague feeling that the Greek word is scientific.

White Guard, etc.) consists largely of words and phrases translated from Russian, German or French; but the normal way of coining a new word is to use a Latin or Greek root with the appropriate affix and, where necessary, the *-ise* formation. It is often easier to make up words of this kind (*deregionalise, impermissible, extramarital, non-fragmentatory* and so forth) than to think up the English words that will cover one's meaning. The result, in general, is an increase in slovenliness and vagueness.

Meaningless words.   In certain kinds of writing, particularly in art criticism and literary criticism, it is normal to come across long passages which are almost completely lacking in meaning.[2] Words like *romantic, plastic, values, human, dead, sentimental, natural, vitality,* as used in art criticism, are strictly meaningless, in the sense that they not only do not point to any discoverable object, but are hardly even expected to do so by the reader. When one critic writes, ''The outstanding features of Mr X's work is its living quality'', while another writes, ''The immediately striking thing about Mr X's work is its peculiar deadness'', the reader accepts this as a simple difference of opinion. If words like *black* and *white* were involved, instead of the jargon words *dead* and *living,* he would see at once that language was being used in an improper way. Many political words are similarly abused. The word *Fascism* has now no meaning except in so far as it signifies ''something not desirable''. The words *democracy, socialism, freedom, patriotic, realistic, justice,* have each of them several different meanings which cannot be reconciled with one another. In the case of a word like *democracy,* not only is there no agreed definition, but the attempt to make one is resisted from all sides. It is almost universally felt that when we call a country democratic we are praising it: consequently the defenders of every kind of régime claim that it is a democracy, and fear that they might have to stop using the word if it were tied down to any one meaning. Words of this kind are often used in a consciously dishonest way. That is, the person who uses them has his own private definition, but allows his hearer to think he means something quite different. Statements like *Marshal Pétain was a true patriot, The Soviet press is the freest in the world, The Catholic Church is opposed to persecution,* are almost always made with intent to deceive. Other words used in variable meanings, in most cases more or less dishonestly, are: *class, totalitarian, science, progressive, reactionary, bourgeois, equality.*

Now that I have made this catalogue of swindles and perversions, let me give another example of the kind of writing that they lead to. This time

---

[2]Example: "Comfort's catholicity of perception and image, strangely Whitmanesque in range, almost the exact opposite in aesthetic compulsion, continues to evoke that trembling atmospheric accumulative hinting at a cruel, an inexorably serene timelessness . . . Wrey Gardiner scores by aiming at simple bullseyes with precision. Only they are not so simple, and through this contented sadness runs more than the surface bitter-sweet of resignation." (*Poetry Quarterly*).

it must of its nature be an imaginary one. I am going to translate a passage of good English into modern English of the worst sort. Here is a well-known verse from *Ecclesiastes:*

> I returned, and saw under the sun, that the race is not to the swift, nor the battle to the strong, neither yet bread to the wise, nor yet riches to men of understanding, nor yet favour to men of skill; but time and chance happeneth to them all.

Here it is in modern English:

> Objective consideration of contemporary phenomena compels the conclusion that success or failure in competitive activities exhibits no tendency to be commensurate with innate capacity, but that a considerable element of the unpredictable must invariably be taken into account.

This is a parody, but not a very gross one. Exhibit 3, above, for instance, contains several patches of the same kind of English. It will be seen that I have not made a full translation. The beginning and ending of the sentence follow the original meaning fairly closely, but in the middle the concrete illustrations—race, battle, bread—dissolve into the vague phrase "success or failure in competitive activities". This had to be so, because no modern writer of the kind I am discussing—no one capable of using phrases like "objective consideration of contemporary phenomena"—would ever tabulate his thoughts in that precise and detailed way. The whole tendency of modern prose is away from concreteness. Now analyse these two sentences a little more closely. The first contains 49 words but only 60 syllables, and all its words are those of everyday life. The second contains 38 words of 90 syllables: 18 of its words are from Latin roots, and one from Greek. The first sentence contains six vivid images, and only one phrase ("time and chance") that could be called vague. The second contains not a single fresh, arresting phrase, and in spite of its 90 syllables it gives only a shortened version of the meaning contained in the first. Yet without a doubt it is the second kind of sentence that is gaining ground in modern English. I do not want to exaggerate. This kind of writing is not yet universal, and outcrops of simplicity will occur here and there in the worst-written page. Still, if you or I were told to write a few lines on the uncertainty of human fortunes, we should probably come much nearer to my imaginary sentence than to the one from *Ecclesiastes.*

As I have tried to show, modern writing at its worst does not consist in picking out words for the sake of their meaning and inventing images in order to make the meaning clearer. It consists in gumming together long strips of words which have already been set in order by someone else, and making the results presentable by sheer humbug. The attraction of this way of writing is that it is easy. It is easier—even quicker, once you have the habit—to say *In my opinion it is a not unjustifiable assumption that* than to say *I think*. If you use ready-made phrases, you not only don't have to hunt about for words; you also don't have to bother with the rhythms of your sentences, since these phrases are generally so arranged as to be more or less euphonious. When you are composing in a hurry—when you are dictating to a stenographer, for instance, or making a public speech—it is natural to fall into a pretentious, latinised style. Tags like *a consideration which we should do well to bear in mind* or *a conclusion to which all of us would readily assent* will save many a sentence from coming down with a bump. By using stale metaphors, similes and idioms, you save much mental effort, at the cost of leaving your meaning vague, not only for your reader but for yourself. This is the significance of mixed metaphors. The sole aim of a metaphor is to call up a visual image. When these images clash—as in *The Fascist octopus has sung its swan song, the jackboot is thrown into the melting-pot*—it can be taken as certain that the writer is not seeing a mental image of the objects he is naming; in other words he is not really thinking. Look again at the examples I gave at the beginning of this essay. Professor Laski (1) uses five negatives in 53 words. One of these is superfluous, making nonsense of the whole passage, and in addition there is the slip *alien* for akin, making further nonsense, and several avoidable pieces of clumsiness which increase the general vagueness. Professor Hogben (2) plays ducks and drakes with a battery which is able to write prescriptions, and, while disapproving of the everyday phrase *put up with,* is unwilling to look *egregious* up in the dictionary and see what it means. (3), if one takes an uncharitable attitude towards it, is simply meaningless: probably one could work out its intended meaning by reading the whole of the article in which it occurs. In (4) the writer knows more or less what he wants to say, but an accumulation of stale phrases chokes him like tea-leaves blocking a sink. In (5) words and meaning have almost parted company. People who write in this manner usually have a general emotional meaning—they dislike one thing and want to express solidarity with another—but they are not interested in the detail of what they are saying. A scrupulous writer, in every sentence that he writes, will ask himself at least four questions, thus: What am I trying to say? What words will express it? What image or idiom will make it clearer? Is this image fresh enough to have an effect? And he will probably ask himself two more: Could I put it more shortly? Have I said anything that is avoidably ugly? But you are not obliged to go to all this trouble. You can shirk it by simply throwing your mind open and letting the ready-made phrases come crowding in. They will construct your sentences for you—even think your thoughts for you, to a certain extent—and at need they will perform the important service of partially concealing your meaning even from yourself. It is at this point that the special connection between politics and the debasement of language becomes clear.

In our time it is broadly true that political writing is bad writing. Where it is not true, it will generally be found that the writer is some kind of rebel, expressing his private opinions, and not a "party line". Orthodoxy, of whatever colour, seems to demand a lifeless, imitative style. The political dialects to be found in pamphlets, leading articles, manifestos, White Papers and the speeches of Under-Secretaries do, of course, vary from party to party, but they are all alike in that one almost never finds in them a fresh, vivid, home-made turn of speech. When one watches some tired hack on the platform mechanically repeating the familiar phrases— *bestial atrocities, iron heel, blood-stained tyranny, free peoples of the world, stand shoulder to shoulder*—one often has a curious feeling that one is not watching a live human being but some kind of dummy: a feeling which suddenly becomes stronger at moments when the light catches the speaker's spectacles and turns them into blank discs which seem to have no eyes behind them. And this is not altogether fanciful. A speaker who uses that kind of phraseology has gone some distance towards turning himself into a machine. The appropriate noises are coming out of his larynx, but his brain is not involved as it would be if he were choosing his words for himself. If the speech he is making is one that he is accustomed to make over and over again, he may be almost unconscious of what he is saying, as one is when one utters the responses in church. And this reduced state of consciousness, if not indispensable, is at any rate favourable to political conformity.

In our time, political speech and writing are largely the defence of the indefensible. Things like the continuance of British rule in India, the Russian purges and deportations, the dropping of the atom bombs on Japan, can indeed be defended, but only by arguments which are too brutal for most people to face, and which do not square with the professed aims of political parties. Thus political language has to consist largely of euphemism, question-begging and sheer cloudy vagueness. Defenceless villages are bombarded from the air, the inhabitants driven out into the countryside, the cattle machine-gunned, the huts set on fire with incendiary bullets: this is called *pacification*. Millions of peasants are robbed of their farms and sent trudging along the roads with no more than they can carry: this is called *transfer of population* or *rectification of frontiers*. People are imprisoned for years without trial, or shot in the back of the neck or sent to die of scurvy in Arctic lumber camps: this is called *elimination of unreliable elements*. Such phraseology is needed if one wants to name things without calling up mental pictures of them. Consider for instance some comfortable English professor defending Russian totalitarianism. He cannot say outright, "I believe in killing off your opponents when you can get good results by doing so". Probably, therefore, he will say something like this:

> While freely conceding that the Soviet régime exhibits certain features which the humanitarian may be inclined to deplore, we must, I think, agree that a certain curtailment of the right to political opposition is an unavoidable concomitant of transitional periods, and that the rigours which the

Russian people have been called upon to undergo have been amply justified in the sphere of concrete achievement.

The inflated style is itself a kind of euphemism. A mass of Latin words falls upon the facts like soft snow, blurring the outlines and covering up all the details. The great enemy of clear language is insincerity. When there is a gap between one's real and one's declared aims, one turns as it were instinctively to long words and exhausted idioms, like a cuttlefish squirting out ink. In our age there is no such thing as "keeping out of politics". All issues are political issues, and politics itself is a mass of lies, evasions, folly, hatred and schizophrenia. When the general atmosphere is bad, language must suffer. I should expect to find—this is a guess which I have not sufficient knowledge to verify—that the German, Russian and Italian languages have all deteriorated in the last ten or fifteen years, as a result of dictatorship.

But if thought corrupts language, language can also corrupt thought. A bad usage can spread by tradition and imitation, even among people who should and do know better. The debased language that I have been discussing is in some ways very convenient. Phrases like *a not unjustifiable assumption, leaves much to be desired, would serve no good purpose, a consideration which we should do well to bear in mind,* are a continuous temptation, a packet of aspirins always at one's elbow. Look back through this essay, and for certain you will find that I have again and again committed the very faults I am protesting against. By this morning's post I have received a pamphlet dealing with conditions in Germany. The author tells me that he "felt impelled" to write it. I open it at random, and here is almost the first sentence that I see: "(The Allies) have an opportunity not only of achieving a radical transformation of Germany's social and political structure in such a way as to avoid a nationalistic reaction in Germany itself, but at the same time of laying the foundations of a co-operative and unified Europe." You see, he "feels impelled" to write—feels, presumably, that he has something new to say—and yet his words, like cavalry horses answering the bugle, group themselves automatically into the familiar dreary pattern. This invasion of one's mind by ready-made phrases (*lay the foundations, achieve a radical transformation*) can only be prevented if one is constantly on guard against them, and every such phrase anaesthetises a portion of one's brain.

I said earlier that the decadence of our language is probably curable. Those who deny this would argue, if they produced an argument at all, that language merely reflects existing social conditions, and that we cannot influence its development by any direct tinkering with words and constructions. So far as the general tone or spirit of a language goes, this may be true, but it is not true in detail. Silly words and expressions have often disappeared, not through any evolutionary process but owing to the conscious action of a minority. Two recent examples were *explore every avenue* and *leave no stone unturned,* which were killed by the jeers of a few journalists. There is a long list of fly-blown metaphors which could similarly be got rid of if enough people would interest themselves in the job; and it should also be possible to laugh the *not un-* formation out of existence,[3] to reduce the amount of Latin and Greek in the average sentence, to drive out foreign phrases and strayed scientific words, and, in general, to make pretentiousness unfashionable. But all these are minor points. The defence of the English language implies more than this, and perhaps it is best to start by saying what it does *not* imply.

To begin with, it has nothing to do with archaism, with the salvaging of obsolete words and turns of speech, or with the setting-up of a "standard English" which must never be departed from. On the contrary, it is especially concerned with the scrapping of every word or idiom which has outworn its usefulness. It has nothing to do with correct grammar and syntax, which are of no importance so long as one makes one's meaning clear, or with the avoidance of Americanisms, or with having what is called a "good prose style". On the other hand it is not concerned with fake simplicity and the attempt to make written English colloquial. Nor does it even imply in every case preferring the Saxon word to the Latin one, though it does imply using the fewest and shortest words that will cover one's meaning. What is above all needed is to let the meaning choose the word, and not the other way about. In prose, the worst thing one can do with words is to surrender to them. When you think of a concrete object, you think wordlessly, and then, if you want to describe the thing you have been visualising, you probably hunt about till you find the exact words that seem to fit it. When you think of something abstract you are more inclined to use words from the start, and unless you make a conscious effort to prevent it, the existing dialect will come rushing in and do the job for you, at the expense of blurring or even changing your meaning. Probably it is better to put off using words as long as possible and get one's meaning as clear as one can through pictures or sensations. Afterwards one can choose—not simply *accept*—the phrases that will best cover the meaning, and then switch round and decide what impression one's words are likely to make on another person. This last effort of the mind cuts out all stale or mixed images, all prefabricated phrases, needless repetitions, and humbug and vagueness generally. But one can often be in doubt about the effect of a word or a phrase, and one needs rules that one can rely on when instinct fails. I think the following rules will cover most cases:

---

[3]One can cure oneself of the *not un-* formation by memorising this sentence: *A not unblack dog was chasing a not unsmall rabbit across a not ungreen field.*

i. Never use a metaphor, simile or other figure of speech which you are used to seeing in print.

ii. Never use a long word where a short one will do.

iii. If it is possible to cut a word out, always cut it out.

iv. Never use the passive where you can use the active.

v. Never use a foreign phrase, a scientific word or a jargon word if you can think of an everyday English equivalent.

vi. Break any of these rules sooner than say anything outright barbarous.

These rules sound elementary, and so they are, but they demand a deep change of attitude in anyone who has grown used to writing in the style now fashionable. One could keep all of them and still write bad English, but one could not write the kind of stuff that I quoted in those five specimens at the beginning of this article.

I have not here been considering the literary use of language, but merely language as an instrument for expressing and not for concealing or preventing thought. Stuart Chase and others have come near to claiming that all abstract words are meaningless, and have used this as a pretext for advocating a kind of political quietism. Since you don't know what Fascism is, how can you struggle against Fascism? One need not swallow such absurdities as this, but one ought to recognise that the present political chaos is connected with the decay of language, and that one can probably bring about some improvement by starting at the verbal end. If you simplify your English, you are freed from the worst follies of orthodoxy. You cannot speak any of the necessary dialects, and when you make a stupid remark its stupidity will be obvious, even to yourself. Political language—and with variations this is true of all political parties, from Conservatives to Anarchists—is designed to make lies sound truthful and murder respectable, and to give an appearance of solidity to pure wind. One cannot change this all in a moment, but one can at least change one's own habits, and from time to time one can even, if one jeers loudly enough, send some worn-out and useless phrase—some *jackboot, Achilles' heel, hotbed, melting pot, acid test, veritable inferno* or other lump of verbal refuse—into the dustbin where it belongs.

Meaning and Idea

1.   What generally assumed premise about the English language does Orwell describe in the opening paragraph? What is his opinion of that premise? What theory about the condition of the English language does he propose in its place?

2.   What is Orwell's analysis of the relation between thought and sloppy language usage?

3.   What does Orwell have to say about the "staleness of imagery" and "lack of precision" in writing? Name the categories of causes that he enumerates for these two conditions.

4. What is Orwell's basic opinion about the connection between politics and language? What does he say is the primary purpose of overtly political use of language? Does he ever express any of his own political leanings in this essay? If so, where? Support your response with specific references from the text.

5. What is Orwell's attitude about the necessity for perfect grammar and syntax? What specific rules does he offer to improve language usage?

Language, Form, Structure

1. The title of this essay promises a connection between politics and language, yet a good deal of the first half of the essay makes no overt mention of politics at all. Where in the first twelve paragraphs does he allude to politics? At what point does he make the connection explicit? Why do you think Orwell follows this structural division of the essay?

2. What is Orwell's purpose in this essay? What is his intended audience? Discuss the relation between purpose and audience in this essay.

3. Analyze Orwell's use of classification in this essay. Are the categories discrete? Do the examples fit the categories appropriately? Orwell relies heavily on process analysis to support his classification of ideas. Outline the process analysis of one particular category that you consider important. What process does he say a "good writer" will undergo for each sentence?

4. Orwell uses quite a few similes throughout this essay. Identify three and comment on their success in terms of the author's thoughts about concrete versus abstract writing.

5. Use a dictionary to define the following words: decadent; hackneyed; profundity; sordid; jargon; superfluous; scrupulous; shirk; orthodoxy; euphemism. Then use each word in a sentence of your own. Explain the following phrases (use a dictionary if necessary): sentimental archaism; mental vices; arresting phrase; sheer humbug.

Ideas for Writing

1. Classify the worst elements of today's commercial advertising. In your classification, include an analysis of the causes behind the conditions you cite.

2. Write an essay in which you classify pornography in our culture. You may want to organize your writing according to the effects or according to the types of media.

3. How closely does *your* evaluation of the connection between politics and language coincide with Orwell's? What do you consider the worst types of politicalization of language? Select three examples from contemporary nonfiction writing or media commentary, and explain how they represent different types of politicalization.

William Golding
THINKING AS A HOBBY

William Golding, born in Cornwall, England, in 1911, was educated at Oxford. He is known for his quiet rebelliousness against the "norms" of society. His novels have often dealt with the darker sides of human nature and experience. Best known among his works is *The Lord of the Flies* (1954), a macabre story of a group of English schoolboys marooned on a desert island. His other works include *The Inheritors* (1955), *The Pyramid* (1967), and *Rites of Passage* (1980). In 1984, Golding received the Nobel Prize for Literature.

"Thinking as a Hobby" first appeared in the August, 1961, edition of *Holiday* magazine. In this tongue-in-cheek essay, Golding divides thinking (*his* favorite hobby and now profession!) into three categories. Read this essay critically, with an eye to the accuracy of Golding's divisions.

While I was still a boy, I came to the conclusion that there were three grades of thinking; and since I was later to claim thinking as my hobby, I came to an even stranger conclusion—namely, that I myself could not think at all.

I must have been an unsatisfactory child for grownups to deal with. I remember how incomprehensible they appeared to me at first, but not, of course, how I appeared to them. It was the headmaster of my grammar school who first brought the subject of thinking before me—though neither in the way, nor with the result he intended. He had some statuettes in his study. They stood on a high cupboard behind his desk. One was a lady wearing nothing but a bath towel. She seemed frozen in an eternal panic lest the bath towel slip down any farther; and since she had no arms, she was in an unfortunate position to pull the towel up again. Next to her, crouched the statuette of a leopard, ready to spring down at the top drawer of a filing cabinet labeled A–AH. My innocence interpreted this as the victim's last, despairing cry. Beyond the leopard was a naked, muscular gentleman, who sat, looking down, with his chin on his fist and his elbow on his knee. He seemed utterly miserable.

Some time later, I learned about these statuettes. The headmaster had placed them where they would face delinquent children, because they symbolized to him the whole of life. The naked lady was the Venus of

Milo. She was Love. She was not worried about the towel. She was just busy being beautiful. The leopard was Nature, and he was being natural. The naked, muscular gentleman was not miserable. He was Rodin's Thinker, an image of pure thought. It is easy to buy small plaster models of what you think life is like.

I had better explain that I was a frequent visitor to the headmaster's study, because of the latest thing I had done or left undone. As we now say, I was not integrated. I was, if anything, disintegrated; and I was puzzled. Grownups never made sense. Whenever I found myself in a penal position before the headmaster's desk, with the statuettes glimmering whitely above him, I would sink my head, clasp my hands behind my back and writhe one shoe over the other.

The headmaster would look opaquely at me through flashing spectacles.

"What are we going to do with you?"

Well, what *were* they going to do with me? I would writhe my shoe some more and stare down at the worn rug.

"Look up, boy! Can't you look up?"

Then I would look up at the cupboard, where the naked lady was frozen in her panic and the muscular gentleman contemplated the hind-quarters of the leopard in endless gloom. I had nothing to say to the headmaster. His spectacles caught the light so that you could see nothing human behind them. There was no possibility of communication.

"Don't you ever think at all?"

No, I didn't think, wasn't thinking, couldn't think—I was simply waiting in anguish for the interview to stop.

"Then you'd better learn—hadn't you?"

On one occasion the headmaster leaped to his feet, reached up and plonked Rodin's masterpiece on the desk before me.

"That's what a man looks like when he's really thinking."

I surveyed the gentleman without interest or comprehension.

"Go back to your class."

Clearly there was something missing in me. Nature had endowed the rest of the human race with a sixth sense and left me out. This must be so, I mused, on my way back to the class, since whether I had broken a window, or failed to remember Boyle's Law, or been late for school, my teachers produced me one, adult answer: "Why can't you think?"

As I saw the case, I had broken the window because I had tried to hit Jack Arney with a cricket ball and missed him; I could not remember Boyle's Law because I had never bothered to learn it; and I was late for school because I preferred looking over the bridge into the river. In fact, I was wicked. Were my teachers, perhaps, so good that they could not understand the depths of my depravity? Were they clear, untormented people who could direct their every action by this mysterious business of thinking? The whole thing was incomprehensible. In my earlier years, I found even the statuette of the Thinker confusing. I did not believe any of my teachers were naked, ever. Like someone born deaf, but bitterly determined to find out about sound, I watched my teachers to find out about thought.

There was Mr. Houghton. He was always telling me to think. With a modest satisfaction, he would tell me that he had thought a bit himself. Then why did he spend so much time drinking? Or was there more sense in drinking than there appeared to be? But if not, and if drinking were in fact ruinous to health—and Mr. Houghton was ruined, there was no doubt about that—why was he always talking about the clean life and the virtues of fresh air? He would spread his arms wide with the action of a man who habitually spent his time striding along mountain ridges.

"Open air does me good, boys—I know it!"

Sometimes, exalted by his own oratory, he would leap from his desk and hustle us outside into a hideous wind.

"Now boys! Deep breaths! Feel it right down inside you—huge draughts of God's good air!"

He would stand before us, rejoicing in his perfect health, an open-air man. He would put his hands on his waist and take a tremendous breath. You could hear the wind, trapped in the cavern of his chest and struggling with all the unnatural impediments. His body would reel with shock and his ruined face go white at the unaccustomed visitation. He would stagger back to his desk and collapse there, useless for the rest of the morning.

Mr. Houghton was given to high-minded monologues about the good life, sexless and full of duty. Yet in the middle of one of these monologues, if a girl passed the window, tapping along on her neat little feet, he would interrupt his discourse, his neck would turn of itself and he would watch her out of sight. In this instance, he seemed to me ruled not by thought but by an invisible and irresistible spring in his nape.

His neck was an object of great interest to me. Normally it bulged a bit over his collar. But Mr. Houghton had fought in the First World War alongside both Americans and French, and had come—by who knows what illogic?—to a settled detestation of both countries. If either country happened to be prominent in current affairs, no argument could make Mr. Houghton think well of it. He would bang the desk, his neck would bulge still further and go red. "You can say what you like," he would cry, "but I've thought about this—and I know what I think!"

Mr. Houghton thought with his neck.

There was Miss Parsons. She assured us that her dearest wish was our welfare, but I knew even then, with the mysterious clairvoyance of childhood, that what she wanted most was the husband she never got. There was Mr. Hands—and so on.

I have dealt at length with my teachers because this was my introduction to the nature of what is commonly called thought. Through them I discovered that thought is often full of unconscious prejudice, ignorance and hypocrisy. It will lecture on disinterested purity while its neck is being remorselessly twisted toward a skirt. Technically, it is about as proficient as most businessmen's golf, as honest as most politicians' intentions, or—to come near my own preoccupation—as coherent as most books that get written. It is what I came to call grade-three thinking, though more properly, it is feeling, rather than thought.

True, often there is a kind of innocence in prejudices, but in those days I viewed grade-three thinking with an intolerant contempt and an incautious mockery. I delighted to confront a pious lady who hated the Germans with the proposition that we should love our enemies. She taught me a great truth in dealing with grade-three thinkers; because of her, I no longer dismiss lightly a mental process which for nine-tenths of the population is the nearest they will ever get to thought. They have immense solidarity. We had better respect them, for we are outnumbered and surrounded. A crowd of grade-three thinkers, all shouting the same thing, all warming their hands at the fire of their own prejudices, will not thank you for pointing out the contradictions in their beliefs. Man is a gregarious animal, and enjoys agreement as cows will graze all the same way on the side of a hill.

Grade-two thinking is the detection of contradictions. I reached grade two when I trapped the poor, pious lady. Grade-two thinkers do not stampede easily, though often they fall into the other fault and lag behind. Grade-two thinking is a withdrawal, with eyes and ears open. It became my hobby and brought satisfaction and loneliness in either hand. For grade-two thinking destroys without having the power to create. It set me watching the crowds cheering His Majesty the King and asking myself what all the fuss was about, without giving me anything positive to put in the place of that heady patriotism. But there were compensations. To hear people justify their habit of hunting foxes and tearing them to pieces by claiming that the foxes liked it. To hear our Prime Minister talk about the great benefit we conferred on India by jailing people like Pandit Nehru and Gandhi. To hear American politicians talk about peace in one sentence and refuse to join the League of Nations in the next. Yes, there were moments of delight.

But I was growing toward adolescence and had to admit that Mr. Houghton was not the only one with an irresistible spring in his neck. I, too, felt the compulsive hand of nature and began to find that pointing out contradiction could be costly as well as fun. There was Ruth, for example, a serious and attractive girl. I was an atheist at the time. Grade-two thinking is a menace to religion and knocks down sects like skittles. I put myself in a position to be converted by her with an hypocrisy worthy of grade three. She was a Methodist—or at least, her parents were, and Ruth had to follow suit. But, alas, instead of relying on the Holy Spirit to convert me, Ruth was foolish enough to open her pretty mouth in argument. She claimed that the Bible (King James Version) was literally inspired. I countered by sying that the Catholics believed in the literal inspiration of Saint Jerome's *Vulgate,* and the two books were different. Argument flagged.

At last she remarked that there were an awful lot of Methodists, and they couldn't be wrong, could they—not all those millions? That was too easy, said I restively (for the nearer you were to Ruth, the nicer she was to be near to) since there were more Roman Catholics than Methodists anyway; and they couldn't be wrong, could they—not all those hundreds of millions? An awful flicker of doubt appeared in her eyes. I slid my arm round her waist and murmured breathlessly that if we were counting heads, the Buddhists were the boys for my money. But Ruth had *really* wanted to do me good, because I was so nice. She fled. The combination of my arm and those countless Buddhists was too much for her.

That night her father visited my father and left, red-cheeked and indignant. I was given the third degree to find out what had happened. It was lucky we were both of us only fourteen. I lost Ruth and gained an undeserved reputation as a potential libertine.

So grade-two thinking could be dangerous. It was in this knowledge, at the age of fifteen, that I remember making a comment from the heights of grade two, on the limitations of grade three. One evening I found myself alone in the schoolhall, preparing it for a party. The door of the headmaster's study was open. I went in. The headmaster had ceased to thump Rodin's Thinker down on the desk as an example to the young. Perhaps he had not found any more candidates, but the statuettes were still there, glimmering and gathering dust on top of the cupboard. I stood on a chair and rearranged them. I stood Venus in her bath towel on the filing cabinet, so that now the top drawer caught its breath in a gasp of sexy excitement. "A-ah!" The portentous Thinker I placed on the edge of the cupboard so that he looked down at the bath towel and waited for it to slip. Grade-two thinking, though it filled life with fun and excitement, did not make for content. To find out the deficiencies of our elders bolsters the young ego but does not make for personal security. I found that grade two was not only the power to point out contradictions. It took the swimmer some distance from the shore and left him there, out of his depth. I decided that Pontius Pilate was a typical grade-two thinker. "What is truth?" he said, a very common grade-two thought, but one that is used always as the end of an argument instead of the beginning. There is a still higher grade of thought which says, "What is truth?" and sets out to find it.

But these grade-one thinkers were few and far between. They did not visit my grammar school in the flesh though they were there in books. I aspired to them, partly because I was ambitious and partly because I now saw my hobby as an unsatisfactory thing if it went no further. If you set out to climb a mountain, however high you climb, you have failed if you cannot reach the top.

I *did* meet an undeniably grade-one thinker in my first year at Oxford. I was looking over a small bridge in Magdalen Deer Park, and a tiny mustached and hatted figure came and stood by my side. He was a German who had just fled from the Nazis to Oxford as a temporary refuge. His name was Einstein.

But Professor Einstein knew no English at that time and I knew only two words of German. I beamed at him, trying wordlessly to convey by my bearing all the affection and respect that the English felt for him. It is possible—and I have to make the admission—that I felt here were two grade-one thinkers standing side by side; yet I doubt if my face conveyed more than a formless awe. I would have given my Greek and Latin and French and a good slice of my English for enough German to communicate. Bu we were divided; he was as inscrutable as my headmaster. For perhaps five minutes we stood together on the bridge, undeniable grade-one thinker and breathless aspirant. With true greatness, Professor Einstein realized that any contact was better than none. He pointed to a trout wavering in midstream.

He spoke: *"Fisch."*

My brain reeled. Here I was, mingling with the great, and yet helpless as the veriest grade-three thinker. Desperately I sought for some sign by which I might convey that I, too, revered pure reason. I nodded vehemently. In a brilliant flash I used up half of my German vocabulary. *"Fisch. Ja. Ja."*

For perhaps another five minutes we stood side by side. Then Professor Einstein, his whole figure still conveying good will and amiability, drifted away out of sight.

I, too, would be a grade-one thinker. I was irreverent at the best of times. Political and religious systems, social customs, loyalties and traditions, they all came tumbling down like so many rotten apples off a tree. This was a fine hobby and a sensible substitute for cricket, since you could play it all the year round. I came up in the end with what must always remain the justification for grade-one thinking, its sign, seal and charter. I devised a coherent system for living. It was a moral system, which was wholly logical. Of course, as I readily admitted, conversion of the world to my way of thinking might be difficult, since my system did away with a number of trifles, such as big business, centralized government, armies, marriage. . . .

It was Ruth all over again. I had some very good friends who stood by me, and still do. But my acquaintances vanished, taking the girls with them. Young women seemed oddly contented with the world as it was. They valued the meaningless ceremony with a ring. Young men, while willing to concede the chaining sordidness of marriage, were hesitant about abandoning the organizations which they hoped would give them a career. A young man on the first rung of the Royal Navy, while perfectly agreeable to doing away with big business and marriage, got as red-necked as Mr. Houghton when I proposed a world without any battleships in it.

Had the game gone too far? Was it a game any longer? In those prewar days, I stood to lose a great deal, for the sake of a hobby.

Now you are expecting me to describe how I saw the folly of my ways and came back to the warm nest, where prejudices are so often called loyalties, where pointless actions are hallowed into custom by repetition, where we are content to say we think when all we do is feel.

But you would be wrong. I dropped my hobby and turned professional.

If I were to go back to the headmaster's study and find the dusty statuettes still there, I would arrange them differently. I would dust Venus and put her aside, for I have come to love her and know her for the fair thing she is. But I would put the Thinker, sunk in his desperate thought, where there were shadows before him—and at his back, I would put the leopard, crouched and ready to spring.

Meaning and Idea

1. In the first paragraph, Golding states that he "came to the conclusion" as a boy that there were three grades of thinking. What is the purpose of that conclusion to this essay?

2. What are the three grades of thinking according to Golding? Summarize each briefly. According to the author, what is the most prevalent grade of thinking? By approximately what percentage?

3. What are the results of "grade two" thinking?

4. On what is the differentiation between grade two and grade one thinking based? Whom does Golding hold up as an example of a grade one thinker?

5. What is Golding's conclusion about the development of his own thinking processes? How does he classify his own mode of thought? How has he changed through the years?

Language, Form, Structure

1. In what order does Golding arrange the three grades of thinking? What is the number of the highest level? How does that arrangement affect the reader's response to the classifications?

2. To which grade of thinking does Golding devote the most discussion? Why? What does this say about Golding's evaluation of the relative importance of his classification?

3.   What is the tone of this essay? How does Golding maintain that tone throughout? Does he ever stray from it? Where? Why?

4.   How does the author accomplish transitions among the three classifications?

5.   What device does Golding use to unify his essay?

6.   Look up and define the following words: writhe; opaquely; depravity; impediments; nape; clairvoyance; proficient; gregarious; libertine; inscrutable. Then, choose five of these terms and use each in a sentence.

Ideas for Writing

1.   Write a short essay in which you classify two or three levels of the activity that is your favorite hobby. Be sure to make clear the basis for their differentiation.

2.   Write an essay in which you classify the instructors from whom you are now taking classes. Base your classification on a principle of education you consider especially important.

3.   To which of Golding's grades of thinking would you assign his own writing in this essay? Why? Using the system of classification he proposes, analyze the level of thinking in "Thinking as a Hobby."

Irwin Shaw

THE GIRLS IN THEIR SUMMER DRESSES

Irwin Shaw (1913–1984) was a novelist, short story writer, playwright, and screenplay writer who was born in Brooklyn, New York, and was educated at Brooklyn College. James Gindin observed that his works "combine sharp commentary and sensitive observation" about the changing social scene, politics, and violence. Shaw was alternately considered a pop or serious writer, and his talents and ironic sense ran the gamut in such works as *Rich Man, Poor Man* (1970), *Nightwork* (1975), and *Beggarman, Thief* (1977).

Irwin Shaw's simple, yet lasting "The Girls in Their Summer Dresses," is set in the New York City of the 1930s, but could easily have been written about a mid-1980s couple. Notice how Shaw develops various levels of affection and response.

*F*ifth Avenue was shining in the sun when they left the Brevoort. The sun was warm, even though it was February, and everything looked like Sunday morning—the buses and the well-dressed people walking slowly in couples and the quiet buildings with the windows closed.

Michael held Frances' arm tightly as they walked toward Washington Square in the sunlight. They walked lightly, almost smiling, because they had slept late and had a good breakfast and it was Sunday. Michael unbuttoned his coat and let it flap around him in the mild wind.

"Look out," Frances said as they crossed Eighth Street. "You'll break your neck."

Michael laughed and Frances laughed with him.

"She's not so pretty," Frances said. "Anyway, not pretty enough to take a chance of breaking your neck."

Michael laughed again. "How did you know I was looking at her?"

Frances cocked her head to one side and smiled at her husband under the brim of her hat. "Mike, darling," she said.

"O.K.," he said. "Excuse me."

Frances patted his arm lightly and pulled him along a little faster toward Washington Square. "Let's not see anybody all day," she said. "Let's just hang around with each other. You and me. We're always up to our neck in people, drinking their Scotch or drinking our Scotch; we only see each other in bed. I want to go out with my husband all day long. I want him to talk only to me and listen only to me."

"What's to stop us?" Michael asked.

"The Stevensons. They want us to drop by around one o'clock and they'll drive us into the country."

"The cunning Stevensons," Mike said. "Transparent. They can whistle. They can go driving in the country by themselves."

"Is it a date?"

"It's a date."

Frances leaned over and kissed him on the tip of the ear.

"Darling," Michael said, "this is Fifth Avenue."

"Let me arrange a program," Frances said. "A planned Sunday in New York for a young couple with money to throw away."

"Go easy."

"First let's go to the Metropolitan Museum of Art," Frances suggested, because Michael had said during the week he wanted to go. "I haven't been there in three years and there're at least ten pictures I want to see again. Then we can take the bus down to Radio City and watch them skate. And later we'll go down to Cavanagh's and get a steak as big as a blacksmith's apron, with a bottle of wine, and after that there's a French picture at the Filmarte that everybody says—say, are you listening to me?"

"Sure," he said. He took his eyes off the hatless girl with dark hair, cut dancer-style like a helmet, who was walking past him.

"That's the program for the day," Frances said flatly. "Or maybe you'd just rather walk up and down Fifth Avenue."

"No," Michael said. "Not at all."

"You always look at other women," Frances said. "Everywhere. Every damn place we go."

"Now, darling," Michael said, "I look at everything. God gave me eyes and I look at women and men and subway excavations and moving pictures and the littleflowers in the field. I casually inspect the universe."

"You ought to see the look in your eyes," Frances said, "as you casually inspect the universe on Fifth Avenue."

"I'm a happily married man." Michael pressed her elbow tenderly. "Example for the whole twentieth century—Mr. and Mrs. Mike Loomis. Hey, let's have a drink," he said, stopping.

"We just had breakfast."

"Now listen, darling," Mike said, choosing his words with care, "it's a nice day and we both felt good and there's no reason why we have to break it up. Let's have a nice Sunday."

"All right. I don't know why I started this. Let's drop it. Let's have a good time."

They joined hands consciously and walked without talking among the baby carriages and the old Italian men in their Sunday clothes and the young women with Scotties in Washington Square Park.

"At least once a year everyone should go to the Metropolitan Museum of Art," Frances said after a while, her tone a good imitation of the tone she used at breakfast and at the beginning of their walk. "And it's nice on Sunday. There're a lot of people looking at the pictures and you get the feeling maybe Art isn't on the decline in New York City, after all—"

"I want to tell you something," Michael said very seriously. "I have not touched another woman. Not once. In all five years."

"All right," Frances said.

"You believe that, don't you?"

"All right."

They walked between the crowded benches, under the scrubby city-park trees.

"I try not to notice it," Frances said, "but I feel rotten inside, in my stomach, when we pass a woman and you look at her and I see that look in your eye and that's the way you looked at me the first time. In Alice Maxwell's house. Standing there in the living room, next to the radio, with a green hat on and all those people."

"I remember the hat," Michael said.

"The same look," Frances said. "And it makes me feel bad. It makes me feel terrible."

"Sh-h-h, please, darling, sh-h-h."

"I think I would like a drink now," Frances said.

They walked over to a bar on Eighth Street, not saying anything, Michael automatically helping her over curbstones and guiding her past automobiles. They sat near a window in the bar and the sun streamed in and there was a small, cheerful fire in the fireplace. A little Japanese waiter came over and put down some pretzels and smiled happily at them.

"What do you order after breakfast?" Michael asked.

"Brandy, I suppose," Frances said.

"Courvoisier," Michael told the waiter. "Two Courvoisiers."

The waiter came with the glasses and they sat drinking the brandy in the sunlight. Michael finished half his and drank a little water.

"I look at women," he said. "Correct. I don't say it's wrong or right. I look at them. If I pass them on the street and I don't look at them, I'm fooling you, I'm fooling myself."

"You look at them as though you want them," Frances said, playing with her brandy glass. "Every one of them."

"In a way," Michael said, speaking softly and not to his wife, "in a way that's true. I don't do anything about it, but it's true."

"I know it. That's why I feel bad."

"Another brandy," Michael called. "Waiter, two more brandies."

He sighed and closed his eyes and rubbed them gently with his finger-tips. "I love the way women look. One of the things I like best about New York is the battalions of women. When I first came to New York from Ohio that was the first thing I noticed, the million wonderful women, all over the city. I walked around with my heart in my throat."

"A kid," Frances said. "That's a kid's feeling."

"Guess again," Michael said. "Guess again. I'm older now, I'm a man getting near middle age, putting on a little fat and I still love to walk along Fifth Avenue at three o'clock on the east side of the street between Fiftieth and Fifty-seventh Streets. They're all out then, shopping, in their furs and their crazy hats, everything all concentrated from all over the world into seven blocks—the best furs, the best clothes, the handsomest women, out to spend money and feeling good about it."

The Japanese waiter put two drinks down, smiling with great hap-piness.

"Everything is all right?" he asked.

"Everything is wonderful," Michael said.

"If it's just a couple of fur coats," Frances said, "and forty-five dollar hats—"

"It's not the fur coats. Or the hats. That's just the scenery for that particular kind of woman. Understand," he said, "you don't have to listen to this."

"I want to listen."

"I like the girls in the offices. Neat, with their eyeglasses, smart, chipper, knowing what everything is about. I like the girls on Forty-fourth Street at lunchtime, the actresses, all dressed up on nothing a week. I like the salesgirls in the stores, paying attention to you first because you're a man, leaving lady customers waiting. I got all this stuff accumulated in me because I've been thinking about it for ten years and now you've asked for it and here it is."

"Go ahead," Frances said.

"When I think of New York City, I think of all the girls on parade in the city. I don't know whether it's something special with me or whether every man in the city walks around with the same feeling inside him, but I feel as though I'm at a picnic in this city. I like to sit near the women in the theatres, the famous beauties who've taken six hours to get ready and look it. And the young girls at the football games, with the red cheeks, and when the warm weather comes, the girls in their summer dresses." He finished his drink. "That's the story."

Frances finished her drink and swallowed two or three times extra. "You say you love me?"

"I love you."

"I'm pretty, too," Frances said. "As pretty as any of them."

"You're beautiful," Michael said.

"I'm good for you," Frances said, pleading. "I've made a good wife, a good housekeeper, a good friend. I'd do any damn thing for you."

"I know," Michael said. He put his hand out and grasped hers.

"You'd like to be free to—" Frances said.

"Sh-h-h."

"Tell the truth." She took her hand away from under his.

Michael flicked the edge of his glass with his finger. "O.K.," he said gently. "Sometimes I feel I would like to be free."

"Well," Frances said, "any time you say."

"Don't be foolish." Michael swung his chair around to her side of the table and patted her thigh.

She began to cry silently into her handkerchief, bent over just enough so that nobody else in the bar would notice. "Someday," she said, crying, "you're going to make a move."

Michael didn't say anything. He sat watching the bartender slowly peel a lemon.

"Aren't you?" Frances asked harshly. "Come on, tell me. Talk. Aren't you?"

"Maybe," Michael said. He moved his chair back again. "How the hell do I know?"

"You know," Frances persisted. "Don't you know?"

"Yes," Michael said after a while, "I know."

Frances stopped crying then. Two or three snuffles into the handkerchief and she put it away and her face didn't tell anything to anybody. "At least do me one favor," she said.

"Sure."

"Stop talking about how pretty this woman is or that one. Nice eyes, nice breasts, a pretty figure, good voice." She mimicked his voice. "Keep it to yourself. I'm not interested."

Michael waved to the waiter. "I'll keep it to myself," he said.

Frances flicked the corners of her eyes. "Another brandy," she told the waiter.

"Two," Michael said.

"Yes, Ma'am, yes, sir," said the waiter, backing away.

Frances regarded Michael coolly across the table. "Do you want me to call the Stevensons?" she asked. "It'll be nice in the country."

"Sure," Michael said. "Call them."

She got up from the table and walked across the room toward the telephone. Michael watched her walk, thinking what a pretty girl, what nice legs.

Meaning and Idea

1. Into what categories does Michael classify women? Does his energetic classification of women make Michael a male chauvinist, or is it just an indication of his general appreciation for the opposite sex and for life in general, as he claims?

2. To what social class do these characters belong? How do you know?

3. In what ways does Frances classify her relation with Michael?

4. What sort of relationship exists between Frances and Michael?

Language, Form, Structure

1. By what method does Michael classify women? Does it follow any system?

2. What is the significance of the title of this story? Could it have been named just as easily "The Girls in the Offices," or "The Salesgirls in the Stores," or "The Girls on Forty-fourth Street at Lunchtime?" Why or why not?

3. At one point in the story, the Japanese waiter is described as "smiling with great happiness." What types or levels of happiness are dealt with in Shaw's story?

4. In what ways can this narrative fiction be read as classification?

5. Look up and write definitions for: excavations; scrubby; battalions; accumulated; mimicked.

Ideas for Writing

1. Write a few paragraphs in which you classify the members of the opposite sex in your school.

2. Select a single emotion and write a classification of the levels of your reactions to it. You might choose jealousy, fear, love, hate, anxiety, or some other emotion important to you.

3. With whom, Frances or Michael, do you think Shaw's sympathies lie most? Why? What elements of the writing give you this opinion?

Dylan Thomas

DO NOT GO GENTLE INTO THAT GOOD NIGHT

Dylan Thomas (1914–1953), one of the most flamboyant of modern poets, was born in Swansea, Wales, the son of a schoolteacher. However, Thomas himself was not particularly enamored of school, and he chose instead the life of a writer, publishing his first volume of poems at the age of 20. In 1936, he began a turbulent and dramatic marriage with Caitlin MacNamara, from whom he was often separated in order to give reading and lecture tours in the United States. Thomas is also known for his drama and prose, among which are the voice-play *Under Milkwood* and the delightful *A Child's Christmas in Wales*. Thomas was an excessive drinker and his alcoholism finally caused his death. Outside the Chelsea Hotel, where he often stayed in New York City, there is a plaque posted to his memory.

"Do Not Go Gentle Into That Good Night" was written in 1952 on the occasion of Thomas's father's final illness and just one year before Thomas's own death. In the poet's categorization of the ways in which different types of men face death, we discern a poignant plea to his father.

$\mathcal{D}$ o not go gentle into that good night,   1
Old age should burn and rave at close of day;
Rage, rage against the dying of the light.

Though wise men at their end know dark is right,
Because their words had forked no lightning they   5
Do not go gentle into that good night.

Good men, the last wave by, crying how bright
Their frail deeds might have danced in a green bay,
Rage, rage against the dying of the light.

Wild men who caught and sang the sun in flight,   10
And learn, too late, they grieved it on its way
Do not go gentle into that good night.

Grave men, near death, who see with blinding sight
Blind eyes could blaze like meteors and be gay,
Rage, rage against the dying of the light.   15

And you, my father, there on the sad height,
Curse, bless, me now with your fierce tears, I pray.
Do not go gentle into that good night.
Rage, rage against the dying of the light.

Meaning and Idea

1. Whom is the speaker addressing in this poem? How is the address different in stanzas one and six? Why?

2. Into what categories does Thomas classify men who are near death? How are they different from one another? How well do these classifications present a full spectrum of types of people? By what principle do you think Thomas made his selection of categories? Why?

3. What does Thomas ask from his dying father? Is there more than one way to interpret his request? Why does he ask for what he does?

Language, Form, Structure

1. This poem is written according to an intricate French structural form called *villanelle*. Without actually diagramming that form, explain, in your own words, how Thomas uses structure as an organizing technique in this poem. What effect does it produce?

2. What is the irony in the use of the word *grave* in line 13? How is that irony achieved? Why do you think Thomas uses irony here?

3. What is the overall purpose of this poem? How well does Thomas fulfill that purpose? How does classification assist that purpose?

4. Select any words that are not familiar to you from this poem, and write definitions for them.

Ideas for Writing

1. Write a short classification in which you group different types of reactions to an important natural event of your choosing, such as birth, maturation, and death, for example. Address your writing to a specific person for a specific reason.

2. Write a classification essay of different types of people in love. Be sure to include reasons why you think they fit into certain categories.

3. In the Author's Prologue to the *Collected Poems of Dylan Thomas* (1957), Thomas writes, "I read somewhere of a shepherd who, when asked why he made from within Fairy rings, ritual observances to the moon to protect his flocks, replied: 'I'd be a damn' fool if I didn't!' These poems, with all their crudities, doubts, and confusions, are written for the love of man and in praise of God, and I'd be a damn' fool if they weren't." Analyze "Do Not Go Gentle Into That Good Night" in light of Thomas's stated purpose. Do you see "crudities, doubts and confusions"? In what way is the poem for the love of man and in praise of God?

Henry Reed
NAMING OF PARTS

Although Henry Reed has written only two volumes of poetry, his earlier one, *A Map of Verona* (1946), is characterized by a fine combination of feeling and form. The volume is divided into four sections. The first, "Naming of Parts," deals with World War II. Reed's observation is sharp and ironic, and his theme is the futility of war. Born in 1914 in Birmingham, England, Henry Reed has been a freelance journalist and teacher. He is best known for his ironic and amusing dramas and radio plays produced by the BBC. His more recent volume of poetry is *Lessons of the War* (1970).

As you read Henry Reed's "Naming of Parts," pay close attention to how the poet intertwines two classifications of simultaneous activities. This poem is a poignant example of Reed's own opinions about war and its activities.

*7*oday we have naming of parts. Yesterday,   1
We had daily cleaning. And tomorrow morning,
We shall have what to do after firing. But today,
Today we have naming of parts. Japonica
Glistens like coral in all of the neighboring gardens,   5
     And today we have naming of parts.

This is the lower sling swivel. And this
Is the upper sling swivel, whose use you will see,
When you are given your slings. And this is the piling swivel,
Which in your case you have not got. The branches   10
Hold in the gardens their silent, eloquent gestures,
     Which in our case we have not got.

This is the safety-catch, which is always released
With an easy flick of the thumb. And please do not let me
See anyone using his finger. You can do it quite easy   15
If you have any strength in your thumb. The blossoms
Are fragile and motionless, never letting anyone see
     Any of them using their finger.

And this you can see is the bolt. The purpose of this
Is to open the breech, as you see. We can slide it   20
Rapidly backwards and forwards: we call this
Easing the spring. And rapidly backwards and forwards
The early bees are assaulting and fumbling the flowers:
     They call it easing the Spring.

They call it easing the Spring: it is perfectly easy   25
If you have any strength in your thumb: like the bolt,
And the breech, and the cocking-piece, and the point of bal-
     ance,
Which in our case we have not got; and the almond-blossom
Silent in all of the gardens and the bees going backwards and   30
     forwards,
     For today we have naming of parts.

Meaning and Idea

1. How is experience categorized in this poem into the "gun world" and the "living world"? Briefly describe the basis of each. What is the relation between the two?

2. What three divisions of activity are mentioned in the first stanza? How does the poet follow through on each division?

3. What is the poet's attitude toward the activities of the training camp? Support your answer with specific references from the poem.

4. To what does the word *parts* in the title refer?

Language, Form, Structure

1. How many speakers are there in this poem? Who are they? How are they different? Where does one voice end and the other begin? Would you call this poem a dialogue? Why or why not?

2. How is time used as a classifying principle in this poem? What are the time periods dealt with?

3. What is the theme of this poem? What is its tone? How do the two affect each other?

4. How is the last stanza structurally different from the others? For what purpose?

Ideas for Writing

1. Classify the various kinds of activities involved in some familiar task. Try to include—in a subtle way—your feelings about the task.

2. Classify the activities or stages which constitute a particular season other than spring.

3. *Double entendre* is a French term meaning "double meaning" and describes a word or expression that simultaneously carries two equally valid meanings and may be used to create irony. How is *double entendre* used in this poem? How does it affect your response to the theme of the poem?

ECCLESIASTES, Chapter 3

Ecclesiastes is the twenty-first book of The Old Testament. It was originally thought to be composed by Solomon, but scholars now place its writing ca. 300–160 B.C.

Ecclesiastes can be read as a philosophical essay whose theme is that all life needs to be lived happily to the fullest because "all is vanity." The certainty of death, the necessities of wisdom and mercy, and ultimate respect for God's judgments form its philosophical core.

Chapter three emphasizes acceptance of the "natural rhythm" of the universe along with enjoyment of one's labors as God's ultimate gift.

To every *thing there is* a season, and a time to every purpose under the heaven:

2 A time to be born, and a time to die; a time to plant, and a time to pluck up *that which is* planted;

3 A time to kill, and a time to heal; a time to break down, and a time to build up;

4 A time to weep, and a time to laugh; a time to mourn, and a time to dance;

5 A time to cast away stones, and a time to gather stones together; a time to embrace, and a time to refrain from embracing;

6 A time to get, and a time to lose; a time to keep, and a time to cast away;

7 A time to rend, and a time to sew; a time to keep silence, and a time to speak;

8 A time to love, and a time to hate; a time of war, and a time of peace.

9 What profit hath he that worketh in that wherein he laboureth?

10 I have seen the travail, which God hath given to the sons of men to be exercised in it.

11 He hath made every *thing* beautiful in his time: also he hath set the world in their heart, so that no man can find out the work that God maketh from the beginning to the end.

12 I know that *there is* no good in them, but for *a man* to rejoice, and to do good in his life.

13 And also that every man should eat and drink, and enjoy the good of all his labour, it *is* the gift of God.

14 I know that, whatsoever God doeth, it shall be for ever: nothing can be put to it, nor any thing taken from it: and God doeth *it,* that *men* should fear before him.

15 That which hath been is now; and that which is to be hath already been; and God requireth that which is past.

16   And moreover I saw under the sun the place of judgment, *that* wickedness *was* there; and the place of righteousness, *that* iniquity *was* there.

17 I said in mine heart, God shall judge the righteous and the wicked: for *there is* a time there for every purpose and for every work.

18 I said in mine heart concerning the estate of the sons of men, that God might manifest them, and that they might see that they themselves are beasts.

19 For that which befalleth the sons of men befalleth beasts; even one thing befalleth them: as the one dieth, so dieth the other; yea, they have all one breath; so that a man hath no preeminence above a beast: for all *is* vanity.

20 All go unto one place; all are of the dust, and all turn to dust again.

21 Who knoweth the spirit of man that goeth upward, and the spirit of the beast that goeth downward to the earth?

22 Wherefore I perceive that *there is* nothing better, than that a man should rejoice in his own works; for that *is* his portion: for who shall bring him to see what shall be after him?

Meaning and Idea

1.   How, according to this chapter, did God order man's relation to time? What attitude about daily life should derive from that relation?

2.   According to the text, are negative emotions and actions permissable? If so, when and why?

Language, Form, Structure

1.   This chapter divides into two structural units. Where does the division take place? What is the change? Why does it occur?

2.   Verses 1–8 give examples of the "natural flow" of life. Do these examples follow any special patterning or classification? Try to group them into general categories.

3.   Make sure you know the definitions for: pluck; refrain; rend; travail.

Ideas for Writing

1. Write a classification of your various emotional ups and downs of the past few years.

2. Classify a typical weekday's activities for you from morning to night. How clearly do you usually uphold this classification of activities?

3. This text derives from the traditional King James translation of the Bible. Yet, within the past ten years or so, many modernized versions of the Bible have appeared—versions that update syntax, try to eliminate the male-oriented language, deal with cultural sensitivities, and so on. How do you feel about the old language versus the new? How do you feel about updated versions of the Bible in general? Why? If possible, find a modified text of this chapter and use specific comparisons to support your opinion.

Henry James
From THE ART OF FICTION

Henry James (1843–1916) was among the most intellectual and productive of modern writers. He wrote novels, short stories, criticism, travel journals, and plays—all of which are read for their acute realism and cultural awareness. James was born in New York City, educated there and in Europe, and dropped out of Harvard Law School in favor of traveling and writing in Europe. In 1915, he gave up his United States citizenship in protest against America's noninvolvement at the beginning of World War I. He took, and kept, British citizenship. His best known novels include *The American* (1877), *The Portrait of a Lady* (1881), *The Bostonian* (1886), *The Ambassadors* (1903), and *The Golden Bowl* (1904).

"The Art of Fiction," published in 1884, is Henry James's still widely read and respected critical essay on fictional craft and creativity. Like most of his writing, the essay focuses a great deal on moral judgment and responsibility. In this essay, reprinted separately in *Partial Portraits* (1886), James dismisses the then accepted distinctions that governed fiction writing.

A novel is a living thing, all one and continuous, like any other organism, and in proportion as it lives will it be found, I think, that in each of the parts there is something of each of the other parts. The critic who over the close texture of a finished work shall pretend to trace a geography of items will mark some frontiers as artificial, I fear, as any that have been known to history. There is an old-fashioned distinction between the novel of character and the novel of incident which must have cost many a smile to the intending fabulist who was keen about his work. It appears to me as little to the point as the equally celebrated distinction between the novel and the romance—to answer as little to any reality. There are bad novels and good novels, as there are bad pictures and good pictures; but that is the only distinction in which I see any meaning, and I can as little imagine speaking of a novel of character as I can imagine speaking of a picture of character. When one says picture one says of character, when one says novel one says of incident, and the terms may be transposed at will. What is character but he determination of incident? What is incident but the illustration of character? What is either a picture or a novel that is not of character? What else do we seek in it and find in it? It is an incident for a woman to stand up with her hand resting on a table and look at you in a certain way; or if it be not an incident I think it will be hard to say what it is. At the same time it is an expression of character. If you say you don't see it (character in *that—allons donc!*), this is exactly what the artist who has reasons of his own for thinking he does see it undertakes to show you. When a young man makes up his mind that he has not faith enough after all to enter the Church as he intended, that is an incident, though you may not hurry to the end of the chapter to see whether perhaps he doesn't change once more. I do not say that these are extraordinary or startling incidents. I do not pretend to estimate the degree of interest proceeding from them, for this will depend upon the skill of the painter. It sounds almost puerile to say that some incidents are intrinsically much more important than others, and I need not take this precaution after having professed my sympathy for the major ones in remarking that the only classification of the novel that I can understand is into that which has life and that which has it not.

The novel and the romance, the novel of incident and that of character—these clumsy separations appear to me to have been made by critics and readers for their own convenience, and to help them out of some of their occasional predicaments, but to have little reality or interest for the producer, from whose pointof view it is of course that we are attempting to consider the art of fiction. The case is the same with another shadowy category which Mr. Besant apparently is disposed to set up— that of the ''modern English novel''; unless indeed it be that in this matter he has fallen into an accidental confusion of standpoints. It is not quite clear whether he intends the remarks in which he alludes to it to be didactic or historical. It is as difficult to suppose a person intending to write a modern English as to suppose him writing an ancient English novel: that is a label which begs the question. One writes the novel, one paints the picture, of one's language and of one's time, and calling it modern English will not, alas! make the difficult task any easier. No more, unfortunately, will calling this or that work of one's fellow-artist a romance—unless it be, of course, simply for the pleasantness of the thing, as for instance when Hawthorne gave this heading to his story of *Blithedale*. The French, who have brought the theory of fiction to remarkable completeness, have but one name for the novel, and have not attempted smaller things in it, that I can see, for that. I can think of no obligation to which the "romancer" would not be held equally with the novelist. The standard of execution is equally high for each. Of course it is of execution that we are talking—that being the only point of a novel that is open to contention. This is perhaps too often lost sight of, only to produce interminable confusions and cross-purposes. We must grant the artist his subject, his idea, his *donnée:* our criticism is applied only to what he makes of it. Naturally I do not mean that we are bound to like it or find it interesting: in case we do not our course is perfectly simple—to let it alone. We may believe that of a certain idea even the most sincere novelist can make nothing at all, and the event may perfectly justify our belief; but the failure will have been a failure to execute, and it is in the execution that the fatal weakness is recorded. If we pretend to respect the artist at all, we must allow him his freedom of choice, in the face, in particular cases, of innumerable presumptions that the choice will not fructify. Art derives a considerable part of its beneficial exercise from flying in the face of presumptions, and some of the most interesting experiments of which it is capable are hidden in the bosom of common things. Gustave Flaubert has written a story about the devotion of a servant-girl to a parrot, and the production, highly finished as it is, cannot on the whole be called a success. We are perfectly free to find it flat, but I think it might have been interesting; and I, for my part, am extremely glad he should have written it; it is a contribution to our knowledge of what can be done—or what cannot. Ivan Turgeniéff has written a tale about a deaf and dumb serf and a lap-dog, and the thing is touching, loving, a little masterpiece. He struck the note of life where Gustave Flaubert missed it—he flew in the face of a presumption and achieved a victory.

Nothing, of course, will ever take the place of the good old fashion of "liking" a work of art or not liking it: the most improved criticism will not abolish that primitive, that ultimate test. I mention this to guard myself from the accusation of intimating that the idea, the subject, of a novel or a picture, does not matter. It matters, to my sense, in the highest degree, and if I might put up a prayer it would be that artists should select none but the richest. Some, as I have already hastened to admit, are much more remunerative than others, and it would be a world happily arranged in which persons intending to treat them should be exempt from confusions and mistakes. This fortunate condition will arrive only, I fear, on the same day that critics become purged from error. Meanwhile, I repeat, we do not judge the artist with fairness unless we say to him, "Oh, I grant you your starting-point, because if I did not I should seem to prescribe to you, and heaven forbid I should take that responsibility. If I pretend to tell you what you must not take, you will call upon me to tell you then what you must take; in which case I shall be prettily caught. Moreover, it isn't till I have accepted your data that I can begin to measure you. I have the standard, the pitch; I have no right to tamper with your flute and then criticise your music. Of course I may not care for your idea at all; I may think it silly, or stale, or unclean; in which case I wash my hands of you altogether. I may content myself with believing that you will not have succeeded in being interesting, but I shall, of course, not attempt to demonstrate it, and you will be as indifferent to me as I am to you. I needn't remind you that there are all sorts of tastes: who can know it better? Some people, for excellent reasons, don't like to read about carpenters; others, for reasons even better, don't like to read about courtesans. Many object to Americans. Others (I believe they are mainly editors and publishers) won't look at Italians. Some readers don't like quiet subjects; others don't like bustling ones. Some enjoy a complete illusion, others the consciousness of large concessions. They choose their novels accordingly, and if they don't care about your idea they won't *a fortiori,* care about your treatment."

So that it comes back very quickly, as I have said, to the liking: in spite of M. Zola, who reasons less powerfully than he represents, and who will not reconcile himself to this absoluteness of taste, thinking that there are certain things that people ought to like, and that they can be made to like. I am quite at a loss to imagine anything (at any rate in this matter of fiction) that people ought to like or to dislike. Selection will be sure to take care of itself, for it has a constant motive behind it. That motive is simply experience. As people feel life, so they will feel the art that is most closely related to it. This closeness of relation is what we should never forget in talking of the effort of the novel. Many people speak of it as a factitious, artificial form, a product of ingenuity, the business of which it is to alter and arrange the things that surround us, to translate them into conventional, traditional moulds. This, however, is a view of the matter which carries us but a very short way, condemns the art to an external repetition of a few familiar *clichés,* cuts short its development, and leads us straight up to a dead wall. Catching the very note and trick, the strange irregular rhythm of life, that is the attempt whose strenuous force keeps

Fiction upon her feet. In proportion as in what she offers us we see life without rearrangement do we feel that we are touching the truth; in proportion as we see it with rearrangement do we feel that we are being put off with a substitute, a compromise and convention. It is not uncommon to hear an extraordinary assurance of remark in regard to this matter of rearranging, which is often spoken of as if it were the last word of art. Mr. Besant seems to me in danger of falling into the great error with his rather unguarded talk about "selection." Art is essentially selection, but it is a selection whose main care is to be typical, to be inclusive. For many people art means rose-colored windowpanes, and selection means picking a bouquet for Mrs. Grundy. They will tell you glibly that artistic considerations have nothing to do with the disagreeable, with the ugly; they will rattle off shallow common places about the province of art and the limits of art till you are moved to some wonder in return as to the province and the limits of ignorance. It appears to me that no one can ever have made a seriously artistic attempt without becoming conscious of an immense increase—a kind of revelation—of freedom. One perceives in that case— by the light of a heavenly ray—that the province of art is all life, all feeling, all observation, all vision. As Mr. Besant so justly intimates, it is all experience. That is a sufficient answer to those who maintain that it must not touch the sad things of life, who stick into its divine unconscious bosom little prohibitory inscriptions on the end of sticks, such as we see in public gardens—"It is forbidden to walk on the grass; it is forbidden to touch the flowers; it is not allowed to introduce dogs or to remain after dark; it is requested to keep to the right." The young aspirant in the line of fiction whom we continue to imagine will do nothing without taste, for in that case his freedom would be of little use to him; but the first advantage of his taste will be to reveal to him the absurdity of the little sticks and tickets. If he have taste, I must add, of course he will have ingenuity, and my disrespectful reference to that quality just now was not meant to imply that it is useless in fiction. But it is only a secondary aid; the first is a capacity for receiving straight impressions.

Mr. Besant has some remarks on the question of "the story" which I shall not attempt to criticise, though they seem to me to contain a singular ambiguity, because I do not think I understand them. I cannot see what is meant by talking as if there were a part of a novel which is the story and part of it which for mystical reasons is not—unless indeed the distinction be made in a sense in which it is difficult to suppose that any one should attempt to convey anything. "The story," if it represents anything, represents the subject, the idea, the *donnée* of the novel; and there is surely no "school"—Mr. Besant speaks of a school—which urges that a novel should be all treatment and no subject. There must assuredly be something to treat; every school is intimately conscious of that. This sense of the story being the idea, the starting-point, of the novel, is the only one that I see in which it can be spoken of as something different from its organic whole; and since in proportion as the work is successful the idea permeates and penetrates it, informs and animates it, so that every word and every punctuation-point contribute directly to the expression, in that proportion do we lose our sense of the story being a blade which may be drawn more or less out of its sheath. The story and the novel, the idea and the form, are the needle and thread, and I never heard of a guild of tailors who recommended the use of the thread without the needle, or the needle without the thread. Mr. Besant is not the only critic who may be observed to have spoken as if there were certain things in life which constitute stories, and certain others which do not. I find the same odd implication in an entertaining article in the *Pall Mall Gazette,* devoted, as it happens, to Mr. Besant's lecture. "The story is the thing!" says this graceful writer, as if with a tone of opposition to some other idea. I should think it was, as every painter who, as the time for "sending in" his picture looms in the distance, finds himself still in quest of a subject—as every belated artist not fixed about his theme will heartily agree. There are some subjects which speak to us and others which do not, but he would be a clever man who should undertake to give a rule—an *index expurgatorius*—by which the story and the no-story should be known apart. It is impossible (to me at least) to imagine any such rule which shall not be altogether arbitrary. The writer in the *Pall Mall* opposes the delightful (as I suppose) novel of *Margot la Balafrée* to certain tales in which "Bostonian nymphs" appear to have "rejected English dukes for psychological reasons." I am not acquainted with the romance just designated, and can scarcely forgive the *Pall Mall* critic for not mentioning the name of the author, but the title appears to refer to a lady who may have received a scar in some heroic adventure. I am inconsolable at not being acquainted with this episode, but am utterly at a loss to see why it is a story when the rejection (or acceptance) of a duke is not, and why a reason, psychological or other, is not a subject when a cicatrix is. They are all particles of the multitudinous life with which the novel deals, and surely no dogma which pretends to make it lawful to touch the one and unlawful to touch the other will stand for a moment on its feet. It is the special picture that must stand or fall, according as it seem to possess truth or to lack it. Mr. Besant does not, to my sense, light up the subject by intimating that a story must, under penalty of not being a story, consist of "adventures." Why of adventures more than of green spectacles? He mentions a category of impossible things, and among them he places "fiction without adventure." Why without adventure, more than without matrimony, or celibacy, or parturition, or cholera, or hydropathy, or Jansenism? This seems to me to bring the novel back to the hapless little *role* of being an artificial, ingenious thing—bring it down from its large, free character of an immense and exquisite correspondence with life. And what is adventure when it comes to that, and by what sign is the listening pupil to recognize it? It is an adventure—an immense one—for me to write this little article; and for a Bostonian nymph to reject an English duke is an adventure only less stirring, I should say, than for an English duke to be rejected by a Bostonian nymph. I see dramas within dramas in that, and innumerable points of view. A psychological reason is, to my imagination, an object adorably pictorial; to catch the tint of its complexion—I feel as if that idea might inspire one to Titianesque efforts. There are few things more exciting to me, in short, than a psychological reason, and yet, I protest, the novel seems to me the most magnificent form of art. I have just been reading, at the same time, the delightful story of *Treasure Island,* by Mr. Robert Louis Stevenson, and, in a manner less consecutive, the last tale from M. Edmond de Goncourt, which is entitled *Chérie.* One of these works treats of murders, mysteries, islands of dreadful renown, hair-breadth escapes, miraculous coincidences and buried doubloons. The other treats of a little French girl who lived in a fine house in Paris, and died of wounded sensibility because no one would marry her. I call *Treasure Island* delightful, because it appears to me to have succeeded wonderfully in what it attempts; and I venture to bestow no epithet upon *Chérie,* which strikes me as having failed deplorably in what it attempts— that is in tracing the development of the moral consciousness of a child. But one of these productions strikes me as exactly as much of a novel as the other, and as having a "story" quite as much. The moral con-sciousness of a child is as much a part of life as the islands of the Spanish Main, and the one sort of geography seems to me to have those "sur-prises" of which Mr. Besant speaks quite as much as the other. For myself (since it comes back in the last resort as I say, to the preference of the individual), the picture of the child's experience has the advantage that I can at successive steps (an immense luxury, near to the "sensual pleasure" of which Mr. Besant's critic in the *Pall Mall* speaks) say Yes or No, as it may be, to what the artist puts before me. I have been a child in fact, but I have been on a quest for a buried treasure only in supposition, and it is a simple accident that with M. De Goncourt I should have for the most part to say No. With George Eliot, when she painted that country with a far other intelligence, I always said Yes.

The most interesting part of Mr. Besant's lecture is unfortunately the briefest passage—his very cursory allusion to the "conscious moral pur-pose" of the novel. Here again it is not very clear whether he be recording a fact or laying down a principle; it is a great pity that in the latter case he should not have developed his idea. This branch of the subject is of immense importance, and Mr. Besant's few words point to considerations of the widest reach, no to be lightly disposed of. He will have treated the art of fiction but superficially who is not prepared to go every inch of the way that these considerations will carry him. It is for this reason that at the beginning of these remarks I was careful to notify the reader that my reflections on so large a theme have no pretention to be exhaustive. Like Mr. Besant, I have left the question of the morality of the novel till the last, and at the last I find I have used up my space. It is a question surrounded with difficulties, as witness the very first that meets us, in the form of a definite question, on the threshold. Vagueness, in such a discussion, is fatal, and what is the meaning of your morality and your conscious moral purpose? Will you not define your terms and explain how (a novel being a picture) a picture can be either moral or immoral? You wish to paint a moral picture or carve a moral statue: will you not tell us how you would set about it? We are discussing the Art of Fiction; questions of art are questions (in the widest sense) of execution; questions of morality are quite another affair, and will you not let us see how it is that you find it so easy to mix them up? These things are so clear to Mr. Besant that he has deduced from them a law which he sees embodied in English Fiction, and which is "a truly admirable thing and a great cause for congratulation." It is a great cause for congratulation indeed when such thorny problems become as smooth as silk. I may add that in so far as Mr. Besant perceives that in point of fact English Fiction has addressed itself preponderantly to these delicate questions he will appear to many people to have made a vain discovery. They will have been positively struck, on the contrary, with the moral timidity of the usual English novelist; with his (or with her) aversion to face the difficulties with which on every side the treatment of reality bristles. He is apt to be extremely shy (whereas the picture that Mr. Besant draws is a picture of boldness), and the sign of his work, for the most part, is a cautious silence on certain subjects. In the English novel (by which of course I mean the American as well), more than in any other, there is a traditional difference between that which people know and that which they agree to admit that they know, that which they see and that which they speak of, that which they feel to be a part of life and that which they allow to enter into literature. There is the great difference, in short, between what they talk of in conversation and what they talk of in print. The essence of moral energy is to survey the whole field, and I should directly reverse Mr. Besant's remark and say not that the English novel has a purpose, but that it has a diffidence. To what degree a purpose in a work of art is a source of corruption I shall not attempt to inquire; the one that seems to me least dangerous is the purpose of making a perfect work. As for our novel, I may say lastly on this score that as we find it in England to-day it strikes me as addressed in a large degree to "young people," and that this in itself constitutes a presumption that it will be rather shy. There are certain things which it is generally agreed not to discuss, not even to mention, before young people. That is very well, but the absence of discussion is not a symptom of the moral passion. The purpose of the English novel—

"a truly admirable thing, and a great cause for congratulation"—strikes me therefore as rather negative.

There is one point at which the moral sense and the artistic sense lie very near together; that is in the light of the very obvious truth that the deepest quality of a work of art will always be the quality of the mind of the producer. In proportion as that intelligence is fine will the novel, the picture, the statue partake of the substance of beauty and truth. To be constituted of such elements is, to my vision, to have purpose enough. No good novel will ever proceed from a superficial mind; that seems to me an axiom which, for the artist in fiction, will cover all needful moral ground: if the youthful aspirant take it to heart it will illuminate for him many of the mysteries of "purpose." There are many other useful things that might be said to him, but I have come to the end of my article, and can only touch them as I pass. The critic in the *Pall Mall Gazette,* whom I have already quoted, draws attention to the danger, in speaking of the art of fiction, of generalising. The danger that he has in mind is rather, I imagine, that of particularising, for there are some comprehensive remarks which, in addition to those embodied in Mr. Besant's suggestive lecture, might without fear of misleading him be addressed to the ingenuous student. I should remind him first of the magnificence of the form that is open to him,which offers to sight so few restrictions and such innumerable opportunities. The other arts, in comparison, appear confined and hampered; the various conditions under which they are exercised are so rigid and definite. But the only condition that I can think of attaching to the composition of the novel is, as I have already said, that it be sincere. This freedom is a splendid privilege, and the first lesson of the young novelist is to learn to be worthy of it. "Enjoy it as it deserves," I should say to him; "take possession of it, explore it to its utmost extent, publish it, rejoice in it. All life belongs to you, and do not listen either to those who would shut you up into corners of it and tell you that it is only here and there that art inhabits, or to those who would persuade you that this heavenly messenger wings her way outside of life altogether, breathing a superfine air, and turning away her head from the truth of things. There is no impression of life, no manner of seeing it and feeling it, to which the plan of the novelist may not offer a place; you have only to remember that talents so dissimilar as those of Alexandre Dumas and Jane Austen, Charles Dickens and Gustave Flaubert have worked in this field with equal glory. Do not think too much about optimism and pessimism; try and catch the colour of life itself. In France to-day we see a prodigious effort (that of Émile Zola, to whose solid and serious work no explorer of the capacity of the novel can allude without respect), we see an extraordinary effort vitiated by a spirit of pessimism on a narrow basis. M. Zola is magnificent, but he strikes an English reader as ignorant; he has an air of working in the dark; if he had as much light as energy, his results would be of the highest value. As for the aberrations of a shallow optimism, the ground (of English fiction especially) is strewn with their brittle particles as with broken glass. If you must indulge in conclusions, let them have the taste of a wide knowledge. Remember that your first duty is to be as complete as possible—to make as perfect a work. Be generous and delicate and pursue the prize.''

Meaning and Idea

1. What is James's attitude toward classifying novels as either "novels of character" or "novels of incident"? What does James describe as the relation between these two types?

2. What is James's theory of classification of novels? What two sets of distinctions will he allow? How do their bases differ from the traditional categorization?

3. What does James say about the division of novel and romance? For what purpose does he say this distinction arose?

4. What determines a "novel" for James? Why does he admit no classifications by either content or form? What examples does he provide to support his judgment? How are they different? How similar?

5. What is James's opinion of Robert Louis Stevenson's *Treasure Island?*

Language, Form, Structure

1. For whom would you say this essay was intended? Why? How does audience affect style in this writing?

2. How is classification an essential strategy in this essay? Are the categories helpful?

3. How does James use exemplification here? What is James's use of comparison in this essay? How does it support his basic theme?

4. Look up and define the following words: transposed; puerile; intrinsically; execution; hairbreadth; doubloons; venture; bestow; epithet.

Ideas for Writing

1. Choose a generally accepted classification of something familiar to you and write a short essay to show that this classification is not really valid. Be sure to include both the general reasoning and your reasons for rebuking it.

2. Write a classification of the most popular films playing this week.

3. What is your approach to reading novels? Generally, are you more interested in character or situation, or, like James, do you feel that those elements are inextricably combined? Give examples from your recent reading experience.

Robert Louis Stevenson

KINDS OF FICTION:
A REPLY TO MR. JAMES

> Robert Louis Stevenson (1850–1894), born in Edinburgh, Scotland, is known for his skillful and delightful combinations of realism and fantasy, psychology and romanticism. He lived a life as adventurous as some of his characters but fought and eventually lost a lifelong battle with tuberculosis. His *Treasure Island* (1883) and *Kidnapped* (1886) set the standard for modern adventure stories, and his *The Strange Case of Dr. Jekyll and Mr. Hyde* (1886) is considered one of the forerunners of the modernist fascination with split personalities in fiction.
>
> This essay, originally titled "A Humble Remonstrance," was published in 1884 as a response to parts of Henry James's "The Art of Fiction," which appeared in the same year. In this excerpt, Stevenson clearly uses classification as a primary technique for ordering opinions about the art of fiction.

We have recently enjoyed a quite peculiar pleasure: hearing, in some detail, the opinions, about the art they practise, of Mr. Walter Besant and Mr. Henry James; two men certainly of very different calibre: Mr. James so precise of outline, so cunning of fence, so scrupulous of finish, and Mr. Besant so genial, so friendly, with so persuasive and humorous a vein of whim: Mr. James the very type of the deliberate artist, Mr. Besant the impersonation of good nature. That such doctors should differ will excite no great surprise; but one point in which they seem to agree fills me, I confess, with wonder. For they are both content to talk about the ''art of fiction;'' and Mr. Besant, waxing exceedingly bold, goes on to oppose this so-called ''art of fiction'' to the ''art of poetry.'' By the art of poetry he can mean nothing but the art of verse, an art of handicraft, and only comparable with the art of prose. For that heat and height of sane emotion which we agree to call by the name of poetry, is but a libertine and vagrant quality; present, at times, in any art, more often absent from them all; too seldom present in the prose novel, too frequently absent from the ode and epic. Fiction is in the same case; it is no substantive art, but an element which enters largely into all the arts but architecture. Homer, Wordsworth, Phidias, Hogarth, and Salvini, all deal in fiction; and yet I do not suppose that either Hogarth or Salvini, to mention but these two, entered in any degree into the scope of Mr. Besant's interesting lecture or Mr. James's charming essay. The art of fiction, then, regarded as a definition, is both too ample and too scanty. Let me suggest another; let me suggest that what both Mr. James and Mr. Besant had in view was neither more nor less than the art of narrative.

But Mr. Besant is anxious to speak solely of "the modern English novel," the stay and bread-winner of Mr. Mudie; and in the author of the most pleasing novel on that roll, *All Sorts and Conditions of Men,* the desire is natural enough. I can conceive then, that he would hasten to propose two additions, and read thus: the art of *fictitious* narrative *in prose.*

Now the fact of the existence of the modern English novel is not to be denied; materially, with its three volumes, leaded type, and gilded lettering, it is easily distinguishable from other forms of literature; but to talk at all fruitfully of any branch of art, it is needful to build our definitions on some more fundamental ground than binding. Why, then, are we to add "in prose"? *The Odyssey* appears to me the best of romances; *The Lady of the Lake* to stand high in the second order; and Chaucer's tales and prologues to contain more of the matter and art of the modern English novel than the whole treasury of Mr. Mudie. Whether a narrative be written in blank verse or the Spenserian stanza, in the long period of Gibbon or the chipped phrase of Charles Reade, the principles of the art of narrative must be equally observed. The choice of a noble and swelling style in prose affects the problem of narration in the same way, if not to the same degree, as the choice of measured verse; for both imply a closer synthesis of events, a higher key of dialogue, and a more picked and stately strain of words. If you are to refuse *Don Juan,* it is hard to see why you should include *Zanoni* or (to bracket works of very different value) *The Scarlet Letter;* and by what discrimination are you to open your doors to *The Pilgrim's Progress* and close them on *The Faery Queen?* To bring things closer home, I will here propound to Mr. Besant a conundrum. A narrative called *Paradise Lost* was written in English verse by one John Milton; what was it then? It was next translated by Chateaubriand into French prose; and what was it then? Lastly, the French translation was, by some inspired compatriot of George Gillillan (and of mine) turned bodily into an English novel; and, in the name of clearness, what was it then?

But, once more, why should we add "fictitious"? The reason why is obvious. The reason why not, if something more recondite, does not want for weight. The art of narrative, in fact, is the same, whether it is applied to the selection and illustration of a real series of events or of an imaginary series. Boswell's *Life of Johnson* (a work of cunning and inimitable art) owes its success to the same technical manoeuvres as (let us say) *Tom Jones:* the clear conception of certain characters of man, the choice and presentation of certain incidents out of a great number that offered, and the invention (yes, invention) and preservation of a certain key in dialogue. In which these things are done wit the more art—in which with the greater air of nature—readers will differently judge. Boswell's is, indeed, a very special case, and almost a generic; but it is not only in Boswell, it is in every biography with any salt of life, it is in every history where events and men, rather than ideas, are presented—in Tacitus, in Carlyle, in Michelet, in Macaulay—that the novelist will find many of his own methods most conspicuously and adroitly handled. He will find besides that he, who is free—who has the right to invent or steal a missing incident, who has the right, more precious still, of wholesale omission—is frequently defeated, and, with all his advantages, leaves a less strong impression of reality and passion. Mr. James utters his mind with a becoming fervour on the sanctity of truth to the novelist; on a more careful examination truth will seem a word of very debateable propriety, not only for the labours of the novelist, but for those of the historian. No art—to use the daring phrase of Mr. James—can successfully "compete with life;" and the art that seeks to do so is condemned to perish *montibus aviis*. Life goes before us, infinite in complication; attended by the most various and surprising meteors; appealing at once to the eye, to the ear, to the mind—the seat of wonder, to the touch—so thrillingly delicate, and to the belly—so imperious when starved. It combines and employs in its manifestation the method and material, not of one art only, but of all the arts. Music is but an arbitrary trifling with a few of life's majestic chords; painting is but a shadow of its pageantry of light and colour; literature does but drily indicate that wealth of incident, of moral obligation, of virtue, vice, action, rapture and agony, with which it teems. To "compete with life," whose sun we cannot look upon, whose passions and diseases waste and slay us—to compete with the flavour of wine, the beauty of the dawn, the scorching of fire, the bitterness of death and separation—here is, indeed, a projected escalade of heaven; here are, indeed, labours for a Hercules in a dress coat, armed with a pen and a dictionary to depict the passions, armed with a tube of superior flake-white to paint the portrait of the insufferable sun. No art is true in this sense: none can "compete with life:" not even history, built indeed of indisputable facts, but these facts robbed of their vivacity and sting; so that even when we read of the sack of a city or the fall of an empire, we are surprised, and justly commend the author's talent, if our pulse be quickened. And mark, for a last differentia, that this quickening of the pulse is, in almost every case, purely agreeable; that these phantom reproductions of experience, even at their most acute, convey decided pleasure; while experience itself, in the cockpit of life, can torture and slay.

What, then, is the object, what the method, of an art, and what the source of its power? The whole secret is that no art does "compete with life.'' Man's one method, whether he reasons or creates, is to half-shut his eyes against the dazzle and confusion of reality. The arts, like arithmetic and geometry, turn away their eyes from the gross, coloured and mobile nature at our feet, and regard instead a certain figmentary abstraction. Geometry will tell us of a circle, a thing never seen in nature; asked about a green circle or an iron circle, it lays its hand upon its mouth. So with the arts. Painting, ruefully comparing sunshine and flake-white, gives up truth of colour, as it had already given up relief and movement; and instead of vying with nature, arranges a scheme of harmonious tints. Literature, above all in its most typical mood, the mood of narrative, similarly flees the direct challenge and pursues instead an independent and creative aim. So far as it imitates at all, it imitates not life but speech: not the facts of human dstiny, but the emphasis and the suppressions with which the human actor tells of them. The real art that dealt with life directly was that of the first men who told their stories round the savage camp-fire. Our art is occupied, and bound to be occupied, not so much in making stories true as in making them typical; not so much in capturing the lineaments of each fact, as in marshalling all of them towards a common end. For the welter of impressions, all forcible but all discreet, which life presents, it substitutes a certain artificial series of impressions, all ineed most feebly represented, but all aiming at the same effect, all eloquent of the same idea, all chiming together like consonant notes in music or like the graduated tints in a good picture. From all its chapters, from all its pages, from all its sentences, the well-written novel echoes and re-echoes its one creative and controlling thought; to this must every incident and character contribute; the style must have been pitched in unison with this; and if there is anywhere a word that looks another way, the book would be stronger, clearer, and (I had almost said) fuller without it. Life is monstrous, infinite, illogical, abrupt and poignant; a work of art, in comparison, is neat, finite, self-contained, rational, flowing and emasculate. Life imposes by brute energy, like inarticulate thunder; art catches the ear, among the far louder noises of experience, like an air artificially made by a discreet musician. A proposition of geometry does not compete with life; and a proposition of geometry is a fair and luminous parallel for a work of art. Both are reasonable, both untrue to the crude fact; both inhere in nature, neither represents it. The novel, which is a work of art, exists, not by its resemblances to life, which are forced and material, as a shoe must still consist of leather, but by its immeasurable difference from life, which is designed and significant, and is both the method and the meaning of the work.

The life of man is not the subject of novels, but the inexhaustible magazine from which subjects are to be selected; the name of these is legion; and with each new subject—for here again I must differ by the whole width of heaven from Mr. James—the true artist will vary his

method and change the point of attack. That which was in one case an
excellence, will become a defect in another; what was the making of one
book, will in the next be impertinent or dull. First each novel, and then
each class of novels, exists by and for itself. I will take, for instance, three
main classes, which are fairly distinct: first, the novel of adventure, which
appeals to certain almost sensual and quite illogical tendencies in man;
second, the novel of character, which appeals to our intellectual appreciation of man's foibles and mingled and inconstant motives; and third, the
dramatic novel, which deals with the same stuff as the serious theatre,
and appeals to our emotional nature and moral judgment.

And first for the novel of adventure. Mr. James refers, with singular
generosity of praise, to a little book about a quest for hidden treasure; but
he lets fall, by the way, some rather startling words. In this book he
misses what he calls the ''immense luxury'' of being able to quarrel with
his author. The luxury, to most of us, is to lay by our judgment, to be
submerged by the tale as by a billow, and only to awake, and begin to
distinguish and find fault, when the piece is over and the volume laid
aside. Still more remarkable is Mr. James's reason. He cannot criticise
the author, as he goes, ''because,'' says he, comparing it with another
work, ''I have been a child, but I have never been on a quest for buried
treasure.'' Here is, indeed, a wilful paradox; for if he has never been on a
quest for buried treasure, it can be demonstrated that he has never been a
child. There never was a child (unless Master James) but has hunted gold,
and been a pirate, and a military commander, and a bandit of the mountains; but has fought, and suffered shipwreck and prison, and imbrued its
little hands in gore, and gallantly retrieved the lost battle, and tri-
umphantly protected innocence and beauty. Elsewhere in his essay Mr.
James has protested with excellent reason against too narrow a conception of experience; for the born artist, he contends, the ''faintest hints of
life'' are converted into revelations; and it will be found true, I believe, in
a majority of cases, that the artist writes with more gusto and effect of
those things which he has only wished to do, than of those which he has
done. Desire is a wonderful telescope, and Pisgah the best observatory.
Now, while it is true that neither Mr. James nor the author of the work in
question has ever, in the fleshly sense, gone questing after gold, it is
probable that both have ardently desired and fondly imagined the details
of such a life in youthful day-dreams; and the author, counting upon that,
and well aware (cunning and low-minded man!) that this class of interest,
having been frequently treated, finds a readily accessible and beaten road
to the sympathies of the reader, addressed himself throughout to the
building up and circumstantiation of this boyish dream. Character to the
boy is a sealed book; for him, a pirate is a beard, a pair of wide trousers
and a liberal complement of pistols. The author, for the sake of circumstantiation and because he was himself more or less grown up, admitted

character, within certain limits, into his design; but only within certain limits. Had the same puppets figured in a scheme of another sort, they had been drawn to very different purpose; for in this elementary novel of adventure, the characters need to be presented with but one class of qualities—the warlike and formidable. So as they appear insidious in deceit and fatal in the combat, they have served their end. Danger is the matter with which this class of novel deals; fear, the passion with which it idly trifles; and the characters are portrayed only so far as they realise the sense of danger and provoke the sympathy of fear. To add more traits, to be too clever, to start the hare of moral or intellectual interest while we are running the fox of material interest, is not to enrich but to stultify your tale. The stupid reader will only be offended, and the clever reader lose the scent.

The novel of character has this difference from all others: that it requires no coherency of plot, and for this reason, as in the case of *Gil Blas*, it is sometimes called the novel of adventure. It turns on the humours of the persons represented; these are, to be sure, embodied in incidents, but the incidents themselves, being tributary, need not march in a progression; and the characters may be statically shown. As they enter, so they may go out; they must be consistent, but they need not grow. Here Mr. James will recognise the note of much of his own work: he treats, for the most part, the statics of character, studying it at rest or only gently moved; and, with his usual delicate and just artistic instinct, he avoids those stronger passions which would deform the attitudes he loves to study, and change his sitters from the humorists of ordinary life to the brute forces and bare types of more emotional moments. In his recent *Author of Beltraffio,* so just in conception, so nimble and neat in workmanship, strong passion is indeed employed; but observe that it is not displayed. Even in the heroine the working of the passion is suppressed; and the great struggle, the true tragedy, the *scène-à-faire,* passes unseen behind the panels of a locked door. The delectable invention of the young visitor is introduced, consciously or not, to this end: that Mr. James, true to his method, might avoid the scene of passion. I trust no reader will suppose me guilty of undervaluing this little masterpiece. I mean merely that it belongs to one marked class of novel, and that it would have been very differently conceived and treated had it belonged to that other marked class, of which I now proceed to speak.

I take pleasure in calling the dramatic novel by that name, because it enables me to point out by the way a strange and peculiarly English misconception. It is sometimes supposed that the drama consists of incident. It consists of passion, which gives the actor his opportunity; and that passion must progressively increase, or the actor, as the piece proceeded, would be unable to carry the audience from a lower to a higher pitch of interest and emotion. A good serious play must therefore be founded on one of the passionate *cruces* of life, where duty and inclination come nobly to the grapple; and the same is true of what I call, for that reason, the dramatic novel. I will instance a few worthy specimens, all of our own day and language; Meredith's *Rhoda Fleming,* that wonderful and painful book, long out of print, and hunted for at bookstalls like an Aldine; Hardy's *Pair of Blue Eyes;* and two of Charles Reade's, *Griffith Gaunt* and *The Double Marriage,* originally called *White Lies,* and founded (by an accident quaintly favourable to my nomenclature) on a play by Maquet, the partner of the great Dumas. In this kind of novel the closed door of *The Author of Beltraffio* must be broken open; passion must appear upon the scene and utter its last word; passion is the be-all and the end-all, the plot and the solution, the protagonist and the *deus ex machina* in one. The characters may come anyhow upon the stage: we do not care; the point is, that, before they leave it, they shall become transfigured and raised out of themselves by passion. It may be part of the design to draw them with detail; to depict a full-length character, and then behold it melt and change in the furnace of emotion. But there is no obligation of the sort; nice portraiture is not required; and we are content to accept mere abstract types, so they be strongly and sincerely moved. A novel of this class may be even great, and yet contain no individual figure; it may be great, because it displays the workings of the perturbed heart and the impersonal utterance of passion; and with an artist of the second class it is, indeed, even more likely to be great, when the issue has thus been narrowed and the whole force of the writer's mind directed to passion alone. Cleverness again, which has its fair field in the novel of character, is debarred all entry upon this more solemn theatre. A far-fetched motive, an ingenious evasion of the issue, a witty instead of a passionate turn, offend us like an insincerity. All should be plain, all straightforward to the end. Hence it is that, in *Rhoda Fleming,* Mrs. Lovel raises such resentment in the reader; her motives are too flimsy, her ways are too equivocal, for the weight and strength of her surroundings. Hence the hot indignation of the reader when Balzac, after having begun the *Duchesse de Langeais* in terms of strong if somewhat swollen passion, cuts the knot by the derangement of the hero's clock. Such personages and incidents belong to the novel of character; they are out of place in the high society of the passions; when the passions are introduced in art at their full height, we look to see them, not baffled and impotently striving, as in life, but towering above circumstance and acting substitutes for fate.

And here I can imagine Mr. James, with his lucid sense, to intervene. To much of what I have said he would apparently demur; in much he would, somewhat impatiently, acquiesce. It may be true; but it is not what he desired to say or to hear said. He spoke of the finished picture and its worth when done; I, of the brushes, the palette, and the north light. He uttered his views in the tone and for the ear of good society; I, with the emphasis and technicalities of the obtrusive student. But the point, I may reply, is not merely to amuse the public, but to offer helpful advice to the young writer. And the young writer will not so much be helped by genial pictures of what an art may aspire to at its highest, as by a true idea of what it must be on the lowest terms. The best that we can say to him is this: Let him choose a motive, whether of character or passion; carefully construct his plot so that every incident is an illustration of the motive, and every property employed shall bear to it a near relation of congruity or contrast; avoid a sub-plot, unless, as sometimes in Shakespeare, the sub-plot be a reversion or complement of the main intrigue; suffer not his style to flag below the level of the argument; pitch the key of conversation, not with any thought of how men talk in parlours, but with a single eye to the degree of passion he may be called on to express; and allow neither himself in the narrative nor any character in the course of the dialogue, to utter one sentence that is not part and parcel of the business of the story or the discussion of the problem involved. Let him not regret if this shortens his book; it will be better so; for to add irrelevant matter is not to lengthen but to bury. Let him not mind if he miss a thousand qualities, so that he keeps unflaggingly in pursuit of the one he has chosen. Let him not care particularly if he miss the tone of conversation, the pungent material detail of the day's manners, the reproduction of the atmosphere and the environment. These elements are not essential: a novel may be excellent, and yet have none of them; a passion or a character is so much the better depicted as it rises clearer from material circumstance. In this age of the particular, let him remember the ages of the abstract, the great books of the past, the brave men that lived before Shakespeare and before Balzac. And as the root of the whole matter, let him bear in mind that his novel is not a transcript of life, to be judged by its exactitude; but a simplification of some side or point of life, to stand or fall by its significant simplicity. For although, in great men, working upon great motives, what we observe and admire is often their complexity, yet underneath appearances the truth remains unchanged: that simplification was their method, and that simplicity is their excellence. . . .

Meaning and Idea

1. Into how many categories does Stevenson classify novels? What are they? In your own words, briefly describe the basis for each category.

2. What is Stevenson's attitude toward Henry James's novel *The Author of Beltraffio?* To which category does he assign it? Why?

3. What is Stevenson's expressed attitude toward his own *Treasure Island*? Do you feel this is his most truthful opinion of the novel? Why? How does his opinion of *Treasure Island* compare with Henry James's opinion of it in the preceding essay, "The Art of Fiction"?

Language, Form, Structure

1. What is Stevenson's purpose in writing this essay? Where and in what tone does he indicate that intention? How does Stevenson order his discussion of the classes of novels? How does that order affect the proportion of attention he devotes to each?

2. What examples does Stevenson use in each category of novel discussed? Why do you think he uses one of his own and one of Henry James's novels? How does he compare the two?

3. How does the role of character serve as an organizing device for Stevenson's classification? How is character used as part of the explanation of each category?

4. How does the author contrast his definition of drama to the generally accepted "strange and peculiarly English misconception" about drama?

5. Write definitions for the following and then use each in a sentence: legion; impertinent; foibles; formidable; insidious; deceit; stultify; nomenclature; ingenious; equivocal.

Ideas for Writing

1. Think about several of the novels, plays, stories, or nonfiction works you have read recently. Classify them according to some principle of your own reasons for reading.

2. What is your opinion of Stevenson's classification of fiction? Does it seem correct to you, or do you feel, like Henry James, that

these separations . . . have been made by critics and readers for their own convenience, and to help them out of some of their difficulties, but have little reality or interest. . . .

Support your opinion with examples from your own reading.

Malcolm Cowley
THE NATIONAL HEARTBEAT: "WE-NESS" AND "ME-NESS"

Malcolm Cowley, born in Pennsylvania in 1898, has stretched his career as literary critic, poet, editor, and social historian from pre-World War I days to the present. He is well known for his studies of the Lost Generation of American expatriate writers in the 1920s, *Exiles' Return* (1934) and *A Second Flowering* (1973). As editor of the liberal *New Republic,* he organized the 1932 Bonus Expeditionary Force to march to President Hoover's doorstep during the Great Depression to demand their army pensions.

"The National Heartbeat: 'We-ness' and 'Me-ness'" carries into the present decade Cowley's fine, sixty-plus–year history of alert social criticism. As you read, pay attention to his social and cultural classifications and how they differ from what he describes as the mainstream opinions.

$\mathcal{S}$ o it has been more or less agreed that America is turning right. One pictures a disciplined army of 200 million persons, not counting toddlers, all, as at a word of command, executing a right face and marching off into John Wayne country.

I should question whether there has been any such unanimity, but undoubtedly there has been a change in mood and direction. Liberals now admit to being qualmish about big government. Conservatives are shouting hallelujah! as they band into national lobbies. The watchword in education is "back to basics." College students, those barometers of the future—if one learns to read the dials—have stopped being rebels; instead they plug for marks, worry about finding jobs after graduation, and one reads that their favorite course is Accounting.

But after the turbulent age group of the 1960's, isn't that what might have been expected? Another age group has appeared with its own standards of the good life, and these were pretty certain to be in conflict with the standards of the group that preceded it.

Age groups and the part they have played in American culture—or indeed in any culture—are a subject that has seldom been thoroughly discussed. It first attracted my attention when I was working on the literary records of the so-called Lost Generation. Soon I noted that this

was only one of several "generations" in 20th-century American literature. Then I observed that the same phenomenon of conflicting age
groups appeared in other fields—art, music, science, public affairs—and
was finally mirrored in the general mood of the country. Each new group
had its own likes, dislikes, and aspirations, its own "consciousness" or
sense of life, and this it tried to impose on older groups and on the future.

But was "generation" the right word for those successive groups?
They seemed to come forward at much shorter intervals than the 30-year
span of a biological generation. American commentators have preferred
to speak in terms of decades, thereby adopting a numerical scheme that
lends itself to simple adjectives: the Roaring 20's, the Depression 30's
(which were not depressed), the silent or shameful 50's, the rebellious
60's. I noted, however, that this counting by tens doesn't often corres-
pond to the true date either for an age group or for changes in the
dominant mood.

I decided to make a chronological table, based on what I remembered
or had learned about our century. The result was something like this:

1904–1918: The Age of Reform. Muckrakers, labor novelists, Bull
Moose, and finally a crusade to make the world safe for democracy.

1919–1930: The Jazz Age. Wall Street follies, the fast buck, bathtub
gin, "The Great Gatsby," expatriation, the crash of '29.

1931–1945: The Depression. Bread lines, the New Deal, Spain, "The
Grapes of Wrath." The Hitler-Stalin Pact, and finally the great war that
was not a crusade.

1946–1960: The Silent Generation. Security, "making it," the baby
boom, the cold war, Joe McCarthy, the New Critics.

1961–1973: The Youth Rebellion. Freedom marches, pot, rock music,
"Make love, not war." Vietnam, "The March on the Pentagon," Watergate.

Others might choose different dates for the beginning and end of each
period (except when the change in mood was abrupt and unmistakable, as
at the end of the two world wars) More often there was a gradual
transition, as when the Silent Generation of the 1950's made way for the
Youth Rebellion. Did the 60's really begin with John F. Kennedy's
Inaugural Address ("Ask what you can do for your country") or only
with the bitter news of his assassination? And what about movements like
Women's Liberation that have already spanned two eras?

One could argue at length about such questions, but I think that two or
three facts might become apparent from my little chart. The first is that
there have been five distinct periods—or six, counting the present era—
since the turn of the century.

They have lasted for an average of a little less than 15 years, or half the
span of a human generation. Finally, one notes that the dominant mood of
the country has gone from one extreme to another, and back again, so that

periods 30 years apart bear some resemblance to each other. The Old Left of the 1930's fathered the New Left of the 1960's. Now, in the late 1970's, we have the New Right, just as in the late 1940's.

Right . . . left . . . right. Hearing those words so often, we picture the country as following the swing of a giant pendulum. The real process, however, is rather an expansion and contraction of interests on the part of influential minorities. "We-ness" and "me-ness" are the two key words. During an expansive period, the general attention is turned outward to broad issues affecting "us," the nation or the world. The leftists are loud and confident. During a contractive period, attention is focused on "my" success in a stable society. The voices we hear are those of conservatives.

One period has followed another in an immensely slow heartbeat rhythm of diastole followed by systole. The Age of Reform, the Depression, the Youth Rebellion of the 1960's—all those were expansive periods. In each case they were succeeded by a contractive period: the Jazz Age, the Silent Generation, and now the "me" years after Watergate.

Of course those alternations were shaped by external events, including wars, a depression, and the baby boom. I believe, however, that they also reveal an inner logic and sequence. Perhaps the guiding concept here is disillusionment. The spokesmen for an expansive period are disillusioned when their dream of the future is shattered by such events as the Treaty of Versailles (1919) or the Hitler-Stalin Pact of 1939. A contractive period, with its hunger for personal achievement, or simply for money, leads to another type of disillusionment, this time connected with stress, alienation, corruption, and nervous breakdown. That was what happened toward the end of the Jazz Age, and it may soon happen again, if we can trust college reports.

And then what is to be expected? Putting on my tall, conical wizard's hat and acting the part of an aged seer, I prophesy that some time in the middle 1980's there will be another reaction from me-ness into we-ness, another cresting and falling wave of popular idealism. I don't know what form it will take, since that will depend on events in the world and the nation, but I am sure it is coming.

Meaning and Idea

1. What is Cowley's basic premise in this essay? What is the focus of his evaluation of the changes which have taken place over the past eighty years? Over the past five years?

2. What is Cowley's opinion of the American political climate of the 1980s? What examples does he offer to support his opinion? What does he say about how present-day college students fit into this political climate?

3. What does the author mean by the phrase "marching off into John Wayne country"? Explain in your own words the meaning of the complete metaphor in the second sentence.

4. What does Cowley mean by *we-ness* and *me-ness*? Why does he identify them as "the two key words"?

5. What does Cowley predict will take place in the mid-1980s? Since we are already there, do you see any evidence of his predictions beginning to come true? How would you characterize Cowley's overall political stance? Do you classify him as a pessimist or an optimist? Why?

Language, Form, Structure

1. According to Cowley, by what classification scheme have most American commentators on culture identified America's consciousness of the twentieth century? What is Cowley's scheme of classification? How are they different? On what basis does he decide to make his categories?

2. What special *connotations* (see page 000) does the author apply to the following words or expressions: right; barometers; consciousness; generation; New Left; New Right.

3. How does this essay combine classification with process analysis? Identify and briefly summarize two process analyses used in this essay.

4. Cowley makes use of numerous allusions to political, social and cultural events. From each of the eras listed on his chart covering the period 1904–1973, choose and explain one fully.

5. Look up the following words in a dictionary and then use each in a sentence: unanimity; qualmish; turbulent; aspirations; expatriation; contractive; diastole; systole; seer; prophesy.

Ideas for Writing

1. Write a classification of the various cliques or social groups in your school. In your prewriting, be sure to decide on basic principles of classification by which to describe the groups.

2. Write a short classification of either "givers" *or* "takers" among people you have known. Include at least three categories.

3. Do you agree with Cowley's basic division of the ages by means of the "we-ness" and "me-ness" factors? Write a further classification of these two groups based on your own observations. Into which group would you place yourself? Into which group would you place the majority of students in your school? Why?

Chapter Seven
CAUSATION

*T*hinking about causes—what produces something—and thinking about effects—what something produces—is an activity both natural and necessary to human life. Questions like, "Why did I do that?", "What happened because I did that?", and "What might happen if I do that?" reflect both our instinctive curiosity and our desire to learn from experience—to explain or control life from our judgments of the past or from our anticipation of the future. Indeed it is hard to think of an hour passing when our minds are not engaged in causal thinking. The whistling we hear: is that the kettle, the wind, the radio? That pulsing headache: is it an emerging cold, tension over an exam, eyestrain, or the day's humidity? And what will result from the headache? Will we miss work, fail a test, finally replace lost eyeglasses, shop for a dehumidifier?

Not surprisingly, great writing throughout history reflects the basic human habit of seeking explanations for why things happen and what occurs after they happen. In almost every culture, early myths explore why the world began and why its inhabitants, human and nonhuman alike, got to be the way they are. Philosophers from Aristotle on have dealt copiously with causal thinking—what it is, how to do it best, how to avoid its traps. For Aristotle, and then for the medieval philosophers who built on his thinking, there existed a taxonomy of causes—*efficient* cause, *material* cause, *formal* cause, *final* cause, to name but a few. For ages most thinkers saw a *necessary* connection between causes and effects, a connection finally controlled by power from a divine source. In the eighteenth century, however, the philosopher David Hume painted a universe as a place of accidents and coincidences, not of absolute connections between causes and effects. Hume helped to change markedly a long-accepted view of causation. By the twentieth century, the philosopher Bertrand Russell declared the idea of cause a "relic of bygone days."

The stance of men like Russell may be extreme and inaccurate; but it is valuable, for it cautions us away from fast and smug interpretations of why things happen. Essential as it is, the whole undertaking of causal thinking can be treacherous. Rushing to judgment, we can assign the wrong cause to an event, or can point to an effect that is no more than a coincidence. Chances are that the notion of causality will be with us for as long as humans think critically about events, but going slowly and carefully as we think about why things happen and what follows when something happens seems the only right way to reach sound and useful judgments. The imaginative writer delves steadily and deeply into causes and effects. The great writer eschews snap judgments, tracing the possibilities for why things occur or for the effects of occurrences, and inviting readers to use their own faculties to validate proposed causes and results.

READING CAUSAL ANALYSIS

Read a tale to a child and the child asks, "Why? Then what?" These questions remain steady ones as we read throughout our lives. In great writing we find minds searching for why things happen—why wars start, why marriages last or fail, why people give up or endure, why kingdoms and civilizations crumble or advance. And great writing takes up the questions beyond these: What happens as a result of certain conditions—*after* wars begin, *after* marriages end, *after* men or women survive, *after* kingdoms fall. What happens then?

The selections in this chapter allow you to see both impulses at work—the search back into causes and the search forward from events into effects. Sophocles' *Oedipus Rex* traces the history of an individual, a family, and a kingdom. The drama lays out a chain of events that precedes and follows human tragedy. Sophocles views the entire sequence in the context of divine decisions as Oedipus seeks to uncover the whys of his life. To the modern mind, Sophocles's world is a world of sharply drawn causes and consequences, but the playwright shows nonetheless the individual human struggling to have an effect on the world, using his wit and his words heroically, if tragically. In the myth of Oedipus, which Sophocles took up for his play, human lives are fated; but in Sophocles' hands, the old story becomes more than just a story of doom. By explaining the consequences of fated actions in human life, he gives us the essence of tragedy.

Reading causation in the masters, we are encouraged to see the subtlety of explanations that guide us away from pat interpretations. Indeed in the hands of great writers, causal analysis is often more an *asking* or a *suggesting* than a certain *stating* of causes and/or effects. Edward Arlington Robinson's poem "Richard Corey" never tells the reader "This is why Richard Corey killed himself"; rather the poet lays out details and patterns that invite the reader to speculate *why*.

Reading causal analyses can teach us much as we approach our own thinking and writing. Great writers remind us to approach the whole undertaking of causation with care, to avoid the quick and facile explanations that lead to error, and to find the explanations that can open our eyes about past events and future possibilities.

WRITING CAUSAL ANALYSIS

Causal thinking is central to much writing. Again and again students receive assignments whose major task is the identification and explanation of the cause of a particular phenomenon, the effects of the phenomenon, or both. History courses might ask you to examine in writing the causes or results of a war. Literature courses might ask you to write on causes or effects of character, events, or places. Science courses might ask you to reflect again and again on events leading to or resulting from some occurrence—how a compound forms from two elements in a test tube, say, or the consequences of unchecked atmospheric pollution.

Causal analysis is the dominant undertaking of a good portion of academic assignments and an important contributor to still more. Most writers undertaking a comprehensive analysis of a subject will pay attention to causality, even if their major concerns lie elsewhere. Explaining how to establish a new lawn, for example, a writer might lay out the consequences of too little watering or too much fertilizer, and would therefore be drawing cause and effect into a paper whose main intent was process analysis. In a comparison between two unequally successful socialist economic systems, you certainly would explore for your reader the causes for the failures of one and the gains of the other. Causal analysis, then, is something you must master as a writer in order to investigate many topics in many fields, and must learn to approach with slow and deliberate thinking beforehand.

AUDIENCE AND PURPOSE

While many causal assignments will require you to discuss causes *and* effects, many will require that you decide for yourself on one or the other. Often, then, the first step in clarifying purpose for your causal writing is to determine which you will be considering—causes or effects. Do you want to consider what led up to an event or phenomenon, or do you want to consider what came after it? Furthermore, what you decide to focus on in causal analysis will depend to a great extent on your interests and point of view. The causes assigned to the same event—World War II, for example—will differ depending on the orientation of the person doing the analysis. A psychologist or a psychologically oriented person may stress the *uber-mensch* mentality of the Third Reich. The economist or economically oriented person might stress the striving for control of world capital. The political scientist or someone interested in the study of government might stress the clash of nations or the political orientations of their leaders. All of these approaches may be valid. Usually important events, like wars, are caused by many conditions and occurrences.

Aside from orientation, you must take into account the scope of discussion within that orientation. Generally the causes leading to something are many and connected, as are the results. You must decide whether you wish to consider far-off causes, or immediate causes, underlying causes, or precipitating events. And for results, too, do you wish to write of immediate or far-reaching results, the most important or the least expected? Will you show that causes or effects usually ascribed to an occurrence are simply wrong or inaccurate? If you decide which kinds of causes and effects you wish to include, you will be able to write with much greater purpose and direction.

In part, your audience may determine both the point of view and the scope you adopt. Does your audience have some special interest or intellectual approach? Does it know a good deal about the subject? If so, do you wish to deepen or rather to challenge their knowledge? Explaining the results of a new gene-splicing technique in a journal for geneticists requires one strategy; explaining it to the educated but not nearly so specialized readership of *Omni* or *Scientific American* requires quite another. Although a writer could assume avid interest from both audiences, the range of materials included in essays to each group would differ drastically. And imagine how those two essays would differ from a piece on the causal analysis of gene-splicing in the Sunday magazine section of your local newspaper.

PROCESS

To help you think about your purpose in causal analysis, write out a sequence of the events or phenomena involved in the topic you're interested in. If you are uncertain about whether you wish to write about causes, effects, or both, try to draft your time line so that your sequence stretches *back* through events and *forward* through results. Then look over your time line or sequential list and decide what interests you most— what *caused* an event or phenomenon, or what resulted from an event or phenomenon, or both. As you look over your page, ask yourself if you have jotted down many causes, for example, that are psychological in nature. If so, that may tell you something about what you wish to stress in your analysis. Use your sequential list as a rough outline and cross out those items that seem uninteresting or illogical and add other items that might make for a fuller discussion. Suppose you've decided to write about the reasons you and your boyfriend broke up last month. You see as you look at your prewriting that the major problem was a raw competitiveness that underlay the relationship despite its passion and mutual respect. You see, too, that you've listed anxiety over pressure to marry as another cause for the end of the relationship. Well, then, the items you've included about your different tastes in clothing, foods, and good times and your different intellectual interests (you're a business major, he's a poet), may not be relevant in this paper. But you might add another item—the psychological stress caused by your frequent separations.

Once you've decided on your focus—causes, effects, or both—and have roughly outlined and revised possible causes and/or effects, you are ready to look even more critically at your analysis. Causality is an extremely valuable tool for a writer, but without sufficient care, we can all too often fall into illogical thinking, assigning cause or effect when there is neither. Therefore you want to review your list of possible causes and effects for problems in logic. Have you called something an effect just because it happened after something else? Have you called something a cause because something else just happens to follow it? Because it snowed the day you got an A on your calculus final, it does not logically follow that the A *resulted* from the snow or that the snow *caused* the A grade. The two events have nothing logically to do with each other. Logicians call this error in logic *post hoc ergo propter hoc* (after this, therefore because of this), and you must be on the lookout for this fallacy as you prepare to write. Also make sure that you have provided a reasonable number of causes and/or effects in your analysis. At times, a single cause or effect is all the writer wishes to convey, but more often than not several causes and/or several results make for a more enlightened discussion. In truth, causation is no simple affair, and a whole chain of events and conditions precedes and follows almost any event.

When you're ready to write, if you wish to focus on effects, you will most likely start with a brief statement of *cause* and then move on to the main concern of your paper—effects of that cause. If, on the other hand, you're primarily interested in discussing effect, then you would do well to start your paper by briefly identifying and explaining the causes leading to this effect. If you're doing both—an ambitious undertaking in a short essay—then identify your phenomenon at the start of your paper and discuss causes and effects in separate sections so as not to confuse the two.

The care and attention you give to planning a paper of causal analysis is worth the effort. Causal thinking is vital, helping us to explain past events and to learn for the future. The well-reasoned causal analysis can teach much to both the writer and the reader.

Bertrand Russell
THE UNHAPPY AMERICAN WAY

Bertrand Russell (1872–1970) was among the most outspoken and candid thinkers of the twentieth century. He earned worldwide respect as a philosopher, mathematician, and social activist. In both his scientific and sociohistorical writings, Russell was ardently devoted to the rational logic of original fact and experience; he was an atheist, yet a profound believer in the basic goodness of the human spirit. He more or less abandoned his career as a mathematician at Cambridge University in favor of social activism—he was a pacifist during World War I, yet he temporarily abandoned his pacifism during the Nazi onslaught. His views were often controversial, and in the 1960s he was one of the guiding forces behind the "Ban the Bomb" antinuclear weapons movement. For such works as *Marriage and Morals* (1929), *A History of Western Philosophy* (1945), and his mathematical philosophies, Russell was awarded the British Order of Merit in 1949 and the Nobel Prize for Literature in 1950.

In his Nobel Prize acceptance speech in 1950, Russell claimed that the fundamental motives of most people are *acquisitiveness, rivalry, vanity,* and *love of power.* In this essay, he analyzes two of the reasons behind the unhappy outcomes of these motives in American life as he viewed it.

*I*t used to be said that English people take their pleasures sadly. No doubt this would still be true if they had any pleasures to take, but the price of alcohol and tobacco in my country has provided sufficient external causes for melancholy. I have sometimes thought that the habit of taking pleasures sadly has crossed the Atlantic, and I have wondered what it is that makes so many English-speaking people somber in their outlook in spite of good health and a good income.

In the course of my travels in America I have been impressed by a kind of fundamental malaise which seems to me extremely common and which poses difficult problems for the social reformer. Most social reformers have held the opinion that, if poverty were abolished and there were no more economic insecurity, the millennium would have arrived. But when I look at the faces of people in opulent cars, whether in your country or in mine, I do not see that look of radiant happiness which the aforesaid social reformers had led me to expect. In nine cases out of ten, I see instead a look of boredom and discontent and an almost frantic longing for something that might tickle the jaded palate.

But it is not only the very rich who suffer in this way. Professional men very frequently feel hopelessly thwarted. There is something that they long to do or some public object that they long to work for. But if they were to indulge their wishes in these respects, they fear that they would lose their livelihood. Their wives are equally unsatisfied, for their neighbor, Mrs. So-and-So, has gone ahead more quickly, has a better car, a larger apartment and grander friends.

Life for almost everybody is a long competitive struggle where very few can win the race, and those who do not win are unhappy. On social occasions when it is *de rigueur* to seem cheerful, the necessary demeanor is stimulated by alcohol. But the gaiety does not ring true and anybody who has just one drink too many is apt to lapse into lachrymose melancholy.

One finds this sort of thing only among English-speaking people. A Frenchman while he is abusing the Government is as gay as a lark. So is an Italian while he is telling you how his neighbor has swindled him. Mexicans, when they are not actually starving or actually being murdered, sing and dance and enjoy sunshine and food and drink with a gusto which is very rare north of the Mexican frontier. When Andrew Jackson conquered Pensacola from the Spaniards, his wife looked out of the window and saw the population enjoying itself although it was Sunday. She pointed out the scandal to her husband, who decreed that cheerfulness must cease forthwith. And it did.

When I try to understand what it is that prevents so many Americans from being as happy as one might expect, it seems to me that there are two causes, of which one goes much deeper than the other. The one that goes least deep is the necessity for subservience in some large organization. If you are an energetic man with strong views as to the right way of doing the job with which you are concerned, you find yourself invariably under the orders of some big man at the top who is elderly, weary and cynical. Whenever you have a bright idea, the boss puts a stopper on it. The more energetic you are and the more vision you have, the more you will suffer from the impossibility of doing any of the things that you feel ought to be done. When you go home and moan to your wife, she tells you that you are a silly fellow and that if you became the proper sort of yes-man your income would soon be doubled. If you try divorce and remarriage it is very unlikely that there will be any change in this respect. And so you are condemned to gastric ulcers and premature old age.

It was not always so. When Dr. Johnson compiled his dictionary, he compiled it as he thought fit. When he felt like saying that oats is food for men in Scotland and horses in England, he said so. When he defined a fishing-rod as a stick with a fish at one end and a fool at the other, there was nobody to point out to him that a remark of this sort would damage the sale of his great work among fishermen. But if, in the present day, you are (let us say) a contributor to an encyclopedia, there is an editorial policy which is solemn, wise and prudent, which allows no room for jokes, no place for personal preferences and no tolerance for idiosyncrasies. Everything has to be flattened out except where the prejudices of the editor are concerned. To these you must conform, however little you may share them. And so you have to be content with dollars instead of creative satisfaction. And the dollars, alas, leave you sad.

This brings me to the major cause of unhappiness, which is that most people in America act not on impulse but on some principle, and that principles upon which people act are usually based upon a false psychology and a false ethic. There is a general theory as to what makes for happiness and this theory is false. Life is concerned as a competitive struggle in which felicity consists in getting ahead of your neighbor. The joys which are not competitive are forgotten.

Now, I will not for a moment deny that getting ahead of your neighbor is delightful, but it is not the only delight of which human beings are capable. There are innumerable things which are not competitive. It is possible to enjoy food and drink without having to reflect that you have a better cook and a better wine merchant than your former friends whom you are learning to cold-shoulder. It is possible to be fond of your wife and your children without reflecting how much better she dresses than Mrs. So-and-So and how much better they are at athletics than the children of that old stick-in-the-mud Mr. Such-and-Such. There are those who can enjoy music without thinking how cultured the other ladies in their women's club will be thinking them. There are even people who can enjoy a fine day in spite of the fact that the sun shines on everybody. All these simple pleasures are destroyed as soon as competitiveness gets the upper hand.

But it is not only competitiveness that is the trouble. I could imagine a person who has turned against competitiveness and can only enjoy after conscious rejection of the competitive element. Such a person, seeing the sunshine in the morning, says to himself, "Yes, I may enjoy this and indeed I must, for it is a joy open to all." And however bored he may become with the sunshine he goes on persuading himself that he is enjoying it because he thinks he ought to.

"But," you will say, "are you maintaining that our actions ought not to be governed by moral principles? Are you suggesting that every whim and every impulse should be given free rein? Do you consider that if So-ad-So's nose annoys you by being too long, that gives you a right to tweak it? Sir, you will continue with indignation, "your doctrine is one which would uproot ll the sources of morality and loosen all the bonds which hold society together. Only self-restraint, self-repression, iron self-control make it possible to endure the abominable beings among whom we have to live. No, sir! Better misery and gastric ulcers than such chaos as your doctrine would produce!''

I will admit at once that there is force in this objection. I have seen many noses that I should have liked to tweak, but never once have I yielded to the impulse. But this, like everything else, is a matter of degree. If you always yield to impulse, you are mad. If you never yield to impulse, you gradually dry up and very likely become mad to boot. In a life which is to be healthy and happy, impulse, though not allowed to run riot, must have sufficient scope to remain alive and to preserve that variety and diversity of interest which is natural to a human being. A life lived on a principle, no matter what, is too narrowly determined, too systematic and uniform, to be happy. However much you care about success, you should have times when you are merely enjoying life without a thought of subsequent gain. However proud you may be, as president of a women's club, of your impeccable culture, you should not be ashamed of reading a low-brow book if you want to. A life which is all principle is a life on rails. The rails may help toward rapid locomotion, but preclude the joy of wandering. Man spent some million years wandering before he invented rails, and his happiness still demands some reminiscence of the earlier ages of freedom.

Meaning and Idea

1.   What implied conditions among Americans is Russell analyzing? Does he focus more on the causes or on the effects of that condition?

2.   Russell identifies two causes of the unhappiness of the American way. What are they? Which does he say is more important?

3.   What is Russell's analysis of a life which is entirely based on principle? What of a life completely governed by impulse? Identify one example he gives for each.

4.   What is Russell's suggestion for a happy way for Americans to lead their lives? What examples does he offer of such a condition?

Language, Form, Structure

1.   How does Russell organize his two causes in this essay? How does he allocate the sections of his discussion?

2.   What is the general tone of this essay? Select three examples in the writing that support your assessment.

3.   What does paragraph six contribute to the essay? What rhetorical tech-

niques does the paragraph make use of? Where else does the essay make use of these techniques?

4. Define the following words and phrases: subservience; invariably; idiosyncracies; felicity; whim; free rein; to run riot; impeccable; lowbrow; on rails; preclude; reminiscence.

Ideas for Writing

1. Write a short causal analysis entitled either "The Happy American" or "The Unhappy American." In it, describe the situation and explore what you consider the two main causes for the situation.

2. Analyze which type of people you consider more successful—those whose life is primarily based on principle or on impulse.

3. Write a short paper in which you evaluate Russell's analysis of Americans. How true is it? How fair? How does the knowledge that Russell is not American (he was British) affect your reading of his analysis?

Kate Chopin
THE STORY OF AN HOUR

Kate Chopin (1851–1904) was reared primarily by her Creole mother and great-grandmother in St. Louis. In her late teens, Chopin married and moved to New Orleans with her cotton broker husband. After he died following fourteen years of marriage, Chopin started life again with her six children. She began her literary career with stories about Creole life, heavily influenced by Maupassant. Her short pieces were published in various magazines, establishing her reputation firmly. *The Awakening* (1899), a forward-thinking novel about the sexual awakening and need for self-fulfilment of a wife, is considered Chopin's masterpiece.

In this short, short narrative, Kate Chopin traces the ironic causal relationships of fate and its strange twists. As you read, look for various levels of meaning and how they affect the causal development of the story.

*K*nowing that Mrs. Mallard was afflicted with a heart trouble, great care was taken to break to her as gently as possible the news of her husband's death.

It was her sister Josephine who told her, in broken sentences, veiled hints that revealed in half concealing. Her husband's friend Richards was there, too, near her. It was he who had been in the newspaper office when intelligence of the railroad disaster was received, with Brently Mallard's name leading the list of "killed." He had only taken the time to assure himself of its truth by a second telegram, and had hastened to forestall any less careful, less tender friend in bearing the sad message.

She did not hear the story as many women have heard the same, with a paralyzed inability to accept its significance. She wept at once, with sudden, wild abandonment, in her sister's arms. When the storm of grief had spent itself she went away to her room alone. She would have no one follow her.

There stood, facing the open window, a comfortable, roomy armchair. Into this she sank, pressed down by a physical exhaustion that haunted her body and seemed to reach into her soul.

She could see in the open square before her house the tops of trees that were all aquiver with the new spring life. The delicious breath of rain was in the air. In the street below a peddler was crying his wares. The notes of a distant song which some one was singing reached her faintly, and countless sparrows were twittering in the eaves.

There were patches of blue sky showing here and there through the clouds that had met and piled above the other in the west facing her window.

She sat with her head thrown back upon the cushion of the chair quite motionless, except when a sob came up into her throat and shook her, as a child who has cried itself to sleep continues to sob in its dreams.

She was young, with a fair, calm face, whose lines bespoke repression and even a certain strength. But now there was a dull stare in her eyes, whose gaze was fixed away off yonder on one of those patches of blue sky. It was not a glance of reflection, but rather indicated a suspension of intelligent thought.

There was something coming to her and she was waiting for it, fearfully. What was it? She did not know; it was too subtle and elusive to name. But she felt it, creeping out of the sky, reaching toward her through the sounds, the scents, the color that filled the air.

Now her bosom rose and fell tumultuously. She was beginning to recognize this thing that was approaching to possess her, and she was striving to beat it back with her will—as powerless as her two white slender hands would have been.

When she abandoned herself a little whispered word escaped her slightly parted lips. She said it over and over under her breath. "Free, free, free!" The vacant stare and the look of terror that had followed it went from her eyes. They stayed keen and bright. Her pulses beat fast, and the coursing blood warmed and relaxed every inch of her body.

She did not stop to ask if it were not a monstrous joy that held her. A clear and exalted perception enabled her to dismiss the suggestion as trivial.

She knew that she would weep again when she saw the kind, tender hands folded in death; the face that had never looked save with love upon her, fixed and gray and dead. But she saw beyond that bitter moment a long procession of years to come that would belong to her absolutely. And she opened and spread her arms out to them in welcome.

There would be no one to live for during those coming years; she would live for herself. There would be no powerful will bending her in that blind persistence with which men and women believe they have a right to impose a private will upon a fellow-creature. A kind intention or a cruel intention made the act seem no less a crime as she looked upon it in that brief moment of illumination.

And yet she had loved him—sometimes. Often she had not. What did it matter! What could love, the unsolved mystery, count for in face of this possession of self-assertion which she suddenly recognized as the strongest impulse of her being.

"Free! Body and soul free!" she kept whispering.

Josephine was kneeling before the closed door with her lips to the keyhole, imploring for admission. "Louise, open the door! I beg; open the door—you will make yourself ill. What are you doing, Louise? For heaven's sake open the door."

"Go away. I am not making myself ill." No; she was drinking in a very elixir of life through that open window.

Her fancy was running riot along those days ahead of her. Spring days, and summer days, and all sorts of days that would be her own. She breathed a quick prayer that life might be long. It was only yesterday she had thought with a shudder that life might be long.

She arose at length and opened the door to her sister's importunities. There was a feverish triumph in her eyes, and she carried herself unwittingly like a goddess of Victory. She clasped her sister's waist, and together they descended the stairs. Richards stood waiting for them at the bottom.

Some one was opening the front door with a latchkey. It was Brently Mallard who entered, a little travel-stained, composedly carrying his grip-sack and umbrella. He had been far from the scene of accident, and did not even know there had been one. He stood amazed at Josephine's piercing cry; at Richards' quick motion to screen him from the view of his wife.

But Richards was too late.

When the doctors came they said she had died of heart disease—of joy that kills.

Meaning and Idea

1. What potential cause and effect sequence is averted by the action described in the opening sentence? Is it really averted after all?

2. How are Mrs. Mallard's immediate reactions to the news of her husband's death different from the norm according to the narrative? What are her subsequent reactions?

3. What is the "something" that was "coming to her and she was waiting for"? How is it possible to read that "something" on more than one level?

4. How does Mrs. Mallard's attitude change after she starts repeating the words—and emotions—"Free, free, free"? What is she free of?

5. What ultimately kills Mrs. Mallard?

Language, Form, Structure

1. Identify three distinct instances of cause and effect in this story. Explain how they relate to one another.

2. How does Chopin's physical description of Mrs. Mallard prepare readers for her exuberance at the sense of new freedom she experiences after her husband's "death"?

3. What are the ironies of this story? To what extent does any one take precedence over the others?

4. What view of marriage is expressed in this story? Whose view of marriage is it—Mrs. Mallard's or the narrator's? Explain your answer.

5. Explain the meanings of the following expressions in this story: veiled hints; hastened to forestall; all aquiver; crying his wares; coursing blood; exalted perception; blind persistence; moment of illumination.

Ideas for Writing

1. Write a causal analysis which explains a sudden change in attitude toward something that recently happened to you. Take into account both immediate and deep-seated causes.

2. Discuss the causation behind a recent joy or happiness you have experienced.

3. Stories are often reflections of the author's opinions about a certain aspect of life. How can you read "Story of an Hour" as an expression of Chopin's opinion about something? What is that opinion? To what extent is it successfully developed in this story?

John Updike
ACE IN THE HOLE

John Updike was born in 1932 in Shillington, Pennsylvania. A *summa cum laude* graduate from Harvard, he went on to study art for a year in Oxford, then joined the staff of *The New Yorker* magazine and for two years wrote "The Talk of the Town" column. He then moved to Ipswich, Massachusetts, to pursue his writing full-time. His work is well-known for its sensitivity and simplicity; his characters are most often concerned with the common things of life—the past, aging, marriages, and relationships. Among his most famous novels are *Rabbit, Run* (1960), *The Centaur* (1965), *Rabbit Redux* (1971), *Bech is Back* (1982), and his most recent, *The Witches of Eastwick* (1984). Among his short story collections are *Pigeon Feathers* (1962) and *Too Far to Go* (1979). He continues to contribute both fiction and criticism to *The New Yorker.*

"Ace in the Hole" first appeared in *The New Yorker* and was included in Updike's 1955 collection of stories, *The Same Door.* Skillfully, with a finely honed realism, Updike weaves together the immediate and deep-seated causes of once-heroic Ace Anderson's life situation and marriage.

*N*o sooner did his car touch the boulevard heading home than Ace flicked on the radio. He needed the radio, especially today. In the seconds before the tubes warmed up, he said aloud, doing it just to hear a human voice, "Jesus. She'll pop her lid." His voice, though familiar, irked him;

it sounded thin and scratchy, as if the bones in his head were picking up static. In a deeper register Ace added, "She'll murder me." Then the radio came on, warm and strong, so he stopped worrying. The Five Kings were doing "Blueberry Hill"; to hear them made Ace feel so sure inside that from the pack pinched between the car roof and the sun shield he plucked a cigarette, hung it on his lower lip, snapped a match across the rusty place on the dash, held the flame in the instinctive spot near the tip of his nose, dragged, and blew out the match, all in time to the music. He rolled down the window and snapped the match so it spun end-over-end into the gutter. "Two points," he said, and cocked the cigarette toward the roof of the car, sucked powerfully, and exhaled two plumes through his nostrils. He was beginning to feel like himself, Ace Anderson, for the first time that whole day, a bad day. He beat time on the accelerator. The car jerked crazily. "On Blueberry Hill," he sang, "my heart stood still. The wind in the wil-low tree"—he braked for a red light—"played love's suh-*weet* melodee—"

"Go, Dad, bust your lungs!" a kid's voice blared. The kid was riding in a '52 Pontiac that had pulled up beside Ace at the light. The profile of the driver, another kid, was dark over his shoulder.

Ace looked over at him and smiled slowly, just letting one side of his mouth lift a little. "Shove it," he said, good-naturedly, across the little gap of years that separated them. He knew how they felt, young and mean and shy.

But the kid, who looked Greek, lifted his thick upper lip and spat out the window. The spit gleamed on the asphalt like a half-dollar.

"Now isn't that pretty?" Ace said, keeping one eye on the light. "You miserable wop. You are *mis*erable." While the kid was trying to think of some smart comeback, the light changed. Ace dug out so hard he smelled burned rubber. In his rear-view mirror he saw the Pontiac lurch forward a few yards, then stop dead, right in the middle of the intersection.

The idea of them stalling their fat tin Pontiac kept him in a good humor all the way home. He decided to stop at his mother's place and pick up the baby, instead of waiting for Evey to do it. His mother must have seen him drive up. She came out on the porch holding a plastic spoon and smelling of cake.

"You're out early," she told him.

"Friedman fired me," Ace told her.

"Good for you," his mother said. "I always said he never treated you right." She brought a cigarette out of her apron pocket and tucked it deep into one corner of her mouth, the way she did when something pleased her.

Ace lighted it for her. "Friedman was O.K. personally," he said. "He just wanted too much for his money. I didn't mind working Saturdays, but until eleven, twelve Friday nights was too much. Everybody has a right to some leisure."

"Well, I don't dare think what Evey will say, but I, for one, thank dear God you had the brains to get out of it. I always said that job had no future to it—no future of any kind, Freddy."

"I guess," Ace admitted. "But I wanted to keep at it, for the family's sake."

"Now, I know I shouldn't be saying this, but any time Evey—this is just between us—any time Evey thinks she can do better, there's room for you *and* Bonnie right in your father's house." She pinched her lips together. He could almost hear the old lady think, *There, I've said it.*

"Look, Mom, Evey tries awfully hard, and anyway you know she can't work that way. Not that *that*—I mean, she's a realist, too . . ." He let the rest of the thought fade as he watched a kid across the street dribbling a basketball around a telephone pole that had a backboard and net nailed on it.

"Evey's a wonderful girl of her own kind. But I've always said, and your father agrees, Roman Catholics ought to marry among themselves. Now I know I've said it before, but when they get out in the greater world—"

"*No,* Mom."

She frowned, smoothed herself, and said, "Your name was in the paper today."

Ace chose to let that go by. He kept watching the kid with the basket-ball. It was funny how, though the whole point was to get the ball up into the air, kids grabbed it by the sides and squeezed. Kids just didn't think.

"Did you hear?" his mother asked.

"Sure, but so what?" Ace said. His mother's lower lip was coming at him, so he changed the subject. "I guess I'll take Bonnie."

His mother went into the house and brought back his daughter, wrapped in a blue blanket. The baby looked dopey. "She fussed all day," his mother complained. "I said to your father, 'Bonnie is a dear little girl, but without a doubt she's her mother's daughter.' You were the best-natured boy."

"Well I *had* everything," Ace said with an impatience that made his mother blink. He nicely dropped his cigarette into a brown flowerpot on the edge of the porch and took his daughter into his arms. She was getting heavier, solid. When he reached the end of the cement walk, his mother was still on the porch, waving to him. He was so close he could see the fat around her elbow jiggle, and he only lived a half block up the street, yet here she was, waving to him as if he was going to Japan.

At the door of his car, it seemed stupid to him to drive the measly half block home. His old coach, Bob Behn, used to say never to ride where you could walk. Cars were the death of legs. Ace left the ignition keys in his pocket and ran along the pavement with Bonnie laughing and bouncing at his chest. He slammed the door of his landlady's house open and shut, pounded up the two flights of stairs, and was panting so hard when he reached the door of his apartment that it took him a couple of seconds to fit the key into the lock.

The run must have tuned Bonnie up. As soon as he lowered her into the crib, she began to shout and wave her arms. He didn't want to play with her. He tossed some blocks and a rattle into the crib and walked into the bathroom, where he turned on the hot water and began to comb his hair. Holding the comb under the faucet before every stroke, he combed his hair forward. It was so long, one strand curled under his nose and touched his lips. He whipped the whole mass back with a single pull. He tucked in the tufts around his ears, and ran the comb straight back on both sides of his head. With his fingers he felt for the little ridge at the back where the two sides met. It was there, as it should have been. Finally, he mussed the hair in front enough for one little lock to droop over his forehead, like Alan Ladd. It made the temple seem lower than it was. Every day, his hairline looked higher. He had observed all around him how blond men went bald first. He remembered reading somewhere, though, that baldness shows virility.

On his way to the kitchen he flipped the left-hand knob of the television. Bonnie was always quieter with the set on. Ace didn't see how she could understand much of it, but it seemed to mean something to her. He found a can of beer in the refrigerator behind some brownish lettuce and those hot dogs Evey never got around to cooking. She'd be home any time. The clock said 5:12. She'd pop her lid.

Ace didn't see what he could do but try and reason with her. "Evey," he'd say, "you ought to thank God I got out of it. It had no future to it at all." He hoped she wouldn't get too mad, because when she was mad he wondered if he should have married her, and doubting that made him feel crowded. It was bad enough, his mother always crowding him. He punched the two triangles in the top of the beer can, the little triangle first, and then the big one, the one he drank from. He hoped Evey wouldn't say anything that couldn't be forgotten. What women didn't seem to realize was that there were things you knew but shouldn't say.

He felt sorry he had called the kid in the car a wop.

Ace balanced the beer on a corner where two rails of the crib met and looked under the chairs for the morning paper. He had trouble finding his name, because it was at the bottom of a column on an inside sports page, in a small article about the county basketball statistics:

"Dusty" Tremwick, Grosvenor Park's sure-fingered center, copped the individual scoring honors with a season's grand (and we do mean grand) total of 376 points. This is within eighteen points of the all-time record of 394 racked up in the 1949–1950 season by Olinger High's Fred Anderson.

Ace angrily sailed the paper into an armchair. Now it was Fred Anderson; it used to be Ace. He hated being called Fred, especially in print, but then the sportswriters were all office boys anyway, Behn used to say.

"Do not just ask for shoe polish," a man on television said, "but ask for *Emu Shoe Gloss,* the *only* polish that absolutely *guarantees* to make your shoes look shinier than new." Ace turned the sound off, so that the man moved his mouth like a fish blowing bubbles. Right away, Bonnie howled, so Ace turned it up loud enough to drown her out and went into the kitchen, without knowing what he wanted there. He wasn't hungry; his stomach was tight. It used to be like that when he walked to the gymnasium alone in the dark before a game and could see the people from town, kids and parents, crowding in at the lighted doors. But once he was inside, the locker room would be bright and hot, and the other guys would be there, laughing it up and towel-slapping, and the tight feeling would leave. Now there were whole days when it didn't leave.

A key scratched at the door lock. Ace decided to stay in the kitchen. Let *her* find *him.* Her heels clicked on the floor for a step or two; then the television set went off. Bonnie began to cry. "Shut up, honey," Evey said. There was a silence.

"I'm home," Ace called.

"No kidding. I thought Bonnie got the beer by herself."

Ace laughed. She was in a sarcastic mood, thinking she was Lauren Bacall. That was all right, just so she kept funny. Still smiling, Ace eased into the living room and got hit with, "What are *you* smirking about? Another question: What's the idea running up the street with Bonnie like she was a football?"

"You saw that?"

"Your mother told me."

"You saw her?"

"Of course I saw her. I dropped by to pick up Bonnie. What the hell do you think?—I read her tiny mind?"

"Take it easy," Ace said, wondering if Mom had told her about Friedman.

"Take it easy? Don't coach *me.* Another question: Why's the car out in front of her place? You give the car to her?"

"Look, I parked it there to pick up Bonnie, and I thought I'd leave it there."

"Why?"

"Whaddeya mean, why? I just did. I just thought I'd walk. It's not that far, you know."

"No, I don't know. If you'd been on your feet all day a block would look like one hell of a long way."

"Okay. I'm sorry."

She hung up her coat and stepped out of her shoes and walked around the room picking up things. She stuck the newspaper in the wastebasket.

Ace said, "My name was in the paper today."

"They spell it right?" She shoved the paper deep into the basket with her foot. There was no doubt; she knew about Friedman.

"They called me Fred."

"Isn't that your name? What *is* your name anyway? Hero J. Great?"

There wasn't any answer, so Ace didn't try any. He sat down on the sofa, lighted a cigarette, and waited.

Evey picked up Bonnie. "Poor thing stinks. What does your mother do, scrub out the toilet with her?"

"Can't you take it easy? I know you're tired."

"You should. I'm always tired."

Evey and Bonnie went into the bathroom; when they came out, Bonnie was clean and Evey was calm. Evey sat down in an easy chair beside Ace and rested her stocking feet on his knees. "Hit me," she said, twiddling her fingers for the cigarette.

The baby crawled up to her chair and tried to stand, to see what he gave her. Leaning over close to Bonnie's nose, Evey grinned, smoke leaking through her teeth, and said, "Only for grownups, honey."

"Eve," Ace began, "there was no future in that job. Working all Saturday, and then Friday nights on top of it."

"I know. Your mother told *me* all that, too. All I want from you is what happened."

She was going to take it like a sport, then. He tried to remember how it *did* happen. "It wasn't my fault," he said. "Friedman told me to back this '51 Chevvy into the line that faces Church Street. He just bought it from an old guy this morning who said it only had thirteen thousand on it. So in I jump and start her up. There was a knock in the engine like a machine gun. I almost told Friedman he'd bought a squirrel, but you know I cut that smart stuff out ever since Palotta laid me off."

"You told me that story. What happens in this one?"

"Look, Eve. I *am* telling ya. Do you want me to go out to a movie or something?"

"Suit yourself."

"So I jump in the Chevvy and snap it back in line, and there was a kind of scrape and thump. I get out and look and Friedman's running over, his arms going like *this*"—Ace whirled his own arms and laughed—"and here was the whole back fender of a '49 Merc mashed in. Just looked like somebody took a planer and shaved off the bulge, you know, there at the back." He tried to show her with his hands. "The Chevvy, though, didn't have a dent. It even gained some paint. But *Friedman,* to *hear* him—Boy, they can rave when their pocketbook's hit. He said"—Ace laughed again—"never mind."

Evey said, "You're proud of yourself."

"No, listen. I'm not happy about it. But there wasn't a thing I could *do*. It wasn't my driving at all. I looked over on the other side, and there was just two or three inches between the Chevvy and a Buick. *Nobody* could have gotten into that hole. Even if it had hair on it." He thought this was pretty good.

She didn't. "You could have looked."

"There just wasn't the *space*. Friedman said stick it in; I stuck it in."

"But you could have looked and moved the other cars to make more room."

"I guess that would have been the smart thing."

"I guess, too. Now what?"

"What do you mean?"

"I mean now what? Are you going to give up?Go back to the Army? Your mother? Be a basketball pro? What?"

"You know I'm not tall enough. Anybody under six-six they don't want."

"Is that so? Six-six? Well, please listen to this, Mr. Six-Foot-Five-and-a-Half: I'm fed up. I'm ready as Christ to let you run." She stabbed her cigarette into an ashtray on the arm of the chair so hard the ashtray jumped to the floor. Evey flushed and shut up.

What Ace hated most in their arguments was these silences after Evey had said something so ugly she wanted to take it back. "Better ask the priest first," he murmured.

She sat right up. "If there's one thing I don't want to hear about from you it's priests. You let the priests to me. You don't know a damn thing about it. Not a damn thing."

"Hey, look at Bonnie," he said, trying to make a fresh start with his tone.

Evey didn't hear him. "If you think," she went on, "if for one rotten moment you think, Mr. Fred, that the be-all and end-all of my life is you and your hot-shot stunts—"

"Look, Mother," Ace pleaded, pointing at Bonnie. The baby had picked up the ashtray and put it on her head for a hat and was waiting for praise.

Evey glanced down sharply at the child. "Cute," she said. "Cute as her daddy."

The ashtray slid from Bonnie's head and she patted where it had been and looked around puzzled.

"Yeah, but watch," Ace said. "Watch her hands. They're really terrific hands."

"You're nuts," Evey said.

"No, honest. Bonnie's great. She's a natural. Get the rattle for her. Never mind, I'll get it." In two steps, Ace was at Bonnie's crib, picking the rattle out of the mess of blocks and plastic rings and beanbags. He extended the rattle toward his daughter, shaking it delicately. Made wary by this burst of attention, Bonnie reached with both hands; like two separate animals they approached from opposite sides and touched the smooth rattle simultaneously. A smile bubbled up on her face. Ace tugged weakly. She held on, and then tugged back. "She's a natural," Ace said, "and it won't do her any good because she's a girl. Baby, we got to have a boy."

"I'm not your baby," Evey said, closing her eyes.

Saying "Baby" over and over again, Ace backed up to the radio and, without turning around, switched on the volume knob. In the moment before the tubes warmed up, Evey had time to say, "Wise up, Freddy. What shall we do?"

The radio came in on something slow: dinner music. Ace picked Bonnie up and set her in the crib. "Shall we dance?" he asked his wife, bowing.

"I want to talk."

"Baby. It's the cocktail hour."

"This is getting us no place," she said, rising from her chair, though.

"Fred Junior. I can see him now," he said, seeing nothing.

"We will have no Juniors."

In her crib, Bonnie whimpered at the sight of her mother being seized. Ace fitted his hand into the natural place on Evey's back and she shuffled stiffly into his lead. When, with a sudden injection of saxophones, the tempo quickened, he spun her out carefully, keeping the beat with his shoulders. Her hair brushed his lips as she minced in, then swung away, to the end of his arm; he could feel her toes dig into the carpet. He flipped his own hair back from his eyes. The music ate through his skin and mixed with the nerves and small veins; he seemed to be great again, and all the other kids were around them, in a ring, clapping time.

Meaning and Idea

1. What was Ace's job? How did he lose it? What is Ace's attitude toward losing his job? Toward work in general?

2. What is Ace's mother's attitude toward his wife, Evey? How does Ace respond to what his mother says of his wife?

3. What is Ace's attitude toward his daughter, Bonnie? What does he do in the story that makes that attitude clear?

4. What is Ace's real name? Why is he called Ace? For what was he famous? What is Evey's attitude toward that fame?

5. Compare Evey's solutions to their current situation to Ace's solutions. Is this the first time they have faced such difficulties? How do you know? How does their past affect their present ideas about solutions?

Language, Form, Structure

1. At what point in the story do we find out that Ace has lost his job? At what point do we find out what his job was? Why do you think Updike arranges this information in this order in the story?

2. In your answer to question 1 in Meaning and Idea you identified the immediate cause for Ace losing his job. What, however, is the underlying cause and effect relationship implied by the story? What other effects does that relationship produce?

3. There are a number of *allusions,* or references, in this story which help place the time period during which it takes place. What is that time period? Identify three such allusions.

4. In the story, the narrator mentions that Evey was "in a sarcastic mood." Sarcasm reflects a sneering or taunting attitude, often with the intent to criticize or hurt. Identify some examples of sarcastic remarks in the story. What do they tell us about characters and relationships?

5. Define the following words and use each in a sentence: irked; static; register; plumes; lurch; measly; virility; rave; whimpered.

Ideas for Writing

1. If you ever lost a job, failed a test or class, or didn't succeed at something important you started out to do, write a causal analysis in which you discuss both obvious and underlying causes for this failure.

2. Write a causal analysis in which you discuss the effects of an unhappy relationship or marriage—either yours or someone else's.

3. The meanings that can be derived from this story's title—either taken as a whole or for its parts—are multiple. Write a short discussion of all the levels of meaning you can think of for the title and their relationships to the story. Include a discussion of why you think Updike would make a title so open to interpretation.
You may want to consider the meanings of the following expressions: "Ace in the hole"; "in the hole"; "Ace." In addition, look at the paragraph on page 381 in which Ace says, "*Nobody* could have gotten into that hole."

Langston Hughes
DREAM DEFERRED

> Langston Hughes (1902–1967) was one of America's foremost poets, essayists, dramatists, and fiction writers, whose self-proclaimed desire as a writer was "to explain and illuminate the Negro condition in America." Once elected class poet in grammar school in Lincoln, Illinois, Hughes first gained adult notoriety as a poet when he was a busboy at a hotel in Washington, D.C. He'd left some poems by the plate of the poet Vachel Lindsay, who fortunately recognized his talent.
>
> "Dream Deferred" has become one of Langston Hughes's best-known poems, especially during the racially turbulent 1960s. In this poem he asks—and perhaps answers—what the results of aspirations unfulfilled are.

*W*hat happens to a dream deferred?

Does it dry up
like a raisin in the sun?
Or fester like a sore—
And then run?
Does it stink like rotten meat?   5
Or crust and sugar over—
like a syrupy sweet?

Maybe it just sags
like a heavy load.   10

Or does it explode?

Meaning and Idea

1. What do you think is the "dream" in this poem? What cause-and-effect relationship is implied concerning this dream?

2. Remembering that Hughes was among the foremost writers about the modern black experience in America, how does this poem relate to that experience as you know it? What "message" is carried by the poem?

Language, Form, Structure

1. Identify the similes and metaphors in this poem. How effective are they? Do you see a logic to their placement in the poem? What effect does the final metaphor have coming where it does? Would a simile there have been as powerful? Why?

2. The poem is a sequence of questions. What effect does this have on the reader? Would the poem be as effective were it built on a series of declarative statements? Why?

3. What is the effect of the rhymes in the poem—sun/run; meat/sweet; load/explode?

4. Make sure you know the meaning of *deferred* and *fester.*

Ideas for Writing

1. Write a short causal analysis about the effects of a time when you "put off" something. Were the results positive or negative? Did they occur naturally, or were they forced?

2. As we noted, Hughes arranges this poem as a series of questions. Write an essay in which you identify what in the writing—choice of language, tone, arrangement on the page, and so on—gives either an implicit or explicit answer to these questions?

Edward Arlington Robinson
RICHARD COREY

Edward Arlington Robinson (1869–1935), described by critic Allen Tate in 1933 as "the most famous of living American poets," led a life of two greatly contrasting halves. Born and raised in a bleak Maine town, he had a depressed childhood. He later devoted himself to his writing, but was often penniless and alcoholic, relying on friends and, at one point, on President Theodore Roosevelt for subsistence. In 1921, his *Collected Poems* was unexpectedly well received, and in rather rapid succession, Robinson won the Pulitzer Prize three times as well as an honorary degree from Yale University.

"Richard Corey" is one of the best-known of modern poems; it has even been rephrased and put to music in Simon and Garfunkel's early song with the same title. In the poem, Edward Arlington Robinson surprises us with the result of a life seemingly headed in one direction, but taking a sharp turn in an opposite one.

*W*henever Richard Corey went down town,
We people on the pavement looked at him:
He was a gentleman from sole to crown,
Clean favored, and imperially slim.

And he was always quietly arrayed,   5
And he was always human when he talked;
But still he fluttered pulses when he said,
"Good-morning," and he glittered when he walked.

And he was rich—yes, richer than a king—
And admirably schooled in every grace: 10
In fine, we thought that he was everything
To make us wish that we were in his place.

So on we worked, and waited for the light,
And went without the meat, and cursed the bread;
And Richard Corey, one calm summer night,   15
Went home and put a bullet through his head.

Meaning and Idea

1.   Before his suicide, what sort of person did Richard Corey appear to be? Was he a fair person? Arrogant? What was his social position? What were the townspeople's impressions of him?

2.   Who is the narrator of this poem? What is his opinion of Richard Corey? To whom does he address the poem? What is the occasion of this poem?

3.   What do you make of Richard Corey's act of suicide? Why do you think he did it? Was it to be expected from the preceding stanzas? Why or why not?

4.   Explain the meaning of lines 13–14:

> So on we worked, and waited for the light,
> And went without meat, and cursed the bread;

Who is the "we"? What is "the light"? Why do they curse the bread?

Language, Form, Structure

1.   *Situational irony* occurs when the results of a situation do not match our expectations of the outcome. How is "Richard Corey" an example of situational irony?

2.   According to the poem, is there any cause-and-effect relationship between the townspeople's impressions of Richard Corey and his suicide? If so, what is it? Is it direct or indirect?

3.   There are a number of descriptive words or phrases in this poem which suggest royalty or regal nature. Identify these and explain how each of them contributes to our understanding of Richard Corey and/or the speaker.

4.   Define the following words as they are used in the poem: sole; crown; grace. Why do you think Robinson chose each of these words over possible synonyms?

Ideas for Writing

1.   If you know personally of a suicide or a suicide attempt, try to write a causal analysis explaining it. If you have no direct knowledge of a suicide, choose another tragic event you know of and explain what caused it.

2.   Choose someone in your school or social group who is greatly admired. Write a causal analysis of the reasons for this admiration.

3.   The narrator tells of the events of this poem from a retrospective (after the fact) point of view. How does that point of view affect his descriptions of Richard Corey? How might the narrative have been different in its feeling and focus if this poem took place before the suicide or if there were no suicide? You may want to try your hand at writing a second version of the poem from either of those points of view. Your version may be prose if you wish.

Sophocles
OEDIPUS REX

Sophocles (c. 496–406 B.C.) and Aechylus, who preceded him, and Euripides, who followed him, form the triumvirate of ancient Greek poets and playwrights with whom we are most familiar. In ancient Greece, Sophocles was well known and respected; he was a statesman, a general, and a priest as well as a poet. Although he is thought to have written approximately 123 plays, few survived to modern times. Among the surviving plays are the Theban trilogy: *Antigone* (441 B.C.), *Oedipus Rex* (c. 429 B.C.), and *Oedipus at Colonus* (405 B.C.). Sophocles, who lived an admirable ninety years, is also credited with widening the scope of Greek tragedy and with introducing painted scenery to western drama.

Oedipus Rex, first produced about 428 B.C., is the second play in Sophocles' Theban trilogy, three plays recounting the Oedipus myth. In this tragedy of patricide, incest, suicide, and self-destruction, Sophocles examined the causal connections between fate and will, the whim of the gods, and individual character flaws. *Oedipus Rex* is thought to exhibit fine examples of well-sustained dramatic irony.

PERSONS REPRESENTED

OEDIPUS   TEIRESIAS   SHEPHERD OF LAÏOS
A PRIEST   IOCASTE   SECOND MESSENGER   CREON
MESSENGER   CHORUS OF THEBAN ELDERS

The Scene: Before the palace of Oedipus, King of Thebes. A central door and two lateral doors open onto a platform which runs the length of the façade. On the platform, right and left, are altars; and three steps lead down into the "orchestra," or chorus-ground. At the beginning of the action these steps are crowded by SUPPLIANTS *who have brought branches and chaplets of olive leaves and who lie in various attitudes of despair.* OEDIPUS *enters.*

PROLOGUE

OEDIPUS: My children, generations of the living
In the line of Kadmos, nursed at his ancient hearth:

Why have you strewn yourselves before these altars
In supplication, with your boughs and garlands?
The breath of incense rises from the city   5
With a sound of prayer and lamentation.
                                Children,
I would not have you speak through messengers,
And therefore I have come myself to hear you—
I, Oedipus, who bear the famous name.
(*To a* PRIEST.) You, there, since you are eldest in the
company,
Speak for them all, tell me what preys upon you,   10
Whether you come in dread, or crave some blessing:
Tell me, and never doubt that I will help you
In every way I can; I should be heartless
Were I not moved to find you suppliant here.
PRIEST: Great Oedipus, O powerful King of Thebes!   15
You see how all the ages of our people
Cling to your altar steps: here are boys
Who can barely stand alone, and here are priests
By weight of age, as I am a priest of God,
And young men chosen from those yet unmarried;   20
As for the others, all that multitude,
They wait with olive chaplets in the squares,
At the two shrines of Pallas, and where Apollo
Speaks in the glowing embers.
                            Your own eyes
Must tell you: Thebes is in her extremity   25
And can not lift her head from the surge of death.
A rust consumes the buds and fruits of the earth;
The herds are sick; children die unborn,
And labor is vain. The god of plague and pyre
Raids like detestable lightning through the city,   30
And all the house of Kadmos is laid waste,
All emptied, and all darkened: Death alone
Battens up the misery of Thebes.

You are not one of the immortal gods, we know;
Yet we have come to you to make our prayer   35
As to the man of all men best in adversity
And wisest in the ways of God. You saved us
From the Sphinx, that flinty singer, and the tribute
We paid to her so long; yet you were never
Better informed than we, nor could we teach you: 40
It was some god breathed in you to set us free.

Therefore, O mighty King, we turn to you:
Find us our safety, find us a remedy,

Whether by counsel of the gods or men.
A king of wisdom tested in the past   45
Can act in a time of troubles, and act well.
Noblest of men, restore
Life to your city! Think how all men call you
Liberator for your triumph long ago;
Ah, when your years of kingship are remembered,   50
Let them not say *We rose, but later fell*—
Keep the State from going down in the storm!
Once, years ago, with happy augury,
You brought us fortune; be the same again!
No man questions your power to rule the land: 55
But rule over men, not over a dead city!
Ships are only hulls, citadels are nothing,
When no life moves in the empty passageways.

OEDIPUS: Poor children! You may be sure I know
All that you longed for in your coming here.   60
I know that you are deathly sick; and yet,
Sick as you are, not one is as sick as I.
Each of you suffers in himself alone.
His anguish, not another's; but my spirit
Groans for the city, for myself, for you.   65

I was not sleeping, you are not waking me.
No, I have been in tears for a long while
And in my restless thought walked many ways.
In all my search, I found one helpful course,
And that I have taken: I have sent Creon,   70
Son of Menoikeus, brother of the Queen,
To Delphi, Apollo's place of revelation,
To learn there, if he can,
What act or pledge of mine may save the city.
I have counted the days, and now, this very day,   75
I am troubled, for he has overstayed his time.
What is he doing? He has been gone too long.
Yet whenever he comes back, I should do ill
To scant whatever hint the god may give.

PRIEST: It is a timely promise. At this instant   80
They tell me Creon is here.

OEDIPUS: O Lord Apollo!
May his news be fair as his face is radiant!

PRIEST: It could not be otherwise: he is crowned with bay,
The chaplet is thick with berries.

OEDIPUS: We shall soon know;
He is near enough to hear us now.

(*Enter* CREON.)

O Prince: 85

Brother: son of Menoikeus:
What answer do you bring us from the god?
CREON: It is favorable I can tell you, great afflications
Will turn out well, if they are taken well.
OEDIPUS: What was the oracle? These vague words   90
Leave me still hanging between hope and fear.
CREON: Is it your pleasure to hear me with all these
Gathered around us? I am prepared to speak,
But should we not go in?
OEDIPUS: Let them all hear it.
It is for them I suffer, more than for myself.   95
CREON: Then I will tell you what I heard at Delphi.

In plain words
The god commands us to expel from the land of Thebes
An old defilement that it seems we shelter.
It is a deathly thing, beyond expiation.   100
We must not let it feed upon us longer.
OEDIPUS: What defilement? How shall we rid ourselves of it?
CREON: By exile or death, blood for blood. It was
Murder that brought the plague-wind on the city.
OEDIPUS: Murder of whom? Surely the god has named him?   105
CREON: My lord: long ago Laïos was our king,
Before you came to govern us.
OEDIPUS: I know;
I learned of him from others; I never saw him.
CREON: He was murdered; and Apollo commands us now
To take revenge upon whoever killed him.   110
OEDIPUS: Upon whom? Where are they? Where shall we find
          a clue
To solve that crime, after so many years?
CREON: Here in this land, he said.
                              If we make enquiry,
We may touch things that otherwise escape us.
OEDIPUS: Tell me: Was Laïos murdered in his house,   115
Or in the fields, or in some foreign country?
CREON: He said he planned to make a pilgrimage.
He did not come home again.
OEDIPUS: And was there no one,
No witness, no companion, to tell what happened?
CREON: They were all killed but one, and he got away   120
So frightened that he could remember one thing only.
OEDIPUS: What was that one thing? One may be the key

To everything, if we resolve to use it.
CREON: He said that a band of highwaymen attacked them,
Outnumbered them, and overwhelmed the King.   125
OEDIPUS: Strange, that a highwayman should be so daring—
Unless some faction here bribed him to do it.
CREON: We thought of that. But after Laïos' death
New troubles arose and we had no avenger.
OEDIPUS: What troubles could prevent your hunting down
the killers?   130
CREON: The riddling Sphinx's song
Made us deaf to all mysteries but her own.
OEDIPUS: Then once more I must bring what is dark to light.
It is most fitting that Apollo shows,
As you do, this compunction for the dead.   135
You shall see how I stand by you, as I should,
To avenge the city and the city's god,
And not as though it were for some distant friend,
But for my own sake, to be rid of evil.
Whoever killed King Laïos might—who knows?—   140
Decide at any moment to kill me as well.
By avenging the murdered king I protect myself.
Come, then, my children: leave the altar steps,
Lift up your olive boughs!
                      One of you go
And summon the people of Kadmos to gather here.   145
I will do all that I can; you may tell them that.

(*Exit a* PAGE.)

So, with the help of God,
We shall be saved—or else indeed we are lost.
PRIEST: Let us rise, children. It was for this we came,
And now the King has promised it himself.   150
Phoibos has sent us an oracle; may he descend
Himself to save us and drive out the plague.

(*Exeunt* OEDIPUS *and* CREON *into the palace by the central door.
The* PRIEST *and the* SUPPLIANTS *disperse R and L. After a short
pause the* CHORUS *enters the orchestra.*)

PARODOS

[STROPHE 1]

CHORUS: What is God singing in his profound
Delphi of gold and shadow?

What oracle for Thebes, the sunwhipped city?
Fear unjoints me, the roots of my heart tremble.
Now I remember, O Healer, your power, and wonder;   5
Will you send doom like a sudden cloud, or weave it
Like nightfall of the past?
Speak, speak to us, issue of holy sound:
Dearest to our expectancy: be tender!

                [ANTISTROPHE 1]
Let me pray to Athenê, the immortal daughter of Zeus,   10
And to Artemis her sister
Who keeps her famous throne in the market ring,
And to Apollo, bowman at the far butts of heaven—

O gods, descend! Like three streams leap against
The fires of our grief, the fires of darkness;   15
Be swift to bring us rest!

As in the old time from the brilliant house
Of air you stepped to save us, come again!

                [STROPHE 2]
Now our afflictions have no end,
Now all our stricken host lies down   20
And no man fights off death with his mind;

The noble plowland bears no grain,
And groaning mothers can not bear—

See, how our lives like birds take wing,   25
Like sparks that fly when a fire soars,
To the shore of the god of evening.

              [ANTISTROPHE 2]
The plague burns on, it is pitiless,
Though pallid children laden with death
Lie unwept in the stony ways,

And old gray women by every path   30
Flock to the strand about the altars

There to strike their breasts and cry
Worship of Phoibos in wailing prayers:
Be kind, God's golden child!

                [STROPHE 3]
There are no swords in this attack by fire,   35
No shields, but we are ringed with cries.
Send the besieger plunging from our homes
Into the vast sea-room of the Atlantic

Or into the waves that foam eastward of Thrace—
For the day ravages what the night spares—   40

Destroy our enemy, lord of the thunder!
Let him be riven by lightning from heaven!

[ANTISTROPHE 3]

Phoibos Apollo, stretch the sun's bowstring,
That golden cord, until it sing for us,
Flashing arrows in heaven!
      Artemis, Huntress,   45
Race with flaring lights upon our mountains!

O scarlet god, O golden-banded brow,
O Theban Bacchos in a storm of Maenads,

(Enter OEDIPUS, *C.)*

Whirl upon Death, that all the Undying hate!   50
Come with blinding cressets, come in joy!

SCENE I

OEDIPUS: Is this your prayer? It may be answered. Come,
  Listen to me, act as the crisis demands,
  And you shall have relief from all these evils.

Until now I was a stranger to this tale,   5
As I had been a stranger to the crime.
Could I track down the murderer without a clue?
But now, friends,
As one who became a citizen after the murder,
I make this proclamation to all Thebans:
If any man knows by whose hand Laïos, son of
  Labdakos,   10
Met his death, I direct that man to tell me everything,
No matter what he fears for having so long withheld it.
Let him stand as promised that no further trouble
Will come to him, but he may leave the land in safety.

Moreover: If anyone knows the murderer to be foreign,   15
Let him not keep silent: he shall have his reward from
  me.
However, if he does conceal it; if any man
Fearing for his friend or for himself disobeys this edict,
Hear what I propose to do:

I solemnly forbid the people of this country,   20
Where power and throne are mine, ever to receive that
        man
Or speak to him, no matter who he is, or let him
Join in sacrifice, lustration, or in prayer.
I decree that he be driven from every house,
Being, as he is, corruption itself to us: the Delphic   25
Voice of Zeus has pronounced this revelation.
Thus I associate myself with the oracle
And take the side of the murdered king.

As for the criminal, I pray to God—
Whether it be a lurking thief, or one of a number—   30
I pray that that man's life be consumed in evil and
        wretchedness.
And as for me, this curse applies no less
If it should turn out that the culprit is my guest here,
Sharing my hearth.
                        You have heard the penalty.
I lay it on you now to attend to this   35
For my sake, for Apollo's, for the sick
Sterile city that heaven has abandoned.
Suppose the oracle had given you no command:
Should this defilement go uncleansed for ever?
You should have found the murderer: your king,   40
A noble king, had been destroyed!
                        Now I,
Having the power that he held before me,
Having his bed, begetting children there
Upon his wife, as he would have, had he lived—
Their son would have been my children's brother,   45
If Laïos had had luck in fatherhood!
(But surely ill luck rushed upon his reign)
I say I take the son's part, just as though
I were his son, to press the fight for him
And see it won! I'll find the hand that brought   50
Death to Labdakos' and Polydoros' child,
Heir of Kadmos' and Agenor's line.
And as for those who fail me,
May the gods deny them the fruit of the earth,
Fruit of the womb, and may they rot utterly!   55
Let them be wretched as we are wretched, and worse!

For you, for loyal Thebans, and for all
Who find my actions right, I pray the favor
Of justice, and of all the immortal gods.

CHORAGOS: Since I am under oath, my lord, I swear   60
    I did not do the murder, I can not name
    The murderer. Might not the oracle
    That has ordained the search tell where to find him?
OEDIPUS: An honest question. But no man in the world
    Can make the gods do more than the gods will.   65
CHORAGOS: There is one last expedient—
OEDIPUS: Tell me what it is.
    Though it seem slight, you must not hold it back.
CHORAGOS: A lord clairvoyant to the lord Apollo,
    As we all know, is the skilled Teiresias.
    One might learn much about this from him, Oedipus.   70
OEDIPUS: I am not wasting time:
    Creon spoke of this, and I have sent for him—
    Twice, in fact; it is strange that he is not here.
CHORAGOS: The other matter—that old report—seems
      useless.
OEDIPUS: Tell me. I am interested in all reports.   75
CHORAGOS: The King was said to have been killed by
      highwaymen.
OEDIPUS: I know. But we have no witnesses to that.
CHORAGOS: If the killer can feel a particle of dread,
    Your curse will bring him out of hiding!
OEDIPUS: No.
    The man who dared that act will fear no curse.   80

(Enter the blind seer TEIRESIAS, *led by a* PAGE.)

CHORAGOS: But there is one man who may detect the
      Criminal.
    This is Teiresias, this is the holy prophet
    In whom, alone of all men, truth was born.
OEDIPUS: Teiresias: seer: student of mysteries,
    Of all that's taught and all that no man tells,   85
    Secrets of Heaven and secrets of the earth:
    Blind though you are, you know the city lies
    Sick with plague; and from this plague, my lord,
    We find that you alone can guard or save us.

    Possibly you did not hear the messengers?   90
    Apollo, when we sent to him,
    Sent us back word that this great pestilence
    Would lift, but only if we established clearly
    The identity of those who murdered Laïos.
    They must be killed or exiled.

                                    Can you use   95
Birdflight or any art of divination
To purify yourself, and Thebes, and me
From this contagion? We are in your hands.

There is no fairer duty
Than that of helping others in distress.   100
TEIRESIAS: How dreadful knowledge of the truth can be
      When there's no help in truth! I knew this well,
      But did not act on it: else I should not have come.
OEDIPUS: What is troubling you? Why are your eyes so cold?
TEIRESIAS: Let me go home. Bear your own fate, and I'll   105
      Bear mine. It is better so: trust what I say.
OEDIPUS: What you say is ungracious and unhelpful
      To your native country. Do not refuse to speak.
TEIRESIAS: When it comes to speech, your own is neither
            temperate
      Nor opportune. I wish to be more prudent.   110
OEDIPUS: In God's name, we all beg
            you—
TEIRESIAS: You are all ignorant.
      No; I will never tell you what I know.
      Now it is my misery; then, it would be yours.
OEDIPUS: What! You do know something, and will not tell
            us?
      You would betray us all and wreck the State?   115
TEIRESIAS: I do not intend to torture myself, or you.
      Why persist in asking? You will not persuade me.
OEDIPUS: What a wicked old man you are!
            You'd try a stone's
      Patience! Out with it! Have you no feeling at all?
TEIRESIAS: You call me unfeeling. If you could only see   120
      The nature of your own feelings . . .
OEDIPUS: Why,
      Who would not feel as I do? Who could endure
      Your arrogance toward the city?
TEIRESIAS: What does it matter!
      Whether I speak or not, it is bound to come.
OEDIPUS: Then, if "it" is bound to come, you are bound to
            tell me.   125
TEIRESIAS: No, I will not go on. Rage as you please.
OEDIPUS: Rage? Why not!
                          And I'll tell you what I think:
      You planned it, you had it done, you all but
      Killed him with your own hands: if you had eyes,

130

I'd say the crime was yours, and yours alone.

TEIRESIAS: So? I charge you, then,
   Abide by the proclamation you have made:
   From this day forth
   Never speak again to these men or to me;
   You yourself are the pollution of this country.   135

OEDIPUS: You dare say that! Can you possibly think you
      have
   Some way of going free, after such insolence?

TEIRESIAS: I have gone free. It is the truth sustains me.

OEDIPUS: Who taught you shamelessness?
         It was not your craft.

TEIRESIAS: You did. You made me speak. I did not want to.   140

OEDIPUS: Speak what? Let me hear it again more clearly.

TEIRESIAS: Was it not clear before? Are you tempting me?

OEDIPUS: I did not understand it. Say it again.

TEIRESIAS: I say that you are the murderer whom you seek.

OEDIPUS: Now twice you have spat out infamy. You'll pay
      for it!   145

TEIRESIAS: Would you care for more? Do you wish to be
      really angry?

OEDIPUS: Say what you will. Whatever you say is worthless.

TEIRESIAS: I say you live in hideous shame with those
   Most dear to you. You can not see the evil.

OEDIPUS: It seems you can go on mouthing like this for ever.   150

TEIRESIAS: I can, if there is power in truth.

OEDIPUS: There is:
   But not for you, not for you,
   You sightless, witless, senseless, mad old man!

TEIRESIAS: You are the madman. There is no one here
   Who will not curse you soon, as you curse me.   155

OEDIPUS: You child of endless night! You can not hurt me
   Or any other man who sees the sun.

TEIRESIAS: True: it is not from me your fate will come.
   That lies within Apollo's competence,
   As it is his concern.

OEDIPUS: Tell me: 160
   Are you speaking for Creon, or for yourself?

TEIRESIAS: Creon is no threat. You weave your own doom.

OEDIPUS: Wealth, power, craft of statesmanship!
   Kingly position, everywhere admired!
         What savage envy is stored up against these,   165
   If Creon, whom I trusted, Creon my friend,
   For this great office which the city once

Put in my hands unsought—if for this power
Creon desires in secret to destroy me!

He has bought this decrepit fortune-teller, this 170
Collector of dirty pennies, this prophet fraud—
Why, he is no more clairvoyant than I am!

Tell us:
Has your mystic mummery ever approached the truth?
When that hellcat the Sphinx was performing here,
What help were you to these people? 175
Her magic was not for the first man who came along:
It demanded a real exorcist. Your birds—
What good were they? or the gods, for the matter of that?
But I came by.
Oedipus, the simple man, who knows nothing—
I thought it out for myself, no birds helped me!
And this is the man you think you can destroy,
That you may be close to Creon when he's king!
Well, you and your friend Creon, it seems to me,
Will suffer most. If you were not an old man, 185
You would have paid already for your plot.
CHORAGOS: We can not see that his words or yours
Have been spoken except in anger, Oedipus,
And of anger we have no need. How can God's will
Be accomplished best? That is what most concerns us. 190
TEIRESIAS: You are a king. But where argument's concerned
I am your man, as much a king as you.
I am not your servant, but Apollo's.
I have no need of Creon to speak for me.

Listen to me. You mock my blindness, do you? 195
But I say that you, with both your eyes, are blind:
You can not see the wretchedness of your life,
Nor in whose house you live, no, nor with whom.
Who are your father and mother? Can you tell me?
You do not even know the blind wrongs 200
That you have done them, on earth and in the world
    below.
But the double lash of your parents' curse will whip you
Out of this land some day, with only night
Upon your precious eyes.
Your cries then—where will they not be heard? 205
What fastness of Kithairon will not echo them?
And that bridal-descant of yours—you'll know it then,
The song they sang when you came here to Thebes

And found your misguided berthing.
All this, and more, that you can not guess at now,   210
Will bring you to yourself among your children.

Be angry, then. Curse Creon. Curse my words.
I tell you, no man that walks upon the earth
Shall be rooted out more horribly than you.
OEDIPUS: Am I to bear this from him?—Damnation   215
    Take you! Out of this place! Out of my sight!
TEIRESIAS: I would not have come at all if you had not asked
      me.
OEDIPUS: Could I have told that you'd talk nonsense, that
    You'd come here to make a fool of yourself, and of me?
TEIRESIAS: A fool? Your parents thought me sane enough.   220
OEDIPUS: My parents again!—Wait: who were my parents?
TEIRESIAS: This day will give you a father, and break your
      heart.
OEDIPUS: Your infantile riddles! Your damned abracadabra!
TEIRESIAS: You were a great man once at solving riddles.
OEDIPUS: Mock me with that if you like; you will find it true.   225
TEIRESIAS: It was true enough. It brought about your ruin.
OEDIPUS: But if it saved this town?
TEIRESIAS (to the PAGE):
                  Boy, give me your hand.
OEDIPUS: Yes, boy; lead him away.
                  —While you are here
We can do nothing. Go; leave us in peace.
TEIRESIAS: I will go when I have said what I have to say.   230
How can you hurt me? And I tell you again:
The man you have been looking for all this time,
The damned man, the murderer of Laïos,
That man is in Thebes. To your mind he is foreignborn,
But it soon will be shown that he is a Theban,   235
A revelation that will fail to please.
                  A blind man,
Who has his eyes now; a penniless man, who is rich now;
And he will go tapping the strange earth with his staff;
To the children with whom he lives now he will be
Brother and father—the very same; to her   240
Who bore him, son and husband—the very same
Who came to his father's bed, wet with his father's
      blood.

Enough. Go think that over.
If later you find error in what I have said,
You may say that I have no skill in prophecy.   245

(*Exit* TEIRESIAS, *led by his* PAGE. OEDIPUS *goes into the palace.*)

ODE I

[STROPHE 1]

CHORUS: The Delphic stone of prophecies
      Remembers ancient regicide
      And a still bloody hand.
      That killer's hour of flight has come.
      He must be stronger than riderless   5
      Coursers of untiring wind,
      For the son of Zeus armed with his father's thunder
      Leaps in lightning after him;
      And the Furies follow him, the sad Furies.

[ANTISTROPHE 1]

      Holy Parnassos' peak of snow   10
      Flashes and blinds that secret man,
      That all shall hunt him down:
      Though he may roam the forest shade
      Like a bull gone wild from pasture
      To rage through glooms of stone.   15
      Doom comes down on him; flight will not avail him;
      For the world's heart calls him desolate,
      And the immortal Furies follow, for ever follow.

[STROPHE 2]

      But now a wilder thing is heard
      From the old man skilled at hearing Fate in the
            wingbeat of a bird.   20
      Bewildered as a blown bird, my soul hovers and can
            not find
      Foothold in this debate, or any reason or rest of mind.
      But no man ever brought—none can bring
      Proof of strife between Thebes' royal house,
      Labdakos' line, and the son of Polybos;   25
      And never until now has any man brought word
      Of Laïos' dark death staining Oedipus the King.

[ANTISTROPHE 2]

      Divine Zeus and Apollo hold
      Perfect intelligence alone of all tales ever told;
      And well though this diviner works, he works in his own
            night;   30
      No man can judge that rough unknown or trust in
            second sight,

For wisdom changes hands among the wise.
Shall I believe my great lord criminal
At a raging word that a blind old man let fall?　　　　　　35
I saw him, when the carrion woman faced him of old,
Prove his heroic mind! These evil words are lies.

SCENE II

CREON:　Men of Thebes:
　　　I am told that heavy accusations
　　　Have been brought against me by King Oedipus.

　　　I am not the kind of man to bear this tamely.

　　　If in these present difficulties　　　　　　　　　　5
　　　He holds me accountable for any harm to him
　　　Through anything I have said or done—why, then,
　　　I do not value life in this dishonor.
　　　It is not as though this rumor touched upon
　　　Some private indiscretion. The matter is grave.　　10
　　　The fact is that I am being called disloyal
　　　To the State, to mý fellow citizens, to my friends.
CHORAGOS:　He may have spoken in anger, not from his
　　　　　　mind.
CREON:　But did you not hear him say I was the one
　　　Who seduced the old prophet into lying?　　　　　15
CHORAGOS:　The thing was said; I do not know how
　　　　　　seriously.
CREON:　But you were watching him! Were his eyes steady?
　　　Did he look like a man in his right mind?
CHORAGOS:　　　　　　　　　　　　　I do not know.
　　　I can not judge the behavior of great men.
　　　But here is the King himself.

　　　(Enter OEDIPUS.)

OEDIPUS:　　　　　　　　　　So you dared come back.　　20
　　　Why? How brazen of you to come to my house,
　　　You murderer!
　　　　　　　　Do you think I do not know
　　　That you plotted to kill me, plotted to steal my throne?
　　　Tell me, in God's name: am I coward, a fool,
　　　That you should dream you could accomplish this?　　25

　　　A fool who could not see your slippery game?
　　　A coward, not to fight back when I saw it?

You are the fool, Creon, are you not? hoping
Without support or friends to get a throne?
Thrones may be won or bought: you could do neither.   30
CREON: Now listen to me. You have talked; let me talk,
            too.
You can not judge unless you know the facts.
OEDIPUS: You speak well: there is one fact; but I find it
            hard
To learn from the deadliest enemy I have.
CREON: That above all I must dispute with you.   35
OEDIPUS: That above all I will not hear you deny.
CREON: If you think there is anything good in being
            stubborn
Against all reason, then I say you are wrong.
OEDIPUS: If you think a man can sin against his own kind
And not be punished for it, I say you are mad.   40
CREON: I agree. But tell me: what have I done to you?
OEDIPUS: You advised me to send for that wizard, did you
            not?
CREON: I did. I should do it again.
OEDIPUS: Very well. Now tell me:
How long has it been since Laïos—
CREON: What of Laïos?
OEDIPUS: Since he vanished in that onset by the road?   45
CREON: It was long ago, a long time.
OEDIPUS: And this prophet,
Was he practicing here then?
CREON: He was; and with honor, as now.
OEDIPUS: Did he speak of me at that time?

CREON: He never did;
At least, not when I was present.
OEDIPUS: But . . . the enquiry?
I suppose you held one?
CREON: We did, but we learned nothing.   50
OEDIPUS: Why did the prophet not speak against me then?
CREON: I do not know; and I am the kind of man
Who holds his tongue when he has no facts to go on.
OEDIPUS: There's one fact that you know, and you could tell
            it.
CREON: What fact is that? If I know it, you shall have it.   55
OEDIPUS: If he were not involved with you, he could not say
That it was I who murdered Laïos.
CREON: If he says that, you are the one that knows it!—
But now it is my turn to question you.

OEDIPUS: Put your questions. I am no murderer.   60
CREON: First, then: You married my sister?
OEDIPUS: I married your sister
CREON: And you rule the kingdom equally with her?
OEDIPUS: Everything that she wants she has from me.
CREON: And I am the third, equal to both of you?
OEDIPUS: That is why I call you a bad friend.   65
CREON: No. Reason it out, as I have done.
    Think of this first. Would any sane man prefer
    Power, with all a king's anxieties,
    To that same power and the grace of sleep?
    Certainly not I.   70
    I have never longed for the king's power—only his
        rights.
    Would any wise man differ from me in this?
    As matters stand, I have my way in everything
    With your consent, and no responsibilities.
    If I were king, I should be a slave to policy.   75

    How could I desire a scepter more
    Than what is now mine—untroubled influence?
    No, I have not gone mad; I need no honors,
    Except those with the perquisites I have now.
    I am welcome everywhere; every man salutes me,   80
    And those who want your favor seek my ear,
    Since I know how to manage what they ask.
    Should I exchange this ease for that anxiety?
    Besides, no sober mind is treasonable.
    I hate anarchy   85
    And never would deal with any man who likes it.

    Test what I have said. Go to the priestess
    At Delphi, ask if I quoted her correctly.
    And as for this other thing: if I am found
    Guilty of treason with Teiresias,   90
    Then sentence me to death! You have my word
    It is a sentence I should cast my vote for—
    But not without evidence!
                            You do wrong
    When you take good men for bad, bad men for good.
    A true friend thrown aside—why, life itself   95
    Is not more precious!
                            In time you will know this well:
    For time, and time alone, will show the just man,
    Though scoundrels are discovered in a day.

CHORAGOS: This is well said, and a prudent man would
          ponder it.

          Judgments too quickly formed are dangerous.   100
OEDIPUS: But is he not quick in his duplicity?
          And shall I not be quick to parry him?
          Would you have me stand still, hold my peace, and let
          This man win everything, through my inaction?
CREON: And you want—what is it, then? To banish me?   105
OEDIPUS: No, not exile. It is your death I want,
          So that all the world may see what treason means.
CREON: You will persist, then? You will not believe me?
OEDIPUS: How can I believe you?
CREON: Then you are a fool.
OEDIPUS: To save myself?
CREON: In justice, think of me.   110
OEDIPUS: You are evil incarnate.
CREON: But suppose that you are wrong?
OEDIPUS: Still I must rule.
CREON: But not if you rule badly.
OEDIPUS: O city, city!
CREON: It is my city, too!
CHORAGOS: Now, my lords, be still. I see the Queen,
          Iocaste, coming from her palace chambers;   115
          And it is time she came, for the sake of you both.
          This dreadful quarrel can be resolved through her.

          (Enter IOCASTE.*)*

IOCASTE: Poor foolish men, what wicked din is this?
          With Thebes sick to death, is it not shameful
          That you should rake some private quarrel up?   120
          (To OEDIPUS.*)* Come into the house.
                              —And you, Creon, go now:
          Let us have no more of this tumult over nothing.
CREON: Nothing? No, sister: what your husband plans for me
          Is one of two great evils: exile or death.
OEDIPUS: He is right.
                         Why, woman I have caught him squarely   125
          Plotting against my life.
CREON: No! Let me die
          Accurst if ever I have wished you harm!
IOCASTE: Ah, believe it, Oedipus!
          In the name of the gods, respect this oath of his
          For my sake, for the sake of these people here!   130
                                                        [STROPHE 1]

CHORAGOS: Open your mind to her, my lord. Be ruled by her,
     I beg you!
OEDIPUS: What would you have me do?
CHORAGOS: Respect Creon's word. He has never spoken like
          a fool,
     And now he has sworn an oath.
OEDIPUS: You know what you ask?
CHORAGOS: I do.
OEDIPUS: Speak on, then.
CHORAGOS: A friend so sworn should not be baited so,   135
     In blind malice, and without final proof.
OEDIPUS: You are aware, I hope, that what you say
     Means death for me, or exile at the least.

                                              [STROPHE 2]

CHORAGOS: No, I swear by Helios, first in Heaven!
     May I die friendless and accurst,   140
  The worst of deaths, if ever I meant that!
     It is the withering fields
        That hurt my sick heart:
     Must we bear all these ills,
        And now your bad blood as well?   145
OEDIPUS: Then let him go. And let him die, if I must,
     Or be driven by him in shame from the land of Thebes.
     It is your unhappiness, and not his talk,
     That touches me.
                    As for him—
     Wherever he is, I will hate him as long as I live.   150
CREON: Ugly in yielding, as you were ugly in rage!
     Natures like yours chiefly torment themselves.
OEDIPUS: Can you not go? Can you not leave me?
CREON: I can.
     You do not know me; but the city knows me,
     And in its eyes I am just, if not in yours.   155

(*Exit* CREON.)

                                          [ANTISTROPHE 1]
CHORAGOS: Lady Iocaste, did you not ask the King to go to
          his chambers?
IOCASTE: First tell me what has happened.
CHORAGOS: There was suspicion without evidence; yet it
          rankled
     As even false charges will.
IOCASTE: On both sides?
CHORAGOS: On both.

IOCASTE: But what was said?
CHORAGOS: Oh let it rest, let it be done with!   160
      Have we not suffered enough?
OEDIPUS: You see to what your decency has brought you:
      You have made difficulties where my heart saw none.

                                            [ANTISTROPHE 2]
CHORAGOS: Oedipus, it is not once only I have told you —
      You must know I should count myself unwise   165
   To the point of madness, should I now forsake you—
         You, under whose hand,
            In the storm of another time,
         Our dear land sailed out free.
         But now stand fast at the helm!   170
IOCASTE: In God's name, Oedipus, inform your wife as well:
      Why are you so set in this hard anger?
OEDIPUS: I will tell you, for none of these men deserves
      My confidence as you do. It is Creon's work,
      His treachery, his plotting against me.   175
IOCASTE: Go on, if you can make this clear to me.
OEDIPUS: He charges me with the murder of Laïos.
IOCASTE: Has he some knowledge? Or does he speak from
            hearsay?
OEDIPUS: He would not commit himself to such a charge,
      But he has brought in that damnable soothsayer   180
      To tell his story.
IOCASTE: Set your mind at rest.
      If it is a question of soothsayers, I tell you
      That you will find no man whose craft gives knowledge
      Of the unknowable.
                         Here is my proof:

An oracle was reported to Laïos once   185
(I will not say from Phoibos himself, but from
His appointed ministers, at any rate)
That his doom would be death at the hands of his own
      son—
His son, born of his flesh and of mine!

Now, you remember the story: Laïos was killed   190
By marauding strangers where three highways meet;
But his child had not been three days in this world
Before the King had pierced the baby's ankles
And left him to die on a lonely mountainside.

Thus, Apollo never caused that child   195
To kill his father, and it was not Laïos' fate

To die at the hands of his son, as he had feared.
This is what prophets and prophecies are worth!
Have no dread of them.
                              It is God himself
Who can show us what he wills, in his own way.   200
OEDIPUS: How strange a shadowy memory crossed my mind,
    Just now while you were speaking; it chilled my heart.
IOCASTE: What do you mean? What memory do you speak
        of?
OEDIPUS: If I understand you, Laïos was killed
    At a place where three roads meet.
IOCASTE: So it was said;   205
    We have no later story.
OEDIPUS: Where did it happen?
IOCASTE: Phokis, it is called: at a place where the Theban
        Way
    Divides into the roads towards Delphi and Daulia.
OEDIPUS: When?
IOCASTE: We had the news not long before you came
    And proved the right to your succession here.   210
OEDIPUS: Ah, what net has God been weaving for me?
IOCASTE: Oedipus! Why does this trouble
                you?
OEDIPUS: Do not ask me yet.
    First, tell me how Laïos looked, and tell me
    How old he was.
IOCASTE: He was tall, his hair just touched
    With white; his form was not unlike your own.   215
OEDIPUS: I think that I myself may be accurst
    By my own ignorant edict.
IOCASTE: You speak strangely.
    It makes me tremble to look at you, my King.
OEDIPUS: I am not sure that the blind man can not see.
    But I should know better if you were to tell me—   220
IOCASTE: Anything—though I dread to hear you ask it.
OEDIPUS: Was the King lightly escorted, or did he ride
    With a large company, as a ruler should?
IOCASTE: There were five men with him in all: one was a
        herald;
    And a single chariot, which he was driving.   225
OEDIPUS: Alas, that makes it plain enough!
                              But who—
    Who told you how it happened?
IOCASTE: A household servant,
    The only one to escape.

OEDIPUS: And is he still
    A servant of ours?
IOCASTE: No; for when he came back at last
    And found you enthroned in the place of the dead king,   230
    He came to me, touched my hand with his, and begged
    That I would send him away to the frontier district
    Where only the shepherds go—
    As far away from the city as I could send him.
    I granted his prayer; for although the man was a slave,   235
    He had earned more than this favor at my hands.
OEDIPUS: Can he be called back quickly?
IOCASTE: Easily.
    But why?
OEDIPUS: I have taken too much upon myself
    Without enquiry; therefore I wish to consult him.
IOCASTE: Then he shall come.
                But am I not one also   240
    To whom you might confide these fears of yours?
OEDIPUS: That is your right; it will not be denied you,
    Now least of all; for I have reached a pitch
    Of wild foreboding. Is there anyone
    To whom I should sooner speak?   245
    Polybos of Corinth is my father.
    My mother is a Dorian: Meropê.
    I grew up chief among the men of Corinth
    Until a strange thing happened—
    Not worth my passion, it may be, but strange.   250

    At a feast, a drunken man maundering in his cups
    Cries out that I am not my father's son!

    I contained myself that night, though I felt anger
    And a sinking heart. The next day I visited
    My father and mother, and questioned them. They
        stormed,   255
    Calling it all the slanderous rant of a fool;
    And this relieved me. Yet the suspicion
    Remained always aching in my mind;
    I knew there was talk; I could not rest;
    And finally, saying nothing to my parents,   260
    I went to the shrine at Delphi.
    The god dismissed my question without reply;
    He spoke of other things.
                Some were clear,
    Full of wretchedness, dreadful, unbearable:
    As, that I should lie with my own mother, breed   265

Children from whom all men would turn their eyes;
And that I should be my father's murderer.

I heard all this, and fled. And from that day
Corinth to me was only in the stars
Descending in that quarter of the sky,   270
As I wandered farther and farther on my way
To a land where I should never see the evil
Sung by the oracle. And I came to this country
Where, so you say, King Laïos was killed.

I will tell you all that happened there, my lady.   275

There were three highways
Coming together at a place I passed;
And there a herald came towards me, and a chariot
Drawn by horses, with a man such as you describe
Seated in it. The groom leading the horses   280
Forced me off the road at his lord's command;
But as this charioteer lurched over towards me
I struck him in my rage. The old man saw me
And brought his double goad down upon my head
As I came abreast.

              He was paid back, and more!
Swinging my club in this right hand I knocked him
Out of his car, and he rolled on the ground.

                        I killed him.

I killed them all.
Now if that stranger and Laïos were—kin,
Where is a man more miserable than I?   290
More hated by the gods? Citizen and alien alike
Must never shelter me or speak to me—
I must be shunned by all.

                And I myself
Pronounced this malediction upon myself!

Think of it: I have touched you with these hands,   295
These hands that killed your husband. What defilement!

Am I all evil, then? It must be so,
Since I must flee from Thebes, yet never again
See my own countrymen, my own country,
For fear of joining my mother in marriage   300
And killing Polybos, my father.

               Ah,
If I was created so, born to this fate,
Who could deny the savagery of God?

O holy majesty of heavenly powers!
May I never see that day! Never!   305
Rather let me vanish from the race of men
Than know the abomination destined me!
CHORAGOS: We too, my lord, have felt dismay at this.
But there is hope: you have yet to hear the shepherd.
OEDIPUS: Indeed, I fear no other hope is left me.   310
IOCASTE: What do you hope from him when he
        comes?
OEDIPUS: This much:
If his account of the murder tallies with yours,
Then I am cleared.
IOCASTE: What was it that I said
Of such importance?
OEDIPUS: Why, "marauders," you said,
Killed the King, according to this man's story.   315
If he maintains that still, if there were several,
Clearly the guilt is not mine: I was alone.
But if he says one man, singlehanded, did it,
Then the evidence all points to me.
IOCASTE: You may be sure that he said there were several; 320
And can he call back that story now? He can not.
The whole city heard it as plainly as I.
But suppose he alters some detail of it:
He can not ever show that Laïos' death
Fulfilled the oracle: for Apollo said   325
My child was doomed to kill him; and my child—
Poor baby!—it was my child that died first.

No. From now on, where oracles are concerned,
I would not waste a second thought on any.
OEDIPUS: You may be right.
                    But come: let someone go   330
For the shepherd at once. This matter must be settled.
IOCASTE: I will send for him.
I would not wish to cross you in anything,
And surely not in this.—Let us go in.

(*Exeunt into the palace.*)

ODE II

                                            [STROPHE 1]

CHORUS: Let me be reverent in the ways of right,
        Lowly the paths I journey on;

Let all my words and actions keep
The laws of the pure universe
From highest Heaven handed down.   5
For Heaven is their bright nurse,
Those generations of the realms of light;
Ah, never of mortal kind were they begot,
Nor are they slaves of memory, lost in sleep:
Their Father is greater than Time, and ages not.   10

[ANTISTROPHE 1]

The tyrant is a child of Pride
Who drinks from his great sickening cup
Recklessness and vanity,
Until from his high crest headlong
He plummets to the dust of hope.   15
That strong man is not strong.
But let no fair ambition be denied;
May God protect the wrestler for the State
In government, in comely policy,
Who will fear God, and on His ordinance wait.   20

[STROPHE 2]

Haughtiness and the high hand of disdain
Tempt and outrage God's holy law;
And any mortal who dares hold
No immortal Power in awe
Will be caught up in a net of pain: 25
The price for which his levity is sold.
Let each man take due earnings, then,
And keep his hands from holy things,
And from blasphemy stand apart—
Else the crackling blast of heaven   30
Blows on his head, and on his desperate heart;
Though fools will honor impious men,
In their cities no tragic poet sings.

[ANTISTROPHE 2]

Shall we lose faith in Delphi's obscurities,
We who have heard the world's core   35
Discredited, and the sacred wood
Of Zeus at Elis praised no more?
The deeds and the strange prophecies
Must make a pattern yet to be understood.
Zeus, if indeed you are the lord of all,   40
Throned in light over night and day,
Mirrors this in your endless mind:
Our masters call the oracle

Words on the wind, and the Delphic vision blind!
Their hearts no longer know Apollo,   45
And reverence for the gods has died away.

SCENE III

(*Enter* IOCASTE.)

IOCASTE: Princes of Thebes, it has occurred to me
To visit the altars of the gods, bearing
These branches as a suppliant, and this incense.
Our King is not himself: his noble soul
Is overwrought with fantasies of dread,   5
Else he would consider
The new prophecies in the light of the old.
He will listen to any voice that speaks disaster,
And my advice goes for nothing.

(*She approaches the altar, R.*)

                                  To you, then, Apollo,
Lycean lord, since you are nearest, I turn in prayer.   10
Receive these offerings, and grant us deliverance
From defilement. Our hearts are heavy with fear
When we see our leader distracted, as helpless sailors
Are terrified by the confusion of their helmsman.

(*Enter* MESSENGER.)

MESSENGER: Friends, no doubt you can direct me: 15
Where shall I find the house of Oedipus,
Or, better still, where is the King himself?
CHORAGOS: It is this very place, stranger; he is inside.
This is his wife and mother of his children.
MESSENGER: I wish her happiness in a happy house,
Blest in the fulfillment of her marriage.
IOCASTE: I wish as much for you: your courtesy
Deserves a like good fortune. But now, tell me:
Why have you come? What have you to say to us?
MESSENGER: Good news, my lady, for your house and
your husband.   25
IOCASTE: What news? Who sent you here?
MESSENGER: I am from
                                             Corinth.
The news I bring ought to mean joy for you,
Though it may be you will find some grief in it.
IOCASTE: What is it? How can it touch us in both ways?   30

MESSENGER: The people of Corinth, they say,
        Intend to call Oedipus to be their king.
IOCASTE: But old Polybos—is he not reigning still?
MESSENGER: No. Death holds him in his sepulchre.   35
IOCASTE: What are you saying? Polybos is dead?
MESSENGER: If I am not telling the truth, may I die myself.
IOCASTE: (*to a* maidservant.) Go in, go quickly; tell this to
        your master.

        O riddlers of God's will, where are you now!
        This was the man whom Oedipus, long ago,   40
        Feared so, fled so, in dread of destroying him—
        But it was another fate by which he died.

        (*Enter* OEDIPUS, center.)

OEDIPUS: Dearest Iocaste, why have you sent for me?
IOCASTE.   Listen to what this man says, and then tell me
        What has become of the solemn prophecies.   45
OEDIPUS: Who is this man? What is his news for me?
IOCASTE: He has come from Corinth to announce your
        father's death!
OEDIPUS: Is it true, stranger? Tell me in your own words.
MESSENGER: I cannot say it more clearly: the King is dead.   50
OEDIPUS: Was it by treason? Or by an attack of illness?
MESSENGER: A little thing brings old men to their rest.
OEDIPUS: It was sickness, then?
MESSENGER: Yes, and his many years.
OEDIPUS: Ah!   55
        Why should a man respect the Pythian hearth, or
        Give heed to the birds that jangle above his head?
        They prophesied that I should kill Polybos,
        Kill my own father; but he is dead and buried,
        And I am here—I never touched him, never,
        Unless he died in grief for my departure,
        And thus, in a sense, through me. No. Polybos   60
        Has packed the oracles off with him underground.
        They are empty words.
IOCASTE: Had I not told you so?
OEDIPUS: You had; it was my faint heart that betrayed me.   65
IOCASTE: From now on never think of those things again.
OEDIPUS: And yet—must I not fear my mother's bed?
IOCASTE: Why should anyone in this world be afraid,
        Since Fate rules us and nothing can be foreseen?
        A man should live only for the present day.
        Have no more fear of sleeping with your mother: 70

How many men, in dreams, have lain with their
    mothers!
No reasonable man is troubled by such things.
OEDIPUS: That is true; only—
If only my mother were not still alive!
But she is alive. I cannot help my dread.   75
IOCASTE: Yet this news of your father's death is wonderful.
OEDIPUS: Wonderful. But I fear the living woman.
MESSENGER: Tell me, who is this woman that you fear?
OEDIPUS: It is Merope, man; the wife of King Polybos.
MESSENGER: Merope? Why should you be afraid of her?   80
OEDIPUS: An oracle of the gods, a dreadful saying.
MESSENGER: Can you tell me about it or are you sworn to
    silence?
OEDIPUS: I can tell you, and I will.
Apollo said through his prophet that I was the man
Who should marry his own mother, shed his father's blood   85
With his own hands. And so, for all these years
I have kept clear of Corinth, and no harm has come—
Though it would have been sweet to see my parents
    again.
MESSENGER: And is this the fear that drove you out of
    Corinth?
OEDIPUS: Would you have me kill my father?   90
MESSENGER: As for that
You must be reassured by the news I gave you.
OEDIPUS: If you could reassure me, I would reward you.
MESSENGER: I had that in mind, I will confess: I thought
I could count on you when you returned to Corinth.   95
OEDIPUS: No: I will never go near my parents again.
MESSENGER: Ah, son, you still do not know what you are
    doing—
OEDIPUS: What do you mean? In the name of God tell me!
MESSENGER: If these are your reasons for not going home.
OEDIPUS: I tell you, I fear the oracle may come true.   100
MESSENGER: And guilt may come upon you through your
    parents?
OEDIPUS: That is the dread that is always in my heart.
MESSENGER: Can you not see that all your fears are
    groundless?
OEDIPUS: How can you say that? They are my parents,
    surely?
MESSENGER: Polybos was not your father.   105
OEDIPUS: Not my father?

MESSENGER: No more your father than the man speaking
            to you.
OEDIPUS: But you are nothing to me!
MESSENGER: Neither was he.
OEDIPUS: Then why did he call me son?   110
MESSENGER: I will tell you:
     Long ago he had you from my hands, as a gift.
OEDIPUS: Then how could he love me so, if I was not his?
MESSENGER: He had no children, and his heart turned to
            you.
OEDIPUS: What of you? Did you buy me? Did you find me
            by chance?
MESSENGER: I came upon you in the crooked pass of
            Kithairon.
OEDIPUS: And what were you doing there?
MESSENGER:.   Tending my flocks.   120
OEDIPUS: A wandering shepherd?
MESSENGER: But your savior, son, that day.
OEDIPUS: From what did you save me?
MESSENGER: Your ankles should tell you that.
OEDIPUS: Ah, stranger, why do you speak of that
            childhood pain?
MESSENGER: I cut the bonds that tied your ankles together.
OEDIPUS: I have had the mark as long as I can remember.   125
MESSENGER: That was why you were given the name you
            bear.
OEDIPUS: God! Was it my father or my mother who did it?
     Tell me!
MESSENGER: I do not know. The man who gave you to me
     Can tell you better than I.   130
OEDIPUS: It was not you that found me, but another?
MESSENGER: It was another shepherd gave you to me.
OEDIPUS: Who was he? Can you tell me who he was?
MESSENGER: I think he was said to be one of Laïos' people.
OEDIPUS: You mean the Laïos who was king here years ago?   135
MESSENGER: Yes; King Laïos, and the man was one of his
            herdsmen.
OEDIPUS: Is he still alive? Can I see him?
MESSENGER: These men here
     Know best about such things.
OEDIPUS: Does anyone here
     Know this shepherd that he is talking about?
     Have you seen him in the fields, or in the town?   140
     If you have, tell me. It is time things were made plain.

CHORAGOS: I think the man he means is that same
            shepherd
        You have already asked to see. Iocaste perhaps
        Could tell you something.
OEDIPUS: Do you know anything
        About him, Lady? Is he the man we have summoned?   145
        Is that the man this shepherd means?
IOCASTE: Why think of him?

        Forget this herdsman. Forget it all.
        This talk is a waste of time.
OEDIPUS: How can you say that,
        When the clues to my true birth are in my hands?
IOCASTE: For God's love, let us have no more questioning!   150
        Is your life nothing to you?
        My own is pain enough for me to bear.
OEDIPUS: You need not worry. Suppose my mother a
            slave,
        And born of slaves: no baseness can touch you.
IOCASTE: Listen to me, I beg you: do not do this thing!   155
OEDIPUS: I will not listen; the truth must be made known.
IOCASTE: Everything that I say is for your
            own good!
OEDIPUS: My own good
        Snaps my patience, then; I want none of it.
IOCASTE: You are fatally wrong! May you never learn who
            you are!
OEDIPUS: Go, one of you, and bring the shepherd here.
        Let us leave this woman to brag of her royal name.   160
IOCASTE: Ah, miserable!
        That is the only word I have for you now.
        That is the only word I can ever have.

        (Exit into the palace.)

CHORAGOS: Why has she left us, Oedipus? Why has she gone   165
        In such a passion of sorrow? I fear this silence:
        Something dreadful may come of it.
OEDIPUS: Let it come!
        However base my birth, I must know about it.
        The Queen, like a woman, is perhaps ashamed
        To think of my low origin. But I   170
        Am a child of Luck; I can not be dishonored.
        Luck is my mother; the passing months, my brothers,

Have seen me rich and poor.
                                      If this is so,
How could I wish that I were someone else?
How could I not be glad to know my birth?   175

ODE III

CHORUS: If ever the coming time were known
          To my heart's pondering,
          Kithairon, now by Heaven I see the torches
          At the festival of the next full moon,
          And see the dance, and hear the choir sing   5
          A grace to your gentle shade:
          Mountain where Oedipus was found,
          O mountain guard of a noble race!
          May the god who heals us lend his aid,   10
          And let that glory come to pass
          For our king's cradling-ground.

          Of the nymphs that flower beyond the years,
          Who bore you, royal child,
          To Pan of the hills or the timberline Apollo,
          Cold in delight where the upland clears,   15
          Or Hermês for whom Kyllenê's heights are piled?
          Or flushed as evening cloud,
          Great Dionysos, roamer of mountains,
          He—was it he who found you there,   20
          And caught you up in his own proud
          Arms from the sweet god-ravisher
          Who laughed by the Muses' fountains?

SCENE IV

OEDIPUS: Sirs: though I do not know the man,
           I think I see him coming, this shepherd we want:
           He is old, like our friend here, and the men
           Bringing him seem to be servants of my house.
           But you can tell, if you have ever seen him.   5

           (*Enter* shepherd *escorted by servants.*)

CHORAGOS: I know him, he was Laïos' man. You can trust
            him.

OEDIPUS: Tell me first, you from Corinth: is this the
           shepherd we were discussing?
MESSENGER: This is the very man.   10
OEDIPUS: (*to* shepherd.) Come here. No, look at me.
           You must answer
        Everything I ask.—You belonged to Laïos?
SHEPHERD: Yes: born his slave, brought up in his house.
OEDIPUS: Tell me: what kind of work did you do for him?   15
SHEPHERD: I was a shepherd of his, most of my life.
OEDIPUS: Where mainly did you go for pasturage?
SHEPHERD: Sometimes Kithairon, sometimes the hills
           near-by.
OEDIPUS: Do you remember ever seeing this man out   20
           there?
SHEPHERD: What would he be doing there? This man?
OEDIPUS: This man standing here. Have you ever seen him
           before?
SHEPHERD: No. At least, not to my recollection.
MESSENGER: And that is not strange, my lord, But I'll   25
           refresh his memory: he must remember when we two
        Spent three whole seasons together, March to
           September,
        On Kithairon or thereabouts. He had two flocks;
        I had one. Each autumn I'd drive mine home   30
        And he would go back with his to Laïos' sheepfold.—
        Is this not true, just as I have described it?
SHEPHERD: True, yes; but it was all so long ago.
MESSENGER: Well, then: so you remember, back in those
           days   35
        That you gave me a baby boy to bring up as my own?
SHEPHERD: What if I did? What are you trying to say?
MESSENGER: King Oedipus was once that little child.
SHEPHERD: Damn you, hold your tongue!
OEDIPUS: No more of that!   40
        It is your tongue needs watching, not this man's.
SHEPHERD: My King, my Master, what is it I have done
           wrong?
OEDIPUS: You have not answered his question about the
           boy.   45
SHEPHERD: He does not know . . . He is only making trouble
OEDIPUS: Come, speak plainly, or it will go hard with you.
SHEPHERD: In God's name, do not torture an old man!
OEDIPUS: Come here, one of you; bind his arms behind
           him.   50

SHEPHERD: Unhappy king! What more do you wish to
          learn?
OEDIPUS: Did you give this man the child he speaks of?
SHEPHERD: I did.
    And I would to God I had died that very day.   55
OEDIPUS: You will die now unless you speak the truth.
SHEPHERD: Yet if I speak the truth, I am worse than dead.
OEDIPUS: Very well; since you insist upon delaying—
SHEPHERD: No! I have told you already that I gave him the
          boy.   60
OEDIPUS: Where did you get him? From your house?
    From somewhere else?
SHEPHERD: Not from mine, no. A man gave him to me.
OEDIPUS: Is that man here? Do you know whose slave
          he was?   65
SHEPHERD: For God's love, my King, do not ask me
          any more!
OEDIPUS: You are a dead man if I have to ask you again.
SHEPHERD: Then . . . Then the child was from the palace
          of Laïos?   70
OEDIPUS: A slave child? Or a child of his own line?
SHEPHERD: Ah, I am on the brink of dreadful speech!
OEDIPUS: And I of dreadful hearing. Yet I must hear.
SHEPHERD: If you must be told, then . . .
                              They said it was Laïos' child,   75
    But it is your wife who can tell you about that.
OEDIPUS: My wife!—Did she give it to you?
SHEPHERD: My lord, she did.
OEDIPUS: Do you know why?
SHEPHERD: I was told to get rid of it.   80
OEDIPUS: An unspeakable mother!
SHEPHERD: There had been prophecies . . .
OEDIPUS: Tell me.
SHEPHERD: It was said that the boy would kill his
          own father.   85
OEDIPUS: Then why did you give him over to this old man?
SHEPHERD: I pitied the baby, my King,
    And I thought that this man would take him far away
    To his own country.
                        He saved him—but for what a fate!   90
    For if you are what this man says you are,
    No man living is more wretched than Oedipus.
OEDIPUS: Ah God!
    It was true!

All the prophecies!   95
                        —Now,
O Light, may I look on you for the last time!
I, Oedipus,
Oedipus, damned in his birth, in his marriage damned,
Damned in the blood he shed with his own hand!   100

(He rushes into the palace.)

ODE IV

[STROPHE 1]

CHORUS: Alas for the seed of men.

What measure shall I give these generations
That breathe on the void and are void
And exist and do not exist?   5

Who bears more weight of joy
Than mass of sunlight shifting in images,
Or who shall make his thought stay on
That down time drifts away?

Your splendor is all fallen.

O naked brow of wrath and tears,   10
O change of Oedipus!
I saw your days call no man blest—
Your great days like ghosts gone.

[ANTISTROPHE 1]

That mind was a strong bow.
Deep, how deep you drew it then, hard archer,   15
At a dim fearful range,
And brought dear glory down!

You overcame the stranger—
The virgin with her hooking lion claws—
And though death sang, stood like a tower   20
To make pale Thebes take heart.

Fortress against our sorrow!

Divine king, giver of laws,
Majestic Oedipus!
No prince in Thebes had ever such renown,   25
No prince won such grace of power.

[STROPHE 2]

And now of all men ever known
Most pitiful is this man's story:
His fortunes are most changed, his state
Fallen to a low slave's   30
Ground under bitter fate.

O Oedipus, most royal one!
The great door that expelled you to the light
Gave at night—ah, gave night to your glory:
As to the father, to the fathering son.   35

All understood too late.

How could that queen whom Laïos won,
The garden that he harrowed at his height,
Be silent when that act was done?

                                          [ANTISTROPHE 2]
But all eyes fail before time's eye,   40
All actions come to justice there.
Though never willed, though far down the deep past,
Your bed, your dread sirings,
Are brought to book at last.
Child by Laïos doomed to die,   45
Then doomed to lose that fortunate little death,
Would God you never took breath in this air
That was my wailing lips I take to cry:

For I weep the world's outcast.

I was blind, and now I can tell why: 50
Asleep, for you had given ease of breath
To Thebes, while the false years went by.

EXODOS

(*Enter, from the palace,* second messenger.)

SECOND MESSENGER: Elders of Thebes, most honored in
      this land,
What horrors are yours to see and hear, what weight
Of sorrow to be endured, if, true to your birth,
You venerate the line of Labdakos!
I think neither Istros nor Phasis, those great rivers,   5
Could purify this place of the corruption
It shelters now, or soon must bring to light—
Evil not done unconsciously, but willed.

The greatest griefs are those we cause ourselves.
CHORAGOS: Surely, friend, we have grief enough already;   10
    What new sorrow do you mean?
SECOND MESSENGER: The Queen is dead.
CHORAGOS: Iocaste? Dead? But at whose hand?
SECOND MESSENGER: Her own
    The full horror of what happened you cannot know,   15
    For you did not see it; but I, who did, will tell you
    As clearly as I can how she met her death.

    When she had left us,
    In passionate silence, passing through the court,
    She ran to her apartment in the house,   20
    Her hair clutched by the fingers of both hands.
    She closed the doors behind her; then, by that bed
    Where long ago the fatal son was conceived—
    That son who should bring about his father's death—
    We heard her call upon Laïos, dead so many years,   25
    And heard her wail for the double fruit of her
        marriage,
    A husband by her husband, children by her child.

    Exactly how she died I do not know:
    For Oedipus burst in moaning and would not let us
    Keep vigil to the end: it was by him   30
    As he stormed about the room that our eyes were
        caught.
    From one to another of us he went, begging a sword,
    Cursing the wife who was not his wife, the mother
    Whose womb had carried his own children and
        himself.   35
    I do not know: it was none of us aided him,
    But surely one of the gods was in control!
    For with a dreadful cry
    He hurled his weight, as though wrenched out
        of himself,
    At the twin doors: the bolts gave, and he rushed in.
    And there we saw her hanging, her body swaying   40
    From the cruel cord she had noosed about her neck.
    A great sob broke from him heartbreaking to hear,
    As he loosed the rope and lowered her to the ground.
    I would blot out from my mind what happened next!
    For the King ripped from her gown the golden brooches   45
    That were her ornament, and raised them, and
        plunged them down

Straight into his own eyeballs, crying, "No more,
No more shall you look on the misery about me,
The horrors of my own doing! Too long you have
        known
The faces of those whom I should never have seen,   50
Too long been blind to those for whom I was
        searching!
From this hour, go in darkness!" And as he spoke,
He struck at his eyes—not once, but many times;
And the blood spattered his beard,   55
Bursting from his ruined sockets like red hail.

So from the unhappiness of two this evil has sprung,
A curse on the man and woman alike. The old
Happiness of the house of Labdakos
Was happiness enough: where is it today?
It is all wailing and ruin, disgrace, death—all   60
The misery of mankind that has a name—
And it is wholly and for ever theirs.

CHORAGOS: Is he in agony still? Is there no rest for him?
SECOND MESSENGER: He is calling for someone to lead him
        to the gates   65
So that all the children of Kadmos may look upon
His father's murderer, his mother's—no,
I cannot say it!
                And then he will leave Thebes,
Self-exiled, in order that the curse
Which he himself pronounced may depart from
        the house.   70
He is weak, and there is none to lead him,
So terrible is his suffering.
                        But you will see:
Look, the doors are opening; in a moment
You will see a thing that would crush a heart of stone.   75

(The central door is opened; Oedipus, *blinded, is led in.)*

CHORAGOS: Dreadful indeed for men to see,
    Never have my own eyes
    Looked on a sight so full of fear.

    Oedipus!
    What madness came upon you, what daemon   80
    Leaped on your life with heavier
    Punishment than a mortal man can bear?
    No: I can not even

Look at you, poor ruined one.   80
And I would speak, question, ponder,
If I were able. No.
You make me shudder.
OEDIPUS: God.   God.
Is there a sorrow greater?   85
Where shall I find harbor in this world?
My voice is hurled far on a dark wind.
What has God done to me?
CHORAGOS: Too terrible to think of, or to see.

[STROPHE 1]

OEDIPUS: O cloud of night,   90
Never to be turned away: night coming on,
I can not tell how: night like a shroud!

My fair winds brought me here.
                          Oh God. Again
The pain of the spokes where I had sight,
The flooding pain   95
Of memory, never to be gouged out.
CHORAGOS: This is not strange.
You suffer it all twice over, remorse in pain,
Pain in remorse.

[ANTISTROPHE 1]

OEDIPUS: Ah dear friend   100
Are you faithful even yet, you alone?
Are you still standing near me, will you stay here,
Patient, to care for the blind?
                          The blind man!
Yet even blind I know who it is attends me,
By the voice's tone—   105
Though my new darkness hide the comforter.
CHORAGOS: Oh fearful act!
What god was it drove you to rake black
Night across your eyes?

[STROPHE 2]

OEDIPUS: Apollo. Apollo. Dear   110
Children, the god was Apollo.
He brought my sick, sick fate upon me.
But the blinding hand was my own!
How could I bear to see
When all my sight was horror everywhere?   115
CHORAGOS: Everywhere; that is true.

OEDIPUS: And now what is left?
     Images? Love? A greeting even,
     Sweet to the senses? Is there anything?
     Ah, no, friends: lead me away.   120
     Lead me away from Thebes.
                              Lead the great wreck
     And hell of Oedipus, whom the gods hate.
CHORAGOS: Your fate is clear, you are not blind to that.
     Would God you had never found it out!

                                                        [ANTISTROPHE 2]
OEDIPUS: Death take the man who unbound   125
     My feet on that hillside
     And delivered me from death to life! What life?
     If only I had died,
     This weight of monstrous doom
     Could not have dragged me and my darlings down.   130
CHORAGOS: I would have wished the same.
OEDIPUS: Oh never to have come here
     With my father's blood upon me! Never
     To have been the man they call his mother's husband!
     Oh accurst! Oh child of evil,   135
     To have entered that wretched bed—
                                   The selfsame one!
     More primal than sin itself, this fell to me.
CHORAGOS: I do not know how I can answer you.
     You were better dead than alive and blind.
OEDIPUS: Do not counsel me any more. This punishment   140
     That I have laid upon myself is just.
     If I had eyes,
     I do not know how I could bear the sight
     Of my father, when I came to the house of Death,
     Or my mother: for I have sinned against them both   145
     So vilely that I could not make my peace
     By strangling my own life.
                              Or do you think my children,
     Born as they were born, would be sweet to my eyes?
     Ah never, never! Nor this town with its high walls,
     Nor the holy images of the gods.
                              For I,   150
     Thrice miserable—Oedipus, noblest of all the line
     Of Kadmos, have condemned myself to enjoy
     These things no more, by my own malediction
     Expelling that man whom the gods declared
     To be a defilement in the house of Laïos.   155

After exposing the rankness of my own guilt,
How could I look men frankly in the eyes?
No, I swear it,
If I could have stifled my hearing at its source,
I would have done it and made all this body   160
A tight cell of misery, blank to light and sound:
So I should have been safe in a dark agony
Beyond all recollection.
                                        Ah Kithairon!
Why did you shelter me? When I was cast upon you,
Why did I not die? Then I should never   165
Have shown the world my execrable birth.

Ah Polybos! Corinth, city that I believed
The ancient seat of my ancestors: how fair
I seemed, your child! And all the while this evil
Was cancerous within me!
                                        For I am sick   170
In my daily life, sick in my origin.

O three roads, dark ravine, woodland and way
Where three roads met: you, drinking my father's
        blood,
My own blood, spilled by my own hand: can you
        remember
The unspeakable things I did there, and the things   175
I went on from there to do?
                                        O marriage, marriage!
The act that engendered me, and again the act
Performed by the son in the same bed—
                                        Ah, the net
Of incest, mingling fathers, brothers, sons,
With brides, wives, mothers: the last evil   180
That can be known by men; no tongue can say
How evil!
                No. For the love of God, conceal me
Somewhere far from Thebes; or kill me; or hurl me
Into the sea, away from men's eyes for ever.

Come, lead me. You need not fear to touch me.   185
Of all men, I alone can bear this guilt.

(*Enter* CREON.)

CHORAGOS: We are not the ones to decide; but Creon
        here
     May fitly judge of what you ask. He only

Is left to protect the city in your place.

OEDIPUS: Alas, how can I speak to him? What right have I   190
    To beg his courtesy whom I have deeply wronged?

CREON: I have not come to mock you, Oedipus,
    Or to reproach you, either.
    (*To* ATTENDANTS.)   —You, standing there:
    If you have lost all respect for man's dignity,
    At least respect the flame of Lord Helios: 195
    Do not allow this pollution to show itself
    Openly here, an affront to the earth
    And Heaven's rain and the light of day. No, take him
    Into the house as quickly as you can.
    For it is proper   200
    That only the close kindred see his grief.

OEDIPUS: I pray you in God's name, since your courtesy
    Ignores my dark expectation, visiting
    With mercy this man of all men most execrable:
    Give me what I ask—for your good, not for mine.   205

CREON: And what is it that you would have me do?

OEDIPUS: Drive me out of this country as quickly as may
        be
    To a place where no human voice can ever greet me.

CREON: I should have done that before now—only,
    God's will had not been wholly revealed to me.   210

OEDIPUS: But his command is plain: the parricide
    Must be destroyed. I am that evil man.

CREON: That is the sense of it, yes; but things are,
    We had best discover clearly what is to be done.

OEDIPUS: You would learn more about a man like me?   215

CREON: You are ready now to listen to the god.

OEDIPUS: I will listen. But it is to you
    That I must turn for help. I beg you, hear me.

    The woman in there—
    Give her whatever funeral you think proper: 220
    She is your sister.
                —But let me go, Creon!
    Let me purge my father's Thebes of the pollution
    Of my living here, and go out to the wild hills,
    To Kithairon, that has won such fame with me,
    The tomb my mother and father appointed for me,   225
    And let me die there, as they willed I should.
    And yet I know
    Death will not ever come to me through sickness
    Or in any natural way: I have been preserved

For some unthinkable fate. But let that be.   230
As for my sons, you need not care for them.
They are men, they will find some way to live.
But my poor daughters, who have shared my table,
Who never before have been parted from their father—
Take care of them, Creon; do this for me.   235
And will you let me touch them with my hands
A last time, and let us weep together?
Be kind, my lord,
Great prince, be kind!
                    Could I but touch them,
They would be mine again, as when I had my eyes.   240

(Enter ANTIGONE *and* ISMENE, *attended.)*

Ah, God!
Is it my dearest children I hear weeping?
Has Creon pitied me and sent my daughters?
CREON: Yes, Oedipus: I knew that they were dear to you
In the old days, and know you must love them still.   245
OEDIPUS: May God bless you for this—and be a friendlier
Guardian to you than he has been to me!

Children, where are you?
Come quickly to my hands: they are your brother's—
Hands that have brought your father's once clear eyes   250
To this way of seeing—
                Ah dearest ones,
I had neither sight nor knowledge then, your father
By the woman who was the source of his own life!
And I weep for you—having no strength to see
       you—,
I weep for you when I think of the bitterness   255
That men will visit upon you all your lives.
What homes, what festivals can you attend
Without being forced to depart again in tears?
And when you come to marriageable age,
Where is the man, my daughters, who would dare   260
Risk the bane that lies on all my children?
Is there any evil wanting? Your father killed
His father; sowed the womb of her who bore him;
Engendered you at the fount of his own existence!
That is what they will say of you.
                     Then, whom   265
Can you ever marry? There are no bridegrooms for
       you,

And your lives must wither away in sterile dreaming.
O Creon, son of Menoikeus!
You are the only father my daughters have,
Since we, their parents, are both of us gone for ever.   270
They are your own blood: you will not let them
Fall into beggary and loneliness;
You will keep them from the miseries that are mine!
Take pity on them; see, they are only children,
Friendless except for you. Promise me this,   275
Great Prince, and give me your hand in token of it.

(CREON *clasps his right hand.*)

Children:
I could say much, if you could understand me,
But as it is, I have only this prayer for you:
Live where you can, be as happy as you can—   280
Happier, please God, than God has made your father!
CREON: Enough. You have wept enough. Now go within.
OEDIPUS: I must; but it is hard.
CREON: Time eases all things.
OEDIPUS: But you must promise—
CREON: Say what you desire.
OEDIPUS: Send me from Thebes!
CREON: God grant that I may!   285
OEDIPUS: But since God hates me . . .
CREON: No, he will grant your wish.
OEDIPUS: You promise?
CREON: I can not speak beyond my knowledge.
OEDIPUS: Then lead me in.
CREON: Come now, and leave your
                                    children.
OEDIPUS: No! Do not take them from me!
CREON: Think no longer
That you are in command here, but rather think   290
How, when you were, you served your own
            destruction.

(*Exeunt into the house all but the* CHORUS; *the* CHORAGOS *chants
directly to the audience.*)

CHORAGOS: Men of Thebes: look upon Oedipus.

This is the king who solved the famous riddle
And towered up, most powerful of men.
No mortal eyes but looked on him with envy,   295
Yet in the end ruin swept over him.

Let every man in mankind's frailty
Consider his last day; and let none
Presume on his good fortune until he find
Life, at his death, a memory without pain.   300

Meaning and Idea

1. What are the conditions in the city of Thebes at the opening of the play? What has caused these conditions to exist? Identify an early passage that descriptively summarizes these conditions.

Who is the oracle of Delphi? How do the oracle's prophesies figure in the conditions in Thebes?

2. How did Oedipus become king of Thebes? What is Oedipus's attitude toward the conditions in Thebes? Has he been aware of them before the opening of the play? What has he done about them up to that point? Why do the people of Thebes think Oedipus can save them from their present state?

3. Who was Laïos? Why didn't the people of Thebes hunt down his killer at the time of the murder? How does Oedipus plan to find the murderers? What does he plan to do with them? What will he do to anyone who withholds information? Who witnessed Laïos's murder? What did he do about it? Why? Why does Oedipus want to locate and question him?

4. Briefly summarize the story of Oedipus's childhood. Who were his real parents? What did they do with him? Why?

5. Who is Teiresias? Why was he sent for? What is his first response to being questioned? What is his secret, and why doesn't he want to reveal it? What is Teiresias's prophesy?

Who is Creon? What is the basis for Oedipus's original suspicions of Creon? What connection does he think exists between Creon and Teiresias? What is Creon's reaction to Oedipus's suspicions? In the end, what does Oedipus want from Creon? What is Creon's response then?

6. Who is Polybus? Why does the news of his death make Oedipus think things will be all right in Thebes?

7. What is the presumed relationship between Laïos, Iocaste, and Oedipus? What is the true relationship? At what point does Iocaste realize the truth about Oedipus? Is this before or after Oedipus knows? What is her first reaction? How does Oedipus realize the truth? What is his first reaction to it? What is Oedipus's condition at the end of the play?

Language, Form, Structure

1. In what ways does Oedipus contribute to the fulfillment of the prophecy? Is there any point in the play at which he could have stopped its fulfillment?

2. What is the main irony of *Oedipus Rex?* Discuss at least two other ironies in this play.

3. Find out the English translation of the word *Oedipus.* Why is Oedipus such an appropriate name for the king?

4. What is the major cause of the tragic ending of this play? Is there more than one cause? If so, identify them, comment on them, and arrange them from least to most important.

5. What are the functions of the choragos in this play? Of the strophe and antistrophe? How do they reveal causal information? How do they progress the action?

6. Eyes are mentioned often throughout the play. Identify some of these references. How does Sophocles combine literal and metaphoric meanings for seeing and blindness in the play?
   Why does Oedipus feel that his taking his own sight more appropriately follows his actions than taking his own life, as Iocaste does?

7. Select at least ten words from this play that were new to you. Use each in a sentence in such a way that you show that you understand the meaning.

Ideas for Writing

1. Describe a recent disaster outside your personal experience. Write an analysis of the causes of this disaster, indicating whether the primary causes derived from nature or from human choice and activity.

2. Analyze the causes and effects of a misunderstanding which occurred recently within a family—either your own or someone else's. Try to shape your essay so that the major source of responsibility is clear to the reader.

3. Write a paper in which you explain what you think was Sophocles's attitude towards prophesy, fate, and human choice. How are they separate or related? Which do you feel the playwright thought was the strongest determinant of the human condition? Support your ideas with specific references to the text of the play.

E. M. Forster
MY WOOD

E. M. Forster (1879–1970) was a member of the Bloomsbury Group—writers, artists, and philosophers living in London who helped shape the modernist movement of the first half of this century. Forster was born in London, but was raised in the countryside of Herfordshire. His fiction often dealt with the effects of social conventions on the natural course of human relationships. Forster's major novels include *Where Angels Fear to Tread* (1905), *A Room With a View* (1908), *Howards End* (1910), *Maurice* (1914), and *A Passage to India* (1924). Forster acquired a well-deserved reputation as a social and literary critic, as well as a short story writer.

"My Wood" is part of Forster's 1936 essay, *Abinger Harvest*. In this piece the author outlines, with a tinge of self-criticism, the effects of property ownership and overly materialistic tendencies.

A few years ago I wrote a book which dealt in part with the difficulties of the English in India. Feeling that they would have had no difficulties in India themselves, the Americans read the book freely. The more they read it the better it made them feel, and a cheque to the author was the result. I bought a wood with the cheque. It is not a large wood—it contains scarcely any trees, and it is intersected, blast it, by a public footpath. Still, it is the first property that I have owned, so it is right that other people should participate in my shame, and should ask themselves, in accents that will vary in horror, this very important question: What is the effect of property upon the character? Don't let's touch economics; the effect of private ownership upon the community as a whole is another question—a more important question, perhaps, but another one. Let's keep to psychology. If you own things, what's their effect on you? What's the effect on me of my wood?

In the first place, it makes me feel heavy. Property does have this effect. Property produces men of weight, and it was a man of weight who failed to get into the Kingdom of Heaven. He was not wicked, that unfortunate millionaire in the parable, he was only stout; he stuck out in front, not to mention behind, and as he wedged himself this way and that in the crystalline entrance and bruised his well-fed flanks, he saw beneath him a comparatively slim camel passing through the eye of a needle and being woven into the robe of God. The Gospels all through couple stoutness and slowness. They point out what is perfectly obvious, yet seldom realized: that if you have a lot of things you cannot move about a lot, that furniture requires dusting, dusters require servants, servants require insurance stamps, and the whole tangle of them makes you think twice before you accept an invitation to dinner or go for a bathe in the Jordan. Sometimes the Gospels proceed further and say with Tolstoy that property is sinful; they approach the difficult ground of asceticism here, where I cannot follow them. But as to the immediate effects of property on people, they just show straightforward logic. It produces men of weight. Men of weight cannot, by definition, move like the lightning from the East unto the West, and the ascent of a fourteen-stone bishop into a pulpit is thus the exact antithesis of the coming of the Son of Man. My wood makes me feel heavy.

In the second place, it makes me feel it ought to be larger.

The other day I heard a twig snap in it. I was annoyed at first, for I thought that someone was blackberrying, and depreciating the value of the undergrowth. On coming nearer, I saw it was not a man who had trodden on the twig and snapped it, but a bird, and I felt pleased. My bird. The bird was not equally pleased. Ignoring the relation between us, it took fright as soon as it saw the shape of my face, and flew straight over the boundary hedge into a field, the property of Mrs. Henessy, where it sat down with a loud squawk. It had become Mrs. Henessy's bird. Something seemed grossly amiss here, something that would not have occurred had the wood been larger. I could not afford to buy Mrs. Henessy out, I dared not murder her, and limitations of this sort beset me on every side. Ahab did not want that vineyard—he only needed it to round off his property, preparatory to plotting a new curve—and all the land around my wood has become necessary to me in order to round off the wood. A boundary protects. But—poor little thing—the boundary ought in its turn to be protected. Noises on the edge of it. Children throw stones. A little more, and then a little more, until we reach the sea. Hapy Canute! Happier Alexander! And after all, why should even the world be the limit of possession? A rocket containing a Union Jack, will, it is hoped, be shortly fired at the moon. Mars. Sirius. Beyond which . . . But these immensities ended by saddening me. I could not suppose that my wood was the destined nucleus of universal dominion—it is so very small and contains no mineral wealth beyond the blackberries. Nor was I comforted when Mrs. Henessy's bird took alarm for the second time and flew clean away from us all, under the belief that it belonged to itself.

In the third place, property makes its owner feel that he ought to do something to it. Yet he isn't sure what. A restlessness comes over him, a vague sense that he has a personality to express—the same sense which, without any vagueness, leads the artist to an act of creation. Sometimes I think I will cut down such trees as remain in the wood, at other times I want to fill up the gaps between them with new trees. Both impulses are pretentious and empty. They are not honest movements towards money-making or beauty. They spring from a foolish desire to express myself and from an inability to enjoy what I have got. Creation, property, enjoyment form a sinister trinity in the human mind. Creation and enjoyment are both very, very good, yet they are often unattainable without a material basis, and at such moments property pushes itself in as a substitute, saying, "Accept me instead—I'm good enough for all three." It is not enough. It is, as Shakespeare said of lust, "The expense of spirit in a waste of shame": it is "Before, a joy proposed; behind, a dream." Yet we don't know how to shun it. It is forced on us by our economic system as the alternative to starvation. It is also forced on us by an internal defect in the soul, by the feeling that in property may lie the germs of self-development and of exquisite or heroic deeds. Our life on earth is, and ought to be, material and carnal. But we have not yet learned to manage our materialism and carnality properly; they are still entangled with the desire for ownership, where (in the words of Dante) "Possession is one with loss."

And this brings us to our fourth and final point: the blackberries.

Blacberries are not plentiful in this meagre grove, but they are easily seen from the public footpath which traverses it, and all too easily gathered. Foxgloves, too—people will pull up the foxgloves, and ladies of an educational tendency even grub for toadstools to show them on the Monday in class. Other ladies, less educated, roll down the bracken in the arms of their gentlemen friends. There is paper, there are tins. Pray, does my wood belong to me or doesn't it? And, if it does, should I not own it best by allowing no one else to walk there? There is a wood near Lyme Regis, also cursed by a public footpath, where the owner has not hesitated on this point. He had built high stone walls each side of the path, and has spanned it by bridges, so that the public circulate like termites while he gorges on the blackberries unseen. He really does own his wood, this able chap. Dives in Hell did pretty well, but the gulf dividing him from Lazarus could be traversed by vision, and nothing traverses it here. And perhaps I shall come to this in time. I shall wall in and fence out until I really taste the sweets of property. Enormously stout, endlessly avaricious, pseudo-creative, intensely selfish, I shall weave upon my forehead the quadruple crown of possession until those nasty Bolshies come and take it off again and thrust me aside into the outer darkness.

Meaning and Idea

1.   British and American usage differ somewhat. What does Forster mean by "a wood"? What is the American English equivalent?

2. What is the primary focus of this essay—causes or effects? Cite the question that establishes the main point of this essay.

3. Trace the cause and effect development that allowed Forster to purchase his wood. What does he suggest as the American involvement in that development? Why does he mention Americans in the first paragraph?

4. What are the four results of property ownership as outlined by Forster? What overall attitude about property ownership do they add up to? Does Forster favor total abandonment of the ownership system? Cite the sentence on which you can base your response.

5. What constitutes for Forster "a sinister trinity in the human mind"? Explain his meaning. What is "the quadruple crown of possession"? Who are "those nasty Bolshies"?

Language, Form, Structure

1. On what basis does Forster arrange the four effects of property ownership? What is the relevance of the fourth effect to the preceding three?

2. How does Forster use allusions (references) in this essay? What, in particular, is the value of the biblical allusions? What are they?

3. Analyze the author's use of transitional techniques in this essay. What is the effect of his single-sentence paragraphs?

4. Discuss how Forster uses personal experience as a way to exemplify his general thesis concerning the effects of ownership.

5. Look up and define the following words: stout; asceticism; antithesis; depreciative; amiss; beset; carnal; meagre; bracken; avaricious.

Ideas for Writing

1. Analyze the effects of the loss of something material on people. Draw on your experience or knowledge of loss of possessions, money, etc. Make clear whether you feel such loss is predominantly a negative or positive occurrence. You may want to make comparisons with nonmaterial losses; for example, death of a loved one, end of a relationship, and so on.

2. Write a causal analysis of why you think most people want *new* things—new cars, new clothes, new houses, new appliances, and so on. Relate your analysis to a general thesis about society's wants or needs.

3. In this essay, Forster uses his own experience with ownership to generalize about society's materialism. Write an essay in which you discuss where you fit into Forster's analysis. Do you consider yourself materialistic? In what ways? Do you consider it a positive or negative trait in yourself or others?

William Shakespeare
WHEN MY LOVE SWEARS THAT SHE IS MADE OF TRUTH

Although William Shakespeare (1564–1616) is considered the world's greatest English-language playwright, some critics feel that his poetry alone would have brought him great fame. He began publishing poetry in 1593, around the same time as his earliest plays, and his 152 *Sonnets,* published in 1609, are considered his greatest poetic achievement. The sonnets, as do the plays, deal with love and death, and with time's effects on each, but, of course, in much more compressed form. Shakespeare was born in Stratford-on-Avon, England, then spent a good deal of his time in London as a playwright-actor before retiring and eventually dying in his hometown.

The full range of Shakespeare's 152 sonnets, written in the 1590s, deals with the universals of change, time, and death, as well as the means by which art and love afford ways for us to face these universals. In "When My Love Swears That She Is Made of Truth," one of Shakespeare's 25 "Dark Lady" sonnets, he explores the cause-and-effect relationship between truth and love.

*W*hen my love swears that she is made of truth,
I do believe her, though I know she lies,
That she might think me some untutored youth,
Unlearned in the world's false subtleties.
Thus vainly thinking that she thinks me young,   5
Although she knows my days are past the best,
Simply I credit her false-speaking tongue;
On both sides thus is simple truth supprest.
But wherefore says she not she is unjust?
And wherefore say not I that I am old?   10
Oh, love's best habit is in seeming trust,
And age in love loves not to have years told:
Therefore I lie with her and she with me,
And in our faults by lies we flattered be.

Meaning and Idea

1. Is the speaker of this poem young or old? Is he younger or older than his beloved?

2. Lines 9 and 10 ask two questions about the main conditions analyzed in this poem. In more modern English, the questions are: "Why doesn't she say she's untrue?" and "Why don't I say that I'm old?" Answer the two questions based on your reading of the poem.

3. What, according to the poem, are the causes for lying between lovers? What is the relationship between the causes and effects of lying?

Language, Form, Structure

1. Explain the meaning of the seeming contradiction of line 2. How else does Shakespeare use contradictions as an explanatory technique in this poem?

2. How is the word *lie* used as a *double entendre* (double meaning) in this poem?

3. What is the effect of Shakespeare writing "When my love swears that *she is made of truth*" rather than ". . . that *she is telling the truth*"? How are the two wordings different? How does the actual wording contribute to the meaning of the poem?

Ideas for Writing

1. Tell about the last lie—or the most important lie—you told. Analyze the reasons for your lying and the effects of it.

2. Write a short causal analysis explaining the main basis of a love (or a close friendship) you have recently been involved in. Because of this basis, did the relationship work better or worse?

3. Shakespeare's sonnet deals with *lying* and *lovers.* In a short paper identify the truths in the poem that seem to you most lasting and universal.

Jack London
TO BUILD A FIRE

Jack London (1876–1916), born to a poor family in San Francisco, built his reputation as an adventurer, a journalist, and, most importantly, as a fiction writer. Many of his brutally realistic stories derive from his gold-seeking exploits in the Yukon Territory and reflect his socialist ideals. Among his novels are *The Call of The Wild* (1903), *The Sea-Wolf* (1904), *The Iron-Heel* (1907), and *Martin Eden* (1909). At the age of 40, London committed suicide through an overdose of narcotics.

By weaving a series of cause-and-effect relations, Jack London patterns an overall, very basic, and very frightening causal development. "To Build a Fire" is an analysis of imagination and survival, instinct and practicality.

*D*ay had broken cold and gray, exceedingly cold and gray, when the man turned aside from the main Yukon trail and climbed the high earth-bank, where a dim and little-travelled trail led eastward through the fat spruce timberland. It was a steep bank, and he paused for breath at the top, excusing the act to himself by looking at his watch. It was nine o'clock. There was no sun nor hint of sun, though there was not a cloud in the sky. It was a clear day, and yet there seemed an intangible pall over the face of things, a subtle gloom that made the day dark, and that was due to the absence of sun. This fact did not worry the man. He was used to the lack of sun. It had been days since he had seen the sun, and he knew that a few more days must pass before that cheerful orb, due south, should just peep above the sky line and dip immediately from view.

The man flung a look back along the way he had come. The Yukon lay a mile wide and hidden under three feet of ice. On top of this ice were as many feet of snow. It was all pure white, rolling in gentle undulations where the ice jams of the freeze-up had formed. North and south, as far as his eye could see, it was unbroken white, save for a dark hairline that curved and twisted from around the spruce-covered island to the south, and that curved and twisted away into the north, where it disappeared behind another spruce-covered island. This dark hairline was the trail—the main trail—that led south five hundred miles to the Chilcoot Pass, Dyea, and salt water; and that led north seventy miles to Dawson, and still on to the north a thousand miles to Nulato, and finally to St. Michael, on Bering Sea, a thousand miles and half a thousand more.

But all this—the mysterious, far-reaching hairline trail, the absence of sun from the sky, the tremendous cold, and the strangeness and weirdness of it all—made no impression on the man. It was not because he was long used to it. He was a newcomer in the land, a *chechaquo,* and this was his first winter. The trouble with him was that he was without imagination. He was quick and alert in the things of life, but only in the things, and not in the significances. Fifty degrees below zero meant eighty-odd degrees of frost. Such fact impressed him as being cold and uncomfortable, and that was all. It did not lead him to meditate upon his frailty as a creature of temperature, and upon man's frailty in general, able only to live within certain narrow limits of heat and cold; and from there on it did not lead him to the conjectural field of immortality and man's place in the universe. Fifty degrees below zero stood for a bite of frost that hurt and that must be guarded against by the use of mittens, ear flaps, warm moccasins, and thick socks. Fifty degrees below zero was to him just precisely fifty degrees below zero. That there should be anything more to it than that was a thought that never entered his head.

As he turned to go on, he spat speculatively. There was a sharp, explosive crackle that startled him. He spat again. And again, in the air, before it could fall to the snow, the spittle crackled. He knew that at fifty below spittle crackled on the snow, but this spittle had crackled in the air. Undoubtedly it was colder than fifty below—how much colder he did not know. But the temperature did not matter. He was bound for the old claim on the left fork of Henderson Creek, where the boys were already. They had come over across the divide from the Indian Creek country, while he had come the roundabout way to take a look at the possibilities of getting out logs in the spring from the islands in the Yukon. He would be in to camp by six o'clock; a bit after dark, it was true, but the boys would be there, a fire would be going, and a hot supper would be ready. As for lunch, he pressed his hand against the protruding bundle under his jacket. It was also under his shirt, wrapped up in a handkerchief and lying against the naked skin. It was the only way to keep the biscuits from freezing. He smiled agreeably to himself as he thought of those biscuits, each cut open and sopped in bacon grease, and each enclosing a generous slice of fried bacon.

He plunged in among the big spruce trees. The trail was faint. A foot of snow had fallen since the last sled had passed over, and he was glad he was without a sled, traveling light. In fact, he carried nothing but the lunch wrapped in the handkerchief. He was surprised, however, at the cold. It certainly was cold, he concluded, as he rubbed his numb nose and cheekbones with his mittened hand. He was a warm-whiskered man, but the hair on his face did not protect the high cheekbones and the eager nose that thrust itself aggressively into the frosty air.

At the man's heels trotted a dog, a big native husky, the proper wolf dog, gray-coated and without any visible or temperamental difference from its brother, the wild wolf. The animal was depressed by the tremendous cold. It knew that it was no time for traveling. Its instinct told it a truer tale than was told to the man by the man's judgment. In reality, it was not merely colder than fifty below zero; it was colder than sixty below, than seventy below. It was seventy-five below zero. Since the freezing point is thirty-two above zero, it meant that one hundred and seven degrees of frost obtained. The dog did not know anything about thermometers. Possibly in its brain there was no sharp consciousness of a condition of very cold such as was in the man's brain. But the brute had its instinct. It experienced a vague but menacing apprehension that subdued it and made it slink along at the man's heels, and that made it question eagerly every unwonted movement of the man as if expecting him to go into camp or to seek shelter somewhere and build a fire. The dog had learned fire, and it wanted fire, or else to burrow under the snow and cuddle its warmth away from the air.

The frozen moisture of its breathing had settled on its fur in a fine powder of frost, and especially were its jowls, muzzle, and eyelashes whitened by its crystalled breath. The man's red beard and mustache were likewise frosted, but more solidly, the deposit taking the form of ice and increasing with every warm, moist breath he exhaled. Also, the man was chewing tobacco, and the muzzle of ice held his lips so rigidly that he was unable to clear his chin when he expelled the juice. The result was that a crystal beard of the color and solidity of amber was increasing its length on his chin. If he fell down it would shatter itself, like glass, into brittle fragments. But he did not mind the appendage. It was the penalty all tobacco chewers paid in that country, and he had been out before in two cold snaps. They had not been so cold as this, he knew, but by the spirit thermometer at Sixty Mile he knew they had been registered at fifty below and at fifty-five.

He held on through the level stretch of woods for several miles, crossed a wide flat of nigger heads, and dropped down a bank to the frozen bed of a small stream. This was Henderson Creek, and he knew he was ten miles from the forks. He looked at his watch. It was ten o'clock. He was making four miles an hour, and he calculated that he would arrive at the forks at half-past twelve. He decided to celbrate that event by eating his lunch there.

The dog dropped in again at his heels, with a tail drooping discouragement, as the man swung along the creek bed. The furrow of the old sled trail was plainly visible, but a dozen inches of snow cvered the marks of the last runners. In a month no man had come up or down that silent creek. The man held steadily on. He was not much given to thinking, and just then particularly he had nothing to think about save that he would eat lunch at the forks and that at six o'clock he would be in camp with the boys. There was nobody to talk to; and, had there been, speech would have been impossible because of the ice muzzle on his mouth. So he continued monotonously to chew tobacco and to increase the length of his amber beard.

Once in a while the thought reiterated itself that it was very cold and that he had never experienced such cold. As he walked along he rubbed his cheekbones and nose with the back of his mittened hand. He did this automatically, now and again changing hands. But, rub as he would, the instant he stopped his cheekbones went numb, and the following instant the end of his nose went numb. He was sure to frost his cheeks; he knew that, and experienced a pang of regret that he had not devised a nose strap of the sort Bud wore in cold snaps. Such a strap passed across the cheeks, as well, and saved them. But it didn't matter much, after all. What were frosted cheeks? A bit painful, that was all; they were never serious.

Empty as the man's mind was of thoughts, he was keenly observant, and he noticed the changes in the creek, the curves and bends and timber jams, and always he sharply noted where he placed his feet. Once, coming around a bend, he shied abruptly, like a startled horse, curved away from the place where he had been walking, and retreated several paces back along the trail. The creek he knew was frozen clear to the bottom—no creek could contain water in that arctic winter—but he knew aso that there were springs that bubbled out from the hillsides and ran along under the snow and on top the ice of the creek. He knew that the coldest snaps never froze these springs, and he knew likewise their danger. They were traps. They hid pools of water under the snow that might be three inches deep, or three feet. Sometimes a skin of ice half an inch thick covered them, and in turn was covered by the snow. Sometimes there were alternate layers of water and ice skin, so that when one broke through he kept on breaking through for a while, sometimes wetting himself to the waist.

That was why he had shied in such panic. He had felt the give under his feet and heard the crackle of a snow-hidden ice skin. And to get his feet wet in such a temperature meant trouble and danger. At the very least it meant delay, for he would be forced to stop and build a fire, and under its protection to bare his feet while he dried his socks and mocassins. He stood and studied the creek bed and its banks, and decided that the flow of water came from the right. He reflected awhile, rubbing his nose and cheeks, then skirted to the left, stepping gingerly and testing the footing for each step. Once clear of the danger, he took a fresh chew of tobacco and swung along at his four-mile gait.

In the course of the next two hours he came upon several similar traps. Usually the snow above the hidden pools had a sunken, candied appearance that advertised the danger. Once again, however, he had a close call; and once, suspecting danger, he compelled the dog to go on in front. The dog did not want to go. It hung back until the man shoved it forward, and then it went quickly across the white, unbroken surface. Suddenly it broke through, floundered to one side, and got away to firmer footing. It had wet its forefeet and legs, and almost immediately the water that clung to it turned to ice. It made quick efforts to lick the ice off its legs, then dropped down in the snow and began to bite out the ice that had formed between the toes. This was a matter of instinct. To permit the ice to remain wouldmean sore feet. It did not know this. It merely obeyed the mysterious prompting that arose from the deep crypts of its being. But the man knew, having achieved a judgment on the subject, and he removed the mitten from his right hand and helped tear out the ice particles. He did not expose his fingers more than a minute, and was astonished at the swift numbness that smote them. It certainly was cold. He pulled on the mitten hastily, and beat the hand savagely across his chest.

At twelve o'clock the day was at its brightest. Yet the sun was too far south on its winter journey to clear the horizon. The bulge of the earth intervened between it and Henderson Creek, where the man walked under a clear sky at noon and cast no shadow. At half-past twelve, to the minute, he arrived at the forks of the creek. He was pleased at the speed he had made. If he kept it up, he would certainly be with the boys by six. He unbuttoned his jacket and shirt and drew forth his lunch. The action consumed no more than a quarter of a minute, yet in that brief moment the numbness laid hold of the exposed fingers. He did not put the mitten on, but, instead, struck the fingers a dozen sharp smashes against his leg. Then he sat down on a snow-covered log to eat. The sting that followed upon the striking of his fingers against his leg ceased so quickly that he was startled. He had had no chance to take a bite of biscuit. He struck the fingers repeatedly and returned them to the mitten, baring the other hand for the purpose of eating. He tried to take a mouthful, but the ice muzzle prevented. He had forgotten to build a fire and thaw out. He chuckled at his foolishness, and as he chuckled he noted the numbness creeping into the exposed fingers. Also, he noted that the stinging which had first come to his toes when he sat down was already passing away. He wondered whether the toes were warm or numb. He moved them inside the moccasins and decided that they were numb.

He pulled the mitten on hurriedly and stood up. He was a bit frightened. He stamped up and down until the stinging returned into the feet. It certainly was cold, was his thought. That man from Sulphur Creek had spoken the truth when telling how cold it sometimes got in the country. And he had laughed at him at the time! That showed one must not be too sure of things. There was no mistake about it, it *was* cold. He strode up and down, stamping his feet and threshing his arms, until reassured by the returning warmth. Then he got out matches and proceeded to make a fire. From the undergrowth, where high water of the previous spring had lodged a supply of seasoned twigs, he got his firewood. Working carefully from a small beginning, he soon had a roaring fire, over which he thawed the ice from his face and in the protection of which he ate his biscuits. For the moment the cold of space was outwitted. The dog took satisfacion in the fire, stretching out close enough for warmth and far enough away to escape being singed.

When the man had finished, he filled his pipe and took his comfortable time over a smoke. Then he pulled on his mittens, settled the ear flaps of his cap firmly about his ears, and took the creek trail up the left fork. The dog was disappointed and yearned back toward the fire. This man did no know cold. Possibly all the generations of his ancestry had been ignorant of cold, of real cold, of cold one hundred and seven degrees below freezing point. But the dog knew; all its ancestry knew, and it had inherited the knowledge. And it knew that it was not good to walk abroad in such fearful cold. It was the time to lie snug in a hole in the snow and wait for a curtain of cloud to be drawn across the face of outer space whence this cold came. On the other hand, there was no keen intimacy between the dog and the man. The one was the toil slave of the other, and the only caresses it had ever received were the caresses of the whip lash and of harsh and menacing throat sounds that threatened the whip lash. So the dog made no effort to communicate its apprehension to the man. It was not concerned in the welfare of the man; it was for its own sake that it yearned back toward the fire. But the man whistled, and spoke to it with the sound of whip lashes, and the dog swung in at the man's heels and followed after.

The man took a chew of tobacco and proceeded to start a new mber beard. Also, his moist breath quickly powdered with white his mustache, eyebrows, and lashes. There did not seem to be so many springs on the left fork of the Henderson, and for half an hour the man saw no signs of any. And then it happened. At a place where there were no signs, where the soft, unbroken snow seemed to advertise solidity beneath, the man broke through. It was not deep. He wet himself halfway to the knees before he floundered out to the firm crust.

He was angry, and cursed his luck aloud. He had hoped to get into camp with the boys at six o'clock, and this would delay him an hour, for he would have to build a fire and dry out his footgear. This was imperative at that low temperature—he knew that much; and he turned aside to the bank, which he climbed. On top, tangled in the underbrush about the trunks of several small spruce trees, was a highwater deposit of dry firewood—sticks and twigs, principally, but also larger portions of sea-soned branches and fine dry last year's grasses. He threw down several

large pieces on top of the snow. This served for a foundation and prevented the young flame from drowning itself in the snow it otherwise
would melt. The flame he got by touching a match to a small shred of
birch bark that he took from his pocket. This burned even more readily
than paper. Placing it on the foundation, he fed the young flame with
wisps of dry grass and with the tiniest dry twigs.

He worked slowly and carefully, keenly aware of his danger. Gradually, as the flame grew stronger, he increased the size of the twigs with
which he fed it. He squatted in the snow, pulling the twigs out from their
entanglement in the brush and feeding directly to the flame. He knew
there must be no failure. When it is seventy-five below zero, a man must
not fail in his first attempt to build a fire—that is, if his feet are wet. If his
feet are dry, and he fails, he can run along the trail for half a mile and
restore his circulation. But the circulation of wet and freezing feet cannot
be restored by running when it is seventy-five below. No matter how fast
he runs, the wet feet will freeze the harder.

All this the man knew. The old-timer on Sulphur Creek had told him
about it the previous fall, and now he was appreciating the advice.
Already all sensation had gone out of his feet. To build the fire he had
been forced to remove his mittens, and the fingers had quickly gone
numb. His pace of four miles an hour had kept his heart pumping blood to
the surface of his body and to all the extremities. But the instant he
stopped, the action of the pump eased down. The cold of space smote the
unprotected tip of the planet, and he, being on that unprotected tip,
received the full force of the blow. The blood of his body recoiled before
it. The blood was alive, like the dog, and like the dog it wanted to hide
away and cover itself up from the fearful cold. So long as he walked four
miles an hour, he pumped that blood, willy-nilly, to the surface; but now it
ebbed away and sank down into the recesses of his body. The extremities
were the first to feel its absence. His wet feet froze the faster, and his
exposed fingers numbed the faster, though they had not yet begun to
freeze. Nose and cheeks were already freezing, while the skin of all his
body chilled as it lost its blood.

But he was safe. Toes and nose and cheeks would be only touched by
the frost, for the fire was beginning to burn with strength. He was feeding
it with twigs the size of his finger. In another minute he would be able to
feed it with branches the size of his wrist, and then he could remove his
wet footgear, and, while it dried, he could keep his naked feet warm by
the fire, rubbing them at first, of course, with snow. The fire was a
success. He was safe. He remembered the advice of the old-timer on
Sulphur Creek, and smiled. The old-timer had been very serious in laying
down the law that no man must travel alone in the Klondike after fifty
below. Well, here he was; he had had the accident; he was alone; and he
had saved himself. Those old-timers were rather womanish, some of
them, he thought. All a man had to do was to keep his head, and he was all

right. Any man who was a man could travel alone. But it was surprising, the rapidity with which his cheeks and nose were freezing. And he had not thought his fingers could go lifeless in so short a time. Lifeless they were, for he could scarcely make them move together to grip a twig, and they seemed remote from his body and from him. When he touched a twig, he had to look and see whether or not he had hold of it. The wires were pretty well down between him and his finger ends.

All of which counted for little. There was the fire, snapping and crackling and promising life with every dancing flame. He started to untie his moccasins. They were coated with ice; the thick German socks were like sheaths of iron halfway to the knees; and the moccasin strings were like rods of steel all twisted and knotted as by some conflagration. For a moment he tugged with his numb fingers, then, realizing the folly of it, he drew his sheath knife.

But before he could cut the strings, it happened. It was his own fault or, rather, his mistake. He should not have built the fire under the spruce tree. He should have built it in the open. But it had been easier to pull the twigs from the brush and drop them directly on the fire. Now the tree under which he had done this carried a weight of snow on its boughs. No wind had blown for weeks, and each bough was fully freighted. Each time he had pulled a twig he had communicated a slight agitation to the tree— an imperceptible agitation, so far as he was concerned, but an agitation sufficient to bring about the disaster. High up in the tree one bough capsized its load of snow. This fell on the boughs beneath, capsizing them. This process continued, spreading out and involving the whole tree. It grew like an avalanche, and it descended without warning upon the man and the fire, and the fire was blotted out! Where it had burned was a mantle of fresh and disordered snow.

The man was shocked. It was as though he had just heard his own sentence of death. For a moment he sat and stared at the spot where the fire had been. Then he grew very calm. Perhaps the old-timer on Sulphur Creek was right. If he had only had a trail mate he would have been in no danger now. The trail mate could have built the fire. Well, it was up to him to build the fire over again, and this second time there must be no failure. Even if he succeeded, he would most likely lose some toes. His feet must be badly frozen by now, and there would be some time before the second fire was ready.

Such were his thoughts, but he did not sit and think them. He was busy all the time they were passing through his mind. He made a new foundation for a fire, this time in the open, where no treacherous tree could blot it out. Next he gathered dry grasses and tiny twigs from the high-water flotsam. He could not bring his fingers together to pull them out, but he was able to gather them by the handful. In this way he got many rotten twigs and bits of green moss that were undesirable, but it was the best he could do. He worked methodically, even collecting an armful of the larger branches to be used later when the fire gathered strength. And all the while the dog sat and watched him, a certain yearning wistfulness in its eyes, for it looked upon him as the fire provider, and the fire was slow in coming.

When all was ready, the man reached in his pocket for a second piece of birch bark. He knew the bark was there, and, though he could not feel it with his fingers, he could hear its crisp rustling as he fumbled for it. Try as he would, he could not clutch hold of it. And all the time, in his consciousness, was the knowledge that each instant his feet were freezing. This thought tended to put him in a panic, but he fought against it and kept calm. He pulled on his mittens with his teeth, and threshed his arms back and forth, beating his hands with all his might against his sides. He did this sitting down, and he stood up to do it; and all the while the dog sat in the snow, its wolf brush of a tail curled around warmly over its forefeet, its sharp wolf ears pricked forward intently as it watched the man. And the man, as he beat and threshed with his arms and hands, felt a great surge of envy as he regarded the creature that was warm and secure in its natural covering.

After a time he was aware of the first faraway signals of sensation in his beaten fingers. The faint tingling grew stronger till it evolved into a stinging ache that was excruciating, but which the man hailed with satisfaction. He stripped the mitten from his right hand and fetched forth the birch bark. The exposed fingers were quickly going numb again. Next he brought out his bunch of sulphur matches. But the tremendous cold had already driven the life out of his fingers. In his effort to separate one match from the others, the whole bunch fell in the snow. He tried to pick it out of the snow, but failed. The dead fingers could neither touch nor clutch. He was very careful. He drove the thought of his freezing feet, and nose, and cheeks, out of his mind, devoting his whole soul to the matches. He watched, using the sense of vision in place of that of touch, and when he saw his fingers on each side of the bunch, he closed them—that is he willed to close them, for the wires were down, and the fingers did not obey. He pulled the mitten on the right hand, and beat it fiercely against his knee. Then, with both mittened hands, he scooped the bunch of matches, along with much snow, into his lap. Yet he was no better off.

After some manipulation he managed to get the bunch between the heels of his mittened hands. In this fashion he carried it to his mouth. The ice crackled and snapped when by a violent effort he opened his mouth. He drew the lower jaw in, curled the upper lip out of the way, scraped the bunch with his upper teeth in order to separate a match. He succeeded in getting one, which he dropped on his lap. He was no better off. He could not pick it up. Then he devised a way. He picked it up in his teeth and scratched it on his leg. Twenty times he scratched before he succeeded in lighting it. As it flamed he held it with his teeth to the birch bark. But the burning brimstone went up is nostrils and into his lungs, causing him to cough spasmodically. The match fell into the snow and went out.

The old-timer on Sulphur Creek was right, he thought in the moment of controlled despair that ensued: after fifty below, a man should travel with a partner. He beat his hands, but failed in exciting any sensation. Suddenly he bared both hands, removing the mittens with his teeth. He caught the whole bunch between the heels of his hands. His arm muscles not being frozen enabled him to press the hand heels tightly against the matches. Then he scratched the bunch along his leg. It flared into flame, seventy sulphur matches at once! There was no wind to blow them out. He kept his head to one side to escape the strangling fumes, and held the blazing bunch to the birch bark. As he so held it, he became aware of sensation in his hand. His flesh was burning. He could smell it. Deep down below the surface he could feel it. The sensation developed into pain that grew acute. And still he endured it, holding the flame of the matches clumsily to the bark that would not light readily because his own burning hands were in the way, absorbing most of the flame.

At last, when he could endure no more, he jerked his hands apart. The blazing matches fell sizzling into the snow, but the birch bark was alight. He began laying dry grasses and the tiniest twigs on the flame. He could not pick and choose, for he had to lift the fuel between the heels of his hands. Small pieces of rotten wood and green moss clung to the twigs, and he bit them off as well as he could with his teeth. He cherished the flame carefully and awkwardly. It meant life, and it must not perish. The withdrawal of blood from the surface of his body now made him begin to shiver, and he grew more awkward. A large piece of green moss fell squarely on the little fire. He tried to poke it out with his fingers, but his shivering frame made him poke too far, and he disrupted the nucleus of the little fire, the burning grasses and tiny twigs separating and scattering. He tried to poke them together again, but in spite of the tenseness of the effort, his shivering got away with him, and the twigs were hopelessly scattered. Each twig gushed a puff of smoke and went out. The fire provider had failed. As he looked apathetically about him, his eyes chanced on the dog, siting across the ruins of the fire from him, in the snow, making restless, hunching movements, slightly lifting one forefoot and then the other, shifting its weight back and forth on them with wistful eagerness.

The sight of the dog put a wild idea into his head. He remembered the tale of the man, caught in a blizzard, who killed a steer and crawled inside the carcass, and so was saved. He would kill the dog and bury his hands in the warm body until the numbness went out of them. Then he could build another fire. He spoke to the dog, calling it to him; but in his voice was a strange note of fear that frightened the animal, who had never known the man to speak in such way before. Something was the matter, and its suspicious nature sensed danger—it knew not what danger, but somewhere, somehow, in its brain arose an apprehension of the man. It flattened its ears down at the sound of the man's voice, and its restless, hunching movements and the liftings and shiftings of its forefeet became more pronounced; but it would not come to the man. He got on his hands and knees and crawled toward the dog. This unusual posture again excited suspicion, and the animal sidled mincingly away.

The man sat up in the snow for a moment and struggled for calmness. Then he pulled on his mittens, by means of his teeth, and got upon his feet. He glanced down at first in order to assure himself that he was really standing up, for the absence of sensation in his feet left him unrelated to the earth. His erect position in itself started to drive the webs of suspicion from the dog's mind; and when he spoke peremptorily, with the sound of whip lashes in his voice, the dog rendered its customary allegiance and came to him. As it came within reaching distance the man lost his control. His arms flashed out to the dog, and he experienced genuine surprise when he discovered that his hands could not clutch, that there was neither bend nor feeling in the fingers. He had forgotten for the moment that they were frozen and that they were freezing more and more. All this happened quickly, and before the animal could get away, he encircled its body with his arms. He sat down in the snow, and in this fashion held the dog, while it snarled and whined and struggled.

But it was all he could do, hold its body encircled in his arms and sit there. He realized that he could not kill the dog. There was no way to do it. With his helpless hands he could neither draw nor hold his sheath knife nor throttle the animal. He released it, and it plunged wildly away, with tail between its legs, and still snarling. It halted forty feet away and surveyed him curiously, with ears sharply pricked forward.

The man looked down at his hands in order to locate them, and found them hanging on the ends of his arms. It struck him as curious that one should have to use his eyes in order to find out where his hands were. He began threshing his arms back and forth, beating the mittened hands against his sides. He did this for five minutes, violently, and his heart pumped enough blood up to the surface to put a stop to his shivering. But no sensation was aroused in the hands. He had an impression that they hung like weights on the ends of his arms, but when he tried to run the impression down, he could not find it.

A certain fear of death, dull and oppressive, came to him. This fear quickly became poignant as he realized that it was no longer a mere matter of freezing his fingers and toes, or of losing his hands and feet, but that it was a matter of life and death with the chances against him. This threw him into a panic, and he turned and ran up the creek bed along the old, dim trail. The dog joined in behind and kept up with him. He ran blindly, without intention, in fear such as he had never known in his life. Slowly, as he plowed and floundered through the snow, he began to see things again—the banks of the creek, the old timber jams, the leafless aspens, and the sky. The running made him feel better. He did not shiver. Maybe, if he ran on, his feet would thaw out; and, anyway, if he ran far enough, he would reach camp and the boys. Without doubt he would lose some fingers and toes and some of his face; but the boys would take care of him, and save the rest of him when he got there. And at the same time there was another thought in his mind that said he would never get to the camp and the boys; that it was too many miles away, that the freezing had too great a start on him, and that he would soon be stiff and dead. This thought he kept in the background and refused to consider. Sometimes it pushed itself forward and demanded to be heard, but he thrust it back and strove to think of other things.

It struck him as curious that he could run at all on feet so frozen that he could not feel them when they struck the earth and took the weight of his body. He seemed to himself to skim along above the surface, and to have no connection with the earth. Somewhere he had once seen a winged Mercury, and he wondered if Mercury felt as he felt when skimming over the earth.

His theory of running until he reached camp and the boys had one flaw in it: he lacked the endurance. Several times he stumbled, and finally he tottered, crumpled up, and fell. When he tried to rise, he failed. He must sit and rest, he decided, and next time he would merely walk and keep on going. As he sat and regained his breath, he noted that he was feeling quite warm and comfortable. He was not shivering, and it even seemed that a warm glow had come to his chest and trunk. And yet, when he touched his nose or cheeks, there was no sensation. Running would not thaw them out. Nor would it thaw out his hands and feet. Then the thought came to him that the frozen portions of his body must be extending. He tried to keep this thought down, to forget it, to think of something else; he was aware of the panicky feeling that it caused, and he was afraid of the panic. But the thought asserted itself, and persisted, until it produced a vision of his body totally frozen. This was too much, and he made another wild run along the trail. Once he slowed down to a walk, but the thought of the freezing extending itself made him run again.

And all the time the dog ran with him, at his heels. When he fell down a second time, it curled its tail over its forefeet and sat in front of him, facing him, curiously eager and intent. The warmth and security of the animal angered him, and he cursed it till it flattened down its ears appeasingly. This time the shivering came more quickly upon the man. He was losing in his battle with the frost. It was creeping into his body from all sides. The thought of it drove him on, but he ran no more than a hundred feet, when he staggered and pitched headlong. It was his last panic. When he had recovered his breath and control, he sat up and entertained in his mind the conception of meeting death with dignity. However, the conception did not come to him in such terms. His idea of it was that he had been making a fool of himself, running around like a chicken with its head cut off—such was the simile that occurred to him. Well, he was bound to freeze anyway, and he might as well take it decently. With this new-found peace of mind came the first glimmerings of drowsiness. A good idea, he thought, to sleep off to death. It was like taking an anesthetic. Freezing was not so bad as people thought. There were lots worse ways to die.

He pictured the boys finding his body next day. Suddenly he found himself with them, coming along the trail and looking for himself. And, still with them, he came around a turn in the trail and found himself lying in the snow. He did not belong with himself any more, for even then he was out of himself, standing with the boys and looking at himself in the snow. It certainly was cold, was his thought. When he got back to the States he could tell the folks what real cold was. He drifted on from this to a vision of the old-timer on Sulphur Creek. He could see him quite clearly, warm and comfortable, and smoking a pipe.

"You were right, old hoss; you were right," the man mumbled to the old-timer of Sulphur Creek.

Then the man drowsed off into what seemed to him the most comfortable and satisfying sleep he had ever known. The dog sat facing him and waiting. The brief day drew to a close in a long, slow twilight. There were no signs of a fire to be made, and, besides, never in the dog's experience had it known a man to sit like that in the snow and make no fire. As the twilight drew on, its eager yearning for the fire mastered it, and with a great lifting and shifting of forefeet, it whined softly, then flattened its ears down in anticipation of being chidden by the man. But the man remained silent. Later the dog whined loudly. And still later it crept close to the man and caught the scent of death. This made the animal bristle and back away. A little longer it delayed, howling under the stars that leaped and danced and shone brightly in the cold sky. Then it turned and trotted up the trail in the direction of the camp it knew, where were the other food providers and fire providers.

Meaning and Idea

1. Where does this story take place? Briefly describe the physical environment. Where is the protagonist headed? What does he imagine awaits him at the end of his journey? What is the reality of that ending?

2. At a number of points in this story, the man welcomes pain. Identify three such instances. Why does he welcome the pain? What condition is he fighting off?

3. What is "the advice of the old-timer on Sulphur Creek"? What was the man's attitude toward this advice? Did it prove to be correct or incorrect advice?

4. What is the man's attitude toward the dog that's with him? How does it change within the story? What is the man's "last resort" use for the dog? Why is it impossible for him to follow through on this?

Language, Form, Structure

1. What is the overall cause-and-effect relationship in this story? This story is made up of many smaller causal relationships that contribute to the overall larger one. Identify ten of these smaller relationships.

2. Discuss the significance of the sentence, "The trouble with him was that he was without imagination." (See page 440.) How does the character flaw implied here become a cause for the man's death?

3. Throughout this story, London writes of both the man's and the dog's knowledge about the cold. Identify a few of those passages. How does London's comparison of the two different experiences (of the man and dog) advance the main point of the story? What is this main point?

4. Explain the final line of the story. Is the final line of this story really an expression of the dog's consciousness? How and what does it reveal about London's attitude about survival? What is the relation of that line to the earlier comment about the man's lack of imagination?

5. Write definitions for the following words: frailty; conjectural; appendage; reiterated; pang; conflagration; excrutiating; acute; nucleus; peremptorily; allegiance; drowsed.

Ideas for Writing

1. Write a causal analysis of an unfortunate result of someone's stubbornness. Attempt to build the overall causal relationship through a series of smaller ones.

2. Analyze the reasons behind a recent decision by the government with which you disagree. Make the effects the basis for your disagreement.

3. Throughout "To Build a Fire" the main character remains nameless; he is only "the man." Perhaps less importantly, the dog also remains simply "the dog." Write a short commentary about the causes and effects of namelessness in this story.

Lewis Thomas
ON WARTS

Dr. Lewis Thomas, born in 1913 in New York City, is president of the Memorial Sloan-Kettering Cancer Center in New York. He was educated at Princeton and Harvard, where he received his medical degree in 1937. He is well-respected for his seemingly tireless work in medical research, administration, and education. In 1970, he began writing a monthly, lay-oriented column for the *New England Journal of Medicine.* These articles have been collected in *The Lives of a Cell: Notes of a Biology Watcher* (published 1974; recipient of the 1975 National Book Award for Arts and Letters) and *The Medusa and the Snail: More Notes of a Biology Watcher* (1979).

In "On Warts," from the collection *The Medusa and the Snail,* Thomas explains what warts are, how they form, and how they may be removed. Perhaps most interesting is his explanation of how and why his attitudes have changed, as well as how he looks toward future results of increased knowledge about such misunderstood "wonderful structures."

*W*arts are wonderful structures. They can appear overnight on any part of the skin, like mushrooms on a damp lawn, full grown and splendid in the complexity of their architecture. Viewed in stained sections under a microscope, they are the most specialized of cellular arrangements, constructed as though for a purpose. They sit there like turreted mounds of dense, impenetrable horn, impregnable, designed for defense against the world outside.

In a certain sense, warts are both useful and essential, but not for us. As it turns out, the exuberant cells of a wart are the elaborate reproductive apparatus of a virus.

You might have thought from the looks of it that the cells infected by the wart virus were using this response as a ponderous way of defending themselves against the virus, maybe even a way of becoming more distasteful, but it is not so. The wart is what the virus truly wants; it can flourish only in cells undergoing precisely this kind of overgrowth. It is not a defense at all; it is an overwhelming welcome, an enthusiastic accommodation meeting the needs of more and more virus.

The strangest thing about warts is that they tend to go away. Fully grown, nothing in the body has so much the look of toughness and permanence as a wart, and yet, inexplicably and often very abruptly, they come to the end of their lives and vanish without a trace.

And they can be made to go away by something that can only be called thinking, or something like thinking. This is a special property of warts which is absolutely astonishing, more of a surprise than cloning or recombinant DNA or endorphy or acupuncture or anything else currently attracting attention in the press. It is one of the great mystifications of science: warts can be ordered off the skin by hypnotic suggestion.

Not everyone believes this, but the evidence goes back a long way and is persuasive. Generations of internists and dermatologists, and their grandmothers for that matter, have been convinced of the phenomenon. I was once told by a distinguished old professor of medicine, one of Sir William Osler's original bright young men, that it was his practice to paint gentian violet over a wart and then assure the patient firmly that it would be gone in a week, and he never saw it again. There have been several meticulous studies by good clinical investigators, with proper controls. In one of these, fourteen patients with seemingly intractable generalized warts on left sides of the body were hypnotized, and the suggestion was made that all the warts on one side of the body would begin to go away. Within several weeks the results were indisputably positive; in nine patients, all or nearly all of the warts on the suggested side had vanished, while the control side had just as many as ever.

It is interesting that most of the warts vanished precisely as they were instructed, but it is even more fascinating that mistakes were made. Just as you might expect in other affairs requiring a clear understanding of which is the right and which the left side, one of the subjects got mixed up and destroyed the warts on the wrong side. In a later study by a group at the Massachusetts General Hospital, the warts on both sides were rejected even though the instructions were to pay attention to just one side.

I have been trying to figure out the nature of the instructions issued by the unconscious mind, whatever that is, under hypnosis. It seems to me hardly enough for the mind to say, simply, get off, eliminate yourselves, without providing something in the way of specifications as to how to go about it.

I used to believe, thinking about this experiment when it was just published, that the instructions might be quite simple. Perhaps nothing more detailed than a command to shut down the flow through all the precapillary arterioles in and around the warts to the point of strangulation. Exactly how the mind would accomplish this with precision, cutting off the blood supply to one wart while leaving others intact, I couldn't figure out, but I was satisfied to leave it there anyhow. And I was glad to think that my unconscious mind would have to take the responsibility for this, for if I had been one of the subjects I would never have been able to do it myself.

But now the problem seems much more complicated by the information concerning the viral etiology of warts, and even more so by the currently plausible notion that immunologic mechanisms are very likely implicated in the rejection of warts.

If my unconscious can figure out how to manipulate the mechanisms needed for getting around that virus, and for deploying all the various cells in the correct order for tissue rejection, then all I have to say is that my unconscious is a lot further along than I am. I wish I had a wart right now, just to see if I am that talented.

There ought to be a better word than "Unconscious," even capitalized, for what I have, so t speak, in mind. I was brought up to regard this aspect of thinking as a sort of private sanitarium, walled off somewhere in a suburb of my brain, capable only of producing such garbled information as to keep my mind, my proper Mind, always a little off balance.

But any mental apparatus that can reject a wart is something else again. This is not the sort of confused, disordered process you'd expect at the hands of the kind of Unconscious you read about in books, out at the edge of things making up dreams or getting mixed up on words or having hysterics. Whatever, or whoever, is responsible for this has the accuracy and precision of a surgeon. There almost has to be a Person in charge, running matters of meticulous detail beyond anyone's comprehension, a skilled engineer and manager, a chief executive officer, the head of the whole place. I never thought before that I possessed such a tenant. Or perhaps more accurately, such a landlord, since I would be, if this is in fact the situation, nothing more than a lodger.

Among other accomplishments, he must be a cell biologist of world class, capable of sorting through the various classes of one's lymphocytes, all with quite different functions which I do not understand, in order to mobilize the right ones and exclude the wrong ones for the task of tissue rejection. If it were left to me, and I were somehow empowered to call up lymphocytes and direct them to the vicinity of my wart (assuming that I could learn to do such a thing), mine would come tumbling in all unsorted, B cells and T cells, suppressor cells and killer cells, and no doubt other cells whose names I have not learned, incapable of getting anything useful done.

Even if immunology is not involved, and all that needs doing is to shut off the blood supply locally, I haven't the faintest notion how to set that up. I assume that the selective turning off of arterioles can be done by one or another chemical mediator, and I know the names of some of them, but I wouldn't dare let things like these loose even if I knew how to do it.

Well, then, who does supervise this kind of operation? Someone's got to, you know. You can't sit there under hypnosis, taking suggestions in and having them acted on with such accuracy and precision, without assuming the existence of something very like a controller. It wouldn't do to fob off the whole intricate business on lower centers without sending along a quite detailed set of specifications, way over my head.

Some intelligence or other knows how to get rid of warts, and this is a disquieting thought.

It is also a wonderful problem, in need of solving. Just think what we would know, if we had anything like a clear understanding of what goes on when a wart is hypnotized away. We would know the identity of the cellular and chemical participants in tissue rejection, conceivably with some added information about the ways that viruses create foreignness in cells. We would know how the traffic of these reactants is directed, and perhaps then be able to understand the nature of certain diseases in which the traffic is being conducted in wrong directions, aimed at the wrong cells. Best of all, we would be finding out about a kind of superintelligence that exists in each of us, infinitely smarter and possessed of technical know-how far beyond our present understanding. It would be worth a War on Warts, a Conquest of Warts, a National Institute of Warts and All.

Meaning and Idea

1. What is the cause of warts? What, according to Thomas, would most people think is the relationship between warts and virus by looking at a microscopic section of a wart? How is this impression different from the actuality?

2. Explain the causal relationship between wart removal and hypnotic suggestion. Why, in one experiment, was painting warts with gentian violet and then suggesting their imminent removal to patients a proof of the power of suggestion? On what basis does Thomas, a respected, responsible physician, believe the power of hypnotic suggestion as it relates to warts?

3. What was Thomas's original opinion about the "Unconscious"? How did that opinion change? Why? How was that change of opinion a result of his investigations on warts?

4. What does Thomas hypothesize as the results of a fuller knowledge about how warts can be "hypnotized away"?

Language, Form, Structure

1. In this essay does Thomas focus mainly on causes or effects? Explain your answer with specific references to the text.

2. What is Thomas's intended audience for this essay? What examples from the essay support your answer? How does his intended audience affect the level of diction in the writing? (*Diction* refers to word choice—among other things, to the level of language used—informal, specialized, colloquial, and so on.)

3. What is the effect of the opening sentence in this essay? What was your response to it? How did that response affect your reading of the essay? How would you characterize the overall tone of the writing? Support your answer with examples from the essay.

4. Identify descriptive sections in the essay. How does the description enhance the writing?

5. Write definitions for these words and then use each in a sentence: turreted; impregnable; exuberant; apparatus; ponderous; cloning; meticulous; intractable; plausible; disquieting.

Ideas for Writing

1. Write a causal analysis of your recent solution to a physical problem (even if that problem was only losing five pounds to look good in a bathing suit). Analyze both causes and effects.

2. Analyze why you recently changed an opinion about something that you had thought of as true for a long time. Why did you change your opinion? What resulted from this change of attitude?

3. The final paragraph strongly suggests a connection between understanding warts and cancer research. Yet, Thomas uses a rather light-hearted tone—even humor at times—in this essay. How appropriate to his subject is the author's levity? Develop your answer with direct references to the text.

Chapter Eight
DEFINITION

*W*illiam Kennedy's 1983 Pulitzer Prize winning novel *Ironweed* opens with a definition that the author adapted from the Audubon Society's *Field Guide to North American Wildflowers*.

> Tall Ironweed is a member of the Sunflower Family (Asteraceae). It has a tall erect stem and bears deep purple-blue flower heads in loose terminal clusters. Its leaves are long and thin and pointed, their lower surfaces downy. Its fruit is seed-like, with a double set of purplish bristles. It flowers from August to October in damp, rich soilfrom New York south to Georgia, west to Louisiana, north to Missouri, Illinois and Michigan. The name refers to the toughness of the stem.

Ironweed is about Francis Phelan, a vagabond wino down on his luck who returns to Albany where he had murdered a strikebreaker many years back and where he accidentally dropped and killed his infant son. The definition of ironweed helps explain the title of the book and establishes the metaphorical relation between the flower and the man. Like "Tall Ironweed," Francis Phelan shows up in lots of places starting with New York and is a lanky, tough-stemmed, off-season bloomer with a soft underbelly. Without the definition, many readers unfamiliar with this special sunflower would have little idea of what Kennedy had in mind in his title and could not make the connections that enrich our understanding of the novel. A dictionary would not have been much help either; *"ironweed"* says *the American Heritage Dictionary,* is "Any plant of the genus Vernonia, having clusters of purple flowers." Period.

A researcher and scientist, Robert Ardrey, in an influential and controversial book of nonfiction called *The Territorial Imperative* (1966), opens his first chapter, "Of Men and Mockingbirds," with these two paragraphs:

> A territory is an area of space, whether of water or earth or air, which an animal or group of animals defends as an exclusive preserve. The word is also used to describe the inward compulsion in animate beings to possess and defend such a space. A territorial species of animals, therefore, is one in which all males, and sometimes females too, bear an inherent drive to gain and defend an exclusive property.
>
> In most but not all territorial species, defense is directed only against fellow members of the kind. A squirrel does not regard a mouse as a trespasser. In most but not all territorial species—not in chameleons, for example—the female is sexually unresponsive to an unpropertied male. As a general pattern of behavior, in territorial species the competition between males which we formerly believed was one for the possession of females is in truth for possession of property.

Understanding the main thesis of the book, the role of territory as an impulse in the human species, depends on our understanding of the word *territory* as Ardrey wishes us to understand its meaning; hence a clear definition of the word early in the text is essential.

William Shakespeare both pleases and jolts us with these humorous, unconventional musings on the word *honor* from Falstaff, the great comic character in *King Henry IV, Part 1* (bracketed information explains unfamiliar idioms):

> Honor pricks me on. [Honor spurs my actions.] Yea, but if honor prick me off when I come on? [What if honor places me on the list of casualties?] How then? Can honor set a leg? No. Or an arm? No. Or take away the grief of a wound? No. Honor hath no skill in surgery then? No. What is honor? A word. What is in that word honor? What is that word honor? Air. A trim reckoning! Who hath it? He that died o'Wednesday. Doth he feel it? No. Doth he hear it? No. Tis insensible then? Yea, to the dead. But will it not live with the living? No. Why? Detraction will not suffer it. Therefore I'll none of it. Honor is a mere scutcheon. And so ends my catechism.

One of the main themes of *King Henry IV, Part I* is honor, the honor human beings show to each other—children to parent, prince to subject, subject to prince, soldier to officer, friend to friend. In those famous lines from act V, scene ii, Shakespeare provides an illuminating, if eccentric, perspective on honor, one that is nonetheless perfectly consistent with Falstaff's nature as a likeable drunk and a coward. Men have killed for honor on the plains of Shrewsbury, and Falstaff's dismissive definition helps us wonder at the madness of war for so frail and yet so compelling a notion. Yet the actions of the male characters are chained to the notion of honor as the core of their existence.

Novelist, nonfiction writer, poet—and essayist, short story writer, biographer, news reporter, technical writer, textbook writer—anyone concerned with and committed to precision in language sooner or later will turn to definition as a strategy for clear writing.

READING DEFINITION

All definitions have as their unswerving purpose to bring meaning to a word, and readers should expect nothing less than to see a word or concept like a specimen under the best microscope—clear, sharply focused, unambiguous. At its most basic level, the definition aims at precise linguistic equivalence: this is that. Readers frequently encounter *lexical* (or dictionary) definitions, no matter what the larger purpose of the piece of writing; words that the writer thinks may be unfamiliar to the reading audience are accompanied by a statement of their meanings. Thus, you can expect to find definitions of foreign, complex, or technical words, or simply definitions of words whose lexical meanings writers wish to call attention to. Santha Rama Rau in her book *Home to India* neatly embeds some succinct yet necessary dictionary definitions as she explains Indian meal times: "*Chota hasari*—the little breakfast—consists of a cup of tea at five thirty or six in the morning, with possibly some fruit or toast served with it. At about eleven or at midday a heavier meal is eaten, *chapatis*—thin unleavened wheat cakes—and curry, with *dal*—a kind of lentil soup—and curds and sweets of some sort." Unaided by these definitions readers would be pretty much in the dark about the italicized words in the selection. In each case just a brief phrase identifies distinguishing characteristics of the word. Rama Rau uses dashes to set off these meanings. Experienced readers know to look for dashes, paired commas, parentheses, italics, quotation marks, the words "that is" or "means" and other language and punctuation clues as signals for definitios.

Sometimes a writer tries to clarify a complex word by providing a *restrictive* meaning, that is, a meaning considerably narrowed from a range of lexical possibilities. Here the writer peels away definitions that are extraneous to his or her purpose and directs readers only to those features of the word that bear upon the discussion at hand. A noted researcher in the acquisition of second languages, Stephen D. Krashen, offers a restrictive definition for *bilingual education* programs before he describes them in an essay written in 1981: "While we could use bilingual education as a cover term for practically all of the programs described below, it will be useful to limit it here. Bilingual education refers to situations in which students are able to study subject matter in their first language while their weaker language skills catch up." Many people who might challenge that as a general definition could accept it provisionally in the context of the essay.

In other cases, a writer will *redefine* a word entirely. The usual effect of this strategy is to make readers look critically at their fundamental assumptions about a word and see it from a new perspective. Ardrey's treatment of *territory* certainly redefines the word.

As you have seen, a simple phrase alone as a synonym is frequently insufficient in suggesting the possibilities of a word. As a result, writers often build to a carefully structured definition sentence with four parts: (1) the term is stated; (2) it is followed by the word *is* or *was*; (3) it is established in a general class or category; (4) and it is then distinguished from other members of its group. Ardrey follows the pattern quite precisely: (1) "A territory (2) is (3) an area of space, whether of water or earth or air, (4) which an animal or group of animals defends as an exclusive preserve." E. E. Cummings's funny and ironical poem in this section is a perfect example of this type of formal definition, run wildly amuck with its startling metaphor.

In addition to occasional brief definitions of important terms—synonyms in a few words or phrases, more formal definitions in a few sentences—writers often turn to extended definitions. An *extended definition* is a rhetorical mode that defines a term in considerable detail. Extended definitions consider the spectrum of issues inherent in a word or concept. True to its name, an extended definition can take paragraphs or pages. It can address not only denotative meanings but also personal, highly subjective, even idiosyncratic views of words or ideas. Without any formal or predictable pattern, the extended definition advances through the use of other rhetorical strategies, alone or in combination, including description, narration, exemplification, process analysis, comparison and contrast, causal analysis, and classification. In this chapter, the essay by Joseph Epstein, ''A Former Good Guy and His Friends,'' draws upon many of the techniques you've studied up to this point.

WRITING DEFINITIONS

This chapter provides opportunities for practice in the various kinds of definitions explained in the previous section, but for the most part you'll be concentrating here on the extended definition when you write. It's a useful activity to practice; the extended definition has many applications, whether you're developing a laboratory report, a research paper, a short story or poem, a business report, or an article for the school newspaper. In one sense, an extended definition is easy to write, it allows you a great deal of freedom to choose from many different rhetorical patterns. In another sense, the task of defining can be rather complicated, especially if you are writing about an abstract term that is rich in connotative meanings. As usual, your purpose and intended audience will help you shape the scope and direction of your definition.

PURPOSE AND AUDIENCE

Choosing a word to define, like choosing any topic for any writing task, demands considerable thought and attention at the outset. How will you select a word or phrase from the hundreds of thousands available in our language? As you think about the various possibilities, as you choose and reject words in an effort to find the one you want to write about, be sure to consider what you intend to do with the term once you select it. Of course it should be one that interests you (for whatever reason)—*love,* perhaps, *heroism, sitcoms, machismo, literacy,* the term *media explosion* or *brotherhood of man* or *a good daughter,* the expression ''Have a good day'' or ''Cool it!''—but unless you're clear on your reasons for writing, you risk a diffuse and fuzzy presentation.

An eye toward purpose will help you shape your topic as you consider some possibilities for your definition. If you selected an abstract term like *love,* for example, you'd soon be lost without some serious thought about why you're writing on this word. You might want to *indicate its particular characteristics* as a human emotion as opposed to other related emotions, like *affection* or *passion*. Here you might choose to dwell on only one essential quality for the term. You might want to *teach* about the various psychological or philosophical definitions of love that key thinkers have used over the last century. You might want to write an *amusing* piece on the foibles of love or a piece that *argues* that love in the 1980s is a vanishing phenomenon. You might want to *explain* the meaning of Christian love.

Your topic is bound to sharpen as your own particular interest in the word interacts with your ideas about purpose. You might feel that the word *love* is too all-encompassing. Perhaps you want to zero in on some particular feature of love. Is your purpose to explore the nonromantic, nonphysical love that one human being, a stranger even, can show toward another? Are you interested in the sexual dimensions of love—man for woman, woman for man, man for man, woman for woman? Are you interested in love of country and its wrenching sacrifices in wartime? Are you interested in the sanctification of love through marriage and its connections to religious ritual? Any one of those approaches would lead you down a path quite different from any other. You might ultimately decide on a different but related term, one better suited to your purpose, like *brotherly love,* say, or *patriotism, fidelity, puppy love,* or *homosexuality*.

Consider, too, your audience's expectations as you shape your topic. Try to imagine the group of readers you want to aim for. A sense of audience will help you determine an appropriate level of language and idiom, of course, but it also will help you focus your definition so that your purpose matches your audience's needs and expectations. Suppose you wanted to define *puppy love,* the adolescent condition of infatuation. You'd take one approach if your intended audience were a group of teenagers you wanted to amuse. You'd use words and you'd present ideas familiar to this age group, and you'd explain any terms you thought your readers would not know, even, perhaps one as basic to your definition as *infatuation*. Surely your jokes would be jokes that adolescents could appreciate. However, if your audience were a group of puzzled parents of junior high school-aged children whom you wanted to instruct about the value of puppy love in an adolescent's maturation, your approach would be quite different. In either case, readers would expect to know the distinguishing features of the concept so that they could recognize it easily.

It's a familiar point, the interaction of audience, purpose, and topic. You want to give these issues your careful attention every time you write.

PROCESS

In advance of writing, spend as much time as you can afford to in deciding on your topic, but don't be surprised if the process of limiting and shaping it continues beyond your early prewriting efforts and through a draft or two. You do have many options, and you want to explore them in depth before you finally decide on any one. A good place to start as a stimulus for ideas is an unabridged dictionary. The range of denotative meanings of a word certainly will stimulate further thought. What has the dictionary excluded? How does the lexical meaning compare with connotative meanings? Depending on your topic, you might wish to consult one of the specialized dictionaries, like the thirteen volume *Oxford English Dictionary* (OED), Eric Partridge's *Dictionary of Slang and Unconventional English,* 7th ed. (New York: Macmillan, 1970), or H. W. Fowler's *A Dictionary of Modern English Usage,* 2nd ed. (New York: Oxford, 1965). A dictionary of synonyms like *Roget's International Thesaurus,* 4th ed. (New York: Crowell, 1977) can show you a galaxy of words and concepts related to your topic.

We said earlier that for your extended definition you can use any of the various rhetorical strategies explained in other chapters of this book, and we want to examine that point a bit further by looking once again at the topic *puppy love*. You'll benefit greatly if you weigh your rhetorical options thoughtfully. You might investigate the meaning of the phrase by *describing* your kid sister's suffering in her most recent infatuation with the high school varsity quarterback. You might *narrate* a firsthand definition of puppy love, based on recollections of the moment your heart leapt at the sight of the green-eyed blonde who joined your tenth-grade algebra class midsemester. You might build towards a definition as you *explain the process* of falling in love for an adolescent. To offer a specialized text-based definition, you might provide *examples* of characters drawn from children's literature who fall in love in their early teens. For some fun with word play you might develop *comparative* or *contrasting* definitions—puppy love with a person's love for puppies, say, or with puppies' love for each other; or, more seriously, you might contrast puppy love with mature love. You might *classify* the various types of puppy love you've observed and so create a multitextured definition. You might *argue* that puppy love is another manifestation of teenage hysteria or peer pressure or emotional immaturity or adult emulation. You might try to *persuade* what you perceive as a reluctant audience of health education teachers to cover puppy love in their courses of study for high school students. For any of these approaches you could draw upon your own personal experiences, your readings in fiction, periodicals, and reference books, or the films or television programs you have seen. The possibilities are far-reaching—we have presented only a few here, of course—and considered along with purpose and audience, the rhetorical strategies provide fruitful areas of exploration in this assignment.

No matter which approach you take, you should be prepared to make your definition clear and specific, to set it off from what may be related but, for your paper, extraneous meanings, and to provide adequate details to make your point comprehensible. You may have to rely upon *negation;*

often a reader will best understand what your word means if you say what the word does not mean. When Emerson complains in his essay ''Gifts'' in this chapter that ''Rings and other jewels are not gifts, but apologies for gifts,'' he startles us with a negative view that few of us hold. Negation, however, helps him move toward an equally surprising affirmation: ''The only gift,'' he insists ''is a portion of thyself. Thou must bleed for me.''

Some writers of definition like to explore the *etymological features* of a term as a technique for developing meanings. Where did the word originate? How has its meaning changed historically? Yet another technique for constructing a concrete definition is to use an *analogy*. By showing your reader point by point how your topic is like something else, you can illustrate the unknown in terms of the known. Analogies can make concrete what may otherwise be hard to visualize. If you tried to define a *singles bar,* for example, by drawing a careful analogy between it and a supermarket or department store where people shop around before settling on a desirable product, you'd be helping readers who had never seen a singles bar to picture the scene with all its tensions, seriousness, and humor.

It seems altogether fitting to end here with a definition. According to the *American Heritage Dictionary, to define* means ''to state the precise meaning of (a word or sense of a word, for example); to describe the nature or basic qualities of; to delineate the outline or form of; to specify distinctly; to serve to distinguish; characterize.'' Your emphasis should be precision, clarity, and specificity—all just challenges for practicing writers.

Ralph Waldo Emerson
GIFTS

Ralph Waldo Emerson (1803–1882), born into a family of Puritan clergy in Boston, was a Unitarian minister at Boston's Old North Church from 1829 to 1832. But he left the ministry because of his distrust of established creeds and his growing belief that an individual's intuition, drawn from nature, was the highest form of knowledge. With this personal philosophy already taking shape, Emerson traveled to Europe where he met Thomas Carlyle, Samuel Taylor Coleridge, and William Wordsworth, all of whom greatly influenced Emerson and his contributions to the literary and philosophical movement of transcendentalism. Emerson was at the core of this movement—along with Thoreau, Alcott, and Fuller—which flourished in New England between 1836 and 1860.

Emerson was a noted lecturer as well as a poet and essayist. His writings include *Nature* (1836), his *Journals* (kept since his Harvard undergraduate days), his *Essays* (1841, 1844), and *Poems* (1847), as well as articles in the magazine *The Dial,* which he edited for two years.

In "Gifts" Emerson defines a term which is usually thought of as being a material object. Yet, he skillfully combines the spiritual with the material in what is ultimately a prescription for allowing others to "feel you and delight in you all the time."

> *Gifts of one who loved me,—*
> *'Twas high time they came;*
> *When he ceased to love me,*
> *Time they stopped for shame.*

It is said that the world is in a state of bankruptcy, that the world owes the world more than the world can pay, and ought to go into chancery, and be sold. I do not think this general insolvency, which involves in some sort all the population, to be the reason of the difficulty experienced at Christmas and New Year, and other times, in bestowing gifts; since it is always so pleasant to be generous, though very vexatious to pay debts. But the impediment lies in the choosing. If, at any time, it comes into my head, that a present is due from me to somebody, I am puzzled what to give, until the opportunity is gone. Flowers and fruits are always fit presents; flowers, because they are a proud assertion that a ray of beauty outvalues all the utilities of the world. These gay natures contrast with the somewhat stern countenance of ordinary nature: they are like music heard out of a workhouse. Nature does not cocker us: we are children, not pets: she is not fond: everything is dealt to us without fear or favor, after severe universal laws. Yet these delicate flowers look like the frolic and interference of love and beauty. Men use to tell us that we love flattery, even though we are not deceived by it, because it shows that we are of importance enough to be courted. Something like that pleasure, the flowers give us: what am I to whom these sweet hints are addressed? Fruits are acceptable gifts, because they are the flower of commodities, and admit of fantastic values being attached to them. If a man should send to me to come a hundred miles to visit him, and should set before me a basket of fine summer-fruit, I should think there was some proportion between the labor and the rewards.

For common gifts, necessity makes pertinences and beauty every day, and one is glad when an imperative leaves him no option, since if the man at the door have no shoes, you have not to consider whether you could procure him a paint box. And as it is always pleasing to see a man eat bread, or drink water, in the house or out of doors, so it is always a great satisfaction to supply these first wants. Necessity does everything well. In our condition of universal dependence, it seems heroic to let the petitioner be the judge of his necessity, and to give all that is asked, though at great inconvenience. If it be a fantastic desire, it is better to leave to others the office of punishing him. I can think of many parts I should prefer playing to that of the Furies. Next to things of necessity, the rule for a gift, which one of my friends prescribed, is, that we might convey to some person that which properly belonged to his character, and was easily associated with him in thought. But our tokens of compliment and love are for the most part barbarous. Rings and other jewels are not gifts, but apologies for gifts. The only gift is a portion of thyself. Thou must bleed for me. Therefore the poet brings his poem; the shepherd, his lamb; the farmer, corn; the miner, a gem; the sailor, coral and shells; the painter, his picture; the girl, a handkerchief of her own sewing. This is right and pleasing, for it restores society in so far to its prmary basis, when a man's biography is conveyed in his gifts, and every man's wealth is an index of his merit. But it is a cold, lifeless business when you go to the shops o buy me something, which does not represent your life and talent, but a goldsmith's. This is fit for kings, and rich men who represent kings, and a false state of property, to make presents of gold and silver stuffs, as a kind of symbolical sin-offering, or payment of black-mail.

The law of benefits is a difficult channel, which requires careful sailing, or rude boats. It is not the office of a man to receive gifts. How dare you give them? We wish to be self-sustained. We do not quite forgive a giver. The hand that feeds us is in some danger of being bitten. We can receive anything from love, for that is a way of receiving it from ourselves: but not from any one who assumes to bestow. We sometimes hate the meat which we eat, because there seems something of degrading dependence in living by it.

Brother, if Jove to thee a present make,
Take heed that from his hands thou nothing take.

We ask the whole. Nothing less will content us. We arraign society, if it do not give us besides earth, and fire, and water, opportunity, love, reverence, and objects of veneration.

He is a good man, who can receive a gift well. We are either glad or sorry at a gift, and both emotions are unbecoming. Some violence, I think, is done, some degradation borne, when I rejoice or grieve at a gift. I am sorry when my independence is invaded, or when a gift comes from such as do not know my spirit, and so the act is not supported; and if the gift pleases me overmuch, then I should be ashamed that the donor should read my heart, and see that I love his commodity and not him. The gift, to be true, must be the flowing of the giver unto me, correspondent to my flowing unto him. When the waters are at level, then my goods pass to him, and his to me. All his are mine, all mine his. I say to him, How can you give me this pot of oil, or this flagon of wine, when all your oil and wine is mine, which belief of mine this gift seems to deny? Hence the fitness of beautiful, not useful things for gifts. This giving is flat usurpation, and therefore when the beneficiary is ungrateful, as all beneficiaries hate all Timons, not at all considering the value of the gift, but looking back to the greater store it was taken from, I rather sympathize with the beneficiary, than with the anger of my lord Timon. For, the expectation of gratitude is mean, and is continually punished by the total insensibility of the obliged person. It is a great happiness to get off without injury and heart-burning, from one who has had the ill luck to be served by you. It is a very onerous business, this of being served, and the debtor naturally wishes to give you a slap. A golden text for these gentlemen is that which I so admire in the Buddhist, who never thanks, and who says, "Do not flatter your benefactors."

The reason of these discords I conceive to be, that there is no commensurability between a man and any gift. You cannot give anything to a magnanimous person. After you have served him, he at once puts you in debt by his magnanimity. The service a man renders his friend is trivial and selfish, compared with the service he knows his friend stood in readiness to yield him, alike before he had begun to serve his friend, and now also. Compared with that good-will I bear my friend, the benefit it is in my power to render him seems small. Besides, our action on each other, good as well as evil, is so incidental and at random, that we can seldom hear the acknowledgments of any person who would thank us for a benefit, without some shame and humiliation. We can rarely strike a direct stroke, but must be content with an oblique one; we seldom have the satisfaction of yielding a direct benefit, which is directly received. But rectitude scatters favors on every side without knowing it, and receives with wonder the thanks of all people.

I fear to breathe any treason against the majesty of love, which is the genius and god of gifts, and to whom we must not affect to prescribe. Let him give kingdoms or flower-leaves indifferently. There are persons, from whom we always expect fairy tokens; let us not cease to expect them. This is prerogative, and not to be limited by our municipal rules. For the rest, I like to see that we cannot be bought and sold. The best of hospitality and of generosity is also not in the will but in fate. I find that I am not much to you; you do not need me; you do not feel me; then am I thrust out of doors, though you proffer me house and lands. No services are of any value, but only likeness. When I have attempted to join myself to others by services, it proved an intellectual trick,—no more. They eat your service like apples, and leave you out. But love them, and they feel you, and delight in you all the time.

Meaning and Idea

1. According to Emerson, what is the greatest cause of difficulty in gift-giving? How can that difficulty be overcome?

2. What is Emerson's attitude about the best source for gifts? What does he mean by "The only gift is a portion of thyself"?

3. Why are beautiful things more "fit" as gifts than useful things?

4. According to Emerson, what is the greatest of all possible gifts? What is the most exalted basis for gift-giving? Why?

Language, Form, Structure

1. Throughout the essay, Emerson continually limits the scope of his definition of *gifts* until he arrives at one critical basis for all gift-choosing and -giving. Trace the process of limitation and identify the conclusion which derives from it.

2. What is the relation in this essay among gift-choosing, gift-giving, and gift-receiving? How do Emerson's discussions of these three categories amount to a definition of *gifts*?

3. What metaphor does Emerson create for gift-giving? How does it help define the term *gifts*?

4. Identify two sections where Emerson uses exemplification to limit the definition.

5. Write definitions for Emerson's use of the following words: chancery; vexations; impediment; countenance; imperative; veneration; onerous; commensurability; rectitude; prerogative.

Ideas for Writing

1. Choose a term that can have both spiritual and materialistic meanings (wealth; success; marriage, for example) and write a definition which blends the two values and shows their relationship to one another.

2. Define the term *generosity.* Focus either on material or spiritual generosity—or both.

3. One critic writes of Emerson's contribution that the philosopher developed "the doctrine of self-reliance, a spirit of optimism, and defiance of tradition and authority: for to the extent that all men are godlike . . . they must trust themselves, can overcome evil, and should regard their fellow men as equal." Write a paper in which you explore the validity of this comment in regard to "Gifts."

Carson McCullers
A TREE. A ROCK. A CLOUD.

Carson McCullers (1917–1967), born in Columbus, Georgia, was an American fiction writer who often focused on an individual's sense of isolation and loneliness in the midst of a malevolent or uncaring society. Her stories were so finely wrought as to lend themselves easily to dramatizations; *The Member of the Wedding* (1946) was made into a play in 1950, and Edward Albee in 1963 dramatized McCullers's novella *The Ballad of the Sad Cafe* (1951). Her earlier well-known work is *The Heart Is a Lonely Hunter* (1940).

A tree, a rock, and a cloud are in this story both the end points of disillusionment and the starting points of love. McCullers's characterization and setting skillfully play against the ultimate happiness (or unhappiness?) she wants to define.

*I*t was raining that morning, and still very dark. When the boy reached the streetcar café he had almost finished his route and he went in for a cup of coffee. The place was an all-night café owned by a bitter and stingy man called Leo. After the raw, empty street the café seemed friendly and bright: along the counter there were a couple of soldiers, three spinners from the cotton mill, and in a corner a man who sat hunched over with his nose and half his face down in a beer mug. The boy wore a helmet such as aviators wear. When he went into the café he unbuckled the chin strap and raised the right flap up over his pink little ear; often as he drank his coffee someone would speak to him in a friendly way. But this morning Leo did not look into his face and none of the men were talking. He paid and was leaving the café when a voice called out to him:

'Son! Hey Son!'

He turned back and the man in the corner was crooking his finger and nodding to him. He had brought his face out of the beer mug and he seemed suddenly very happy. The man was long and pale, with a big nose and faded orange hair.

'Hey Son!'

The boy went toward him. He was an undersized boy of about twelve, with one shoulder drawn higher than the other because of the weight of the paper sack. His face was shallow, freckled, and his eyes were round child eyes.

'Yeah Mister?'

The man laid one hand on the paper boy's shoulders, then grasped the boy's chin and turned his face slowly from one side to the other. The boy shrank back uneasily.

'Say! What's the big idea?'

The boy's voice was shrill; inside the café it was suddenly very quiet.

The man said slowly: 'I love you.'

All along the counter the men laughed. The boy, who had scowled and sidled away, did not know what to do. He looked over the counter at Leo, and Leo watched him with a weary, brittle jeer. The boy tried to laugh also. But the man was serious and sad.

'I did not mean to tease you, Son,' he said. 'Sit down and have a beer with me. There is something I have to explain.'

Cautiously, out of the corner of his eye, the paper boy questioned the men along the counter to see what he should do. But they had gone back to their beer or their breakfast and did not notice him. Leo put a cup of coffee on the counter and a little jug of cream.

'He is a minor,' Leo said.

The paper boy slid himself up onto the stool. His ear beneath the upturned flap of the helmet was very small and red. The man was nodding at him soberly. 'It is important,' he said. Then he reached in his hip pocket and brought out something which he held up in the palm of his hand for the boy to see.

'Look very carefully,' he said.

The boy stared, but there was nothing to look at very carefully. The man held in his big, grimy palm a photograph. It was the face of a woman, but blurred, so that only the hat and the dress she was wearing stood out clearly.

'See?' the man asked.

The boy nodded and the man placed another picture in his palm. The woman was standing on a beach in a bathing suit. The suit made her stomach very big, and that was the main thing you noticed.

'Got a good look?' He leaned over closer and finally asked: 'You ever seen her before?'

The boy sat motionless, staring slantwise at the man. 'Not so I know of.'

'Very well.' The man blew on the photographs and put them back into his pocket. 'That was my wife.'

'Dead?' the boy asked.

Slowly the man shook his head. He pursed his lips as though about to whistle and answered in a long-drawn way: 'Nuuu—' he said. 'I will explain.'

The beer on the counter before the man was in a large brown mug. He did not pick it up to drink. Instead he bent down and, putting his face over the rim, he rested there for a moment. Then with both hands he tilted the mug and sipped.

'Some night you'll go to sleep with your nose in a mug and drown,' said Leo. 'Prominent transient drowns in beer. That would be a cute death.'

The paper boy tried to signal to Leo. While the man was not looking he screwed up his face and worked his mouth to question soundlessly: 'Drunk?' But Leo only raised his eyebrows and turned away to put some pink strips of bacon on the grill. The man pushed the mug away from him, straightened himself, and folded his loose crooked hands on the counter. His face was sad as he looked at the paper boy. He did not blink, but from time to time the lids closed down with delicate gravity over his pale green eyes. It was nearing dawn and the boy shifted the weight of the paper sack.

'I am talking about love,' the man said. 'With me it is a science.'

The boy half slid down from the stool. But the man raised his forefinger, and there was something about him that held the boy and would not let him go away.

'Twelve years ago I married the woman in the photograph. She was my wife for one year, nine months, three days, and two nights. I loved her. Yes . . .' He tightened his blurred, rambling voice and said again: 'I loved her. I thought also that she loved me. I was a railroad engineer. She had all home comforts and luxuries. It never crept into my brain that she was not satisfied. But do you know what happened?'

'Mgneeow!' said Leo.

The man did not take his eyes from the boy's face. 'She left me. I came in one night and the house was empty and she was gone. She left me.'

'With a fellow?' the boy asked.

Gently the man placed his palm down on the counter. 'Why naturally, Son. A woman does not run off like that alone.'

The café was quiet, the soft rain black and endless in the street outside. Leo pressed down the frying bacon with the prongs of his long fork. 'So you have been chasing the floozie for eleven years. You frazzled old rascal!'

For the first time the man glanced at Leo. 'Please don't be vulgar. Besides, I was not speaking to you.' He turned back to the boy and said in a trusting and secretive undertone: 'Let's not pay any attention to him. O.K.?'

The paper boy nodded doubtfully.

'It was like this,' the man continued. 'I am a person who feels many things. All my life one thing after another has impressed me. Moonlight. The leg of a pretty girl. One thing after another. But the point is that when I had enjoyed anything there was a peculiar sensation as though it was laying around loose in me. Nothing seemed to finish itself up or fit in with the other things. Women? I had my portion of them. The same. Afterwards laying around loose in me. I was a man who had never loved.'

Very slowly he closed his eyelids, and the gesture was like a curtain drawn at the end of a scene in a play. When he spoke again his voice was excited and the words came fast—the lobes of his large, loose ears seemed to tremble.

'Then I met this woman. I was fifty-one and she always said she was thirty. I met her at a filling station and we were married within three days. And do you know what it was like? I just can't tell you. All I had ever felt was gathered together around this woman. Nothing lay loose in me any more but was finished up by her.'

The man stopped suddenly and stroked his long nose. His voice sank down to a steady and reproachful undertone: 'I'm not explaining this right. What happened was this. There were these beautiful feelings and loose little pleasures inside me. And this woman was something like an assembly line for my soul. I run these little pieces of myself through her and I come out complete. Now do you follow me?'

'What was her name?' the boy asked.

'Oh,' he said. 'I called her Dodo. But that is immaterial.'

'Did you try to make her come back?'

The man did not seem to hear. 'Under the circumstances you can imagine how I felt when she left me.'

Leo took the bacon from the grill and folded two strips of it between a bun. He had a gray face, with slitted eyes, and a pinched nose saddled by faint blue shadows. One of the mill workers signaled for more coffee and Leo poured it. He did not give refills on coffee free. The spinner ate breakfast there every morning, but the better Leo knew his customers the stingier he treated them. He nibbled his own bun as though he grudged it to himself.

'And you never got hold of her again?'

The boy did not know what to think of the man, and his child's face was uncertain with mingled curiosity and doubt. He was new on the paper route; it was still strange to him to be out in the town in the black, queer early morning.

'Yes,' the man said. 'I took a number of steps to get her back. I went around trying to locate her. I went to Tulsa where she had folks. And to Mobile. I went to every town she had ever mentioned to me, and I hunted down every man she had formerly been connected with. Tulsa, Atlanta, Chicago, Cheehaw, Memphis . . . For the better part of two years I chased around the country trying to lay hold of her.'

'But the pair of them had vanished from the face of the earth!' said Leo.

'Don't listen to him,' the man said confidentially. 'And also just forget those two years. They are not important. What matters is that around the third year a curious thing begun to happen to me.'

'What?' the boy asked.

The man leaned down and tilted his mug to take a sip of beer. But as he hovered over the mug his nostrils fluttered slightly; he sniffed the staleness of the beer and did not drink. 'Love is a curious thing to begin with. At first I thought only of getting her back. It was a kind of mania. But then as time went on I tried to remember her. But do you know what happened?'

'No,' the boy said.

'When I laid myself down on a bed and tried to think about her my mind became a blank. I couldn't see her. I would take out her pictures and look. No good. Nothing doing. A blank. Can you imagine it?'

'Say Mac!' Leo called down the counter. 'Can you imagine this bozo's mind a blank!'

Slowly, as though fanning away flies, the man waved his hand. His green eyes were concentrated and fixed on the shallow little face of the paper boy.

'But a sudden piece of glass on a sidewalk. Or a nickel tune in a music box. A shadow on a wall at night. And I would remember. It might happen in a street and I would cry or bang my head against a lamppost. You follow me?'

'A piece of glass . . .' the boy said.

'Anything. I would walk around and I had no power of how and when to remember her. You think you can put up a kind of shield. But remembering don't come to a man face forward—it corners around sideways. I was at the mercy of everything I saw and heard. Suddenly instead of me combing the countryside to find her she begun to chase me around in my very soul. *She* chasing *me,* mind you! And in my soul.'

The boy asked finally: 'What part of the country were you in then?'

'Ooh,' the man groaned. 'I was a sick mortal. It was like smallpox. I confess, Son, that I boozed. I fornicated. I committed any sin that suddenly appealed to me. I am loath to confess it but I will do so. When I recall that period it is all curdled in my mind, it was so terrible.'

The man leaned his head down and tapped his forehead on the counter. For a few seconds he stayed bowed over in this position, the back of his stringy neck covered with orange furze, his hands with their long warped fingers held palm to palm in an attitude of prayer. Then the man straightened himself; he was smiling and suddeny his face was bright and tremulous and old.

'It was in the fifth year that it happened,' he said. 'And with it I started my science.'

Leo's mouth jerked with a pale, quick grin. 'Well none of we boys are getting any younger,' he said. Then with sudden anger he balled up a dishcloth he was holding and threw it down hard on the floor. 'You draggle-tailed old Romeo!'

'What happened?' the boy asked.

The old man's voice was high and clear: 'Peace,' he answered.

'Huh?'

'It is hard to explain scientifically, Son,' he said. 'I guess the logical explanation is that she and I had fleed around from each other for so long that finally we just got tangled up together and lay down and quit. Peace. A queer and beautiful blankness. It was spring in Portland and the rain came every afternoon. All evening I just stayed there on my bed in the dark. And that is how the science come to me.'

The windows in the streetcar were pale blue with light. The two soldiers paid for their beers and opened the door—one of the soldiers combed his hair and wiped off his muddy puttees before they went outside. The three mill workers bent silently over their breakfasts. Leo's clock was ticking on the wall.

'It is this. And listen carefully. I meditated on love and reasoned it out. I reasoned it out. I realized what is wrong with us. Men fall in love for the first time. And what do they fall in love with?'

The boy's soft mouth was partly open and he did not answer.

'A woman,' the old man said. 'Without science, with nothing to go by, they undertake the most dangerous and sacred experience in God's earth. They fall in love with a woman. Is that correct, Son?'

'Yeah,' the boy said faintly.

'They start at the wrong end of love. They begin at the climax. Can you wonder it is so miserable? Do you know how men should love?'

The old man reached over and grasped the boy by the collar of his leather jacket. He gave him a gentle little shake and his green eyes gazed down unblinking and grave.

'Son, do you know how love should be begun?'

The boy sat small and listening and still. Slowly he shook his head. The old man leaned closer and whispered:

'A tree. A rock. A cloud.'

It was still raining outside in the street: a mild, gray, endless rain. The mill whistle blew for the six o'clock shift and the three spinners paid and went away. There was no one in the café but Leo, the old man, and the little paper boy.

'The weather was like this in Portland,' he said. 'At the time my science was begun. I meditated and I started very cautious. I would pick up something from the street and take it home with me. I bought a goldfish and I concentrated on the goldfish and I loved it. I graduated from one thing to another. Day by day I was getting this technique. On the road from Portland to San Diego———'

'Aw shut up!' screamed Leo suddenly. 'Shut up! Shut up!'

The old man still held the collar of the boy's jacket; he was trembling and his face was earnest and bright and wild. 'For six years now I have gone around by myself and built up my science. And now I am a master. Son. I can love anything. No longer do I have to think about it even. I see a street full of people and a beautiful light comes in me. I watch a bird in the sky. Or I meet a traveler on the road. Everything, Son. And anybody. All stranger and all loved! Do you realize what a science like mine can mean?'

The boy held himself stiffly, his hands curled tight around the counter edge. Finally he asked: 'Did you ever really find that lady?'

'What? What say, Son?'

'I mean,' the boy asked timidly, 'have you fallen in love with a woman again?'

The old man loosened his grasp on the boy's collar. He turned away and for the first time his green eyes had a vague and scattered look. He lifted the mug from the counter, drank down the yellow beer. His head was shaking slowly from side to side. Then finally he answered: 'No, Son. You see that is the last step in my science. I go cautious. And I am not quite ready yet.'

'Well!' said Leo. 'Well well well!'

The old man stood in the open doorway. 'Remember,' he said. Framed there in the gray damp light of the early morning he looked shrunken and seedy and frail. But his smile was bright. 'Remember I love you,' he said with a last nod. And the door closed quietly behind him.

The boy did not speak for a long time. He pulled down the bangs on his forehead and slid his grimy little forefinger around the rim of his empty cup. Then without looking at Leo he finally asked:

'Was he drunk?'

'No,' said Leo shortly.

The boy raised his clear voice higher. 'Then was he a dope fiend?'

'No.'

The boy looked up at Leo, and his flat little face was desperate, his voice urgent and shrill. 'Was he crazy? Do you think he was a lunatic?' The paper boy's voice dropped suddenly with doubt. 'Leo? Or not?'

But Leo would not answer him. Leo had run a night café for fourteen years, and he held himself to be a critic of craziness. There were the town characters and also the transients who roamed in from the night. He knew the manias of all of them. But he did not want to satisfy the questions of the waiting child. He tightened his pale face and was silent.

So the boy pulled down the right flap of his helmet and as he turned to leave he made the only comment that seemed safe to him, the only remark that could not be laughed down and despised:

'He sure has done a lot of traveling.'

Meaning and Idea

1. What is being defined in this story?

2. How old is the boy in this story? What does he do? Approximately what area of the country is the setting for this story? How do you know?

3. What is the man's "science"? Is it really an exact measure of things? Look at the line where he says the woman was his wife for "one year, nine months, three days, and two nights." Does that exactitude derive from scientific thought or from something else?

4. Has the man ever really given up his love for his wife? Where does he state a specific answer to that? Do you know the answer before he says it? How?

5. Why does the man choose to tell this story to the boy rather than to the other adult patrons in the café? Does he really "love" the boy? Why does he tell him he does?

Language, Form, Structure

1. How would you characterize the boy's attitude toward the man? How does it serve the definition being formulated?

2. Why is the name of the man's wife "immaterial"? If he loved her so, why wouldn't he say her name? What is the effect of that omission on the definition?

3. How is process analysis used at various points to develop the definition in this story? In the process of love, how is "A tree. A rock. A cloud" the correct starting point?

4.   What is the purpose of Leo in this story? What is his attitude toward the man? How does it serve as a contrast to the man? How does that contrast contribute to the definition?

5.   Look up and define the following words from the story; then use each in an original sentence: scowled; sidled; transient; floozie; undertone; immaterial; mania; tremulous.

Ideas for Writing

1.   Write your own definition of *love,* arranging your definition in three stages: the beginning point of love; the point at which you know for sure; the point at which you are satisfied.

2.   Write a definition for *loneliness.* Use experience as the main basis for your definition; in other words, try to avoid abstraction.

3.   McCullers's great strength as a writer is her ability to evoke a rich human sensibility, to treat emotionally fragile people who are lonely and love-starved, and to honor individualism and sensitivity. To what degree does "A Tree. A Rock. A Cloud." support that judgment? In your essay response, make specific references to the text.

Carl Sandburg
PRIMER LESSON

Carl Sandburg (1878–1967) was born in Galesburg, Illinois, of Swedish immigrant parents. Many have considered him as a kind of bardic successor to Walt Whitman; both poets celebrated the common people and their activities and experiences. Sandburg himself never did well in school, but received his "education" as a laborer, soldier, wanderer, and journalist. In addition, he was active in the 1907–1908 presidential campaign of Eugene V. Debs, the candidate of the Social Democratic Party; Sandburg himself maintained his socialist politics throughout his life. By his old age, he was well respected for collections such as *Chicago Poems* (1916), *The People, Yes* (1936), and the Pulitzer Prize winning *Complete Poems* (1950). Between 1926 and 1939, he also wrote a six-volume biography of Abraham Lincoln. In 1964, President Lyndon Johnson awarded Sandburg the Presidential Medal of Freedom.

This poem is as simple as any primer book lesson, while its message carries much more complex meanings. Though Sandburg never actually defines the term *proud words,* we end up knowing its meaning.

Look out how you use proud words.
When you let proud words go, it is
　　not easy to call them back.
They wear long boots, hard boots; they
　　walk off proud; they can't hear you
　　calling—
Look out how you use proud words.

5

Meaning and Idea

1. Whom is the poet addressing in this poem? How do you know?

2. What is meant by "proud words"? Give examples of what might be considered "proud words." What might be an occasion to use them?

3. Why does Sandburg say that you can't call back proud words? Do your own personal experiences support that statement? Explain.

Language, Form, Structure

1. How does Sandburg use *personification* as a technique in this poem? How does it effectively serve the definition?

2. What is a *primer?* Why is the poem titled "Primer Lesson" and not "Proud Words"?

3. The first and last lines of this poem are the same, but how is their impact different? Why? How has implied definition changed their impact and value?

Ideas for Writing

1. Write a short definition of a lie. You may want to concentrate on the feelings that lies engender for both speaker and receiver.

2. Write a definition entitled "Famous Last Words." Use examples, but make sure you come to a clear dfinition of the term.

3. Sandburg never actually defines or gives examples of *proud words,* yet it is legitimate to say that the reader has a clear meaning of the term at the end of the poem. How does Sandburg achieve that? Write a definition of *proud words* as you understand it from "Primer Lesson" and then explain how the poem brings you to that understanding.

Robert Graves
THE NAKED AND THE NUDE

Robert Graves, born in 1895 near London, gained a reputation as a novelist, poet, and literary critic. Graves saw considerable action as a member of the Royal Welsh Fusiliers during World War I, during which time he befriended the poet Siegfried Sassoon. After the war, he studied at Oxford, where he later taught. Graves's novel *I, Claudius* (1934) is familiar to British and American television audiences as the basis for a critically acclaimed series. His war memoir *Good-bye to All That* (1929) is a haunting chronicle of the physical and social destruction of World War I. *The White Goddess* (1948), Graves's "historical grammar of poetic myth," delves into the matriarchal basis of history and artistic creation.

In reading Graves's "The Naked and the Nude" pay special attention to the ways in which the poet separates then synthesizes the denotative and connotative values of two seemingly similar words.

For me, the naked and the nude
(By lexicographers construed
As synonyms that should express
The same deficiency of dress
Or shelter) stand as wide apart   5
As love from lies, or truth from art.

Lovers without reproach will gaze
On bodies naked and ablaze;
The hippocratic eye will see
In nakedness, anatomy;   10
And naked shines the Goddess when
She mounts her lion among men.

The nude are bold, the nude are sly
To hold each treasonable eye.
While draping by a showman's trick   15
Their dishabille in rhetoric,
They grin a mock-religious grin
Of scorn at those of naked skin.

The naked, therefore, who compete
Against the nude may know defeat;   20
Yet when they both together tread
The briary pastures of the dead,
By Gorgons with long whips pursued,
How naked go the sometime nude!

Meaning and Idea

1. Check a dictionary to find the denotation of the word *naked*. What, according to Graves, does the word *naked* connote? What details does he offer to show what he means by the word? What do lines 11–12 mean?

2. What is the denotation of the word *nude*? What images support the connotation Graves is trying to present for the word?

3. How do the two compare? Explain the last stanza in your own words.

Language, Form, Structure

1. The first stanza of the poem establishes Graves's main point. What is that point? What is the purpose of the statement in parentheses in lines 2–5? Why is the language there so much more formal and scholarly than the language in the rest of the stanza? What in general is the tone (see Glossary) of the poem.

2. Graves's definitions progress through a series of images. Which images are most vivid? Why does he use exemplification (see Glossary) to define the words? How does the repetition of the words *naked* and *nude* serve as a transitional device? What other transitional devices are apparent?

3. In stanza two Graves explains what he means by *naked*, in stanza three what he means by *nude*. Then in stanza four he presents the two words together. How do you think this organizational pattern serves the meaning of the poem? Why does he choose comparison and contrast as a strategy for defining the words? What is the surprise in the last line?

4. What are the "briary pastures of the dead"? What is Graves's purpose in using the phrase "dishabille in rhetoric"? Check your dictionary for the meanings of the following words: lexicographers (line 2); deficiency (4); hippocratic (9); Gorgon (23).

Ideas for Writing

1. Write a paragraph in which you define the words *naked* and *nude* with images based upon your own connotations for the words.

2. Select any two synonyms that have similar denotations but different connotations and write an essay in which you explore the definitions of those words. Provide details in order to make your meanings of the words clear.

3. Write a paragraph in which you comment upon Graves's use of language in this poem. Consider, for example, his choice of words. Why does he select *deficiency* (line 4) instead of *lack? Gaze* (7) instead of *stare? Mount* (12) instead of *climb? Bold* instead of *daring* or *brave?* You might also comment on Graves's use of nouns and verbs, his use of classical references (lines 11–12 and 24), his use of rhyme, rhythm, and meter.

E. E. Cummings
A POLITICIAN

> Born in Cambridge, Massachusetts, in 1894, E. E. Cummings took his B.A. and M.A. Degrees at Harvard, lived in Paris in the 1920s, then settled in New York's bohemian Greenwich Village. His travels spurred him to write the semifictional, semi-sociological *The Enormous Room* (1922) and *Eimi* (1933). Cummings is best known, however, for his poetry, for his whimsical play with typography and syntax, as well as for his near abhorrence of capital letters (he did not use capitals even for his name). He died in New Hampshire in 1962.
>
> Notice how in this very brief poem, Cummings manages to evoke various levels of meaning.

a politician is an arse upon
which everyone has sat except a man

Meaning and Idea

1. What is an *arse?* Why does Cummings choose this spelling and pronunciation over the more common one?

2. What can you say about the poet's attitude toward politicians? Do his feelings seem to be general or specific? Explain.

Language, Form, Structure

1.   What are the various meanings of the word *arse* in this poem? Explain how "everyone" can have sat on this arse, but not one man has. What various levels of meaning of *man* are implied?

2.   Explain the metaphorical structure of this definition.

Ideas for Writing

1.   Write an essay in which you define the word *politician*. Draw upon your personal experiences or upon what you have read or observed about politicians. Be specific.

2.   Select a profession and write a series of two-line definitions of it following Cummings's plan.

3.   Write a few paragraphs in which you respond to the simplicity (seemingly so) of Cummings's statement. Do you think this definition is sufficient? Do you think it is a poem? Explain your responses.

Joseph Epstein

A FORMER GOOD GUY AND HIS FRIENDS

> Joseph Epstein is an editor, essayist, and short story writer who has a keen perception of American culture and lifestyles. Born in Chicago in 1937, Epstein has contributed regularly to such magazines as *Commentary, The New Yorker,* and *Harper's.*
>
> In "A Former Good Guy and His Friends," which appeared in the Spring 1985 volume of The *American Scholar,* author Joseph Epstein, writing under the pen name "Aristides," offers an engrossing extended definition of *friendship.* Pay close attention to the ways in which Epstein uses almost all the expository techniques you've studied earlier in this book— classification, narration, exemplification, process analysis, and so on.

I recently saw a copy of the high-school newspaper that appeared the week of my class's graduation and found myself a bit miffed to discover that I was not voted Most Popular or Best Liked or Most Friendly or Best Personality or any other of the categories that speak to the ideal, vivid in the days of my youth, of being a Good Guy. It may seem immodest of me to talk about myself in this way, and normally I should refrain from doing so, but the plain fact is that I worked sedulously at being thought not merely a Good Guy but an extraordinarily Good Guy and felt that I had greatly succeeded. Whence this interest on my part in being such a devilishly Good Guy, you may ask. I suppose it came about as a matter of elimination. Since I was neither a first-rate athlete, nor a notably successful Lothario, nor even a half-serious student, all that was left on the buffet of roles for me to choose from was Good Guy or thug, and since I hadn't the wardrobe for thug I went for Good Guy—and I went for it in a big way. Almost anyone who attended Nicholas Senn High School in Chicago when I did will, I feel confident, tell you, "Sure, I remember Aristides. He was a Good Guy"

What is a Good Guy turns out not to be so simple a question. If Aristotle had gone to Nicholas Senn High School—a notion it gives me much delight to contemplate—he would doubtless have been able to posit no fewer than eleven kinds of Good Guy and compose an ample disquisition on the nature of the Good Guy, or Good-Guyness. Perhaps a disquisition is required, for there is apparently some disagreement about what constitutes a Good Guy. Not long ago, for example, when I remarked to a friend from my high-school days that I thought I used to be a fine specimen of the type known as Good Guy, he replied that he thought I had not quite made it. I was very popular, he allowed, but I wasn't bland enough. The pure Good Guy, he argued, should be very bland. Your true Good Guy should never give offense, or even hint at the potentiality for giving offense, and I, who was locally famous for an above-average sharpness of tongue, was considered verbally too dangerous to qualify as a pure Good Guy. Very well. I can accept that. Let me, then, revise my earlier statement: Almost anyone who attended Nicholas Senn High School when I did will, I feel confident, tell you, "Sure, I remember Aristides. He was a Good Guy—only don't cross him."

Does the ideal of the Good Guy still exist? For all I know, it may have gone the way of the Cute Girl, which, I gather, no self-respecting female above the age of ten nowadays cares to be thought. But as I construed it then, a Good Guy was someone whom vast numbers of people felt to be a Good Guy. I thus set out to convince vast numbers of people. It proved no very complex task. Ben Franklin, whom I did not read until years later, remarks in his autobiography that, if you wish to insinuate yourself in the good graces of another person, the trick is not to do that person a favor but to have him do one for you. So the trick of making many friends, at least on the superficial level on which the Good Guy operates, is not to charm them but to let them charm you.

It was many friends I wanted: multitudes, large assemblages, whole hordes. To acquire them I was ready to turn off the charm. I was, in those days, the reverse of a snob; I looked up my nose at everyone. No one was too lowly for me to court. I became a boredom-proof listener, a full-time dispenser of bonhomie. Sashaying through the halls of our high school, greeting my innumerable conquests in the Good Guy sweepstakes, I uttered a stream of babblesome salutations not to be equaled for inanity outside a major league infield: "Hi babes," "What say," "How're you makin' it," "Take it easy," "Hang in there," "How's it goin'," "Be good," "Yo!" and fifteen or twenty other utterances of equal profundity that I have since forgotten.

In cultivating friends, I was calculating but not altogether insincere. If one way to make friends is to show a great interest in other people, showing such an interest, however artificial it might be at the outset, can before long issue in genuine interest. Besides, I not only collected but liked people; I liked their oddness and idiosyncrasy. As a good listener, I was taken into many a confidence and vouchsafed many a glance into secret desires, passions, fears—all of which the incipient if still quite unknown writer in me found fascinating. As a Good Guy, I knew how to keep a secret, never to betray a trust, and was, withal, a ready and reliable confidant. "Kids say the darndest things," a smarmy radio "personality" named Art Linkletter used to remark. They do indeed, and I like their saying many of them to me, which was one of the minor fringe benefits of being thought such a corking Good Guy. A larger benefit was the small number of people who, initially captured by my Good Guy maneuvers, have thus far remained lifelong friends.

Still, I may have exulted too much, albeit secretly, in this knack I had for making friends easily. Sometimes I would try this knack out, like a professional tenor singing in the shower at home, for the sheer pleasure of exercising it. I would choose a young thug ("hoods" we then called them), or a shy girl, or someone whose background was utterly different from my own, and set out to win him or her over to my ever-enlarging stable of friends. Almost always I succeeded. It was pure art, really— friends for friends' sake. In those days, had I had a reasonable grasp of grammar and syntax, I could have written a book entitled *How to Win Friends Without Caring in the Least About Influencing People*.

I merely wished to be liked, and only by everybody I met. To be thought a Good Guy by all—this didn't seem too much to ask. Occasionally it would get back to me that someone or other didn't understand what lay behind my considerable popularity. I felt my appeal ought to have been self-evident to him; I was, self-evidently, a Good Guy. Then there was small band of people around whom I stepped gingerly. They were insensate to my blandishments, these people—most of them boys but also a few girls—whom I thought of, even in high school, as "in business for themselves." In a rough sense, each of us is in business for himself—each of us, that is, is pre-eminently concerned about his own preservation and rise in the world and has a necessary and probably sensble selfishness— but these people were rather more selfish than was either necessary or sensible. They were generally rather intense and (no rather about it) humorless. The very notion of the Good Guy, with all his airy friend- liness, was alien to them, and so, consequently, was I. It only now occurs to me that I was also possibly in business for myself in those days. My business was being popular. It was a pleasant enough line of work, requiring no character whatsoever.

I can write all this now chiefly because I am—as a great many people will tell you—no longer a Good Guy. I may not even be, to shift at last to lowercase spelling, a nice fellow. I have not yet arrived at the stage of Evelyn Waugh's character Gilbert Pinfold, who of himself asks, "Why does everyone except me find it so easy to be nice?" but I find I do not much mind making enemies. Some enemies seem to me eminently worth having. This is something that the old Good Guy in me failed to under- stand. Chiefly through writing a good deal of journalism and literary criticism, I have by now acquired, I feel certain, an ample supply of enemies. If the people I have written critically about feel as I do about the people who have written critically about me, my guess is that they have not altogether forgotten me and that, should my name ever crop up in their presence, it is cause for them to murmur a brief Bulgarian curse or a stirring undeleted epithet.

Perhaps because, as a former Good Guy, it has taken me so long to acquire enemies, I like to dwell upon them and on occasion I have even dreamed of them. In one such dream the people I have written harshly about are gathered together in a large room in a Manhattan hotel to throw a party for me. There they stand, as in a drawing out of *Esquire:* Joseph Heller, John Updike, Norman Mailer, William F. Buckley, Jr., Gore Vidal, Renata Adler, Philip Roth, Ann Beattie, Gabriel García Márquez, and others too numerous to mention. In this dream I sit alone, in white tie and tails, at a long dais. Everyone in the room is standing, champagne glasses raised in my direction, waiting for me to speak. "Sorry, gang," I announce at last, a wide smile plastered across my face, "but no more Mr. Good Guy."

If early life taught me how to gather a wide acquaintanceship, and later life how not to fear enemies, the great mystery remains friendship. Aristo- tle, who devotes fully two books of the *Nicomachean Ethics* to the subject of friendship, begins by remarking that "without friends no one would choose to live," which seems to me quite true. Yet the quality and variety of friendship are nearly inexhaustible, and, as Aristotle says, "not a few things about friendship are matters of debate." The first matter for debate, perhaps, is one's own interest in friendship—or, more precisely, one's own devotion to friendship. "The only way to have friends," writes Joubert, "is to throw everything out the window, to keep your door unlocked, and never to know where you will be sleeping at night. You will tell me there are few people mad enough to act like this. Well then, they shouldn't complain about not having any friends. They don't want any." I suspect Joubert is correct about this, even though it means that I, who value my friends, do not qualify as someone absolutely devoted to friendship. I want to have friends, but on my terms—and, as I grow older, these terms grow more and more strict.

Although not usually at its center, friendship plays a part in many of the greatest literary works. Straightaway there is the friendship of Achilles and Patroclus. Cervantes presents, in Don Quixote and Sancho Panza, a lovely instance of a friendship between unequals and opposites. Dickens provides many of his young heroes with charming, self-effacing friends—Tommy Traddles, Herbert Pocket, etc.—of a kind we could all use in our corner. The friendship that develops between Huck Finn and Jim is of course one of Mark Twain's great touches—perhaps his greatest touch. The delicacy and subtlety required in friendship—almost always referred to as "personal relations"—is nearly the entire subject of E. M. Forster. In Henry James it is not so much friendship as the betrayal of friendship that looms so large. But the novelist of friendlessness is Joseph Conrad, whose heroes are among the loneliest figures in literature and among the most moving in part because of their solitariness, which gives them their tragic dimension.

Possibly the greatest literary friendship on record, and the most literarily consequential, was that between Montaigne and the poet and the magistrate Étienne de La Boétie. The two men met when Montaigne was thirty, La Boétie thirty-three. Their rapport was immediate and perfect; each was able, in letters and in person, to reveal his soul to the other. In 1563, four years after they met, La Boétie came down with an intestinal ailment from which he died, with Montaigne at his bedside. Montaigne was permanently bereft. Donald M. Frame, Montaigne's biographer and translator, believes that "there is much to show that the *Essays* themselves are—among other things—a compensation for the loss of La Boétie." With Étienne de La Boétie gone, Montaigne had no one to speak with and write for but himself—and the world. La Boétie is the friend, and theirs the single dominant friendship, referred to when, in his essay "Of friendship," Montaigne writes: "In the friendship I speak of, our souls mingle and blend with each other so completely that they efface the seam that joined them, and cannot find it again. If you press me to tell why I loved him, I feel that this cannot be expressed, except by answering: Because it was he, because it was I." The void left by the death of La Boétie was never to be filled by Montaigne; references to him in the *Essays* are frequent; eighteen years after his friend's death, Montaigne can still be troubled by thoughts about him. Which is greater, having known such a friendship or its loss, is a question that troubled Montaigne his life long.

Such a friend is rare at any time, in any life. I have never known such a friend in my own life, and I am not at all sure I should want one. (I exclude my wife, whom I consider to be in the realm above that of friendship.) As a boy, I recall how important it seemed to have a best friend; and I, as someone who had made friends rather easily, had, seriatim, several best friends. I might have a best friend for a summer, or a school term, but gradually we would drift not quite apart but to a friendship of lesser intensity. In a best friend I desired someone to pal around with, someone to rely on, someone occasionally to confide in. I required no full communion of souls, not being myself a very soulful character. The notion of the best friend carries over into adulthood with marriage, where, traditionally, the groom appoints a best man, who is presumably his best friend. I have been married twice—I believe I got it right the second time—but the combined total attendance at both my weddings was two; I had witnesses in place of best men. Even now I do not feel the want of a best friend, but I do have a number of good friends whom I cherish.

Was it Plutarch who said that one didn't need more than seven friends? Until this moment I have never counted mine, but—dead on, Plutarch—it turns out I can think of exactly seven friends, very good friends, whose death or disappearance from my life would devastate me. I can think of a second tier of ten or so friends who enrich my life but with whom the same degree of easy intimacy and depth of feeling does not quite exist. I can think of a third tier of twenty or so people whom I am always pleased to see or hear from, in whose company I feel perfectly comfortable, and with whom I believe I share a reciprocal regard. (Although they are more than acquaintances, are the people in this third tier truly friends? There ought to be a word to denote relationships that fall between that of acquaintance and friend, but there is not; the language—as Flaubert once remarked in attempting to express his love for his mistress—is inept.) After this third tier, in the stadium of my social life, we next move up to the grandstand of acquaintances and the bleachers of business associates. The first tier has not changed, and some members of it I have known for forty years. Some come down from the third tier to sit in the second; and a few from both the second and third tiers have departed, either through death or disagreement, before the game (my game) is done.

"How many intelligent people do you know in this city?" a famous writer once asked me. Ours is a city of roughly seven million people, of whom he said he had discovered three who were intelligent. High standards, these, and behind these standards was the clear implication that he valued intelligence above all else in friends. I hope I don't insult my friends when I say that it is not chiefly for their intelligence that I value them, even though all are intelligent. Some I value for their point of view; some for their loyalty and steadfastness; some for their seriousness and integrity; and two or three for their goodness, by which morally freighted word I mean to imply a combination of all these qualities.

When I think of the qualities that might unite the first tier of my friends, I am hard-pressed to come up with any persuasive pattern. I share interests with all of them, but they are not the same interests. Three of the seven are not bookish; four of them have politics different from mine. These same four are my exact contemporaries and indeed were high-school classmates; the other three are older than I, one of them more than twenty-five years older. Sexist swine that I am, all seven are men. (About women as friends, more presently.) None is orthodox in his religious views, and from two of them I have never heard any talk of religion at all; and although one would think one ought to know this about good friends, for all I know these two are atheists. (Must make a mental note to ask.) Two—not the same two—do not live in the same city as I do. Some among these seven good friends of mine have never even heard the names of the others. All seven are united in two things: first, none is what I think of as a high-maintenance friend—someone, that is, who requires regular ministering to in the form of visits, daily telephone calls, or lengthy letters; and, second, all have agreed to appreciate me.

Along with appreciation of me, we also, my close friends and I, do not disagree strongly on any important subject. I am not certain how much disagreement a close friendship can bear. I don't think I could have a close friend who is a racist or an anti-Semite. I am not sure I could have a close friend who despised my politics; yet agreement on politics, though pleasing in a friend, is not for me, I like to think, decisive. I have found myself among fairly large groups in which nearly everyone agreed with my political views, and a most comforting feeling such an atmosphere can provide. But I have always been impressed by Tocqueville's remark, made in his *Recollections,* that in politics "shared hatreds are almost always the basis for friendship." Hatreds, even cozily shared ones, are not a good basis for friendship; they too soon lead to one's having to accept the enemy of one's enemy as one's friend. The enemy of one's enemy, after all, can turn out to be himself a terrible character. Politics may make strange bedfellows but finally not very good friends, as witness John Reed, he of *Ten Days That Shook the World,* writing to H. J. Whigham, his editor on the *Metropolitan Magazine:* "You and I call ourselves friends, but we are not really friends, because we don't believe in the same things, and the time will come when we won't speak to each other."

Perhaps the reason the number of people I currently call friend seems so large has to do with my age, which is pretty near smack-dab middle age. Being middle-aged, I am able to have friends chronologically on either side of my own age: friends ten or twenty or even thirty years older than I and friends ten or now even twenty years younger. Meanwhile I retain my contemporaries, upon whom death has thus far made no inroads. With older friends, my age sometimes seems to dissolve, and in some cases I have felt something akin to experiential seniority to people twenty or so years older. I have been lucky in having some of the most interesting older people I have met take me seriously.

I had a friend whom I much admired, a man in his middle-eighties, whom I never met but knew only through correspondence. He first wrote to me about something I had written in this magazine; I answered his letter; and each time I wrote anything in this or any other magazine he would write to comment upon it and to dilate upon the same subject, usually turning out something much more interesting than I had written. In his business life he had been in advertising, and as the editor of the leading trade publication for the advertising industry he told me he saw it as his job to try to make advertising less vulgar. "You have only to look about you to see how successful I have been," he added. He had delicious irony and, being of an advanced age, he felt no need to dawdle over clichés or empty pieties. He seemed to read all the intellectual magazines, loved Trollope, closed out each evening with a page or two of Burton's *Anatomy of Melancholy* "because I find a page or two of his magnificent prose gives me a fitting way to end the day," and he even took the icy plunge into contemporrry philosophy. He described himself to me as a compulsive reader, and once, before a national election, noted:

> Are you inflicted these days with fervid pleas to save the country? I get at least one in every mail. I will, for the sake of something to read, read an invitation to attend the opening of a new cleaning establishment but I will not punish myself by reading campaign letters. After all, even a compulsive reader has limits.

I soon found that art of the pleasing afterglow of publication was receiving a letter from him. Thinking to deepen our relationship, I once wrote to him when I was planning a visit to a large city near his own smaller one to invite him and his wife to lunch. He wrote back to say that his eyesight was no longer good enough for him to drive on freeways, his hearing was all but shot, and, since he went out less and less, he really didn't have any fit clothes for dining out. He thanked me for my invitation but would have to refuse. Besides, he said, nowadays he was much at his best in his letters. I never made another such invitation and we continued to exchange letters for a year or so more, when, one early summer's day,

I received a letter from his daughter that began, "My father . . . died June 15th after a three-day illness. I know how much his correspondence with you meant to him. When he came home from the hospital last fall, the first thing he did was to have me sit down and type a letter to you on the horrors of modern baseball." A friend unmet but still missed.

Friendships with the young are very different. I have a number of such friendships, almost all of which have derived from my work as a teacher and a writer. I never set out to make them. But over a decade as a university teacher I have found eight or so students to whom, in spite of myself, my heart has gone out. All of them wish to be writers or to do one or another kind of literary work, and they, I assume, have found my acquaintance useful. I am a touch flattered by these friendships, for they function in the way that Aristotle prescribed for friendships between the young and the older—that is, these young friends honor me and I in my turn try to be helpful to them. With one exception, I do not have what Aristotle termed "friendship of the complete type with them." This is in part because we do not share a common past; in part because they, being young, live largely in the future while I try to live in the present; but in greatest part because, for now, we are not equals. I hope I do not treat them with condescension, yet the fact is that thus far along I have achieved more in the line of work to which they aspire, and it is this, ahievement, that makes us unequal. (As they grow older and achieve more, this inequality narrows.) I have been on the other side of such relationships, the younger man who pays homage to the older who repays him in the coin of utility: by advice, by helping through his connections, by permitting conversational intimacies. Perhaps because I have benefited from such relationships, I feel gratified to enter into similar ones myself, now in he role of senior man. I feel as if I am passing on the baton that had earlier been passed on to me.

I have found the most delightful of such unequal friendships to be the most unequal of all—that between a parent and his children. Here, again, Aristotle is my guide; he notes that the inequality derives from the fact that a parent may disown a son or daughter for dishonorable behavior but, because his or her debt is too great, a son or daughter may not disown a parent. Is it possible, though, to declare one's child one's friend? Is blood thicker than friendship? I have felt something very akin to friendship with both my sons, and felt it fairly early in their lives. I remember an autumn afternoon on which I went with my eldest son, then fourteen, to Sears, Roebuck to get new tires for my car. I thought the job could be done in an hour; it turned out to take four. We had lunch in a Chinese restaurant. We walked the streets of the neighborhood. We babbled away to each other on all sorts of subjects. Because the car was still not ready, we sojourned to the appliance section of the Sears store to watch a bit of the U.S. Open tennis tournament while we sat on rolled-up rugs. "What a boon companion this kid is,'' I thought. ''If he weren't my son, I can imagine him, when grown older, as my friend.''

There have been times in my life when I felt I required no further friends; I said to myself, as one says when dealt a set hand in draw poker, I'll play with these. But this hasn't been so, and I am pleased that it hasn't. Even now, in middle life, I continue to gain friendships while I watch other friendships lapse or otherwise fall away. I am not quite up to the ratio of Evelyn Waugh, who in this connection reported: ''In the first ten years of adult life I made a large number of friends. Now [Waugh was forty-three when he wrote this] on the average I make one new one a year and lose two.'' My own efficiency is not so high. I say ''efficiency'' because there are times when those of us who are promiscuous in our choice of friends feel we could do with many fewer. These are the times when the duties of friendship seem greatly to outweigh its pleasures. Lunches to attend, phone calls to return, letters to answer, obligations to repay—sometimes the duties of friendship (and these are the lighter duties) seem all too much. And they are often too much, unless, of course, one is friendless, in which case one pines for lunches to attend, phone calls to return, letters to answer, and obligations to repay. Friendship may know no happy medium.

Not everyone has the same appetite for friendship. P. G. Wodehouse once claimed that he required few friends. But then he was happily married and happy in his work, and this combination of good fortune doubtless lessens the need for friends. Friends are more important to the unmarried or the less-than-happily married, I think. That very social being, Henry James, who was a good friend to so many people and who always took the obligations of friendship with the utmost seriousness, nonetheless seemed, for much of his later life, a friendless man; and toward the end he remarked, plaintively, that he felt himself quite without contemporaries. Mencken claimed not to care much for the company of writers, yet for a long stretch he befriended, and championed, that otherwise lonely figure, Theodore Dreiser. Max Brod was a supremely good friend to Kafka. One senses that Melvile did not get anywhere near the spiritual sustenance he had hoped for from his friendship with Hawthorne. The friendship award in American literature, however, ought to go to William Dean Howells, who proved so good a friend to Henry James and Mark Twain, two writers who had very little use for each other.

Howells never had to introduce James to Twain, luckily enough for him, for introducing two of one's friends to each other can produce a tense moment. How delightful when they turn out to appreciate each other! How dreadful when they don't! Then there is the tricky terrain when one of your friends attacks another of your friends to you. Obviously, one must stage a defense; just as obviously, it must be a careful one, so that in defending your attacked friend you do not seem to attack the attacker. I have a close friend many of whose own friends I heartily despise and at whom, in lulls in our conversation, I sometimes like to toss verbal darts. I sympathize with my friend—I have been placed in this position myself—but not enough to let up on him. Why does it bother me that a man I like so much has friends I so dislike? Do I see it as a judgment on me? How, after all, can I have so good a friend who has such miserable taste in choosing friends?

What kind of friend am I? I try to be good but know I am not great. Perhaps it is that I am able to live very comfortably within my family, that my work fills up larger and larger portions of my days, including weekends; but I think it is accurate to say that I do not so much depend upon as enjoy my friends. Certainly, I am less and less aggressive in friendship; increasingly, I hang back and wait for friends to get in touch with me. I allow long stretches to pass in which I do not see people I care a good deal about. More and more I feel at greater ease as a guest than as a host. Apart from a small circe of very dear friends, the effort required of friendship seems to me harder and harder to make. Not long ago I let a close friendship die because I had heard that this friend had said things behind my back that were painful to me; more recently, I informed a friend who had moved to another, distant country that I could not keep up my end of our correspondence; since then a business associate with whom I was on my way to forming a friendship accused me of sharp dealing in a publishing matter, and so I suggested to him that, if he really believed what he said, we cease to speak to each other for a period of five years (we still have two years to go). Fifteen or twenty years ago I would have acted differently in each case: confronted my friend with what he said, kept up my end of the correspondence, argued my innocence with meticulous care. No longer.

As one grows older, one realizes better the limits of friendship. In my case, I have begun to realize how far I wish to go with my friendships, which is to differing limits with different friends. At the lowest end of the scale, I have false friends: I deem them false not because of any hypocrisy on their part or mine but because our friendship is made up of pretense on both sides, and it is the taste for cordiality that makes this pretense possible. As a former Good Guy, I retain a special weakness for entering into this kind of friendship, which is, like a magician's trunk, hollow at bottom.

Next on the scale are casual friendships, such as the one I have with the salesman at the shop where over the years I have bought my suits. This man and I have never addressed each other by any but our last names. Since I sometimes go two or three or four years without buying a new suit or jacket, the time between our meetings is ample. Yet when we do meet a fine feeling prevails, and I believe that this feeling is not owing to salesmanship alone. We have a certain regard for each other; we enjoy talking together about nothing in particular: my work, his travels, the city in which we both live. The last time I was in the shop I learned that, within the same month, his wife had died of cancer and he had had a stroke. People I have known better than he have died or suffered affliction, and yet their troubles have affected me less—or at least I have thought less about them. In friendship "casual" can be a tricky term.

I have other friends whom I don't think of as casual at all, whom I genuinely like, yet whom I am perfectly content to see on the most limited basis. I have a friend from college days with whom I go to one, sometimes two baseball games a year; we do not meet in winter. I have some friends I see only for lunch (and one or two with whom I am always planning to meet but never do meet for lunch). I have friends whom I see only when their wives are along; I have other friends whose husbands or wives I have never met. I have a friend who lives a mere two miles from where I do and whom I generally meet but once a year and sometimes less frequently than that. I have a category of friends whom I am pleased to run into but do not wish necessarily to see again soon; there is always a slightly embarrassed silence when we part without either of us saying, "We must get together again soon."

At a high-school reunion I recently attended—this was for the school at which I was not voted Most Popular, Best Liked, Most Friendly, etc.— I felt an odd mixture of elation and sadness, for such events, I realized, are really graveyards of dead friendships. It was lovely to see all these friends from my past. As Logan Pearsall Smith once put it, "The mere process of growing old together will make the slightest acquaintance seem a bosom friend." Hence the elation. The sadness came from the knowledge that there was no real hope of renewing any of these relationships, that at such meetings we jump back to our youth for this one night, but that by morning we shall recall why we haven't stayed friends through the years—because, that is, life has dragged us elsewhere and there is no point in pretending that we can drag ourselves back.

I number more than a few women in the second and third tiers of my friends, and yet I must add that I think of women as belonging in a different category of friends. Montaigne thought women incapable of friendship: "Besides, to tell the truth, the ordinary capacity of women is inadequate for that communion and fellowship which is the nurse of this sacred bond; nor does their soul seem firm enough to endure the strain of so tight and durable a knot." From such remarks are movements such as Women's Liberation made. One of the nicest consequences of the current Women's Liberation movement, I should say, is that it has brought out the fellowship (Flaubert is correct; the language is frequently inept) between women, making friendships between women seem, to pick up Montaigne's phrase, "tight and durable" indeed. But friendships between men and women are something else again. La Bruyère speaks interestingly to this point:

> Friendship may exist between a man and a woman, quite apart from any influence of sex. Yet a woman always looks upon man as a man, and so a man regards a woman. This intimacy is neither pure friendship nor pure love. It is a sentiment which stands alone.

I once asked Lillian Hellman about Edmund Wilson, a writer I much admired but never met and who, from his letters and diaries, seemed damned unpleasant. "You have to realize," she said, "that there were really two Edmund Wilsons: the man's and the woman's Edmund Wilson. If you were a man, Edmund had to prove his superiority to you by demonstrating that he was smarter than you. He was the intellectual equivalent of the playground bully. But if you were a woman, he could be very gentle, sweet, *galant,* even when he had no sexual interest in you. I of course knew him as a woman, and so have nothing but nice thoughts about him."

This seems to me very penetrating, and not alone about Edmund Wilson. I suspect we are all a bit two-faced in this regard, depending upon which sex we are facing. In discussing friendship, the moralists almost invariably contrast it with erotic love, holding friendship to be on a different level because of its disinterestedness, a quality to which erotic love can never lay claim. Too often when even the most decorous men and women are together the sound of flutes can be heard off in the forest, albeit neither party is prepared to gambol to them. Still, the gentlest wind of Eros can give an odd twist to a friendship between a man and a woman. Is it correct to say that when men and women are together they find t difficult to be themselves? Or is it more correct to say instead that they are most like themselves?

Let the flutes resound, let the winds of Eros blow the roof down, I know I am not ready to give up any of my female friends. I am not, in fact, ready to give up any of my friends. Aristotle says that a happy man has need of friends; I am not sure I qualify as his happy man, but I know I have need of mine: for the delight and support and affection they give. He also says that "it would seem actually impossible to be a great friend to many people," adding later, when considering the question of whether we need friends more in good fortune or in bad, that "the presence of friends . . . seems desirable in all circumstances." I agree on both points, while recognizing that I for one may have more friends than the philosophical limit allows. Still, this comes under a category that Aristotle, for all his marvelous comprehensibility, does not consider—that which I think of as the Happy Problem. For now I am fully prepared to live with mine.

Meaning and Idea

1. What is Epstein's definition of a *best friend?* Does he have a best friend? Does he feel he needs one?

2. What are the basic similarities among Epstein's friends? What are the basic differences? Which are more important to the author? What does he consider the primary necessities of friendship?

3. What does the author mean by an "unequal friendship"? What is the highest form of such a friendship? On what is it based? Is it always a negative condition as the name implies?

4. How does Epstein feel about friendships between men and women in general? How does he feel about his own such friendships? Are they as important to him as friendships between men and men? Why?

5. Toward the end of the essay, Estein asks the question, "What kind of friend am I?" Briefly summarize his response to that question.

Language, Form, Structure

1. How does Epstein's opening discussion of "Good Guys" lead him into an extended definition of *friendship?* How was Epstein a "Good Guy"? In what ways did he fail as one? How are these successes and failures related to his definition of *friendship?*

2. The beginning tone of this essay is a little smug, even a little sarcastic. Yet, the tone seems to change considerably as the essay proceeds. What does it change to? Can you identify a particular point at which that change occurs? What tone dominates the essay once the sarcasm fades?

3. Throughout the essay, the author makes use of classification to help organize his definitions. What is his categorical breakdown of the types and activities of "Good Guys"? How does he classify his various "tiers" of friends? Toward the end of the essay, how does Epstein use his understanding of the "limits of friendship" to define different types of friends? What are those types?

4. Epstein writes of himself at one point in this essay: "Sexist swine that I am." Identify examples of what you consider to be sexist language or a sexually biased organization of ideas used to formulate his definition of friendship.

5. Select ten words unfamiliar to you in this essay, look them up in a dictionary, and write sentences of your own for each.

Ideas for Writing

1. Write a definition of *a best friend.* You may want to define this term in general or to focus your definition on a qualitative analysis of your own best friend.

2. In a thesis statement and introductory paragraph, answer for yourself Epstein's question, "What kind of friend am I?" Then continue your essay as an extended definition of that particular type of friend.

3. Throughout this essay, Epstein makes numerous literary allusions, both to famous writers' works and friendships. Comment on their appropriateness—both in choice and scope—to this essay. What is their purpose? Are they all necessary? In general, do you feel they enhance or detract from the writing? In what ways?

Julio Cortázar
AXOLOTL

> Julio Cortázar is an Argentine writer born in Belgium in 1914. He is known for the surrealism of his fiction—life is often a barely decipherable puzzle filled with strange images. His novels, translated into English, include *The Winners* (1960), *Hopscotch* (1963), and *Sixty-Two: A Model Kit* (1968), and his short story collections include *End of the Game* (1956) and *A Change of Light and Other Stories* (1980). His story, "Blow-Up," was the basis for a critically acclaimed film by the Italian director Michelangelo Antonioni in 1966.
>
> A narrator becomes an ancient fish, and author Julio Cortázar defines for us not only a thing, but also its existential essence and the process of discovering that essence. In reading this intriguing story, pay close attention to uses of description and analogy.

There was a time when I thought a great deal about the axolotls. I went to see them in the aquarium at the Jardin des Plantes and stayed for hours watching them, observing their immobility, their faint movements. Now I am an axolotl.

I got to them by chance one spring morning when Paris was spreading its peacock tail after a wintry Lent. I was heading down the boulevard Port-Royal, then I took Saint-Marcel and L'Hôpital and saw green among all that grey and remembered the lions. I was friend of the lions and panthers, but had never gone into the dark, humid building that was the aquarium. I left my bike against the gratings and went to look at the tulips. The lions were sad and ugly and my panther was asleep. I decided on the aquarium, looked obliquely at banal fish until, unexpectedly, I hit it off with the axolotls. I stayed watching them for an hour and left, unable to think of anything else.

In the library at Sainte-Geneviève, I consulted a dictionary and learned that axolotls are the larval stage (provided with gills) of a species of salamander of the genus Ambystoma. That they were Mexican I knew already by looking at them and their little pink Aztec faces and the placard at the top of the tank. I read that specimens of them had been found in Africa capable of living on dry land during the periods of drought, and continuing their life under water when the rainy season came. I found their Spanish name, *ajolote,* and the mention that they were edible, and that their oil was used (no longer used, it said) like cod-liver oil.

I didn't care to look up any of the specialized works, but the next day I went back to the Jardin des Plantes. I began to go every morning, morning and afternoon some days. The aquarium guard smiled perplexedly taking my ticket. I would lean up against the iron bar in front of the tanks and set to watching them. There's nothing strange in this, because after the first minute I knew that we were linked, that something infinitely lost and distant kept pulling us together. It had been enough to detain me that first morning in front of the sheet of glass where some bubbles rose through the water. The axolotls huddled on the wretched narrow (only I can know how narrow and wretched) floor of moss and stone in the tank. There were nine specimens, and the majority pressed their heads against the glass, looking with their eyes of gold at whoever came near them. Disconcerted, almost ashamed, I felt it a lewdness to be peering at these silent and immobile figures heaped at the bottom of the tank. Mentally I isolated one, situated on the right and somewhat apart from the others, to study it better. I saw a rosy little body, translucent (I thought of those Chinese figurines of milky glass), looking like a small lizard about six inches long, ending in a fish's tail of extraordinary delicacy, the most sensitive part of our body. Along the back ran a transparent fin which joined with the tail, but what obsessed me was the feet, of the slenderest nicety, ending in tiny fingers with minutely human nails. And then I discovered its eyes, its face. Inexpressive features, with no other trait save the eyes, two orifices, like brooches, wholly of transparent gold, lacking any life but looking, letting themselves be penetrated by my look, which seemed to travel past the golden level and lose itself in a diaphanous interior mystery. A very slender black halo ringed the eye and etched it onto the pink flesh, onto the rosy stone of the head, vaguely triangular, but with curved and irregular sides which gave it a total likeness to a statuette corroded by time. The mouth was masked by the triangular plane of the face, its considerable size would be guessed only in profile; in front a delicate crevice barely slit the lifeless stone. On both sides of the head where the ears should have been, there grew three tiny sprigs red as coral, a vegetal outgrowth, the gills, I suppose. And they were the only thing quick about it; every ten or fifteen seconds the sprig pricked up stiffly and again subsided. Once in a while a foot would barely move, I saw the diminutive toes poise mildly on the moss. It's that we don't enjoy moving a lot, and the tank is so cramped—we barely move in any direction and we're hitting one of the others with our tail or our head—difficulties arise, fights, tiredness. The time feels like it's less if we stay quietly.

It was their quietness that made me lean toward them fascinated the first time I saw the axolotls. Obscurely I seemed to understand their secret will, to abolish space and time with an indifferent immobility. I knew better later; the gill contraction, the tentative reckoning of the delicate feet on the stones, the abrupt swimming (some of them swim with a simple undulation of the body) proved to me that they were capable of escaping that mineral lethargy in which they spent whole hours. Above all else, their eyes obsessed me. In the standing tanks on either side of them, different fishes showed me the simple stupidity of their handsome eyes so similar to our own. The eyes of the axolotls spoke to me of the presence of a different life, of another way of seeing. Glueing my face to the glass (the guard would cough fussily once in a while), I tried to see better those diminutive golden points, that entrance to the infinitely slow and remote world of these rosy creatures. It was useless to tap with one finger on the glass directly in front of their faces; they never gave the least reaction. The golden eyes continued burning with their soft, terrible light; they continued looking at me from an unfathomable depth which made me dizzy.

And nevertheless they were close. I knew it before this, before being an axolotl. I learned it the day I came near them for the first time. The anthropomorphic features of a monkey reveal the reverse of what most people believe, the distance that is traveled from them to us. The absolute lack of similarity between axolotls and human beings proved to me that my recognition was valid, that I was not propping myself up with easy analogies. Only the little hands . . . But an eft, the common newt, has such hands also, and we are not at all alike. I think it was the axolotls' heads, that triangular pink shape with the tiny eyes of gold. That looked and knew. That laid the claim. They were not *animals*

It would seem easy, almost obvious, to fall into mythology. I began seeing in the axolotls a metamorphosis which did not succeed in revoking a mysterious humanity. I imagined them aware, slaves of their bodies, condemned infinitely to the silence of the abyss, to a hopeless meditation. Their blind gaze, the diminutive gold disc without expression and nonetheless terribly shining, went through me like a message: "Save us, save us.'' I caught myself mumbling words of advice, conveying childish hopes. They continued to look at me, immobile; from time to time the rosy branches of the gills stiffened. In that instant I felt a muted pain; perhaps they were seeing me, attracting my strength to penetrate into the impenetrable thing of their lives. They were not human beings, but I had found in no animal such a profound relation with myself. The axolotls were like witnesses of something, and at times like horrible judges. I felt ignoble in front of them; there was such a terrifying purity in those transparent eyes. They were larvas, but larva means disguise and also phantom. Behind those Aztec faces, without expression but of an implacable cruelty, what semblance was awaiting its hour?

I was afraid of them. I think that had it not been for feeling the proximity of other visitors and the guard, I would not have been bold enough to remain alone with them. "You eat them alive with your eyes, hey," the guard said, laughing; he likely thought I was a little cracked. What he didn't notice was that it was they devouring me slowly with their eyes, in a cannabalism of gold. At any distance from the aquarium, I had only to think of them, it was as though I were being affected from a distance. It got to the point that I was going every day, and at night I thought of them immobile in the darkness, slowly putting a hand out which immediately encountered another. Perhaps their eyes could see in the dead of night, and for them the day continued indefinitely. The eyes of axolotls have no lids.

I know now that there was nothing strange, that that had to occur. Leaning over in front of the tank each morning, the recognition was greater. They were suffering, every fiber of my body reached toward that stifled pain, that stiff torment at the bottom of the tank. They were lying in wait for something, a remote dominion destroyed, an age of liberty when the world had been that of the axolotls. Not possible that such a terrible expression which was attaining the overthrow of that forced blankness on their stone faces should carry any message other than one of pain, proof of that eternal sentence, of that liquid hell they were undergoing. Hopelessly, I wanted to prove to myself that my own sensibility was projecting a non-existent consciousness upon the axolotls. They and I knew. So there was nothing strange in what happened. My face was pressed against the glass of the aquarium, my eyes were attempting once more to penetrate the mystery of those eyes of gold without iris, without pupil. I saw from very close up the face of an axolotl immobile next to the glass. No transition and no surprise, I saw my face against the glass, I saw it on the outside of the tank, I saw it on the other side of the glass. Then my face drew back and I understood.

Only one thing was strange: to go on thinking as usual, to know. To realize that was, for the first moment, like the horror of a man buried alive awaking to his fate. Outside, my face came close to the glass again, I saw my mouth, the lips compressed with the effort of understanding the axolotls. I was an axolotl and now I knew instantly that no understanding was possible. He was outside the aquarium, his thinking was a thinking outside the tank. Recognizing him, being him himself, I was an axolotl and in my world. The horror began—I learned in the same moment—of believing myself prisoner in the body of an axolotl, metamorphosed into him with my human mind intact, buried alive in an axolotl, condemned to move lucidly among unconscious creatures. But that stopped when a foot just grazed my face, when I moved just a little to one side and saw an axolotl next to me who was looking at me, and understood that he knew also, no communication possible, but very clearly. Or I was also in him, or all of us were thinking humanlike, incapable of expression, limited to the golden splendor of our eyes looking at the face of the man pressed against the aquarium.

He returned many times, but he comes less often now. Weeks pass without his showing up. I saw him yesterday, he looked at me for a long time and left briskly. It seemed to me that he was not so much interested in us any more, that he was coming out of habit. Since the only thing I do is think, I could think about him a lot. It occurs to me that at the beginning we continued to communicate, that he felt more than ever one with the mystery which was claiming him. But the bridges were broken between him and me, because what was his obsession is now an axolotl, alien to his human life. I think that at the beginning I was capable of returning to him in a certain way—ah, only in a certain way—and of keeping awake his desire to know us better. I am an axolotl for good now, and if I think like a man it's only because every axolotl thinks like a man inside his rosy stone resemblance. I believe that all this succeeded in communicating something to him in those first days, when I was still he. And in this final solitude to which he no longer comes, I console myself by thinking that perhaps he is going to write a story about me, that, believing he's making up a story, he's going to write all this about axolotls.

Meaning and Idea

1. What is an *axolotl?* Look up the term in an encyclopedia so that you have a clear picture of what Cortázar is writing about.

2. How did the narrator come to look at axolotls? What first attracted him to them? How did his interest grow? Which of their physical features most concerned him? Why?

3. Who is the "He" who is first mentioned in the next-to-the-last paragraph? What does the narrator think of himself at the end of the story?

Language, Form, Structure

1. What abstract concepts is Cortázar attempting to define in this story? Does he succeed in defining them for you? How?

2. At one point the narrator insists, "I was not propping myself up with easy analogies." What is an *analogy?* How in fact is analogy used as a major technique in this story?

3. The narrator uses personification throughout the story, yet there is a curious two-way process taking place: At some points, he imparts human characteristics to the axolotls; at others, he transfers axolotl features to humans. Find instances of each process in the story.

4. Identify the point in the narrative development (not in the first paragraph) at which the narrator believes he has become an axolotl. How is description used to accomplish this transformation?

5. Make sure you know the definitions of the following words from this story: obliquely; banal; placard; translucent; diaphanous; diminutive; lethargy; unfathomable; anthropomorphic; abyss; ignoble; metamorphosed; lucidly. Choose any five of these words and use them in original sentences.

Ideas for Writing

1. Write a definition of the term *self-image.* Begin with a technical definition (perhaps from a psychology textbook) and then develop your own less technical definition.

2. Define the concept of *metamorphosis.* You may want to attempt to deal with the various levels of metamorphoses: the technical/scientific; the emotional; the surreal (as in Franz Kafka's story *The Metamorphosis*). Organize your essay of extended definition by using analogies.

3. An old adage states that "The eyes are the mirror of the soul." Write an essay in which you discuss to what extent Cortázar's story supports that adage. Does "Axolotl" go beyond our usual understanding of that saying? How?

Marianne Moore
POETRY

> Marianne Moore (1887–1972) was born near St. Louis a year before another famous American poet, T. S. Eliot, was born there. Moore and her mother later moved to Carlisle, Pennsylvania, where she attended the Metzger Institute, then took her degree at Bryn Mawr College. She originally considered being a painter, but abandoned that pursuit to try writing poetry and to teach stenography at the U.S. Indian School in Carlisle from 1911 to 1915. In 1918, she moved to New York City where she worked as a tutor and as an assistant in the New York Public Library, and where she became one of the most ardent Brooklyn Dodgers fans. For three years, Moore edited *The Dial,* an established literary review of the time.
>
> "Poetry" is a classic example of Marianne Moore's straightforward style of poetry. She defines for us that most elusive of terms, effecting a synthesis of the abstract and the concrete, which she considered so vital.

I, too, dislike it: there are things that are important beyond
      all this fiddle.
  Reading it, however, with a perfect contempt for it, one
      discovers in
  it after all, a place for the genuine.
    Hands that can grasp, eyes
      that can dilate, hair that can rise
        if it must, these things are important not because a   5
high-sounding interpretation can be put upon them but
      because they are
  useful. When they become so derivative as to become
      unintelligible,
  the same thing may be said for all of us, that we
    do not admire what   10
      we cannot understand: the bat
        holding on upside down or in quest of something to

eat, elephants pushing, a wild horse taking a roll, a tireless
      wolf under
a tree, the immovable critic twitching his skin like a
   horse that feels a flea, the base-   15
ball fan, the statistician—
   nor is it valid
      to discriminate against 'business documents and

school-books'; all these phenomena are important. One
      must make a distinction   20
however: when dragged into prominence by half poets,
      the result is not poetry,
nor till the poets among us can be
   'literalists of
   the imagination'—above   25
      insolence and triviality and can present

for inspection, imaginary gardens with real toads in them,
      shall we have
it. In the meantime, if you demand on the one hand,
the raw material of poetry in
   all its rawness and   30
   that which is on the other hand
      genuine, then you are interested in poetry.

Meaning and Idea

1. What is the "it" of stanza one? What is "all this fiddle"? What is "the genuine"?

2. Summarize, in your own words, Marianne Moore's definition of poetry. What ideal combination of elements makes up genuine poetry? How is the image "imaginary gardens with real toads in them" an example of this ideal combination?

3. What do you suppose Moore meant by "half poets"?

4. What is Moore's attitude toward critics? Do you think that she was expressing her feelings about critics in general or about one specific critic? Why?

Language, Form, Structure

1. How would you characterize Moore's poem—as essentially concrete or abstract? Why? Which is more important to Moore?

2. How is the technique of exemplification important to stanzas two and three? What is exemplified in each? What examples are offered?

3. For whom did Moore intend this definition? How do you know? How does her audience affect her style here?

4. The phrases "business documents and school-books" and "literalists of the imagination" refer to writings by two of the world's greatest writers—Tolstoy and Yeats. What value do such references add to Moore's definition of poetry?

5. Be sure you understand how Moore uses the following words: dilate; derivative; quest; phenomena; insolence; triviality.

Ideas for Writing

1. Write a definition of the term *satisfaction*. Distinguish between abstract and concrete manifestations of the term, and integrate them to form your definition.

2. Write your own prose definition of *poetry*. You may use references to specific poems or poets, or you may make your definition more general in nature.

3. In the final edition of her *Collected Poems,* Moore ended this poem at the word *genuine* in line 3. What do you think of that version of the poem? Why do you think she might have done that? Is it as effective as a definition (or as a poem) in that severely abridged version? Write an essay in which you compare the two versions.

Archibald MacLeish
ARS POETICA

Archibald MacLeish (1892–1982) was among the more controversial of modern American poets—for his political and social concerns, though, rather than for his poetry. MacLeish was born in Glencoe, Illinois, and took his B.A. at Yale and his law degree at Harvard. He served in World War I (an experience that deeply affected him), and he later was in the forefront of the modernist movement in Paris. He was the recipient of three Pulitzer Prizes for *Conquistador* (1932), a long narrative poem for which MacLeish retraced Cortez's route through Mexico; for *Collected Poems 1917–1952* (1952); and for *J. B.* (1958), a verse drama about the biblical Job. His writing in the 1930s reflected his concern with the rise of fascism and what he saw as his fellow poets' "softness" on this issue. In 1939, he was appointed Librarian of Congress by Franklin Roosevelt, and he served in that post for five years. MacLeish was an Assistant Secretary of State from 1944 to 1945, and a founder and chairman of the first UNESCO conference in 1946.

Archibald MacLeish's "Ars Poetica" defines a process, rather than the thing itself. As you read this poem, be aware of how closely MacLeish follows his own advice about poetry-making.

A poem should be palpable and mute
As a globed fruit,

Dumb
As old medallions to the thumb,

Silent as the sleeve-worn stone
Of casement ledges where the moss has grown—   5

A poem should be wordless
As the flight of birds.

A poem should be motionless in time
As the moon climbs,   10

Leaving, as the moon releases
Twig by twig the night-entangled trees,

Leaving, as the moon behind the winter leaves,
Memory by memory the mind—

A poem should be motionless in time   15
As the moon climbs.

A poem should be equal to:
Not true.

For all the history of grief
An empty doorway and a maple leaf.   20

For love
The leaning grasses and two lights above the sea—

A poem should not mean
But be.

Meaning and Idea

1. Translated from the Latin, *Ars Poetica* means "the art of poetry." What is MacLeish's definition, in summary, of the art of poetry?

2. Explain the meaning of lines 17–18:

A poem should be equal to:
Not true.

"Equal to" what? Why, or how, "Not true"?

3. Explain how a poem can "be" but "not mean" (lines 23–24).

4. Has MacLeish defined *poetry* in this poem? If not, what is the focus of his definition?

Language, Form, Structure

1. Analyze MacLeish's use of *similes* in the opening stanza, his use of *repetition* in stanza two, and his use of *negation* (see Chapter introduction, page 465) in various places.

2. Which pair of lines exemplifies the process of image-making in poetry? Explain each.

3. A *paradox* is a statement that is seemingly contradictory or opposed to logic, yet also appears to be true. How is line 7, "A poem should be wordless," paradoxical? How *can* a poem be wordless?

4. Know the meanings of these words: palpable; medallions; casement.

Ideas for Writing

1. Choose a process which you know well and write a definition essay entitled, "The Art of _____" (fill in the blank with the process).

2. Define *marriage* by outlining what it *should be* or what effects it *should* have. Use some negation as a part of your development.

3. Write a short essay on how the mood and effect of this poem would be different had MacLeish used *is* instead of *should be* throughout the poem. How does the latter choice affect the poet's relationship with the reader? Which do you prefer? Why?

4. Write an essay in which you compare Marianne Moore's definition of poetry (in "Poetry," pages 504–505) and MacLeish's. In your paper make specific references to the text.

William Blake
THE TIGER

William Blake (1757–1827) was an English poet, artist, and mystic. Despite the fact that he was virtually unknown in his time, and only one early volume of his poetry, *Poetical Sketches* (1783), was published during his lifetime, Blake's written and visual works greatly influenced the English romantics and subsequent generations. His work expresses a mixture of naive lack of sentimentality (as in *Songs of Innocence,* 1789, and *Songs of Experience,* 1794) with mythological imagination (as in *The Marriage of Heaven and Hell,* 1790, and *Jerusalem,* 1804–1820).

Blake's well-known poem, "The Tiger," perhaps on first sounding seems to be an innocent rhyme about an animal. But, on closer reading, "The Tiger" exposes the many levels of meaning that define this "fearful symmetry."

*7*iger! Tiger! burning bright
In the forests of the night,
What immortal hand or eye
Could frame thy fearful symmetry?

In what distant deeps or skies   5
Burnt the fire of thine eyes?
On what wings dare he aspire?
What the hand dare seize the fire?

And what shoulder, and what art,
Could twist the sinews of thy heart?   10
And when thy heart began to beat,
What dread hand forged thy dread feet?

What the hammer? what the chain?
In what furnace was thy brain?
What the anvil? what dread grasp   15
Dare its deadly terrors clasp?

When the stars threw down their spears,
And watered heaven with their tears,
Did he smile his work to see?
Did he who made the Lamb make thee?   20

Tiger! Tiger! burning bright
In the forests of the night,
What immortal hand or eye,
Dare frame thy fearful symmetry?

Meaning and Idea

1. Describe Blake's tiger in your own words.

2. What is meant by the tiger's "fearful symmetry"?

3. Who is the "he" of stanza five? Why does Blake question "his" work?

Language, Form, Structure

1. A *symbol* is a word that stands for something else so that its meaning reaches beyond the literal. Of what is the tiger a symbol in this poem? What animal expresses its opposite symbolic value in this poem? Explain how symbolism is used as a basis of definition in this poem. How is context important for symbolic value here?

2. Blake attempts to define *the tiger* through a series of questions. How does he organize those questions? How do they form the basis of a definition in this poem?

3. Why is the word and punctuation, *Tiger!* repeated at the beginning of the poem? Why does the last stanza repeat the first? How? What is the purpose of the repetition in this poem?

4. What mood does the poem evoke? How does Blake accomplish the mood?

5. Briefly comment on the uses and types of metaphor in this poem.

6. Write definitions for: immortal; aspire; sinews; anvil.

Ideas for Writing

1. Write a definition of a particular animal or object. Try to introduce symbolic elements in your definition so that it reflects a feeling or condition.

2. Write a definition of *fear* or *bravery* organizing your material in the framework of a series of questions. However, unlike Blake, you should use your questions as departure points for explicit answers that will aid your definition.

3. Earlier in this chapter, you read a poem by Marianne Moore, "Poetry," in which she refers to a criticism written about Blake by the poet W. B. Yeats. Yeats wrote:

The limitation of his view was from the very intensity of his vision; he was a too literal realist of imagination as others are of nature; and because he believed that the figures seen by the mind's eye, when exalted by inspiration, were 'eternal existences,' symbols of divine essences, he hated grace of style that might obscure their lineaments.

Comment on "The Tiger" in light of Yeats's criticism. Specific to this poem, do you agree or disagree with Yeats?

Richard Rodriguez
COMPLEXION

Richard Rodriguez was born in San Francisco in 1944, and held a variety of jobs, including janitor, before becoming a full-time writer in 1981, a transition which was facilitated by the publication and positive reception of *Hunger of Memory: The Education of Richard Rodriguez* in 1982. He has received a Fullbright Fellowship and a National Endowment for the Humanities Fellowship. Rodriguez's work often chronicles his (and others') alienation from their own cultures; he has led a strong campaign against affirmative action which he views as yet another form of cultural alienation. He claims George Orwell as his prose model.

In this selection from *Hunger of Memory: The Education of Richard Rodriguez* (1982), the author defines for us what is essentially an objective, physical term. However, the nature of his personal definition of the physical takes us beneath the surface to the emotional roots of the term.

*C*omplexion. My first conscious experience of sexual excitement concerns my complexion. One summer weekend, when I was around seven years old, I was at a public swimming pool with the whole family. I remember sitting on the damp pavement next to the pool and seeing my mother, in the spectators' bleachers, holding my younger sister on her lap. My mother, I noticed, was watching my father as he stood on a diving board, waving to her. I watched her wave back. Then saw her radiant, bashful, astonishing smile. In that second I sensed that my mother and father had a relationship I knew nothing about. A nervous excitement encircled my stomach as I saw my mother's eyes follow my father's figure curving into the water. A second or two later, he emerged. I heard him call out. Smiling, his voice sounded, buoyant, calling me to swim to him. But turning to se him, I caught my mother's eye. I heard her shout over to me. In Spanish she called through the crowd: 'Put a towel on over your shoulders.' In public, she didn't want to say why. I knew.

That incident anticipates the shame and sexual inferiority I was to feel in later years because of my dark complexion. I was to grow up an ugly child. Or one who thought himself ugly. (*Feo.*) One night when I was eleven or twelve years old, I locked myself in the bathroom and carefully regarded my reflection in the mirror over the sink. Without any pleasure I studied my skin. I turned on the faucet. (In my mind I heard the swirling voices of aunts, and even my mother's voice, whispering, whispering incessantly about lemon juice solutions and dark, *feo* children.) With a bar of soap, I fashioned a thick ball of lather. I began soaping my arms, I took my father's straight razor out of the medicine cabinet. Slowly, with steady deliberateness, I put the blade against my flesh, pressed it as close as I could without cutting, and moved it up and down across my skin to see if I could get out, somehow lessen, the dark. All I succeeded in doing, however, was in shaving my arms bare of their hair. For as I noted with disappointment, the dark would not come out. It remained. Trapped. Deep in the cells of my skin.

Throughout adolescence, I felt myself mysteriously marked. Nothing else about my appearance would concern me so much as the fact that my complexion was dark. My mother would say how sorry she was that there was not money enough to get braces to straighten my teeth. But I never bothered about my teeth. In three-way mirrors at department stores, I'd see my profile dramatically defined by a long nose, but it was really only the color of my skin that caught my attention.

I wasn't afraid that I would become a menial laborer because of my skin. Nor did my complexion make me feel especially vulnerable to racial abuse. (I didn't really consider my dark skin to be a racial characteristic. I would have been only too happy to look as Mexican as my light-skinned older brother.) Simply, I judged myself ugly. And, since the women in my family had been the ones who discussed it in such worried tones, I felt my dark skin made me unattractive to women.

Thirteen years old. Fourteen. In a grammar school art class, when the assignment was to draw a self-portrait, I tried and I tried but could not bring myself to shade in the face on the paper to anything like my actual tone. With disgust then I would come face to face with myself in mirrors. With disappointment I located myself in class photographs—my dark face undefined by the camera which had clearly described the white faces of classmates. Or I'd see my dark wrist against my long-sleeved white shirt.

I grew divorced from my body. Insecure, overweight, listless. On hot summer days when my rubber-soled shoes soaked up the heat from the sidewalk, I kept my head down. Or walked in the shade. My mother didn't need anymore to tell me to watch out for the sun. I denied myself a sensational life. The normal, extraordinary, animal excitement of feeling my body alive—riding shirtless on a bicycle in the warm wind created by furious self-propelled motion—the sensations that first had excited in me a sense of my maleness, I denied. I was too ashamed of my body. I wanted to forget that I had a body because I had a brown body. I was grateful that none of my classmates ever mentioned the fact.

I continued to see the *braceros,* those men I resembled in one way and, in another way, didn't resemble at all. On the watery horizon of a Valley afternoon, I'd see them. And though I feared looking like them, it was with silent envy that I regarded them still. I envied them their physical lives, their freedom to violate the taboo of the sun. Closer to home I would notic the shirtless construction workers, the roofers, the sweating men tarring the street in front of the house. And I'd see the Mexican gardeners. I was unwilling to admit the attraction of their lives. I tried to deny it by looking away. But what was denied became strongly desired.

In high school physical education classes, I withdrew, in the regular company of five or six classmates, to a distant corner of a football field where we smoked and talked. Our company was composed of bodies too short or too tall, all graceless and all—except mine—pale. Our conversation was usually witty. (In fact we were intelligent.) If we referred to the athletic contests around us, it was with sarcasm. With savage scorn I'd refer to the 'animals' playing football or baseball. It would have been important for me to have joined them. Or for me to have taken off my shirt, to have let the sun burn dark on my skin, and to have run barefoot on the warm wet grass. It would have been very important. Too important. It would have been too telling a gesture—to admit the desire for sensation, the body, my body.

Fifteen, sixteen. I was a teenager shy in the presence of girls. Never dated. Barely could talk to a girl without stammering. In high school I went to several dances, but I never managed to ask a girl to dance. So I stopped going. I cannot remember high school years now with the parade of typical images: bright drive-ins or gliding blue shadows of a Junior Prom. At home most weekend nights, I would pass evenings reading. Like those hidden, precocious adolescents who have no real-life sexual experiences, I read a great deal of romantic fiction. 'You won't find it in your books,' my brother would playfully taunt me as he prepared to go to a party by freezing the crest of the wave in his hair with sticky pomade. Through my reading, however, I developed a fabulous and sophisticated sexual imagination. At seventeen, I may not have known how to engage a girl in small talk, but I had read *Lady Chatterley's Lover*.

It annoyed me to hear my father's teasing: that I would never know what 'real work' is; that my hands were so soft. I think I knew it was his way of admitting pleasure and pride in my academic success. But I didn't smile. My mother said she was glad her children were getting their educations and would not be pushed around like *los pobres*. I heard the remark ironically as a reminder of my separation from *los braceros*. At such times I suspected that education was making me effeminate. The odd thing, however, was that I did not judge my classmates so harshly. Nor did I consider my male teachers in high school effeminate. It was only myself I judged against some shadowy, mythical Mexican laborer—dark like me, yet very different.

Language was crucial. I knew that I had violated the ideal of the *macho* by becoming such a dedicated student of language and literature. *Machismo* was a word never exactly defined by the persons who used it. (It was best described in the 'proper' behavior of men.) Women at home, nevertheless, would repeat the old Mexican dictum that a man should be *feo, fuerte, y formal*. 'The three F's,' my mother called them, smiling slyly. *Feo* I took to mean not literally ugly so much as ruggedly handsome. (When my mother and her sisters spent a loud, laughing afternoon determining ideal male good looks, they finally settled on the actor Gilbert Roland, who was neither too pretty nor ugly but had looks 'like a man.') *Fuerte,* 'strong,' seemed to mean not physical strength as much as inner strength, character. A dependable man is *fuerte*. *Fuerte* for that reason was a characteristic subsumed by the last of the three qualities, and the one I most often considered—*formal*. To be *formal* is to be steady. A man of responsibility, a good provider. Someone *formal* is also constant. A person to be relied upon in adversity. A sober man, a man of high seriousness.

I learned a great deal about being *formal* just by listening to the way my father and other male relatives of his generation spoke. A man was not silent necessarily. Nor was he limited in the tones he could sound. For example, he could tell a long, involved, humorous story and laugh at his own humor with high-pitched giggling. But a man was not talkative the way a woman could be. It was permitted a woman to be gossipy and chatty. (When one heard many voices in a room, it was usually women who were talking.) Men spoke much less rapidly. And often men spoke in monologues. (When one voice sounded in a crowded room, it was most often a man's voice one heard.) More important than any of this was the fact that a man never verbally revealed his emotions. Men did not speak about their unease in moments of crisis or danger. It was the woman who worried aloud when her husband got laid off from work. At times of illness or death in the family, a man was usually quiet, even silent. Women spoke up to voice prayers. In distress, women always sounded quick ejaculations to God or the Virgin; women prayed in clearly audible voices at a wake held in a funeral parlor. And on the subject of love, a woman was verbally expansive. She spoke of her yearning and delight. A married man, if he spoke publicly about love, usually did so with playful, mischievous irony. Younger, unmarried men more often were quiet. (The *macho* is a silent suitor. *Formal*.)

At home I was quiet, so perhaps I seemed *formal* to my relations and other Spanish-speaking visitors to the house. But outside the house—my God!—I talked. Particularly in class or alone with my teachers, I chattered. (Talking seemed to make teachers think I was bright.) I often was proud of my way with words. Though, on other occasions, for example, when I would hear my mother busily speaking to women, it would occur to me that my attachment to words made me like her. Her son. Not *formal* like my father. At such times I even suspected that my nostalgia for sounds—the noisy, intimate Spanish sounds of my past—was nothing more than effeminate yearning.

High school English teachers encouraged me to describe very personal feelings in words. Poems and short stories I wrote, expressing sorrow and loneliness, were awarded high grades. In my bedroom were books by poets and novelists—books that I loved—in which male writers published feelings the men in my family never revealed or acknowledged in words. And it seemed to me that there was something unmanly about my attachment to literature. Even today, when so much about the myth of the *macho* no longer concerns me, I cannot altogether evade such notions. Writing these pages, admitting my embarrassment or my guilt, admitting my sexual anxieties and my physical insecurity, I have not been able to forget that I am not being *formal*.

So be it.

Meaning and Idea

1.   In the incident by the swimming pool when the author is 12, why does his mother tell him to put a towel over his shoulders? Why does she say it in Spanish? What was the effect of the comment on Rodriguez?

2.   What two expected results of his dark complexion did Rodriguez not fear? Why? What result did he fear most? How does he develop that fear?

3.   What does Rodriguez mean when he says he was *feo*? What were the effects of the author's considering himself *feo* during his adolescence? What were the longer-lasting effects?

4.   How does Rodriguez compare himself to the *braceros,* construction workers, and Mexican gardeners? Why does he envy them?

5.   What is Rodriguez's definition of *machismo*? What were the "three F's"? How did Rodriguez arrive at his own definition of each? How did he see himself in relation to the "three F's"? What is his present view of himself in relation to them?

Language, Form, Structure

1.   What is the main term defined in this essay? How does Rodriguez use various lesser definitions to build up support for the whole definition? Why does the author define both English and Spanish words? How does he connect them?

2.   What is the connection between the use of language and the definition of character traits or feelings according to this essay? Explain fully at least two examples.

3. In the paragraph that begins "Thirteen years old. Fourteen." Rodriguez writes about his class photographs. He says: "I located myself . . . my dark face undefined by the camera." What is the meaning of the word *undefined* here? How does it relate to the overall definitional context of this essay?

4. How does Rodriguez use narration as an integral part of his definition? How does he arrange his narrations?

5. Write definitions for these words from the essay: buoyant; menial; vulnerable; precocious; pomade; effeminate; subsumed.

Ideas for Writing

1. Write an extended definition of the term *cultural* or *racial stereotype*. You may choose to focus on the stereotypes you know about your own cultural or racial group and develop your definition through personal narrative.

2. Write a definition of the term *ugly*. Use negation as your main development technique.

3. At the end of this essay, Rodriguez writes:

> Writing these pages, admitting my embarrassment or my guilt, admitting my sexual anxieties and my physical insecurity, I have not been able to forget that I am not being *formal*.

Do you feel that men exposing their emotions so publicly in writing is "unmanly" as Rodriguez fears it may be? Do you feel Rodriguez's writing in this essay is in any way effeminate? On a broader scale, do you feel there are appropriate differences in subject and tone in writing for male and female writers? Why?

Chapter Nine
ARGUMENTATION AND PERSUASION

*W*e devote a good deal of our daily thinking and talking time to reasoning, often reasoning with someone or other to convince the person to believe something that we ourselves believe, or to take some particular action we believe necessary. *X* is the best place to go; *Y* is the worst choice for mayor; plan *B* is the most reasonable solution to problem *Z*; course 1 is the only valid course to follow. In writing, too, we take positions and defend them, and this undertaking, stemming in the most formal sense from ancient Greek oratory, we call *argumentation.*

Although some logicians make a precise distinction between arguing and persuading, the two frequently work together. Strictly speaking, the essence of *argumentation* is a coolly rational presentation of statement and support, eschewing emotional appeals and prejudicial language and aiming instead for a person's intellectual faculty. The arguer's goal is to get you to agree. *Persuasion,* on the other hand, reaches for feelings; based in logic too, it usually aims to arouse emotion, even passion, so that you act. The persuader's goal is to get you to agree—and then to do something about it. When you say "You're right" to a friend who marshals statistics—batting averages, win-loss records, runs batted in—to convince you that the Astros are a better team than the Mets, he's won the argument. When you buy a new breakfast cereal because of a 30-second commercial spot on television, you're not only convinced, you're convinced strongly enough to take action.

Good written argumentation and persuasion, designed to appeal to reasonable readers, will be grounded in reason. The writer asserts something, takes a position (when stated formally, this is often called the *proposition*), and then advances this position point by point. But like effective argumentation in life, written argumentation usually provides more than direct logical proof. Readers and writers alike are complex creatures, feeling and thinking at once. No wonder then that throughout history, writers have developed argumentative approaches to convince readers both through reasoning and through emotional evocation.

READING ARGUMENTATION

From early literature to modern novels, stories, dramas, and essays, argumentation abounds. From Job's remonstrance to God to the polemics of Brecht, Lawrence, and Woolf in our century, we note lively evidence of the impulse to argue well so that others see important issues as we do.

Effective argumentation will not only move the reader through logic but will move the reader to "feel" the writer's position as well. In effective argumentative essays the reader sets in force a whole arsenal of strategies—comparison, classification, causation, description, narration, and so on. A sharp anecdote, a lambent sensory description, an explanation of ghastly or wonderful effects, an extended analogy, an apt comparison—all of these can help persuade the reader to accept the writer's particular position or point of view. But fiction writers, poets, dramatists, and satirists also employ argumentation and persuasion. The essayist may dwell more on aspects of logic and the imaginative writer more on emotional appeals; but the good writer in any genre will draw on techniques that sway both intellect and emotions, yoking in the work both sense and sensibility. Indeed, writers from Aristotle, to Austen to T. S. Eliot have recommended this joining in life and in literature.

In this chapter, Swift's satire, "A Modest Proposal," argues against popular policy and attitudes toward Ireland not by saying outright, "The British treatment of Ireland should be altered," but by using a variety of expository techniques that move us not only intellectually but emotionally. His comparison of babies to livestock, for example, to be bred, killed, "stewed, roasted, baked, or boiled," and put on the table for dinner alarms the reader, convincing us of the *narrator's* madness and of the *writer's* good sense. Point by point Swift has his speaker argue for the wisdom of killing babies as a solution to "the Irish problem," and through well-chosen details, examples, facts and figures—"I compute that Dublin would take off annually about twenty thousand carcasses, and the rest of the kingdom (where they will be sold somewhat cheaper) the remaining eighty thousand"—makes readers see British proposals to maintain domination of impoverished Ireland as cruelty and madness in the name of reason and logic. Indeed the whole superlogical structure of Swift's satire encourages in the reader an *emotional* acceptance of the victims and an *emotional* aversion to the oppressor. The "Proposal" encourages the reader to say, "No more proposals, no more propositions. Just kindness, just love."

Good argumentation, then, can move not only our minds but also our hearts. Martin Luther King's "I Have a Dream" speech, included here, points out the folly and danger of America turning her back on blacks and forgetting the promise of democracy laid down in the Constitution. But the speech wins us over through more than logic alone. The resonant repetitions, the carefully chosen metaphors ("manacles of segregation," "chains of discrimination") move the readers' emotions in assent to King's proposition that the promise of democracy is a promise to all Americans.

Perhaps the most remarkable balance between logic and emotion in literature resides in Marvel's "To His Coy Mistress," one of the poems in this chapter. The poet appeals to his mistress's reason so that she'll accept his propositions; yet his language, fraught with subtle sensuality, aims for emotional appeal ("The grave's a fine and private place,/But none, I think, do there embrace"). The speaker's objective is to persuade his demure lady through reason and feeling to love him now, not later. He wants action, and he wants it today!

As we read argumentation we can see, too, the choices of logical strategies. Will the writer start with a proposition and then support it point by point, or will the writer lay down points and let the proposition emerge? The former approach we call *deduction,* the latter, *induction.* King works deductively; he comes right out with his proposition, then his entire speech supports this through example, analysis of causes and effects, and so on. Swift's essay, in contrast, works inductively. Readers, after experiencing the *speaker's* proposition, supporting details, and calculations, grasp on their own the *writer's* proposition—a rejection of the basic assumptions laid down in the "Proposal."

While reading argumentation, then, we can observe a rich play of the writer's options. Max Schulman's story "Love Is a Fallacy" pokes fun at the rigors of formal argumentation. But even in humorous fictional writing, we can see the wide range of possibilities for argumentative ploys. To get us to embrace a proposition, writers will use a variety of dramatic and expository techniques. They may appeal to our reason and to our emotions, probably both. Writers may work deductively, guiding us from proposition to support, or inductively from detail and example until their handiwork frames the larger proposition. In short, reading argumentation provides a blueprint of strategies in logic that have already been used to win many readers and that remain useful as we ourselves write to argue or persuade.

WRITING ARGUMENTATION

The ancient Greeks developed certain rules that strictly governed formal argumentation and debate, and orators and writers followed these rules for centuries. Today we tend to approach argumentation with fewer rules. Still, it is useful to keep certain guidelines in mind as you develop your own argumentative essays, and to keep certain thoughts in mind even before you select your topic. Argumentation will require a good deal of you—your most careful reasoning, an energetic marshaling of support, extreme sensitivity to the emotional issues of your topic, and exact use of language. The first question you want to ask yourself is "What issue do I care strongly enough about to be able to take an emphatic position on?" This is no occasion for reticence; you must take a stand and stick by it. Also, before you choose your topic, you'll want to ask yourself "What do I know about?" You don't necessarily want your first argumentation papers to end up being extensive research undertakings, and so a topic that you not only care about but also know something about will be a good place to start.

AUDIENCE AND PURPOSE

Argumentative essays have as their goal the logical presentation of ideas in order to convince the reader of a sound point of view. A further purpose may be to get their readers to act once they accept the essay's proposition. In either case, you want to take readers with you from proposition to supporting points to conclusion. And to do so you must think carefully about *who* your readers are, what they know, and what information, data, illustrations, or other supporting details are likely to get them to think as you do. Your level of usage, your choice of vocabulary, your tone and style all must serve your ultimate purpose. To argue against the excessive use of living animals for scientific experiments, you might present readers with a dispassionate paper that lays out statistics and cases drawn from reliable sources. Numbers have their own drama, and a careful, rational presentation could win over your readers. If your purpose were to recruit demonstrators for a march in Washington next month to support the Animal Protection League, you might spark your essay with your own bias, individualizing the cases, emphasizing the particular suffering of animals in selected examples, and exhorting your readers with emotionally charged language to meet you on the steps of the capitol.

One point to keep in mind is that readers are more often than not rational people. You will want then to build a sound argument and to avoid name-calling that might alienate your audience. As you develop your proposition, try for a statement that will respect your audience's diversity. If you say anyone who doesn't support school busing is "a Nazi and a right-wing hoodlum," you will prevent any readers inclined toward opposing busing from reading your essay with an open mind.

Of course, certain audiences tend to be in agreement on certain subjects. But more often than not an academic audience—generally your main readership—holds diverse views. As you write, try to imagine what a reader with opposing views might say. An excellent strategy is to include these opposing views somewhere in your essay and either acknowledge their viability before you go on to make your own points or refute them one by one. This *refutation,* a requirement in classical argumentation, is still useful for persuading readers on the other side or for convincing readers sitting on the fence. As for readers who agree with your position, the refutation and the good argumentation in general can help them to test their beliefs and to sharpen and strengthen their thinking.

As you prepare to write, think about the knowledge level of your readers. If they know very little about the subject, then your argument will have to cover some very basic points. What is *vivisection*? What is its history in the American scientific community? What are other options for researchers? If, on the other hand, your readers are specialists on your topic, then you will need to pitch your essay to their high level, avoid telling them what they already know, and include sophisticated thinking and information.

Think of your audience as you organize the points that support your proposition. If you put your strongest points first, most readers will lose interest as the essay moves on to weaker arguments. If you put all your strong points last, your readers may never be interested enough to get to them. A balanced strategy is to put your second strongest point first, then proceed to your less strong points, and end your argument with your strongest point—the point you most want your readers to remember.

Being especially clear about your own purpose and about your audience is critical as you develop essays designed to change minds.

PROCESS

Identify the issue you want to write about. Consider the matters raised in the selections in this chapter. If you have trouble identifying a strong belief or conviction, look at a news magazine or a newspaper. Study editorial pages; read a political column; listen to a commentator's opinion on radio or television. No doubt your thinking on different matters will perk up even if it's just to *oppose* what you read or hear. Once you've chosen a topic that you care about and perhaps even know a good deal about, you can turn to developing your argument.

First, you must shape your topic into a proposition, the thesis sentence in argumentation. Whether the logical plan of your essay is deductive or inductive, you will need a clear statement of proposition to work with. Not every essay states its thesis outright—writers sometimes leave you to figure it out on your own—but a clear statement of proposition helps a reader straight off to determine where the essay intends to go. Even an inductive essay can benefit from such a statement at the end so that readers can check their perceptions against the writer's. At any rate, a clear idea of the main position the essay will assert directs you as you plan and as you write. An argumentative essay builds on a strong proposition (*Y* must be upheld; *B* should be abolished). Write your proposition and edit any language that could bait or alienate your audience.

Prewrite on your topic in order to generate the major points of your argument. Even the most fair-minded proposition needs strong supporting points in order for readers to accept it fully. Through jottings, lists, freewriting—whatever technique works for you—generate the points that will hold up your position. And before you write, generate examples, facts, figures, descriptions that make each point convincing and alive.

Also before you write, check your argument for logic. Logic, of course, plays a part in most writing, but in argumentation it plays an especially important role. If your logic is faulty, reasonable readers will reject your entire premise, however worthy it in itself may be. Look to see that your essay does not *oversimplify* complicated matters. Consider cautiously the value of calling for the end to *all* biological investigations that employ living animals. Many advances in human health care have followed such experimentation, and you might lose readers if you overlook the advantages stemming from such scientific research. Also look to see that your conclusions logically follow the proposition and its supporting points. The Latin phrase *non sequitur,* meaning *"doesn't follow,"* refers to a statement that does not logically follow another statement, although we intend it to. "Opposing vivisection will improve the lot of helpless animals everywhere" risks being a a *non sequitur* if you do not develop the issues in your paper carefully. What about the cruelty inflicted upon pets in some households? About animals abandoned every September as resort areas close down all over America and families return home? Look as well to see that the authorities you invoke are truly authorities. Your brother's report of outrageous experiments with frogs in a summer camp nature program would not convince anyone that vivisection abuse is widespread throughout the scientific community. Another way to strengthen the logic of your position is to make sure that you've argued the issues and have not just attacked people connected with your "opposition." Such a personal attack is called *ad hominem,* from the Latin "to the person." The *ad hominen* approach is easy to fall into in argumentation involving us emotionally, but readers can easily dismiss it as beside the issue.

Good logic can work for you and so can good language. Solid argumentation relies on good writing. As you write and as you edit, try for the most alive language and the most alive examples and descriptions. The well-turned phrase will attract your readers' attention and incline them toward your position more than will dull phrases or repetitive syntax. Fresh figurative language, sensory description, lively comparison, lively example—all the rhetorical devices that you have at your command as a writer—will serve you well as you argue for your proposition, making logical and emotional appeals to your reader.

In arguing it's easy to overdo the use of transitions by linking ideas frequently with logical connectors—*therefore, thus, and so, as a result, then, consequently,* and many others like them. These transitions are useful certainly to connect points here and there; but the logic in a well-reasoned essay has its own flow that requires few guideposts. In most cases readers will know on their own when point *A* follows point *B* intelligently and will not need the added push of *therefore.*

Finally, the conclusion of your argumentative essay is particularly important. It's what readers "hear" last and it can often clinch or lose their support. There are no hard and fast rules for concluding argumentation. In a fairly long paper a restatement of your proposition, one that presents your point with fresh language, will impress readers with what is most important to the essay without being boring. In a short paper your conclusion might set a new frame of reference by generalizing from your stated proposal to an even larger, more relevant issue.

Throughout your college career and on the job your skills at argumentation will serve you well. Spend time here in practicing these skills: presenting your points honestly, avoiding the overstatement of emotional appeals, and weighing the logic of your positions carefully.

How did he prove his idea

Martin Luther King, Jr.
I HAVE A DREAM

Martin Luther King, Jr. (1929–1968), was born in Atlanta, Georgia, the son of a Baptist minister. King followed his father's lead into the ministry and soon became known for his inspiring oratorical abilities. He became the most prominent leader of the early civil rights movement in the United States: In 1955, he organized the year-long, successful boycott of the segregated Montgomery, Alabama, bus system; he subsequently organized and led the Southern Christian Leadership Council, which promoted other boycotts, marches, and demonstrations in favor of civil rights for blacks. King was an instrumental organizer of the 1963 March on Washington and the 1965 voter-registration drive in Selma, Alabama. Staunchly devoted to Gandhian-style nonviolent resistence, the Reverend Dr. King received the 1968 Nobel Prize for Peace. In 1968, he was assassinated.

On August 28, 1963, nearly a quarter of a million people of all races converged on Washington, D.C., to take part in the historic March on Washington at the height of the American civil rights movement. In front of the Lincoln Memorial, on the one hundredth anniversary of the Emancipation Proclamation, the Reverend Dr. Martin Luther King, Jr., delivered the spellbinding "I Have a Dream" speech in which he outlined his vision of a better, more peaceful country.

*F*ive score years ago, a great American, in *whose symbolic shadow we stand,* signed the Emancipation Proclamation. This momentous decree came as a great beacon light of hope to millions of Negro slaves who had been seared in the flames of withering injustice. It came as a joyous daybreak to end the long night of captivity.

Thesis

But one hundred years later, we must face the tragic fact that the Negro is still not free. One hundred years later, the life of the Negro is still sadly crippled by the manacles of segregation and the chains of discrimination. One hundred years later, the Negro lives on a lonely island of poverty in the midst of a vast ocean of material prosperity. One hundred years later, the Negro is still languishing in the corners of American society and finds himself an exile in his own land. So we have come here today to dramatize an appalling condition.

In a sense we have come to our nation's capital to cash a check. When the architects of our republic wrote the magnificent words of the Constitution and the Declaration of Independence, they were signing a promissory note to which every American was to fall heir. This note was a promise that all men would be guaranteed the unalienable rights of life, liberty, and the pursuit of happiness.

It is obvious today that America has defaulted on this promissory note insofar as her citizens of color are concerned. Instead of honoring this sacred obligation, America has given the Negro people a bad check; a check which has come back marked "insufficient funds." But we refuse to believe that the bank of justice is bankrupt. We refuse to believe that there are insufficient funds in the great vaults of opportunity of this nation. So we have come to cash this check—a check that will give us upon demand the riches of freedom and the security of justice. We have also come to this hallowed spot to remind America of the fierce urgency of *now*. This is no time to engage in the luxury of cooling off or to take the tranquilizing drugs of gradualism. *Now* is the time to make real the promises of Democracy. *Now* is the time to rise from the dark and desolate valley of segregation to the sunlit path of racial justice. *Now* is the time to open the doors of opportunity to all of God's children. *Now* is the time to lift our nation from the quicksands of racial injustice to the solid rock of brotherhood.

It would be fatal for the nation to overlook the urgency of the moment and to underestimate the determination of the Negro. This sweltering summer of the Negro's legitimate discontent will not pass until there is an invigorating autumn of freedom and equality. 1963 is not an end, but a beginning. Those who hope that the Negro needed to blow off steam and will now be content will have a rude awakening if the nation returns to business as usual. There will be neither rest nor tranquillity in America until the Negro is granted his citizenship rights. The whirlwinds of revolt will continue to shake the foundations of our nation until the bright day of justice emerges.

But there is something that I must say to my people who stand on the warm threshold which leads into the palace of justice. In the process of gaining our rightful place we must not be guilty of wrongful deeds. Let us not seek to satisfy our thirst for freedom by drinking from the cup of bitterness and hatred. We must forever conduct our struggle on the high plane of dignity and discipline. We must not allow our creative protest to degenerate into physical violence. Again and again we must rise to the majestic heights of meeting physical force with soul force. The marvelous new militancy which has engulfed the Negro community must not lead us to a distrust of all white people, for many of our white brothers, as evidenced by their presence here today, have come to realize that their destiny is tied up with our destiny and their freedom is inextricably bound to our freedom. We cannot walk alone.

And as we walk, we must make the pledge that we shall march ahead. We cannot turn back. There are those who are asking the devotees of civil rights, "When will you be satisfied?" We can never be satisfied as long as the Negro is the victim of the unspeakable horrors of police brutality. We can never be satisfied as long as our bodies, heavy with the fatigue of travel, cannot gain lodging in the motels of the highways and the hotels of the cities. We cannot be satisfied as long as the Negro's basic mobility is from a smaller ghetto to a larger one. We can never be satisfied as long as a Negro in Mississippi cannot vote and a Negro in New York believes he has nothing for which to vote. No, no, we are not satisfied, and we will not be satisfied until justice rolls down like waters and righteousness like a mighty stream.

I am not unmindful that some of you have come here out of great trials and tribulations. Some of you have come fresh from narrow jail cells. Some of you have come from areas where your quest for freedom left you battered by the storms of persecution and staggered by the winds of police brutality. You have been the veterans of creative suffering. Continue to work with the faith that unearned suffering is redemptive.

Go back to Mississippi, go back to Alabama, go back to South Carolina, go back to Georgia, go back to Louisiana, go back to the slums and ghettos of our northern cities, knowing that somehow this situation can and will be changed. Let us not wallow in the valley of despair.

I say to you today, my friends, that in spite of the difficulties and frustrations of the moment I still have a dream. It is a dream deeply rooted in the American dream.

I have a dream that one day this nation will rise up and live out the true meaning of its creed: "We hold these truths to be self-evident; that all men are created equal."

I have a dream that one day on the red hills of Georgia the sons of former slaves and the sons of former slaveowners will be able to sit down together at the table of brotherhood.

I have a dream that one day even the state of Mississippi, a desert state sweltering with the heat of injustice and oppression, will be transformed into an oasis of freedom and justice.

I have a dream that my four little children will one day live in a nation where they will not be judged by the color of their skin but by the content of their character.

I have a dream today.

I have a dream that one day the state of Alabama, whose governor's lips are presently dripping with the words of interposition and nullification, will be transformed into a situation where little black boys and black girls will be able to join hands with little white boys and white girls and walk together as sisters and brothers.

I have a dream today.

I have a dream that one day every valley shall be exalted, every hill and mountain shall be made low, the rough places will be made plain, and the crooked places will be made straight, and the glory of the Lord shall be revealed, and all flesh shall see it together.

This is our hope. This is the faith with which I return to the South. With this faith we will be able to hew out of the mountain of despair a stone of hope. With this faith we will be able to transform the jangling discords of our nation into a beautiful symphony of brotherhood. With this faith we will be able to work together, to pray together, to struggle together, to go to jail together, to stand up for freedom together, knowing that we will be free one day.

This will be the day when all of God's children will be able to sing with new meaning

My country, 'tis of thee,
Sweet land of liberty,
    Of thee I sing:
Land where my fathers died,
Land of the pilgrims' pride,
From every mountain-side
    Let freedom ring.

And if America is to be a great nation this must become true. So let freedom ring from the prodigious hilltops of New Hampshire. Let freedom ring from the mighty mountains of New York. Let freedom ring from the heightening Alleghenies of Pennsylvania!

Let freedom ring from the snowcapped Rockies of Colorado!

Let freedom ring from the curvaceous peaks of California!

But not only that; let freedom ring from Stone Mountain of Georgia!

Let freedom ring from Lookout Mountain of Tennessee!

Let freedom ring from every hill and molehill of Mississippi. From every mountainside, let freedom ring.

When we let freedom ring, when we let it ring from every village and every hamlet, from every state and every city, we will be able to speed up that day when all of God's children, black men and white men, Jews and Gentiles, Protestants and Catholics, will be able to join hands and sing in the words of the old Negro spiritual, "Free at last! free at last! thank God almighty, we are free at last!"

Meaning and Idea

1. Who is the "great American" to whom King refers at the opening of his speech? What was the Emancipation Proclamation?

2. What comparisons does King make between the conditions of blacks in 1863 and 1963? Are these conditions always stated explicitly? What is the point of the comparison?

3. What examples does King offer of the daily conditions of blacks which lead him to the conclusion that satisfaction cannot be achieved "until justice rolls down like waters and righteousness like a mighty stream"? What does he mean by the term *satisfied* in this context?

4. What does King say of the relations between blacks and whites? What are the potential difficulties? What is his suggestion?

Language, Form, Structure

1. For what position is King arguing? Does he ever directly state a thesis for this speech? In a single sentence in your own words, state what his main proposition is. Is King's intention merely to convince the audience of his opinion, or does he also want to persuade them to action? Explain your answer.

2. King uses numerous metaphors in the development of his argument. Which do you find most impressive? Explain the extended metaphor (an *extended metaphor* sustains a figurative comparison through a number of related images) that begins with the first sentence of the third paragraph: "In a sense we have come to our nation's capital to cash a check."

3. What is the role of repetition in this speech? How does King use repetition to compound his opinions? How does he use it to move his argument forward?

4. One of the most impressive features of this speech is the full range of vision and audience that King demonstrates. How does he cover descriptive, geographic, and social range? How does he make his words appeal to the widest possible audience?

5. Toward the end of the speech, King introduces the litany of "Let freedom ring." Analyze the meaning and use of the transitional phrase, "But not only that," in the middle of that section.

6. Make sure you know the meanings of the following words: manacles; languishing; degenerate; inextricably; wallow; interposition; nullification; exalted; prodigious. Select five for use in your own sentences.

Ideas for Writing

1. Write a speech in which you argue strongly a position and a plan for action concerning an important issue at your school. Try to use language as dramatically as possible.

2. Write your opinion of the present conditions of one aspect of black (or any other minority's) life in the country today.

3. As you know, Martin Luther King, Jr., like his father, was a Baptist minister. As such, he grew up on and practiced the art of stirring, emotional oratory. How is the language of this speech influenced by a "preacher style"? Do you feel it is effective as an essay alone, or is it written specifically to be orated? Explain your response.

Joseph Conrad
Preface to LORD JIM

Joseph Conrad (1857–1924), whose real name was Josef Teodor Konrad Nalecz Korzeniowski, was born in Poland. Although his second language was French, and he did not learn English until he was 21, he became one of the greatest English novelists. Conrad's father was a Polish writer and nationalist who was exiled to Russia for his political activities, together with his wife and son. Conrad was orphaned at 11, became a sailor at 17, and a few years later joined a British freighter. He subsequently served in eastern seas and elsewhere, receiving his Master's Certificate in 1886, the year he became a naturalized British subject. Many of his novels draw on his experience in the East. Quite popular in his own lifetime, he left a legacy of works such as *The Nigger of the "Narcissus"* (1897), *Heart of Darkness* (1899), *Lord Jim* (1900), *Nostromo* (1904), *The Secret Agent* (1907), *Victory* (1915), and a number of short story collections.

Told in a long, recursive narrative by the character Marlow, *Lord Jim* (1900) is one of the great masterpieces of twentieth-century literature. Jim is an officer on board an unseaworthy ship filled with Moslem pilgrims. When Jim incorrectly identifies impending disaster, the captain orders all the officers into the only lifeboat. Jim's sense of honor (and guilt) initially prevents his joining them, but at the last moment he jumps overboard and is saved by the other officers. Jim wanders the globe, searching for absolution, and finally becomes an adviser to a native chieftain in the East Indies, where he is renamed Tuan Jim, or Lord Jim. His lost honor haunts him, however, and, indirectly responsible for the shooting of the chief's son, Jim begs the old chief to shoot him.

In his Preface to *Lord Jim,* Conrad argues against the literary critics who at first thought he'd entirely lost control as a writer, and against a personal critic who thought the story "morbid" rather than spiritually uplifting.

*W*hen this novel first appeared in book form a notion got about that I had been bolted away with. Some reviewers maintained that the work starting as a short story had got beyond the writer's control. One or two discovered internal evidence of the fact, which seemed to amuse them. They pointed out the limitations of the narrative form. They argued that no man could have been expected to talk all that time, and other men to listen so long. It was not, they said, very credible.

After thinking it over for something like sixteen years I am not so sure about that. Men have been known, both in thee tropics and in the temperate zone, to sit up half the night "swapping yarns." This, however, is but one yarn, yet with interruptions affording some measure of relief; and in regard to the listeners' endurance, the postulate must be accepted that the story *was* interesting. It is the necessary preliminary assumption. If I hadn't believed that it *was* interesting I could never have begun to write it. As to the mere physical possibility we all know that some speeches in Parliament have taken nearer six than three hours in delivery; whereas all that part of the book which is Marlow's narrative can be read through aloud, I should say, in less than three hours. Besides—though I have kept strictly all such insignificant details out of the tale—we may presume that there must have been refreshments on that night, a glass of mineral water of some sort to help the narrator on.

But, seriously, the truth of the matter is, that my first thought was of a short story, concerned only with the pilgrim ship episode; nothing more. And that was a legitimate conception. After writing a few pages, however, I became for some reason discontented and I laid them aside for a time. I didn't take them out of the drawer till the late Mr. William Blackwood suggested I should give something again to his magazine.

It was only then that I perceived that the pilgrim ship episode was a good starting-point for a free and wandering tale; that it was an event, too, which could conceivably colour the whole "sentiment of existence" in a simple and sensitive character. But all these preliminary moods and stirrings of spirit were rather obscure at the time, and they do not appear clearer to me now after the lapse of so many years.

The few pages I had laid aside were not without their weight in the choice of subject. But the whole was re-written deliberately. When I sat down to it I knew it would be a long book, though I didn't foresee that it would spread itself over thirteen numbers of "Maga."

I have been asked at times whether this was not the book of mine I liked best. I am a great foe to favouritism in public life, in private life, and even in the delicate relationship of an author to his works. As a matter of principle I will have no favourites; but I don't go so far as to feel grieved and annoyed by the preference some people give to my Lord Jim. I won't even say that I "fail to understand. . . .." No! But once I had occasion to be puzzled and surprised.

A friend of mine returning from Italy had talked with a lady there who did not like the book. I regretted that, of course, but what surprised me was the ground of her dislike. "You know," she said, "it is all so morbid."

The pronouncement gave me food for an hour's anxious thought.

Finally I arrived at the conclusion that, making due allowances for the subject itself being rather foreign to women's normal sensibilities, the lady could not have been an Italian. I wonder whether she was European at all? In any case, no Latin temperament would have perceived anything morbid in the acute consciousness of lost honour. Such a consciousness may be wrong, or it may be right, or it may be condemned as artificial; and, perhaps, my Jim is not a type of wide commonness. But I can safely assure my readers that he is not the product of coldly perverted thinking. He's not a figure of Northern Mists either. One sunny morning in the commonplace surroundings of an Eastern roadstead, I saw his form pass by—appealing—significant—under a cloud—perfectly silent. Which is as it should be. It was for me, with all the sympathy of which I was capable, to seek fit words for his meaning. He was "one of us."

Meaning and Idea

1.   What does Conrad identify as the early critical reactions to the book form of *Lord Jim?* Does he agree or disagree with them? What evidence does he offer to support his reaction to the criticisms?

2.   What is "the necessary preliminary assumption" Conrad would like readers to have about *Lord Jim?* What other assumptions does he presume? What is his attitude about those assumptions?

3.   What opinion does Conrad express about the book? How has he reacted to others' opinions of it? What particular opinion disturbs Conrad? Why? On what basis does he refute that disturbing opinion?

4.   What does Conrad identify as the inception of the character of Lord Jim? From what does the character derive? From what does he *not* derive?

Language, Form, Structure

1.   At one point, Conrad identifies what he thinks of as the *theme* of *Lord Jim.* Quote the exact phrase in which he does this.

2.   *Refutation* is an argumentative technique that counters opposing arguments to a position. How does refutation structure this essay? Does Conrad prove his opposition's argument wrong or false to your satisfaction?

3.   According to this preface, by what *process* was the book *Lord Jim* composed?

4.   Look up the meaning of the word *preface.* What is the purpose of this preface to the novel *Lord Jim?* Is it meant to give the reader details about the story? On what basis is it meant to prepare the reader?

5.   Look up the following words: credible; yarn; postulate; lapse; morbid; acute.

Ideas for Writing

1. Reread the last paper you wrote (for this class or any other) for which you received criticism you feel was unjustified. Write a short refutation of that criticism. Cite examples directly from your paper.

2. Think of a misinformed comment you recently heard about a current issue. Write a response in which you propose a more correct or informed opinion.

3. Write a paper in which you outline the process Conrad says he followed in writing *Lord Jim*. Pay particular attention to the last two sentences. Do you agree with Conrad's notion of process? How closely does it match your own writing procedures? How would you summarize your own writing process?

Jonathan Swift
A MODEST PROPOSAL

Jonathan Swift (1667–1745) is rightfully afforded the title "greatest of English satirists." He was born in Dublin, Ireland, and educated at Trinity College there. Swift was politically as well as literarily productive; originally a liberal Whig, he turned to Tory politics and wrote numerous political pamphlets. Appointed Dean of St. Patrick's Cathedral in Dublin in 1713, he remained at that post until 1736. His private life was secretive and somewhat complex. His *Journals to Stella* are a three-year series of letters to a young woman, Esther Johnson, whom he may or may not have secretly married. His early *Battle of the Books* and *Tale of a Tub* (1704) were satires on contemporary thought and religious excess. *Gulliver's Travels* (1726) and *A Modest Proposal* (1729) revealed the depth of Swift's social and political insights along with his venomous satirical skills. He began experiencing terrifying bouts with mental illness around 1736, suffered a mental breakdown in 1741, and died four years later.

Next to *Gulliver's Tavels*, "A Modest Proposal," written in 1729, is perhaps best known among Jonathan Swift's writings. It was directed at the British ruling class because of their oppressive treatment of the Irish. Clearly full of biting satire, this essay has its very serious side as well, easily discernible through careful reading of Swift's seemingly outlandish argument.

*I*t is a melancholy object to those who walk through this great town or travel in the country, when they see the streets, the roads, and cabin doors, crowded with beggars of the female-sex, followed by three, four, or six children, all in rags and importuning every passenger for an alms. These mothers, instead of being able to work for their honest livelihood, are forced to employ all their time in strolling to beg sustenance for their helpless infants, who, as they grow up, either turn thieves for want of work, or leave their dear native country to fight for the Pretender in Spain, or sell themselves to the Barbadoes.

I think it is agreed by all parties that this prodigious number of children in the arms, or on the backs, or at the heels of their mothers, and frequently of their fathers, is in the present deplorable state of the kingdom a very great additional grievance; and therefore whoever could find out a fair, cheap, and easy method of making these children sound, useful members of the commonwealth would deserve so well of the public as to have his statue set up for a preserver of the nation.

But my intention is very far from being confined to provide only for the children of professed beggars; it is of a much greater extent, and shall take in the whole number of infants at a certain age who are born of parents in effect as little able to support them as those who demand our charity in the streets.

As to my own part, having turned my thoughts for many years upon this important subject, and maturely weighed the several schemes of other projectors, I have always found them grossly mistaken in their computation. It is true, a child just dropped from its dam may be supported by her milk for a solar year, with little other nourishment; at most not above the value of two shillings, which the mother may certainly get, or the value in scraps, by her lawful occupation of begging; and it is exactly at one year old that I propose to provide for them in such a manner as instead of being a charge upon their parents or the parish, or wanting food and raiment for the rest of their lives, they shall on the contrary contribute to the feeding, and partly to the clothing, of many thousands.

There is likewise another great advantage in my scheme, that it will prevent those voluntary abortions, and that horrid practice of women murdering their bastard children, alas, too frequent among us, sacrificing the poor innocent babes, I doubt, more to avoid the expense than the shame, which would move tears and pity in the most savage and inhuman breast.

The number of souls in this kingdom being usually reckoned one million and a half, of these I calculate there may be about two hundred thousand couples whose wives are breeders; from which number I subtract thirty thousand couples who are able to maintain their own children, although I apprehend there cannot be so many under the present distresses of the kingdom; but this being granted, there will remain an hundred and seventy thousand breeders. I again subtract fifty thousand for those women who miscarry, or whose children die by accident or disease within the year. There only remain an hundred and twenty thousand children of poor parents annually born. The question therefore is, how this number shall be reared and provided for, which, as I have already said, under the present situation of affairs, is utterly impossible by all the methods hitherto proposed. For we can neither employ them in handicraft or agriculture; we neither build houses (I mean in the country) nor cultivate land. They can very seldom pick up a livelihood by stealing till they arrive at six years old, except where they are of towardly parts; although I confess they learn the rudiments much earlier, during which time they can however be looked upon only as probationers, as I have been informed by a principal gentlemen in the county of Cavan, who protested to me that he never knew above one or two instances under the age of six, even in a part of the kingdom so renowned for the quickest proficiency in that art.

I am assured by our merchants that a boy or girl before twelve years old is no salable commodity; and even when they come to this age they will not yield above three pounds, or three pounds and half a crown at most on the Exchange; which cannot turn to account either to the parents or the kingdom, the charge of nutriment and rags having been at least four times that value.

I shall now therefore humbly propose my own thoughts, which I hope will not be liable to the least objection.

I have been assured by a very knowing American of my acquaintance in London, that a young healthy child well nursed is at a year old a most delicious, nourishing, and wholesome food, whether stewed, roasted, baked or boiled; and I make no doubt that it will equally serve in a fricassee or a ragout.

I do therefore humbly offer it to public consideration that of the hundred and twenty thousand children, already computed, twenty thousand may be reserved for breed, whereof only one fourth part to be males, which is more than we allow to sheep, black cattle, or swine; and my reason is that these children are seldom the fruits of marriage, a circumstance not much regarded by our savages, therefore one male will be sufficient to serve four females. That the remaining hundred thousand may at a year old be offered in sale to the persons of quality and fortune through the kingdom, always advising the mother to let them suck plentifully in the last month, so as to render them plump and fat for a good table. A child will make two dishes at an entertainment for friends; and when the family dines alone, the fore or hind quarter will make a reasonable dish, and seasoned with a little pepper or salt will be very good boiled on the fourth day, especially in winter.

I have reckoned upon a medium that a child just born will weigh twelve pounds, and in a solar year if tolerably nursed increaseth to twenty-eight pounds.

I grant this food will be somewhat dear, and therefore very proper for landlords, who, as they have already devoured most of the parents, seem to have the best title to the children.

Infant's flesh will be in season throughout the year, but more plentiful in March, and a little before and after. For we are told by a grave author, an eminent French physician, that fish being a prolific diet, there are more children born in Roman Catholic countries about nine months after Lent than at any other season: therefore, reckoning a year after Lent, the markets will be more glutted than usual, because the number of popish infants is at least three to one in this kingdom; and therefore it will have one other collateral advantage, by lessening the number of Papists among us.

I have already computed the charge of nursing a beggar's child (in which list I reckon all cottagers, laborers, and four fifths of the farmers) to be about two shillings per annum, rags included: and I believe no gentleman would repine to give ten shillings for the carcass of a good fat child, which, as I have said, will make four dishes of excellent nutritive meat, when he hath only some particular friend or his own family to dine with him. Thus the squire will learn to be a good landlord, and grow popular among the tenants; the mother will have eight shillings net profit, and be fit for work till she produces another child.

Those who are more thrifty (as I must confess the times require) may flay the carcass; the skin of which artifically dressed will make admirable gloves for ladies, and summer boots for fine gentlemen.

As to our city of Dublin, shambles may be appointed for this purpose in the most convenient parts of it, and butchers we may be assured will not be wanting; although I rather recommend buying the children alive, and dressing them hot from the knife as we do roasting pigs.

A very worthy person, a true lover of his country, and whose virtues I highly esteem, was lately pleased in discoursing on this matter to offer a refinement upon my scheme. He said that many gentlemen of this kingdom, having of late destroyed their deer, he conceived that the want of venison might be well supplied by the bodies of young lads and maidens, not exceeding fourteen years of age nor under twelve, so great a number of both sexes in every county being now ready to starve for want of work and service; and these to be disposed of by their parents, if alive, or otherwise by their nearest relations. But with due deference to so excellent a friend and so deserving a patriot, I cannot be altogether in his sentiments; for as to the males, my American acquaintance assured me from frequent experience that their flesh was generally tough and lean, like that of our schoolboys, by continual exercise, and their taste disagreeable; and to fatten them would not answer the charge. Then as to the females, it would, I think with humble submission, be a loss to the public, because they soon would become breeders themselves: and besides, it is not improbable that some scrupulous people might be apt to censure such a practice (although indeed very unjustly) as a little bordering upon cruelty; which, I confess, hath always been with me the strongest objection against any project, how well soever intended.

But in order to justify my friend, he confessed that this expedient was put into his head by the famous Psalmanazar, a native of the island Formosa, who came from thence to London above twenty years ago, and in conversation told my friend that in his country when any young person happened to be put to death, the executioner sold the carcass to persons of quality as a prime dainty; and that in his time the body of a plump girl of fifteen, who was crucified for an attempt to poison the emperor, was sold to his Imperial Majesty's prime minister of state, and other great mandarins of the court, in joints from the gibbet, at four hundred crowns. Neither indeed can I deny that if the same use were made of several plump young girls in this town, who without one single groat to their fortunes cannot stir abroad without a chair, and appear at the playhouse and assemblies in foreign fineries which they never will pay for, the kingdom would not be the worse.

Some persons of a desponding spirit are in great concern about that vast number of poor people who are aged, diseased, or maimed, and I have been desired to employ my thoughts what course may be taken to ease the nation of so grievous an encumbrance. But I am not in the least pain upon that matter, because it is very well known that they are every day dying and rotting by cold and famine, and filth and vermin, as fast as can be reasonably expected. And as to the younger laborers, they are now in almost as hopeful a condition. They cannot get work, and consequently pine away for want of nourishment to a degree that if at any time they are accidentally hired to common labor, they have not strength to perform it; and thus the country and themselves are happily delivered from the evils to come.

I have too long digressed, and therefore shall return to my subject. I think the advantages by the proposal which I have made are obvious and many, as well as of the highest importance.

For first, as I have already observed, it would greatly lessen the number of Papists, with whom we are yearly overrun, being the principal breeders of the nation as well as our most dangerous enemies; and who stay at home on purpose to deliver the kingdom to the Pretender, hoping to take their advantage by the absence of so many good Protestants, who have chosen rather to leave their country than to stay at home and pay tithes against their conscience to an Episcopal curate.

Secondly, the poorer tenants will have something valuable of their own, which by law may be made liable to distress, and help to pay their landlord's rent, their corn and cattle being already seized and money a thing unknown.

Thirdly, whereas the maintenance of an hundred thousand children, from two years old and upwards, cannot be computed at less than ten shillings a piece per annum, the nation's stock will be thereby increased fifty thousand pounds per annum, besides the profit of a new dish introduced to the tables of all gentlemen of fortune in the kingdom who have any refinement in taste. And the money will circulate among ourselves, the goods being entirely of our own growth and manufacture.

Fourthly, the constant breeders, besides the gain of eight shillings sterling per annum by the sale of their children, will be rid of the charge of maintaining them after the first year.

Fifthly, this food would likewise bring great custom to taverns, where the vinters will certainly be so prudent as to procure the best receipts for dressing it to perfection, and consequently have their houses frequented by all the fine gentlemen, who justly value themselves upon their knowledge in good eating; and a skillful cook, who understands how to oblige his guests, will contrive to make it as expensive as they please.

Sixthly, this would be a great inducement to marriage, which all wise nations have either encouraged by rewards or enforced by laws and penalties. It would increase the care and tenderness of mothers toward their children, when they were sure of a settlement for life to the poor babes, provided in some sort by the public, to their annual profit instead of expense. We should see an honest emulation among the married women, which of them could bring the fattest child to the market. Men would become as fond of their wives during the time of their pregnancy as they are now of their mares in foal, their cows in calf, or sows when they are ready to farrow; nor offer to beat or kick them (as is too frequent a practice) for fear of a miscarriage.

Many other advantages might be enumerated. For instance, the addition of some thousand carcasses in our exportation of barreled beef, the propagation of swine's flesh, and improvement in the art of making good bacon, so much wanted among us by the great destruction of pigs, too frequent at our tables, which are no way comparable in taste or magnificence to a well-grown, fat yearling child, which roasted whole will make a considerable figure at a lord mayor's feast or any other public entertainment. But this and many others I omit, being studious of brevity.

Supposing that one thousand families in this city would be constant customers for infants' flesh, besides others who might have it at merry meetings, particularly weddings and christeninngs, I compute that Dublin would take off annually about twenty thousand carcasses, and the rest of the kingdom (where probably they will be sold somewhat cheaper) the remaining eighty thousand.

I can think of no one objection that will possibly be raised against this proposal, unless it should be urged that the number of people will be thereby much lessened in the kingdom. This I freely own, and it was indeed one principal design in offering it to the world. I desire the reader will observe, that I calculate my remedy for this one individual kingdom of Ireland and for no other that ever was, is, or I think ever can be upon earth. Therefore let no man talk to me of other expedients: of taxing our absentees at five shillings a pound: of using neither clothes nor household furniture except what is of our own growth and manufacture: of utterly rejecting the materials and instruments that promote foreign luxury: of curing the expensiveness of pride, vanity, idleness, and gaming in our women: of introducing a vein of parsimony, prudence, and temperance: of learning to love our country, in the want of which we differ even from Laplanders and the inhabitants of Topinamboo: of quitting our animosities and factions, nor acting any longer like the Jews, who were murdering one another at the very moment their city was taken: of being a little cautious not to sell our country and conscience for nothing: of teaching landlords to have at least one degree of mercy toward their tenants: lastly, of putting a spirit of honesty, industryy, and skill into our shopkeepers; who, if a resolution could be now taken to buy only our native goods, would immediately unite to cheat and exact upon us in the price, the measure and the goodness, nor could ever yet be brought to make one fair proposal of just dealing, though often and earnestly invited to it.

Therefore I repeat, let no man talk to me of these and the like expedients, till he hath at least some glimpse of hopee that there will ever be some hearty and sincere attempt to put them in practice.

But as to myself, having been wearied out for many years with offering vain, idle, visionary thoughts, and at length utterly despairing of success, I fortunately fell upon this proposal, which, as it is wholly new, so it hath something solid and real, of no expense and little trouble, full in our own power, and whereby we can incur no danger in disobliging England. For this kind of commodity will not bear exportation, the flesh being of too tender a consistence to admit a long continuance in salt, although perhaps I could name a country which would be glad to eat up our whole nation without it.

After all, I am not so violently bent upon my own opinion as to reject any offer proposed by wise men, which shall be found equally innocent, cheap, easy, and effectual. But before something of that kind shall be advanced in contradiction to my scheme, and offering a better, I desire the author or authors will be pleased maturely to consider two points. First, as things now stand, how they will be able to find food and raiment for an hundred thousand useless mouths and backs. And secondly, there being a round million of creatures in human figure throughout this kingdom, whose sole subsistence put into a common stock would leave them in debt two millions of pounds sterling, adding those who are beggars by profession to the bulk of farmers, cottagers, and laborers, with their wives and children who are beggars in effect; I desire those politicians who dislike my overture, and may perhaps be so bold to attempt an answer, that they will first ask the parents of these mortals whether they would not at this day think it a great happiness to have been sold for food at a year old in the manner I prescribe, and thereby have avoided such a perpetual scene of misfortunes as they have since gone through by the oppression of landlords, the impossibility of paying rent without money or trade, the want of common sustenance, with neither house nor clothes to cover them from the inclemencies of the weather, and the most inevitable prospect of entailing the like or greater miseries upon their breed forever.

I profess, in the sincerity of my heart, that I have not the least personal interest in endeavoring to promote this necessary work, having no other motive than the public good of my country, by advancing our trade, providing for infants, relieving the poor, and giving some pleasure to the rich. I have no children by which I can propose to get a single penny; the youngest being nine years old, and my wife past childbearing.

Meaning and Idea

1. Outline the six advantages Swift discusses as the results of enactment of his proposal. By what principle does he arrange them? What two types of "national profit" does he suggest?

2. How does the next to the last paragraph express Swift's genuine concern for the conditions of his native Ireland? What were some of those conditions?

3. What is the purpose of Swift's disclaimer at the end of the essay?

Language, Form, Structure

1. What is the main *proposition* of Swift's "modest proposal"? What are the *minor propositions* (a *minor proposition* is a less generalized, though related, statement of opinion that supports the main proposition)?

2. The introduction in this essay spans a good many paragraphs. Identify the scope of the introduction. How does Swift begin establishing a fairly serious tone and purpose for his proposal? Where and how in the introduction does the reader begin to recognize the satire. (*Satire* is a literary form that uses wit, humor, irony, and sarcasm to criticize human behavior). What satirical elements do you find in this essay?

3. Why does Swift repeatedly use words such as *modest, humbly,* and *sincerity?* Look up the etymology of the word *modest,* and check the *Oxford English Dictionary* for its various range of usages.

4. As in any well-written argumentation, Swift adequately deals with opposing arguments, although he does write: "I can think of no one objection that will possibly be raised against this proposal." What, in fact, is the purpose of his discussion of opposition arguments in this essay? What are some of the most important of these?

5. How does Swift use the "logic" of mathematics in support of his proposal?

6. As discussed in the introduction to this chapter (pages 523–524), *logical fallacies* are errors in logical development of an argument. What major logical fallacies do you discern in Swift's argument? Was he aware of them as well? How do you know?

7. Define the following words from "A Modest Proposal": alms; bastard; rudiments; liable; prolific; repine; deference; prudent; contrive; emulation; parsimony; inclemencies.

Ideas for Writing

1. Write a "modest proposal" of your own in which you use satire to argue about an important issue in society today. Make sure to deal with potential opposition arguments.

2. Write an argumentative essay in which you propose specific means by which someone in your immediate family could make your family life better. Make your audience that particular person. Be sure to include some historical background to the present situation, as well as your vision of what future conditions will be if your proposal is adopted.

3. Check an unabridged dictionary or some other source for a complete definition of *satire.* Using the definition, comment upon Swift's use of satire. How is it an effective tool in Swift's argument? Do you feel that satire makes his discussion of the Irish condition more or less effective than, say, a straightforward causal analysis? Do you find the satire in any way detrimental to your understanding of the issue, or do you find it enhances your understanding? Explain with specific references to the text.

William Shakespeare
PUT MONEY IN THY PURSE

William Shakespeare was born the son of a businessman in Stratford-on-Avon, England, in 1564, and he received his grammar school education there. Except for his marriage to Anne Hathaway in 1582, we know little of Shakespeare's life until his appearance as an actor and playwright in London in 1592. By 1599, he was a part owner of the famous Globe Theatre where many of his most famous plays—including *Hamlet, King Lear,* and *Othello*—are thought to have been first produced. Shakespeare's great plays are complemented by his *Sonnets* (written in the 1590s, but published in 1609) to the unknown "W. H." and the "dark lady." He returned to Stratford in 1613, and he died there in 1616.

Othello is Shakespeare's tragedy of the conflict between love and honor. This scene is a discussion between Iago, Othello's aged lieutenant (whom Othello mistakenly considers "Honest Iago") and Roderigo, Iago's stupid, servile follower. Othello, the Moorish general of Venice, has eloped with Desdemona, the daughter of a Venetian senator, and only Othello's high-standing and respect in Venetian society has saved him from prosecution. Iago and Roderigo are clearly jealous—Iago for reasons of his evil nature; Roderigo because of his love for Desdemona. In this scene, Iago attempts to convince Roderigo not to follow what the lieutenant considers an unprofitable course of action. Cassio, one of Othello's trusted soldiers, is a good friend of Desdemona; Iago will use Cassio, without his knowing, to arouse Othello's jealousy.

RODERIGO: Iago,—

IAGO: What say'st thou, noble heart?

RODERIGO: What will I do, think'st thou?

IAGO: Why, go to bed and sleep.

RODERIGO: I will incontinently drown myself.   5

IAGO: If thou dost, I shall never love thee after. Why, thou silly gentleman?

RODERIGO: It is silliness to live when to live is torment; and then have we a prescription to die when death is our physician.   10

IAGO: O villainous! I have looked upon the world for four
times seven years; and since I could distinguish betwixt a
benefit and an injury, I never found man that knew how
to love himself. Ere I would say I would drown myself for
the love of a guinea hen, I would change my humanity   15
with a baboon.

RODERIGO: What should I do? I confess it is my shame to be
so fond, but it is not in my virtue to amend it.

IAGO: Virtue? a fig! 'Tis in ourselves that we are thus or thus.
Our bodies are our gardens, to the which our wills are   20
gardeners; so that if we will plant nettles or sow lettuce,
set hyssop and weed up thyme, supply it with one gender
of herbs or distract it with many—either to have it sterile
with idleness or manured with industry—why, the power
and corrigible authority of this lies in our wills. If the   25
balance of our lives had not one scale of reason to poise
another of sensuality, the blood and baseness of our
natures would conduct us to most preposterous conclusions. But we have reason to cool our raging motions, our
carnal stings, our unbitted lusts; whereof I take this that 30
you call love to be a sect or scion.

RODERIGO: It cannot be.

IAGO: It is merely a lust of the blood and a permission of the
will. Come, be a man! Drown thyself? Drown cats and
blind puppies! I have professed me thy friend, and I   35
confess me knit to thy deserving with cables of perdurable toughness. I could never better stead thee than now.
Put money in thy purse. Follow these wars; defeat thy
favor with an usurped beard. I say, put money in thy
purse. It cannot be that Desdemona should long continue   40
her love to the Moor—put money in thy purse—nor he
his to her. It was a violent commencement, and thou
shalt see an answerable sequestration—put but money in
thy purse. These Moors are changeable in their wills—fill
thy purse with money. The food that to him now is as   45
luscious as locusts shall be to him shortly as bitter as
coloquintida. She must change for youth: when she is
sated with his body, she will find the error of her choice.
She must have change, she must. Therefore put money in
thy purse. If thou wilt needs damn thyself, do it a more   50
delicate way than drowning. Make all the money thou
canst. If sanctimony and a frail vow betwixt an erring
barbarian and a supersubtle Venetian be not too hard for
my wits and all the tribe of hell, thou shalt enjoy her.

Therefore make money. A pox of drowning! 'Tis clean   55
out of the way. Seek thou rather to be hanged in compassing thy joy than to be drowned and go without her.

RODERIGO: Wilt thou be fast to my hopes, if I depend on the
issue?

IAGO: Thou art sure of me. Go, make money. I have told thee   60
often, and I retell thee again and again, I hate the Moor.
My cause is hearted; thine hath no less reason. Let us be
conjunctive in our revenge against him. If thou canst
cuckold him, thou dost thyself a pleasure, me a sport.
There are many events in the womb of time, which will   65
be delivered. Traverse, go, provide thy money! We have
more of this to-morrow. Adieu.

RODERIGO: Where shall we meet i' th' morning?

IAGO: At my lodging.

RODERIGO: I'll be with thee betimes.   70

IAGO: Go to, farewell.—Do you hear, Roderigo?

RODERIGO: What say you?

IAGO: No more of drowning, do you hear?

RODERIGO: I am changed.

IAGO: Go to, farewell. Put money enough in your purse.   75

RODERIGO: I'll sell my land.

IAGO: Thus do I ever make my fool my purse;
For I mine own gained knowledge should profane

RODERIGO: Where shall we meet i' th' morning?

IAGO: At my lodging.   80

RODERIGO: I'll be with thee betimes.

IAGO: Go to, farewell.—Do you hear, Roderigo?

RODERIGO: What say you?

IAGO: No more of drowning, do you hear?

RODERIGO: I am changed.   85

IAGO: Go to, farewell. Put money enough in your purse.

RODERIGO: I'll sell my land.

IAGO: Thus do I ever make my fool my purse;
For I mine own gained knowledge should profane
If I would time expend with such a snipe   90
But for my sport and profit. I hate the Moor;
And it is thought abroad that 'twixt my sheets
H'as done my office. I know not if't be true;
Yet I, for mere suspicion in that kind,
Will do as if for surety. He holds me well;   95
The better shall my purpose work on him.
Cassio's a proper man. Let me see now:
To get his place, and to plume up my will

In double knavery—How, how?—Let's see:—
After some time, to abuse Othello's ear   100
That he is too familiar with his wife.
He hath a person and a smooth dispose
To be suspected—framed to make women false.
The Moor is of a free and open nature
That thinks men honest that but seem to be so;   105
And will as tenderly be led by th' nose
As asses are.
I have't! It is engendered! Hell and night
Must bring this monstrous birth to the world's light.

Exit.

Meaning and Idea

1.   What has Roderigo decided to do as a result of Desdemona's marriage to Othello? What does Iago tell Roderigo to do instead? What is the meaning of the words "put money in thy purse"? Why does Iago keep talking about money?

2.   Iago's definition of love appears in lines 33–34. What does he mean?

3.   What does Iago predict to the gullible Roderigo about the fate of Desdemona and Othello's marriage?

4.   How does Iago *really* feel about Roderigo? How does he feel about Othello? Which lines support your belief?

Language, Form, Structure

1.   Iago makes many references to animals here. What are these references? How do they reflect the nature of Iago's mind? Who is the guinea hen in line 315?

2.   The two speeches by Iago, lines 19–31 and 33–57, are superb examples of persuasive prose used for evil ends. How does Iago manage to persuade Roderigo to take his advice? What techniques of persuasion has Iago used?

3.   Iago's arguments have the semblance of clear logic. What, however, has Iago omitted in his discussion of will and lust? In his explanation of what will happen to Othello and Desdemona's relationship?

4.   Explain the comparison in lines 19–25.

5.   Check the meanings of these words and explain them in the context of the selection: incontinently; nettles; hyssop; corrigible; sensuality; baseness; carnal; perdurable; sanctimony; barbarian; compassing; snipe.

Ideas for Writing

1. Write an essay in which you try to persuade someone to do something for himself or herself but which ultimately is to your benefit. Assume your primary reason for being persuasive is that your own benefit is served.

2. Write a persuasive essay in which you convince someone to take some action for the course of love.

3. Write a brief analysis of Shakespeare's use of language and imagery in this selection.

Andrew Marvell
TO HIS COY MISTRESS

> Andrew Marvell (1621–1678) is among the best known of the English metaphysical poets. He was a friend and assistant to John Milton, though he was somewhat more diplomatic and tolerant than his mentor. Marvell is best remembered for his biting wit and satire, some of it aimed directly at the Commonwealth, even though he remained a loyal member of Parliament until his death. Among his fine lyrical poetry is "The Garden," "Horatian Ode upon Cromwell's Return from Ireland," "The Nymph Complaining for the Death of her Faun," and "To His Coy Mistress."
>
> Marvell makes an age-old argument the basis of this poem, but he gives it an energy and universality that have earned for him respect and admiration from readers for over three hundred years. As you read "To His Coy Mistress," pay special attention to Marvell's balance of subject, tone, and form in order to derive the full force of his argument.

*H*ad we but world enough, and time,
This coyness, lady, were no crime.
We would sit down, and think which way
To walk, and pass our long love's day.

Thou by the Indian Ganges' side 5
Shouldst rubies find; I by the tide
Of Humber would complain. I would
Love you ten years before the Flood,
And you should, if you please, refuse
Till the conversion of the Jews. 10
My vegetable love should grow
Vaster than empires, and more slow;
An hundred years should go to praise
Thine eyes, and on thy forehead gaze;
Two hundred to adore each breast, 15
But thirty thousand to the rest;
An age at least to every part,
And the last age should show your heart.
For, lady, you deserve this state.
Nor would I love at lower rate. 20
    But at my back I always hear
Time's winged chariot hurrying near;
And yonder all before us lie
Deserts of vast eternity.
Thy beauty shall no more be found, 25
Nor, in thy marble vault, shall sound
My echoing song; then worms shall try
That long-preserved virginity,
And your quaint honor turn to dust,
And into ashes all my lust: 30
The grave's a fine and private place,
But none, I think, do there embrace.
    Now therefore, while the youthful hue
Sits on thy skin like morning dew,
And while thy willing soul transpires 35
At every pore with instant fires,
Now let us sport us while we may,
And now, like amorous birds of prey,
Rather at once our time devour
Than languish in his slow-chapped power. 40
Let us roll all our strength and all
Our sweetness up into one ball,
And tear our pleasures with rough strife
Thorough the iron gates of life.
Thus, though we cannot make our sun 45
Stand still, yet we will make him run.

Meaning and Idea

1.   Why does the speaker call his mistress *coy?* How is her coyness a "crime" to him?

2.   Of what is the speaker attempting to persuade his mistress? Approximately what age is the mistress?

3.   How does the speaker use the element of time as a part of his argument?

4.   The last two lines of the poem refer to a myth about Zeus, the Greek king of the gods: Zeus made the sun stand still so that his night of lovemaking with Alcmene would last all the longer. With that information, discuss the meaning of the last two lines of this poem.

Language, Form, Structure

1.   What is the main point of the poem? Is it a poem about seduction, innocence, love, fleeting time, the mortality of the human race—any or all of these? Explain your answer.

2.   Outline the three stages of the speaker's argument in his effort to convince his mistress. What transitions help Marvell connect the various argumentative strands?

3.   What two contrasting views of seduction and sexuality does the speaker present? Which does he seem to prefer? Why?

4.   Lines 29–32 form the end of the midpart of the speaker's argument. Would you say that his attitude has shifted from one of patience to one of slight sarcasm? Why? What words and phrases indicate his growing impatience? Do you feel he was *ever* really patient with his mistress? Why?

5.   Marvell's use of language is extraordinary. Identify the most outstanding examples of original sensory images. Identify as many allusions as possible in the poem, especially in lines 5–20. Of what benefit to the argument are these allusions?

6.   Identify and define at least five words that are new to you in this poem.

Ideas for Writing

1.   Write an ironic argument in which you attempt to persuade a specific member of the opposite sex to do something. In the beginning of your argument, pay close attention to the other person's point of view, then refute it before proposing your own plan of action.

2.   Write a narration of a time when you convinced *yourself* to do something

you thought you didn't want to do. Arrange your narration/argumentation chronologically.

3. One critic calls some of the lines in this poem "as fine an example as
English poetry can show of wit blended with imagination" and, referring to lines
31–32, says they are "the perfection of tragic whimsicaliity." Write a paper in which
you support this assessment of "To His Coy Mistress." Make specific references to
the poem.

Wilfred Owen
DULCE ET DECORUM EST

> Wilfred Owen (1893–1918) was among the English "war
> poets" of World War I, the most notable of whom was Siegfried
> Sassoon. Owen was born in Oswestry, England, and had a
> checkered education. He partially rejected Christianity in the
> midst of studying for the priesthood, then moved to Bordeaux,
> France. He returned to England in 1915 to enlist in the Man-
> chester Regiment of the British Army. While recuperating in a
> hospital in Edinburgh, he met Sassoon, who encouraged
> Owen's poetry writing. Owens was killed a week before the
> Armistice in 1918, and his poems were published by Sassoon in
> 1920.
>
> In "Dulce et Decorum Est" a young soldier pleads against the
> romanticization of war. The poet makes his case all the more
> convincing by the pointed contrast of his realistic description of a
> dying fellow soldier against an abstract and distant call to arms.
> The poem gains power from our knowledge that Owen himself
> died in that war. *Dulce et decorum est pro patria mori,* a line
> from Horace, the Roman poet who lived in the first century B.C.,
> means "It is sweet and becoming to die for one's country."

Bent double, like old beggars under sacks,
Knock-kneed, coughing like hags, we cursed through sludge,
Till on the haunting flares we turned our backs,
And towards our distant rest began to trudge.
Men marched asleep. Many had lost their boots,   5

But limped on, blood-shod. All went lame, all blind;
Drunk with fatigue; deaf even to the hoots
Of gas-shells dropping softly behind.

Gas! GAS! Quick, boys!—An ecstasy of fumbling,
Fitting the clumsy helmets just in time,   10
But someone still was yelling out and stumbling
And flound'ring like a man in fire or lime.—
Dim through the misty panes and thick green light,
As under a green sea, I saw him drowning.

In all my dreams before my helplesss sight   15
He plunges at me, guttering, choking, drowning.

If in some smothering dreams, you too could pace
Behind the wagon that we flung him in,
And watch the white eyes writhing in his face,
His hanging face, like a devil's sick of sin,   20
If you could hear, at every jolt, the blood
Come gargling from the froth-corrupted lungs
Bitter as the cud
Of vile, incurable sores on innocent tongues,—
My friend, you would not tell with such high zest   25
To children ardent for some desperate glory,
The old lie: *Dulce et decorum est*
Pro patria mori.

Meaning and Idea

1. Briefly describe, in your own words, the setting and action of this poem. How is the one soldier's experience different from the others'?

2. What are the "gas shells" and the "Gas!" that Owens writes about? What war do those references clearly place this poem in?

3. How does Owen use the quotation from Horace to establish his own idea? Why does he call Horace's opinion "The old lie"? What attitude does that description express?

4. Explain the double meaning of line 4. What is the "distant rest"?

Language, Form, Structure

1. What would you say is the position Owen is arguing here? Who is being addressed in this poem? What clue does the "you" of line 17 provide? Is the intended audience fighting in the war as the narrator is? How are the narrator and audience linked by dreams in this poem?

2. Given the narrative context of the poem, does *ecstasy* seem like a strange word choice in line 9? Why? Why does Owen use that word?

3. What descriptive details are most powerful in making Owen's argument? Comment on Owen's use of similes in this poem. Identify each. How do they enhance the description of "Dulce et Decorum Est"?

4. Explain Owen's use of the following descriptions: blood-shod (line 6); helpless sight (15); desperate glory (26).

5. Make sure you know the meanings of the following words: hags, sludge (line 2); guttering (16); cud (23); vile (24); ardent (26).

Ideas for Writing

1. Write an essay in which you express your opinion of a current United States military involvement. Limit your argument to a specific part of the world rather than attempting to deal with United States military involvement generally. Try to make your argument as personalized as possible.

2. Write your own argumentation in response to the quotation from Horace.

3. Owen was only 25 years old when he actually did "die for one's country." Referring to the language and style of this poem, do you think that Owen would have felt that his death was "sweet and becoming"? Does it seem possible, based on your interpretation of this poem, that Owen could have these antiwar sentiments yet still be proud of his fate? Explain your answer.

Max Shulman

LOVE IS A FALLACY

Max Shulman was born in 1919 in St. Paul, Minnesota, and attended the University of Minnesota where, as a writer for the campus humor magazine, he was discovered by an editor from Doubleday. That "discovery" led to Shulman's first book, *Barefoot Boy with Cheek,* and since then, he has made his career as a writer whose humor is almost always aligned with recognizable situations and facts. He has written numerous books, screenplays, and plays, and he was the creator and writer for the popular television series "The Many Loves of Dobie Gillis," which aired from 1959 to 1962.

In this comic essay—replete with comic dialogue—humorist Max Shulman classifies the very same logical fallacies of which any writer needs to be aware in serious argumentative writing.

---

*C*ool was I and logical. Keen, calculating, perspicacious, acute and astute—I was all of these. My brain was as powerful as a dynamo, as precise as a chemist's scales, as penetrating as a scalpel. And—think of it!—I was only eighteen.

It is not often that one so young has such a giant intellect. Take, for example, Petey Burch, my roommate at the University of Minnesota. Same age, same background, but dumb as an ox. A nice enough fellow, you understand, but nothing upstairs. Emotional type. Unstable. Impressionable. Worst of all, a faddist. Fads, I submit, are the very negation of reason. To be swept up in every new craze that comes along, to surrender yourself to idiocy just because everybody else is doing it—this, to me, is the acme of mindlessness. Not, however, to Petey.

One afternoon I found Petey lying on his bed with an expression of such distress on his face that I immediately diagnosed appendicitis. "Don't move," I said. "Don't take a laxative. I'll get a doctor."

"Raccoon," he mumbled thickly.

"Raccoon?" I said, pausing in my flight.

"I want a raccoon coat," he wailed.

I perceived that his trouble was not physical, but mental. "Why do you want a raccoon coat?"

"I should have known it," he cried, pounding his temples. "I should have known they'd come back when the Charleston came back. Like a fool I spent all my money for textbooks, and now I can't get a raccoon coat."

"Can you mean," I said incredulously, "that people are actually wearing raccoon coats again?"

"All the Big Men on Campus are wearing them. Where've you been?"

"In the library," I said, naming a place not frequented by Big Men on Campus.

He leaped from the bed and paced the room. "I've got to have a raccoon coat," he said passionately, "I've got to!"

"Petey, why? Look at it rationally. Raccoon coats are unsanitary. They shed. They smell bad. They weigh too much. They're unsightly. They—"

"You don't understand," he interrupted impatiently. "It's the thing to do. Don't you want to be in the swim?"

"No," I said truthfully.

"Well, I do," he declared. "I'd give anything for a raccoon coat. Anything!"

My brain, that precision instrument, slipped into high gear. "Anything?" I asked, looking at him narrowly.

"Anything," he affirmed in ringing tones.

I stroked my chin thoughtfully. It so happened that I knew where to get my hands on a raccoon coat. My father had had one in his undergraduate days; it lay now in a trunk in the attic back home. It also happened that Petey had something I wanted. He didn't *have* it exactly, but at least he had first rights on it. I refer to his girl, Polly Espy.

I had long coveted Polly Espy. Let me emphasize that my desire for this young woman was not emotional in nature. She was, to be sure, a girl who excited the emotions, but I was not one to let my heart rule my head. I wanted Polly for a shrewdly calculated, entirely cerebral reason.

I was a freshman in law school. In a few years I would be out in practice. I was well aware of the importance of the right kind of wife in furthering a lawyer's career. The successful lawyers I had observed were, almost without exception, married to beautiful, gracious, intelligent women. With one omission, Polly fitted these specifications perfectly.

Beautiful she was. She was not yet of pin-up proportions, but I felt sure that time would supply the lack. She already had the makings.

Gracious she was. By gracious I mean full of graces. She had an erectness of carriage, an ease of bearing, a poise that clearly indicated the best of breeding. At table her manners weere exquisite. I had seen her at the Kozy Kampus Korner eating the specialty of the house—a sandwich that contained scraps of pot roast, gravy, chopped nuts, and a dipper of sauerkraut—without even getting her fingers moist.

Intelligent she was not. In fact, she veered in the opposite direction. But I believed that under my guidance she would smarten up. At any rate, it was worth a try. It is, after all, easier to make a beautiful dumb girl smart than to make an ugly smart girl beautiful.

"Petey," I said, "are you in love with Polly Espy?"

"I think she's a keen kid," he replied, "but I don't know if you'd call it love. Why?"

"Do you," I asked, "have any kind of formal arrangement with her? I mean are you going steady or anything like that?"

"No. We see each other quite a bit, but we both have other dates. Why?"

"Is there," I asked, "any other man for whom she has a particular fondness?"

"Not that I know of. Why?"

I nodded with satisfaction. "In other words, if you were out of the picture, the field would be open. Is that right?"

"I guess so. What are you getting at?"

"Nothing, nothing," I said innocently, and took my suitcase out of the closet.

"Where are you going?" asked Petey.

"Home for the weekend." I threw a few things into the bag.

"Listen," he said, clutching my arm eagerly, "while you're home, you couldn't get some money from your old man, could you, and lend it to me so I can buy a raccoon coat?"

"I may do better than that," I said with a mysterious wink and closed my bag and left.

"Look," I said to Petey when I got back Monday morning. I threw open the suitcase and revealed the huge, hairy, gamy object that my father had worn in his Stutz Bearcat in 1925.

"Holy Toledo!" said Petey reverently. He plunged his hands into the raccoon coat and then his face. "Holy Toledo!" he repeated fifteen or twenty times.

"Would you like it?" I asked.

"Oh yes!" he cried, clutching the greasy pelt to him. Then a canny look came into his eyes. "What do you want for it?"

"Your girl," I said, mincing no words.

"Polly?" he said in a horrified whisper. "You want Polly?"

"That's right."

He flung the coat from him. "Never," he said stoutly.

I shrugged. "Okay. If you don't want to be in the swim, I guess it's your business."

I sat down in a chair and pretended to read a book, but out of the corner of my eye I kept watching Petey. He was a torn man. First he looked at the coat with the expression of a waif at a bakery window. Then he turned away and set his jaw resolutely. Then he looked back at the coat, with even more longing in his face. Then he turned away, but with not so much resolution this time. Back and forth his head swiveled, desire waxing, resolution waning. Finally he didn't turn away at all; he just stood and stared with mad lust at the coat.

"It isn't as though I was in love with Polly," he said thickly. "Or going steady or anything like that."

"That's right," I murmured.

"What's Polly to me, or me to Polly?"

"Not a thing," said I.

"It's just been a casual kick—just a few laughs, that's all."

"Try on the coat," said I.

He complied. The coat bunched high over his ears and dropped all the way down to his shoe tops. He looked like a mound of dead raccoons. "Fits fine," he said happily.

I rose from my chair. "Is it a deal?" I asked, extending my hand.

He swallowed. "It's a deal," he said and shook my hand.

I had my first date with Polly the following evening. This was in the nature of a survey; I wanted to find out just how much work I had to do to get her mind up to the standard I required. I took her first to dinner. "Gee, that was a delish dinner," she said as we left the restaurant. Then I took her to a movie. "Gee, that was a marvy movie," she said as we left the theater. And then I took her home. "Gee, I had a sensaysh time," she said as she bade me good night.

I went back to my room with a heavy heart. I had gravely underestimated the size of my task. This girl's lack of information was terrifying. First she had to be taught to *think*. This loomed as a project of no small dimensions, and at first I was tempted to give her back to Petey. But then I got to thinking about her abundant physical charms and about the way she entered a room and the way she handled a knife and fork, and I decided to make an effort.

I went about it, as in all things, systematically. I gave her a course in logic. It happened that I, as a law student, was taking a course in logic myself, so I had all the facts at my finger tips. "Polly," I said to her when I picked her up on our next date, "tonight we are going over to the Knoll and talk."

"Oo, terrif," she replied. One thing I will say for this girl: you would go far to find another so agreeable.

We went to the Knoll, the campus trysting place, and we sat down under an old oak, and she looked at me expectantly. "What are we going to talk about?" she asked.

"Logic."

She thought this over for a minute and decided she liked it. "Magnif," she said.

"Logic," I said, clearing my throat, "is the science of thinking. Before we can think correctly, we must first learn to recognize the common fallacies of logic. These we will take up tonight."

"Wow-dow!" she cried, clapping her hands delightedly.

I winced, but went bravely on. "First let us examine the fallacy called Dicto Simpliciter."

"By all means," she urged, batting her lashes eagerly.

"Dicto Simpliciter means an argument based on an unqualified generalization. For example: Exercise is good. Therefore everybody should exercise."

"I agree," said Polly earnestly. "I mean exercise is wonderful. I mean it builds the body and everything."

"Polly," I said gently, "the argument is a fallacy. *Exercise is good* is an unqualified generalization. For instance, if you have heart disease, exercise is bad, not good. Many people are ordered by their doctors *not* to exercise. You must *qualify* the generalization. You must say exercise is *usually* good, or exercise is good *for most* people. Otherwise you have committed a Dicto Simpliciter. Do you see?"

"No," she confessed. "But this is marvy. Do more! Do more!"

"It will be better if you stop tugging at my sleeve," I told her, and when she desisted, I continued. "Next we take up a fallacy called Hasty Generalization. Listen carefully: You can't speak French. I can't speak French. Petey Burch can't speak French. I must therefore conclude that nobody at the University of Minnesota can speak French."

"Really?" said Polly, amazed. *"Nobody?"*

I hid my exasperation. "Polly, it's a fallacy. The generalization is reached too hastily. There are two few instances to support such a conclusion."

"Know any more fallacies?" she asked breathlessly. "This is more fun than dancing even."

I fought off a wave of despair. I was getting nowhere with this girl, absolutely nowhere. Still, I am nothing if not persistent. I continued. "Next comes Post Hoc. Listen to this: Let's not take Bill on our picnic. Every time we take him out with us, it rains."

"I know somebody just like that," she exclaimed. "A girl back home—Eula Becker, her name is. It never fails. Every single time we take her on a picnic—"

"Polly," I said sharply, "it's a fallacy. Eula Becker doesn't *cause* the rain. She has no connection with the rain. You are guilty of Post Hoc if you blame Eula Becker."

"I'll never do it again," she promised contritely. "Are you mad at me?"

I sighed deeply. "No, Polly, I'm not mad."

"Then tell me some more fallacies."

"All right. Let's try Contradictory Premises."

"Yes, let's," she chirped, blinking her eyes happily.

I frowned, but plunged ahead. "Here's an example of Contradictory Premises: If God can do anything, can He make a stone so heavy that He won't be able to lift it?"

"Of course," she replied promptly.

"But if He can do anything, He can lift the stone," I pointed out.

"Yeah," she said thoughtfully. "Well, then I guess He can't make the stone."

"But He can do anything," I reminded her.

She scratched her pretty, empty head. "I'm all confused," she admitted.

"Of course you are. Because when the premises of an argument contradict each other, there can be no argument. If there is an irresistible force, there can be no immovable object. If there is an immovable object, there can be no irresistible force. Get it?"

"Tell me some more of this keen stuff," she said eagerly.

I consulted my watch. "I think we'd better call it a night. I'll take you home now, and you go over all the things you've learned. We'll have another session tomorrow night."

I deposited her at the girls' dormitory, where she assured me that she had had a perfect terrif evening, and I went glumly home to my room. Petey lay snoring in his bed, the raccoon coat huddled like a great hairy beast at his feet. For a moment I considered waking him and telling him that he could have his girl back. It seemed clear that my project was doomed to failure. The girl simply had a logic-proof head.

But then I reconsidered. I had wasted one evening; I might as well waste another. Who knew? Maybe somewhere in the extinct crater of her mind, a few embers still smoldered. Maybe somehow I could fan them into flame. Admittedly it was not a prospect fraught with hope, but I decided to give it one more try.

Seated under the oak the next evening I said, "Our first fallacy tonight is called Ad Misericordiam."

She quivered with delight.

"Listen closely," I said. "A man applies for a job. When the boss asks him what his qualifications are, he replies that he has a wife and six children at home, the wife is a helpless cripple, the children have nothing to eat, no clothes to wear, no shoes on their feet, there are no beds in the house, no coal in the cellar, and winter is coming."

A tear rolled down each of Polly's pink cheeks. "Oh, this is awful, awful," she sobbed.

"Yes, it's awful," I agreed, "but it's no argument. The man never answered the boss's question about his qualifications. Instead he appealed to the boss's sympathy. He committed the fallacy of Ad Misericordiam. Do you understand?''

"Have you got a handkerchief?" she blubbered.

I handed her a handkerchief and tried to keep from screaming while she wiped her eyes. "Next," I said in a carefully controlled tone, "we will discuss False Analogy. Here is an example: Students should be allowed to look at their textbooks during examinations. After all, surgeons have X-rays to guide them during an operation, lawyers have briefs to guide them during a trial, carpenters have blueprints to guide them when they are building a house. Why, then, shouldn't students be allowed to look at their textbooks during an examination?''

"There now," she said enthusiastically, "is the most marvy idea I've heard in years."

"Polly," I said testily, "the argument is all wrong. Doctors, lawyers, and carpenters aren't taking a test to see how much they have learned, but students are. The situations are altogether different, and you can't make an analogy between them."

"I still think it's a good idea," said Polly.

"Nuts," I muttered. Doggedly I pressed on. "Next we'll try Hypothesis Contrary to Fact."

"Sounds yummy," was Polly's reaction.

"Listen: If Madame Curie had not happened to leave a photographic plate in a drawer with a chunk of pitchblende, the world today would not know about radium."

"True, true," said Polly, nodding her heead. "Did you see the movie? Oh, it just knocked me out. That Walter Pidgeon is so dreamy. I mean he fractures me."

"If you can forget Mr. Pidgeon for a moment," I said coldly, "I would like to point out that the statement is a fallacy. Maybe Madame Curie would have discovered radium at some later date. Maybe somebody else would have discovered it. Maybe any number of things would have happened. You can't start with a hypothesis that is not true and then draw any supportable conclusions from it."

"They ought to put Walter Pidgeon in more pictures," said Polly. "I hardly ever see him any more."

One more chance, I decided. But just one more. There is a limit to what flesh and blood can bear. "The next fallacy is called Poisoning the Well."

"How cute!" she gurgled.

"Two men are having a debate. The first one gets up and says, 'My opponent is a notorious liar. You can't believe a word that he is going to say.' . . . Now, Polly, think. Think hard. What's wrong?''

I watched her closely as she knit her creamy brow in concentration. Suddenly a glimmer of intelligence—the first I had seen—came into her eyes. "It's not fair," she said with indignation. "It's not a bit fair. What chance has the second man got if the first man calls him a liar before he even begins talking?"

"Right!" I cried exultantly. "One hundred percent right. It's not fair. The first man has *poisoned the well* before anybody could drink from it. He has hamstrung his opponent before he could even start. . . . Polly, I'm proud of you."

"Pshaw," she murmured, blushing with pleasure.

"You see, my dear, these things aren't so hard. All you have to do is concentrate. Think—examine—evaluate. Come now, let's review everything we have learned."

"Fire away," she said with an airy wave of her hand.

Heartened by the knowledge that Polly was not altogether a cretin, I began a long, patient review of all I had told her. Over and over and over again I cited instances, pointed out flaws, kept hammering away without letup. It was like digging a tunnel. At first everything was work, sweat, and darkness. I had no idea when I would reach the light, or even *if* I would. But I persisted. I pounded and clawed and scraped, and finally I was rewarded. I saw a chink of light. And then the chink got bigger and the sun came pouring in and all was bright.

Five grueling nights this took, but it was worth it. I had made a logician out of Polly; I had taught her to think. My job was done. She was worthy of me at last. She was a fit wife for me, a proper hostess for my many mansions, a suitable mother for my well-heeled children.

It must not be thought that I was without love for this girl. Quite the contrary. Just as Pygmalion loved the perfect woman he had fashioned, so I loved mine. I determined to acquaint her with my feelings at our very next meeting. The time had come to change our relationship from academic to romantic.

"Polly," I said when next we sat beneath our oak, "tonight we will not discuss fallacies."

"Aw, gee," she said, disappointed.

"My dear," I said, favoring her with a smile, "we have now spent five evenings together. We have gotten along splendidly. It is clear that we are well matched."

"Hasty Generalization," said Polly brightly.

"I beg your pardon," said I.

"Hasty Generalization," she repeated. "How can you say that we are well matched on the basis of only five dates?"

I chuckled with amusement. The dear child had learned her lessons well. "My dear," I said, patting her hand in a tolerant manner, "five dates is plenty. After all, you don't have to eat a whole cake to know that it's good."

"False Analogy," said Polly promptly. "I'm not a cake. I'm a girl."

I chuckled with somewhat less amusement. The dear child had learned her lessons perhaps too well. I decided to change tactics. Obviously the best approach was a simple, strong, direct declaration of love. I paused for a moment while my massive brain chose the proper words. Then I began:

"Polly, I love you. You are the whole world to me, and the moon and the stars and the constellations of outer space. Please, my darling, say that you will go steady with me, for if you will not, life will be meaningless. I will languish. I will refuse my meals. I will wander the face of the earth, a shambling, hollow-eyed hulk."

There, I thought, folding my arms, that ought to do it.

"Ad Misericordiam," said Polly.

I ground my teeth. I was not Pygmalion; I was Frankenstein, and my monster had me by the throat. Frantically I fought back the tide of panic surging through me. At all costs I had to keep cool.

"Well, Polly," I said, forcing a smile, "you certainly have learned your fallacies."

"You're darn right," she said with a vigorous nod.

"And who taught them to you, Polly?"

"You did."

"That's right. So you do owe me something, don't you, my dear? If I hadn't come along you never would have learned about fallacies."

"Hypothesis Contrary to Fact," she said instantly.

I dashed perspiration from my brow. "Polly," I croaked, "you mustn't take all these things so literally. I mean this is just classroom stuff. You know that the things you learn in school don't have anything to do with life."

"Dicto Simpliciter," she said, wagging her finger at me playfully.

That did it. I leaped to my feet, bellowing like a bull. "Will you or will you not go steady with me?"

"I will not," she replied.

"Why not?" I demanded.

"Because this afternoon I promised Petey Burch that I would go steady with him."

I reeled back, overcome with the infamy of it. After he promised, after he made a deal, after he shook my hand! "The rat!" I shrieked, kicking up great chunks of turf. "You can't go with him, Polly. He's a liar. He's a cheat. He's a rat."

"Poisoning the well," said Polly, "and stop shouting. I think shouting must be a fallacy too."

With an immense effort of will, I modulated my voice. "All right," I said. "You're a logician. Let's look at this thing logically. How could you choose Petey Burch over me? Look at me—a brilliant student, a tremendous intellectual, a man with an assured future. Look at Petey—a knot-head, a jitterbug, a guy who'll never know where his next meal is coming from. Can you give me one logical reason why you should go steady with Petey Burch?''

"I certainly can," declared Polly. "He's got a raccoon coat."

Meaning and Idea

1. Briefly compare the narrator with his roommate. On whose opinion have you based your comparison? Can that opinion be trusted as a sufficient basis for the comparison? Why?

2. For what reasons does the narrator want Polly Espy? How does he describe her? What element of that description comes back to haunt him in the end?

3. On what basis does the narrator arrange to "take over" his roommate's girlfriend?

4. How would you categorize the nature of Polly's conversation up to the point when the narrator "comes on" to her? After that point?

Language, Form, Structure

1. Develop your own definition of the term *logical fallacy.* List and briefly describe the eight fallacies Shulman identifies in this essay. Make up an example of your own for each of the fallacies.

2. Identify the author's allusions to Pygmalion and Frankenstein. How is each appropriate to the theme of this essay?

3. Define the following words from the essay: perspicacious; astute; acme; coveted; gamy; waxing; waning; trysting; cretin; grueling. Choose five and use them in sentences.

Ideas for Writing

1. Think of a recent action by one of your friends, which you thought was inappropriate or wrong in some way. Write an essay describing that action and explaining why it was wrong.

2. Of the eight fallacies described in Shulman's essay, which do you think is the most serious error in writing? Write an argumentative paper to answer this question.

3. In this essay, Shulman actually defines the same logical fallacies that you would find described in a rhetorical textbook. Which way would you prefer to learn about logical fallacies—in a story such as this or in a textbook essay? Why? Do you find this story entertaining? Why or why not? Do you find it informative? How so?

Adrienne Rich
CLAIMING AN EDUCATION

> Adrienne Rich was born in 1929 in Baltimore. She graduated from Radcliffe College in 1951, the same year W. H. Auden chose her volume of poems, *A Change of World,* for the prestigious Yale Younger Poet series. Rich's later poetry concentrates quite a bit on feminist issues. *Diving into the Wreck* (1973) won the 1974 National Book Award, and *Of Woman Born: Motherhood as Experience and Institution* (1976) is a fascinating prose study of motherhood. The voluume of poetry *The Dream of Common Language* (1978) delves into Rich's other major theme, the need for communication. In 1981, she published the volume of poems *A Wild Patience Has Taken Me this Far.*
>
> Adrienne Rich delivered this speech to entering students at Douglass College, New Jersey, in 1977. The speech argues about the unfairness in our treatment of women in American higher education. More generally, the speech is about the intellectual subjugation of women, and thus becomes her part of "our shared commitment toward. . . . the inborn potentialities of so many women's minds."

*F*or this convocation, I planned to separate my remarks into two parts: some thoughts about you, the women students here, and some thoughts about us who teach in a women's college. But ultimately, those two parts are indivisible. If university education means anything beyond the processing of human beings into expected roles, through credit hours, tests, and grades (and I believe that in a women's college especially it *might* mean much more), it implies an ethical and intellectual contract between teacher and student. This contract must remain intuitive, dynamic, unwritten, but we must turn to it again and again if learning is to be reclaimed from the depersonalizing and cheapening pressures of the present-day academic scene.

The first thing I want to say to you who are students, is that you cannot afford to think of being here to *receive* an education, you will do much better to think of yourselves as being here to *claim* one. One of the dictionary definitions of the verb "to claim" is: *to take as the rightful owner, to assert in the face of possible contradiction.* "To receive" is *to come into possession of; to act as receptacle or container for; to accept as authoritative or true.* The difference is that between acting and being acted-upon, and for women it can literally mean the difference between life and death.

One of the devastating weaknesses of university learning, of the store of knowledge and opinion that has been handed down through academic training, has been its almost total erasure of women's experience and thought from the curriculum, and its exclusion of women as members of the academic community. Today, with increasing numbers of women students in nearly every branch of higher learning, we still see very few women in the upper levels of faculty and administration in most institutions. Douglass College itself is a women's college in a university administered overwhelmingly by men, who in turn are answerable to the state legislature, again composed predominantly of men. But the most significant fact for you is that what you learn here, the very texts you read, the lectures you hear, the way your studies are divided into categories and fragmented one from the other—all this reflects, to a very large degree, neither objective reality, nor an accurate picture of the past, nor a group of rigorously tested observations about human behavior. What you can learn here (and I mean not only at Douglass but any college in any university) is how *men* have perceived and organized their experience, their history, their ideas of social relationships, good and evil, sickness and health, etc. When you read or hear about "great issues," "major texts," "the mainstream of Western thought," you are hearing about what men, above all white men, in their male subjectivity, have decided is important.

Black and other minority peoples have for some time recognized that their racial and ethnic experience was not accounted for in the studies broadly labeled human; and that even the sciences can be racist. For many reasons, it has been more difficult for women to comprehend our exclusion, and to realize that even the sciences can be sexist. For one thing, it is only within the last hundred years that higher education has grudgingly been opened up to women at all, even to white, middle-class women. And many of us have found ourselves poring eagerly over books with titles like: *The Descent of Man; Man and His Symbols; Irrational Man; The Phenomenon of Man; The Future of Man; Man and the Machine; From Man to Man; May Man Prevail?; Man, Science and Society;* or *One-Dimensional Man*—books pretending to describe a "human" reality that does not include over one-half the human species.

Less than a decade ago, with the rebirth of a feminist movement in this country, women students and teachers in a number of universities began to demand and set up women's studies courses—to *claim* a woman-directed education. And, despite the inevitable accusations of "unscholarly," "group therapy," "faddism," etc., despite backlash and budget cuts, women's studies are still growing, offering to more and more women a new intellectual grasp on their lives, new understanding of our history, a fresh vision of the human experience, and also a critical basis for evaluating what they hear and read in other courses, and in the society at large.

But my talk is not really about women's studies, much as I believe in their scholarly, scientific, and human necessity. While I think that any Douglass student has everything to gain by investigating and enrolling in women's studies courses, I want to suggest that there is a more essential experience that you owe yourselves, one which courses in women's studies can greatly enrich, but which finally depends on you, in all your interactions with yourself and your world. This is the experience of *taking responsibility toward yourselves.* Our upbringing as women has so oftenn told us that this should come second to our relationships and responsibilities to other people. We have been offered ethical models of the self-denying wife and mother; intellectual models of the brilliant but slapdash dilettante who never commits herself to anything the whole way, or the intelligent woman who denies her intelligence in order to seem more "feminine," or who sits in passive silence even when she disagrees inwardly with everything that is being said around her.

Responsibility to yourself means refusing to let others do your thinking, talking, and naming for you; it means learning to respect and use your own brains and instincts; hence, grappling with hard work. It means that you do not treat your body as a commodity with which to purchase superficial intimacy or economic security; for our bodies and minds are inseparable in this life, and when we allow our bodies to be treated as objects, our minds are in mortal danger. It means insisting that those to whom you give your friendship and love are able to respect your mind. It means being able to say, with Charlotte Brontë's *Jane Eyre:* "I have an inward treasure born with me, which can keep me alive if all the extraneous delights should be withheld or offered only at a price I cannot afford to give."

Responsibility to yourself means that you don't fall for shallow and easy solutions—predigested books and ideas, weekend encounters guaranteed to change your life, taking "gut" courses instead of ones you know will challenge you, bluffing at school and life instead of doing solid work, marrying early as an escape from real decisions, getting pregnant as an evasion of already existing problems. It means that you refuse to sell your talents and aspirations short, simply to avoid conflict and confrontation. And this, in turn, means resisting the forces in society which say that women should be nice, play safe, have low professional expectations, drown in love and forget about work, live through others, and stay in the places assigned to us. It means that we insist on a life of meaningful work, insist that work be as meaningful as love and friendship in our lives. It means, therefore, the courage to be "different"; not to be continuously available to others when we need time for ourselves and our work; to be able to demand of others—parents, friends, roommates, teachers, lovers, husbands, children—that they respect our sense of purpose and our integrity as persons. Women everywhere are finding the courage to do this, more and more, and we are finding that courage both in our study of women in the past who possessed it, and in each other as we look to other women for comradeship, community, and challenge. The difference between a life lived actively, and a life of passive drifting and dispersal of energies, is an immense difference. Once we begin to feel committed to our lives, responsible to ourselves, we can never again be satisfied with the old, passive way.

Now comes the second part of the contract. I believe that in a women's college you have the right to expect your faculty to take you seriously. The education of women has been a matter of debate for centuries, and old, negative attitudes about women's role, women's ability to think and take leadership, are still rife both in and outside the university. Many male professors (and I don't mean only at Douglass) still feel that teaching in a women's college is a second-rate career. Many tend to eroticize their women students—to treat them as sexual objects—instead of demanding the best of their minds. (At Yale a legal suit [*Alexander v. Yale*] has been brought against the university by a group of women students demanding a stated policy against sexual advances toward female students by male professors.) Many teachers, both men and women, trained in the male-centered tradition, are still handing the ideas and texts of that tradition on to students without teaching them to criticize its antiwoman attitudes, its omission of women as part of the species. Too often, all of us fail to teach the most important thing, which is that clear thinking, active discussion, and excellent writing are all necessary for intellectual freedom, and that these require *hard work*. Sometimes, perhaps in discouragement with a culture which is both antiiintellectual and antiwoman, we may resign ourselves to low expectations for our students before we have given them half a chance to become more thoughtful, expressive human beings. We need to take to heart the words of Elizabeth Barrett Browning, a poet, a thinking woman, and a feminist, who wrote in 1845 of her impatience with studies which cultivate aa "passive recipiency" in the mind, and asserted that "women want to be made to *think actively:* their apprehension is quicker than that of men, but their defect lies for the most part in the logical faculty and in the higher mental activities." Note that she implies a defect which can be remedied by intellectual training; *not* an inborn lack of ability.

I have said that the contract on the student's part involves that you demand to be taken seriously so that you can also go on taking yourself seriously. This means seeking out criticism, recognizing that the most affirming thing anyone can do for you is demand that you push yourself further, show you the range of what you *can* do. It means rejecting attitudes of "take-it-easy," "why-be-so-serious," "why-worry-you'll-probably-get-married-anyway." It means assuming your share of responsibility for what happens in the classroom, because that affects the quality of your daily life here. It means that the student sees herself engaged *with* her teachers in an active, ongoing struggle for a real education. But for her to do this, her teachers must be committed to the belief that women's minds and experience are intrinsically valuable and indispensable to any civilization worthy the name; that there is no more exhilarating and intellectually fertile place in the academic world today than a women's college—*if* both students and teachers in large enough numbers are trying to fulfill this contract. The contract is really a pledge of mutual seriousness about women, about language, ideas, methods, and values. It is our shared commitment toward a world in which the inborn potentialities of so many women's minds will no longer be wasted, raveled-away, paralyzed, or denied.

Meaning and Idea

1. What is the occasion for Rich's speech? Where is she?

2. What is the "contract" that Rich proposes? What is the nature of that contract? What does she set forth in the very beginning as the potential benefits of fulfilling that contract?

3. State in your own words Rich's main proposition in this essay. Identify any *minor propositions* as well.

4. In this speech, what does Rich state or imply about the relation between men and women generally? Specifically, what does she say about that relation as it concerns higher education? As it concerns the shaping of history?

Language, Form, Structure

1. How does Rich announce that she will organize her speech? What does she indicate is the relation between the different parts of that organization? How well does she balance her discussion of the parts?

2. What, according to Rich, is the difference between *receiving* and *claiming* an education? How does she use lexical (dictionary) definition to support her own definitions? How does she use definition as a way to express opinion? Where else in the essay does she use definition as the basis for opinion?

3. Trace the way in which Rich refines her interpretation of the expression "taking responsibility toward yourselves." How does that refining process form a core for the argumentation in this essay?

4. What literary allusions does Rich use in this speech? What is their significance?

5. In many arguments, writers will combine both emotional and logical appeals to the reader. Where does Rich use logical appeal most effectively? Where does she use emotional appeal?

6. Check the definitions of the following words: poring; slapdash; dilettante; commodity; superficial; extraneous; dispersal; rife; intrinsically; raveled.

Ideas for Writing

1. Write an essay in which you argue for the necessity of a fresh approach to some aspect of the education you are receiving—or claiming. Give the background to the present situation as well as suggestions for improvements.

2. Write an argument concerning the portrayal of women in a film you have seen recently. Perhaps you have seen a 1950s film on television that can help you develop a thesis. What attitudes about women were expressed in the film? Would you categorize them as sexist or not? Did they confirm or deny any expectations you may have had about the film?

3. Clearly, Rich takes a feminist approach in this essay. First, develop for yourself (with lexical aids) a working definition of the adjective *feminist*. Then, read through Rich's essay once again and try to discern where specific word choice or logical connections can be termed *feminist*.

Write a short essay in which you argue about the appropriateness of the word choice to the subject of Rich's essay.

John Stuart Mill
ON LIBERTY

> John Stuart Mill (1806–1873), the Victorian British philosopher and economist, was one of the major influences on the direction of modern political, economic, and philosophical thought. Schooled in the Utilitarianism of Jeremy Bentham and of his father, James Mill, John Stuart Mill liberalized that doctrine considerably. Mill's advocacy of *laissez-faire* economics is still highly-touted, though Mill himself was an early advocate of such socialist movements as labor unions, women's rights, and farm cooperatives. His base of logic lay in induction and empiricism (the doctrine that all knowledge derives from experience) and can be found in such works as *Principles of Political Economy* (1848), *On Liberty* (1859), and *Utilitarianism* (1863).
>
> "On Liberty" comes from Mill's *On Liberty; and Thoughts on Parliamentary Reform,* published in 1859. There are those who consider Mill's arguments in that collection the basis for liberal individualism, while others consider it the direct ancestor of the conservative *laissez-faire* doctrines of contemporary political leaders. In reading Mill's argument, postulate your own opinion about its contemporary importance, and pay close attention to the structure of his argumentative development.

The subject of this Essay is not the so-called Liberty of the Will, so unfortunately opposed to the misnamed doctrine of Philosophical Necessity; but Civil, or Social Liberty: the nature and limits of the power which can be legitimately exercised by society over the individual. A question seldom stated, and hardly ever discussed, inn general terms, but which profoundly influences the practical controversies of the age by its latent presence, and is likely soon to make itself recognized as the vital question of the future. It is so far from being new, that, in a certain sense, it has divided mankind, almost from the remotest ages; but in the stage of progress into which the more civilized portions of the species have now entered, it presents itself under new conditions, and requires a different and more fundamental treatment.

The struggle between Liberty and Authority is the most conspicuous feature in the portions of history with which we are earliest familiar, particularly in that of Greece, Rome, and England. But in old times this contest was between subjects, or some classes of subjects, and the Government. By liberty, was meant protection against the tyranny of the political rulers. The rulers were conceived (except in some of the popular governments of Greece) as in a necessarily antagonistic position to the people whom they ruled. They consisted of a governing One, or a governing tribe or caste, who derived their authority from inheritance or conquest, who, at all events, did not hold it at the pleasure of the governed, and whose supremacy men did not venture, perhaps did not desire, to contest, whatever precautions might be taken against its oppressive exercise. Their power was regarded as necessary, but also as highly dangerous; as a weapon which they would attempt to use against their subjects, no less than against external enemies. To prevent the weaker members of the community from being preyed upon by innumerable vultures, it was needful that there should be an animal of prey stronger than the rest, commissioned to keep them down. But as the king of the vultures would be no less bent upon preying on the flock than any of the minor harpies, it was indispensable to be in a perpetual attitude of defence against his beak and claws. The aim, therefore, of patriots was to set limits to the power which the ruler should be suffered to exercise over the community; and this limitation was what they meant by liberty. It was attempted in two ways. First, by obtaining a recognition of certain immunities, called political liberties or rights, which it was to be regarded as a breach of duty in the ruler to infringe, and which, if he did infringe, specific resistance, or general rebellion, was held to be justifiable. A second, and generally a later expedient, was the establishment of constitutional checks, by which the consent of the community, or of a body of some sort, supposed to represent its interests, was made a necessary condition to some of the more important acts of the governing power. To the first of these modes of limitation, the ruling power, in most European countries, was compelled, more or less, to submit. It was not so with the second; and, to attain this, or when already in some degree possessed, to attain it more completely, became everywhere the principal object of the lovers of liberty. And so long as mankind were content to combat one enemy by another, and to be ruled by a master, on condition of being guaranteed more or less efficaciously against his tyranny, they did not carry their aspirations beyond this point.

   A time, however, came, in the progress of human affairs, when men ceased to think it a necessity of nature that their governors should be an independent power, opposed in interest to themselves. It appeared to them much better that the various magistrates of the State should be their tenants or delegates, revocable at their pleasure. In that way alone, it seemed, could they have complete security that the powers of government would never be abused to their disadvantage. By degrees this new demand for elective and temporary rulers became the prominent object of the exertions of the popular party, wherever any such party existed; and superseded, to a considerable extent, the previous efforts to limit the power of rulers. As the struggle proceeded for making the ruling power emanate from the periodical choice of the ruled, some persons began to think that too much importance had been attached to the limitation of the power itself. *That* (it might seem) was a resource against rulers whose interests were habitually opposed to those of the people. What was now wanted was, that the rulers should be identified with the people; that their interest and will should be the interest and will of the nation. The nation did not need to be protected against its own will. There was no fear of its tyrannizing over itself. Let the rulers be effectually responsible to it, promptly removable by it, and it could afford to trust them with power of which it could itself dictate the use to be made. Their power was but the nation's own power, concentrated, and in a form convenient for exercise. This mode of thought, or rather perhaps of feeling, was common among the last generation of European liberalism, in the Continental section of which it still apparently predominates. Those who admit any limit to what a government may do, except in the case of such governments as they think ought not to exist, stand out as brilliant exceptions among the political thinkers of the Continent. A similar tone of sentiment might by this time have been prevalent in our own country, if the circumstances which for a time encouraged it, had continued unaltered.

But, in political and philosophical theories, as well as in persons, success discloses faults and infirmities which failure might have concealed from observation. The notion, that the people have no need to limit their power over themselves, might seem axiomatic, when popular government was a thing only dreamed about, or read of as having existed at some distant period of the past. Neither was that notion necessarily disturbed by such temporary aberrations as those of the French Revolution, the worst of which were the work of an usurping few, and which, in any case, belonged, not to the permanent working of popular institutions, but to a sudden and convulsive outbreak against monarchical and aristocratic despotism. In time, however, a democratic republic came to occupy a large portion of the earth's surface, and made itself felt as one of the most powerful members of the community of nations; and elective and responsible government became subject to the observations and criticisms which wait upon a great existing fact. It was now perceived that such phrases as "self-government," and "the power of the people over themselves," do not express the true state of the case. The "people" who exercise the power are not always the same people with those over whom it is exercised; and the "self-government" spoken of is not the government of each by himself, but of each by all the rest. The will of the people, moreover, practically means the will of the most numerous or the most active *part* of the people; the majority, or those who succeed in making themselves accepted as the majority; the people, consequently, *may* desire to oppress a part of their number; and precautions are as much needed against this as against any other abuse of power. The limitation, therefore, of the power of government over individuals loses none of its importance when the holders of power are regularly accountable to the community, that is, to the strongest party therein. This view of things, recommending itself equally to the intelligence of thinkers and to the inclination of those important classes in European society to whose real or supposed interests democracy is adverse, has had no difficulty in establishing itself; and in political speculations "the tyranny of the majority" is now generally included among the evils against which society requires to be on its guard.

Like other tyrannies, the tyranny of the majority was at first, and is still vulgarly, held in dread, chiefly as operating through the acts of the public authorities. But reflecting persons perceived that when society is itself the tyrant—society collectively, over the separate individuals who compose it—its means of tyrannizing are not restricted to the acts which it may do by the hands of its political functionaries. Society can and does execute its own mandates: and if it issues wrong mandates instead of right, or any mandates at all in things with which it ought not to meddle, it practices a social tyranny more formidable than many kinds of political oppression, since, though not usually upheld by such extreme penalties, it leaves fewer means of escape, penetrating much more deeply into the details of life, and enslaving the soul itself. Protection, therefore, against the tyranny of the magistrate is not enough: there needs protection also against the tyranny of the prevailing opinion and feeling; against the tendency of society to impose, by other means than civil penalties, its own ideas and practices as rules of conduct on those who dissent from them; to fetter the development, and, if posssible, prevent the formation, of any individuality nnot in harmony with its ways, and compel all characters to fashion themselves upon the model of its own. There is a limit to the legitimate interference of collective opinion with individual independence: and to find that limit, and maintain it against encroachment, is as indispensable to a good condition of human affairs, as protection against political despotism.

But though this proposition is not likely to be contested in general terms, the practical question, where to place the limit—how to make the fitting adjustment between individual independence and social control—is a subject on which nearly everything remains to be done. All that makes existence valuable to any one, depends on the enforcement of restraints upon the actions of other people. Some rules of conduct, therefore, must be imposed, by law in the first place, and by opinion on many things which are not fit subjects for the operation of law. What these rules should be, is the principal question in human affairs; but if we except a few of the most obvious cases, it is one of those which least progress has been made in resolving. No two ages, and scarcely any two countries, have decided it alike; and the decision of one age or country is a wonder to another. Yet the people of any given age and country no more suspect any difficulty in it, than if it were a subject on which mankind had always been agreed. The rules which obtain among themselves appear to them self-evident and self-justifying. This all but universal illusion is one of the examples of the magical influence of custom, which is not only, as the proverb says, a second nature, but is continually mistaken for the first. The effect of custom, in preventing any misgiving respecting the rules of conduct which mankind impose on one another, is all the more complete because the subject is one onn which it is not generally considered necessary that reasons should be given, either by one person to others, or by each to himself. People are accustomed to believe, and have been encouraged in the belief by some who aspire to the character of philosophers, that their feelings, on subjects of this nature, are better than reasons, and render reasons unnecessary. The practical principle which guides them to their opinions on the regulation of human conduct, is the feeling in each person's mind that everybody should be required to act as he, and those with whom he sympathizes, would like them to act. No one, indeed, acknowledges to himself that his standard of judgement is his own liking; but an opinion on a point of conduct, not supported by reasons, can only count as one person's preference; and if the reasons, when given, are a mere appeal to a similar preference felt by other people, it is still only many people's liking instead of one. To an ordinary man, however, his own preference, thus supported, is not only a perfectly satisfactory reason, but the only one he generally has for any of his notions of morality, taste, or propriety, which are not expressly written in his religious creed; and his chief guide in the interpretation even of that. Men's opinions, accordingly, on what is laudable or blameable, are affected by all the multifarious causes which influence their wishes in regard to the conduct of others, and which are as numerous as those which determine their wishes on any other subject. Sometimes their reason—at other times their prejudices or superstitions: often their social affections, not seldom their anti-social ones, their envy or jealousy, their arrogance or contemptuousness: but most commonly, their desires or fears for themselves—their legitimate or illegitimate self-interest. Wherever there is an ascendant class, a large portion of the morality of the country emanates from its class interests, and its feelings of class superiority. The morality between Spartans and Helots, between planters and negroes, between princes and subjects, between nobles and roturiers, between men and women, has been for the most part the creation of these class interests and feelings: and the sentiments thus generated, react in turn upon the moral feelings of the members of the ascendant class, in their relations among themselves. Where, on the other hand, a class, formerly ascendant, has lost its ascendancy, or where its ascendancy is unpopular, the prevailing moral sentiments frequently bear the impress of an impatient dislike of superiority. Another grand determining principle of the rules of conduct, both in act and forbearance, which have been enforced by law or opinion, has been the servility of mankind towards the supposed preferences or aversions of their temporal masters, or of their gods. This servility, though essentially selfish, is not hypocrisy; it gives rise to perfectly genuine sentiments of abhorrence; it made men burn magicians and heretics. Among so many baser influences, the general and obvious interests of society have of course had a share, and a large one, in the direction of the moral sentiments: less, however, as a matter of reason, and on their own account, than as a consequence of the sympathies and antipathies which grew out of them: and sympathies and antipathies which had little or nothing to do with the interests of society, have made themselves felt in the establishment of moralities with quite as great force.

The likings and dislikings of society, or of some powerful portion of it, are thus the main thing which has practically determined the rules laid down for general observance, under the penalties of law or opinion. And in general, those who have been in advance of society in thought and feeling, have left this condition of things unassailed in principle, however they may have come into conflict with it in some of its details. They have occupied themselves rather in inquiring what things society ought to like or dislike, than in questioning whether its likings or dislikings should be a law to individuals. They preferred endeavouring to alter the feelings of mankind on the parrticular points on which they were themselves heretical, rather than make common cause in defence of freedom, with heretics generally. The only case in which the higher ground has been taken on principle and maintained with consistency, by any but an individual here and there, is that of religious belief: a case instructive in many ways, and not least so as forming a most striking instance of the fallibility of what is called the moral sense: for the *odium theologicum,* in a sincere bigot, is one of the most unequivocal cases of moral feeling. Those who first broke the yoke of what called itself the Universal Church, were in general as little willing to permit difference of religious opinion as that church itself. But when the heat of the conflict was over, without giving a complete victory to any party, and each church or sect was reduced to limit its hopes to retaining possession of the ground it already occupied; minorities, seeing that they had no chance of becoming majorities, were under the necessity of pleading to those whom they could not convert, for permission to differ. It is accordingly on this battlefield, almost solely, that the rights of the individual against society have been asserted on broad grounds of principle, and the claim of society to exercise authority over dissentients, openly controverted. The great writers to whom the world owes what religious liberty it possesses, have mostly asserted freedom of conscience as an indefeasible right, and denied absolutely that a human being is accountable to others for his religious belief. Yet so natural to mankind is intolerance in whatever they really care about, that religious freedom has hardly anywhere been practically realized, except where religious indifference, which dislikes to have its peace disturbed by theological quarrels, has added its weight to the scale. In the minds of almost all religious persons, even in the most tolerant countries, the duty of toleration is admitted with tacit reserves. One person will bear with dissent in matters of church government, but not of dogma; another can tolerate everybody, short of a Papist or a Unitarian; another, every one who believes in revealed religion; a few extend their charity a little further, but stop at the belief in a God and in a future state. Wherever the sentiment of the majority is still genuine and intense, it is found to have abated little of its claim to be obeyed.

In England, from the peculiar circumstances of our political history, though the yoke of opinion is perhaps heavier, that of law is lighter, than in most other countries of Europe; and there is considerable jealousy of direct interference, by the legislative or the executive power, with private conduct; not so much from any just regard for the independence of the individual, as from the still subsisting habit of looking on the government as representing an opposite interest to the public. The majority have not yet learnt to feel the power of the government their power, or its opinions their opinions. When they do so, individual liberrty will probably be as much exposed to invasion from the government, as it already is from public opinion. But, as yet, there is a considerable amount of feeling ready to be called forth against any attempt of the law to control individuals in things in which they have not hitherto been accustomed to be controlled by it; and this with very little discrimination as to whether the matter is, or is not, within the legitimate sphere of legal control; insomuch that the feeling, highly salutary on the whole, is perhaps quite as often misplaced as well grounded in the particular instances of its application. There is, in fact, no recognized principle by which the propriety or impropriety of government interference is customarily tested. People decide according to their personal preferences. Some, whenever they see any good to be done, or evil to be remedied, would willingly instigate the government to undertake the business; while others prefer to bear almost any amount of social evil, rather than add one to the departments of human interests amenable to governmental control. And men range themselves on one or the other side in any particular case, according to this general direction of their sentiments; or according to the degree of interest which they feel in the particular thing which it is proposed that the government should do, or according to the belief they entertain that the government would, or would not, do it in the manner they prefer; but very rarely on account of any opinion to which they consistently adhere, as to what things are fit to be done by a government. And it seems to me that in consequence of this absence of rule or principle, one side is at present as often wrong as the other; the interference of government is, with about equal frequency, improperly invoked and improperly condemned.

The object of this Essay is to assert one very simple principle, as entitled to govern absolutely the dealings of society with the individual in the way of compulsion and control, whether the means used be physical force in the form of legal penalties, or the moral coercion of public opinion. That principle is, that the sole end for which mankind are warranted, individually or collectively, in interfering with the liberty of action of any of their number, is self-protection. That the only purpose for which power can be rightfully exercised over any member of a civilized community, against his will, is to prevent harm to others. His own good, either physical or moral, is not a sufficient warrant. He cannot rightfully be compelled to do or forbear because it will be better for him to do so, because it will make him happier, because, in the opinions of others, to do so would be wise, or even right. These are good reasons for remonstrating with him, or reasoning with him, or persuading him, or entreating him, but not for compelling him, or visiting him with any evil in case he do otherwise. To justify that, the conduct from which it is desired to deter him, must be calculated to produce evil to some one else. The only part of the conduct of any one, for which he is amenable to society, is that which concerns others. In the part which merely concerns himself, his independence is, of right, absolute. Over himself, over his own body and mind, the individual is sovereign.

It is, perhaps, hardly necessary to say that this doctrine is meant to apply only to human beings in the maturity of their faculties. We are not speaking of children, or of young persons below the age which the law may fix as that of manhood or womanhood. Those who are still in a state to require being taken care of by others, must be protected against their own actions as well as against external injury. For the same reason, we may leave out of consideration those backward states of society in which the race itself may be considered as in its nonage. The early difficulties in the way of spontaneous progress are so great, that there is seldom any choice of means for overcoming them; and a ruler full of the spirit of improvement is warranted in the use of any expedients that will attain an end, perhaps otherwise unattainable. Despotism is a legitimate mode of government in dealing with barbarians, provided the end be their improvement, and the means justified by actually effecting that end. Liberty, as a principle, has no application to any state of things anterior to the time when mankind have become capable of being improved by free and equal discussion. Until then, there is nothing for them but implicit obedience to an Akbar or a Charlemagne, if they are so fortunate as to find one. But as soon as mankind have attained the capacity of being guided to their own improvement by conviction or persuasion (a period long since reached in all nations with whom we need here concern ourselves), compulsion, either in the direct form or in that of pains and penalties for noncompliance, is no longer admissible as a means to their own good, and justifiable only for the security of others.

It is proper to state that I forgo any advantage wwhich could be derived to my argument from the idea of abstract right, as a thing independent of utility. I regard utility as the ultimate appeal on all ethical questions; but it must be ulitity in the largest sense, grounded on the permanent interests of man as a progressive being. Those interests, I contend, authorize the subjection of individual spontaneity to external control, only in respect to those actions of each, which concern the interest of other peoplle. If any one does an act hurtful to others, there is a prima facie case for punishing him, by law, or, where legal penalties are not safely applicable, by general disapprobation. There are also many positive acts for the benefit of others, which he may rightfully be compelled to perform; such as, to give evidence in a court of justice; to bear his fair share in the common defence, or in any other joint work necessary to the interest of the society of which he enjoys the protection; and to perform certain acts of individual beneficence, such as saving a fellow creature's life, or interposing to protect the defenceless against ill-usage, things which whenever it is obviously a man's duty to do, he may rightfully be made responsible to society for not doing. A person may cause evil to others not only by his actions but by his inaction, and in either case he is justly accountable to them for the injury. The latter case, it is true, requires a much more cautious exercise of compulsion than the former. To make any one answerable for doing evil to others, is the rule; to make him answerable for not preventing evil, is, comparatively speaking, the exception. Yet there are many cases clear enough and grave enough to justify that exception. In alll things which regard the external relations of the individual, he is *de jure* amenable to those whose interests are concerned, and if need be, to society as their protector. There are often good reasons for not holding him to the responsibility; but these reasons must arise from the special expediencies of the case: either because it is a kind of case in which he is on the whole likely to act better, when left to his own discretion, than when controlled in any way in which society have it in their powwer to control him; or because the attempt to exercise control would produce other evils, greater than those which it would prevent. When such reasons as these preclude the enforcement of responsibility, the conscience of the agent himself should step into the vacant judgement-seat, and protect those interests of others which have no external protection; judging himself all the more rigidly, because the case does not admit of his being made accountable to the judgement of his fellow creatures.

But there is a sphere of action in which society, as distinguished from the individuaal, has, if any, only an indirect interest; comprehending all that portion of a person's life and conduct which affects only himself, or if it also affects others, only with their free, voluntary, and undeceived consent and participation. When I say only himself, I mean directly, and in the first instance: for whatever affects himself, may affect others through himself; and the objection which may be grounded on this contingency will receive consideration in the sequel. This, then, is the appropriate region of human liberty. It comprises, first, the inward domain of consciousness; demanding liberty of conscience, in the most comprehensive sense; liberty of thought and feeling; absolute freedom of opinion and sentiment on all subjects, practical or speculative, scientific, moral, or theological. The liberty of expressing and publishing opinions may seem to fall under a different principle, since it belongs to that part of the conduct of an individual which concerns other people; but, beiing almost of as much importance as the liberty of thought itself, and resting in great part on the same reasons, is practically inseparable from it. Secondly, the principle requires liberty of tastes and pursuits; of framing the plan of our life to suit our own character; of doing as we like, subject to such consequences as may follow: without impedimeent from our fellow creatures, so long as what we do does not harm them, even though they should think our conduct foolish, perverse, or wrong. Thirdly, from this liberty of each individual, follows the liberty, within the same limits, of combination among individuals; freedom to unite, for any purpose not involving harm to others: the persons combining being supposed to be of full age, and not forced or deceived.

No society in which these liberties are not, on the whole, respected, is free, whatever may be its form of government; and none is completely free in which they do not exist absolute and unqualified. The only freedom which deserves the name, is that of pursuing our own good in our own way, so long as we do not attempt to deprive others of theirs, or impede their efforts to obbtain it. Each is the proper guardian of his own health, whether bodily, or mental and spiritual. Mankind are greater gainers by suffering each other to live as seems good to themselves, than by compelling each to live as seems good to the rest.

Meaning and Idea

1.   What basic definition does Mill ascribe to the term *liberty*? How is that definition modified throughout the essay? On what "practical question" does Mill's argument about liberty hinge? What is the "principal question in human affairs"?

2.   Trace the historical change in attitude toward rulers as outlined by Mill in this essay. Why did it occur?

3. According to Mill, why may it be necessary to limit the power of the majority opinion? What does he mean by "the tyranny of the majority"? What, according to Mill, is the difference between the right of the society to persuade and to compel its citizens to act in certain ways? Which is preferable? What acts *may* be compelled? On what basis?

4. What is Mill's attitude toward the connection between religions and liberty?

5. What, according to Mill, is the relation between personal preference and rules of conduct or propriety? Which class has usually determined morality? What examples of this does he offer? Can you offer a few more examples from present-day societies?

Language, Form, Structure

1. Mill's first paragraph is almost a model introduction to argument because of the elements it includes. Analyze how Mill: (1) identifies the focus of the essay; (2) establishes a definition for his argument; (3) focuses on the contemporary importance of his discussion; (4) provides a historical context for his argument. Also, identify any other element of the first paragraph that you feel is especially important.

2. The introduction to this chapter discusses the difference between *inductive* and *deductive* reasoning (see page 521). You may want to clarify your understanding of these terms further by looking in a dictionary, encyclopedia, or basic philosophy textbook. Would you characterize Mill's logic in this essay as primarily inductive or deductive? Explain.

3. Where does Mill place his thesis statement in this essay? Identify it. Why is it placed where it is?

4. Analyze Mill's use of transitions in this essay. Is it significant to the logical development that three of the essay's thirteen paragraphs beggin with the word *But*? How do the other transitions affect the development of Mill's argument?

5. What sentence signals the beginning of the essay's conclusion? How does Mill use *summary* as a part of his conclusion? What generalization does he derive from this summary?

6. Would you classify this piece more as an *argumentation* or a *persuasion* essay (see chapter introduction, page 519)? Where does Mill include specific suggestions for action?

7. Check the meanings of the following words from the essay: infringe; efficaciously; superseded; axiomatic; despotism; formidable; fetter; multifarious; fallibility; tacit.

Ideas for Writing

1. Select an aspect of life over which you feel the government exerts too much—*or* too little—control. Write an argument in favor of reversing the current trend. Be sure to include a blend of objective analysis and personal preference.

2. Write an argument for or against a greater voice by students in the shaping of curriculum at your school. Include a discussion of the relation between students' goals at your school and the present curriculum's ability to fulfill those goals.

3. John Stuart Mill is known for his advocacy of the doctrine of *laissez-faire* both in economics and in personal life. Very basically, *laissez-faire* is characterized by complete lack of, or at least minimal, government regulation. For further clarification, look up *laissez-faire* in an encyclopedia and pay close attention to how it relates to ideas about individualism.

How is Mill's argument in "On Liberty" a reflection of laissez-faire? What do you think of this attitude? Is it applicable to the 1980s? How so?

Acknowledgments

Melville Cane, "Snow toward Evening." Copyright 1926 by Harcourt Brace Jovanovich, Inc.; renewed 1954 by Melville Cane. Reprinted from *So That It Flower* by Melville Cane by permission of the publisher.

Raymond Carver, "My Father's Life." Reprinted by permission of the author. Copyright © 1984 by Raymond Carver. First appeared in *Esquire.*

Willa Cather, "A Wagner Matinee." Reprinted from *The Troll Garden,* by Willa Cather, edited by James Woodress, by permission of University of Nebraska Press. Copyright © 1983 by the University of Nebraska Press.

Lucille Clifton, "Good Times." From *Good Times,* by Lucille Clifton. Copyright © 1969 by Lucille Clifton. Reprinted by permission of Random House, Inc.

Joseph Conrad, "The Secret Sharer" and preface to *Lord Jim.* "The Secret Sharer" by Joseph Conrad copyright 1910 by Harper & Bros. from the book *Twixt Land and Sea* published by Doubleday & Company, Inc. Preface to *Lord Jim* by Joseph Conrad copyright © 1920 by Doubleday & Company, Inc. Reprinted by permission of the publisher.

Julio Cortázar, "Axolotl." From *A Change of Light and Other Stories,* translated by Gregory Rabassa. Copyright © 1980 by Alfred A. Knopf, Inc. Reprinted by permission of Alfred A. Knopf, Inc.

Malcolm Cowley, "The National Heartbeat: 'We-ness' and 'Me-ness.' " Reprinted by permission of Malcolm Cowley.

Countee Cullen, "Incident." From *Color,* copyright 1925 by Countee Cullen. Reprinted by permission of Harper & Row, Publishers, Inc.

E. E. Cummings, "In Just Spring" from *Tulips and Chimneys* (1922); "Nobody Loses All the Time" from IS 5 (1926); and "A Politician" from 1 X 1 (1944). Reprinted by permission of Liveright Publishing Corporation.

Emily Dickinson, "There's Been a Death in the Opposite House," "Crumbling Is Not an Instant's Act." Reprinted by permission of the publishers and the Trustees of Amherst College from *The Poems of Emily Dickinson,* edited by Thomas H. Johnson, Cambridge, Mass.: The Belknap Press of Harvard University Press, copyright 1951, © 1955, 1979, 1983 by the President and Fellows of Harvard College.

Joseph Epstein (Aristides), "A Former Good Guy and His Friends." Reprinted from *The American Scholar,* volume 54, number 2, Spring, 1985. Copyright © 1985 by the United Chapters of Phi Beta Kappa. By permission of the publishers.

William Faulkner, "A Rose for Emily." From *Collected Stories of William Faulkner,* by William Faulkner. Copyright 1930, 1958 by William Faulkner. Reprinted by permission of Random House, Inc.

E. M. Forster, "My Wood." From *Abinger Harvest,* copyright 1936, 1964 by Edward Morgan Forster. Reprinted by permission of Harcourt Brace Jovanovich, Inc. and by Edward Arnold Publishers Ltd.

Sigmund Freud, "Libidinal Types." From Volume 21 of *The Standard Edition of the Complete Psychological Works of Sigmund Freud,* translated and edited by James Strachey. Reprinted by permission of Sigmund Freud Copyrights, Ltd.; The Institute of Psycho-Analysis; The Hogarth Press, Ltd.; and Basic Books.

permission of Houghton Mifflin Company.

Paule Marshall, "From the Poets in the Kitchen." From *The New York Times,* January 9, 1983. Copyright © 1983 by The New York Times Company. Reprinted by permission.

Ved Mehta, "The Baby Myna." From *Vedi.* Copyright © 1982 by Ved Mehta. Reprinted by permission of Ved Mehta and Georges Borchardt, Inc.

Marianne Moore, "Poetry." Reprinted with permission of Macmillan Publishing Company from *Collected Poems* by Marianne Moore. Copyright 1935 by Marianne Moore, renewed 1963 by Marianne Moore and T. S. Eliot.

Toni Morrison, "A Slow Walk of Trees." From *The New York Times,* July 4, 1976. Copyright © 1976 by The New York Times Company. Reprinted with permission.

Ogden Nash, "Very Like a Whale." From *Verses from 1929 on* by Ogden Nash. Copyright 1934 by The Curtis Publishing Company. Reprinted by permission of Little, Brown and Company.

George Orwell, "Marrakech," "Politics and the English Language." "Marrakech" from *Such, Such Were The Joys* by George Orwell, copyright 1953 by Sonia Bronwell Orwell; renewed 1981 by Mrs. George K. Perutz, Mrs. Miriam Gross, Dr. Michael Dickson, Executors of the Estate of Sonia Bronwell Orwell. Reprinted by permission of Harcourt Brace Jovanovich, Inc. "Politics and the English Language" from *Shooting an Elephant and Other Essays* by George Orwell, copyright 1950 by Sonia Bronwell Orwell; renewed 1978 by Sonia Pitt-Rivers. Reprinted by permission of Harcourt Brace Jovanovich, Inc. and by the estate of the late Sonia Bronwell Orwell and Secker & Warburg Ltd.

Wilfred Owen, "Dulce et Decorum Est." From *Collected Poems* by Wilfred Owen. Copyright © 1963 by Chatto & Windus Ltd. Reprinted by permission of New Directions Publishing Corp.

Sylvia Plath, "A Comparison." Copyright © 1962 by Sylvia Plath. Reprinted by permission of Olwyn Hughes.

Henry Reed, "Naming of Parts." From *A Map of Verona.* Reprinted by permission of Jonathan Cape Ltd.

Adrienne Rich, "Claiming an Education." From *On Lies, Secrets, and Silence.* Copyright © 1979 by Adrienne Rich. Reprinted by permission of W. W. Norton & Co., Inc.

Edward Arlington Robinson, "Richard Corey." Originally published by Charles Scribner's Sons. Reprinted by permission of the publisher.

Richard Rodriguez, "Complexion." From *Hunger of Memory* by Richard Rodriguez. Copyright © 1981 by Richard Rodriguez. Reprinted by permission of David R. Godine, Publisher, Boston.

Bertrand Russell, "The American Way (a Briton Says) Is Dour." From *The New York Times,* June 15, 1952. Copyright © 1952 by The New York Times Company. Reprinted with permission.

Carl Sandburg, "Primer Lesson." From *Slabs of the Sunburnt West* by Carl Sandburg, copyright 1922 by Harcourt Brace Jovanovich, Inc.; renewed 1950 by Carl Sandburg. Reprinted by permission of the publisher.

Max Shulman, "Love Is a Fallacy." Reprinted by permission of the Harold Matson Company, Inc.

Susan Sontag, From *Illness As Metaphor,* copyright © 1978 by Susan Sontag. Reprinted by permission of Farrar, Straus & Giroux.